AUTOCOURSE

OFFICIAL HISTORY OF THE
INDIANAPOLIS 500®

AUTOCOURSE
OFFICIAL HISTORY OF THE
INDIANAPOLIS 500®
DONALD DAVIDSON & RICK SHAFFER

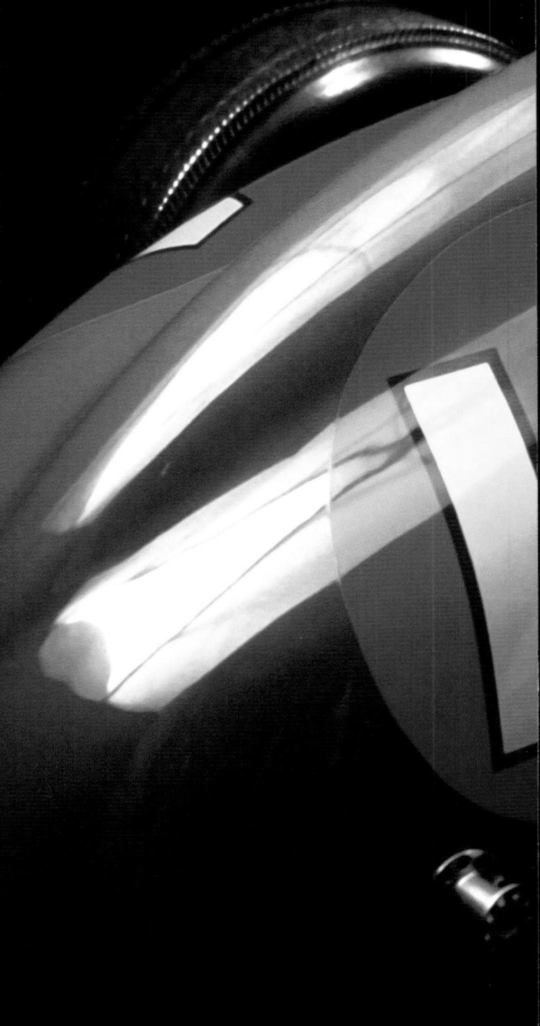

AUTOCOURSE OFFICIAL HISTORY OF
THE INDIANAPOLIS 500
is published by: Crash Media Group Ltd
Number One, The Innovation Centre, Silverstone Circuit,
Silverstone, Northants NN12 8GX, United Kingdom

Tel: +44 (0)870 3505044
Fax: +44 (0)870 3505088
Email: info@crash.net
Website:www.crashmediagroup.com

Printed in China through
World Print Ltd.

ISBN: 1-905334-20-6

ACKNOWLEDGMENTS

The authors would like to thank the following people for their invaluable assistance and support in this project: Ron McQueeney, IMS director of photography (who personally shot many of the post-1960s photographs used in this publication), and his staff, namely MaryEllen Loscar, Shawn Payne, and Jim Haines. For their extraordinary copyediting skills: Sherry Smith Davidson and Timothy L. Davidson. For being kind enough to read either all or part of the manuscript and offer suggestions: Nigel Roebuck, Terry Reed, David Scoggan, John Chuhran, and Ron Rose. For his work in helping "purify" the "box scores" of the 500-Mile Races in the rear of the book: Tim Sullivan of the Indianapolis Motor Speedway. For their general support: Fred Nation, Ron Green, and Ellen K. Bireley, also of IMS. And finally, all the gratitude in the world to the heroes of the "500," and the many ladies and gentlemen over the last century who have contributed in some way to the success of "The Greatest Spectacle in Racing," the Indianapolis 500.

Donald Davidson and Rick Shaffer

publisher
BRYN WILLIAMS

house editor (US)
TIM DAVIDSON

photo captions
DONALD DAVIDSON

art editor
STEVE SMALL

production
MIKE WESTON

sales promotion
DEBBIE THOMAS

office manager
WENDY SALISBURY

photography
Indianapolis Motor Speedway
LAT Photographic

DISTRIBUTORS

NORTH AMERICA
Motorbooks International
PO Box 1
729 Prospect Avenue
Osceola
Wisconsin 54020, USA
Tel: (1) 715 294 3345
Fax: (1) 715 294 4448

Gardners Books,
1 Whittle Drive, Eastbourne,
East Sussex, BN23 6QH
Tel: +44 (0)1323 521555
Email: sales@gardners.com

Menoshire Ltd
Unit 13
21 Wadsworth Road
Perivale
Middlesex UB6 7LQ
Tel: +44 (0)20 8566 7344
Fax: +44 (0)20 8991 2439

Every vehicle we build comes equipped with our racing spirit.

Indianapolis Motor Speedway®

HONDA
The Power of Dreams

INTRODUCTION

THE Indianapolis 500-Mile Race, undoubtedly the best-known automobile racing contest in the world, is far, far more than just that. It transcends all of motorsports. It is a cherished institution, attended by a massive audience, many of whom have been drawn to the track virtually for the span of their entire lives. Millions upon millions of people have watched it on television or listened to the radio broadcasts, legions of the latter having developed traditions of their own in the 1950s and 1960s, by annually spending Memorial Day cleaning out the garage, painting a fence, or attending a picnic... always with one ear being tuned to the radio.

Of those who go, a large number perhaps attend no other automobile race during the entire year. But they wouldn't dream of missing this one. To them, it is almost a religious experience, the memories of all of their past visits pouring forth as they walk through the gates for yet another race morning. Entire families will attend en masse, encompassing several generations, while those who have gone for 40 consecutive years or more are surprisingly not at all uncommon.

The pre-race ceremonies are of the utmost importance to the regulars, and the hush which falls over the several hundred thousand-strong crowd at the appropriate times never fails to astound those who experience it for the first time.

And the start, of course, is indescribable.

The beloved Speedway is much older than most people realize. It was built as a combination race track and testing facility in 1909, with the 500-Mile Race being held for the first time on May 30, 1911. That's almost one hundred years ago. At the time the track opened, the automobile industry was in its infancy, the first powered flight by the Wright brothers had taken place less than six years earlier, and Louis Blériot had not yet flown the English Channel. Many in attendance had yet to purchase their first automobiles, women were not permitted to vote, and Arizona and New Mexico (which between them would eventually produce five drivers who would win the "500" a total of eleven times) weren't even states yet.

In 2006, the "500" was conducted for the 90th time, the only occasions on which it has not been held being two years during America's involvement in World War I and four more years during World War II. Other than that, the race has carried on through major conflicts like Vietnam and Korea. It continued to be held throughout the crippling Great Depression of the 1930s, and through various other difficult times, whether involving depressions, recessions, or even the "energy-crunch" scares of the 1970s. It has had to overcome much criticism, controversy, public outcry, and political strife, even enduring the efforts of a U.S. senator in the 1950s who sought to have automobile racing banned completely.

But the "500" has always kept its position at the pinnacle of U.S. open-wheel racing and as its most potent symbol.

For more than half a century the *AUTOCOURSE* name has been synonymous with producing motor racing publications to the highest standards of both writing and presentation. We are proud to have been involved with the Indianapolis Motor Speedway staff, who have helped us in our quest to produce the most pictorially lavish, and historically accurate, account of the "world's most famous motor race."

It makes fascinating reading.

Bryn Williams
Publisher
Crash Media Group
November 2006

1911 MAR
WINNER OF THE 1st

32

HALL OF FAME
MUSEUM

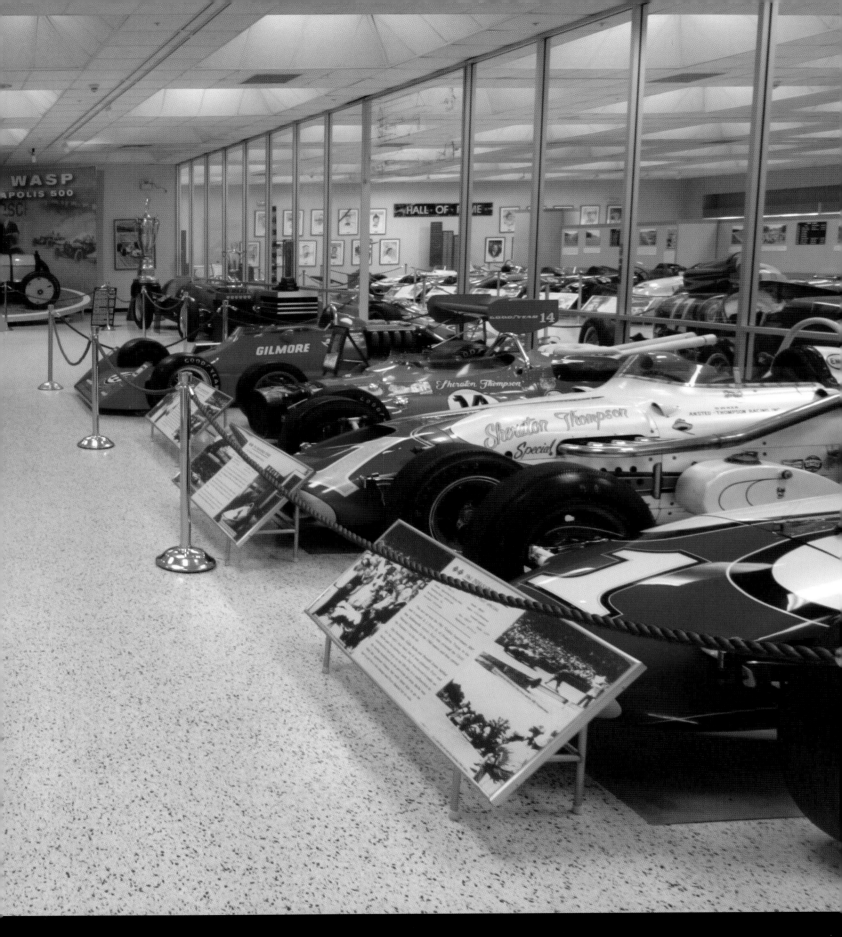

The history of the Indianapolis "500" is well represented in the Hall of Fame Museum, which is actually inside the 2.5-mile oval, located between turns one and two. The Museum is open every day of the year except for Christmas Day, and normally has on display approximately 90 vehicles, in addition to a variety of trophies, helmets, and uniforms, many of which have been donated either by the drivers themselves, or by their families. The vehicles are not restricted merely to Indianapolis "500" cars number of European sports cars and Formula One cars, motorcycles and early-day American passenger vehicles. On the right, in this shot, are all four of A. J. Foyt's winning cars, while off in the distance is the Marmon "Wasp" which won the very first Indianapolis "500" in 1911. The admission is a very nominal $3 per adult, $1 per student (ages 6-15), and no charge at all for accompanied children of five and under. Rides around the track in a bus are also offered, contingent upon weather conditions,

PART 1
THE EARLY YEARS

1911
1960

BY DONALD DAVIDSON

Chapter 1
HOW IT ALL BEGAN

T is entirely possible that, had it not been for a gentleman named Carl Graham Fisher, there never would have been an Indianapolis Motor Speedway.

He was an extraordinary man, who, with very limited formal education, not only gave the world the legendary racetrack, but also developed Miami Beach from swamplands into an exotic resort area, and spearheaded the Lincoln Highway Commission, which raised the massive funds necessary to build the first drivable highway across the United States.

Fisher was heavily involved in the automobile business, not as a manufacturer per se, but as one of the industry's strongest advocates. A self-made man who came from less-than-easy beginnings in southern Indiana, he had opened a bicycle repair shop virtually at the center of Indianapolis, the state's capital, when he was only 17, running it with two brothers who were even younger than he. Within months, it had been transformed into a fully fledged dealership. In 1898, when he was 24, he caused quite a commotion by driving a noisy, backfiring French De Dion motor tricycle through the bustling downtown streets, notable because it is believed to have been the very first gasoline-powered vehicle many of the locals had ever seen.

Two years later, Fisher traveled by train to New York's Madison Square Garden in order to attend the nation's first-ever automobile show.

There was, at that time, no such thing as a large automobile company, but rather dozens and dozens of small ones. Very shortly, there would soon be literally hundreds of them. Early automobiles were little more than motorized versions of horse-drawn buggies, and to this point, virtually everything available had been individually built "one-offs." Typically they would either be the work of a start-up company or else a firm already in business as a coachbuilder of horse-drawn vehicles, painstakingly turning them out one at a time.

Ransom E. Olds, however, had developed and perfected a buggy-like gasoline-powered vehicle, which he planned to produce in quantity, something no one had yet done. It didn't take long for it to become known as, quite simply, the "curved-dash" Olds, and its creator was in attendance at the New York show, seeking regional distributors, or "agents," as dealers were known in the early days. Olds and Fisher met, struck up a friendship, and, not surprisingly, Carl rode the train home, clutching the contract for the Indianapolis area.

It wasn't long before Fisher began to take on other makes, bicycles constituting less and less of his inventory. Needing more space, he moved to the 300 block of North Illinois Street and formed the Fisher Automobile Company, phasing out bicycles completely. He gained considerable notoriety over the next few years as a tireless promoter and executor of stunts, leading to his sometime nickname, "Crazy Carl Fisher."

In spite of the fact that he preferred to stay out of the limelight himself – he had an aversion to being photographed – he

enthusiastically took to producing such publicity-seeking stunts as dropping one of the newfangled horseless carriage vehicles from a second-floor roof and demonstrating that it could still be driven away. Another was to construct a steep wooden ramp outside one of his buildings in order to show that an Overland automobile could be driven up the steep 134-foot-long gradient to the third-floor rooftop in nine seconds.

Perhaps his most famous stunt took place several years later, when late on the afternoon of October 30, 1908, city folk ran out into the city streets in time to see a huge gas-filled balloon floating across the Indianapolis sky. That sight, in itself, was not *that* unusual except for the fact that instead of a basket rigged below it, there hung an *automobile!*

Piloted by Capt. George Bumbaugh, a well-known early balloonist from Springfield, Illinois, and a close friend of Fisher, the balloon had been filled at the Indianapolis Gas Company, just north of the city, and, accompanied by Fisher, the pair were bound for Southport, a few miles to the south. The automobile was a Stoddard-Dayton, a make for which Fisher had recently become agent, and the scenario was that after landing in Southport, it would supposedly be driven back to Indianapolis, drawing attention along the way and finally arriving back at Fisher's showroom potentially with a huge Pied Piper of Hamelin-inspired procession in tow.

The stunt was successfully completed, but it was not quite as it had appeared. The Stoddard which floated across the sky was not the same one which was driven back. The flown version was, for reasons of weight, "less engine." It was rolled into some bushes upon landing, and a few moments later, out came a motorized look-alike, driven down earlier in the day by one of Fisher's brothers.

The "stunt" worked. A large photograph appeared in the following morning's newspapers, and there, in huge letters on the side of the airborne balloon, was emblazoned the name "Stoddard–Dayton." No standard display advertisement in the paper would have been anywhere near as effective.

By this time, Indianapolis had thoroughly embraced the automobile and a number of factories had long since opened up and gone into production. The company heads were all cronies of Fisher and it seemed that everybody knew everybody else. They would frequently gather for discussions over lunch, the regular haunt being the back room of a restaurant run by Horace T. "Pop" Haynes at 114 North Pennsylvania Street, right next door to where Fisher's bicycle shop had been.

In "talking shop," the biggest challenge, they all agreed, was the increasing difficulty of trying to test their vehicles. With potential speeds having increased from a bare crawl, to 15 mph, to 20, to 30, to 40 and beyond, the city and county roads, which they had been using, were no longer suited for the task. While some states had begun appropriating funds for the development of roads, Indiana was not among them, and West Washington Street, the main thoroughfare through Indianapolis – later designated as part of Highway 40, but then known as The Old National Road – was still *dirt*. In spite of regular grading, ruts were constantly developing, and when it rained to any extent, vehicles would become hopelessly mired axle-deep in mud.

With the open roads no longer suited for the purpose of testing to the fullest, the one-mile dirt track at the Indiana State Fairgrounds had been put into use. But even that had become outmoded. With speeds of 50 and 60 miles per hour

and even faster now obtainable, top-heavy vehicles would slue and careen around the turns, placing great strain on the tires but never really allowing the engines to be stressed to their fullest.

Fisher believed that something much larger was needed: perhaps a five-mile circle, or at least something with long straights and gradual turns so that out-and-out speed could be obtained, something where vehicles could be pushed and strained to their absolute maximum. Then, when something failed, it would be up to the engineers to determine *what* had failed, *why* it had failed, and then produce something more substantial.

Obviously, the building of a facility of this magnitude would incur great expense, but at least part of the cost could be offset by potential income derived in at least two ways. Not only would the manufacturers be able to rent the track on an individual basis for private testing throughout the year, but occasional automobile *races* could be held at which the paying general public would have an opportunity to see, in competition, stripped-down versions of the very vehicles they could purchase at the downtown showrooms.

In 1907, a wealthy Englishman named Hugh Fortescue Locke–King spent a considerable amount of money to build, on his estate in Weybridge, Surrey, a futuristic racecourse called Brooklands. Virtually but not quite an oval, it featured steeply banked parabolic turns made out of concrete sections, and flat straights, plus a series of airstrip-like roads laid out through the infield which could be linked up to form any number of different combinations of road course.

When a number of multi-course racetracks began to emerge in the United States in the 1960s, it was thought to be a revolutionary concept. Locke–King's Brooklands had offered such a facility some *60 years* before.

It has occasionally been suggested that it was the creation of Brooklands which gave Fisher the idea for building the Indianapolis Motor Speedway. While he certainly did eventually visit Brooklands and was greatly impressed by it, there is proof that a racetrack/test track had been on his mind for years before Brooklands was even started.

In the November 15, 1906, issue of *Motor Age* magazine, the following letter appeared:

Advantages of a Big Circular Track

INDIANAPOLIS, IND. – Editor Motor Age – I note with considerable interest that you are taking up individual opinions regarding the advisability of track racing on large tracks. As you are probably aware, a large track of 3 to 5 miles in diameter, with a width of 100 to 150 feet, has been a hobby of mine for the past 3 years, and I have done a great deal of work toward a track of this kind. The proposed track at French Lick fell through, for the reason that enough level ground could not be secured for a track of sufficient size. After considerable time and investigation arrangements were made with our fair board in Indianapolis for the ground for a 3-mile track, but after a careful survey it was found impossible to put more than a 2-mile track on it.

Very few people understand what an immense difference there is between a mile track and a 3-mile track,

and to do this it will be necessary to have a drawing to scale of 1, 3 and 5-mile tracks in order to convey properly to the average driver the respective sizes. I have been an interested spectator in most of the big track meets and road races in this country and France – including the Vanderbilt and Bennett – and it is my opinion that the only successful racing course, and the one which will ultimately find favor with both drivers and the public, will be a 3 or 5-mile circular course.

There is no question in my mind that track racing on mile tracks is doomed. The average horse track is narrow, has fences that are dangerous, and is always dusty or muddy, and with high speed cars, where wide skids are necessary, racing becomes so dangerous that frequently the fastest cars, from a slow start or other temporary delay, gets off in the rear without chances of ever gaining the front on account of continuous seas of dust and skidding cars ahead that would make it too dangerous to attempt to pass. This condition would not exist on a 3 or 5-mile track.

To the spectators there is very little enjoyment in seeing a 25 or 50-mile road race, where immense crowds throng the course and where only fleeting glimpses can be had of the cars as they come and go down the road. There is no accommodation for the public in a race of

this kind, and the thousands of dollars spent in advertising and for special privileges that go to private individuals could well come into the purse of the management of a 3 or 5-mile track. The American manufacturers annually spend thousands of dollars in building high speed racing cars to compete with French cars and without possible chance of winning, and I think this is largely due to the fact that American drivers do not have a chance to thoroughly test their cars continuously at high speed for weak spots in construction, or to become entirely familiar with and have their car under perfect control at very high speeds.

There is no question in my mind that it takes weeks and months of practice handling a car at 75, 80 and 90 miles an hour to be able to properly gauge distances, numerous road conditions, and the response of the car to such conditions. It has been my experience that quite a number of racing cars, when tested over the best roads we had in this country, seemed to have wonderful speed. There was no accurate way to time them for any distance, and the best anybody could do was to guess at what the cars were doing.

It seems to me a 5-mile track, properly laid out, without fences to endanger drivers, with proper grandstands, supply stores for gasoline and oil, and other accommodations would net for one meet such as the Vanderbilt cup race a sufficient amount to pay half of the entire cost of the track. With the present record at 52 seconds on a mile track, I am confident a 3-mile track 100 feet wide will stand a speed of 100 miles an hour, and that a 5-mile track will stand a speed of 2 miles a minute.

In diagrams I have seen of a 5-mile track it is possible at any point of the curve to see in a direct line 800 feet ahead, and a curve of this kind, when gradual and continuous, is not nearly so severe as some of the short, choppy curves at Ormond beach, where a speed of 2 miles a minute was made by a couple of the contestants in the meet in the south last winter. – C. G. Fisher.

While he obviously meant "circumference" in the opening paragraph instead of "diameter," and he fell a little short of the mark with his prediction that one-mile tracks were "doomed," the letter clearly proves that such a track had been on his mind as early as 1903. It is interesting, also, that even in 1906, at a time when the recognized world record for the flying mile was just under 110 mph, Fisher was already suggesting the potential of a car being able to lap a circular five-mile track at 10 mph faster than that.

The mention of "the track at French Lick" refers to a proposed venture with Tom Taggart, an Irish-born former mayor of

Indianapolis who owned quite a bit of land at the famed southern-Indiana resort. While Taggart thought it would serve as an excellent added attraction, and it is certainly possible that Fisher and Taggart received negative response from the locals and the more conservative sometime guests, it was the futility of trying to build on the fairly hilly terrain in that neck of the woods which brought months of planning to an end.

The consideration given at around the same time to utilizing the handily located Indiana State Fairgrounds no doubt came after several of the various tests held on the one-mile track there as early as 1903, the downside being, as Fisher states in his letter, that he was striving for at least a three-mile track, whereas no more than two miles would fit onto the available land.

The point is that all of these conclusions had been arrived at long before Brooklands was even started, let alone completed.

It is most interesting that Fisher and Locke–King, who came from different parts of the world and from such vastly different upbringings, should both come to the same conclusion at approximately the same time. Locke–King and his wife had attended some early motor-racing events on the Continent and had been dismayed at the poor showing of the British teams against the Europeans. He determined that with Britain's very restrictive speed limits and its narrow and twisting roads, not to mention a complete lack of any testing venue, there was no opportunity for the development of automobiles of the quality he had seen demonstrated by the French, Germans, and Italians.

But whereas Locke–King had the wherewithal to underwrite the project himself, Fisher, while well on his way to becoming exceedingly wealthy, needed some help.

Fisher was born in Greensburg, Indiana, a rural town some 80 miles southeast of Indianapolis, not far from the borders of Kentucky and Ohio. His father, a lawyer, is said to have had difficulty with alcohol and ended up leaving Mrs. Fisher and their three sons. As the oldest, Carl found himself effectively the head of the household at about the age of 12. His mother took in sewing and eventually moved the family to Indianapolis, where Carl learned the basics of earning a living. He started out in a grocery store but soon began hopping on trains to shine shoes and sell newspapers and candy. He added further items, was taken into the confidence of men many years his senior, and later graduated to selling

"naughty" postcards to those he knew he could trust. The tips were good.

In spite of extremely poor eyesight, he was quite athletic. He had a penchant for speed and became drawn in by the bicycle craze which began to sweep America in the late 1880s. While the "high wheels," similar in appearance to "penny farthings," were popular for touring, pure racing bikes were starting to come into vogue. Carl obtained a bicycle and began to engage in competition. In 1891, the Fisher brothers opened a repair shop, and just a short time later, they moved to another location at 112 North Pennsylvania Street, just one block from the city center. Never one to miss an opportunity, Carl would show up to compete at a race meet, bringing along with him an assortment of spare frames, chains, and other parts for sale to his colleagues.

Still only in his teens, Fisher traveled to Columbus, Ohio, where he managed to talk manufacturer George C. Erland into providing him with bicycles on consignment. He was able to do the same thing in Toledo with the renowned Colonel Albert Pope.

Main photograph: Although frequently identified as Carl Fisher, this is, in fact, Lewis Strang, who was destined to start from the pole in the first Indianapolis 500, held more than two years after this photograph was taken in March, 1909. Strang, on his way to participating in an event at Savannah, Georgia, stopped off to visit the work in progress. The scale model of the track was displayed right next to the Georgetown Pike (now West 16th Street) outside of turn two, approximately the location of the parking lot for the Brickyard Crossing Golf Resort and Inn (formerly the Speedway Motel).
Photograph: IMS

An organization known as the Zig-Zag Cycling Club was actually much larger and more prestigious than it sounded, and it included among its membership some of the city's most influential citizens. Many became longtime associates of Fisher, and it is fascinating to learn just "who knew who, when." There was an extraordinary crossover in the early days of the automobile industry, bicycles, motorcycles, powerboats, and aviation, many of the same names on the business side and in engineering continuously cropping up as if everybody had a connection with everybody else.

The Zig-Zag club was founded on August 8, 1890, by Arthur Newby, destined to become one of Fisher's partners in the Indianapolis Motor Speedway venture. A onetime office boy at Nordyke & Marmon, Newby eventually became that firm's bookkeeper. He later left to help start a business called the Indianapolis Stamping Company, a manufacturer of bicycle parts and chains. He also ran a bicycle shop located within walking distance of Fisher's. A great advocate of bicycle racing, Newby is credited with having created the then extremely popular six-day events.

In 1898, very possibly at Fisher's urging, Newby opened up a 15,000-seat, quarter-mile, steeply banked wooden velodrome north of town, close to what eventually became 30th Street and Central Avenue. The League of American Wheelmen booked its national convention there in July of that year.

One of the riders against whom Fisher was regularly competing during these days was a friend from Cleveland, Ohio, named Berna Eli Oldfield, who later graduated from bicycles, took up smoking cigars, and allowed his given name to develop into "Barney."

The bicycle craze was already winding down by this point, and Newby closed down his oval at the end of 1899. He and his partners then sold the Indianapolis Stamping Company to the American Bicycle Company, where it was later reorganized

as the enormously successful Diamond Chain Company.

Newby's attention had turned to the National Automobile & Electric Company, of which he was a director, and which was to be reorganized in 1904 as the National Motor Vehicle Company, with himself as president.

Fisher quickly went from bicycles to motorized tricycles to automobiles and a brief attempt at becoming a racing driver. He spent a couple of summers racing at county fair dirt-track programs, and engaging in an endeavor known as "barnstorming." This involved visiting country fairs and participating on a half-mile horse track in a series of short events which may not necessarily have been completely aboveboard. He would agree, for a fee, to show up and engage in "best-of-three" one-lap contests against a horse or an aircraft. Because he had control of the throttle, it was up to him to gauge the closeness of the finishes.

The absolute master at this was his old friend Barney Oldfield, a flamboyant showman who went on to amass a fortune out of such escapades. Three or four of them would show up as a "troupe," complete with an aircraft, and astonish the crowd with their bravery. More often than not, the aircraft would be flown by another friend, the famed stunt pilot, Lincoln Beachey. At the end of the day, the more affluent in the crowd would be offered flights by Beachey and "hot laps" around the dirt oval by Fisher and Oldfield, Carl pointing out at the conclusion that he also *sold* such vehicles.

Hampered by his poor eyesight, Fisher did not stay with it very long. He did pursue "serious" motorsport briefly – and even powerboat racing – but after traveling to the Gordon Bennett trials in France in 1905 as a potential relief driver for the Pope–Toledo team, and having an Indianapolis-built Premier end up being too heavy to meet the requirements for the elimination trials for the 1905 Vanderbilt Cup on Long Island, he decided to retire.

By this time, he was well on his way to becoming a very

wealthy man. About a year earlier, one day in 1904, a life-changing opportunity came to him in the form of an inventor named Percy C. Avery. There are two or three conflicting versions of how and where Fisher and Avery first met, but the result is that a partnership was formed.

One of the many not-yet-solved problems of early-day motoring was how to illuminate sufficiently the way at night. No light had yet been developed, safely, that would enable a motorist to clearly see the road ahead. Avery believed he had a solution. He produced a cylinder containing carbide gas, and when a lighted match was held to a pair of tiny jets at one end, just above a valve, a bright white light was produced by the fed gas.

Fisher was typically enthusiastic and could see the potential. Avery, having exhausted all of his available capital, needed backing. Fisher explained that much of his money was "tied up" at the moment but that he had a friend whom he believed would be interested in becoming involved.

That friend was James A. Allison.

A native of Marcellus, Michigan, Jim Allison was the proprietor of the Indianapolis-based Allison's Perfect Fountain Pens, as well as a printing concern, the Allison Coupon Company, which over the years was to produce coupons and rolls of tickets by the millions. Allison, too, had been a member of Newby's Zig-Zag Cycling Club. Although quite a bit different in nature, Fisher and Allison had become good friends. While Fisher was constantly hatching ideas and jumping from project to project with unbridled boyish enthusiasm, Allison was much more cautious in his approach and insiders felt that he was the ideal stabilizing force in their various partnerships. While Fisher would put his arm around an associate's shoulder and exclaim, "If only I had your education," Allison would prefer to stand at a distance.

The gigantic Allison Engineering Company, which would eventually become one of America's most famous entities, was not yet even a gleam in Jim Allison's eye.

While a lot less demonstrative than Fisher, Allison was nevertheless suitably impressed by Avery's invention. They listened to Avery's reasoning that the sum of $5,000 should be sufficient for starting up a company, and Fisher and Allison are understood to have immediately pledged $1,000 apiece. On September 6, 1904, the three men formed the Concentrated Acetylene Company, officially recorded six days later as having $10,000 of capital stock.

A catchy name was sought for the product, and based on an exclamation Fisher is reported to have made upon the initial demonstration they agreed to call it Prest-O-Lite.

The men acquired a shed at the corner of 28th and Pennsylvania streets, and with just one assistant to begin with, Avery went to work. Several moves were made in quick succession as the business expanded, eventually to the creation of a fair-sized factory at 211 East South Street, immediately south of the Union Station railroad terminal. There were plenty of trials and tribulations, not the least of which was the occasional explosion. It was here on June 6, 1908, that an enormous blast rocked the surrounding area. After reports that a number of frightened patients had fallen from their beds in the old St. Vincent's Hospital at the corner of Delaware and South streets and that the contents of several vats in a nearby sauerkraut factory had been dumped over the workers, the city fathers requested that Fisher and Allison find a new location outside of the city limits. Before long, they had set up a plant on the banks of White River, a little southwest of the city.

With distractions like that, it was easy to see why Fisher's plan for a "motor parkway" kept getting pushed aside.

Fisher had another friend and business associate named Lem Trotter, who was very much involved in real estate and local politics. According to Trotter (who died in May 1966 at the age of 96), he and Fisher took a trip by automobile to Dayton, Ohio, one autumn day in 1908. On the return journey, yet another punctured tire forced them to the side of the road in the little village of Dublin, Indiana, very close to the birthplace of Wilbur Wright, the Dayton resident whose inaugural powered flight with his brother had taken place less than five years earlier.

Fisher, who was known to blaspheme as a matter of course during a regular conversation, began cursing and swearing about the state of the roads, the quality of the tires, the quality of the automobiles and everything else in general.

Paraphrasing Trotter's version, Fisher went on to elaborate how his proposed track would help solve all of these problems. Trotter, equally plain-speaking, rejoined that since Carl had been *talking* about it so much over the previous few years, why didn't he simply go ahead and *do* it. Fisher replied that if the right property were to be available, then, by golly, he would.

The puncture was fixed, and the two friends pressed on back to Indianapolis.

A day or two later, Trotter arrived at Fisher's office and suggested they go for a ride. He had something to show Fisher which he thought might be of interest. They left the city limits

Above: **Arthur Newby: Fisher associate from the bicycle days, and philanthropist extraordinaire.**
Photograph: IMS

Main photograph: Now resurfaced with
street paving bricks, the track is as it will be
for the next 25 years. The steeper-banked
ten-foot "outer lip" will be removed after
the 1935 race, and a second wall, placed at
a 90-degree angle to the nine-degree angle
of the remaining banking, will be placed in
front of this existing wall, which is at a 90-
degree angle to the ground.
Photograph: IMS

Above: The only known photograph of the
four original owners together, very likely
taken on the morning of the inaugural
"500" on May 30, 1911, shows, left to
right, Arthur Newby, Frank Wheeler, Carl
Fisher, and James Allison. Their
personalities definitely come forth.
Photograph: IMS

via the northwest edge and motored west through the countryside for about five miles until they arrived at the corner of the Crawfordsville Pike and a little cart track that would eventually become Georgetown Road. They were surrounded by farmland. The Crawfordsville Pike turned gently at that point and continued on, slightly northwest, off into the distance. Alongside of it ran a railroad which was part of the Ben Hur traction line, headed for Crawfordsville. A glance in the opposite direction revealed that the tracks went straight downtown, southeast to Union Station. The pair pulled up next to the little station located on the south side of the corner – a stop for the local farming community – and Trotter proudly pointed across the way, telling Fisher, "This farmland is for sale."

What they were looking at was four adjoining 80-acre tracts, relatively flat and measuring approximately one mile from north to south and a half mile from east to west. Presumably roamed at one time by Indians, it had been referred to for years by the locals as "the old Pressley farm."

Trotter suggested that the main entrance could be erected right on the corner and that the many potential spectators not arriving on foot, on horseback, or by automobile could easily be transported to and from downtown by train.

Fisher needed little convincing.

The next thing was to establish a price and arrange for the purchase. As it turned out, there were two owners involved. Daniel Chenoweth, an insurance executive, owned three of the four tracts, which he agreed to sell for $200 per acre, a total of $48,000. Unfortunately, this did not include the 80-acre tract on the corner. This belonged to Kevi Munter, the owner of a downtown livery stable. Mr. Munter either was a little hard-nosed, or got wind of what was being proposed for his 80 acres, or both, but $200 per acre was not enough for him.

He wanted $300.

And he eventually got it.

A substantial amount of money had to be raised, and Fisher knew he could not do it alone. There was the matter of $72,000 to purchase the property, plus a great deal more for the building of the track.

He excitedly shared the news with his cronies, and legend has it that he drew a sketch of what he had in mind in pencil, either on a Pop Haynes napkin or a tablecloth. After determining that $250,000 should be the goal, it didn't take long for him to line up four friends who were willing to join him in putting up $50,000 apiece. Allison was one, and Arthur Newby was another.

The other two were Frank Wheeler and Stoughton Fletcher, although the latter was not a partner for long. Fletcher was a member of a well-known local banking family of many years' standing, and its conservative approach did not encompass being involved in anything so frivolous as a racetrack. Within a matter of days, "Stoat," as they called him, had to tell his friends, with his tail between his legs, that while the various loans they had discussed would still be approved, his family had strongly suggested that he *not* be personally involved.

Iowa-born Frank Wheeler was probably more like Fisher than the other two partners, although he was described as bluff. While everyone else called Newby either "Art" or "A.C.," to Wheeler he was merely "Newby." He was fairly outgoing and flamboyant, with an aptitude for sales. His fortunes are said to have risen and fallen on several occasions, and he happened to be riding high when the track project presented itself. He was George Schebler's partner in the now hugely successful Wheeler–Schebler Carburetor Company, Schebler being the reserved inventor/engineer who once built musical instruments, Wheeler the freewheeling gambler with the finances.

As further evidence of just how everybody seemed to be involved with everybody else, Wheeler and Schebler had been brought together by a mutual friend who was aware Schebler needed a financial partner. That friend was Harry C. Stutz, who was still several years away from creating the legendary Stutz Motor Company.

Before they had time to either find someone to take up Fletcher's share, or else up the ante to $62,500 each, Fisher determined that the whole job could be completed for a mere $220,000. With $36,000 borrowed against the land from Fletcher's bank, it was now necessary to raise only $46,000 each. Allison and Wheeler agreed to this, but Newby had second thoughts and asked to hold his involvement to $25,000. It ended up that Fisher and Allison split the balance of Newby's share between them, thus becoming the senior partners.

It was an interesting quartet, Fisher and Wheeler being outgoing while Allison and Newby were much more reserved. It has been suggested that Allison did not care for Wheeler. Newby, who was never in the best of health, lived a quiet life and never married. He was kindly and extremely philanthropic, giving away, without fanfare during his lifetime, several million dollars.

The land was purchased in mid-December of 1908, and on December 12, the local newspapers revealed the plans for the "Indiana Motor Parkway." By the time the Indianapolis Motor Speedway Company had officially been formed on March 20, 1909—there had been a delay of the intended February 8 filing – Fisher's original plan had been slightly modified. Still seeking the five-mile track he had always strived for, the first plan here was for a three-mile rectangular-shaped oval, inside of which would be a two-mile road course, which when linked up with the oval would produce a five-mile lap. When included, the road course would require making a tight left turn shortly after entering the backstretch and then twisting and turning through the infield for two miles, eventually returning to the backstretch just a few yards further to the north of where the exit had taken place.

Clearly, Fisher imagined presenting races which would rival the Vanderbilt Cup on Long Island and the American Grand Prize in Savannah, or perhaps even *landing* those very prestigious events.

P. T. Andrews, the civil engineer from New York who was hired to oversee the project, soon came back to report that the dimensions Fisher sought could certainly be achieved, but at a price.

Andrews commenced his task – legend has it – by drawing, to scale, a one-mile circle on a piece of cardboard. He then cut out the circle, divided it into quarters, and laid the four pieces on a map of the property, pushing them to each corner and finishing up by drawing in the straights. A three-mile

"outer" track was certainly attainable, but the outer edges of the straights would be pushed so close to the perimeters of the property that there would be no room for grandstands. By reducing the length of each of the straights and pulling the "corners" closer together, Andrews suggested, a track of 2½ miles instead would fit perfectly.

And so it was.

Under the direction of the King Brothers of Montezuma, Indiana, grading began around the end of March. This included the road-course section – now increased to 2½ miles in order to still achieve the five-mile total – but because of a variety of difficulties with the oval, it was soon abandoned.

There was one other piece of engineering which required time and expense.

A creek ran through the southwestern portion of the property, and because of the size of the oval, it was necessary to build two bridges to span it.

To this very day, the creek runs underneath Georgetown Road, about 350 yards north of West 16th Street, then immediately enters the Speedway grounds, briefly turning south and then east again, at which point it flows beneath the main straight just at the entrance to turn one. It then heads south once more and continues on around the inside of the turn, arcing back to the east as it goes, before heading south yet again, this time leaving the grounds by flowing out under the south "short chute."

It presented quite a challenge for the engineers at the time, but the challenge was met, and virtually a full century later the creek is still there, flowing unobtrusively under the track at those same two points.

Construction was underway, but it soon became obvious that Fisher's proposed opening date of July 4 for automobile racing was a little on the ambitious side. But just because the 2½-mile track wasn't going to be ready by that time, it didn't mean there couldn't be some *other* form of competition.

Above: **Frank Wheeler: Always willing to take a chance, he is said to have made and lost more than one fortune.**

Below: **The original plan was to link an infield road course with the oval, giving the potential of a five-mile track. Difficulties with the surface of the oval placed the road course concept on hold... for about 90 years.**
Photographs: IMS

Indianapolis Motor Speedway.
The Greatest Race Course in the World.

1909: Competition begins... with a balloon race

On top of all of his numerous other time-consuming activities, the tireless Fisher had founded the Aero Club of Indiana a few months earlier and had immediately begun taking balloon-ascension lessons from George Bumbaugh. Fisher is believed to have been only the 21st person in the United States to qualify as a balloon pilot. Now envisioning the track as a proving ground for aviation as well as for automobiles, he had gone to considerable lengths and expenditure to outbid several cities for the honor of hosting the Aero Club of America's U.S. National Balloon Championships.

Thus on Saturday, June 5, 1909, the Indianapolis Motor Speedway presented its first competitive event.

Ever the showman, and wanting visitors to be suitably impressed on the journey out to the track from downtown, Fisher had pledged to foot the bill himself for the cost of laying oil on the dirt-based Georgetown Pike in return for the farmers agreeing to plant shade trees and apply white paint to their wooden picket fences.

The balloon race was a great success from a publicity point of view and it drew a huge crowd. Many problems were caused, however, by the fact that the majority of those in attendance were not actually on the property. While somewhere between 3,500 and 4,000 dutifully paid the admission at either the $1.00 gate or the 50-cent gate, at least ten times that many reasoned that the greater part of a balloon ascent could be witnessed from *outside* the grounds.

Indiana Governor Thomas R. Marshall, who four years later would be serving as vice-president of the United States, was due to participate in the ceremonial sendoff. Unfortunately, the traffic was so horribly entangled on the Georgetown Pike that he was obliged to park his vehicle about a mile away on a farmer's property and complete the balance of his journey on foot. He was still gamely trudging across the fields when, at shortly before 4:00 P.M., his heart sank. Off in the western sky, he could see the first balloons departing.

A total of nine gas-filled balloons participated, six qualifying for the National Championship, and the three which did not being given a handicap event of their own. Bumbaugh and Fisher drew the largest cheer when their *Indiana* rose into the air, adorned with six American flags attached to the webbing and with Fisher dropping red roses on the crowd as the balloon floated over them.

Dr. Goethe Link and Russ Irvin of Indianapolis won the handicap division by making it down to Westmoreland, Tennessee, a distance of 235 miles, by 11 o'clock the following morning. It took a little while longer to determine the winner of the National Championship, mainly because the final landing points were not a fair indication of the exact distance the changing winds had carried each contestant. Several had landed after finding themselves being carried back north and seeing landmarks they had passed over hours earlier. It was finally determined that *University City,* a St. Louis entry, was the winner, 61-year-old John Berry and his aide, Paul McCullough, having covered a zigzagging 382 miles on their way to Fort Payne, Alabama.

Fisher and Bumbaugh ended up fourth.

In the meantime, there were serious problems with the track surface.

It had been decided to use a mixture of crushed stone or powdered rock and what was variously described as tar, macadam and asphaltum oil. This was a combination which was being employed more and more for the paving of public roads, although *not,* as Fisher would point out with a dig at every opportunity, in Indiana. But while reasonably acceptable for the latter, it would soon prove to be totally inadequate for the rigorous punishment inflicted by competition. A leisurely drive on city streets or out in the countryside was one thing. A powerful, wheel-spinning vehicle, clawing to gain traction, and slipping and sliding through turns as fast as it could go, was quite another.

The weather was not cooperating either. Throughout June and July, it seemed as if it was either pouring with rain, or else was so hot and muggy that the surface would refuse to harden, remaining for much of the time as a sea of spongy and sticky goo.

With the July 4 program cancelled, the new schedule called for a series of motorcycle races to be held on Friday and Saturday, August 13 and 14, followed a week later by three days of automobile racing.

On Friday, August 6, a number of riders and officials, on their way to an event in Cleveland, Ohio, stopped by to look the place over. They were not impressed. The riders had hoped to take a few laps, but the facility was far from ready. They departed with Fisher assuring them that plenty of practice time would be available to them the following Thursday.

Main photograph: An aircraft is still such a curiosity in 1910 (the first powered flight having taken place only six and a half years earlier) that many of the people flocking around this one, parked on IMS's main straight, have never been so close to one before.

Below: The first competitive event ever held at the track is the U.S. National Championship for gas-filled balloons, held on June 5, 1909.
Photographs: IMS

Motorcycles... on a surface of crushed rock and tar

The motorcycle races were to conclude a four-day-long convention of the Federation of American Motorcyclists, expected to draw several hundred members to the city for a variety of activities and meetings. All of motorcycling's leading officials and supporters would be in attendance.

Came Thursday, August 12, and further problems resulted in the track not being ready until late in the afternoon. Ed Lingenfelder, one of motorcycle racing's leading riders, took a few practice laps but was not happy when he returned. The track was abrasive and the riders expressed concern that blown tires would result in many injuries. There were even pleas to move the races to the one-mile dirt track at the Indiana State Fairgrounds, but officials agreed to give Fisher a chance to work out the problems.

Race day, ominous Friday the 13th, came and went, but not a wheel was to turn, the two-day program being postponed to Saturday and Monday.

It hadn't taken long for the management of the Indianapolis Motor Speedway to experience its first rainout!

Saturday dawned clear, but no sooner had practice commenced than the surface began causing further problems. Riders would return from runs covered with white powdered dust. Oil would be applied to the surface in an attempt to settle the dust and the next practice session would conclude with riders coming in covered with oil.

The races got underway, but with several modifications to the order of the day. The 10-event program was reduced to eight, and even then, few of them went as planned. Many riders would either decline to start an event, or else pull in well before its conclusion.

After yet another delay, caused by the refusal of many riders to come out for one of the events, a little psychology was used on two leading riders, resulting in an "East–West" championship match race between Ed Lingenfelder, a Californian, and colorful Jake de Rosier, a Springfield, Massachusetts, rider who wore red tights and had an American flag stitched to his back. They battled virtually side by side for almost two of the scheduled four laps, until just before the conclusion of the halfway point, when, in full view of the sparse audience on the main straight, de Rosier's front tire blew, wrapping itself around the forks and sending him flying over the handle-

bars to land on his back. Lingenfelder soloed to win.

The seventh event of the day turned out to be the last. The officials announced that not only would the 10-lap, 25-mile professional championship *not* be held, but that they would be cancelling the balance of the event and not returning on Monday.

And that, for the time being, was the end of motorcycle racing at the Indianapolis Motor Speedway.

There was one interesting footnote concerning the day's events. The final race held, the 10-mile FAM amateur championship, was won by the Springfield, Massachusetts-built Indian of local rider Erwin G. Baker. He would later gain considerable notoriety by setting numerous records for crossing the country in passenger cars in ever-decreasing elapsed times, causing an impressed New York newspaperman in 1914 to give him the nickname "Cannonball."

Above: The motorcycle races, planned as a two-day event for August 13–14, are postponed by rain and then cancelled completely before the conclusion of the first day, due to the track conditions.
Photograph: IMS

Main photo: Ray Harroun "hot laps" with the single-seat Marmon "Wasp" he helped to design, approximately five miles from the track. By race day, 1911, the famous rear-view mirror will be in place.
Photograph: IMS

Above: An entrant in the 1909 motorcycle races, as well as all of the pre-"500" automobile events, Charlie Merz competed in four 500-Mile Races between 1911 and 1916, served as chief steward (1935-39) and was briefly Speedway's assistant general manager in 1940. A company he started, Merz Engineering, sponsored cars in the "500" between 1950 and 1955.
Photographs: IMS

Bring on the automobiles

Less than a week after the motorcycles, it was time for the automobiles to take over. A full program of 18 events was planned over the three-day period, a series of short races to be held each day with a much longer event to wind up the proceedings.

Needless to say, all events were conducted on the oval, the planned infield road course now all but forgotten.

Practice periods were conducted on Tuesday and Wednesday, and it wasn't long before the Chadwick of Len Zengle got around in two minutes and two seconds. On Wednesday, Barney Oldfield took out the mighty Blitzen Benz and was the first to beat two minutes, turning a lap in 1:58 for an average speed of 76.2 mph.

Every one of the 65 cars entered for the various events made practice laps, but the problems of the previous week still had not yet been solved. During one session it would be so dusty that the drivers would hardly be able to see where they were going. During the next, after spirited attempts to lay the dust, they would come in covered from head to toe with oil and tar. Not only that, but several drivers and riding mechanics would return from runs with broken goggles, plus cuts and gashes from jagged rocks hurled back from churning wheels in front of them.

The center part of the track was in reasonable shape, hav-

ing been fairly evenly covered over with tar and oil, and then packed down by numerous passes with heavy rollers. But an excursion too far either to the left or right was cause for considerable concern, because the surface would make an unpleasant transition into an uneven pile of boulder-like rocks.

On the positive side, there was plenty of good publicity in the form of support from all three of the local newspapers, *The Indianapolis Star* publishing, on its front page, a thrilling account by one of its reporters, who told of having been driven around on several "hot laps" at about 60 mph by Buick team driver Bob Burman. This was especially noteworthy for the time considering that the reporter was a *lady*, Betty Blythe.

Thursday, August 19, arrived and crowds began to file into the Speedway. Every few minutes, another train from downtown would drop people off at the depot directly across from the main entrance, just as Lem Trotter had envisioned the year before. There was infield parking space set aside to accommodate 10,000 automobiles, and in recognition of the fact that not everybody had yet adapted to the automotive age, there were no less than 3,000 hitching posts in place for those who arrived on horseback or by horse-drawn vehicle.

The proceedings began promptly at noon, with five cars taking off to contest a two-lap, five-mile, standing-start dash for cars of stock chassis, powered by engines measuring between 161 and 230 cubic inches. The winner, in a time of

Inset left: Approximately 3,200,000 street paving bricks (weighing about 9½ pounds each) are laid down in the autumn of 1909, the majority being Culver Blocks from the Wabash Clay Company in Veedersburg, Indiana. Many of them are still there to this day, beneath several layers of asphalt.
Photograph: IMS

five minutes, 18.40 seconds, was a Stoddard–Dayton, driven by Austrian-born Louis Schwitzer, who would later gain quite a reputation as an industrialist, and who would serve for several years as the Technical Chairman for the Indianapolis 500-Mile Race.

Of the three other "short" races, two were won by drivers who were on their way to becoming exceedingly well known. Louis Chevrolet, then a driver/engineer for Buick, won a four-lap, 10-mile dash for cars of between 231 and 300 cubic inches, while Ray Harroun, who would make history in less than two years' time, was the victor in a four-lap "free-for-all" handicap event.

The third winner did not fare so well. The huge Knox of Wilfred "Billy" Bourque beat Buick drivers Louis Chevrolet and Bob Burman in a two-lap dash for cars of between 301 and 450 cubic inches, but poor Bourque did not have long to cherish his victory. Sadly, he did not even make it through the same afternoon.

Just past the halfway mark of the featured 250-mile race for the Prest-O-Lite trophy, Bourque spun out of turn four, hit an infield ditch, flipped over several times, and ended up hitting a fence post. Bourque and his luckless riding mechanic, Harry Holcomb, both perished.

It was nearly 7:00 P.M. when Burman was flagged in as the winner, the race having taken almost four hours and 40 minutes to run. Officials of the Contest Board of the American Automobile Association, sanctioning body for the events, threatened to cancel the final two days because of the deteriorating surface, but once again, the persuasive Fisher was able to talk them out of it.

Although there were more races on the second day than there had been on the first – eight – the program was concluded by 5:30 P.M., largely due to the main event having been for only 100 miles. Thankfully, there were no injuries. Several drivers made attempts at what was announced as "the world's record" for the flying mile. The Blitzen Benz of Barney Oldfield flew through it in 43 1/10 seconds, a speed of 83.5 mph.

A huge crowd turned out for the third and final day, the feature being a 300-mile marathon for the enormous, seven-and-a-half-foot-tall Wheeler–Schebler trophy, which Frank Wheeler had commissioned from Tiffany's. Crafted out of silver, it was said to have cost Wheeler's company $10,000.

The day began with attempts at breaking the "world's" record for the flying kilometer. Walter Christie, of front-drive fame, posted a time of 29 7/10 seconds, but he was clearly upstaged by the colorful Oldfield, who clamped down on his cigar and thundered through the kilometer with his Benz in 26 2/10 seconds to claim the record at 86.5 mph.

The maximum cubic-inch displacement for the Wheeler–Schebler contest was a very generous 600 cid, and many top names came out for it. In addition to Oldfield, Chevrolet, Burman, and Harroun, there were Herb Lytle and Lewis Strang (Walter Christie's nephew), plus future stars Johnny Aitken, Charlie Merz, and Ralph de Palma.

The race did not go the full distance.

At 175 miles, young Charlie Merz, driving a National, had his right front tire blow as he was negotiating turn one. He crashed through the outer fencing and into an area where several spectators were standing. The car came to rest within just a matter of feet of where the creek flows out beneath the track.

Merz escaped, but his riding mechanic did not, and neither did two of the spectators.

There was some confusion at first over the identity of the riding mechanic. Thought to be Herb Lyme, it turned out to be Claude Kellum, who had been mechanic for Merz's teammate, Johnny Aitken. Earlier in the race, Merz had been forced to stop on the backstretch with a dead battery. Lyme then ran through the infield to the pits to get a replacement and was so exhausted when he arrived that Kellum, now at leisure due to Aitken's car already being out for the day, was pressed into service to make the fateful return trip.

No sooner had the Merz disaster struck at the south end of the track than the Marmon of Bruce Keen hit a pedestrian bridge at the north end and turned upside down.

The race had already been going on for almost four and a quarter hours and still had another 65 miles remaining.

Even while the AAA officials were meeting to discuss halting the race, Fisher, Allison, Newby, and Wheeler were doing the same. All were in agreement, and the crusty, outspoken starter, Fred "Pop" Wagner, brought it to an end by waving the checkered flag.

Leigh Lynch was declared the winner for the Jackson Motor Car Company, but controversy would reign for several weeks over whether or not the Michigan firm had any claim to the trophy, since the race had not gone the full distance.

Wagner, who was frequently to butt heads with Fisher, told the partners that AAA would be sanctioning no further events until the problem of the deteriorating surface had been solved.

Emergency meetings were quickly held and it was obvious that something had to be done. Several new surfaces were considered, including concrete, but the latter was dismissed because of the anticipated problem of constant patching after the inevitable winter freezes.

Down go the bricks

After much consideration, it was decided to accept the recommendation of the National Paving Brick Manufacturers Association and resurface the track with street-paving bricks. Contact was made with the Wabash Clay Company in Veedersburg, Indiana, located about a dozen miles this side of the Illinois border, and on September 18, two rail-car loads of bricks were unloaded by workmen at the station across the street and transported over to the track by horse and cart. A layer of sand was spread on top of the existing surface, into which were placed a few hundred bricks, laid on their sides, staggered in rows and separated on each side by about a

Inset above: It was "Happy" Johnny Aitken, the first person ever to lead the "500," who conducted the vigorous tests on the first portion of bricks and mortar laid down in September 1909. The winning pit manager for Joe Dawson in 1912 and Jules Goux in 1913, Aitken was vice president of the infant Allison Engineering concern when he died on October 15, 1918, a victim of the influenza epidemic.

Inset top: Bob Burman, one of the more successful drivers in the pre-"500" events of 1909–10, took part in the first five 500-Mile Races. His run of 141.732 mph on the sands of Daytona Beach, Florida, on April 27, 1911, was claimed by the Americans as the World Land Speed Record for the flying mile.
Photographs: IMS

quarter of an inch. They were actually designed to lie face-to-face, but in this case it was agreed that a much stronger surface could be obtained by placing them slightly apart and then pouring mortar between them.

Once the section was completed, several tests were conducted by National's Aitken in an attempt to disturb the surface. After making a series of aggressive standing starts, his colleagues then drove a couple of poles into the ground, anchored them in cement, and then ran ropes from the front axle back to the poles. For the next several minutes, the air was filled with the acrid smell of burning rubber as Aitken held down the accelerator, the car's rear end swaying from side to side as the spinning wheels hopelessly tried to gain traction. When upon inspection no damage appeared to have been inflicted, the Wabash Valley officials were given the word to prepare for an order numbering around three and a half million bricks.

As it turned out, due to the narrow strip of mortar being inserted every three or so inches, the total number required ended up being "only" 3,200,000. Nevertheless, it was quite an order to fill, and while the company was normally producing about one million per month and might have twice that many in stock at any one time, *three* million was a little beyond them. They subcontracted with several neighboring firms, but the estimate is that approximately 90 percent of the bricks used were Culver Blocks, bearing the wording, "Pat May 21, 1901," which refers to the date on which Ruben Culver's patent was granted, rather than the date on which they were cast.

The rate at which the bricks were laid was truly impressive, the entire job being completed in only 63 days. The report was that on one day, 140,000 were laid during a 24-hour period, the average being well over 50,000 per day. By the time the job was completed on December 10, the nickname "The Brickyard" had already been coined by the locals.

One week later, on a freezing-cold December 17, Governor Marshall was back to participate in the dedication ceremonies, this time there being no traffic jams to impede his arrival. One of his duties was to lay the final brick, the publicity staff claiming it to be solid gold. Although it weighed a hefty 52 pounds, it was later revealed to be gold-plated *brass,* the brass having been obtained from a melted-down Wheeler–Schebler carburetor.

It was far too cold to reasonably conduct any races, although an eight-lap "free-for-all" was attempted. Seven hardy souls tried it and Johnny Aitken, wearing a balaclava helmet borrowed from a boy spectator, completed the distance, frozen to the marrow in 16 minutes, 18.41 seconds. His average speed was 73.59 mph.

Lewis Strang was by far the fastest of those who braved the cold. The following day being a couple of degrees warmer, he powered his enormous 120-horsepower Fiat through the flying quarter mile at an amazing 111.8 mph. He turned a complete lap at 91.81 mph and made two consecutive laps at an average speed of 91.04 mph.

1910: A summer of speed on the Brickyard... and in the air

An ambitious schedule was announced for 1910, including a trio of three-day meets of automobile racing over the holiday weekends of Memorial Day, July 4, and Labor Day, plus a week-long aviation meet in June and even a 24-hour race scheduled to commence on August 12. The latter was never held, being cancelled on July 4.

The Memorial Day weekend program called for 10 events on Friday, May 27, seven on Saturday, and 14 more on Monday. The longest were to be the 100-mile Prest-O-Lite race on Friday and the Wheeler–Schebler event, now reduced to 200 miles, on Saturday.

The new surface held up and the meeting was a huge success. About 25,000 people showed up on Saturday, and on Monday there were an estimated 50,000, many of them making their way to the infield because every available seat in the grandstands had been taken. Other than veteran Herb Lytle breaking his left leg on day two, there were no injuries to speak of. Barney Oldfield blazed through the flying mile in 35.63 seconds for an average speed of 101.04 mph and track records fell left, right, and center.

The big winners were Ray Harroun, who claimed both the Wheeler–Schebler trophy and the Remy Grand Brassard for Marmon; Tommy Kincade, the 100-mile Prest-O-Lite race for National; and Bob Burman, the five-mile Speedway Helmet dash for Buick. Following Harroun in the Wheeler–Schebler contest were 1909 winner Lynch on a Jackson, Aitken on a National, and Louis Chevrolet's brother, Arthur, on a Buick.

Fisher, Allison, Newby, and Wheeler could finally relax.

But not for long.

Only two weeks later came aviation week, kicking off on Monday, June 13. The main talking point this time was the presence of several aircraft brought over from Dayton, Ohio, by the Wright brothers. One of the craft, flown by 21-year-old Walter Brookins, temporarily put Indianapolis on the aviation map by twice breaking the apparent "world" record for altitude. On opening day, using a short monorail temporarily laid down for the purpose, he took off from the infield and soared to a height of 4,384 feet. Four days later he tried again. This time he returned to earth by landing in a nearby field, where he claimed that the onboard equipment had given him a reading of 5,300 feet. It was later determined by several engineers to be 4,938 feet, which still broke his previous record by 554 feet.

The automobiles were back in early July, with a total of 28 events scheduled. There were to be 10 each on Friday and Saturday, and eight on Monday (July 4), with, as usual, none scheduled for Sunday. The longest race this time was Monday's 200-mile event for the Cobe trophy. Originally put up by Ira M. Cobe, president of the Chicago Automobile Club, this magnificent cup had debuted one year earlier at a 23.27-mile course of county roads laid out between the northern-Indiana towns of Crown Point and Lowell. The race, won by Louis Chevrolet in a Buick, had been a 17-lap, 395-mile marathon which took over four hours to complete. A huge crowd watched the proceedings from various points around the course, but only a handful actually purchased seats in the bleachers at the start/finish line. A financial disaster, the event was not renewed, and Fisher bid for the trophy to move to Indianapolis.

Unfortunately, the July meet was not nearly as successful as that of May. While the racing was certainly entertaining and safe, the turnouts were generally disappointing, no doubt due to the oppressive heat and the fact that the womenfolk probably had plans for the holiday weekend which did not include going to any noisy racetrack.

Then, three weeks after the meet, a major story broke with the announcement that AAA had decided to disqualify all of the cars which had been entered as Marquette–Buicks and strip them of everything they had won. The sanctioning body had always been pretty adamant about "stock" meaning precisely that. In May, Buick's Model-16 had been ruled ineligible (along with a few others) because it had not yet been manufactured in sufficient numbers to qualify as "stock." It had since met the requirements, but it had now been decided to enter the cars for the July meet as Marquette–Buicks, inasmuch as they had been manufactured at Buick's Marquette Motor Company plant in Saginaw, Michigan. Even as the cars had begun to win on the first day, there were rumblings that they were not exactly as represented. When a newspaper advertisement appeared soon afterwards, heralding the victories as being accomplished by Buicks rather than

Marquette–Buicks, AAA decided to take fairly drastic action.

The chief benefactor was Marmon's Joe Dawson, who had gone home believing he had captured only the Cobe Cup. Three weeks later, he learned he had won three more, including the 100-mile Remy event.

In spite of Monday's temperature having been cooler, due to a morning shower, the track activities still only drew an estimated 20,000, leading management to reconsider its plans for the Labor Day meet. In addition to cancelling the 24-hour race, scheduled for August 12–13, it was announced that the Labor Day meet would be reduced from three days to two.

There were 20 events on tap for the late-summer program, 11 planned for Saturday, September 3, headlined by the 100-mile race for the Remy trophy, and nine for Labor Day, concluding with a 50-mile "free-for-all" and a 200-mile race for "stock" chassis with engines measuring up to 600 cubic inches. Eddie Hearne of Chicago won both the Remy on Saturday and the "free-for-all" on Monday with a Benz, while Aitken won Monday's 200-miler over National teammate Al Livingstone in just over two and three quarters hours, for an average speed of 71.466 mph.

The estimated crowd of 18,000 on the grounds on Monday was actually quite reasonable considering that a huge parade was being held downtown, coupled with the fact that there had been a substantial shower in the morning. Rain threatened again later in the day, and it was almost dark when Aitken took the checkered flag in the 200-miler.

Once again, the racing had been both close and relatively injury-free, Lytle's broken leg in May having been the only one

of a serious nature during any of the three meets. Even so, the crowds had appeared to be dropping off. Nothing in July or September had come anywhere near to rivaling Memorial Day's 50,000. Perhaps, reasoned Fisher, Allison, Newby, and Wheeler, there had been *too much* racing.

On Tuesday, September 6, the newspapers revealed that the partners were considering for 1911 one major event which would pay a huge purse in an attempt to draw entries from all over the world. Apparently, they had started out by considering either a 1,000-mile race or one of 24 hours' duration as favored by many of the larger manufacturers. Further discussion led to the consideration of the spectators and that something lasting in the region of six or seven hours would be more appropriate, something that could start at around 10:00 A.M. and be concluded in time for everyone to be able to leave the grounds in time to relax over their evening meals. The answer appeared to be a distance of between 300 and 500 miles. The total purse would be in the region of $30,000, while the winner could expect to win as much as $12,000.

For a specific date, Memorial Day was being strongly considered, as recommended by Lem Trotter, who suggested that while they certainly planned to draw from far beyond merely that of the local farming community, there was, nevertheless, a late-May farming procedure known as "haying," following which the farmers had a two-week break and could attend to other matters.

A day or so later came the formal announcement: Memorial Day it was to be, and the race distance would be 500 miles.

Bottom right: The 100-mile "free-for-all," held September 3, 1910, is won by Eddie Hearne in the pole-sitting number three Benz. Runner-up Harry Knight, (number 27, starting third) drives a Westcott, manufactured in Richmond, Indiana.

Inset below: For the benefit of the large crowd as well as the participants, a capable medical staff is on hand from the very beginning.
Photographs: IMS

Chapter 2
A 500-MILE RACE IT IS

1911: The Marmon Wasp, the little professor, and a rearview mirror

JUST as the partners had hoped, the announcement of the inaugural Indianapolis 500-Mile Race was met with considerable enthusiasm, causing the newspaper and magazine writers to have to search for new superlatives.

It seemed as if everybody was talking about it.

Entry blanks were quickly prepared and mailed out, and in no time at all, the first one was returned. On October 22, 1910, paperwork was received from the J. I. Case Threshing Machine Company of Racine, Wisconsin, nominating Lewis Strang as the driver for one of its Case automobiles.

For the majority of the races in 1909 and 1910, management had charged extremely nominal entry fees, in some cases requiring only five or ten dollars for the two- and four-lap affairs. Because of the potential of a massive entry list for this one, however, and wanting to ensure that each entry was only of the most serious nature, they decided to set the fee at a hefty $500.

It didn't seem to make a lot of difference.

It was certainly a gamble on the part of the manufacturers, considering that no prize money at all was offered beyond the first 10 finishers. There was $10,000 (plus accessory prizes) posted for the winner, followed by $5,000 for second and $3,000 for third, on down to $500 for 10th, after which there was nothing.

Even so, the entries just kept on coming, and when the May 1 closing date arrived there *was* a most impressive total of 46 cars.

May 1 was also the day on which the track was made available for practice, a gesture offered by management to provide teams unfamiliar with the 2½-mile track with as much practice time as they wished. Not surprisingly, it was the local teams which took advantage, many of those from far away not even setting out for the track until well on into the second half of the month.

The most admirable of the latter was the Pope–Hartford team, which came all the way from Springfield, Massachusetts. The two cars to be driven in the race were loaded down with toolboxes and as many spares as they could hold. They were then driven across country, stopping overnight in New York, Buffalo, Cleveland, and Columbus, Ohio, before finally pulling into Indianapolis, where they were met out on East Washington Street by Frank Fox, the local Pope–Hartford agent who was to drive one of the cars in the race.

A qualification of sorts was put in place, requiring that each car demonstrate a reasonable showing of speed. Time trials were scheduled for May 27 and 28, at which point contestants would be required to average 75 miles per hour, from a flying start, down a quarter-mile section of the main straight. Considering that a few had been able to turn complete laps in practice at up to 88 mph, the stipulation did not appear overly demanding. Cars able to complete the distance in 12 seconds or under, therefore, would be included in the field. Those unable would be allowed two additional tries, failure after three resulting in exclusion.

Although there have been various claims over the years as to a certain entry's spectacular qualifying time, there were, in

Main photograph: History is about to be made as Carl Fisher (right) prepares to lead the field away with the Stoddard–Dayton passenger car for what may well be the first mass rolling start ever for an automobile race, and quite possibly, the first ever use of a "pace" car. Next to Fisher (right to left) are Lewis Strang, Ralph de Palma, Harry Endicott, and Johnny Aitken, who will be the first person ever to lead the "500."

Inset below left: A society crowd, decked out in all its finery, occupies the choice seats across from the pits.

Photographs: IMS

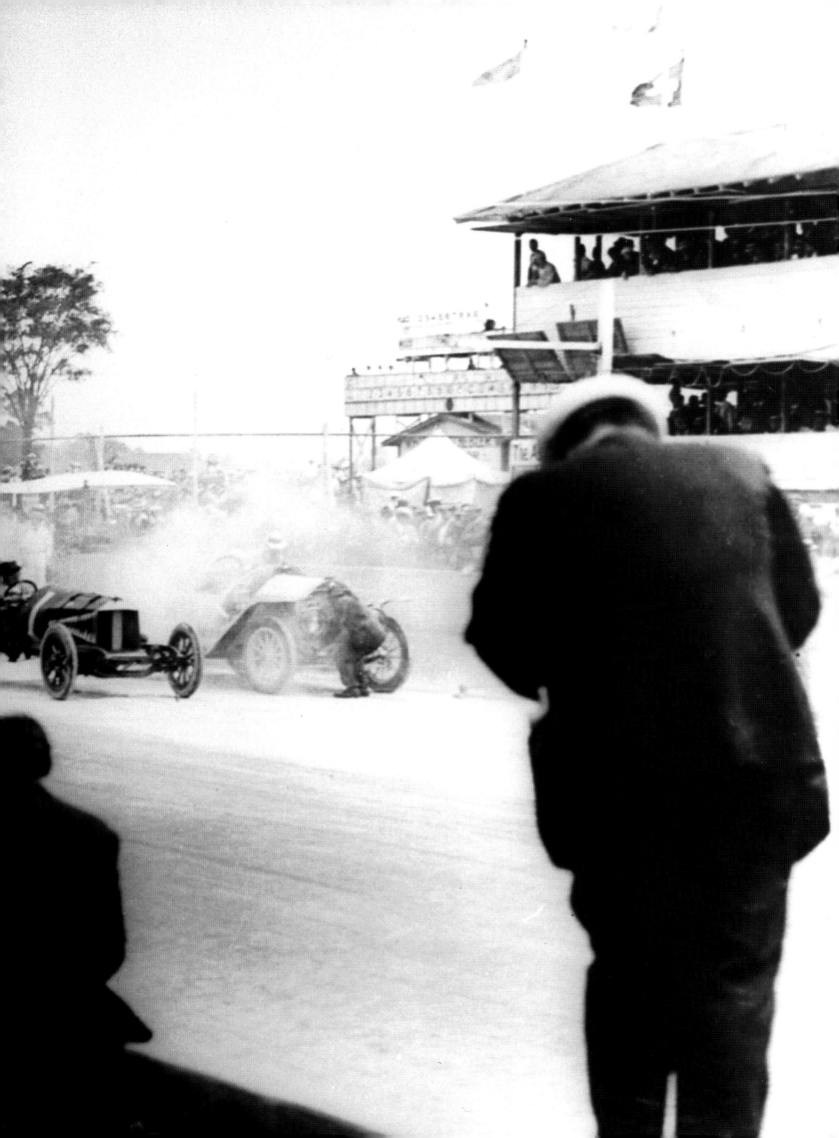

RAY HARROUN

Born in Spartansburg, Pennsylvania, on January 12, 1879, Ray Harroun, winner of the inaugural "500" in 1911, always thought of himself more as an engineer and inventor than a racing driver. He claimed the prime reason he had engaged in competition was to observe and analyze at close quarters the performance of implements he had helped develop. Very professor-like in his speech and demeanor (one of his nicknames was "The Little Professor"), his mind was constantly creating, even into his eighties.

Even at the time of his death, on January 19, 1968 (one week past his 89th birthday), a bomb carrier he had designed was still being used in the Vietnam War. This was by a gentleman who had served with the Navy in the Spanish-American war. By the time he designed and built his first racing car in 1905, he had been involved in such diversified occupations as dental technician, typewriter repairman, and even chauffeur for William Thorne, the Chicago-based president of Montgomery Ward.

While a project engineer for Nordyke & Marmon in Indianapolis, he was declared by *Motor Age* magazine to be the most successful racing driver in the United States for the 1910 season, there being no official American Automobile Association national champion until 1916. During this same year, not only did he work with Howard Marmon in the design and creation of the Marmon "Wasp" (which would win the 1911 "500"), but he also built two monoplanes which he test flew from the infield of the Indianapolis Speedway.

While gently pooh-poohing any suggestion that he had "invented" the rearview mirror, he is, nevertheless, believed to have been the very first person ever to have used one on an automobile when he silenced critics by installing such a device on the winning "Wasp" in 1911.

He left Marmon to head up Maxwell's racing team in 1914 and 1915, while concurrently serving as an engineer on the Maxwell passenger car side. In 1917, he moved to Wayne, Michigan, and realized a long-time ambition by creating his own passenger car firm, set up to produce automobiles, designed entirely by himself, at the rate of 500 per month. The timing was most unfortunate. He was almost immediately obliged to take on government contract work, manufacturing munitions as part of the war effort. Harroun Motors Corporation struggled along and eventually went into receivership in 1922.

Four years later, he was general manager for Carl Fisher's short-lived Fulford-By-The-Sea board track speedway, which was flattened by the Miami hurricanes after just one event. The rather impish Harroun lived his final years in a trailer court on the south side of Anderson, Indiana, where, in one corner of a tiny room, sat a box containing dozens of his blueprints and drawings from the 'teens, twenties, and thirties.

He had the honor of driving the Marmon "Wasp," not only before the start of the 25th running of the "500" in 1937, but also as an 82-year-old on the morning of the 1961 race, half a century to the very day after his history-making win.

fact, no records kept or even announced at the time, the beating of the minimum being the only matter of importance. The successful qualifiers were then lined up according to the order of their entry – and numbered accordingly – number one starter Lewis Strang merely having been the first to enter some months earlier.

Surprisingly, with such a large entry list, only two of the 46 failed to arrive, the pair of Falcars from Moline, Illinois, unable to secure some crucial parts in time. Of the 44 cars which did arrive, only four failed to meet the qualifying requirements, one being involved in an accident, one suffering mechanical problems, and the remaining two being unable to meet the 75-mph minimum.

A few days before the race, Carl Fisher made yet another of his many unintended landmark decisions, this one pioneering a procedure which is not only a widely employed staple of motor racing in the United States to this day, but which has become one of its most lucrative marketing opportunities. Typically, all of the races at the Speedway to that point had employed standing starts, usually eight or nine cars wide, and with 20 having been the largest number of contestants to line up for any single event. Now faced with twice that many, Fisher decided it would be safer instead to employ a rolling start. His plan was to use a passenger car for the purpose of leading the field steadily around on one unscored lap and then pull into the pit area at the conclusion of the lap, releasing the field to the flagman.

On the day before the race, once the field had been set, Fisher carried out several experiments at varying speeds, using 12, 18, and finally 25 cars. Allison rode with him. The first couple of attempts were a little on the ragged side, but eventually things smoothed out and everyone headed downtown for that evening's drivers' meeting at the old Tomlinson Hall.

The agreed-upon speed was 40 mph.

On race morning, a stately Stoddard–Dayton, of which Fisher just happened to be the local agent, was placed in the "pole" position (number one spot). It is entirely possible that it was the personal vehicle of either Fisher or Allison. The first four successfully qualified entries were placed directly to Fisher's right, followed by seven rows of five, with the 40th and final starter bringing up the rear by itself in row nine.

At 10:00 A.M., an aerial bomb announced that it was time for the engines to be fired, and shortly thereafter, Fisher led the field away on what is believed to have been the very first occasion on which a major event employed a rolling start, and very likely the birth of the now time-honored tradition of "the pace car."

Starter "Pop" Wagner greeted the accelerating mass at the

conclusion of the lap by waving his red flag (green was not used to start the race until 1930), and from the outside of the front row, Johnny Aitken led the roaring pack into the first turn with his National. Aitken stayed in front for four laps, thus becoming the first driver ever to lead the Indianapolis 500.

On lap five, wealthy young Spencer Wishart took over with an imported Mercedes Grand Prix car, and five laps after that there was a minor surprise when Wishart bowed to unheralded Fred Belcher at the wheel of a chain-driven Knox. The competition was fierce as a fourth contestant took over on lap 14, this time the Grand Prix Fiat of David Bruce-Brown, another East Coast "Ivy Leaguer," whose family was in the social registers as a member of New York's "fashionable 400."

Unfortunately, tragedy had already struck by this time. While coming nowhere close to the holocaust predicted by detractors – one of the newspapers predicted that between ten and 20 men would lose their lives – a fatal accident did occur on lap 13 when the Amplex of Art Greiner turned over, inflicting fatal injuries on the riding mechanic, Sam Dickson of Chicago.

At 20 laps, a fifth leader emerged, as up to the front went the Simplex of Italian-born Ralph de Palma, a leader of only four laps on this day but destined to become by far the most dominant performer of the event's early years.

Plodding along, not far behind, at a predetermined 75 mph, was Nordyke & Marmon's Ray Harroun, who had helped design and build a most controversial entry.

While there was no rule requiring that a riding mechanic accompany the driver – in a long race at least – this was the common practice. In March of 1910, Marmon had unveiled a purpose-built single-seat competition car which had gone on to enjoy quite a bit of success during the season, including in a few of the races at Indianapolis. Now outfitted with an even more streamlined body, it drew the attention and the concern of the numerous participants who had not previously been faced with racing against it. The contention was that without a riding mechanic to keep him apprised of upcoming cars which may be attempting to pass, Harroun represented a safety hazard. Apparently this concern had not been raised during the previous year, when Harroun had driven basically the same car in shorter races and against fewer competitors.

The wily Harroun (who, with a twinkle in his eyes, had told reporters he was of Arabian descent, whereas his ancestors were really Irish), silenced the complaints by installing four rods above the cowling to which he fixed a three-by-eight-inch mirror. Presumably, he could look up and have a fine panoramic view of what was taking place behind him.

He later admitted that it shook so badly at speed on the bricked surface that he was unable to see anything anyway.

But the storm had been curbed.

It is believed to have been the very first use of a rearview mirror on any automobile anywhere in the world, and while there is evidence of the idea having been proposed before this, there has yet to be any proof that it was ever put into practice.

Harroun has frequently been credited with having "invented" the rearview mirror, an honor over which he always chuckled. The concept had, in fact, been planted in his memory bank seven years earlier in Chicago, during the period he had served as chauffeur for William Thorne, president of Montgomery Ward. While waiting in front of a building one day for Mr. Thorne, who was inside attending a meeting, Harroun found himself entertained by all of the commotion on the busy street. A handful of automobiles were puttering along amidst a sea of horse-drawn vehicles, people on bicycles darting in and out of traffic, and defiant pedestrians attempting to cross from one side of the street to the other. Along came a horse-drawn taxicab, piloted by a gentleman wearing a multilayered cloak and a top hat. On the end of a pole, which stuck out at an angle near his seat, hung a mirror.

Main photograph: The "auto" bridge at the entrance to turn two, for the access of automobiles from the Georgetown Pike (later West 16th Street) to the infield, will be replaced by a tunnel in 1912 and soon dismantled.

Inset far left: Ray Harroun relaxes after winning. The rods above the cowling carry what may well have been the first rearview mirror ever used on an automobile.

Inset below: Starter Fred "Pop" Wagner waves the checkered flag across the hood of the Marmon "Wasp" as Harroun finally completes the 500 miles.
Photographs: IMS

Main photograph: **The Lozier of genial Ralph Mulford, hampered by numerous tire problems, finishes second.**

Inset below left: **The Benz of Bob Burman stops for a time-consuming tire change.**
Photographs: IMS

The cab driver would glance into it every few seconds in order to make sure he was not about to knock someone from his bicycle.

And that is where Harroun got the idea.

The car he was now driving in the "500" was, of course, the Marmon "Wasp." Painted yellow, it had originally been nicknamed by local newspaper writers "The Yellow Jacket," mainly because of the appearance of its sweeping tail, and especially after the mandatory placement, at the back end of it, of a raised disc bearing the car's number on either side. "Yellow Jacket" was soon shortened simply to "Wasp."

During the previous year's events, plus in practice for this one, Harroun had literally been running "tire" tests in order to determine the best compromise between speed and wear. He

discovered that by reducing his lap speeds from 80 mph to 75 mph, he could *double* the distance covered before a change became necessary. Thus he set out with a plan.

How to save the cumbersome amount of time required for pit stops?

Make as few as possible.

Harroun's plan was to disregard what everyone else was doing and simply maintain his calculated pace. Originally, Harroun had not even wanted to drive in this event. He had announced his retirement at the end of the 1910 season, telling Walter and Howard Marmon he preferred to concentrate on the engineering side and let others drive. He felt young Joe Dawson was perfectly capable of driving "The Wasp." They kept pressing and he finally relented. He insisted, however, that he didn't believe he could drive the distance alone, and while a journeyman Marmon engineer and test driver named William Studebaker was nominated for both the Harroun car and the more standard Marmon "4" assigned to Dawson, it was a disciplined long-distance specialist who was brought in. Cyrus Patschke, of Lebanon, Pennsylvania, had been the co-driver on several East Coast 24-hour marathons, and it was he who took the wheel of the Marmon near the halfway mark while Harroun rested for about an hour.

During the second half, Harroun led effectively the whole way, giving up the lead twice for a total of 10 laps to genial Ralph Mulford, the bow tie-wearing Sunday school teacher who had driven his Lozier down from Detroit with his wife occupying the riding mechanic's seat. Mulford led for the final time on lap 181, at which time he came in to change yet another tire, and Harroun sailed on to the checkered flag from there, beating out Mulford and the Fiat of David Bruce–Brown.

Unfortunately, Harroun's victory was somewhat clouded in controversy. Not every contestant who came to race with a stripped-down passenger car was happy that he had been beaten by a car built strictly for competition. The "Wasp" was powered by a six-cylinder engine at a time when all of Marmon's passenger cars came with a "four." Marmon cylinders

were cast in pairs, and with "500" entries being permitted up to 600 cubic inches, the engineering staff reasoned that the addition of a third "pair" would still displace only 477 cid.

There were also rumblings in some quarters that Mulford may have really won the race because of his greater pace. There were several logical arguments for and against this.

The finishing order was indeed revised several times, but always with Harroun the winner. Finally, after a couple of days, Fisher called an end to the proceedings and ordered all of the scoring records destroyed.

The main problem was believed to have stemmed from a multi-car accident which took place about one third of the way through the event. While greatly exaggerated over the years – one version even suggesting that a slewing car hit the timing-and-scoring stand, which it absolutely did NOT – what happened was this: A tie rod broke on the Case of Vienna-born Joe Jagersberger (who later developed the Rajo head) as he was coming down the main straight. As he prepared to slow to a safe halt, next to the outer wall near the entrance to turn one, his riding mechanic misjudged the speed at which the car was still traveling and he attempted to hop off and run along side. He lost his footing, and the left rear wheel ran over him. He suffered relatively minor injuries, but Harry Knight in a Westcott (from Richmond, Indiana) locked up behind him and swerved into the Kokomo-built Apperson of Herb Lytle, which was stationary at its pit. The Apperson was flipped upside down.

It is believed that it was during the aftermath of this accident that the continuity of the scoring procedure may have been interrupted, a number of Fisher, Allison, Wheeler, and Newby associates having enthusiastically offered their services without having previously been involved in the scoring of an automobile race. There is another report that the mechanical timing device may have malfunctioned briefly.

While the exceedingly polite and sporting Mulford never officially protested, he always felt he had won and believed so until the day he died, October 23, 1973. He always emphasized that he didn't wish any bad feeling on anyone and that he had nothing but absolute reverence for Ray Harroun,

whom he outlived by five and a half years. He also said he appreciated the fact the current Speedway management was continuing to "remember him" every Christmas, leading some to assume that he was being paid off in some way. He was, in fact, referring merely to being an annual recipient of a small set of drinking glasses management began sending out in the early 1950s to friends and acquaintances each December. The list soon grew to several thousand.

Publications of the day reported that Harroun stopped four times, three of which were to change the right rear tire, the other three tires going the entire distance. While the number of stops made by the quicker-running Mulford does not appear to have been recorded, one contemporary account states that he changed 14 tires, several of which had blown out on the course. Some sources report one particular failure having taken place as he entered turn one, requiring that he nurse the car around for two miles... on the rim... and on the rough brick surface. The resulting stop, not to mention the time lost while driving around at a reduced pace, ran to two minutes and 30 seconds, the damaged rim having to be hammered out before the tire could be changed.

In the meantime, Harroun was still motoring steadily along, trouble free at 75 mph.

He took the checkered flag in just over six hours and 42 minutes, having averaged 74.602 mph.

In spite of the controversy, the race was a huge success. The crowd was estimated by the local newspapers at 80,000, while officials downtown at Union Station, the city's railroad terminal, declared it to have been the busiest day in its history, with approximately 75,000 people having passed through there.

Above: Highly regarded David Bruce–Brown, twice winner of the American Grand Prize, finished third in the 1911 "500" and was the fastest qualifier, at 88.45 mph, in 1912.

Below: Boyish Joe Dawson, whose father, uncle, and other relatives were Marmon engineers (as was he), was loaned to National for the 1912 "500." He remained with Marmon for many years and later became a highly respected member of the AAA Contest Board.

Photographs: IMS

A delighted Fisher soon announced that the purse for 1912 would be doubled to $50,000 for the first 12 finishers, rather than 10, with $20,000 going to the winner. There would also, no doubt, be an increase in posted contingency prizes offered by accessory firms, the winning Marmon's prize of $10,000 having been boosted to $14,250 by such postings in 1911.

In the meantime, Nordyke & Marmon had an announcement of its own. Because the demand for its passenger cars had increased dramatically since the victory – which was the motivation for the various firms to be involved in racing to begin with – it had decided to rest on its laurels and retire from the sport.

Marmon had pulled off a most ingenious marketing ploy a few months before the race. No sooner had its two entries been filed as the 11th and 12th to be submitted than somebody hit upon a brilliant idea. The current vehicle being offered to the public was the Marmon Model-32. Realizing the cars in the "500" were to be numbered according to the order of entry, it was requested that track management "hold back" the pair of Marmons until 30 had been received. The request was granted, and Marmon was ultimately assigned numbers 31 and 32.

Another firm was just getting started. The Ideal Motor Company was about to start producing automobiles for the public but hadn't quite ready in May. A prototype took part in the "500," ran the whole distance and finished 11th. Having decided to name the cars for the company's president, Harry C. Stutz, a soon-to-be-famous slogan was coined, "Stutz: The Car That Made Good In A Day."

1912: De Palma's big push: Extraordinary sportsmanship in the face of defeat

Many of the 1911 participants elected not to return the following year, either because of the expense involved, because they felt they had gained the attention they sought, because they no longer wished to contend with the form of some of the entries (eight of the 40 starters could hardly have been considered as the intended stripped-down passenger cars) or even because their firm was no longer in business. Struggling automobile companies seemed to be either merging or falling into receivership almost by the week.

Because the Contest Board of the American Automobile Association (AAA) – the event's sanctioning body – felt that 40 starters were too many, new restrictions were placed on the number of cars which could participate in an event. A formula was devised, with safety in mind, requiring that cars spread equally around a track be entitled to a distance of 400 feet between each.

This was the formula which determined that the number of starters on a 2½-mile track should be limited to 33, although Carl Fisher had already decided to restrict the 1912 starting field to 30.

Fisher also announced that no more than two cars per make could start, but that thinking soon had to be amended, and shortly before the deadline, teams were advised that a third car would be acceptable after all. Even then, only 29 entries were received and two of those were "no-shows." Two were unable to meet the new qualifying requirements – one full lap at above 75 mph, rather than merely over one quarter of a mile – and a third did not try.

So race day saw only 24 starters, although all were of excellent quality in spite of the fact that one completely dominated. Teddy Tetzlaff led laps one and two with a Fiat, but the 1908 Grand Prix Mercedes of Ralph de Palma took over on lap three and proceeded to run away with the event.

Hour after hour de Palma led, until by 475 miles he was five and a half laps ahead, and his advantage, in terms of time, was over 11 minutes.

With about five laps to go, and with large numbers of the sun-baked crowd already heading for the exits, word spread that de Palma was beginning to slow down. Could it really be? Indeed, thick smoke could be seen pouring from the engine compartment and he was obviously in trouble.

Four laps to go and then three, and he was going slower and slower. Finally, approximately at the entry to turn four, and with about one and a quarter laps remaining, the Mercedes ground to a halt.

A connecting rod had snapped, punching a hole in the crankcase. Within the next few minutes, all of the remaining oil had been deposited onto the track.

To the admiration of the spectators at the north end, de Palma and his riding mechanic, an Australian named Rupert Jeffkins, then got out and proceeded to push the heavy car through the turn. (Riding mechanics were now

required in all of the cars, by the way, AAA having ruled that a second person had to be on board for any event scheduled for more than 100 miles in duration.)

Joe Dawson, Harroun's teammate in 1911 and a full-time employee of Marmon's engineering department, was on loan for this race to Arthur Newby's National Motor Vehicle Company. It was the 22-year-old, boyish-looking Dawson who was running second, but obviously now making up the deficit by leaps and bounds. A steadily building ovation began to reach the ears of de Palma and Jeffkins as they pushed down the main straight. They were still a couple of hundred yards short of the start/finish line when Dawson unlapped himself for the final time and roared past to take the checkered flag. Attention then turned back to de Palma. To everyone's amazement, he was seen to be smiling as he pushed, acknowledging the ovation with an occasional wave.

It later transpired that de Palma believed he was in his final lap, rather than the penultimate, and that he could still push home to finish. In fact, there was still another lap to go. By the time the officials had advised de Palma of this, Dawson had already taken two extra "precautionary" laps (to ensure against a possible scoring error) and had pulled up at his pit, there being no designated "winner's enclosure" at the time. De Palma and Jeffkins leaned against the side of their Mercedes, defeated, exhausted and bathed in perspiration. A few moments later, the utterly charming and beautifully mannered de Palma caught his breath, broke into a wide grin and strolled over to shake the hand of the new winner, a gesture the bashful Dawson never forgot.

The rule in 1912, as it had been in 1911, was that in order to claim one of the posted prizes, a car had to complete the entire 500 miles. The race did not end with the winner crossing the line. Instead, cars contesting for the balance of the prize-paying positions would still be circulating for a considerable time thereafter.

The extreme example took place in 1912.

Ralph Mulford, the previous year's runner-up, had switched from Lozier to Knox and had suffered a number of mechanical delays throughout the day. Long after the Fiat of Teddy Tetzlaff and relief driver Caleb Bragg had finished second, and the Mercer of British-born Hughie Hughes had arrived in third, there came a point when nine cars had completed their individual versions of 500 miles and Mulford's was the only one

still out there running.

Greatly exaggerated interpretations of what took place next have Mulford "marching up to a concession stand to order a hot dog" while "the crowd was rolling in the aisles." The reality is that hot dogs were not sold at the track in 1912, and even if they *had* been, all of the concession stands would have long since closed up for the day. And there was no crowd still around to *roll* in the aisles. All that remained as evening approached were Mulford's crew, plus a few officials and timing-and-scoring personnel who were obliged to remain behind until the run was finally over.

What did take place, according to the journals of the day and other eyewitness accounts, is that on yet another pit stop with about 17 laps to go, a hamper of food was produced

Above: In one of the most dramatic moments in the entire history of the "500," Ralph de Palma and Rupert Jeffkins (de Palma's riding mechanic) push their stricken Mercedes in after having led 196 of the 200 laps. In the foreground, taking a well-earned stretch is Joe Dawson, who took over the lead for the last two laps to win. Moments after this photograph was taken, the extraordinarily sporting de Palma walked over to congratulate Dawson, a gesture the bashful Dawson could never get over.
Photograph: IMS

from the personal car of one of the crew, and that chicken and sandwiches were passed around.

When an official went down to point out that the sun would soon be setting and that Mulford might not even have a chance to finish before dark, the driver requested that since he was the only person still running, why couldn't 10th place simply be awarded to him?

After being shown the clearly written rule, Mulford was ready to throw in the towel, but with $1,200 just sitting there waiting to be claimed, the crew wouldn't hear of it. So Mulford and his riding mechanic climbed back on board. In their laps, however, they cradled some of the food from the hamper, and while turning the next couple of laps at a fairly leisurely 60 mph, they took turns at eating while the other one steered. Mulford then picked up the pace a notch and finally completed the 500 miles in a time of eight hours and 53 minutes. His average speed was 56.29 mph, and the elapsed time between Dawson winning the race and Mulford finishing 10th was two and a half hours.

The following year, the finishing positions offering prize money were reduced from 12 to 10, as they had been in 1911, and officials would no longer insist that the full distance be completed.

Because the 11th- and 12th-place positions had not been earned, Fisher and his associates agreed to pay it out regardless in the form of a consolation to all of those who had not finished. The total number of laps completed by the non finishers were added together and an amount was calculated for the value of each completed lap, so that everyone who dropped out would be paid proportionally according to the distance each had traveled. Len Ormsby, who completed only five laps, was subsequently consoled with a princely $9.61. This has been reported, incorrectly, as having been the smallest prize ever awarded for a "500," whereas, in fact, it was almost double that of an amount paid to a contestant in 1924.

When Dawson had come on to the National team at the last moment, he had effectively "bumped" Don Herr, who was actually assigned to drive what would ultimately become the winner and who had spent much of the winter preparing it. Although relief drivers have generally received little or no credit down through the years, Herr nevertheless did get to drive the car. Just as Harroun had been relieved by Cyrus Patschke in 1911, so Herr spelled Dawson between laps 108 and 144 in 1912, Dawson coming back in for the finish.

National's victory rewarded the company much as had Marmon's the year before. Sales figures jumped and Arthur Newby found himself in an awkward situation. As both head of National and a partner in the track, he had to report to Fisher, Allison, and Wheeler that National's board of directors had voted to withdraw from racing.

1913: "Sans le bon vin..."

Although foreign cars and drivers had competed in the first two 500-Mile Races, none of them had come strictly for the event, the drivers from overseas, so far, having been either in the country on an extended basis or else on their way to applying for citizenship. Striving for the "500" to be a truly international affair from the very beginning, overseas entries had always been sought, with spirited but unsuccessful efforts to lure for 1911 Victor Hemery, Felice Nazzaro, Christian Lautenschlager, Ferenc Szisz, Louis Wagner, and others.

For 1913, with the maximum cubic-inch displacement now reduced to 450 cid, several teams decided to try it. Peugeot, winner of the 1912 French Grand Prix in the hands of Georges Boillot, sent two cars, for Jules Goux and Paolo Zuccarelli, while the Italian Isotta–Fraschini concern entrusted three in the care of Vincenzo Trucco, winner of the 1908 Targa Florio, one for himself and two for American drivers. Also making the trip was a Belgian, Theodore Pilette, the Mercedes representative in Brussels who brought over a Knight-powered Mercedes.

The chief hopes for America appeared to be the three-car team from Stutz Motor Company, located about four miles from the track, and a three-car team from Mercer of

Trenton, New Jersey.

There was a real scramble in the early laps, due to the fact that many of the faster cars were starting in the back. Rather than lining up the cars according to the order of entry, a blind draw was now being employed.

Caleb Bragg led the opening lap for Mercer, but was passed the very next time around by the Mason of Bob Evans. Goux took over on lap four and stayed in front until the 15th circuit, at which point the Keeton of Bob Burman assumed the lead for the next 100 miles. After that, Goux pretty much had things in command for the entire last three quarters of the race, bowing twice to a member of the Stutz brigade for a total of 18 laps while making pit stops. Shared by Norwegian-born Gil Anderson and West Coast driver Earl Cooper, the local entry was only 13 laps away from finishing second when a broken crankshaft forced it out.

Instead of leaving the foreigners to their own ends, every effort had been made to make sure they had plenty of help. National's Johnny Aitken, who had retired as a driver after leading the 1911 race and had served as pit manager and race strategist for Joe Dawson's win in 1912, was asked by Fisher to perform a similar duty for Peugeot. He evidently did a creditable job, considering that Goux won the race by a massive margin of 13 minutes and eight seconds.

There is a famous story concerning Goux's victory, which over the years spawned several greatly exaggerated versions.

Faced with six and a half hours of continuous shuddering over the all-brick surface while unprotected from a blazing hot sun, Goux had sought a way to refresh himself along the way. It was duly recorded that he did so by consuming, of all things, a little champagne!

Goux made six pit stops, and the legend is that he and his riding mechanic, Emil Begin, consumed some "bubbly" on each stop. While questioned by some in later years as having ever really happened, it was clearly reported in all three of the Indianapolis daily newspapers at the time, plus in all of the respected weekly motoring journals. Much was made of the story, and Goux was quoted the following day as having

Inset above left: Winner Jules Goux, with riding mechanic Emil Begin.

Above: Peugeot teammates Paulo Zuccarelli and Jules Goux wash up after a day of practice in 1913.
Photographs: IMS

Above: A Japanese-style pagoda replaces the twin judges' stands for 1913. Japanese architecture is extremely popular in the United States at the time.

Main photograph: The Peugeot of Arthur Duray negotiates a turn at the delightfully rural and rustic-looking Indianapolis Motor Speedway.
Photographs: IMS

proclaimed, "Sans le bon vin, Je ne serais pas été en état de faire la victoire," which, roughly translated, meant, "Without the good wine, I could not have won."

The great American historian Charles Lytle, who passed away in 1978, visited Goux in Paris on several occasions after World War II and received a slightly different response to the inevitable question each time, ranging from denial that it taken place at all to smiling and recalling that the champagne had been of the finest vintage.

The conclusion, based on a variety of opinions, including from some who were there, is that champagne was indeed consumed, but in restricted quantity. The containers were small "half-bottles," containing just under half a pint each, and it is believed that Goux requested one on four of his stops rather than all six. While Goux and Begin apparently did finish all of the first half-bottle between them, the other three occasions merely consisted of either just a swallow or two, or perhaps mere use of the champagne as a form of mouthwash.

One way or another, the newspapers did give the story quite a bit of play and AAA soon introduced a new rule, forbidding the consumption of any alcoholic beverage by a participant during a motor race.

Goux, who was on the engineering staff at Peugeot and whose father was an executive there, spoke very little English at first. He became more fluent during four subsequent visits and, in 1922, married an Indianapolis lady named Ruth Davis.

With Goux having already completed the race and being surrounded by the press, an epic duel was taking place on the track for the honor of finishing second. The advantage was held by a Mercer, which had been shared by Wishart and de Palma. Another Stutz, driven by Charlie Merz and also by Cooper, who had shared with Anderson, was not far behind. The Mercer took the flag with one lap to go about the time the Stutz appeared in turn four.

The only problem was that the Stutz *was on fire!*

Harry Stutz, serving as his own pit manager, walked out onto the track and signaled for the car to be driven to the pits. His order was ignored. A minute or so later, the Mercer came around to claim the runner-up honors, followed about 35 seconds after that by the slowing local entry, literally in a

blaze of glory, and with Harry Martin, the riding mechanic on the winning Dawson/Herr National of the year before, bravely lying out over the hood in a valiant attempt to beat out the flames!

Needless to say, the ovation was considerable.

In the spring of 1913, one of the track's most famous landmarks had made its debut. It had been decided to replace the twin judges' stands at the start/finish line with a single construction, and, completed just a few days before the race it took the form of a Japanese pagoda. Whether or not a smaller version at the Indiana State Fairgrounds was the influence has never been determined, but Japanese architecture was very popular in America at that time, and it may well have been Frank Wheeler who suggested such a design. The original pagoda was razed after the 1925 race in order to make way for a similar version which was placed further back from the edge of the track, this one surviving until June 20, 1956.

1914: One–Two–Three–Four for the tri-colour

The French returned in 1914 and trounced the Americans, the visitors this time occupying the first four finishing positions. René Thomas and Albert Guyot, both very much involved in early aviation, finished first and third for Delage, while Peugeots placed second and fourth, driven by Arthur Duray and Goux. The runner-up was a private entry, its engine displacing only 183 cubic inches, driven by Duray, a Belgian national, born in New York to French parents!

Once again, there was plenty of entertainment for the spectators in the opening laps, the "blind draw" setting up a situation in which there were to be six lead changes between five drivers in the first 13 laps alone.

As with the year before, the foreign competitors were made to feel most welcome and they expressed much relief. They had come for the prestige of the race and for the massive purse. But they also had come with much reservation. They were provided with a separate set of garages (outside of turn two), and at first, they were very reclusive. They would tend to rise very early and take practice laps at daybreak, long before the Americans arrived for work. They treated visitors with much suspicion until they realized that the visits were all in admiration and friendship.

And there was much laughter when they revealed the vicious rumors which had been circulating Europe concerning racing in America. If one did not have a spectacular accident, they had been told, one did not get paid!

The highest-finishing American was the fifth-placed Stutz driven by the famed Barney Oldfield, competing in his first of only two 500s, and sharing the wheel with Gil Anderson,

whose own car had dropped out earlier.

Probably partly due to the fact that the entry fee had been reduced from $500 to $200 for this year, a total of 45 cars had been entered and all but six of them made at least one time trial, meaning that nine posted times but missed the cut for the 30-car field.

Immediately after qualifying was complete, a certain withdrawal had taken place which may not have seemed to be overly significant at the time, but which indirectly led to a career-ending accident for a former winner, and the creation of a term which for quite a number of years came to be widely used in the United States.

Complaining of "excessive vibration" with his six-cylinder Mercedes after earning a spot, Ralph de Palma elected to withdraw. This would have allowed Eddie Pullen to move back into the field, except that his Mercer had already been loaded up and shipped back to Trenton. Eagerly ready to take his place was the 32nd-fastest qualifier, the Isotta–Fraschini of Ray Gilhooly, a driver who had already gained an unfortunate reputation for being rather erratic. On the 42nd lap of the race, the poor fellow subsequently lost control on the back-stretch and went into an elaborate series of spins and pirouettes. Joe Dawson, the 1912 winner, who was coming up to lap him for the third time, took evasive action and crashed upside down as a result.

Dawson was hospitalized for several weeks but recovered to return to Marmon's engineering department, and eventually become one of AAA's most respected senior officials.

In the meantime, for many years thereafter, any spectacular accident, whether on a racetrack, or involving an out-of-control snow skier, or even somebody merely falling from a ladder or a bicycle, might well be referred to as "doing a Gilhooley," although, technically speaking, the driver's name was not spelled with an "e" before the "y."

Ray Harroun, the retired 1911 winner, was now on the engineering staff for the Maxwell Motor Company and was heading up its racing effort. One of the Maxwells finished ninth, doing so with by far the most economic run in motor-racing history. For this one car only, Harroun had developed a special carburetor which would run on kerosene. Considering that the total consumption for 500 miles was 30 gallons, and that kerosene sold for the time at six cents per gallon, it meant that the entire fuel bill was only $1.80.

Why kerosene was not used by others after that is not known.

On a more dramatic note, during time trials, Georges Boillot, now a two-time winner of the French Grand Prix who had

declined to come over the year before, *almost* broke 100 mph. He pushed his 345-cubic-inch Peugeot around in one minute, 30.13 seconds, for an average speed of 99.85 mph. He never did lead, but ran second for a while and dropped out with a broken frame after 148 laps.

Sadly, the clouds of war were quickly gathering over Europe, and France was about to be drawn into it. Most of the foreign drivers and riding mechanics could not return in 1915 because they were in uniform. Goux, Thomas, Duray,

INDIANAPOLIS MOTOR SPEEDWAY
FOURTH INTERNATIONAL 500-MILE SWEEPSTAKES RACE MAY 30TH 1914

OFFICIAL PROGRAM
PRICE TEN CENTS
PAY NO MORE

Guyot, and other notables were all on the front, some of them chauffeuring generals while others were directly involved in combat.

On May 20, 1916, the great Boillot perished when his fighter plane was shot down over Verdun, near the German border.

1915: De Palma prevails

The maximum allowable cubic-inch displacement for 1915 was lowered yet again to 300. The field was increased to AAA's maximum of 33, and a limit of three cars per make was imposed. This resulted in a minor controversy when Bob Burman's entry, a modified Peugeot called a Burman Special, was ruled as a Peugeot, thus leading to three privately entered Peugeot drivers having to decide among themselves which one was going to give up an earned spot. And in spite of the fact that one of the four Sunbeams had to forfeit as well, and a couple more withdrawals left only 24 starters, the officials still did not relent.

After two years of lining the cars up according to the order of entry, and two more of using a blind draw, speed finally became the factor. Stutz driver Howdy Wilcox, who believed he could win the pole, started eyeing the diamond stickpin which was sparkling in the jacket lapel of Harry Stutz. A friendly wager was made, and when Wilcox returned with a pole-winning lap of 98.90 mph, Stutz handed over the pin.

Because May 30, 1915, fell on a Sunday, the 500-Mile Race had been scheduled instead for Saturday, May 29. The weather forecast was not good. It rained almost constantly for four straight days, and the prognostication for Saturday was no better. The creek inside of turn one had broken its banks and many of the roads leading to the track were under water. At around 10 o'clock on Friday morning, the partners announced that the race was being postponed until Monday.

The majority of the race was led by Ralph de Palma, driving one of the cars Mercedes had fielded for the politically overshadowed French Grand Prix of the previous July. Boillot, trying desperately to win his country's Grand Prix for Peugeot for the third consecutive year, had lost the lead with one lap to go and then dropped out with a mechanical failure as Mercedes swept to a one–two–three finish. De Palma, who had gone over to drive an English Vauxhall, traveled to Stuttgart after the race on behalf of the wealthy Chicago

sportsman E. C. Patterson, in order to purchase the Mercedes which had been driven by Louis Wagner to second. De Palma later reported that he had been working on the car in the factory when some of the German mechanics suddenly came running in, pleading, "Herr de Palma, Herr de Palma, you must leave at once."

War had broken out.

De Palma was barely able to get the Mercedes to Le Havre and on board a ship bound for home.

Carl Fisher, vacationing in Europe with his wife, had a similar experience, as did Johnny Aitken, who was in Paris on behalf of Fisher and Allison to purchase a couple of Peugeots. All of them left immediately and made it home safely.

De Palma's chief opposition during the 1915 race was a Peugeot driven by Dario Resta, a dark-complexioned Italian-born driver who had been raised in London and spoke with an aristocratic English accent. Originally down to drive a Sunbeam, Resta had recently taken leave of his exotic-car business near Piccadilly Circus and had moved to New York as a representative of the Peugeot Auto Import Company. And he had just married an American. Some years earlier, he had met Miss Mary Wishart while delivering a car from England to her father in Connecticut. Her famous brother, Spencer, had driven in the first four Indianapolis 500s but had been fatally injured during the 1914 Elgin (Illinois) road races. Mary was now Mrs. Resta.

And so the race became a battle between two Italian-born drivers who had not lived in the country of their birth since childhood. De Palma won by the fairly narrow margin of just under three and a half minutes over Resta, while third place was a Stutz shared by Gil Anderson and Johnny Aitken, who had now come out of retirement.

Fisher, who from the very beginning had wanted the "500" to be a truly international affair, certainly had been granted his wish. First was an Italian-born American resident, driving a German car, followed by an Italian-born English citizen, now living in America and driving a French car, followed by an American car shared by a Norwegian and an American.

The finish was not without its excitement. Resta had fallen back in the late stages after his steering had begun to develop more and more play. He was exhausted at the finish and could barely lift his arms.

De Palma, in the meantime, had the unthinkable occur.

In a virtual repeat of his 1912 dilemma, another connecting

Ralph de Palma takes the checker from starter Tom Hay. The precarious-looking rope bridge will not be used after 1924.
Photograph: IMS

INDIANAPOLIS MOTOR SPEEDWAY
FIFTH INTERNATIONAL 500-MILE SWEEPSTAKES RACE MAY 29TH 1915

OFFICIAL PROGRAMME

PRICE TEN CENTS
PAY NO MORE

rod had snapped with about three laps to go. This time, however, the fates were with him and he was able to nurse the car to the finish line. Instead of stopping at his pit or at the south end, as had become the custom for the winners, de Palma drove his smoking and clattering mount straight back to the brand-new garage area behind the pits, secured the car behind a locked door, and then returned for his accolades on foot.

The Mercedes had been somewhat modified, incidentally, having spent several of the winter months at the Packard factory in Detroit under the care of Chief Engineer Colonel Jesse Vincent. The car had sprouted a long sweeping tail and there were allegedly other Packard refinements beneath the hood.

In terms of speed, de Palma posted a record which would stand for several years. By completing the 500 miles in just under five hours and 34 minutes, at an average speed of 89.84 mph, he had sliced a full half hour from Thomas's record of the year before, while beating Harroun's 1911 time by one hour and eight minutes.

The 1915 race was quite noteworthy in that for the very first time, the winning entrant was an individual car owner rather than an automobile company. It was a growing trend. E. C. Patterson was in racing purely for the sport, being the advertising director and later managing editor for the famed *Collier's* magazine.

Shortly after the race, a well-deserved promotion was given to a rising Speedway figurehead. Already nicknamed "Pop" due to his rapidly graying hair, in spite of being only in his mid-thirties, T. E. Myers had been on the staff almost from the very beginning. An accountant for Fisher, Allison, and Trotter's Globe Realty Company, which was located within the same office building as the track's on North Capitol Avenue, Myers had been asked to come over and help with ticket sales for the pre-"500" events in 1910. He quickly took on more and more responsibilities until he was effectively the general manager. The partners recognized this and, in the days following the 1915 race, they made it official.

During the majority of Myers's lengthy tenure at the track, his personal secretary was Miss Eloise Dallenbach, otherwise known as the beloved "Miss Dolly." For better than 30 years, it was the inseparable team of "Pop" and "Dolly" which ran the day-to-day affairs at IMS.

It was certainly not very difficult, by this time, for the four partners to get together for a meeting, since three of them lived within walking distance of each other. Fisher had built a

RALPH de PALMA

Although his claim that he won 2,557 races out of 2,889 starts over a 25-year career is generally accepted by historians as being vastly exaggerated, the beautifully mannered and always immaculately dressed Italian-born Ralph de Palma (Troia, December 19, 1882) is nevertheless considered as unquestionably the most accomplished of all of the early-day drivers who raced on American soil. (His combined total of heat wins and match races during his numerous years of dirt-track "barnstorming" after he had fallen on financially difficult times is believed to be only a fraction of his claim).

It would be tempting to refer to de Palma as the most successful *American* of the early days, except that he did not become a citizen until 1920, having arrived in the United States as a 10-year-old immigrant in 1893. Most notable among his numerous major victories were the Elgin National trophy three times (1912, 1914, and 1920), the Vanderbilt Cup in 1912 (at Milwaukee) and 1914 (Santa Monica), and the Indianapolis 500 in 1915.

He was considered by the journalists of the respected weekly magazine, *Motor Age,* to be the national champion of 1912 and 1914, there being no official points champion until 1916. De Palma was also runner-up to Jimmy Murphy in the 1921 French Grand Prix at Le Mans, driving a Ballot, just as he had in the 1920 event at Elgin, Illinois. All of the other major victories came at the wheel of Mercedes Grand Prix cars owned by American privateers.

Although never recognized in Europe, his run of 149.875 mph with a V-12 Packard on the sands of Daytona Beach on February 12, 1919, was considered by the Americans as the World Land Speed Record until beaten 14 months later. For all of de Palma's accomplishments, he is best known not for any victory, but for the sportsmanship he displayed in perhaps the most crushing defeat ever in American motorsports.

He led 196 of the 200 laps at Indianapolis in 1912, the only four he didn't lead being the first two and the last two. After a snapped connecting rod smashed its way through the crankcase and led to the car grinding to a halt with barely 1$\frac{1}{4}$ laps remaining, de Palma and his riding mechanic, Australian Rupert Jeffkins, proceeded to push the heavy car through turn four and down the main straight in an attempt to complete the 199th lap.

The cheering by the admiring crowd only increased as the sporting de Palma smiled and waved to acknowledge the heartfelt ovation. He then went over to shake the hand of Joe Dawson, who had led the last two laps to win.

With the total of de Palma's laps led at Indianapolis now increased to 200 (he had led four in 1911), the two-time pole winner ultimately added 412 more (132 in 1915, 93 in 1919, 79 in 1920, and 108 out of 112 completed in 1921), eventually to reach 612, a record which survived until Al Unser finally surpassed it in 1987.

One of motor racing's most elegant ambassadors, the great de Palma passed away in Pasadena, California, on March 31, 1956, at the age of 73.

1916: The rest bested by Resta

The 1916 race was scheduled, not for 500 miles, but rather only 300.

The popular version of the motive behind this change is that this had been done in order to support the war effort by cutting back on the expenditure of fuel, tires, and other materials. In fact, Fisher had begun to believe that the race was too long and that the general public would prefer something shorter. He would quickly discover that he had misread them, but, upon reflection, history shows that the shorter race was politically the correct thing to do.

At the time, however, no sooner had the event concluded than Fisher announced that for 1917, the race would return to 500 miles.

Because of the reduced distance for 1916, the starting time had been moved from 10:00 A.M. to 1:00 P.M., and a couple of cars were even still trying to qualify at around the time the race normally would be starting.

In an effort to encourage the participants to refrain from waiting until the last possible moment to qualify, an incentive was put in place which survives to this day. Single-lap qualifying was still in effect, but the cars were now lined up according to the day on which each had qualified, the first-day qualifiers, in order of speed, placed ahead of the second-day qualifiers, and so on.

Of the 30 cars on the entry list, a couple of last-minute withdrawals, various mechanical failures, and a few "no-shows" resulted in the smallest field ever to face the starter. Only 21 cars lined up, and one-third of *those* were fielded by

Above: Dario Resta, an Italian-born Englishman, temporarily living on the East Coast and married to an American (the sister of the late Spencer Wishart), lines up for 1916's 300-mile race with an entry from New York's Peugeot Auto Import Company.

Right: Eventual fifth-placed finisher Barney Oldfield between practice runs.

Below: Before he ever learned how to fly a plane, WWI flying "ace" Eddie Rickenbacker was a "500" driver. He leads the first nine laps of the 1916 race, driving a Maxwell owned by Carl Fisher and Jim Allison for which he is team manager.

Photographs: IMS

home northeast of the track on Cold Springs Road, and shortly thereafter, Allison (to the north) and Wheeler (to the south) erected mansions which were considerably more grandiose than that of Fisher's. All three homes have survived to this day and are located on the campus of Marian College.

teams set up by track management.

Concerned by the diminishing number of entries, due to fewer automobile manufacturers choosing to be involved, along with the curtailment of foreign entries due to the war, Fisher and Allison had begun to acquire race cars. Under the banner of the Indianapolis Speedway Team Company, they had purchased a pair of Peugeots, plus had commissioned the local Premier Motor Company to build three copies.

There was one other.

The Prest-O-Lite company had made Fisher and Allison into multimillionaires, and they were already involved in the lengthy process of selling the company to Union Carbide. An ultramodern factory – which, previously unheard of in factory life, actually allowed sunlight to pour through enormous windows – had been completed right across the street from the track in 1913. One day in the fall of 1915, a young fellow came to visit them there. His name was Eddie Rickenbacher (spelled then with an "h" rather than a "k"), and while he was soon to become world famous as America's World War I flying "ace," he was, at this time, a "500" driver who had not yet learned how to fly a plane.

Rickenbacher (to use the spelling he adopted after being held in England late in 1916 as a suspected German spy) had been the number one driver for the prestigious Maxwell Motor Company. But Maxwell had just become yet another firm to discontinue its racing effort. When Rickenbacher learned that the quartet of competition cars was for sale, he rushed to meet with Fisher and Allison. A deal was quickly made. The cars were moved into the factory, Rickenbacher was retained as driver and team manager, and the Prest-O-Lite Racing team was in business.

Things started out rather well for the track owners. On the pole for the race was Aitken in an Indianapolis Speedway Team Company Peugeot, followed by Rickenbacher in a Prest-O-Lite Maxwell, then Gil Anderson in one of the Premier-built Peugeot copies. Dario Resta, who went on to win with a New York-entered Peugeot, started on the outside of the front row, the lineups since 1913 having been reduced from five per row to four.

Not in the lineup was defending winner de Palma. He had withheld his entry, seeking a substantial $5,000 in appearance money. Management refused to pay it, arguing that no other track was offering the huge purse posted by IMS and that to pay de Palma even one cent would create a terrible precedent. De Palma waited it out and so did they. The closing date passed; de Palma relented and subsequently asked to be included as a post-entrant. All of the others were asked to sign waivers to allow this, and at least one declined, the rumor being that it may have been de Palma's great nemesis, Barney Oldfield. One way or another, de Palma was forced to sit it out.

Oldfield, by the way, had accepted Fisher's invitation to make a demonstration run on May 28 with the ancient and massive front-drive Christie. With it, Barney recorded a lap at 102.623 mph, the first 100-mph lap ever turned at the

Speedway, although the engine was far too large for the car to be eligible for any Indianapolis race.

Rickenbacker led the first nine laps of the 1916 event and then promptly dropped out. He took over a second Maxwell from George "Pete" Henderson, a Canadian, eventually to finish sixth. Second, behind Resta, was the somewhat mysterious "Wilbur D'Alene," who was, in reality, Ed Aleon from Evansville, Indiana. "D'Alene" was driving a car fielded by a pair of German immigrants who were on their way to establishing one of the most respected names in American automobile history, Fred and Augie Duesenberg.

For the first time since the introduction of the 500-Mile Race (this time, of course, a "300"), track management decided to hold a second program. On September 9, the Harvest Day Classic was held, consisting of three events in one afternoon. A 10-lap (25-mile) sprint was followed by a 50-mile race, and finally a 100-mile race, using the same cars. In spite of a spirited effort by Rickenbacker, who spun out while trying to take the lead with just over a lap to go in the finale, Johnny Aitken kept the prize money in the family by winning all three events for the Indianapolis Speedway Team Company.

It would be quite a while before the next time racing cars would be heard circulating the track.

1917–1918: War clouds... from racetrack to aerodrome

Actually, there was to have been a "500" in 1917 but it was not immediately announced. Fisher was at odds with the local hoteliers, and he was insisting that they discontinue their policy of doubling and tripling the normal rates at race time.

Based on the success of the Indianapolis Motor Speedway, numerous other racetracks had sprung up around the country, including one which had just opened approximately 120 miles to the southeast, in Cincinnati, Ohio. Although slightly smaller – two miles to the lap instead of 2½ – Fisher was threatening to transfer the Indianapolis classic to Cincinnati!

The dispute carried all the way into the early part of 1917, and it was not until March that a compromise was finally reached. In the meantime, the long-rumored entry of the United States into the Great War had been dominating the headlines for months, and no sooner had Fisher announced that the 1917 race would be held after all, than on Friday, March 23, he was obliged to cancel.

Even then, the track was not completely silent. With the facility being offered to the government as part of the war effort, a couple of aviation maintenance battalions established themselves on the grounds. For the next two years, the sound of racing engines was to be replaced by that of aircraft as the infield became, among other things, a refueling point between military establishments in Dayton, Ohio, and Rantoul, Illinois. In addition, several experimental aircraft were tested at the track, flown by leading test pilots of the day.

The sound of racing cars would return in 1919.

Below: Dario Resta.
Photograph: IMS

Below: Aviation maintenance battalions are housed on the infield for much of 1917 and 1918.
Photograph: IMS

Chapter 3
EXIT THE AUTO MANUFACTURERS, ENTER THE RACING CAR SPECIALISTS

1919: Back home again in Indiana

NO sooner had Armistice been signed on November 11, 1918, than plans for a 1919 "500" were underway.

Frank Wheeler, in the meantime, was no longer a part of the operation.

While the Wheeler–Schebler concern was certainly continuing to flourish, other investments had not gone so well. New racetracks, hoping to duplicate the success of the Indianapolis Motor Speedway, had seemingly been popping up left, right, and center. In the summer of 1914, much to the surprise of his colleagues, Wheeler had become heavily involved in a two-mile speedway to be built at Fort Snelling, Minnesota, which is now the site of Minneapolis–St. Paul International Airport. The choice of surface was concrete, and the project was beset with problems from the very beginning.

An ambitious 500-mile race was held at the completed track in the fall of 1915 and the Stutz team scored a resounding one–two finish, crossing the line in a virtual dead heat while enjoying a lead of half an hour over the third-placed Duesenberg. Unfortunately, the event was poorly attended and was a financial disaster.

The picture became more dismal as the months wore on, and the bills kept piling up. Wheeler, as track president, felt personally responsible for the growing debt and he kept pouring money into the facility in an attempt to save it. In April 1916, he gave up the struggle, resigned, and a few months later, the place went bankrupt.

In the meantime, with additional capital being required for taxes and for general upkeep at Indianapolis, it was suggested that the partners agree to a cash assessment in order to "carry them through the war years." Not only did Wheeler feel he was temporarily too financially strapped to chip in, he even offered up all of his IMS shares. Allison suggested to Fisher that the two of them could jointly assume Wheeler's holdings, but with Fisher now heavily involved in the development of Miami Beach, Allison, on May 10, 1917, ended up purchasing the whole lot. Six weeks later, Wheeler gave up his seat on the board.

With no racing to speak of in war-torn Europe, a fair number of entries came from overseas, including a four-car team from Ballot. One of them, driven by René Thomas, won the pole at 104.70 mph, the 1914 winner being one of seven drivers who were able to exceed 100 mph during qualifications.

Riding with Thomas was Robert Laly, his mechanic from 1914, who, like Thomas, was making his first appearance at the track in five years. While just about all of the foreign drivers and mechanics had hair-raising stories to tell about their experiences since last appearing at the Speedway, none had had a tougher time of it than Laly. The poor fellow had been forced to endure several months as a prisoner of war.

Also on the grounds, with a Peugeot, was ex-fighter pilot André Boillot, the younger brother of Georges Boillot, who had given his life for his country.

Quite a number of the Americans had their stories to tell as well, but there was one who clearly stood out from all of the others.

Shortly after the September 1916 Harvest Day Classic, ex-Duesenberg and -Maxwell driver Eddie Rickenbacher had left for Europe, where, after changing one letter in his surname, he totally ignored "red tape" and refused to accept that his lack of formal education would preclude his becoming a pilot. Within a very short time, he was flying combat missions and downing enemy aircraft, the total eventually reaching 26. By the time the hostilities were settled and he had returned home to a hero's welcome, Captain Eddie Rickenbacker was known to millions as America's highly decorated World War I flying "ace."

He was also no longer a race driver.

Rickenbacker was on hand at Indianapolis this time to serve as referee, but this would be only the beginning. In just a few short years he would be totally in control of the Indianapolis Motor Speedway.

Prior to the record-breaking run by Thomas, the first person to officially break 100 mph in qualifying was Howdy Wilcox, driving a Peugeot which had been prepared within walking distance of the track. With the selling of Prest-O-Lite to Union Carbide, Fisher and Allison had been obliged to find another place in which to store their racing cars. Allison solved the problem by putting up a new building, just a block or so down on the other side of Main Street, in the development now known as Speedway City.

Yet another ambition of Fisher had been to create what he believed would be the world's first "horseless city." Through a pair of real-estate companies he owned jointly with Allison and Lem Trotter, the three of them had begun acquiring property near the track in 1912. The modernistic Prest-O-Lite factory was soon joined by others, the theory being that industry would operate on one side of an exceptionally wide north-and-south street (Main Street) while housing would be erected on the other. It began to take shape in 1913, and soon became known as Speedway City. Incorporated in 1926 as the Town of Speedway, it continues to operate 80 years later, quite independently from the City of Indianapolis, a town board overseeing its own school system, police and fire departments, and water company. Many of the streets are named for early automobile companies, and the four grade schools are named Fisher, Allison, Wheeler, and Newby for the track's founders.

Nobody could have known it at the time, but the very

Above: Nineteen-nineteen winner Howdy Wilcox outside of the Indianapolis Speedway Team Company headquarters, later Allison Engineering's Plant One, and, decades after that, the home of Riley & Scott.

Right: Pole winner René Thomas, with Robert Laly, his winning riding mechanic of 1914, who in the meantime had served as a prisoner of war.
Photographs: IMS

moving of the racing cars across the street to Allison's new building planted the seeds for what was to become one of America's most famous industrial dynasties. With plenty of sophisticated machining equipment acquired by Allison for the race shop, he began taking on engineering assignments for local firms. Word spread quickly, and it wasn't long before government jobs followed. In just a matter of months, the Indianapolis Speedway Team Company transformed into the Allison Experimental Company, and shortly thereafter, to the legendary Allison Engineering.

A pair of Peugeots were prepared in that new building – later Allison's Plant One – and, driven by Wilcox and 1913 winner Jules Goux, they finished first and third. In fact, Goux's car on race day was not entirely "Peugeot." After suffering mechanical trouble a couple of days earlier, the team had replaced the Peugeot engine with one of the 1916 copies by Premier.

Finishing second in the 1919 "500" was Eddie Hearne in a Durant Special, which was in reality one of the 1915 Stutz entries now owned by Cliff Durant, the son of Billy Durant, the founder of General Motors. In fact, Cliff made his first of several starts as a driver in this race, his Chevrolet Special also being a 1915 Stutz.

A healthy total of 42 cars had been entered, and for the first time since 1914, there was a full field, this being the first ever to be flagged away with 33 starters. Unfortunately, the race was marred by tragedy, with two separate accidents resulting in fatal injuries. On lap 45, Arthur Thurman, an attorney from Washington, D.C., became the first driver to lose his life in a "500" when his car crashed and caught fire. About an hour and a half later, Iowa-born Louis Le Cocq became the second. Thurman's mechanic, Robert Bandini, perished along with him, while LeCocq's Nicolas Molinaro was able to overcome his injuries and survive.

Towards the end of the race, and with local driver Howdy Wilcox heading for the checkered flag, a trackside band began performing a song which had been published just two years earlier. Released quite simply as "Indiana," it would later take on the longer title of "Back Home Again in Indiana," and, starting in 1946, would become part of one of the track's most beloved traditions by being sung on race morning.

When Wilcox pulled into the winner's enclosure at the

Below: Contrary to popular belief, Jules Goux is drinking water from this glass during practice in 1919, not champagne.

Bottom: Thirty-three cars are ready to leave on the 1919 pace lap behind the V-12 Packard of Colonel Jesse Vincent.
Photographs: IMS

south end of the track, the riding mechanic alongside him was not Maurice Becker, who had held the position all month. While it was officially reported that Becker had taken sick on race morning, it was, in fact, major objection from his new wife which caused him to have to step down. Pressed into service was eager young Leo Banks, whose dazed look at the conclusion was due to the fact that he was trying to figure out how he could break the news to his mother before she would learn, through her neighbors, of his unexpected adventure.

1920: When is a Chevrolet not a Chevrolet?

For 1920, the limit on engine sizes was reduced, yet again, to 183 cubic inches. The reason for this rather random-sounding figure – the previous limitations of 600, 450, and 300 had all ended in nice round numbers – was because Speedway management had decided to adopt the new European Grand Prix racing formula of three liters. Ironically, because Europe was still recovering from the war and no Grand Prix events were held in either 1919 or 1920, the first international race to be conducted under the new formula was the 1920 Indianapolis 500.

Another long-standing "500" tradition was established with the introduction of a new system for qualifying. Four consecutive laps were now required instead of one, while up to three attempts could be made, providing neither the first nor the second had been run to completion. A "reasonable" number of warm-up laps were permitted (amended several years later to a maximum of three), during which time a driver would make the decision as to when he wished his timing process to commence. He would indicate this by raising one hand as he came down the main straight, a procedure which, in spite of some gentle criticism, would remain unchanged until 1974!

It is interesting, also, that for the first few years, a car making a qualifying attempt did not necessarily have to be on the track by itself. The commonly used technique, today, of running directly behind another driver during the race or in practice in order to achieve a slightly faster lap speed by "copping a tow" is nothing new. In the early 1920s, prior to the rule being changed, more than one driver *qualified* that way.

The first person to register a four-lap qualifying run on the opening day of time trials was Art Klein, a pre-World War I driver, who, as Lt. Arthur H. Klein, had fought in aerial combat in France along with Rickenbacker. He completed his 10-mile run in just a little under 6½ minutes to average 92.7 mph. Continuing to race up through 1922, Klein eventually would become involved in the motion picture industry, and for over 20 years he would head up the transportation department at the Warner Brothers studio, employing, during his tenure, several leading Indianapolis 500 chief mechanics.

On the pole, at 99.15 mph, was Ralph de Palma, driving one of the Ernest Henry-designed straight-eight Ballots. With it, de Palma proceeded to dominate yet another race. After being delayed by a flat tire at the very start, even as the pace car was pulling into the pits, he had fought his way back to the front and remained there between laps 113 and 186. He had held the lead for about two consecutive hours when the old de Palma misfortune befell him yet again. He slowed to a halt at the north end of the track, believing he was out of fuel. His riding mechanic took off running several hundred yards

down to their pit in order to obtain some fuel, and before returning, the poor fellow made the mistake of drinking some cold water. There would be happier days ahead for this young man. The son of de Palma's sister, he would soon become a race driver himself and exactly five years from this day, Peter de Paolo would join his uncle Ralph as a winner of the "500."

As it turned out, Peter's several-hundred-yard trot had been for naught. His uncle had discovered that one of the engine's two magnetos had failed and that by unhooking one, he could still motor along on four of the eight cylinders. Already fired up and motoring south, de Palma slowed down in order for Peter to climb on board, after which they went on to salvage fifth. Peter later recalled that he felt as if his stomach were filled with freezing-cold barbed wire.

Into the lead and on to the victory cruised Gaston Chevrolet, the 23-year-old younger brother of the Swiss-born Louis and Arthur. Several years their junior, Gaston had been born after the family had moved to France.

Now residents of Indianapolis, the brothers had moved around quite a bit since coming to the United States, Louis and Arthur having been race drivers and engineers for several firms. Strong-willed, they were anything but patient men, especially Louis. No sooner had the Chevrolet Motor Company been formed in 1912 than the brothers had had a major argument with Billy Durant over design, after which they stormed out and gave up their shares, which, in just a few years' time, would have made them multimillionaires.

They had built some cars for the 1916 and 1919 Indianapolis races, known as Frontenacs, and they were now associated with the William Small Company, which had just taken over the assets of the financially troubled Monroe Motor Company.

The brothers fielded seven uniquely streamlined cars in the 1920 race, four as Monroe Specials and three as Frontenacs. Only two of the cars finished, the other five all being victims of a steering-arm failure which caused all but one of them to crash. Only Louis Chevrolet himself was able to avoid an accident, withdrawing when he sensed a failure was about to occur. Teammate Roscoe Sarles was bitten twice. After a steering malfunction sent him into the turn-four wall on his 58th lap, he came back to the pits, took over as a relief driver for Bennett Hill, and later had exactly the same thing occur in exactly the same place.

It is said that after the trackside victory celebration had been completed and the winning team had returned to its garage, Louis began lamenting the elimination of so many of his cars due to the same problem. He concluded his emotional outpouring by executing a swift kick to the side of the winning car – whereupon its steering arm fell clattering to the ground.

Although the Chevrolet brothers were foreign-born, it was claimed as an American victory, the first since 1912. René Thomas was second in a Ballot, while Duesenbergs took third and fourth, driven by rising American stars Tommy Milton and Jimmy Murphy.

Another long-standing tradition debuted in 1920 with the creation of the Citizens of Indianapolis Lap Prize Fund. Believed to be the very first such fund ever established for an automobile race, the goal was to raise the then considerable sum of $20,000 and pay it out to the race leader at the rate of $100 per lap. This meant that the driver who could lead every lap (to this day no one ever has) would have the potential of *doubling* the posted total for winning, regardless of whatever else could be earned in accessory prize money.

Although it would be achieved only once more during the next 25 years, the entire amount was raised this first time, and the $3,000 de Palma earned for finishing fifth paled next to the $8,600 he piled up purely by leading. Joe Boyer, who crashed out in the late stages after leading almost half of the entire race and who otherwise would have come away with nothing, consoled himself with $9,200 for his laps in front.

While generally credited to George M. Dickson – Arthur Newby's successor at the National Motor Vehicle Company – insiders later revealed that credit for the idea of the lap prize fund should really have gone to a lady, Pop Myers's personal assistant, Miss Eloise "Dolly" Dallenbach.

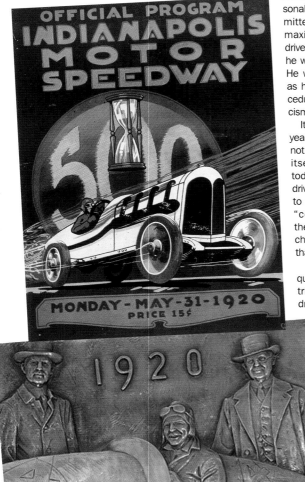

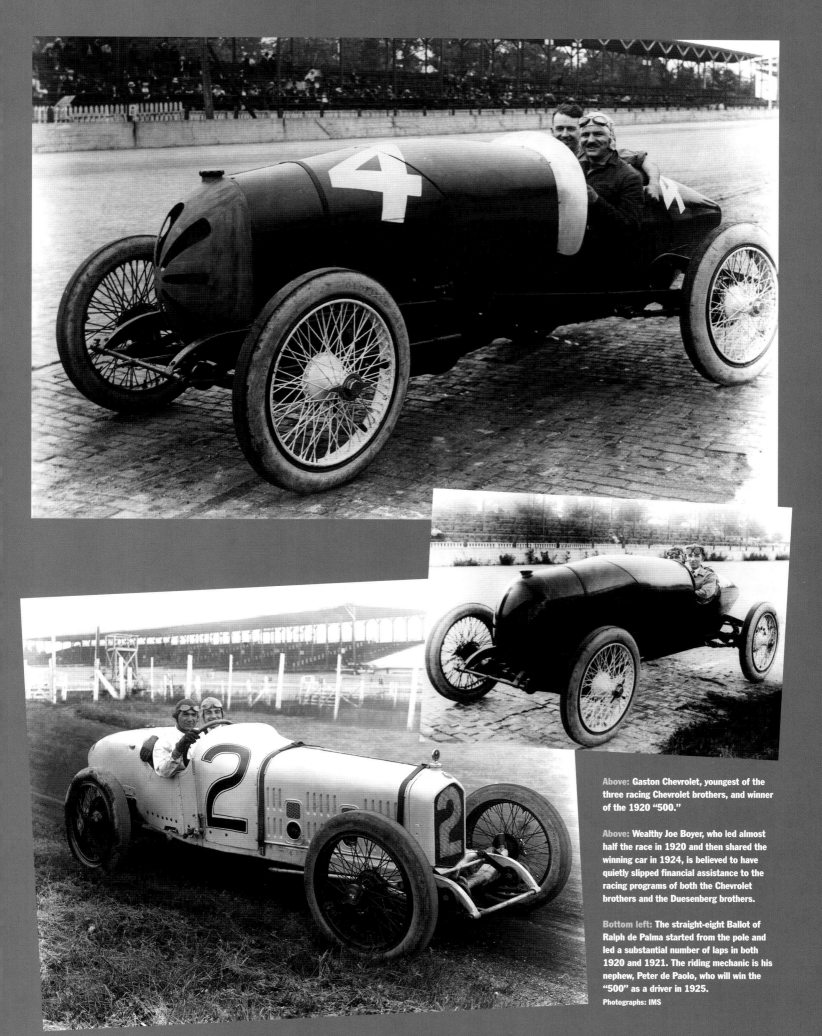

Above: Gaston Chevrolet, youngest of the three racing Chevrolet brothers, and winner of the 1920 "500."

Above: Wealthy Joe Boyer, who led almost half the race in 1920 and then shared the winning car in 1924, is believed to have quietly slipped financial assistance to the racing programs of both the Chevrolet brothers and the Duesenberg brothers.

Bottom left: The straight-eight Ballot of Ralph de Palma started from the pole and led a substantial number of laps in both 1920 and 1921. The riding mechanic is his nephew, Peter de Paolo, who will win the "500" as a driver in 1925.

Photographs: IMS

1921: The brothers Chevrolet versus the brothers Duesenberg

Louis and Arthur returned to the Speedway in 1921 with heavy hearts. In the final race of the 1920 season, a 250-mile event at the steeply banked wooden board track at Beverly Hills, California, on Thanksgiving Day, young Gaston had been fatally injured. He was the first Indianapolis 500 winner to lose his life in a racing accident.

There was one other notable passing. Despondent over the loss of a friend to diabetes, the diabetic Frank Wheeler had taken his life on the morning of May 27. Although no longer a partner in the track, he was still a neighbor of Fisher and Allison on Cold Spring Road, and was the man who may well have been responsible for the judge's stand taking the form of a Japanese pagoda.

Although there had been 32 entries in 1920, several had been withdrawn and only 23 started. This time, there were only 25 entries to begin with. Of these, one was withdrawn and another was not permitted to compete because the full entry fee was never paid. Fortunately, the other 23 were able to meet the minimum four-lap qualifying speed of 80 mph.

Once again, de Palma completely dominated for as long as he lasted, following a nip-and-tuck battle at the start. Evidently comfortable with the new four-lap qualifying format, he won the pole for the second consecutive year, this time at 100.75 mph.

The lineup had a new look this year. After five-abreast starts in 1911 and 1912, and four-abreast starts thereafter, it was decided for 1921 to reduce the number of cars per row to three. With all of the other modifications made over the years, the three-abreast start is one tradition which has remained totally unchanged ever since.

De Palma led the opening lap with his Ballot but was passed the next time around by wealthy Joe Boyer, who was now a member of the Duesenberg team. De Palma was back to lead laps three, four, and five, after which Roscoe Sarles, now a Boyer teammate, went to the front. Sarles was there for just one lap before de Palma grabbed it back, hanging on to it thereafter for the next two and a half hours.

The Ballot finally faltered at 110 laps and dropped out two laps later with a broken connecting rod, giving up a

Main photograph: Jimmy Murphy takes the checker with his experimental Miller-engined Duesenberg as the first to win while driving a car he owns himself.

Below: The brothers Duesenberg (Augie and Fred); Fred on the right.
Photographs: IMS

5½-minute lead and having led for all but four of the 112 laps. It increased de Palma's career total of laps led to 612, a record which would remain unbroken until 1987. In fact, with 200 laps to his credit after the 1912 race (four in 1911 and 196 in 1912), no name other than de Palma's would lead that category for the next three quarters of a century.

During the winter, the Chevrolet brothers had developed an eight-cylinder version of their Frontenac engine, and they had two of them ready in time for the race. One of them, driven by Tommy Milton, went into the lead when de Palma was eliminated, and it remained in front for the remainder of the distance.

It was the second win in succession for Louis and Arthur, although Milton had not qualified without a struggle, mechanical trouble forcing him to line up 20th in the 23-car field. He later claimed that he was down on power and that he had employed a little psychology to beat Roscoe Sarles. A rather reserved, somber, and quite secretive man, who tried without success to hide the fact that he had sight in only one eye, Milton stated that at one point during the race, he had found himself side by side with Sarles. He was able to stay there only by really extending his equipment. He claimed he looked over at Sarles, grinned, and then gestured as if to indicate that things were coming easily for him. Milton believed he broke the Duesenberg driver's spirit with this tactic.

Whether or not the story is true is purely a matter of conjecture, but the result was that Sarles was almost four minutes behind at the finish.

There was much discussion throughout the month concerning the fact that the French Grand Prix was being revived after seven years, and that Duesenberg was sending over a four-car team. The rumor mill had de Palma driving one of the cars, as it did Milton, Ralph Mulford, Howdy Wilcox, and several others. It ended up being Jimmy Murphy and Joe Boyer, plus Frenchmen Albert Guyot and Louis Ingelbert, the latter suffering injuries during practice and being replaced with André Dubonnet of apéritif fame.

It was rather like old home week, with nine of the 13 starters having competed in a "500," and to the astonishment of just about everyone, it was Murphy who won the race. Ernest Ballot was said to have been furious, his much-favored cars finishing second and third in the hands of de Palma (with de Paolo as his riding mechanic) and Goux.

Shortly after returning to America, or perhaps even on the homeward-bound steamship, Murphy arranged to purchase his winning car from the Duesenberg brothers. Fred and Augie had recently relocated from Elizabeth, New Jersey, to Indianapolis, and had entered the passenger-car business, erecting a factory barely four miles from the track. Still placing their faith in the original theory that success on the racetrack would translate into success in the showroom, they were delighted that Murphy would be racing one of their products. As an independent, surely his anticipated victories would only help bolster the prestige of their company to even greater heights – without them having to underwrite the expense!

That euphoria soon faded, however, when it was learned that the very likable Murphy and his faithful mechanic, Ernie Olson, were in the process of removing the Duesenberg engine, replacing it with a straight-eight Miller (then a little-known entity), and calling the result the Murphy Special. The well-meaning Jimmy certainly never intended to antagonize the brothers. He was merely trying to protect his investment by doing what he felt was necessary to win.

Below: Eddie Hearne, affectionately nicknamed "Grandpa," participated in many of the pre-"500" events, plus the "500" itself off and on between 1911 and 1927. He finished second in 1919 (with soon-to-be-great Harry Hartz as his riding mechanic) and third in 1922.
Photograph: IMS

Main photograph: Four of the five privately entered Bugattis sit in the pits on race morning 1923.

Right: The straight-eight Miller, powerhouse of the 1920s.

Below right: Camera-shy Harry Miller, considered by contemporaries to have been a genius.

Below: Just before the start in 1922. Jimmy Murphy will be the first to win from the pole, his car now correctly numbered 35. Most photos show the car bearing number eight, which it carried when he arrived for practice.
Photographs: IMS

1922: The Roaring Twenties keep on Roaring

One 1922 entry which caused quite a few raised eyebrows, but which was quickly withdrawn, was a Duesenberg to be driven by Wallace Reid, the famed silent film actor! A leading matinee idol, Reid had recently starred in four consecutive features with racing backgrounds and had become enamored of the sport through his various doubles and stuntmen. There is no record or indication of him ever having participated in competition anywhere. Regardless, Lasky Studios, to whom he was contracted, immediately objected and he was obliged to withdraw. Just which Duesenberg Reid had acquired or who his mechanics were to have been is unknown.

In spite of there being seven Duesenberg Straight-8 Specials in the lineup – five of them finishing within the first seven – it was Murphy who won. He led the first 74 laps and stayed out in front for 153 of the 200 laps, as the first driver ever to win from the pole. He knocked a quarter of an hour from de Palma's seven-year-old record, averaging 94.484 mph on *his* way to winning in five hours 17 1/2 minutes.

Harry Hartz, the riding mechanic for Eddie Hearne in the previous three years, finished second in his debut as a "500" driver, beating his former employer by one position, while de Palma's nephew, Peter de Paolo, also led briefly in his "500" debut as a driver.

The combined products of the Duesenberg Brothers and of Harry Miller would be dominating the "500" for the next several years, with Miller eventually having virtually the entire field to himself. How ironic it should be that the first victory by either one would be an unintended collaboration instituted by neither of them, a Miller engine being placed in a Duesenberg chassis by an independent.

This was the beginning of the amazing Miller dynasty, a company which, later passing through the hands of Fred Offenhauser, Louis Meyer, and Dale Drake – and finally John Drake – would still be turning out winning engines in the "500" four decades hence.

JIMMY MURPHY

One of more than two dozen people who had at least one "500" start as both a driver and riding mechanic, Jimmy Murphy, the upset winner of the 1921 French Grand Prix at Le Mans (the summer before he won the "500"), remains as one of only two Americans who won a European Grand Prix, driving an American car. The only other occasion came 45 years later when Dan Gurney's Eagle captured the 1967 Belgian Grand Prix at Spa–Francorchamps.

The son of Irish immigrants, who were both deceased by the time he was ten years old, James Anthony Murphy was born in San Francisco on September 12, 1894. His already widowed father, a San Francisco fireman, perished (while a hospital patient) during the famous 1906 earthquake. Murphy was raised by his mother's sister and her husband, Martin O'Donnell, who eventually became a Los Angeles County judge.

Jimmy opened a garage in the Los Angeles area while still a teenager and somehow became connected with the Duesenberg team at some 1916 West Coast events, serving as a riding mechanic for Eddie O'Donnell, who was not related to Jimmy's uncle. In the Vanderbilt Cup race at Santa Monica, he rode with the wealthy amateur William Weightman, who finished a surprising third.

Murphy rode in the Duesenberg of O'Donnell at Indianapolis in 1919 (they did not finish), shortly before being named to the driver lineup. He was fourth in the 1920 "500" and fourth again the following year after taking over a team car started by Eddie Miller.

Following the 1921 French Grand Prix, Murphy purchased the car from the Duesenberg brothers and then replaced the engine with a straight-eight Miller. Not only was his subsequent "500" win the first by either a Duesenberg or a Miller (the car being a combination of both), but Murphy was the first person to win from the pole, and the first to win while driving a car entered by himself. He drove Millers to third in the "500" in 1923 and 1924, and between 1920 and 1924, won 18 board track events, including 13 over distances of 200 miles and more.

He won the AAA National Championship in 1922 and 1924, slipping to second in 1923, mainly due to missing several races while traveling to and from Europe, where he drove a Miller to third in the Italian Grand Prix. Front-drive, while by no means a new idea, had never been tried in a "500." Murphy approached Harry Miller about the concept and commissioned such a car for the 1925 "500."

He died before it was completed, crashing fatally in a 150-mile race at Syracuse, New York, on September 15, 1924, in what may have been his only race ever on a dirt track. The following May, the front-drive car placed second. Of a sunny disposition, and said to have possessed a "pleasing golden tenor," the usually smiling Murphy appeared as himself opposite Agnes Ayres in a 1922 silent film called "Racing Hearts."

Above: The three Mercedes which compete in 1923 (the company will not become Mercedes–Benz until 1926) are the very first cars ever in a "500" to be boosted by a supercharger. They are gear-driven rather than centrifugal.
Photographs: IMS

Below: John de Palma (left), who competed in the 1915 "500" won by his brother, Ralph, chats during 1923 practice with Ralph (right) and sportsman car owner/driver Cliff Durant, son of Billy Durant, who founded General Motors.

Bottom: A Durant Miller, sans engine cover.
Photographs: IMS

INDIANAPOLIS MOTOR SPEEDWAY COMPANY
Eleventh International Sweepstakes Distance 500 Miles
May 30th 1923
OFFICIAL MOTOR PROGRAM
Price 25¢ PAY NO MORE

1923: Downsizing to single-seaters; It's Paradise Won for Milton

The 1922 race wound up a three-year run of the 183-cubic-inch formula. For 1923, a further reduction had been announced, restricting engines to two liters, or 122 cubic inches. In addition, riding mechanics were no longer mandatory for the first time since 1912, the result being the arrival of a number of sleek-looking downsized single-seaters.

The 1923 lineup was as intriguing as just about any other in history. Daimler Motoren Gesellschaft sent three Mercedes, this being three years before the company's merger with Benz. Led by Christian Lautenschlager, two-time winner of the French Grand Prix, these were the first cars ever entered for a "500" boosted by superchargers.

Five Bugattis came over in the hands of as sophisticated and as colorful a group of sportsmen as ever appeared at Indianapolis. It was never clear who spearheaded this effort, but the drivers were Louis Zborowski, Pierre de Vizcaya, Prince Bertrand de Cystria, Raul Riganti, and Martin de Alzaga. Zborowski, a British citizen, who was the son of a Polish count and a wealthy American lady, was the man who fielded the famous "Chitty Chitty Bang Bang" Higham Specials at Brooklands, and who helped finance the Aston–Martin company. Riganti and de Alzaga were Argentinians, the latter once owning a Hollywood night club and being married to Kay Williams, who later married actor Clark Gable. De Vizcaya was the son of a banker who helped finance Ettore Bugatti.

On the American side, there was a trio of Packards, powered by six-cylinder engines and built in virtual secrecy for Ralph de Palma, Joe Boyer, and Dario Resta, under the direction of de Palma and Colonel Jesse Vincent. Harry Stutz entered a pair of Millers, while Cliff Durant either entered or sponsored no fewer than eight. The Stutz entries were called HCS Specials (Harry's initials) for the passenger-car firm he had formed after losing control of the Stutz Motor Company. It has occasionally been reported that these were HCS-based cars and that they contained much Stutz engineering. They were, in fact, pure Millers which merely displayed the HCS logo on either side of the cowling.

One other entry of considerable local and general interest was the lone Barber–Warnock special. Built mostly out of Ford Model-T parts, it had been put together by Louis and Arthur Chevrolet and was outfitted with one of their Frontenac heads. With Monroe's savior, the William Small Company, having also gone into receivership, the latest venture for Louis and Arthur was the Chevrolet Brothers Manufacturing Company. Louis didn't stay around for long, but over a period of about eight years, Arthur was to turn out many dozen examples of the "Fronty–Ford" Specials, which were extremely successful on half-mile dirt tracks in the forerunner of what today is called sprint car racing.

This was by far the most competitive "500" yet held. The previous record for lead changes had been 12 in 1911. This time there were 28, of which 27 came during the first 110 laps. Murphy, who did not qualify until the second day, came all the way from 9th to lead the first lap, after which he and Milton were to alternate five times in seven laps. There were 13 separate occasions on which a driver would hold the lead for one lap only, and three others on which it would be held for a mere two laps in succession. Even Cliff Durant duked it out with Milton and managed to lead for a total of four laps.

Unfortunately, one of Durant's cars was involved in a most regrettable accident soon after the start. Veteran Earl Cooper had been obliged to make a pit stop at the end of the very first lap, and after several minutes, he climbed out and turned the car over to a more eager Tom Alley. The problem was fixed and Alley took off. A few laps later, Alley spun through turn two and smashed through a tall wooden fence which lined part of the backstretch, killing a 15-year-old boy named Bert Shoup who was standing on the other side, peeping through a hole. It turned out that the youngster had snuck onto a train in Lafayette, had ridden down to Union Station, and then had been able to sneak into the track and work his way around to an area where no spectators were supposed to be.

Just as Duesenberg's huge onslaught had failed to produce a win in 1922, so Durant came up short this time, his cars finishing second, third, fourth, sixth, and seventh, just ahead of the first of two Mercedes which finished.

It was Milton who took the win, thereby becoming the first driver ever to enter Victory Lane for a second time. He did not do it alone, however, as pinched feet from a pair of brand-new shoes, plus some badly blistered hands, forced him to seek a relief driver. In jumped teammate Howdy Wilcox, winner of the 1919 race, who had already been sidelined by clutch trouble. Wilcox, who spelled Milton between laps 103 and 151, became the first of three drivers in "500" history who led the same race in two different cars.

A "complete" Miller had won for the first of many times.

Originally a manufacturer of carburetors, Harry Miller had become involved with engine development just before WWI. A straight-eight Miller engine had made its "500" debut in 1921, finishing seventh in the hands of Ira Vail. In 1922, two "complete" Millers—engine and chassis—had started, while Jimmy Murphy, of course, had won with the Miller engine in the Duesenberg chassis. Before long, Harry Miller's products would be dominating.

All three of the Packards had fallen by the wayside in the 1923 race, as had all but one of the Bugattis, and while two of the closely watched supercharged entries from Mercedes did manage to complete the full distance in eighth and eleventh positions, the third one was out early. In spite of the fact that riding mechanics were no longer mandatory, the veteran Lautenschlager decided to take one along with him anyway. Only 15 laps into the race, poor Jacob Krauss had to be carted away to the hospital when Lautenschlager hit the turn-one wall, marking the last occasion on which a mechanic

would go along for the journey until they were made mandatory again in 1930.

A huge cheer went up from the crowd about 33 minutes after Milton had taken the checkered flag, when Arthur Chevrolet's little Barber–Warnock Fronty–Ford finally completed its 200th lap. Driven by the very bashful Lora Corum, who helped prepare it, and fielded for just a fraction of the cost of every other car in the race, it ran all day, stopped only twice, never changed a tire, and motored home a very popular fifth.

Some 37 minutes after Corum had finished, a Duesenberg crossed the line to claim 10th.

It was the only one in the field.

Faced with a variety of growing pains concerning its fledgling passenger-car business, the Duesenberg racing program had fallen horribly behind. In spite of the fact that only three entries had been submitted this time, allotted qualifying time was about to run out and the brothers had yet to get a single car in the race. Qualifications were positively to end at sundown on the day before the race, and a late-afternoon

TOMMY MILTON

Articulate, studious, and usually quite somber, the rather private Tommy Milton was the first driver to win the Indianapolis 500 for a second time. An engineer for much of his life, he gave the appearance in his later years of being a bank manager. Born in St. Paul, Minnesota, on November 14, 1893, he came from a family of dairy farmers.

He claimed that as a 15-year-old, he had driven with several friends to witness races at the Indianapolis Speedway even before there was a "500." He competed in eight 500-Mile Races between 1919 and 1927, finishing third for the Duesenberg brothers in 1920, winning in 1921 with a Chevrolet Brothers-built and -entered Frontenac Special, and then winning again in 1923 with an HCS Miller fielded by Harry Stutz.

Winner of the 1919 Elgin, Illinois, road race, Milton was victorious in a number of board track speedway events, the major ones being two at Uniontown, Pennsylvania, and one at Tacoma, Washington, in 1920; a 250-mile race at Tacoma in 1921; a 250-miler at Beverly Hills, California, and a 300-miler at Kansas City, Missouri, in 1922; a 250-miler at Charlotte, North Carolina, in 1924; and 250-milers at Culver City, California, and again at Charlotte in 1925.

He won the 1921 AAA National Championship, and while he was later credited by well-meaning friends as having won the 1920 title as well, he always stated,

"That is very kind of you, but I have a medal on which is engraved 'second.'" On April 27, 1920, driving a streamlined Duesenberg he had helped finance, he roared through the measured mile on the sands of Daytona Beach at an average speed of 156.046 mph, recognized by the Americans as the World Land Speed Record.

All of this was quite remarkable in that Milton had been born with no sight in his right eye, a fact he was generally able to keep secret. It probably accounted for the fact that whenever he was not smiling (which was most of the time), he appeared to be scowling. Never a mixer, he was nevertheless greatly respected by the other drivers, and when one veteran was asked if he thought Milton had the equivalent of only one eye, the response was, "Are you kidding? He's got at least five in the back of his head." Very methodical and intelligent in his approach, Milton was courted by Carl Fisher when Fisher and Allison were considering selling the Indianapolis Speedway. Milton declined, but he did invest in Fisher's unsuccessful Montauk Point project.

Chief steward for the 500-Mile Race between 1949 and 1952, it was Milton who, as a Packard engineer in 1936, fathered the tradition of awarding the "500" pace car to the winning driver. Sadly, he fell into ill health in later years and he died by his own hand in Mount Clemens, Michigan, on July 11, 1962.

telephone call was placed from the factory to the track, informing the officials that at least one car would soon be on its way. The sun was already near the horizon when Phil Shafer, cap on backwards, went flying out onto West Washington Street. Children, cats, dogs, and chickens scattered in every direction as he thundered through the dirt back roads to get to the track. By the time he arrived, in a cloud of dust, the officials had already been obliged to close down for the day.

A compromise was made. Considering that the field was several short of the desired 33, a special concession was made whereby the team would be allowed to qualify the following morning – race morning, that is – at sunrise.

No doubt to the utter joy of the slumbering neighborhood, Shafer drove the car back through the streets at daybreak, arriving in time to take some practice laps at shortly after 5:00 A.M. At 5:45, he made his four-lap run and qualified for the race.

Because the crew had not had time to install an upholstered seat, poor Shafer had ridden the rough bricks while sitting on bare metal. So severely skinned up was he after it was over, that he had to make his way over to the infield hospital for some attention. He later drove the car during the race, but it was teammate Wade Morton who started... *with* a seat. Morton and another driver named Jerry Wonderlich, who was once married to silent-film actress Agnes Ayres, had also set out to qualify their Duesenbergs that morning. Unfortunately, they left much later than Shafer and became so horribly entangled in track-bound traffic that by the time they pulled in, it was far too late to make a run.

Duesenberg would enjoy much better fortune in the "500" in 1924 and 1925.

In the meantime, there was a major development behind the scenes in the days following the 1923 race.

While passenger-car firms were still utilizing the Speedway for private testing during the off-season, the 500-Mile Race itself had become less and less of an event for the manufacturers. Duesenberg was certainly using it for the original purpose – to try to sell automobiles – but the cars the brothers were now racing had virtually no connection at all with what they were offering for sale. The majority of the entries were now being constructed by racing specialists and purchased by wealthy sportsmen who probably owned a yacht and race-

horses. In the eyes of some, the "500" had steadily transformed from being a test of automobiles into a sporting event for drivers, in which the cars they were piloting were of secondary importance.

Among those who felt this way was none other than Carl Fisher.

Spending less and less time with track matters, Fisher had recently given up his home in Indianapolis and had moved permanently down to Miami Beach. Not only were things flourishing down there, but he was now focused on yet another development project, this one at Montauk Point on Long Island. He startled many by making the statement during May that he might even be willing to sell his share in the track – and while he didn't quite go to *that* extent, he did, nevertheless, relinquish the reins.

On June 11, 1923, Carl Graham Fisher, the man who had started it all, stepped down and turned the presidency over to his friend, James A. Allison.

1924: Co-winners, and the dawning of the supercharger

Greatly impressed by the gear-driven superchargers on the three Mercedes entries in 1923, Fred and Augie Duesenberg had installed Roots-type centrifugal "blowers" on three of their four cars for 1924. For the second consecutive year, a driver managed to lead the race with two different cars. This time it was Joe Boyer. Starting on the inside of the second row with one of the supercharged Duesenbergs, Boyer blew by everybody to lead the opening lap. But he didn't stay there for long. He was repassed by the Miller of Jimmy Murphy before the end of lap two, and just a couple of laps later he came gliding into the pits – with supercharger trouble.

Boyer stayed with the car for quite a number of laps after that, but eventually turned it over to other drivers. Just past the halfway mark, steadily running teammate Lora Corum, running about 2½ minutes behind in fourth position, came in to make his only scheduled stop of the day. The decision was made to change drivers, and Corum was obliged to step out in favor of Boyer.

Once back underway, it didn't take long for Boyer to make up ground, and when veteran Earl Cooper ran into tire trouble at 177 laps, Boyer sailed into the lead. It took just a little over five hours and five minutes for the Duesenberg to complete 500 miles, breaking Jimmy Murphy's 1922 mark by 12 minutes and raising the record average speed to 98.23 mph.

Boyer was a true sportsman who certainly wasn't racing for a living. Son of the head of the Burroughs Adding Machine Company, the friendly and athletic Joe was of the country club set, and is believed to have discreetly slipped financial aid to the recent racing programs of both the Chevrolets and the Duesenbergs. Alvin Macauley, now the president of Packard, had once been an employee of Boyer's father.

Throughout history, the relief drivers were to receive little or no mention, the starting driver normally being the only one credited. In the cases of Cyrus Patschke for Ray Harroun in 1911, Don Herr for Joe Dawson in 1912, and Howdy Wilcox for Tommy Milton in 1923, each had driven the winning car during the race but had turned the wheel back over to the original driver before the finish. In this case, however, with Corum starting and Boyer finishing, it was decided to declare them co-winners, the first of two occasions on which this would occur.

For the first time since 1912, there had been an increase in basic prize money, this time from $50,000 to $60,000. The additional amount went into a consolation fund for cars which did not place within the top 10. Eventually, a posted amount was worked out for each position, but in 1924, it was paid proportionally according to the distance each car had completed. With the unfortunate Ernie Ansterburg having crashed his Duesenberg on the backstretch of only his second lap, his share for one trip past the start/finish line resulted in the smallest amount ever paid to a "500" contestant: $5.25.

One other footnote is that there were three Barber–Warnock Fronty–Fords in the lineup and all three were still running at the end, although some distance behind. One of them, flagged off after 176 laps, was driven by an outgoing young Englishman named Alfred Moss, who was temporarily in the area to study dentistry. Three decades later, car owners at Indianapolis would be clamoring for the services of his son, all of whom he politely declined. It seems rather ironic that while the famed Stirling Moss was never to compete in a "500," his father did.

Below: Early arriving motorists have an excellent view of the pits because they could drive right up to the fence. There were no grandstands behind the pits until 1946.

Bottom: From 1911 until 1957, race personnel would pose on race morning for a panoramic photograph. The group would stand in a semi-circle (although it would appear in the end result as if they were in a straight line) and then hold still for several seconds while the camera, on a motorized winch, would "pan" the group.
Photographs: IMS

1925: Home in under five hours

Nineteen twenty-five was to be the third and final year for the 122-cubic-inch engines, the announced specifications for 1926 reducing the size of the power plants to only 1½ liters, a mere 91½ cubic inches.

The recent fields had been of excellent quality but had fallen quite a bit short of the maximum of 33 starters. Only 24 had faced the flagman in 1923, while the starting lineups of 1924 and 1925 comprised a mere 22 cars. Supercharging had grabbed everyone's attention, and only six of the 22 cars in 1925 were "unblown."

Assisted considerably by refinements in supercharging, speeds took a substantial leap. On the pole was Miller driver "Leon Duray," who, in spite of being nicknamed "The Flying Frenchman," was really a Philadelphian named George Stewart. (The name had been coined while he was part of a "barnstorming" troupe of dirt-track racers organized by showman J.

PETER de PAOLO

One of racing's finest-ever spokesmen, 1925 Indianapolis 500 winner Peter de Paolo (April 6, 1898– November 26, 1980) was the first to win the race in under five hours and therefore the first to average better than 100 mph. He was also the only person ever to lead the "500" as both a driver and riding mechanic.

Apprenticed to his uncle Ralph de Palma, he rode from the pole in both 1920 and 1921, placing a delayed fifth after leading as late as the 186th lap in 1920, and breaking down after leading 108 out of 112 laps completed in 1921. When de Palma finished second to Jimmy Murphy in the 1921 French Grand Prix for Ballot, Peter was on board. By 1922, Peter was driving himself, leading laps 84, 85, and 86 in a Chevrolet brothers Frontenac at Indianapolis shortly before crashing.

In 1925, as team leader for Duesenberg, he won the "500" (with 22 laps of relief from Norman Batten) at a record average speed of 101.13 mph. He followed that up with four more major board track wins to capture the 1925 AAA National Championship. During that summer, he traveled to Europe for the purpose of driving a Duesenberg in the Italian Grand Prix, but when those plans failed to materialize, he was invited by the mighty Alfa Romeo team to compete anyway. He was up to second near the end, but ran into a delay and finished fifth.

He slipped to third in AAA rankings in 1926 but

roared back the following year to three more major wins and another title. He never found top form again after an accident during qualifying at Indianapolis in 1928, although he did race for several more years, including in the 1934 Grand Prix of Tripoli and a handful of European events. In 1935, he managed the pit for winner Kelly Petillo, and in 1937, authored "Wall Smacker," his very entertaining memoir.

He had a distinguished military career during WWII, serving in Europe as a lieutenant colonel under General Jimmy Doolittle, and in the late 1940s, wrote a May column for *The Indianapolis News*. He also wrote about the board tracks during a 1950s series for the magazine, *Speed Age*.

A thoroughly entertaining storyteller, he was in much demand as a toastmaster and after-dinner speaker, milking his racing stories for all they were worth, skillfully pausing for the laughs and telling jokes in a mock Italian dialect. In fact, he would really play up the Italian angle for a fresh group and then get a huge laugh when he would press his finger and thumb together and reveal, "I was-a born in Pheeeel-adelphia, Penysl-VAIN-ia."

In spite of standing only about five-foot-seven, he possessed a surprisingly basso voice and he enjoyed singing a cappella. Even into his eighties, he would enter a building singing his interpretation of operatic arias.

Alex Sloan). "Duray" beat the old record by five miles per hour, turning his four-lap qualifying run at 113.196 mph.

Two cars in particular received a great deal of attention because of their extremely low profiles.

While the concept of front-drive was by no means a new one, no such car had ever been entered in a "500." Sometime during the previous summer, Jimmy Murphy had suggested to Harry Miller that front-drive might have quite an advantage at Indianapolis, especially after an abundance of oil had been deposited on the bricks. Miller agreed. Now a fairly wealthy man, thanks to his numerous successes in high-paying AAA Championship board-track events during the carefree, pre-tax days of the 1920s, Murphy commissioned such a car.

There was a shocking period in 1924 when no fewer than *three* Indianapolis 500 winners lost their lives within two weeks of each other. On September 2, Joe Boyer, who had shared the winning car barely three months earlier, succumbed to injuries suffered the previous day in a board-track accident at Altoona, Pennsylvania. The very next day, Boyer's 1923 Packard teammate, Dario Resta, lost his life while trying to break some distance records for Sunbeam at Brooklands in England.

And on September 15, the great Jimmy Murphy perished in a dirt-track accident at Syracuse, New York.

He had already solidified his second AAA National Championship in three years.

With work having already commenced on the front-drive, the sporting Cliff Durant stepped in to underwrite its completion, after which Miller decided to build a slightly different second version for himself.

Veteran driver Dave Lewis, who was Miller's brother-in-law, qualified the Murphy/Durant car for the middle of the second row, but Bennett Hill was not at all happy with the handling of the other one. Although he did qualify it, he stepped out, and rumors had de Palma replacing him. In the end, Harry Miller withdrew it completely.

For those people unable to attend the race, it was no longer necessary to wait for newspaper descriptions in order to learn what had taken place. There had been experimentation with radio at the track as early as 1922, but merely by amateurs who delivered well-intentioned, crackle-punctuated reports for the handful of locals who actually owned receivers. By 1925, the concept of radio had really begun to catch on, and there were now a couple of considerably more formidable outlets offering broadcasts on race day. *The Indianapolis News* had debuted radio station WFBM six months earlier, at a studio on one of the top floors of the Indianapolis Athletic Club building. The new station had a crew on hand to file reports as did the *Chicago Tribune*'s eventual powerhouse, WGN.

Much of the 1925 race was led by Duesenberg's Peter de Paolo, but badly blistered hands forced him to turn the wheel over to Norman Batten for about 35 minutes while the blisters received attention.

Between laps 127 and 173, Dave Lewis led with the front-drive, but when he came in for the final time for fuel and tires, he was so exhausted he couldn't get the car fully stopped. He overshot his pit and had to go on around. He was still leading when he came in to try it again, but the refreshed de Paolo was about to overhaul him. Lewis climbed out of the car in order to make way for a relief driver, and of all the people it could have been, in scrambled Bennett Hill, the very person who had said "no thanks" to the other front-drive.

Whether or not there was a major difference in the handling characteristics between the two cars is not known, but Hill proceeded to chase after de Paolo. Because of the time lost by the aborted stop, plus the driver change, Hill was now 1½ laps behind. Apparently he had no misgivings about driving *this* car. Closer and closer he came to de Paolo, eventually catching up and unlapping himself with just about a dozen laps remaining. De Paolo wisely let him go.

The Duesenberg held on for the win, the fast-closing Hill coming across the line just 53.9 seconds later for what had been by far the closest finish up to that point.

De Paolo's time sliced nine minutes from the old record as he came home in four hours, 56 minutes, and 39.46

seconds. As the first to finish in under five hours, he was also the first to win the race at an average speed in excess of 100 mph, doing so at 101.13 mph.

The Lewis/Hill combination also topped 100 mph, as did the third-placed Duesenberg of Phil Shafer and Wade Morton.

This second consecutive win by the Duesenberg brothers was a huge boost for their prestigious passenger-car firm, although in reality, the company was no longer strictly theirs. It had been struggling financially for some time, and a couple of its major shareholders had come in to run it, Fred and Augie being retained as engineers. The brothers were still running the racing team, but all of their expenditure had to be approved. In fact, the racing operation wasn't even in the factory anymore but rather directly across the street, on the upper floor of the Thompson Pattern Company, a building which did not have an elevator! Anytime a car had to be moved in or out, it was necessary to remove a quantity of bricks from the wall and then gently edge the car either up or down on several sturdy wooden planks! The building was finally demolished after a substantial fire in 2004, but even into the 1970s, de Paolo would still take an occasional leisurely drive down there in May, walk round to the back, and chuckle to himself as he looked up to see the telltale signs of where the bricks had been removed and replaced on numerous occasions half a century earlier.

In tenth position in the 1925 race was an Italian Fiat driven by Pietro Bordino, a highly respected Grand Prix driver, who had been befriended by de Paolo and who was staying in the same private residence just a short distance from the track. In fact, it was so close that after the post-race celebrating had been completed and the crowd had thinned out, de Paolo and his wife, Sally, returned there *on foot.*

They did make one stop along the way, visiting Rosner's drugstore on the corner of West 16th Street and Main Street in order to treat themselves to a double chocolate malt. From there, they strolled the remaining block or so back to the house on 15th Street, where there was a joyous welcoming by friends and neighbors. After a while, Peter excused himself from the celebration and eased his aching and beaten body into a steaming-hot bath, taking with him a glass of wine. Far into the night, the house was filled with the glorious sound of his strong, surprisingly basso voice as he delivered renditions of various operatic arias.

A famous landmark came down a day or two after the race. Because of the steadily rising speeds, since it had been erected in 1913, there had been growing concerns that the pagoda had probably been built a little too close to the edge of the track. It took only a few minutes for it to be burned to the ground, and its successor, similar in appearance but many feet further back, was in place by the following May and ready to serve for the next 30 years.

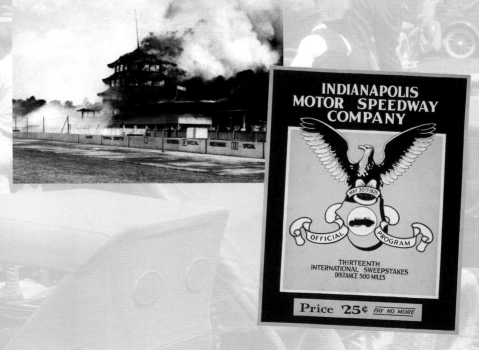

SUPERCHARGED SCREAMERS

OFFICIAL PROGRAM
INDIANAPOLIS
MOTOR SPEEDWAY
COMPANY.
Fourteenth International Sweepstakes Distance 500 Miles
May 31st 1926

Price 25¢ PAY NO MORE

Left: Judging by the puddles, this photograph was taken during the period the 1926 race was stopped (after 71 laps) due to a rain shower.

Bottom: Frank Lockhart arrives in 1926 with the promise of serving as relief driver for Bennett Hill, if needed. When driver/owner Peter Kreis has to be hospitalized with pneumonia, Lockhart receives the break of a lifetime.
Photographs: IMS

1926: From hopeful relief driver to race winner

IN spite of engine sizes having been further reduced from 122 cubic inches to only 91½ for 1926, the early indications in practice were that the cars would be lapping just as quickly as ever. This was the fifth reduction since the original cut from 600 cubic inches to 450 in 1913, and it stood as a fitting tribute to the engineers that lap speeds had increased by 25 mph in just 13 years, this being achieved with engines that were now less than one-sixth the size permissible at the beginning.

The sensation of qualifications was a young dirt-track driver who wasn't even on the entry list. Bashful 23-year-old Dayton, Ohio-born Frank Lockhart had gained quite a reputation among the West Coast racers for his amazing prowess on Californian dirt tracks, and he had been encouraged by colleagues to try Indianapolis. His initial assignment was to serve as a potential relief driver for Bennett Hill, and it wasn't long before he was turning very respectable lap times.

He was about to receive the break of a lifetime.

Peter Kreis, a teammate of de Paolo at Duesenberg the year before, had now acquired one of a growing number of rear-drive Millers, but just a couple of days before qualifications were to begin on May 27, Kreis came down with a serious bout of pneumonia and had to be admitted to Methodist Hospital.

Largely through the efforts of Ernie Olson, the late Jimmy Murphy's mechanic, Lockhart was invited to try out the Miller in Kreis's absence.

The results were extraordinary. The single-lap track record at the time was 114.285 mph, set the year before by de Paolo in a 122-cid Duesenberg. With very little practice, Lockhart went to the qualifying line in his "91" and proceeded to shatter the mark, running through his first official lap at 115.488 mph.

With lap two just a fraction under 115, Lockhart appeared headed for the four-lap record as well. Instead, he was headed for the pits. Still in the process of trying to "unlearn" his dirt-track techniques, his exuberant cornering had resulted in the shredding of the right rear tire.

Lockhart went out again a short time later to make a second attempt at a slightly reduced rate – 111 mph – but this time a valve broke after one lap, damaging the block.

He was down to one "strike."

On the day before the race, Lockhart made his third and final attempt. Fully aware that the chances of a full field of 33 were looking slim, he took the advice of Olson and others and cruised through at a conservative 95.782 mph. He would start 20th.

Rain clouds were hovering when the field of 28 lined up on race morning. Every single car was supercharged, including an Arthur Chevrolet-fielded Fronty–Ford which also featured front-drive. All but 10 of the cars were straight-eight Millers, and two of those were Miller-based.

Phil Shafer jumped from fifth starting position to lead the first lap with a rear-drive Miller, and remained there for 15 laps until Dave Lewis took over with a front-drive. Other than for Shafer moving in front briefly on lap 22, the low-slung car of Lewis controlled the race up through lap 59.

At that point, who should come to the front but Lockhart!

Seven laps later, it rained, and for the first time ever, the "500" was halted.

The storm passed, and after about an hour and five minutes, the 16 surviving cars were pushed off for a restart. It was pretty much all Lockhart from that point on. Harry Hartz did manage to lead for six laps while Lockhart made a pit stop at just past halfway, but when rain stopped the proceedings for a second time at 400 miles, Lockhart had a two-lap lead over Hartz.

There was no question of a restart this time. Assessing in advance that it would have been impossible to dry the track a second time before dark, Chief Steward W. D. "Eddie" Eden-burn had had the forethought to have starter Seth Klein standing by with the checkered flag. If rain were to halt the proceedings again anytime after 300 miles, he would end it. Thus, when a steady drizzle began to increase, Edenburn looked at his watch and then ordered Klein to throw the flag. Lockhart was declared the winner.

In spite of the fact that the race had been stopped and restarted, the timing and scoring crew had been able to calculate an elapsed time for the race. The oddity was that Lockhart's average speed for 400 miles—95.885 mph—was slightly faster than the speed at which he had qualified, the same situation having occurred two years earlier with the Corum/Boyer Duesenberg.

Of the 13 cars flagged off when the rains came, de Paolo's fifth-place-finishing Duesenberg was the only non-Miller still running. It was seven laps behind.

The three overseas entries which started each had fallen by the wayside, the Anzani-powered cars of Brooklands standouts E. A. D. Eldridge and W. D. Hawkes having lasted 45 and 91 laps, respectively, while pre-World War I veteran Albert Guyot's fifth and final Indianapolis attempt was over in only eight laps. This was the second appearance for Hawkes, husband of the famed lady racer, the former Gwenda Glubb Stewart. In 1922, Douglas Hawkes had been at Indianapolis with a TT Bentley – basically a sports car – and had completed the entire 500 miles in six hours and 40 minutes, some one hour and 23 minutes after Jimmy Murphy had taken the checker. No sooner had the race been completed than he was obliged to sail for England in order to have the Bentley readied in time for the Tourist Trophy, on the Isle of Man, only three weeks later.

Also at the track in 1926 was a longtime Eldridge and Hawkes associate, Captain John Duff, co-winner of the second running of the 24-Hours of Le Mans two years earlier. He ended up as a most unlikely participant in the "500." On May 27, the first day of qualifications, young Herbert Jones, who had only just turned 22, crashed an Elcar Motor Company-sponsored Miller while trying to qualify for his second "500." The car had turned upside down and then landed on its wheels, snuffing out the life of the driver. It was the track's first fatality since 1919, and the first one ever during a qualifying attempt.

The decision was made to repair the damaged car, and Duff, who had already landed the assignment as Jones's relief driver, jumped in to assist with the job. It was completed the day before the race, and Duff made the qualifying run. His speed was sufficient, but the engine dropped a valve at the end of the run and damaged a cylinder in the process, necessitating yet another "all-nighter."

While Duff did run a steady race and was running ninth when the rains came, there was still the sobering reality that just four days earlier, the very cockpit in which he rode had taken a driver's life.

1927: Lockhart breaks 120

Any intentions officials may have had regarding a reduction in engine size translating into lower speeds were dashed by the time practice began in 1927. The four-lap qualifying record was broken four times on the opening day of time trials, and defending winner Frank Lockhart ended up on the pole at an amazing 120.100 mph. His fastest lap had been just a shade under 121.

Lockhart – who, in spite of his very humble beginnings and limited education, was now in a position to own his own car – continued to be full of surprises. Most experts had assumed that all of the fastest qualifiers would be of the lower-sitting front-drive variety. Most of them were, except that Lockhart's pole sitter was rear-drive.

Lockhart took the lead at the start and remained there for almost two hours, not relinquishing it until he came in for fuel and tires after 81 laps. It would be 63 years before any driver would break *that* record. Other than for nine laps led by dirt-track driver "Dutch" Baumann, after Lockhart had come in to make his stop, the defending winner was in front for almost 300 miles.

On the 121st lap, just when it was beginning to appear that, for the first time, a driver was going to win for the second time in succession, a connecting rod broke and Lockhart's run was over.

Nineteen twenty-five winner Peter de Paolo went to the front at this point, driving a car he had taken over from Bob McDonough after his own had dropped out. It was one of three virtual Miller front-drive copies built under the direction of the now retired Earl Cooper.

De Paolo led for 30 laps until the 149th lap, at which time he had to pit for a lengthy change of sparkplugs, dropping him to an eventual sixth-place finish.

The new leader was somewhat of a surprise. Driving in the "500" for the first time, George Souders, a Lafayette, Indiana, native and Purdue University undergraduate, had spent the last couple of seasons living in Abilene, Texas, and had done quite well racing on dirt tracks down there. He had been befriended during that period by a young sportsman named Bill White, who eventually would become quite a prominent figure as a car owner and racing promoter. Later known as "Hollywood" Bill White, he had purchased for Souders a Duesenberg, allegedly (but never proven to be) the same one with which de Paolo had won the 1925 "500." It was, at the very least, of the same type.

This was the combination now leading.

While car after car stopped for a change of driver, Souders just kept on motoring. In fact, every car finishing from second on down through 17th employed at least one relief driver, while several cars required a second and even a third relief. The cars which finished seventh and eighth were shared by

OFFICIAL PROGRAM

INDIANAPOLIS MOTOR SPEEDWAY CO.

15th INTERNATIONAL SWEEPSTAKES 500 MILES

MAY 30th 1927

Price — 25¢ PAY NO MORE

1st Place — Winner
INDIANAPOLIS MOTOR SPEEDWAY 15TH ANNUAL 500 MILE RACE 1927.
George Souders Duesenberg Special

Inset top left: The front-drive version of the Miller straight-eight requires that the engine be mounted in the opposite direction, placing the supercharger practically over the driver's feet.

Above: Norman Batten, who drove relief for Peter de Paolo in the 1925-winning Duesenberg, bravely steers his blazing Miller past the fuel-laden pits in 1927.
Photographs: IMS

four drivers each, and more than one driver turned laps in three different cars.

The margin of victory for Souders was the second-largest ever: just over 12 minutes. It would have been closer to seven minutes had it not been for a devastating example of misfortune, which, along with several others in those days, never seemed to be afforded the attention it perhaps warranted. A Duesenberg, shared by first-time starters Benny Shoaff and Babe Stapp, completed its 198th lap in second place. The crew eagerly awaited the completion of the 199th lap, but it never came, the drive gears giving way within sight of the finish and unable to propel the car for its final three or four miles.

All the youngsters could do was watch helplessly as car after car passed by, headed for the checkered flag.

While the combination of Earl Devore and "Zeke" Meyer shared a Miller to second place and earned prize money amounting to $12,800, Shoaff and Stapp had to console themselves with $550.

There was a bit of an irony in the winner's enclosure. The track's publicist for the last several years had been Steve Hannagan, who was well on his way to becoming one of the best-known public-relations people in the country. Now spending the majority of his time with Fisher in Miami, Hannagan was, like Souders, a native of Lafayette. Not only that, but they had even attended the same high school, Hannagan having been ahead of Souders by just one year.

Finishing fourth was a pair of young drivers who were each participating in their first "500," but who eventually would become two of the track's most notable icons. The 24-year-old Wilbur Shaw, who had never before driven in a race of lengthier than 100 miles (and typically over much shorter distances than that), sought relief at the midpoint of the race. He handed over, for a while, to his 22-year-old mechanic, who had also been a frequent rival of his in Midwestern dirt-track events, and who in fact had been in line to drive this very car

himself. His name was Louis Meyer.

Who could have known that not only would Meyer and Shaw become the first two drivers to win the "500" three times, but that in 20 years' time, Shaw would be the president and general manager of the track and Meyer would be co-owner of the company producing the most successful engine in the track's history.

There was one major piece of excitement in the early stages of the race when, on the 24th lap, a huge shout went up from the crowd. A car was coming down the main straight with flames pouring from its rear end. It was later determined that fuel dripping from a split fuel tank had somehow become ignited, turning the rapidly moving car into a rolling blowtorch. Driver Norman Batten, who had briefly shared de Paolo's winning Duesenberg in 1925, was standing up in the cockpit, leaning forward and steering as best he could.

Batten guided the car over to the inside of the track and continued, at a moderate speed, past the pits, bravely remaining at the helm in spite of crew members from the various other teams yelling at him to jump for safety. Only after he had taken it past the final pit at the south end did he finally leap out. The slowing car came to a rest on the inside of turn one, no longer a blowtorch, but rather now a steadily burning bonfire.

Batten, who was hospitalized for several weeks, was hailed as a hero for averting what could have been a catastrophe in the fuel-laden pits. He would recover to compete in the 1928 race, finishing fifth, but he was only months away from losing his life in a rather bizarre fashion. In November 1928, Batten and his friend Earl Devore, the 1927 runner-up, loaded their Millers onto a ship and sailed down for a winter of racing in South America. The ship was the ill-fated S. S. Vestris. It was caught in a violent storm off the coast of Virginia, and sank many hours later after the hold had filled up with thousands of gallons of seawater. Both drivers were lost.

Cars In Position For Start
Indianapolis Motor Speedway.
16th Annual 500 Mile Race 1928.

1928: So long Fisher and Allison, Hello Rickenbacker: The track changes hands

By the time the 1928 "500" was held, the track was under new ownership.

After returning from World War I as an American hero, Eddie Rickenbacker had turned down numerous lucrative offers to go on the lecture circuit, to appear in vaudeville and in motion pictures and various other money-making ventures, choosing instead to enter industry. The Rickenbacker Motor Company was formed in Detroit in 1922, with Captain Eddie overseeing every aspect of it. The Rickenbacker automobiles were technically advanced, luxurious machines of the highest quality, the firm gaining even more prestige when one of its products was invited to serve as the "500" pace car in 1925, with Eddie, himself, at the wheel. Unfortunately, times were difficult, and largely due to a substantial depression which preceded the more famous one of the 1930s, the company began to struggle and Rickenbacker was obliged to close everything down in late 1926.

In the meantime, Rickenbacker had been invited to serve as a member of the AAA Contest Board, and no sooner had he accepted than the organization underwent a major revamping. While a few of the members did have connections with the automobile industry, the majority were businessmen who knew little or nothing about automobile *racing*. The

names of several who had been serving for years disappeared from the roster, and in no time at all, Rickenbacker was elevated to board chairman.

In spite of the failure of the Rickenbacker Motor Company, Eddie still had faithful backers in Detroit who believed in him and pledged they would be willing to support in him in any future endeavor of merit.

Rickenbacker traveled to Main Street in Speedway, Indiana, in order to pay a visit to Jim Allison, his partner/boss from 1916. Would Allison, Eddie wanted to know, be interested in selling Allison Engineering?

No, he would not. But Allison did come back with a counterproposal Rickenbacker had not anticipated.

How about putting in a bid for the Indianapolis Motor Speedway?

Rickenbacker rushed back to Detroit as fast as he could get there, raving to his backers about the possibility of purchasing the track from Fisher and Allison. Newby had retired from industry and was not in the best of health. Wheeler, out of the picture since 1917, had died six years earlier. Fisher had all but completely lost interest in the track, and Allison wasn't far behind him.

Fisher, who was very enthusiastic about Rickenbacker taking over, was dealing with the beginnings of a devastating reversal of fortune.

One of his numerous ventures in Miami – at a time when

Rickenbacker was finally able to generate the necessary amount by floating bonds through Frank Blair of the Union Guardian Trust Company in Detroit. On August 31, 1927, application was filed for the formation of the Indianapolis Motor Speedway *Corporation,* the track having been held, up to this point, by the Indianapolis Motor Speedway *Company.*

Rickenbacker now found himself in an extraordinary position. In just a matter of months, he had risen from being drafted on to the AAA Contest Board, to becoming its chairman, to suddenly being the owner of title of the Indianapolis Motor Speedway. A persuasive man to begin with, one can only assume that any rule or regulation Rickenbacker cared to implement would have met with little opposition.

For the next several years, Rickenbacker would prove to be an extremely hands-on owner, but the challenges would be many.

The name on everybody's lips as the track opened for practice in 1928 was Frank Lockhart. Strongly favored as a potential winner of the upcoming race, he had crashed to his death on April 25 while trying to break the world land speed record on the sands of Daytona Beach, Florida.

Just three days earlier, fellow American Ray Keech had taken the record from England's Malcolm Campbell by recording a two-way average of 207.552 mph with an enormous 8,000-pound contraption, powered by *three* Aero Liberty V-12 aircraft engines displacing a whopping 4,950 cubic inches. Lockhart had developed a considerably lighter streamliner, utilizing a pair of supercharged straight-eight Millers forming a V-16 and displacing only 181 cubic inches. He recorded 203 mph on the southern run and was believed to be traveling in excess of 210 mph on the return when a tire blew with catastrophic results.

Months earlier, Lockhart had entered two rear-drive Millers for the "500," and no sooner had the track opened than his friendship and camaraderie with Keech came to light, when Lockhart's widow arranged for the sale of the car Frank had planned to drive himself to a backer of Keech.

In 1927, Wilbur Shaw had landed a driving assignment at the expense of Louis Meyer. Now, the roles were reversed. Shaw was down to pilot a rear-drive Miller for owner/driver Phil Shafer, but when an anticipated sponsorship fell through, Shafer decided he would place one of his two cars up for sale.

The previous year at Atlantic City, New Jersey, Meyer had become good friends with a quiet young man about his own age named Alden Sampson II, who came from a wealthy family and dearly wanted to become a race driver himself. Meyer

OFFICIAL PROGRAM
The INDIANAPOLIS MOTOR SPEEDWAY CORPORATION
16th INTERNATIONAL SWEEPSTAKES
DISTANCE 500 MILES
MAY-30, 1928
PRICE PAY 25 CENTS NO MORE.

he had already started a massive development project at Montauk Point on Long Island – was to build a magnificent, steeply banked, 1½-mile board-track speedway. These incredibly fast, but short-lived facilities were the forerunner of the modern American "superspeedways." Located at Fulford-by-the-Sea, just north of Miami, this one had opened on February 22, 1926, under the direction of General Manager Ray Harroun. At a time when the single-lap record at Indianapolis had not yet reached 115 mph, Peter de Paolo was able to win a full 300-mile race at Miami at a phenomenal *average* of almost 130 mph!

Before a second event could be held, however, a hurricane smashed its way through Miami, all but flattening everything in its path. If solid buildings were unable to withstand its impact, a wooden board-track certainly had little chance, and down it went.

In an effort to try to save Miami and begin rebuilding as quickly as possible, work on Montauk Point was halted. The bills mounted rapidly and Fisher's massive empire was in trouble.

Rickenbacker had a few more hurdles to overcome than he had anticipated, and his 30-day option on the track soon ran out. He had tried, without success, to raise the asking price (believed to have been in the region of $700,000) through business interests in Indianapolis. Allison granted him an extension of another 30 days.

convinced "Sam" that the rear-drive was the opportunity of a lifetime, and to the surprise of Shafer, who thought he was dealing with a couple of starry-eyed dreamers, Sampson paid for the car in full.

Shaw, for the time being, was out of a "ride."

On the pole was "Leon Duray" (George Stewart), who laid down a set of laps that, largely due to a major change in specifications, would stand as records for several years to come. Methanol, a wood grain-based alcohol, recently had become the fuel of choice and Duray used it to the fullest advantage. He completed his four-lap run with a record average speed of 122.391 mph, after an earlier "wave-off" similar to that of Lockhart's in 1926. Prior to having to come in with a right rear tire problem, Duray had turned a lap at a truly amazing 124.018. Only one other driver, Cliff Woodbury, was able to exceed 120, and many an oldtimer would claim years later that Duray's was the greatest driving feat they had ever witnessed at the track.

Shaw did manage to qualify a car, but literally at the very last moment. Peter de Paolo, trying to knock Duray from the pole late on May 26, had crashed in turn three of his second lap and severely damaged his car. It was repaired in the shops of Arthur Chevrolet, and Shaw was hired to replace the injured de Paolo. He successfully qualified the car – but on race morning.

That Shaw was able to do so at all is quite remarkable, in that rain had fallen overnight and the track was still slippery. The final practice session for qualified cars – otherwise known as "carburetion runs" – also was held on race morning and two qualifiers, Lora Corum and Dutch Baumann, both crashed their Duesenbergs and had to withdraw.

Shortly before the start, an ambulance pulled up in the pits near the start/finish line, and to the delight of the crowd, out was wheeled a stretcher bearing de Paolo. He was carried to a seat inside the pagoda.

The majority of the first 150 miles was led by Duray with his front-drive Miller, but he began to fade and the car eventually dropped out, while fellow front-row qualifier Cliff Bergere, already eliminated, was at the wheel as a relief driver.

A Duesenberg, shared by Jimmy Gleason and Russ Snowberger, led a total of 56 laps and was in contention until the very end, while also up front during the latter half was Tony Gulotta at the wheel of the second Lockhart entry. Sharing the wheel with Dutch Baumann, who had crashed his Duesenberg a couple of hours before the start, Gulotta was leading as late as lap 181, with Gleason second and the steadily running Louis Meyer, who had started 13th, in third.

In quick succession, Gulotta was forced in with a fuel-feed problem and Gleason had to pit with a failing magneto, whereupon, to the dismay of Phil Shafer, who had sold the car to Sampson just a few days earlier, into the lead for the final 19 laps went the 23-year-old Meyer.

Youth had been served again. Although he had driven relief the year before, Meyer had had no previous "500" starts. Finishing second, also having started for the first time, was another famous name of the future, Lou Moore, who eventually would become the first owner to win five times, three of them with the famous Blue Crown Specials in the 1940s. Moore shared the wheel on this day with Louis Schneider, who was destined to win in 1931. Schneider had one previous start under his belt. Third was defending winner George Souders, also with one previous start, while fourth was the combination of newcomer Ray Keech in the other Lockhart car sharing the wheel with second-time-starting Shaw, whose de Paolo Miller had dropped out early.

Left: Ray Keech had just lost his World Land Speed Record of 207.552 mph to Britain's Major Henry Segrave when he won the 1929 "500," in Maude Yagle's ex-Frank Lockhart Miller.

Photograph: IMS

Public awareness of the race – beyond merely realizing that it existed – was enhanced to an even greater extent this year by the fact that the National Broadcasting Company devoted a full half an hour of air time to covering the finish by radio. Evidently, it was of enough importance to NBC that they sent in Graham McNamee, who was their lead announcer, not only for major sporting events like the Jack Dempsey/Gene Tunney prize fights and major league baseball's World Series, but for events like the 1924 National Republican Convention. Before long, CBS started covering the race as well, reports being filed by another famous commentator, Ted Husing.

On August 4, 1928, came the surprising news that the seemingly robust Jim Allison had passed away within a few days of his 56th birthday. He had divorced his wife of many years and had traveled to Fisher's retreat on Montauk Point for the purpose of marrying his longtime personal assistant. He contracted pneumonia while there and returned home by train. His condition worsened, and he succumbed less than one week after the marriage had taken place.

1929: Hollywood comes to the Speedway

One of the items Fisher and Allison had discussed with Rickenbacker during the period of the potential purchase of the track had been a suggestion that a golf course be installed on the grounds in order to generate additional revenue throughout the rest of the year. Designed by William H. Diddel, an Indianapolis architect, such a course was opened in 1929, with nine holes on the infield and nine more on the other side of the backstretch, accessed by a bridge spanning the track, just north of the exit of turn two.

In 1929, nobody could match the records Duray had set the previous year – not even Duray himself. Cliff Woodbury, who had qualified second in 1928, won the pole, this time at 120.599 mph with Duray second.

It was Duray who led at the start, Woodbury in hot pursuit ahead of Duray's teammate, former motorcycle-racing great Ralph Hepburn.

Woodbury's challenge was short-lived. Coming onto the main straight on only his fourth lap, he spun around and hit the outer wall with force, the pole sitter being eliminated with only three laps on the board.

The fact that the wrecked car was up against the wall, and that corner workers were trying to remove it by sliding it up over the wall on planks, apparently didn't warrant a very long caution. Duray and his rivals just kept on charging.

To the surprise of just about everybody, the leader at the end of lap eight was a rear-drive Miller, driven by a friendly giant of a man named "Deacon" Litz.

It later came to light that the third-running Deacon had reached for the handbrake upon entering turn three, only to discover to his horror that it had fallen off. In a desperate attempt to keep from hitting second-placed Ralph Hepburn, he had wrenched the car onto the apron and then "dirt-tracked" through the turn, coming out of it ahead of not only Hepburn, but Duray as well.

He stayed in front for 56 laps.

The race was being filmed by the MGM motion-picture company, a full crew on hand to make a silent comedy entitled "Speedway," starring William Haines, Anita Page, Ernest Torrence, and Karl Dane, much of it being shot in and around the garage area. The search for a car/driver combination to serve as a "double" for the role of "the villain" had been easy. The solidly built, gruff, and usually scowling Leon Duray, with his trademark black uniform, was precisely what they were looking for. For "the hero," the car they chose was the white #26 Miller of Deacon Litz.

It appeared that Louis Meyer was going to be able to successfully defend his title, at least until his final pit stop on lap 157. The engine stalled at that point, and by the time it could be refired, Louis had lost an excruciating seven minutes. Ray Keech passed him with the ex-Lockhart Miller, and so did the Miller of Lou Moore, the latter sharing the wheel with yet another newcomer, Barney Kloepfer. Just as fate had knocked out the Shoaff/Stapp Duesenberg in 1927, so, two years later, the second-placed runner was eliminated again, the Moore/Kloepfer Miller breaking a connecting rod on its 199th lap.

The Moore/Kloepfer car was one of the first to carry a sponsorship of a product not directly tied to the automobile business. While there were now cars running as Boyle Valve

Below: The view south from the pagoda in 1929 shows that since the previous May a second bank of garages has been erected in order to house the growing number of entries.
Photograph: IMS

Specials, Packard Cable Specials, Elgin Piston Pin Specials, and even State Auto Insurance Specials, Lou Moore's Miller carried the backing of Majestic Radios.

Keech went on to win (with his Simplex Piston Ring Special), and some six minutes later, Meyer was able to take advantage of Moore's misfortune by taking second. Jimmy Gleason, who had so nearly won the year before, co-drove a Duesenberg with Thane Houser and Ernie Triplett to third place.

The winning entrant – the backer of Keech who had purchased the Miller from Frank Lockhart's widow in 1928 – was M. A. Yagle. It turned out that the "M" stood for "Maude" and that M. A. Yagle was actually a lady. She and her husband continued entering a car in the "500" up through 1932 and were quite active in racing on the East Coast for several years.

Finishing seventh was a French Delage, driven by the debonair Louis Chiron from the Principality of Monaco, who was near the beginning of a long and illustrious career. Accompanying him was a female interpreter, Alice Hoffman Trobeck, who just a few years later would marry the great German driver Rudolf Caracciola. Extremely handy with a stopwatch, she was surprised to learn that, at American tracks, women were not permitted in the pits or garage area. She used her considerable charms to prevail upon Tom Beall, owner of the trackside lunch counter, to allow a small platform to be erected on the roof, where, armed with a pair of stopwatches, she was able to keep Chiron informed of his position throughout the race.

The garage area, to which a second bank of garages had been added due to the growing number of entries, had taken on the nickname "Gasoline Alley." Originally, this had applied only to the one corner where the fuel depot was located, but it was now being used for the entire garage complex. A very popular newspaper strip cartoon by that name had debuted in 1919, and it has never been determined whether or not one may have influenced the other.

Once again, relief drivers were used quite extensively, and Cliff Woodbury led a most eventful day. After crashing the pole-winning car within five minutes of the start, he came back to serve as a relief driver on no fewer than three other cars, one of them finishing eighth and another twelfth. He remains as the only person ever to drive four different cars in the same "500."

Sadly, the race was not without its tragedy; shortly after the start, young Bill Spence lost his life when his car hit the turn two inside wall and overturned. It was the first fatality involving a driver in the race itself since 1919.

The true perils of the sport were rammed home yet again only two weeks later on June 15, when, in a 200-mile event on the board track at Altoona, Pennsylvania, "500" winner Ray Keech met his end on the very same track which had taken the lives of fellow "500" victors Howdy Wilcox (in 1923) and Joe Boyer (in 1924).

For 1930, there was a drastic change in the specifications.

Rickenbacker was among many people who lamented that the Indianapolis "500" was no longer an event for products of the automobile companies, but rather had become a sporting event for drivers, whose mounts were now sophisticated thoroughbred racing cars, owned by individual sportsmen, and built by specialists who had no direct stake or involvement in the automobile industry. Some companies were still using the track for testing, but Indianapolis-based firms were diminishing. A number had relocated to Detroit and many more were no longer in existence. In an attempt to encourage a return to the Speedway by the automobile firms, Rickenbacker drew up a set of specifications which opened engine sizes all the way up from 91½ cubic inches to a full 366 (six liters) and eliminated supercharging except on two-cycle engines.

There was also a weight-versus-engine-size ratio imposed to discourage the practice of placing large engines in small, light cars, and for some reason never quite made clear, riding mechanics once again would become mandatory. Apparently, it was an attempt to have the cars at least look like something which would be driven on the street.

The latter would come under much criticism until finally dropped after 1937.

There is a myth which has persisted for almost 80 years, suggesting that these specifications were brought about by necessity due to the Wall Street "crash" of October 31, 1929. In fact, Rickenbacker first drew up the beginnings of these specs during the summer of 1928 and worked with various committees for technical input to perfect them by September. The rules were passed by the AAA Contest Board in January 1929 and were immediately announced as going into effect for 1930.

This was a full *ten months* before the Wall Street stock market "crash," and yet the myth persists to this day.

Chapter 5
DEALING WITH THE GREAT DEPRESSION

1930: Sweeping changes: Superchargers out, back in with the riding mechanics

DESPITE Rickenbacker's well-intentioned efforts, the manufacturers never did embrace the theory that they could gain attention for their products by engaging in competition at Indianapolis. Only Studebaker of South Bend, Indiana, in 1932 and 1933 and Ford in 1935 took advantage of the new specifications with major efforts, the former with reasonable success, the latter with an episode which was to cause quite a bit of embarrassment for the firm. Instead, the general makeup of the field for the next few years was to be a conglomeration of pre-existing single-seat racing cars modified to accommodate a second person, a few brand-new two-seaters, and a collection of home-built "specials" created out of production cars or at least powered by production engines; either way, at very little cost.

The quality varied greatly.

As an added incentive for the encouragement of entries, the size of the starting field was increased from 33 cars to 40 for 1930, but because so many entrants were running behind schedule, only 38 were able to complete four-lap runs at above the minimum of 85 mph.

The class of the field was 23-year-old Billy Arnold, who stepped in at the last moment for Harry Hartz. The 1926 AAA national champion had suffered a severe leg injury in a crash near the end of the 1927 season, and was just now attempting to make his return to competition. Driving a brand-new (nonsupercharged) 152-cubic-inch front-drive Miller which he had commissioned during the winter, Hartz had given plenty of practice time both to Arnold and to Ralph Hepburn in anticipation of needing a relief driver. Both had driven in the last couple of 500-Mile Races, but neither yet had an assignment for this one.

Hartz even made a qualifying attempt, turning a lap at 110.429 mph, which, had he completed the run, would have

been fast enough to start on the front row. Instead, he came in, determining that he just hadn't recovered enough to be able to do the car justice. Unlike Hepburn, who had suggested making a variety of changes after driving the car, Arnold seemed happy with things as they were. So it was Arnold who got the call, and out went the Chicago youth to put the car on the pole at 113.268 mph.

It is the only occasion in the track's history on which a driver has won the pole position while driving a car which had just made an incomplete attempt in the hands of another driver.

There had been a complete revision in the flag code, and for the first time, green was now to be used to start the race rather than to indicate "one lap to go." Red, which had been used to start races since before the first running of the "500," now meant "stop," while white, for the time being, meant "stop for consultation." The flag indicating "one lap to go" was of king's blue.

The race was a complete runaway, Arnold dominating to an extent even greater than that of the luckless de Palma in 1912. Louis Meyer did manage to get ahead at the start, but Arnold had passed him by the end of lap three for what turned out to be the only lead change of the entire race. Arnold led 198 consecutive laps to win by seven minutes over second place.

Throughout much of the second half, Hartz tried without success to get Arnold to slow down and protect his lead, gesturing, at times, in quite animated fashion. Billy reasoned that to slow down might spoil his rhythm, so he just kept on charging. He was home in just under five hours to average 100.448 mph, as the first driver to exceed 100 mph for the distance without the aid of a relief driver.

In second place was a Miller, shared by William "Shorty" Cantlon and Herman Schurch, this particular Miller being one with a difference. It was powered by a "marine" engine (designed for boat racing) of four cylinders rather than eight. It was quick. Financed by "Hollywood Bill" White, the car had been taken up to Muroc Dry Lake on April 10, and Cantlon had established a four-cylinder record for the flying mile at almost 145 mph. While it may not have drawn a great deal of attention at the time, it was actually the forerunner of the famed "four-banger" Offenhauser engine which would enjoy immeasurable success over the next several decades.

Third, in a straight-eight Miller, was Louis Schneider, a former Indianapolis motorcycle policeman and dirt-track racer whose rather antagonistic demeanor would frequently land him in trouble with officialdom. His Miller carried the sponsorship of a brand-new company, one which would be involved in racing for the majority of the next 35 years: Bowes Seal Fast.

Fourth, with Alden Sampson going along for the ride, was Louis Meyer, leader of the only two laps not claimed by Arnold. Hardly going with the status quo, two straight-eight,

91-cubic-inch Millers had been bored out to 100.5 cid each and then mounted side by side, the two crankshafts being geared together to drive a propeller shaft which ran between them. This arrangement has often been mistaken for Frank Lockhart's approach of taking two straight-eights to form a V-16. The Meyer/Sampson engines both were horizontal.

Because the Great Depression had not yet grabbed the country and money was still reasonably plentiful, there was an abundance of accessory prize money and lap prizes attached to Arnold's win. The total earned by the winning entry was $50,350, a huge amount for the time. It later came to light that Arnold had been so anxious to drive the car for the frugal Hartz that he had been happy to forgo the standard 40 percent of the prize money and had driven for approximately half that amount. There were no complaints on either side.

A reporter in the victory enclosure reminded the new winner that just the night before, Arnold had come out of his hotel with his mother and younger brother to discover that his personal passenger car had been stolen. "Tell that guy (the car thief) to come round to my room," drawled the nonchalant Arnold in response, "and I'll give him the title." Later that evening, Arnold received an anonymous call at the hotel, telling him where his stolen Chrysler was parked. He sent his younger brother over to retrieve it, and when it came back with part of the windshield missing, Billy told the brother to keep the car for himself.

Early in the race there had been a gigantic chain-reaction accident at the north end, involving seven cars, fortunately without any substantial injury. The incident was captured on film by a newsreel company and was to appear numerous times over the years, both in documentaries and in inexpensively made Hollywood "epics" about racing.

In a separate accident, however, a riding mechanic did lose his life. His name was Paul Marshall and the cruel irony is that Cy Marshall, with whom he was riding, was his own brother.

Once again, foreign entries had been sought by management, but the only starters were a pair of Italian Maseratis, one from the factory and the other by an independent. Letterio Piccolo Cucinotta, whom the crowd predictably nicknamed "Piccolo Pete," finished twelfth, while Baconin Borzacchini, who would win the grueling Mille Miglia in Italy in 1932, lasted only seven laps with a temperamental 16-cylinder entry fielded by the Maserati brothers themselves.

One story, which easily could have seemed to be the product of somebody's imagination, and which has been greatly exaggerated over the years, was in fact reported in detail at the time. Chet Miller, who eventually would become one of the track's most enduring veterans, was making his debut, driving a Detroit-entered Fronty–Ford built largely out of Ford Model "T" parts and fielded at very little cost.

Following a lap-92 pit stop, an eagle-eyed official would not allow Miller to return to the track because the car's right front spring was broken. While Miller tried to assure the official that he had been able to overcome the handling difficulties, the official stood firm. The story went on to describe that, with no spare on hand, a couple of the crew members had gone into the infield behind the pits, where they quickly located a Model "T" which was unattended. They are reported to have removed the spring and installed it on Chet Miller's racing car, and after being stationary for 41 minutes, Miller went back into the race ultimately to finish a rather distant 13th place. Not only that, but when the mechanics returned after the race, the Model "T" was still unattended and the spring reportedly was reinstalled without the owner ever having been aware of the transaction.

1931: Five hundred miles without a stop? In a diesel?

A record 70 entries were received for the 1931 race, 24 more than the previous high, but there was not the participation by Detroit that Rickenbacker had envisioned.

The danger factor was still very much in evidence. Joe Caccia, a 1930 race participant, and his riding mechanic, Clarence Grove, both perished during practice when their

"home-built" special hit the wall in the second turn with considerable force.

The start of the race was delayed by a couple of hours due to morning rainstorms, but once it was underway, defending winner Billy Arnold was just as dominant as he had been the year before, at least for the first 400 miles. Arnold originally had won the pole at an average speed of 113.848 mph, but the run was disallowed when the car failed a post-qualification test. Not all of the brakes had been hooked up. He went out again on the second day of time trials and qualified even faster, at 116.080 mph, but had to start all the way back in 18th starting position.

It took the defending winner just seven laps to get to the front, and he was to stay there all the way until lap 162, when, with a lead of about five laps, he tangled with another car, driven by Luther Johnson. They hit the turn-four wall, and in one of the strangest occurrences ever at the track, a dislodged wheel from Arnold's car cleared the outer wall, bounced at an angle across Georgetown Road and into the front yard of a private home, where it mowed down and fatally injured an 11-year-old boy named Wilbur Brink.

Arnold and his riding mechanic, a colorful Hollywood stuntman named William "Spider" Matlock, both were hospitalized, Arnold suffering from a broken pelvis and some burns, and Matlock with a broken shoulder blade.

Because of the huge advantage Arnold had built, he continued to be the leader for the next several minutes. Running second, now four laps behind, was Tony Gulotta, driving a car called the Hunt Special, powered by a Studebaker President straight-eight passenger-car engine.

The year before, six Studebaker engineers had tried to talk their management into supporting an entry in the "500," but with management declining, they had gone ahead and done it on their own. The car's name, the Romthe Special, was actually an acronym comprising the first letter of each of their surnames.

This year, they were back with two cars. One had just been eliminated in the Arnold accident, Studebaker employee Luther Johnson being knocked out with the Bill Richards Special. Richards, who was also the riding mechanic, was the "R" in Romthe. The other car was Gulotta's Hunt Special, Hunt being the "H" in Romthe.

All Gulotta had to do now was unlap himself four times and he would be leading.

He didn't quite make it. At the very moment he was passing Arnold's wrecked car for the fourth time, he slid on some oil and spun into the outer wall. Technically, he had taken the lead, but it never showed in the official records because he hadn't made it down to the start/finish line.

Into first position and on to the victory went steadily running Louis Schneider, the former Indianapolis motorcycle policeman and son of a local tailor.

It appeared, for a few laps, as if products of the Indianapolis Public Schools system were going to finish first *and* second, Bill Cummings running close behind Schneider after having taken over as a relief driver for Deacon Litz. Cummings had only 22 laps to go when he hit the outer wall between turns one and two.

Coming home second was Fred Frame, in a Duesenberg owned by Harry Hartz, while third was a Miller shared by Ralph Hepburn and Peter Kreis.

The fifth-place finisher (and the person who had inherited the pole upon Arnold's original run being disallowed) was Russ Snowberger, who drove a Studebaker-powered car he had built the year before. He claimed to have had less than $1,500 wrapped up in the car, yet he had earned an estimated $10,000 in prize money during the 1930 AAA Championship season and from this latest showing.

Finishing 13th, and completing the 500 miles about 38 minutes after Schneider had taken the checker, was an enormous specially built Duesenberg chassis containing a Cummins Diesel truck engine.

Months earlier, Clessie Cummins had traveled up from Columbus, Indiana, for the purpose of talking with Rickenbacker about the new specs. Cummins believed one of his engines could last the distance but he was a little concerned

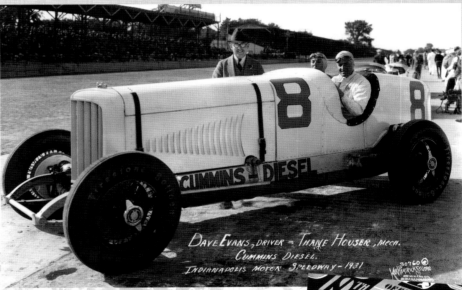

Dave Evans, driver – Thane Houser, mech.
Cummins Diesel.
Indianapolis Motor Speedway – 1931

about the speed necessary to qualify. Rickenbacker offered a special concession, ruling that if the car could complete four qualifying laps in excess of 80 mph, it would be included in the field regardless.

Driver Dave Evans made it with plenty to spare, at 96.871 mph.

The car gained considerable attention at the time, not only by completing the full distance, but by being able to do so without making a single pit stop. It burned 31 gallons of crude oil, at a total expenditure of only $2.55.

There was a little excitement along the way. Evans and his mechanic, Thane Houser, became aware that the water temperature was beginning to rise. Houser signaled to the pits for an indication of whether to come in, but no response was forthcoming. The procedure was repeated on several subsequent laps, still with no response.

They just kept on running.

After the race was over and the team was back in the garage, Evans and Houser cornered the fellow in charge of hand signals, in order to find out what had happened. The poor fellow had misplaced the piece of paper on which the "key" to the signals had been written. The Cummins mechanics were outfitted with factory shop coats, secured by belts tied around the waist, and when the still-puzzled crew member removed his coat, the mystery was solved. Out fell the missing piece of paper, which he had jammed down into his belt during the morning's rain delay.

This red-faced crew member had already become quite well known for his accomplishments in air racing but would gain even greater notoriety as a general during World War II.

His name was Jimmy Doolittle.

General Doolittle, who was still attending the "500" as a special guest well into the 1970s, would often laugh with the oldtimers when needled about that embarrassing incident.

There was a growing problem with a safety issue during these days, which Rickenbacker eventually would address. There was, at the outer edge of the turns, a steeper angle of banking that was approximately ten feet wide. The intent when it was designed was that its saucer-like characteristic would enable a car drifting too high in the turns to be able to veer onto the outer lip and then "diamond" back down.

A situation the designers had not foreseen concerned the fact that the outer walls had been installed at an angle of 90 degrees to the ground, rather than 90 degrees to the angle of the outer banking. While lap speeds of 80 and 90 mph had not presented any particular problems, cars slightly missing a

turn, or else spinning through one at well over 100, very likely would hit the outer wall either headfirst or tailfirst and invariably vault completely over the top, sometimes with devastating results.

In 1931, however, there was a lighter moment involving Wilbur Shaw, the eventual three-time winner who at this time was still trying to earn his spurs. Shaw had not been able to qualify the car to which he was assigned, and Fred Duesenberg retained him to drive relief in one of the two cars Fred had entered independently from brother Augie.

Driver Phil Pardee had been instructed to come in and hand over to Shaw soon after the start, but he waited until lap 26 before doing so. Shaw jumped in and began to chase after the leaders, but was faced with a further challenge by the fact that he was quite a bit shorter than Pardee. He found it necessary to hang out of the left side in order to be able to see what was up ahead. On lap 60, while racing with several other cars into turn three, Shaw lost control, hit the wall, and the car flew completely over the top.

Relatively uninjured, Shaw and his mechanic were piled into an ambulance and driven at speed through the bumpy infield, Shaw later claiming that he suffered more bruises during the ambulance ride than he had in the accident.

He returned to the pits with his tail between his legs, only to be surprised by Fred Duesenberg's fatherly welcome. Shaw was further surprised when Duesenberg asked if he felt like taking over the team car. Shaw subsequently jumped into Jimmy Gleason's machine, which was painted identically but displayed a different number – 33 instead of 32.

Shaw drove the car for some distance and finally gave it back to Gleason, who finished sixth.

With the race over and Shaw back in the garage area, he was approached by Terry Curley, the riding mechanic who had been with Shaw in the car which had not qualified. Having lined himself up with another, driven by Phil Shafer, Curley had been horrified to see Shaw flying over the wall. Fearing for his friend's life, he was astounded, about an hour later, to be passed by what appeared to be Wilbur at the wheel of the same car. He thought he had seen a ghost. Only after Shaw explained what had happened could poor Terry Curley finally calm himself down.

1932: Three in a row for owner Hartz

An even greater number of entries were filed for 1932, the previous year's record of 70 being topped by two.

There was further tragedy during practice, with two separate accidents involving fatalities. Dirt-track driver Benny Benefiel crashed during practice on May 25, and while he survived, Harry Cox, his riding mechanic, did not. Two days later, former motorcycle stunt man and "wall of death" circus performer Milton Jones, owner of two cars and a riding mechanic in the 1930 race, crashed and later succumbed to his injuries. His riding mechanic was able to escape.

Lou Moore pulled a bit of a surprise by being able to edge Billy Arnold for the number one starting position, but the race quickly turned into another Arnold runaway, at least for the first 150 miles. The 1930 winner grabbed the lead by the end of lap two and stayed there all the way up until lap 60. At that point, he swerved to avoid a slower car at the exit of turn two, lost control, and hit the outer wall, vaulting completely over the top.

Arnold and Matlock were luckier than most of the others who had "gone over the top," but they did sustain injuries; ironically, the exact reverse of the year before, Arnold receiving the broken shoulder blade and Matlock, the broken pelvis.

Arnold had recently married, and the new bride was far from enamored with racing. She pressured him to retire, and he relented, going on to become a very successful businessman. He became an area representative for the De Soto division of Chrysler Corporation in several Southwestern states, and eventually became a building contractor in Oklahoma City. He also had a very distinguished military career during WWII, serving for a while as engineering officer for the 8th Air Force in England and rising to the rank of lieutenant colonel.

With Arnold eliminated, the lead went to muscular Bob Carey, a highly regarded newcomer from nearby Anderson, Indiana, who was driving a Miller owned by Louis Meyer. With the Sampson "16" already on the sidelines, Louis was supervising the Carey pit. Carey led until lap 95, when he blew a right rear tire at the south end of the track. He spun around but kept on going, making it back to the pit, but not without blowing another tire and damaging the frame. A few laps after his lengthy stop, he was flagged in for an inspection many felt was unnecessary. But in spite of all the time lost, Carey refused to be beaten, climbing from 12th to fourth at the finish. He had driven the last 200 miles without goggles.

The winner was Billy Arnold's teammate, Fred Frame. The always very serious Frame had not expected to be driving the car he was in. After the 1931 race, Frame had purchased the second-placed Duesenberg from Harry Hartz and entered it for himself. The veteran Cliff Durant was down to drive yet another brand-new front-drive Miller for Hartz, but when he changed his mind, Frame turned his Duesenberg over to fellow dirt-track specialist Billy Winn and jumped into the Hartz front-drive himself.

Finishing second was a very popular local driver who was appearing in the "500" for the first time, and, like Frame, was in a car he had not expected to be driving. His name was Howdy Wilcox, and there was plenty of confusion because while he was assumed to be the son of the 1919 winner, the

Above: **Bob Carey (from nearby Anderson, Indiana) loses many minutes due to blown tires after leading 36 laps just before halfway, but still recovers to finish fourth in his only "500" start.**
Photograph: IMS

Above: The five Studebaker entries line up in front of the pagoda in 1932. The "sunburst" radiator design was a trademark of body fabricator Herman Rigling.

Inset right: There were no failures on any of the five factory-entered Studebaker President passenger-car engines, two of the cars eliminated by wheel bearing problems late in the 1932 race, and all five cars completing the full 500 miles in 1933.
Photographs: IMS

Bottom left: Fans enjoy the shade under the grandstand.

Below: Trucks and cars provide impromptu vantage points from the infield.
Photographs: IMS

two were not even distantly related. In fact, friends and family of the "original" Howdy Wilcox theorized that the newcomer had merely assumed the name in order to further his career. It has since been documented as being his given name at birth in 1907, a couple of years before the 1919 winner had even begun to race.

Howdy Wilcox II, as the press referred to him, had been very successful in local dirt-track racing and was a colleague of Wilbur Shaw, Bill Cummings, Dutch Baumann (by this time deceased), Billy Arnold, Shorty Cantlon, Louis Schneider, and Bob Carey, most of whom lived in and around Indianapolis. Several of them had migrated to the West Coast for the winter of 1931/32, mostly to compete at the famed Legion Ascot Speedway, and when Cantlon broke his leg in an accident at El Centro in February 1932, he hired Wilcox to drive his Indianapolis car.

Wilcox was not the only person who was substituting for an injured owner/driver. Wilbur Shaw subbed for Ralph Hepburn and led 27 laps before a broken rear axle knocked him out after 157 laps.

The second-place finish by Wilcox was even more remarkable considering that not only had he been able to hide a diabetic condition from the medical staff, but they had not detected that due to an accident a couple of years earlier, he had sight in only one eye.

The diabetic condition, however, would come to the fore the following year in very dramatic fashion.

In the meantime, Rickenbacker was delighted by the fact that an automobile company had finally decided to become officially involved. Studebaker had commissioned, from the Indianapolis-based firm of Rigling and Henning, a team of four frames and bodies to match that of the 1931 Hunt car, all five to be powered by standard Studebaker President straight-eight passenger-car engines.

All qualified handily, and it appeared that all five would finish until a wheel-bearing problem knocked out two of the cars late in the race. Of the survivors, Cliff Bergere finished an excellent third, while Zeke Meyer (not related to Louis) took sixth and Gulotta was flagged off at the end with 184 laps to his credit. Peter Kreis and Luther Johnson were the unlucky pair who had the wheel-bearing failures late in the going.

Russ Snowberger, who had fielded a Studebaker for very little outlay in the previous two years, tried it this time with a Hupmobile Hupp Comet engine in the same frame. He finished fifth.

Racing had been the theme of quite a number of motion pictures over the years, normally lighthearted affairs in which drivers like Barney Oldfield, Teddy Tetzlaff, Earl Cooper, Jimmy Murphy, and Peter de Paolo appeared as themselves. In 1932, however, there was a fairly major production starring James Cagney, Joan Blondell, Ann Dvorak, and Frank

BILLY ARNOLD

Billy Arnold competed in the "500" only five times, but he set a pace in the early 1930s nobody could match. Born in Chicago on December 16, 1905, the baby-faced Arnold had a pair of top-ten finishes to his credit (seventh in 1928 and eighth in 1929, both times assisted by relief drivers) when he showed up in 1930 without "a ride." Harry Hartz, the 1926 AAA national champion and three-time "500" runner-up, was attempting a comeback after having suffered severe leg injuries in an accident at Salem, New Hampshire, in 1927.

Driving a brand-new front-drive car he had commissioned, Hartz went out to qualify on the opening day of time trials, but returned after one lap at 110 mph (which would have been good enough for the front row) with the realization that he still wasn't up to the task. Arnold, who had practiced in the car in anticipation of Hartz needing a relief driver, went out soon after and won the pole at 113.268 mph. On race day, Louis Meyer led at the start, but when Arnold took over on lap three, that was, in fact, the last lead change of the entire race. He went on to lead a record 198 consecutive laps and win by a full seven minutes.

The following year, Arnold won the pole again, but the run was disallowed due to a technical infraction. He re-qualified on the second day, this time at a much faster 116.080 mph, but he was obliged to start back in 18th. It took him precisely seven laps to get to the front, after which he led for 155 consecutive laps until crashing – while enjoying a five-lap lead – with less than 100 miles to go.

In 1932, he qualified second to Lou Moore, took the lead at the end of the second lap, and was not headed until he crashed while trying to avoid a sliding car on lap 60. Of the 421 laps he had completed over the three-year period, he had led 410, for an incredible percentage of 97.39. He was second only to Ralph de Palma in terms of laps led. His new bride, however, was not impressed with racing, and Billy retired, never to drive again.

He became associated with Chrysler Corporation as a field rep for De Soto, eventually overseeing several Southwestern states, and he had a very distinguished military career during WWII, stationed in England and rising to the rank of lieutenant colonel. He was, by all accounts, exceedingly affable as a young man, and he certainly comes across that way in the 1931/32 Hollywood motion picture, "The Crowd Roars," in which he plays himself. A pleasantly capable actor, he greets "Joe Greer" (James Cagney) with a lazy Chicago drawl, and then suddenly appears to have leaped four decades into the future. Sitting on the pit wall, he wraps his left arm around Cagney's shoulder in a partial bear hug and then shakes hands with an upturned clasp, as if he were a flower child of the 1970s.

Reports are that the friendliness wore off during his military career and that he was somewhat mysterious and reclusive in his final years, which were spent in Oklahoma City as a building contractor. He never visited the Speedway after 1955, although he did remain in contact with Hartz, and he attended a military reunion in Indianapolis shortly before he died on November 10, 1976.

McHugh. Entitled "The Crowd Roars," it was directed by Howard Hawks. While none of the principals came to the track, several participants spent time there staging choreographed "mock" shots. If there is something about these sequences which don't appear to be quite right, it is probably due to the fact that they were shot during the dead of winter and the tree branches are completely devoid of leaves! Among those participants who appeared as themselves and had speaking parts were Billy Arnold, Fred Frame, Louis Schneider, Harry Hartz, Shorty Cantlon, and Spider Matlock.

Left: Fred Frame, the previous year's runner-up, jumps at the opportunity to drive Harry Hartz's new car after Cliff Durant, for whom it was intended, decides not to compete.
Photograph: IMS

Main photograph: For many years, Tom
Beall's diner was a home away from home
for the racing crowd. It was located at the
southwest corner of the garage area, just
inside the fence behind the pits. "Bench
racing" sessions were a daily occurrence.
The benevolent Beall would allow down-on-
their-luck participants to "put it on the
slate" during the month of May, the general
rule of thumb during the 1930s being that
the winning driver would pay off all the
outstanding debts.
Photographs: IMS

1933: The Great Depression hits home, but the "500" just keeps on going

By 1933, the country was fully plunged into the Great Depression.

In efforts to keep the 500-Mile Race going, and to keep people coming through the turnstiles, it was necessary to make a number of concessions.

The ticket prices were reduced, and so was the purse. The traditional $50,000 for the top ten finishers, unchanged since 1912, was reduced to $30,000, with first place dropping from $20,000 to $12,000 and tenth from $1,400 to $840.

The participants were less than happy, but they had little choice in the matter. Thousands upon thousands of Americans had lost their jobs, with many losing everything they owned. At least the 500-Mile Race was still going and there was some prize money to be won.

A number of new rules were in effect. On-board fuel tanks were limited to a capacity of only 15 gallons, leading many to believe that up to three pit stops might be required instead of as few as one in recent years. There was a restriction on oil as well. No more than six gallons could be carried, and more importantly, for the first time ever, no oil could be added during the race.

The qualification procedure took on an entirely new dimension, with endurance becoming a major factor. Instead of four laps, a completed qualifying run now consisted of ten laps, so that when Bill Cummings won the pole at 118.530 mph, it took him just under 12 minutes and 40 seconds to complete the distance.

Because the 40-car lineup of the previous two years had resulted in 13 rows of three, followed by a single car, it had been decided to fill out the 14th row, thus calling for 42 starters. The run of the slowest successful qualifier – Gene Haustein at 107.603 mph – required just under 14 minutes to complete. Coupled with the extra time required for warm-up laps prior to taking the green flag, plus the cool-off laps after the checker, it meant that almost a full hour would be used up by qualifying just four cars. Because of this, it was wisely decided to expand the "run for the pole" to both Saturday, May 20, and Sunday, May 21.

The majority of the participants were not at all happy about

having to drive such a distance in order to qualify.

The month of May 1933 was filled with drama and tragedy and by the time the race was over, five men had lost their lives.

On the lap before he was expected to take the green flag for a qualifying attempt, Bill Denver (real name: William Orem) crashed at the south end of the track and died, along with his riding mechanic, Hugh "Bob" Hurst.

During the race, yet another local dirt-track driver making his debut, Mark Billman, crashed in turn two after making his way up to ninth position. Elmer Lombard, his riding mechanic, lived to tell the tale, but Billman did not. About an hour later, East Coast driver Malcolm Fox took evasive action to avoid another car and Lester Spangler, running sixth and coming up to lap him, ran up over Fox's right rear wheel. Runner-up in the hotly contested 1932 Pacific Coast championship, Spangler was helpless. The car landed upside down and bounced back onto its wheels, both Spangler and his mechanic, Glen "Monk" Jordan, perishing instantly.

Before the start, there had been a major episode involving Howdy Wilcox II, the runner-up of the year before. A couple of days before the race, Louis Schneider, who was being sponsored by Edelweiss beer, had brought over a couple of cases of the product to Tom Beall's trackside diner and a bench racing party had ensued. Suddenly, Wilcox collapsed. Bill Cummings and Wilbur Shaw, knowing of his secret diabetic condition, rushed to grab candy from the lunch counter and started forcing it down their friend's throat.

The incident came to the attention of the track's physician, Dr. Horace Allen, who determined, erroneously, that Wilcox was susceptible to epileptic fits. He ruled that Wilcox, who had qualified sixth, could not start.

A number of pleas were made and friends of Wilcox – there were many – began circulating a petition requesting that he be reinstated. There was an attempt to present it to Chief Steward Eddie Edenburn on race morning, but Edenburn would not accept it.

About half an hour before the start, everything came to a head. Wilcox apparently still believed he was going to be competing. Officials insisted that he would not. A second petition was drafted, this one worded more strongly. The drivers, some with their helmets already in place, surrounded Eddie Edenburn and the other officials, declaring that if Wilcox was not

permitted to start, they wouldn't be doing so either.

Edenburn deferred to Rickenbacker, and it was common knowledge that Captain Eddie Rickenbaker was not in the habit of bowing to ultimatums. Nor did he on this occasion. Rickenbacker announced that while he was not a physician, Dr. Allen was, and Dr. Allen had recommended that Wilcox not be permitted to start. That was good enough for him. The race would start without Wilcox. Any participant wishing to withdraw was welcome to do so, but if the majority refused to climb into their cars within the next few moments, the gates to the track probably would be padlocked and there might not ever be an Indianapolis 500 again.

It is understood that Louis Meyer was the voice of reason who settled the troops, later suggesting that it was the general state of the world, the cutting of the purse, the oil rule, and the longer qualification runs which had combined to cause tempers to flare. It was quite remarkable that at the age of only 28, Meyer would be considered the respected elder statesman who could calm the waters.

The situation was not completely resolved. The car's owner, Joe Marx, who had actually purchased it from Meyer (it was the one driven to fourth by Carey the year before), chose Mauri Rose as the replacement. Rose would go on to become one of the most accomplished drivers ever at the Speedway. At this time, however, he had only driven in practice and had never had a start. There were immediate objections from others over this "novice" starting on the outside of the second row. A compromise was reached whereby the car would be rolled all the way to the back, but in the interests of time, instead of moving everyone else up one position, the cars on the outside of each row were pushed forward to fill the space in front of them, so that ninth became sixth, 12th became ninth, and so forth.

All 42 cars did push off for the pace lap, but by the time they did, it was about 10:15 A.M., marking the first time ever that the start had been delayed for a reason other than rain.

Rose, who had won the 100-mile National Championship

race at Detroit the previous year, was about to raise a few eyebrows. Confiding, in later years, that he had always been driven by aggression, he took off like the wind at the start, and at the end of ten laps had passed 30 cars. He was running 12th and still coming. He had made it all the way up to fourth when the timing gear broke at 48 laps, but not before he had passed the cars of every single person who had objected to him starting at the front.

The first 32 laps were led by Bill Cummings, after which Fred Frame and Babe Stapp traded the number one position several times up through lap 129. It was Louis Meyer from

Above: Louis Meyer, driving a car he entered himself but which actually belongs to fellow driver Ralph Hepburn, is the first ever to win twice without the aid of a relief driver.
Photograph: IMS

that point on, Louis joining Tommy Milton as a two-time winner and becoming the first ever to win twice without the aid of a relief driver.

It was not the most financially rewarding of days. Whereas Billy Arnold had won $50,350 in 1930, Louis's total take this time, including accessory awards and lap prize money, was only $18,000. The lap prize fund had fallen far short of its $20,000 goal, with only $3,150 being raised, the majority of the second half of the race carrying no postings at all. Instead of earning $7,100, at the rate of $100 per lap, Meyer took in only $850.

Wilbur Shaw, who finished second (his best so far), earned a total of $9,100, while third-placed Lou Moore ended up with $4,100.

On the other end of the scale, Louis Schneider, out on the very first lap for the dubious distinction of being the only driver ever to finish 42nd in the "500," came away with a mere $200.

This was the final appearance for Schneider. He had always claimed to have a preference for the number 13, but AAA had been refusing to issue it for several years. In 1933, Schneider pushed the issue by showing up for practice with his beautifully painted red car adorned with "13" in silver on either side of the tail. Officials insisted he change it to 22, which he did, but not without some muttered verbal abuse and digs wherever possible. The following year, after several more run-ins, his "500" entry was rejected and he was never permitted to compete again. He continued racing with what AAA referred to as "outlaw" organizations, and after a 1937 midget car accident greatly affected his health, he succumbed to tuberculosis, in an Indianapolis mission on September 22, 1942.

Fourth in the race was Alden Sampson's "16," which was outfitted with a two-way radio system. The car even had the call letters WOXAC painted on the side. Radio communication was not a new thing at the track, already having been tried several times without success, but this one was said to have worked quite well until a battery cable broke at 340 miles. Driver Chet Gardner was not privy to the conversations, riding mechanic Herschel McKee wearing a special aviation helmet which housed the earphones. A pair of batteries were bolted to the cross members of the frame, the receiving set was under the mechanic's seat, and a brass rod, mounted on a bracket on the left side of the frame, served as the antenna. The microphone rested in a cradle on the instrument panel. McKee was a most interesting person, having been a bona fide member of the Lafayette Escadrille Flying Corp in World War I. An Indianapolis native, he rode as a mechanic several times right after the war, typically alongside foreign drivers. He even drove relief for E. A. D. Eldridge in 1926.

The Studebaker team had returned for the second and final time and had solved its wheel-bearing problem, all five cars completing the full 500 miles and finishing seventh, ninth, 10th, 11th, and 12th. Four of the five cars had been outfitted with streamlined bodies, a feature the disgruntled Cliff Bergere said actually hampered their performance.

On August 1, Howdy Wilcox II was back in the news.

Apparently prevented from ever racing in the "500" again, and objecting to the suggestion that he suffered from epilepsy, he sued the track and various parties for $100,000. The case went to trial two years later, and he was awarded $42,000. He is believed to have collected only a fraction of that amount.

1934: Conservative William

Not only did the 10-lap qualifying-run procedure remain for 1934, but now there was a fuel consumption ruling imposed as well. For 500 miles, the entire allotment was 45 gallons. For qualifications, it was a mere three gallons, anything above that causing the run to be disallowed and charged as a "strike." Everyone agreed there would be no multiple warm-up laps. They would be taking the green flag the first time around.

The fastest qualifier was the fiery and diminutive Kelly Petillo, a leading West Coast driver whose third lap at 122.166 mph was the fastest since Leon Duray's 1928 record run and the fastest ever by a nonsupercharged "two-man" car.

There was another dreadful accident during practice when popular Peter Kreis, the Knoxville, Tennessee, contractor, perished along with Bob Hahn, another hopeful driver who was serving as a riding mechanic primarily as a way of being involved.

The rate of accidents was coming under increasing fire, and it had already been decided, following the 1933 race, that 42 cars were just too many. The limit for 1934 was returned to 33, and it has remained thus ever since. Further, Rickenbacker was already considering a complete reconfiguration of the turns, although the implementation of this was still over a year away.

Times were still tough, but amazingly the race-day crowds, even if down a little from the late 1920s and very early 1930s, were still enormous. Somehow or other, people still managed to find a way to scrape together enough to be able to spend Memorial Day at the track. Others used various forms of ingenuity.

One of the features of race morning for many years was the marching past of the massed bands. The fact that it seemed to get bigger every year was no illusion. Word had circulated that anyone willing to participate would be admitted to the grounds at no charge. All they needed to do was bring an instrument. By around 1937, estimates were that somewhere in the region of 1,000 people would march up the straight, always from south to north for some reason. Just how many of those 1,000 could actually *play* an instrument was quite another matter.

Others who were low on funds employed a more basic approach.

Ever since the track had opened in 1909, all of the policing and security had been performed by the Indiana National Guard. One of the Guard's duties was to try to deal with the annual challenge of the gate-crashers on Georgetown Road. This had been a ritual for years, especially during the Great Depression. There was a fairly tall wooden fence to mark the western boundary of the property, and people would start gathering up and down the other side of the narrow two-lane road a few minutes before the start, trying to look as nonchalant as possible. Guardsmen would be posted every few feet on the other side of the fence inside the track, waiting for the inevitable. At a certain point, usually at the moment the engines were fired, a shout would be heard and upwards of two or three hundred people would scamper across the road and scale the fence, the guardsmen all but helpless to stop them. Once inside the grounds, with the cars already having departed on the pace lap, the gate-crashers still had about three minutes in which to find a vantage point from which they could witness the start.

Frank Brisko led 69 laps of the 1934 "500" with a car which employed four-wheel-drive, a concept first tried out in a "500" in 1932. This one was fielded by the Four Wheel Drive Auto Company of Clintonville, Wisconsin, precisely the type of firm Rickenbacker had hoped would come for the purpose of using the track as a proving ground. The car, which started on the front row for the second consecutive year, eventually finished ninth, driven for the last third by a West Coast driver making his first appearance. Just 21 years old, Rex Mays was destined never to win the "500" but was on his way to becoming one of racing's most respected and beloved stars.

The winner was the exceedingly popular and boisterous Bill

Cummings, who recalled having heard the roar of the engines as a boy playing in his front yard barely four miles from the track before WWI. For much of his life, he carried the nickname "Wild Bill," a moniker which apparently bothered him. It has been suggested that he inherited it from his namesake father, a former Marmon employee who was said to have had a freewheeling style. While nobody enjoyed life to a greater extent *off* the track than the new winner, he was deadly serious about his racing. After pulling into the victory enclosure at the conclusion of what he felt was a very disciplined, fuel-saving 500 miles, he suggested to the press, "Perhaps, after this, they'll start calling me 'Conservative William' instead."

In second position was Mauri Rose, driving the same Leon Duray-entered car Shaw had driven to second the year before. Finishing third was the steady Lou Moore, who took relief from Shaw (who, after starting in the middle of the front row, had dropped out early). Moore, incidentally, did not even arrive at the track until May 26, having just returned from the Grand Prix of Tripoli in North Africa, where he had finished eighth with the very same Miller he drove at Indianapolis.

Cummins Engine Company had returned for the first time since 1931, this time with two diesels. A four-cycle version, driven by Dave Evans, fell out with a failed transmission after 81 laps, while a two-cycle experimental placed 12th, with Evans relieving H. W. "Stubby" Stubblefield.

While the safety issue concerning the outer banking was growing steadily more serious, there was a rather bizarre lighter moment during the early stages. In fact, two drivers – George Bailey and Chet Miller – went over the wall early in the race but escaped injury. When rescue workers rushed to the aid of Miller on the other side of the wall between turns one and two, he was nowhere to be found. Although the car was substantially damaged, it was still drivable. With neither Miller nor his riding mechanic having been hurt except for a few scratches, Miller proceeded to drive the car around to the turn two tunnel and then make his way back to the garage area.

During May of 1935, the issue of safety would come to a head and finally be addressed.

ADDRESSING THE ISSUE OF SAFETY

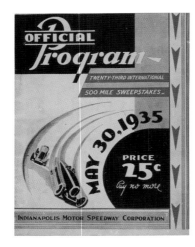

1935: Helmets, warning lights, and Kelly's folly

IN the spring West Coast races of 1932, Wilbur Shaw had begun to wear an item of headgear which rather resembled a pudding basin. It was, in fact, a helmet which had been worn a couple of years earlier by Britain's Sir Henry Segrave, during one of his world land speed record attempts at Daytona Beach. Shaw, who had been there to try for records in a smaller class at the same time, had been so fascinated by the helmet that Segrave had given it to him as a gift. Although he took quite a bit of needling, Shaw continued to wear it, this being at a time when he was winning a lot of races and participating in pre-race publicity "shoots" with great frequency. While not the first to wear a helmet at Indianapolis (Rickenbacker experimented with a helmet in 1916 and Louis Chiron wore one in the 1929 race), he appeared, for a while in 1932, as if he was going to be the first to *win* with one, a rear axle knocking him out of the lead with just over 100 miles to go.

In 1933, Shaw's riding mechanic was Billy Devore, the son of Earl Devore, the 1927 runner-up who had gone down on the S.S. Vestris with Norman Batten. Billy (who later qualified for seven Indianapolis races himself) wore a helmet as well, and the pair finished second.

By 1934, upwards of a dozen drivers were wearing them, Louis Meyer included.

In April 1935, AAA made the use of helmets mandatory.

In addition, the subject of caution periods received attention, and it was determined that the display of a yellow flag at the start/finish line was no longer sufficient. Warning lights were erected at six points around the track, green to be displayed at all times the course was clear, and yellow whenever it was not. One complaint for several years had been that unless the chief starter witnessed a problem for himself, the only indication he had that a caution period was needed was when he would see a yellow flag being waved at one of the other

stations. The complaint from the drivers was that it sometimes took a while for a yellow to "come around" to the starter. This same situation prevailed in 1935. The lights (believed to be Marmon passenger car headlights) were operated from the starter's stand, but with no radio communication yet, the yellow would be turned on only after the displaying of a flag at another post. This was later changed so that a switch could be thrown from any of the other observer posts, thus alerting all of the participants at the same time.

Not only did the fuel restrictions remain in place for 1935, but they were made even tougher. The allotment for 500 miles was reduced from 45 gallons to only 42$\frac{1}{2}$.

There was a new chief steward this year, Eddie Edenburn having passed away the previous September. Assuming his duties was Charlie Merz, the National and Stutz driver from the track's earliest days. He was now the proprietor of his own engineering business, and he would go on to a very distinguished military career in Europe during World War II.

Rex Mays ended up on the pole at 120.736 mph, and not only was he the youngest-ever pole winner thus far, at 22, he was to remain so even up through the 2006 "500." Because Art Sparks, the car's co-owner and co-chief mechanic, was currently on an AAA suspension and not allowed in the pits or garage area, he was obliged to direct operations from the spectator side of the pit fence. He even examined the sparkplugs from there.

Kelly Petillo, who now was fielding his own car, appeared to have beaten Mays by blazing through 10 laps at 121.687 mph, with one at 122.416 mph. Unfortunately, the run was disallowed and a "strike" assessed because he had exceeded the fuel limit by 5/8 of a pint.

Kelly was confused when he came in, not realizing that he had run so quickly. He had asked his crew to keep him apprised of his "time," but what he had intended to ask for was his "speed." When they showed him the pit board bearing the chalked numbers "1.14," he misread it as 114 mph. He picked up the pace, only to see "1.13." It was only after

Main photograph: Turn one is still very rustic-looking in 1935. Note how the creek winds its way through the infield on its way to flowing out beneath West 16th Street.

Inset below: Time is running out for 1935 time trials, and all four of the cars seen in line are late-arriving Ford V-8 Millers that the team is desperately trying to get qualified.

Photographs: IMS

they chalked him the message "slow down" that he was able to gauge himself, by which time the consumption damage had been done.

He came back for a second try and took it a little steadier this time, with nine safe laps at 117 mph. On the very last lap, a connecting rod broke, cracking three cylinders, breaking the crankcase in two, and wrecking the engine.

He was down to his last strike and just about out of money.

Help came from several quarters, and the proprietor of a near-Eastside Indianapolis machine shop came to his aid, assigning several people to the repair job. Kelly was finally able to make it in at a very conservative 115.095 mph on May 26, good enough for 22nd starting position.

There has been a long-held myth that Petillo ran in the race with his engine held together by baling wire, which is not even close to being true. There certainly had been quite a bit of patching and welding involved, using a variety of borrowed parts and some last-minute machining, but the engine never could have held together unless the workmanship was first-rate.

A few nights before the race, a dinner was held at the Indianapolis Athletic Club to recognize a handful of drivers who were being inducted into a new club. After Dave Evans had finished sixth in the 1933 race at an average speed of 100.425 mph, it occurred to him that he was one of only 12 drivers who had been able to complete the entire 500 miles averaging 100 mph or better, and without the aid of a relief driver.

Evans discussed this with a number of people during May 1934, and the result was the formation of the Champion Spark Plug Company 100 Mile an Hour Club. Of the 14 drivers eligible for membership by the time the first dinner was held on May 25, 1935, two were already deceased, but 11 of the 12 still living all were in attendance and impeccably dressed. Starting in 1951, members were presented with brown leather "bomber" jackets which displayed the 100 Mile an Hour club logo over the heart, and these were to become the envy of all drivers who had not earned one. It was a sad day when the club was discontinued in 1970.

Dignitaries had always been drawn to the "500," and Rickenbacker made it a point to invite distinguished notables, giving them honorary titles. In 1935, the invitation to serve as "honorary referee" was accepted by a well-known aviator who was currently on the faculty of Purdue University as a student counselor. It was Rickenbacker's pleasure to escort Amelia Earhart through the pit area on race morning, along with her husband, George Putnam, of the publishing firm.

Earlier in the month, author Laura Ingalls Wilder had spent a day at the track, but for reasons which may have come as quite a surprise to those who were familiar with her only through her classics such as "Little House on the Prairie." In complete contrast with the lifestyle one would generally have associated with her, Ingalls was a very accomplished pilot. She was at the track only because engine trouble, just this side of St. Louis, had forced her to land at Indianapolis, thereby aborting her attempt on the nonstop coast-to-coast flying record, held at that time by none other than Amelia Earhart.

Mays took the lead at the start of the race and remained in front for the next one and a half hours. Babe Stapp and Petillo led briefly before Mays took over again, leading all the way until the 99th lap. During the second half it was all Petillo, with the exception of five laps led by Shaw while Petillo stopped. Rain fell in the latter stages, quite heavily at times, but never enough for the officials to call for a red flag or an early checker.

It was a stirring win by Petillo, and it would have continued to be one of the great stories of the Speedway had he not been such a controversial character off the track. Emotional and engaging, he had a winning grin and the ability to charm people. He also could be a real thorn in the side of the officials, and was not the most conscientious person when it came to repaying loans. Although referred to by some sources as an Irish–Italian, there was nothing Irish about Kelly. The son of an Italian grocer, his full name was Cavino Michelle

Above: Paid for largely out of prize money earned by winning the 1934 AAA National Championship race at Mines Field, California (now the site of Los Angeles International Airport), Kelly Petillo financed his own car for the 1935 "500." He suffers trials and tribulations during qualifications but enjoys a relatively trouble-free race.

Main photograph: The view looking across from turn one to turn two (in the spring of 1936) shows how the original application of asphalt was only to the particularly deteriorated portions of the brick surface. Note also that the troublesome inside wall has been removed.

Photographs: IMS

Petillo. He went by his middle name, and when a school teacher mistook "Michelle" for "Me Kelly," he was given a nickname he eventually adopted professionally.

Petillo did not handle success particularly well, and a variety of off-track activities led to him becoming a persona non grata. It was a shame, because it completely overshadowed his not-inconsiderable skills behind the wheel of a racing car.

Kelly's riding mechanic was a well-spoken 23-year-old engineer named Jimmy Dunham, whose career was quite unique in that he had never ridden in a race of any kind before and never would again. He would be very much the center of attention when attending the race as a special guest in 2005, that being the first time he had set foot on the property in 70 years! His memory was truly remarkable.

Wilbur Shaw and "Conservative William" Cummings placed second and third in 1935, while fourth was Floyd Roberts, another Legion Ascot standout who had started from the front row in his first "500."

Perhaps the story gaining the most attention was the much-anticipated entry by the Ford Motor Company. Spear-

headed by the entrepreneurial efforts of Preston Tucker, Edsel Ford (who was forever trying to please his hard-to-please father), had entered into an arrangement whereby Harry Miller would design and build a team of cars to be powered by the new Ford V8 flathead engine. Tucker would be the team manager. The seeds of the plan had been planted during a visit to the track by Tucker and the Ford family in 1932, when the five-car Studebaker team had been there for the first time.

If Studebaker had done it with five cars, then by golly, Ford should have ten.

And that was the number of cars Miller and Ford entered, although it was never clear as to whether the tenth car was ever completed. But nine certainly *did* go to the track. The lead drivers were to have been Peter de Paolo and Cliff Bergere, but no sooner had the first couple of cars shown up for their initial runs on May 13 than both drivers discreetly withdrew. De Paolo cited a design flaw which had the steering box located right next to the block. He contended that as soon as the engine heated up, the car would become harder and harder to steer.

He was correct.

By May 25, eight of these beautiful cars had arrived, but none had qualified. A ninth finally arrived, and after a frantic last-minute scramble, four were able to make it in, while a fifth, driven by Dave Evans, missed the 33-car field by one position. The other four each made a qualifying run but did not run to completion. The four drivers who made it were Ford test driver George Bailey, former motorcycle racer-turned-"500" driver Johnny Seymour, and two newcomers from the dirt-track circuit, Bob Sall and Ted Horn. Sall would appear in only this year, but Horn would join Rex Mays as one of the greatest-ever "500" drivers who never were able to win.

One by one the Miller–Fords fell by the wayside, each with the very malady de Paolo predicted would occur. Horn lasted the longest, finally giving up after 145 laps when his car became impossible to steer. In his next nine starts over the next 13 years, Horn would complete 1,799 out of a possible 1,800 laps.

Henry Ford was said to have been furious over the outcome – he had not been in favor of the program to begin with – and he ordered all of the cars destroyed. None of them were, and after a couple of years, they began to resurface in various forms, typically with Offenhauser engines in place of the Fords.

Sadly, the track was still haunted by tragedy, 1935 being a dreadful year in that respect.

After the accidents of 1933, it had been decided that lack of driver experience might be partially at the root of the problem. Although the testing of all drivers – later known as the "rookie" test – became mandatory in 1936, there was a similar program in place in 1934. It required that any driver whose reputation was not particularly strong should have to undergo a scrutinized evaluation, while newcomers *with* a sufficient reputation would not.

One driver who was waived was Johnny Hannon, the defending East Coast champion. The car to which he was assigned did not arrive and he was ultimately hired by Leon Duray, the now-retired driver who owned two cars. Both Duray and Tony Gulotta, Duray's other driver, worked with Hannon and both drove him around for several laps, Hannon riding in the mechanic's seat.

When it was time for Hannon to move behind the wheel, Oscar "Shorty" Reeves jumped into the mechanic's seat. Before taking off, Gulotta and Duray cautioned Hannon against gathering speed too quickly. The confident newcomer did not heed their advice. He picked up speed on the backstretch, barreled into turn three, and then spun and hit the outer wall tailfirst with enough force to break completely through, leaving behind a large, triangular-shaped gap.

Shorty Reeves, a local musician, would eventually recover; but Hannon, without having completed an entire lap at speed, was injured fatally.

Later on the very same day, May 21, Hartwell W. ("Stubby") Stubblefield, trying to qualify for his fifth "500," had the right-side steering arm fail on his eighth of 10 qualifying laps and he crashed over the outer wall at the exit of turn one. He and his riding mechanic, Leo Whittaker, both perished.

It wasn't over yet.

The Hannon car was repaired, and just six days after the accident, eager young Clay Weatherly qualified it. Coming out of turn four on the way to completing his 10th lap of the race, Weatherly crashed through the outer protective fencing. He did not survive.

Things simply could not continue in this manner, and in spite of the severe financial strain during an already difficult time, Rickenbacker called for a major redesign of the track.

1936: An economy drive, and a fistful of firsts

As soon as the 1935 race was over, bulldozers moved in immediately to begin digging out the steep outer lip in the turns. In addition, a new outer retaining wall was installed, this one placed at a 90-degree angle to the track, rather than at 90 degrees to the ground. Instead of removing the pre-existing wall, it remained in place, concrete being poured down into the wedge-shaped separation between the two. As late as 1992, spectators in the turns could look down from their seats and see the tops of two walls rather than one.

Some portions of the brick surface had deteriorated and crumbled quite seriously over the years, especially in the turns, where several huge gouges had developed. It was decided that some asphalt should be applied, but only to the most troublesome areas, the result being a rather patchy-looking affair for the 1936 event. Within a couple of years, the turns had been paved in full, as had the north and south short straights, and in 1939, the backstretch as well. By 1940, the only bricks still exposed were approximately 650 yards of the main straight, which, as a nostalgic link with the past, would remain so until October 1961.

Inset below: This view shows just how steep the outer banking was in the turns up through 1935. The ten-foot-wide "outer lip" was removed that summer, many of the Culver Block "Speedway bricks" in private collections today having become available as a result of this track modification.

Inset below center: A perfect example of the deterioration of the bricks, just prior to the initial application of asphalt. Imagine being a riding mechanic when an inside pass required racing through that gouge in the foreground.
Photographs: IMS

Above: This aerial view of the track in 1936 shows that the surroundings are still pretty much farmland.

Centre right: With the Great Depression coming to an end, the crowds pick up again. This shot (looking north) was taken approximately at the location of Victory Lane. This was also the route taken by cars, after taking the checker, back to the garage area. The presence of a similar gate further north, at the point where cars would enter the pits from the garage area, may well be where the term "pit gate" came from.

Photographs: IMS

No longer would it be acceptable for just any driver to go out and practice.

Every single newcomer, regardless of background and accomplishments at other tracks, would be required to undergo a rigorous evaluation, later known as the "rookie" test. For 1936, it comprised five phases, with 10 laps each to be completed at 80, 90, 100, 105, and 110 mph. A committee of veteran drivers would then decide whether the newcomer should be permitted to make a qualification attempt.

Perhaps the most important upgrade of all was the removal of the inside wall in the turns. Many a car over the years had spun through a turn, hit the inside wall, sustained damage and then ricocheted back out into the path of oncoming cars, potentially to be faced with further damage. Not only was the wall now gone, but so was the bank of earth behind it, with a flat and very wide apron in its place. This modification was universally applauded by the drivers.

The old Wheeler–Schebler trophy, which dated all the way back to 1909, had been closeted for a brief period after the introduction of the "500," and then had been brought out again, along with several of the other more elaborate 1909–10 trophies, to be given as prizes for various distances. The Wheeler–Schebler was designated as the award for leading at 400 miles, with an original clause still in place specifying that the company winning it for a third time would "retire" it permanently. This article had been modified to read "car owner" rather than "company," and it became the property of Harry Hartz by virtue of his cars having led at 400 miles in 1930, 1931, and 1932.

In the summer of 1935, it was announced that a brand-new trophy had been commissioned from Spaulding–Gorham of Chicago. Designed by Robert Hill, creator of the 1932 Gordon Bennett balloon trophy, it would be symbolic of victory in the "500" each year and was to be called the "Men of Motors" trophy. It wasn't long before the name was modified to reflect that of the company underwriting it, and it would be known forever after as the Borg–Warner trophy.

At a dinner in New York in February 1936, the Borg–Warner

trophy was unveiled, emblazoned with bas-relief sculptures of every 500-Mile Race winner up to that point and said to have contained $10,000 worth of silver.

There was a further reduction in the amount of fuel allowable for 1936, but instead of lowering the amount by an additional 2½ gallons, it was reduced by a whopping five gallons. The total amount for 500 miles would now be only 37½ gallons.

Only one car had run out of fuel before the end of the race in 1935, and there had been none at all in 1934. In 1936, there would be seven.

Rex Mays won the pole for the second year in a row, and led the first 12 laps. Babe Stapp took over for 25 laps, and then Wilbur Shaw became the leader.

In 1932, Art Sparks and Paul Weirick had come to the track with a uniquely designed, streamlined car driven by Stubby Stubblefield. The fact that it started 25th and finished 14th does not begin to tell the story. It had made a run at the Muroc Dry Lake at over 147 mph that April, and until a wheel-bearing problem slowed it way down on its last qualifying lap at the Speedway, it had been making a run for the pole.

Nicknamed "The Catfish" because of its shape, it was actually the work of some students at Stanford University. Sparks had a friend there who taught engineering. The university had a one-eighth-scale wind tunnel, and it ended up that the students were given the job of designing a racing car as a class project.

The Catfish, which was later owned by Fred Frame and showed up in "mock" racing scenes in several Hollywood racing epics, never did live up to its potential. But the design intrigued Wilbur Shaw, and during the winter of 1935/36, he and former driver (now car builder) Myron Stevens constructed a version of their own.

Shaw, with Stevens as his riding mechanic, was now leading the race. As they approached the halfway point, an unnerving development began to take place. The streamlined

body was shaking loose. The situation worsened, and it became necessary to come in.

Almost 12 minutes were lost while the cowling was secured, and 15 laps later they had to come in for another five minutes. They dropped all the way to 17th place, 14 minutes behind the leader.

Shaw was furious.

In the meantime, the leader was Louis Meyer, who was just trying to make the best of a really challenging month. He had been plagued by various engine problems and had not been able to post his 10-lap qualifying run until May 27, forcing him to start back in 28th.

Everything held together during the race, and except for 16 laps led by sophomore Ted Horn, now driving for Harry Hartz, Louis held on for the remainder of the distance.

Below: Based on the Art Sparks/Paul Weirick "Catfish" of 1932, Wilbur Shaw and Myron Stevens (also the riding mechanic) built this streamliner in Los Angeles during the winter of 1935/36.
Photograph: IMS

LOUIS MEYER

All kinds of famous "firsts" were registered when Louis Meyer turned into Victory Lane at Indianapolis in 1936. Not only was he the first driver to have won the "500" for a third time, but he was the first to be presented with the brand-new Borg–Warner trophy, the first to be presented with the keys to the pace car, and he unintentionally sparked off a famous tradition by drinking what appeared to be milk in the winner's enclosure. It was, in fact, BUTTER-milk (his drink of choice on a hot day since childhood), but with excited executives within the dairy industry believing that the newspaper photographs were showing him drinking regular milk, milk it would be from that point.

Born in Yonkers, New York, on July 21, 1904, Louis relocated to the Los Angeles area with his family at an early age. He first appeared at Indianapolis in 1926 as a mechanic for his mentor, Frank Elliott, and in 1927, he believed he would be driving a car owned by Elliott until it was sold a few days before the race to another owner, who chose newcomer Wilbur Shaw as his driver. Meyer stayed on as mechanic and ended up driving relief for Shaw on his way to fourth place. In 1928, the roles were reversed, and a car to which Shaw was assigned was put up for sale.

Meyer, now just short of his 24th birthday, had Alden Sampson II, a friend of his own age, purchase

the car. In his first start, Louis won the race. He almost won it again in 1929, finishing second to Ray Keech after a stalled engine during a pit stop cost him seven minutes. He finished fourth (after starting on the front row) in 1930, was fourth in 1931 as a relief driver on a car he owned, and was first again in 1933.

He was trying for an unprecedented fourth win in 1939 when he spun out while trying to catch Shaw with only three laps remaining. Easygoing and friendly, but possessing a strong business sense, Louis entered into a venture with eventual Novi owner Lew Welch for the purpose of rebuilding Ford passenger car engines on the West Coast. It was fabulously successful.

In the winter of 1945/46, Louis and Dale Drake purchased Fred Offenhauser's engine business, Louis remaining as a partner in the ownership of the "Offy" until 1964, when he sold out to Drake to become the Speedway, Indiana-based distributor for Ford's new V-8 double-overhead camshaft racing engine.

An avid golfer throughout his life (and even jet-skiing into his late eighties), the delightful and fatherly Louis (whose gravelly pronunciation of the race track was something along the lines of 'der Schpeedway'), was 91 years old when he passed away on October 7, 1995.

Everybody had his fingers crossed in the closing laps, knowing that fuel consumption was going to be critical.

One by one, cars started rolling to a stop at the side of the track, and by the time the race ended, seven had exhausted their fuel supplies, including four which had been running within the first 10. The worst hit was Shorty Cantlon, who had been holding on to third just before running dry with a little over five laps to go.

Meyer and Horn were able to baby their cars home to the finish, Meyer becoming the first driver ever to win the "500" for a third time. By starting back in 28th, Meyer tied 1911 winner Ray Harroun for having come from the deepest within the pack to win, a record still unbroken 70 years later.

Meyer was unknowingly about to usher in one of the most time-honored and cherished traditions at the Indianapolis Motor Speedway. When he was a youngster growing up in the New York City district of Yonkers, his mother had told him that he could refresh himself on a hot day by drinking buttermilk. Thus, buttermilk became his drink of choice. A crew member handed him a bottle in the victory enclosure – he was going to drink it regardless of the outcome – and Louis held it up, along with three fingers, for the benefit of the photographers.

The following day, an executive with the milk industry saw a photograph of the celebration in the sports section of his newspaper, and, thinking it was milk rather than buttermilk, he vowed to have milk available the following year. Milk became a part of the post-race celebration and was continued up through 1941, and then again after the revival of the race in 1946, following WWII. It was dropped between 1947 and 1955, but was returned in 1956 and has been a major part of the event ever since.

One of the major racing stories during the spring and on into the month of May was the claim by defending winner Kelly Petillo that he had retired as a driver. Nobody really believed him. He claimed number 1 for his car, but then announced that the dashing and dapper East Coast dirt-track champion George "Doc" MacKenzie was to be his driver. AAA informed Petillo that MacKenzie would have to carry number 10.

The arguments continued but Petillo relented, and to the surprise of just about everybody, the race started without him in the lineup. He drove anyway. On lap 142, MacKenzie came in for fuel and tires and Kelly jumped in to replace him.

MacKenzie had run an excellent race and had kept the car well within the first ten. But the diminutive Petillo proceeded to go to work with his most unorthodox style of actually lifting his posterior from the seat, leaning at an angle with his back braced against the top of the seat, and driving with his right leg fully extended. He went from sixth at 180 laps to third at 190, passing Cantlon just before the latter expended his fuel supply.

It was Meyer first (at a record 109.069 mph), Horn second, and Petillo, driving for MacKenzie, third. Fourth was taken by Mauri Rose for the Four Wheel Drive Company, while Shaw was able to salvage seventh.

There was yet another "first" for Meyer, in addition to having been the first to win three times, the first to win the Borg–Warner trophy, and the first to drink what had *appeared* to be regular milk.

Tommy Milton, who a decade earlier had seemed to be on

the verge of becoming the first three-time winner himself, had long since retired and was now an engineer with Packard. When company executives invited him to drive the Packard pace car at the start of the 1936 "500," he agreed, with the suggestion that it would be rather a fitting gesture to present the pace car to the winner of the race at its conclusion.

They concurred, and Meyer was the first to benefit from the continued tradition of presenting the winning driver with either the actual pace car, or at least something very similar.

Victory Lane, as the winner's celebration area had long since become known, had taken on a slightly different appearance this year. It had been in the same location for about 20 years, although apparently never at anyone's particular direction. In the very early years, each car, after finishing the distance, would either stop at its own pit or else continue on down to the very end of the pits, and then, after making a sharp left turn, be driven back over to the garage area. Evidently, it wasn't long before it became standard for the winning car to stop as soon as it had made the left turn, the driver being surrounded right there and then by crew, press, and well-wishers, even while the cars finishing second, third, fourth, and so on, would still be motoring past the scene, just inches away, on their way back to the garage area.

Because the victory area had become so crowded in recent years, an eight-foot-high fence of wooden posts and wire had been erected, creating a rectangular-shaped area which became nicknamed "The Bull Pen." It was a lot easier to police just who was in the enclosure and who was not, and it even had a gate, which would be pulled shut by the security guards as soon as the winning car had been driven in.

Main photograph: Pace car driver Ralph de Palma (the 1915 winner) poses with the La Salle Series 50 on the bricks before the start of the 1937 "500."

Inset below: Jimmy Snyder, the fastest in 1937 and 1939, and the first over 130.
Photograph: IMS

1937: Wilbur pulls it off... by two seconds

Mercifully, for 1937, the fuel limit was lifted.

There was one other factor to be considered, however. It was mandated that the only fuel permissible would be "pump" gasoline. For the last several years, many of the participants had been using various blends of fuel, the most popular being methanol.

In 1936, the ban on supercharging (except on two-cycle engines) had been lifted, but only one supercharged car, an American-owned French Bugatti, had been entered. It was never presented for a qualifying attempt.

While no winning engine in recent years had been larger than 260 cubic inches (and *without* a supercharger), cagey Art Sparks had carefully read the rule book and determined that there was nothing to preclude using an engine of at least 100 cubic inches greater than that *with* one.

He set about building what he felt would be the ultimate racing car, and not surprisingly, he ran low on funds. He joined forces with the young, wealthy, and exceedingly eccentric Joel Thorne, and the job was completed.

Bill Cummings sped through his 10-lap qualifying run to win the pole at 123.445 mph, and on his final lap, he recorded 125.139 mph, finally to exceed the single-lap mark held by Leon Duray ever since 1928. And Cummings was doing it with a riding mechanic on board; not that this had

been evident at the time. Ever since lap three, diminutive Frankie Del Roy, one of the most colorful of all the onboard mechanics, had been "down in the basement" in an attempt to keep the car from jumping out of gear.

Track closing time in those days was normally either 7:00 P.M. (rather than the 6:00 P.M. it eventually became) or precisely at "sundown," this, of course, becoming later as the month wore on. Just as the sun was touching the horizon on Saturday, May 23, the third day of qualifications, Jimmy Snyder, a onetime Chicago milkman and University of Illinois pre-med student, went out with the massive "blown" six-cylinder Sparks Special.

Oldtimers recalled standing on the top floor of the pagoda, looking out across the infield in the fading light and seeing the flames flowing from the exhaust pipe as Snyder would back off for the third turn.

The Cummings lap of 125.139 mph, a week earlier, had required one minute, 11.92 seconds to complete.

There was about to be an audible gasp.

Snyder's first lap was under that by THREE SECONDS, at an absolutely incredible 130.492 mph.

Needless to say, a 366-cubic-inch engine with a supercharger was a formidable combination.

The speed dropped just a little the second time around, at 129.422 mph, while lap three was 127.334. The run then came to an end, Snyder slowing and heading for the pits. It had become too dark to continue.

Snyder tried it again on May 26, and this time ran the distance, exceeding the Cummings speed by a couple of miles per hour at 125.287, and becoming the first person to complete the 25-mile distance in less than 12 minutes.

The second-fastest qualifier, also making it on May 26, was a bit of a surprise. Still claiming he was retired, Kelly Petillo had begun the month with Floyd Roberts as his driver. But after a dispute, followed by Rex Mays declining an invitation to replace Roberts, the never-unobtrusive Kelly jumped in and qualified the car himself.

There were two separate accidents on May 28, which resulted in the loss of three more lives. Shortly before the track closed for the day, Frank McGurk had a connecting rod break during a qualifying attempt, causing him to spin into the turn one infield and flip. Riding mechanic Albert Opalko, who had been on the pole with Petillo in 1934, died on the way to the hospital. Earlier in the day, Overton "Bunny" Phillips, later of Bugatti restoration fame, had a crankshaft break just south of the start/finish line, throwing his car out of control. He spun across to the pit wall and hit a stationary car, next to which were standing Otto Rohde, an engineer for Champion Spark Plug Company, and George Warford, a dirt-track driver who was serving as a fireman. Phillips and his mechanic were uninjured, but neither Rohde nor Warford had a chance.

Both issues were addressed. From that point on, no car was permitted to sit on the racetrack side of the pit wall at any time except during the race, while the era of the riding mechanic was about to come to an end.

A historical footnote took place during practice with the arrival of a car built by pre-World War I driver Lee Oldfield, a longtime member of the AAA Technical Committee who was extremely active with the Society of Automotive Engineers. Greatly impressed by the showing of the German Auto Unions in recent Grand Prix events, Oldfield had constructed a car in which the engine, a V-16 Marmon, was mounted *behind* the driver.

It was the first rear-engined car ever entered at Indianapolis.

Oldfield made a number of practice runs with the car, and it is believed that Fred Frame may also have driven some laps. It never made a qualifying attempt, however, and never did return. Oldfield (who was in no way related to Barney Oldfield, against whom he often raced) said later that the infamous Joel Thorne had agreed to put up part of the money to develop the car, but, not surprisingly for him, failed to do so.

Thorne, who was still only 22 years old at this time, became embroiled in quite a controversy after qualifying was completed. He had entered no less than six cars for the race and had tried to qualify one himself. He ended up the slowest of 35 qualifiers, thus missing "the cut" by two positions. The first alternate car,

Inset below: **Pre-WWI driver Lee Oldfield (not related to the famed Barney, against whom he raced) makes a brief appearance during practice in 1937 with a V-16 Marmon-powered car with its engine located behind the driver. Influenced by the German Auto Union Grand Prix cars, Oldfield creates the first rear-engined car ever to appear at the track. That is him in the white shirt.**
Photograph: IMS

Above: Off in the distance, due south, on race morning 1937 can be seen the smoke stack of Fisher and Allison's old Prest-O-Lite factory. All the way up until the mid-1950s (when double-decker grandstands began to block the view), veteran drivers during practice would use the flow of the smoke as a form of windsock.

Photograph: IMS

just ahead of him, was owned by Phil Shafer and driven by Emil Andres. When Shafer withdrew the car because of mechanical problems, Thorne became the first alternate.

That gave him an idea.

When he learned from Cliff Bergere and car owner George Lyons that they felt confident of no better than a fifth-place finish, Thorne offered to pay them fifth-place money in return for their withdrawing the car. Another version had him also purchasing it.

One way or another, word of this transaction reached the AAA officials, and Thorne was summoned to a meeting. He was advised that no alternates would be permitted to start, and that while he would be allowed to serve as a relief driver on one of his *own* cars, he would not be permitted to start in any of them or drive for anybody else.

Thorne (who stood a breathtaking six feet, six inches tall at a time when anything over about six feet would draw a second look) did not take this well. He stormed out of the office, threatening to buy up the entire field and then withdraw everybody.

The officials huddled as soon as he was gone, and quickly decided that they had better go around the garage area and warn car owners that Thorne might be paying them a visit. In several cases he had beaten them there, each owner believing he had made an exclusive arrangement.

Thorne was called back for another meeting, at which time the point was raised that AAA had the power to hand out suspensions, and frequently did. Assuming he planned to drive in the "500" at some point in the future, he might be well advised to cease all of this nonsense and concentrate on supporting his previously qualified entries from the sidelines. Thorne rethought the situation and returned to qualify for the next four years, placing ninth in 1938, seventh in 1939, and fifth in 1940. His eccentricity, however, would continue.

What was not generally known was that several of the members of the AAA Contest Board would have occasional dealings with Thorne's aunt, who was none other than Frances Perkins, Franklin D. Roosevelt's Secretary of Labor between 1933 and 1945.

In recognition of this being the 25th running of the Indianapolis 500, the color silver was predominant on the cover of the souvenir program, and on race morning, longtime racing enthusiasts were afforded a real treat. The winning Marmon "Wasp" from 1911 and the winning National from 1912 both were on hand, courtesy of Fred Holliday, who owned both cars. Driving the Marmon on a lap of honor shortly before the start was a slightly greying Ray Harroun, while behind the wheel of the National was the still-rather-bashful Joe Dawson. Riding in the mechanic's seat next to Joe was none other than Don Herr, the man who had *thought* he was going to be the driver of this car in 1912, but who ended up driving it anyway as Dawson's relief.

As a further indication of the passing of time, former riding mechanic Billy Devore, son of the 1927 runner-up, was in the lineup, thus becoming the first second-generation driver to qualify for a "500."

There had been a slight revision in the flag system. White, which had been used as the "stop for consultation" flag since 1930, now replaced king's blue for indicating "one lap to go," while black was replacing white as the consultation flag. This now conformed with the European flag system, the exception being that "one lap to go" has never been used in international competition.

Jimmy Snyder and the Sparks "big six" could not be restrained. Because of his late qualifying run, he had to start all the way back in 19th, but by the end of the very first lap, he was all the way up to fifth.

At the end of the second lap, he was third and about to take second.

By the end of the third lap he was leading.

Snyder ran away with the event for 27 amazing laps, but the strain on the transmission was just too great. He came rolling in and was out of the race.

Wilbur Shaw, who was back with his Catfish-influenced streamliner and had qualified second, went to the lead when Snyder pitted. From that point on, Shaw pretty much had the race in his control, except for 43 laps in two segments while he was making pit stops. It was the same car which inherited the lead both times – Louis Meyer's winner of the previous year – but it led with two different drivers.

Starting and finishing on this murderously hot day was Ralph Hepburn, Shaw's very close friend. Spelling Hepburn between laps 108 and 163 had been a newcomer by the name of Bob Swanson.

By 1936, the brand-new sport of midget car racing was on its way to becoming extremely popular, but midget car drivers were not yet being given very serious consideration by the AAA officials at the Speedway. Swanson had been assigned to a car in 1936, but was turned down without even having been given an opportunity to display his skills in a test. He had better luck in 1937, when he returned with the car in which Rex Mays had started from the pole the previous two years, and after starting 21st, he was all the way up to seventh in 10 laps and fifth by lap 30. He was sidelined at 52 laps but then was asked to fill in for Hepburn. He led from lap 130, and when he came in at 163 to hand back to Hepburn, he was still leading.

At lap 180, Shaw was almost two minutes ahead and averaging over 114 mph. But he

Bottom: Driving the car with which Louis Meyer had won in 1936, close friend Ralph Hepburn scores a very close second in 1937.

Below: With all due regard to Ralph Hepburn, who had suffered a major leg injury five years earlier, many felt that had relief driver Bob Swanson been left in the car at the last pit stop, winner Wilbur Shaw might have been caught before the finish.
Photographs: IMS

Below: Ten years after making his "500" debut, Wilbur Shaw finally enters Victory Lane, driving a car he helped build himself. Riding mechanic John W. "Jigger" Johnson (left) had been here before, having ridden with Louis Schneider in 1931. Jigger would also be the last on-board mechanic to win, the riding mechanics no longer being required from 1938 on.
Photograph: IMS

was starting to slow. He had noticed that his oil pressure was dropping to zero in the turns and that the needle would barely waver on the straights. He was going to have to baby it home to save the engine. Leon Duray, whose two cars had both dropped out, had taken over Shaw's pit board and was advising Shaw that Hepburn was gaining many seconds per lap.

Five laps to go, four, three, two, and then the white flag.

The closest margin of victory up to this point had been 27 seconds, by Bill Cummings over Mauri Rose in 1934, but Shaw was only an estimated 14 seconds ahead of Hepburn at the start of the final lap.

With riding mechanic John W. "Jigger" Johnson constantly looking over his shoulder and Shaw's mental calculations working out perfectly, they beat Hepburn across the line by just 2.16 seconds.

This would remain as the closest finish ever in a "500" for the next 45 years, not to be broken until 1982.

In spite of slowing down in the closing laps, Shaw had knocked 11 minutes from Meyer's 1936 record, upping the average speed to 113.580 mph.

Years later, more than one insider would be suggesting that with all due respect to Hepburn, who had suffered a serious leg injury in 1932, the result might have been different had Swanson been allowed to stay in the cockpit. Ironically, when Hepburn had been forced to miss the 1932 "500" because of that leg injury, it was Shaw whom Hepburn had hired as a replacement.

During the midpoint of the race, Shaw's crew had repeatedly shown him a chalked message reading simply, "Frame?" Somewhat confused, Shaw yelled over the roar of the engine to Jigger Johnson, and Jigger began searching around, inside and out, in an attempt to locate some kind of a problem with the frame. None could be found. They shrugged at each other and kept going. The mystery was solved after the race was over. Believing he might be in need of a relief driver, the crew was inquiring of Shaw as to whether or not he would like Fred *Frame* to take over!

The euphoria displayed by the winners in the victory enclosure does not always indicate that *all* is well. The combination of oil constantly splashed on his shins and a severely burned right foot, courtesy of a piping-hot accelerator, was such that the crew later carried Shaw, in a sitting position, over to the infield hospital for medical attention. He climbed on the scales while he was there and discovered that since breakfast, he had dropped from 138 pounds to 127.

This was the last year for Rickenbacker's "366" formula, referred to so unkindly by many as "The Junk Era," because starting in 1938 the new European Grand Prix formula would be adopted for the "500." The specs called for a limit of three liters (183 cubic inches) for supercharged engines and 4½ liters (274) for those which were unsupercharged. Exotic blends of fuel could now be used, with gasoline still an option.

The best news of all, for many people, came later in the summer when it was finally ruled that for 1938, riding mechanics no longer would be mandatory.

They were a hearty bunch, the riding mechanics. Many of them aspired to be "500" drivers and were regular competitors at other tracks, entrusting their lives to others at Indianapolis as a way of "getting a foot in the door." There were probably about 75 people who took laps in practice at various times as both drivers and riding mechanics, while 24 are documented to have had at least one start in the race in both capacities, with several more having performed in relief roles as either or both.

The most prominent of those who appeared in both roles were: Peter de Paolo (the only person to *lead* the race in both categories); Jimmy Murphy, who rode with Eddie O'Donnell in 1919; and Harry Hartz, who not only was the only driver ever (through 2006) to finish second three times and never win, but had also been runner-up as a mechanic for Eddie Hearne in 1919. The only winning riding mechanic who also drove in the "500" was Ralph de Palma's 1915 partner, Louis Fontaine, who lasted for 33 laps in 1921; and while 1935 winner Kelly Petillo was a riding mechanic in 1930, it is unclear whether he actually rode in the race.

One way or another, it would be single-seaters from here on.

Chapter 7
SINGLE-SEATERS, THE EUROPEAN FORMULA, AND GATHERING WARCLOUDS

1938: *"Mrs. Roberts, Mrs. Roberts, we just heard on the radio that your husband has won the 500"*

WHILE the new specifications did curb the speeds somewhat in 1938, it was not by a great deal. Floyd Roberts won the pole for the now retired Lou Moore at 125.506 mph. Kelly Petillo went out for an attempt shortly after Roberts and had a nine-lap average of 126.3 going thanks to several laps at 127, but a worn tire forced him in before he could take the checker.

Clyde Adams had built two new cars for Art Sparks and Joel Thorne, based on the 1937 "big six." The engines for these were 183-cid supercharged versions. On the second day of time trials, Ronney Householder did ten laps at 125.769 mph with one of them, slightly faster than Roberts, who just happened to be Ronney's neighbor in Van Nuys, California. The cars were quite unique in that the engine was placed in the frame at a slight angle, the driveshaft angling across to the right rear corner. The cockpit, which was far to the left, allowed the driver to sit extremely close to the ground and offered a perfect view of the all-left-hand turns.

The early stages of the race featured a battle between front-row starter Rex Mays, driving a Bill White-owned Alfa Romeo, and Jimmy Snyder with the other new Sparks/Thorne car. White had acquired the Alfa at the 1936 Vanderbilt Cup road race on Long Island, and after it was temporarily converted to a "two-man" car, Mays had driven it at Indianapolis in 1937. Mays opened a lot of eyes and really impressed the Europeans when the combination returned to Long Island that summer, finishing third in the 300-mile race behind the Auto Union of Bernd Rosemeyer and the Mercedes–Benz of Britain's Dick Seaman.

With the Alfa converted back to a single-seater (and now re-bodied by Ernie Weil), Mays set the pace for the first 14 laps. Snyder came up through the pack from the fifth row, and except for a couple of laps led by Mays while Snyder pitted, the Chicago driver remained in front until Roberts took over at lap 75.

There was an unfortunate accident just past the 100-mile mark when Snyder's mentor, Emil Andres of Chicago, crashed in the second turn, dislodging a wheel. The errant wheel bounced through the crowded infield, scattering people in every direction. Everett Spence of Terre Haute could not avoid it, and if there was any positive side to the tragic outcome, it would be that almost half a century would pass before the next time a spectator would be fatally injured as the result of an on-track incident.

Master strategist Lou Moore had Floyd Roberts running a typically well-thought-out race by having him stop only once, for fuel and a tire change at 105 laps. It was still the rule (as it would be until 1947) that the driver was obliged to climb out of the car during a stop. Even so, Roberts was back in and on his way in just over one minute, an extremely rapid stop for the time.

Snyder led again, but his supercharger began to give trouble and he was knocked out after 151 laps. Householder, who took relief from Billy Winn, hero of the 1936 Vanderbilt Cup, ran regularly between second and third positions until the same problem knocked him out a short time later.

Roberts, whose average speed of 117.200 mph would stand as the distance track record for the next ten years, made a very compelling winner. Born in North Dakota, he had struggled for breaks for years on the West Coast until suddenly blossoming in 1934, finishing second to Rex Mays in the Pacific Coast championship. Until recently a factory worker on the assembly line at a Lockheed Aircraft plant, he once had recuperated from a racing injury by operating a steam shovel. His wife and family were not at the track when he won. Mrs. Roberts had listened to the early stages of the race on the radio in Van Nuys until it was time to depart for

her job at the phone company, where she was going to take advantage of working a Memorial Day holiday shift paying extra money. When people started coming in to tell her that her husband had won, co-workers insisted she go home to celebrate.

Chet Miller had been running second until the 197th lap, when he had to duck in for fuel. Inexplicably, he did not return to the track for two full minutes, thus giving up the position to defending winner Wilbur Shaw, whose streamliner now had a piece of body paneling covering the riding mechanic's seat. Miller was fortunate to salvage third.

It had been Shaw's intention to drive an Italian Maserati in this race. He had been invited to drive a privately owned model at the last minute in the 1937 Vanderbilt Cup (after withdrawing his Indianapolis winner), and he was so impressed after finishing ninth that he told Chicago sportsman Mike Boyle that he thought he could win at Indianapolis with one. A deal was made, and Boyle placed an order with the factory. Unfortunately, there was a misunderstanding over specifications, and while the Maserati which was delivered was certainly supercharged, the engine displaced only 90 cubic inches, less than half of the size allowable. Shaw decided to stick with his 1937 winner and have his friend, Mauri Rose, drive the Maserati. Rose was running fourth when the supercharger packed up after 165 laps.

A new Maserati would be ordered for 1939, and Harry "Cotton" Henning, Boyle's chief mechanic, would sail for Italy that February to receive it and to make certain that this time there were no misunderstandings.

In the meantime, much pre-race interest in 1938 had centered on the entries of Italian driver Tazio Nuvolari (down to drive an Alfa Romeo), and four new cars being built under the direction of Harry Miller. Constructed in Pittsburgh, the Millers had been commissioned by Gulf Oil Company. Two were front-engined and two were rear-engined, although only one of the latter was completed in time to make the trip. No doubt inspired by Billy Winn's spirited performance in the 1936 Vanderbilt Cup, in which he had run third before dropping out near the end, Miller was contemplating making Winn part of a team he envisioned taking to Europe. This dream soon faded. There were a variety of mechanical problems with the cars and none of them qualified, Ralph Hepburn rolling out for a last-ditch attempt with the rear-engined car at the very moment time trials were being shut off.

During practice for the Pau Grand Prix in April, the very first race held in Europe under the new regulations, the Alfa which Nuvolari had planned to bring over caught fire. He arrived anyway, five days before the race, without a car, and amidst all kinds of rumors. He was said to be asking a fairly hefty retainer for his services as a driver, and, not surprisingly, there were no takers. He ended up being named honorary starter and actually did wave the green at the start. He hopped into a couple of cockpits during practice, but strictly for photographic purposes, and he accepted one invitation for a "guest drive," although this proved to be decidedly short-lived. He was invited by Lew Welch to take out the car Herb Ardinger had qualified (Welch would be renowned later as the owner of the Novi racing cars). An eyewitness reported that no sooner had the engine been fired than Nuvolari jammed it in gear and took off just as he would have in a Grand Prix car. The car shuddered along for a few yards until stalling with stripped gears, never having reached the racing surface. Nuvolari is said to have climbed out and walked back defiantly, while Welch and a couple of mechanics headed down to the aid of the abandoned car, with no acknowledgement by anyone as they passed in opposite directions.

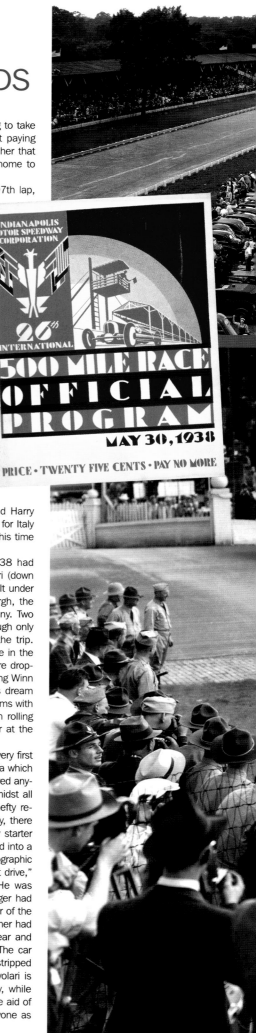

Far left: Looking north, up the main straight from the pagoda.

Left: Only one of the two revolutionary Harry Miller-designed rear-engined cars is completed in time, Ralph Hepburn managing some practice laps but pulling into the pit area for a qualifying run just as time trials are ending.

Below: The Alfa Romeo of Tazio Nuvolari does not arrive, but the great Italian driver (pictured with winner Roberts) comes anyway. He serves as honorary starter, waving the green flag at the start.
Photographs: IMS

Left: Floyd Roberts pulls in at the conclusion of the 1938 race, the now fenced-off Victory Lane having taken on the nickname "The Bull Pen" due to the fact that there is even a gate to shut after the winning car has entered.
Photograph: IMS

1939: Almost (but not quite) a fourth win for Louis

The Maserati Henning brought back from Italy for the 1939 "500" was just as had been hoped for, a straight-eight, dual-supercharged "183," which was, in fact, two "fours," mounted in line with a supercharger on each. A couple of weeks before he had left to go over, there had been considerable sadness in the Boyle camp due to the fact that the very popular 1934 winner, Bill Cummings, had lost his life in an automobile accident on the southeast side of Indianapolis. Shaw, Cummings, and Chet Miller were to have been teammates.

Just as there had been much cheering in 1937 when it was no longer mandatory for cars to carry a riding mechanic, there was now further cause for celebration when it was announced that the length of a qualification run was being cut from ten laps back to four.

Jimmy Snyder won the pole at 130.138 mph with one of the Sparks/Thorne cars, and he was joined on the front row by Shaw's Maserati, and by Louis Meyer, who was driving a Bowes Seal Fast-sponsored car built in 1938 by Myron Stevens. Powered by a straight-eight Winfield engine, it strongly resembled, unpainted, a 1934 Grand Prix Mercedes. Bitterly disappointed was Rex Mays, who, having joined the Sparks/Thorne team for just this one year, turned a lap during practice at an unofficial record of 131.5 mph. Strongly favored for another pole, he had difficulty in qualifying and later dropped out of the race at 145 laps after having run second for many laps.

To spectators who had not attended practice in 1937 or 1938, the car George Bailey had qualified for the outside of row two looked decidedly odd. It was one of the Gulf Millers with the engine located *behind* the driver, and while it would be around for only 47 laps in this race, another historical landmark had been recorded. There were actually three of these cars by 1939. In spite of numerous revolutionary approaches – slant-six supercharged engines, four-wheel drive, and independent suspension – they were beset with problems. Johnny Seymour was severely burned in one of them when he crashed, the gasoline contained in the side-mounted pontoon tanks having been ignited when a tank split upon impact. The following May, George Bailey would have a similar accident soon after practice began and would succumb to his injuries. The pontoon tanks would disappear by 1941, and while one of the cars was still appearing at the track ten years later, Harry Miller's last hurrah had not been a success.

Thus, life for the car owners had now been further complicated with yet another decision to be made. Should one place one's faith in a production engine or racing engine, supercharged or nonsupercharged, four-cylinder, six, eight, 12 or 16, or front-drive, rear-drive, or even four-wheel-drive?

And now, front-engined or rear-engined?

A dilemma indeed.

On hand in 1939 as honorary referee was Gene Tunney, the articulate former world heavyweight boxing champion, forever linked with Jack Dempsey. Tunney was now serving as chairman of the board of directors for the American Distilling Company. In 1938, the honorary referee had been another female aviatrix following in the footsteps of Amelia Earhart, namely Jacqueline Cochran, holder of numerous speed and distance records and, later, the first woman to break the sound barrier.

Between them, the three members of the front row – Snyder, Shaw, and Meyer – led all but five laps of the race, Meyer striving to become the first person ever to win the "500" for a fourth time. On the 182nd lap, after having led since lap 135, he blew a right front tire and spun out in turn one. By the time he made it back to the pits, Shaw had taken the lead. Meyer sped after him and, in uncharacteristic desperation, spun out of turn two on his 198th lap and crashed through the inside wooden fence, thrown onto the track as the car hit.

Louis immediately picked himself up and walked to the side of the track, where an ambulance was ready to take him over for a checkup at the infield hospital. He later stated that by the time he climbed into the ambulance, he had already told himself that he had retired as a race driver! No sooner had his wife come into the hospital and been assured that he was virtually uninjured, than she asked him why he wasn't wearing any shoes. He looked down with surprise, not having been aware that he wasn't. They were found a few minutes later, lying in the belly pan of the car, where they had remained behind when he suddenly exited.

In the meantime, Shaw had gone on to his second win in three years, a foreign car having won for the first time since the Fisher and Allison-owned Peugeot had taken the prize in 1919. The supercharged Sparks/Thorne car of Jimmy Snyder ran smoothly all day, leading for 65 laps and being in a solid third, ready to take advantage of Meyer's misfortune at the finish. Cliff Bergere finished in the number three position.

A huge pall was cast over the day when a three-car accident brought out the caution for a lengthy period just past the halfway point. Bob Swanson had just taken over for Ralph Hepburn in the now-re-bodied 1937 second-place-finishing car, when he spun coming out of the second turn. The car flipped over and Swanson was deposited onto the racetrack. Both the first- and third-placed finishers of the previous year, Floyd Roberts and Chet Miller, came upon the scene, with Miller turning left and Roberts turning right. Miller's car swerved into the infield grass, dug in, and turned upside down. Roberts vaulted over the low-sitting outer wooden fence but remained upright as he went over.

Swanson and Miller, both of whose accidents had looked extremely serious, were hospitalized – but both recovered to race again the following year. Roberts was not so fortunate. In spite of the fact that the car had barely left the ground, the former Sunday school teacher and devout churchgoer had received a jolting blow to the head upon landing. Shockingly, the defending winner died of a basal skull fracture.

Another chapter in track history was closed on August 15, when word was received that Carl Fisher, the man who had started it all, had passed away in a Miami hospital at the age of 65.

Left: Shaw wins for the second time in three years.

Below: It is the third year for rear-engined cars and the second year for Harry Miller's version, now totaling three in number. Two of them do not make a qualifying attempt, but George Bailey lines up on the outside of the second row as the first person ever to drive a rear-engined car in the "500."

Bottom: Local studio photographer Charles Bell prepares to take the traditional pre-race panoramic photo of all the participants, the motorized winch mechanism bearing the camera, requiring about 15 seconds to complete the "pan."
Photographs: IMS

Bottom: Mike Boyle's privately entered 1938 dual-supercharged Grand Prix Maserati is undefeated at Indianapolis as Wilbur Shaw becomes the first driver ever to win in consecutive years. In his last four starts he has finished first, second, first, and first.
Photograph: IMS

1940: Two in a row and three out of four for Shaw

Spectators and public alike began to wonder whether there would even *be* a "500" in 1940. The situation in Europe had been deteriorating for some time, and on September 7, 1939, war was declared.

In spite of the concerns, Rickenbacker did press ahead, and Wilbur Shaw accomplished something never before achieved. He became the first person to win the "500" in consecutive years, and with the very same car, the Mike Boyle-owned Maserati. In fact, Shaw had now finished first, second, first, and first in four consecutive years, not to mention second-place finishes in 1933 and 1935.

Second in the 1940 race was pole sitter Rex Mays in the Louis Meyer-vacated Bowes–Winfield, while third was Mauri Rose in a Lou Moore-owned car which the late Floyd Roberts had helped Louis "Curly" Wetteroth and Moore build during the winter of 1938/39. During practice, Mays had lapped at an unofficial 132.4 mph.

Shaw had received somewhat of a break, not that he wouldn't have won anyway. Rain began to fall with about 100 miles to go, and while the officials never did feel it was necessary to completely stop the race, the yellow-flag caution situation did preclude any advancement of a position other than for cars being eliminated. The fact that Shaw's teammate, Ted Horn, was a lap down when the caution began, and that the race was halted as soon as Shaw won, is the reason why Horn's amazing nine-race record, between 1936 and 1948, shows him completing one lap short of a possible 1,800 laps.

Finishing tenth was a Maserati shared by René LeBegue and René Dreyfus, both of whom were on leave from the French Army. Lucy O'Reilly Schell, an American lady living in Monte Carlo and married to a Frenchman who had just lost his life in an automobile accident, had managed to convince the French government that it would do wonders for the morale of the war-torn country if two native sons could be permitted to compete at Indianapolis. There was, of course, by this time, a complete ban on all of motorsports in Europe.

Permission was granted and two Maseratis, painted in the French national racing color of blue, were shipped over, accompanied by LeBegue and Dreyfus. Also making the trip were Lucy's son, a then-18-year-old Harry Schell (who would become a Grand Prix star in the 1950s), and Luigi Chinetti, the eventual three-time winner of the 24-Hours of Le Mans and a major importer of Ferraris to the United States after the war.

There was an apparent misunderstanding over the qualifying procedure, and in spite of repeated attempts by the officials to explain it, Dreyfus accepted a speed which did not hold up as one of the fastest 33. Pleas were made by several of the Americans, including Shaw, to allow Dreyfus to start anyway, but officials did not feel they should bend the rules. As it happened, LeBegue's engine blew during the final practice session, so the engine from the Dreyfus car was dropped in. The drivers then shared the wheel for the race, alternating every 50 laps or so, putting in two equal shifts apiece.

Dreyfus, who was supposed to return to France as soon as the race was over, decided to defect and settle in New York, where he was to run a very prestigious and elegant French restaurant for the next several decades.

1941: Will there even be a race next year?

Despite the war raging in Europe, the "500" was held again in 1941. Amazingly, René LeBegue received permission from the French government to come back. This time, he brought a pair of French Talbots, but did so with extreme difficulty, having to truck them over the Pyrenees and then wind down through an authorized "corridor" in order to reach Lisbon. He managed to get them onto a ship, after which he and his other driver, Jean Trevoux, arranged for air passage. He was faced with numerous other challenges after arriving, and his

luck was even worse than the year before. The cars, which had beautiful lines, were basically sports cars, still being out-fitted with mudguards and headlights when they arrived. In spite of help and encouragement from the Americans, neither car was able to qualify.

There was a new chief steward by this time, Charlie Merz having been called to service in Europe before the track had opened for practice in 1940. His replacement was Ted Doescher, an impressive-looking ex-college football star who was only 36 years of age.

And Eddie Rickenbacker was absent. In 1934, he had become involved with Eastern Air Lines, and in 1938 he had taken it over, preventing him from spending much time at the track. On February 26, 1941, while on a business trip, he had been lucky to escape with his life when the private plane on which he was flying crashed just outside of Atlanta. Because he was still confined to a hospital bed on race morning, a special hookup was arranged so that he could speak over the public address system and the radio broadcast.

Rex Mays, the only three-time pole sitter at this point, was denied a fourth when Mauri Rose grabbed it away from him with a Maserati owned by Lou Moore. With Shaw starting on the outside, it marked the second year in a row that the same three drivers had qualified for the front rank. Not only that, but they were the one–two–three finishers of the 1940 race.

Mays led the first 38 laps before bowing to Rose for six. Shaw then took over and appeared well on his way to winning, not only for a third consecutive time (a feat not yet accomplished through 2006) but also to be the first to win for a fourth time. On his 152nd lap, while easily in the lead, he spun through turn one and hit the outside wall tailfirst, sustaining a substantial back injury.

A wire wheel had collapsed, and Shaw had a theory for the reason.

At around seven o'clock on race morning, there had been a huge explosion in the garage area, followed by a fire. By the time it was contained, the eastern third of the south bank (a second bank of garages had been erected in 1929) had burned to the ground. It transpired that a member of the Thorne Engineering team had been doing some last-minute welding at the same time as George Barringer's rear-engine slant-six supercharged Miller was being fuelled with gasoline. Fumes apparently drifted through cracks in the wall and into the Thorne garage. The Thorne cars were not damaged, but Barringer's Miller was reduced to a burnt-out shell.

During the ensuing excitement, race cars, tools, equipment, and all other belongings had to be hurriedly moved out of the garage area, people ducking to avoid the lids of exploding 55-gallon drums of fuel as they flew through the air like frisbees.

A day or two before the race, Shaw had been balancing his wheels and one of them had given him some difficulty, never quite balancing properly. He had been chalking the letters "OK" on each tire as the wheel on which it was mounted was checked out, but he chalked the words "use last" on the one which had given trouble. Shaw's theory was that this may well have been the wheel which collapsed during the race, the chalk lettering having been washed away by the water from the hoses during the fire.

Into the lead, following Shaw's accident, went Cliff Bergere, who was driving the car in which Floyd Roberts had lost his life the year before. Bergere had purchased it from Lou Moore and repaired it, but Moore was still very much involved. Not far behind, and closing, was Mauri Rose, but not in the pole-winning Maserati. Instead, he was handling the car with which he had finished third in 1940, also owned by Moore.

The Maserati had dropped out after 60 laps, by which time Moore had become steadily less pleased with the current placing of his other driver, Floyd Davis. One wonders whether there may have been some sort of personality conflict going on between Moore and Davis, both of whom were known to be quite strong-headed. Although most versions of this story have Davis being far, far behind, he was, in fact, running 11th, only two and a half minutes out of first and just over half a minute behind Bergere.

Nevertheless, Davis, who presumably was on a one-stop

A true icon of the Indianapolis Motor Speedway, Wilbur Shaw ranks as one of the three or four most important figures in the track's entire history. Had it not been for his persistence in trying to find someone who would purchase the shuttered race track from the Eddie Rickenbacker interests in the immediate post-WWII years, one wonders whether the Speedway would have even survived.

With three firsts, three seconds, and a shared third-place finish (with Lou Moore in 1934) in just eight races (1933–40), Shaw's record was the most outstanding of any driver in the "500" until A. J. Foyt, Al Unser and Rick Mears came along decades later. Making his "500" debut in 1927, he led 508 laps between 1932 and 1941 (only Ralph de Palma had led more at that time); he was the first person to win twice in succession (1939-40); and he was leading substantially at the three-quarter distance in 1941, apparently destined for a history-making third consecutive win (and fourth overall) when a wire wheel collapsed, causing him to hit the first-turn outer wall. (While Foyt finally became a four-time winner 36 years later in 1977, the feat of "three in a row" has, of this writing, *still* not yet been achieved.)

Born in Shelbyville, Indiana, on October 31, 1902, Shaw came from very humble beginnings. Described as terrier-like in his approach, the feisty five-foot, seven-inch Shaw was a firm believer in "anything you can do, I can do better," whether it be on the golf course, at a card table, mastering conjuring tricks, or anything requiring athletic ability.

Driving racing cars was a given, especially when prize money for success by a hungry young man could translate into food on the dining table. The sport was to make him exceedingly wealthy. And when his beloved Indianapolis Speedway seemed destined to become a housing development, Shaw would have *none* of that. In what has been described as a one-man campaign for saving the track, he was eventually paired with Tony Hulman, who purchased it and installed Shaw as president and general manager.

With the shy and retiring Hulman happy to remain in the shadows for the first few years, the outgoing and universally respected Shaw (looking for all the world like a Hollywood leading man) was perfect in his role as the track's dynamic figurehead.

He was two weeks away from celebrating the ninth anniversary of the track's purchase when, on October 30, 1954, the eve of his 52nd birthday, the small aircraft in which he was returning from a business trip to Detroit went down near Decatur, Indiana.

strategy anyway, was called in a little earlier than expected, at lap 72. With an eager Rose standing by and ready to go, Davis was ordered by Moore to step out. Davis did so with reluctance, feeling that he was pacing himself for the long haul and that he would be in the hunt at the end regardless.

By the time Rose sped off, the car had dropped two more positions. Hanging out of the left side of the cockpit in order to see, the diminutive Rose started to go to work. He was eighth by lap 100, fifth at lap 110, and fourth by lap 120. When Shaw crashed on his 152nd lap, Rose climbed to third, and when Rex Mays promptly pitted to take on fuel, Rose went to second.

Only Bergere was ahead of Rose now, but Bergere was

Above: The eastern third of the south bank of garages burns to the ground on the morning of the 1941 race, the casualties including the rear-engined V-6 supercharged four-wheel-drive Miller which George Barringer had qualified 15th. Deacon Litz (left) and Wilbur Shaw console Barringer upon the loss of his car.
Photograph: IMS

slowing. He and Moore had been working on a straightforward plan to save time on pit stops: don't make any. Using an enormous fuel tank, Bergere was trying to duplicate the Dave Evans Cummins Diesel run of a decade earlier and go the distance nonstop. The difference here was that Lou Moore had always insisted on running gasoline whenever he could for better mileage, and for the last many laps, Bergere had been feeling the effects of the fumes. On the 162nd lap, the two cars came down the main straight side by side, with the flying Rose on the inside. He took the lead and was never headed after that, Bergere refusing to come in but fading to fifth by the finish.

Although Moore had nothing complimentary to say about Davis at the finish—and before long a lifelong rift would develop between the two drivers as well – the fact remains that Rose did everything he could at the time to give Davis equal credit. Instead of driving straight to Victory Lane, he slowed down at the pit and looked around for Davis. It was his intention to turn the wheel back to Davis and let him drive the car on down to Victory Lane, an extremely thoughtful gesture. Davis had already headed south on foot. Throughout the celebration, the animated Rose appeared to have gone out of his way to include the usually somber Davis in everything, the two of them posing together, grinning and shaking hands.

When the official photos of the winning team were shot at the start/finish line the following morning, however, Rose was sitting in the cockpit, with Moore standing next to him, and Davis nowhere to be seen. At the prize giving later in the day, Davis was excluded again, Moore going up with Rose to accept the checks from Pop Myers. It was a great shame, but the meticulous and deep-thinking Moore was not a very forgiving person.

Unfortunately, the drivers soon fell out as well. The problem is believed to have been disagreements over endorsements following the race.

There was one further irony. Davis had not even been the original driver assigned to the car. Instead, it had been a 28-year-old star of the future, Dennis "Duke" Nalon, a beautifully mannered and always immaculately turned-out crowd favorite from Chicago who had made two previous "500" starts. When Duke was offered a chance to drive a Maserati instead,

he asked Moore to be released. The Maserati finished 15th.

While many a driver relied strictly on prize money for income and would seek employment only if absolutely necessary during the off-season, Rose was now a full-fledged engineer. A "troubleshooter" on the engineering staff at a nearby Allison plant, he prided himself in having worked it out so that he could qualify and drive in the race on accrued days off, thus having been able to win the Indianapolis 500 without losing a single day of work.

In fourth place was one of the 1935 Ford–Miller chassis containing a one-of-a-kind engine, developed by Bud Winfield and designed by the legendary Leo Goosen, a truly unsung hero who had a major part in just about every American engine at the Speedway for over 40 years. The engine was the result of a conversation between Winfield and Lew Welch.

Legend has it that on a rainy day a couple of years earlier, Welch had wandered into the Bowes–Meyer garage, curious about Winfield's new straight-eight. The conversation developed, and eventually Welch is alleged to have asked Winfield, if money were no object, what would he build? When Winfield chuckled and revealed what had already been on his mind, Welch surprised him by saying, "Well, let's do it."

The result was a supercharged V-8 Winfield power plant, which after World War II would be renamed for the tiny location northwest of Detroit, Michigan where industrialist Welch's factory was producing optional and non-optional equipment for Ford Motor Company. The name of the place, not yet large enough even to qualify as a village, was Novi. (Now a large city, the name is said to have derived from once having been "stop number six" on a late-19th century wooden plank toll way which ran northwest to Howell, Michigan. The abbreviation of "No.," for "number," combined with "VI," the Roman numeral for "six," eventually transformed into Novi).

The two extra years of racing the Americans had been able to enjoy while Europe was at war were about to come to an end. The United States was drawn into the hostilities on December 7, 1941, and when war was declared the following day, the eyes and ears of the racing world were poised in anticipation of an announcement from Eddie Rickenbacker.

It did not come immediately, as many had expected, but rather three weeks later, on December 29. Entries for the

Left: A look down the main straight circa 1941. While a number of safety issues have been addressed by this time, note the height of the wooden "retaining" rail. Also note the Prest-O-Lite chimney off in the distance. The tree apparently was taken down between the races of 1946 and 1947.

Bottom: Because co-winners Floyd Davis and Mauri Rose are not photographed together on the morning after the 1941 race, the "official" photograph shows Floyd Davis (who started the race) sitting in the car after having qualified, with Mauri Rose (who finished) being shown as an inset above the engine cover.
Photographs: IMS

Co-Winners-
Mauri Rose and Floyd Davis-
Indianapolis Motor Speedway-
1941.

© 8 5 4
Charles J. Bell
Indpls. I. Itd.

1942 Indianapolis 500 had already been mailed out and six (the four nominated drivers being Mauri Rose, Cliff Bergere, Frank Wearne and Joel Thorne) had been filed with Pop Myers when the word came. The 500-Mile Race was being called off and would be suspended until after the war was over.

Not surprisingly, the patriotic Rickenbacker immediately did what Fisher and Allison had in 1917 by offering up the Speedway to the government. To his considerable surprise and disappointment, the offer was politely declined. During World War I, the infield had served as a more-than-adequate facility for the landing and takeoff of aircraft, but time had moved on, and the government inspectors who paid a visit quickly determined that it was simply too small for the larger and faster aircraft of the current day.

Rickenbacker, living in New York, instructed Pop Myers to close down the operation at 444 North Capitol Avenue (there was still no year-round office at the track itself), and he nominated one of his brothers, Al Rickenbacker, to oversee everything in the interim. Also named manager of the golf course, Al would be taking care of any racetrack business from out there.

On July 15, 1942, motor racing of all types was brought to a halt by federal mandate, and the amount of maintenance to be carried out at the Speedway during the next three and a half years would be exactly zero.

1942–1945: The track is shuttered

In 1940, Wilbur Shaw had curtailed his racing activities to the point of competing only in the "500" each year, largely due to the fact that he had taken a position with Firestone Tire and Rubber Company as general manager of its new aircraft division. He had temporarily relocated to Akron, Ohio. Firestone, meanwhile, had been experimenting for quite some time with a synthetic-rubber tire. Looking forward to the time when the war would be over and the national speed limit of only 35 mph would be lifted, the company wanted to prove that the new tire would be able to exceed that speed, not only by a considerable amount, but also over long distances. Firestone sought permission from the government to conduct the tests (using Shaw) at the Indianapolis Motor Speedway, and permission was granted.

Although the tests took place with much secrecy, it is believed that one or more passenger cars made runs at speeds of approximately 30 mph in late November 1944 and that on the 29th of the month, Shaw took to the track in the Firestone test car, a Miller formerly owned by Mike Boyle.

In what he described in his excellent memoir, *Gentlemen, Start Your Engines*, as "the longest, coldest 500-mile high speed run I ever made in my life," Shaw is understood to have averaged 100.34 mph, finishing in just under five hours

and stopping only for replenishments.

But the *condition* in which Shaw found the Speedway was of considerable alarm to him. One version of the story has attempts at opening the locked entry gate resulting in the entire *thing* collapsing to the ground. Literally ignored since the day the facility had been shut down, the infield had grown into a virtual jungle, and the old wooden grandstands were rotting and on the verge of collapse. Weeds had forced their way up through the crumbling mortar between the bricks on the main straight, and a few of the locals told of recently having been able to hunt rabbits in the waist-high overgrowth of the pit area.

It was apparently necessary to "weed the groove" before the tests could even begin.

Shaw also learned from the locals that the track was generally thought to be done for and that as soon as the war was over, it probably would be sold to developers and subdivided in preparation for the anticipated post-war housing boom.

As soon as the test was over, Shaw arranged to travel to New York to meet with Eddie Rickenbacker. Although it is understood that there had been several bondholders to begin with, including at least a couple with far larger holdings than that of Rickenbacker, it is further understood that he had been steadily buying up the shares of his colleagues over the years and that, on paper at least, he was now the sole owner.

Shaw quickly determined that while Rickenbacker had been quoted as saying that the track would be opened for business as soon as the hostilities were over, he would not, in fact, be averse to entertaining proposals of sale. For several months during 1944, in fact, it was known that a group from the American Legion had been making overtures, believing that as local owners, they could return the 500-Mile Race to its former glory. Nothing came of it. Another plan suggested Rickenbacker would continue to own the track, but that it would be operated by Seth Klein, the longtime chief starter for the "500" who had been employed for some time by the Indianapolis-based Marmon–Herrington Company, producer of military vehicles.

Shaw, who had risen from fairly meager beginnings to become quite comfortably fixed, thanks to his success on the track and numerous product endorsements (not to mention his executive position with Firestone), evidently did not, at this point, envision attempting to make the purchase himself.

Shaw sent out approximately 30 letters to a variety of companies and individuals involved in racing, and he was thrilled to receive immediate enthusiastic responses. It is understood that Rickenbacker was asking quite a bit in excess of $600,000, but that Shaw believed he might be able to get it for $500,000. With that in mind, Wilbur reasoned that 20 partners putting in $25,000 apiece would be enough to raise the amount.

His enthusiasm over the responses began to cool, however, when he read between the lines and sensed what has been referred to as "product exclusivity." In other words, he realized that certain companies saw themselves taking over the track, making it their own, and then preventing any rival company from participating. What he sought, instead, was someone who would be prepared to operate the track in a more benevolent fashion so that no reasonable participant would be excluded.

1945: Shaw finds a savior

Among Shaw's many friends and associates was an investment broker named Homer Cochran, about whom little is known. That was apparently by Cochran's own choice. A very quiet and private individual, he had a longtime interest in racing and is believed to have briefly tried racing on dirt tracks himself. This was during the early 1920s, when a very young Wilbur Shaw was just starting out and working at Bill Hunt's Speedway Engineering Company on North Illinois Street in Indianapolis. The two had met at that time and had remained friends.

Cochran had been telling Shaw for quite some time of a gentleman in Terre Haute, Indiana, with whom he had been involved in several deals, and who in recent years had been gaining a reputation for purchasing potentially successful companies which had fallen on hard times, then building them up.

The gentleman to whom he referred was Anton Hulman, Jr.

The grandson of a German immigrant, whose wholesale grocery company owned the now extremely successful Clabber Girl Baking Powder products, "Tony" Hulman, as he preferred to be called, turned out to be just the person Shaw had been looking for.

While no specific date has been established, the meeting is believed to have taken place early in October 1945. Shaw and Cochran drove over to Terre Haute to meet in Tony's office at Hulman and Company. Along with Tony were: Joseph R. Cloutier, the company's treasurer; Leonard Marshall, an attorney; Joseph Quinn, head of the Hulman-owned Terre Haute Gas Company; and Tom Doherty, a real-estate broker who was a longtime friend of the family.

Shaw was delighted to find that the remarkably shy but polite Hulman had an almost boyish enthusiasm for the track. He spoke fondly of having attended the 1914 race with his father, and he was to recall on numerous occasions in later years the once rather challenging journey to and from Terre Haute on Highway 40, to which Tony *always* referred as The Old National Road. And he seemed especially nostalgic about the stop on the way home, after each year's race, at what he called "The Halfway House."

He certainly knew who Wilbur Shaw was, and there was one other irony: Tony's father had known Carl Fisher.

Tony proved to be an extremely proud Hoosier, and associates always marveled at the knack he seemed to possess for being able to look into the future when it came to business ventures. He expressed great interest in seeing the track and the 500-Mile Race return to its former glory and become to Indiana what the Derby at Churchill Downs was to Kentucky. An ironic side note is that around this same time, Hulman is understood to have been approached with a view to *purchasing* Churchill Downs during a particularly difficult period of its existence.

Hulman told Shaw that *should* he be involved, he would not plan to take any profits out of the track, but rather would apply them toward renovation and improvements. He also stated that, on the other hand, as a businessman, he did not wish to enter a situation in which the track would *lose* money. He was assured, both by Shaw and later by Pop Myers, that the track, properly run, should prove to be a sound and wise investment.

At his first opportunity, Tony made the trip over to take a look. What he found did not seem to discourage him in any way. He is believed to have made several more visits in quick succession to show friends, and when they would look over at him with alarm and concern, the grin on his face was telling them that his mind was already made up.

Things began to come together in a hurry.

Shaw quickly contacted Paul Y. Davis, an Indianapolis attorney and Rickenbacker confidant who had been the IMS Board secretary throughout the Rickenbacker regime. A meeting involving all of the principals was set up for 11:30 A.M. on Wednesday, November 14, 1945, in the privacy of Parlor D at the Indianapolis Athletic Club.

Details of the sale have never been made public; but it is believed that by the time Shaw originally went to meet Hulman, Wilbur had begun to see himself as owner of the track after all, with a sizeable investment of his own, plus the help of others. Thus, Hulman originally was considered as merely the principal backer.

It is believed that Rickenbacker was prepared to sell the track for what he had raised to pay for it – approximately $700,000 – thereby waiving all of the not inconsiderable amount that had been spent during his stewardship, namely the installation of the golf course in 1929 and, immediately after the Great Depression, the vast amounts pumped into the area of track safety innovations.

Rickenbacker had planned to fly in a day early to meet privately with Davis, but the flight was delayed and he did not arrive until about 9:00 P.M. Instead, Rickenbacker spent all of Wednesday morning with Davis, and he was an hour late to the luncheon meeting.

Negotiations began in earnest.

Shortly before 5 o'clock, Rickenbacker, who just days earlier had come to accept that he probably would be reopening the track himself, came out of the meeting and prepared to head for the airport, indicating that a deal had been made and only a few final details were still being worked out by the others. A formal announcement could be expected about any time.

Whatever the advance speculation on what the new setup might be, the end result was that Hulman reportedly had purchased the track himself, and that Shaw had been named president and general manager, with Hulman as chairman of the board. Pop Myers, whom some had believed would be offered the presidency, was given the title of vice-president. The fact that he had served as general manager effectively since about 1910, and officially since 1915, put both Shaw and Myers in awkward positions. Myers even offered to resign on more than one occasion during the next few years, but it was never accepted, and he was still on the staff when he passed away on March 13, 1954, at the age of 80.

Hulman, in the meantime, generally could move around town without being approached, because even for quite some time after the purchase, many people in Indianapolis did not even know who he was. Instead, he seemed perfectly happy to remain in the wings and have the internationally known and positively dynamic Shaw "front" the management team and begin the seemingly impossible task of getting the track into shape for the reopening... which was due to take place in less than six months' time.

Main photograph: Weeds are growing up through the pit boxes, and the facility is generally in pretty sad condition after four years of neglect.

Inset below: Overseeing part of the monumental task of getting the track ready for a 1946 race are Superintendent of the Grounds Jack Fortner, Tony Hulman, and the colorful Joseph L. Quinn, Jr., who will serve as the track's safety director for the next 30 years.

Photographs: IMS

Chapter 8:
BACK UP AND RUNNING AGAIN

Main photograph: Swerving to avoid hitting another car on lap 41, Mauri Rose careens into the car of Paul Russo, which had crashed 24 laps earlier, but which had not yet been removed from the track. Passing by them is the stunning-looking Novi of Ralph Hepburn, which is leading at the time.

Inset below: Of the several Europeans who tackle the "500" in 1946, Luigi Villoresi fares by far the best, driving a Maserati to seventh place.

Photographs: IMS

1946: The dawning of the Hulman era

NO sooner had Tony Hulman assumed ownership than began the Herculean task of getting the track ready for a 1946 race. It was a massive undertaking merely to clear the tangled overgrowth from the infield, remove the rotted and fallen trees, and rip out the weeds and bushes which had sprung up through the grandstands.

Any misgivings Hulman may have harbored over how the revival of the event might be received by participants and the public, after such a long layoff, began to diminish when the entries started to roll in almost immediately. Entries closed with 56 cars, including nine from overseas.

The office phones at 444 North Capitol Avenue were ringing, the tickets were selling, and even the lap prize fund sold out for the first time since 1927, plus for only the third time ever. But time was running out. May 1 arrived and the facility was nowhere near ready to accommodate the general public. The track surface itself was in reasonable condition, and so it was decided to allow the participants to start practicing, but to hold off opening the gates until May 15. As it turned out, not much was lost because the weather was generally cold and very few cars were ready to run anyway.

The early spectators were astounded at the amount of work that had been carried out in just five months' time, a brand-new iron-and-steel paddock having been built across from the pagoda. There were also new bleachers in turn two, and fans were especially taken aback by the fact that platforms designed to carry 12 rows of parquet seating had been erected on either side of the pagoda. Surprisingly, this was the first seating ever offered at this location, early-arriving motorists for the first 30 years of operation having been able to drive right up to the fence and witness all of the pit work from just feet away while sitting atop their own vehicles. That was no longer possible, but the new arrangement was to become extremely popular.

Out on the West Coast, the Offenhauser engine business had changed hands. It had been acquired by Louis Meyer and Dale Drake, Dale having been Louis's riding mechanic in 1932. In 1931, the car Louis owned, which he had taken over from Myron Stevens to finish fourth, had been called the Jadson Special, named for the valves produced by J. A. Drake & Sons. Dale was one of the "sons."

The AAA Contest Board had a new chairman, Rickenbacker having resigned. Now at the helm was British-born Colonel Arthur Herrington, an Indianapolis resident who had acquired the old Marmon firm. A prolific producer of military vehicles, the Marmon–Herrington Company was operating out of the old Duesenberg plant on West Washington Street.

Much interest had been generated by the entry of Rudolf Caracciola, the great pre-war Mercedes–Benz driver who had won the European championship in 1935, 1937, and 1938. A German in spite of his Italian surname, Caracciola had moved to Switzerland and eventually would become a Swiss citizen. He was down to drive one of the 1½-liter Type-165 cars which Mercedes had built in complete secrecy for the 1939 Grand Prix of Tripoli. There had been a plan for Caracciola to take charge of both cars in 1941 but they could not leave Germany and were subsequently hidden. A frequent visitor to the Caracciola home in Lugano was none other than Colonel Peter de Paolo, currently stationed with the Air Force in Zurich. It was de Paolo who called up one day in early 1945 with the astonishing news that the cars had just arrived at a Zurich Mercedes-Benz dealership. He had seen them there. Caracciola caught the next train and after much difficulty, was able to take the cars into his custody, one of them being in poor condition. The entry for the good car was filed for the 1946 "500" but the difficulties with customs eventually became insurmountable and he finally had to throw up his hands.

He decided to come anyway, accompanied by his wife, the former Alice Hoffman Trobeck, who had been at the track in 1929 with Louis Chiron. Shortly after arriving, Caracciola was contacted by Joel Thorne, who had entered two cars but was unable to drive one himself because he had been injured in a motorcycle accident and was temporarily confined to a wheelchair. The car Thorne was offering was the old Sparks "big six," long since outfitted with a 183-cubic-inch engine.

With just a few days remaining before the race, Caracciola took the car out for practice, but soon was flagged in because he was wearing only a cloth helmet. Hard helmets would not be required in Europe until 1952, and he did not own one. Colonel Herrington produced a British Army tank driver's helmet, and the problem was solved. On May 28, while out for practice and attempting to build up to qualifying speed, Caracciola lost control in turn two, flipped, and was thrown from the car. It was extremely windy on that day, but the general theory is that he hit a bird and was momentarily stunned. One way or another, the consensus was that Colonel Herrington's helmet had saved his life.

Caracciola remained in Methodist Hospital for many days and was visited frequently by the very concerned Mr. and Mrs. Hulman. A great friendship developed between the two couples, and after Rudolf was released from the hospital, the Caracciolas were invited to spend as long as was needed in Terre Haute while Rudolf convalesced. They spent the

summer at the family lodge on the outskirts of town, and the Caracciolas must have thought they were back in Germany. The lodge was next to a lake and surrounded by heavily wooded areas which were quite Wagnerian in character.

The other members of the foreign contingent all arrived late, and the only one to qualify was the Maserati of Luigi Villoresi. Tazio Nuvolari, entered as a Villoresi teammate, sent his regrets due to the accidental death of his son, and many were surprised when the renowned Achille Varzi was unable to get the third car up to speed. Duke Nalon qualified the Maserati originally intended for Nuvolari.

The pole was won at just over 126 mph by Cliff Bergere in the ex-Lou Moore 1938 Floyd Roberts winner, and with no cars currently owned by him, Moore was serving as Bergere's chief mechanic. Next to them was a pair of really unconventional machines. Starting second was Paul Russo in a car called the Fageol's Twin Coach Special, its rather bulbous but aerodynamic body sporting a little tailfin. It was powered by not one but two 90-cubic-inch Offenhauser midget car engines, both supercharged, one in front of the driver and the other behind. Both throttles were operated by the same pedal, and it was effectively four-wheel-drive, employing two of the 1935 Ford Miller front-drive units.

It was quite an arrangement.

Next to Russo was young Sam Hanks, driving a car Myron Stevens had built for Gordon Schroeder in 1939 in order to house the V-16 "twin Miller" engine Frank Lockhart had developed for his land speed record car. As unlikely as it may seem, the engine from the car in which Lockhart had met his end on the sands of Daytona Beach in 1928 was now on the front row at Indianapolis *eighteen years later!* The car was called the Spike Jones Special and was actually sponsored by the zany band leader himself.

Filling the field was a slow process, with ill-prepared cars arriving late and the weather just not cooperating. Only six cars made it in on the first day. Work was still being frantically performed in the attempt to get the place in decent shape, and even on qualifying days electricians could be seen balancing on ladders while stringing telephone wires.

The requirements for driver tests had been relaxed quite a bit, and no less than 26 hopefuls started out, 13 of them either giving up or running out of time before the test could be completed. One of them, who attracted quite a little cheering section, was Zenon "Bud" Bardowski, a dirt-track driver from Gary, Indiana, who had just purchased a car with the three and a half years of back pay he had accrued while serving as a Japanese P.O.W. He called his car the U.S. Army Recruiting Special.

The sensation of qualifying was the now 50-year-old Ralph Hepburn, the runner-up from 1937 and the legendary leader of the Harley–Davidson motorcycle team before he ever turned his attention to racing cars. The car Hepburn drove was a low-slung, cigar-shaped Frank Kurtis creation containing the V-8 Winfield supercharged engine from 1941.

It had now been renamed "Novi."

The Novi legend truly began on May 26 (the sixth of eight qualifying days), when Hepburn came screaming down the main straight to start his official time trial. The current track record was the late Jimmy Snyder's 130.492-mph lap from his pole-winning qualifying run in 1939.

Hepburn's first lap was an incredible 134.288!

He dropped slightly into the 133 range for the next two laps but came blazing back to finish with one at 134.449 mph.

The four-lap record, previously 130.138 mph, was now 133.944.

Inset left: Paul Russo's Fageol's Twin Coach Special is powered by a pair of 90-cubic-inch Offenhauser midget car engines – each supercharged – one being in front of the driver and the other behind. Both throttles are linked to a common pedal. Technically, it is also a four-wheel-drive affair since a pair of the 1935 Ford front-drive units are utilized, one driving the front wheels and the other the rear wheels. As unlikely as it may seem, the car qualifies second!

Inset below left: With the Mercedes–Benz of Rudolf Caracciola being held up by customs in Europe, the great three-time pre-war Grand Prix champion accepts an offer to drive for the injured Joel Thorne. Owner Thorne is the man in the wheelchair.
Photographs: IMS

For quite a number of years, Hepburn and Bergere had shared a little tradition of their own during qualifying, in which one would hold the pit board displaying the speeds while the other was making a run. Just as Hepburn had held the board while Bergere was winning the pole, so Bergere held the board during the time the new records were being set.

About 45 minutes before the start of the race, which for the first time had been moved from the traditional 10:00 A.M. to 11:00 A.M., the many thousands of people on the infield who had not been paying full attention to the announcements over the public address system quieted when they realized the most glorious sound was floating from the speakers. It was the voice of James Melton, a leading tenor with the New York Metropolitan Opera Company. He was singing the song "Indiana," which has since become better known by its longer title, "Back Home Again in Indiana."

Melton, a friend of Tony Hulman, was a collector of vintage and veteran automobiles and was, for a time, president of the Antique Automobile Club of America. A number of cars from his collection were among those vehicles on hand to be driven down the main straight as part of the pre-race ceremonies, their occupants dressed in period costume. How Melton came to perform the song over the public address is not known, but the seeds of a tradition had been planted. He returned to sing it in subsequent years and it was so well received that in 1950, it was moved to its approximate placing in the program today, just moments before the firing of the engines.

Unfortunately, many ticket holders and potential general

admission customers never did hear the song the first year because they were still trying to enter the grounds. Clambering for entertainment of any kind, and in particular seeking to rekindle the nostalgic memories of peacetime and past visits to the track, the largest crowd so far was attempting to cram its way onto the grounds. Traffic jams, which caught everyone unaware, gridlocked the main thoroughfares for miles around, and long after the race had started, people were still trying to get in. This situation became further complicated during the second half of the race, when those attempting to get an early start for home were trying to get out!

The attrition of race cars began almost immediately, and management realized they had an additional problem concerning the logistics of trying to clean up in the aftermath of an accident. Mauri Rose, who vaulted all the way from ninth starting position to lead the first lap, was on his 41st circuit when he crashed into Paul Russo's wrecked Fageol's twin Offy midget job, which had hit the wall 24 laps earlier. The safety crew still hadn't figured out what to do with the Russo car when Rose suddenly had to take evasive action to avoid hitting another, and plowed into Russo's.

Most of the action was provided by Hepburn, whose screaming Novi leaped from 19th at the start to third by lap 10 and into the lead on lap 12. His twelfth circuit was turned at 129.73 mph, the fastest ever in competition up to that point. He was leading by over a minute when he came in at lap 56 and then had to remain in the pit for almost nine minutes because of a brake problem. He had fallen back to 13th by the time he got going, but was clearly the fastest in the field. While the leaders were pacing themselves at 115 mph, he was lapping at 124, eventually to make his way back up to fourth before coming to a rest on the backstretch of his 123rd lap with a dropped valve.

The winner was steadily running George Robson, driving one of the six-cylinder Thorne Engineering cars. Robson, who was born in the Northern England town of Newcastle-upon-Tyne but raised in southern California, took the lead when Hepburn made his first stop and was never headed after lap 93.

Second, only 34 seconds behind, was former riding mechanic Jimmy Jackson, who, during the early part of practice, had purchased a Cotton Henning-prepared car which Mike Boyle had entered for George Connor. With very little experience outside of a few seasons of midget car racing in Michigan just before World War II, Jackson ran a steady race and held second for most of the last 300 miles.

Jackson gained quite a bit of attention because he was defying the long-held belief that the color green around a racetrack was considered unlucky. Not only was his car painted bright kelly green, but his uniform, helmet, and gloves all were of that color as well. Not only that, but his crew wore T-shirts and pith helmets which had been dyed green. This was all for a reason. An Indianapolis native, Jackson had attended Arsenal Technical High School and played football there, green being the school's color.

Finishing third was Ted Horn, driving the ex-Wilbur Shaw Maserati. This was yet another combination which could well have won. Horn had to stop after only nine laps and lost almost seven minutes while a magneto was replaced, dropping him back to dead last. Because of his speed thereafter, combined with the extraordinary high rate of attrition, he was able to make it up to tenth by lap 90 and third at the finish.

Another driver who endeared himself to the crowd that day was Californian Bill Sheffler, a onetime UCLA pole-vaulter who was on the verge of entering the top ten at 30 laps when he had to pit with an oil leak. He lost 13½ minutes while having it repaired. Then, at around 300 miles, he started to lose the clutch, but refused to give up, turning lap after lap on the inside of the track at barely 60 mph. Luigi Villoresi suffered from magneto problems and made four stops totaling over half an hour. In spite of the fact that it took him 36½ minutes longer than Robson to complete the full 500 miles, he still did so, finishing seventh. At this point, only two other cars were still running, and both were flagged in. Sheffler had logged only 139 laps, but because cars still running at the end were scored ahead of those which had dropped out, regardless of the lap count, Sheffler was awarded ninth!

1947: ASPAR, The Blue Crowns, and the "EZY" signal

There was, in 1947, a most unfortunate episode which had begun to develop even before the 1946 race. A number of drivers, owners, and chief mechanics had formed an organization on the West Coast which was incorporated on March 25, 1946, as the American Society of Professional Auto Racing.

ASPAR, as it quickly became known, is understood to have been started with the very best of intentions, and certainly, the list of officers would indicate that. Rex Mays was president, Ralph Hepburn was first vice-president, and Chet Miller was the treasurer, while others involved were Peter de Paolo, Louis Meyer, Babe Stapp, and Duke Nalon.

As with many organizations, the profile and general attitude began to change as more and more revolutionary types became involved. General conditions and treatment at the nation's racetracks apparently had been the original issue, but not surprisingly, the matter of prize money soon came to the fore.

Virtually all AAA-sanctioned events were conducted on the basis of a minimum guaranteed purse or 40 percent of the gate, whichever was larger. The Indianapolis 500 had always been run for a flat purse plus accessory money, and some of the participants, long since upset that IMS had never released attendance figures or any financial information, began to demand that this be changed.

During practice in 1946, owners and drivers had been asked to sign a form stating that they were willing to compete for the purse as posted. Several refused to sign. As soon as the race was over, Hulman announced that the minimum purse for 1947 would be raised from $60,000 to $75,000 and that this would be made retroactive for 1946, the result being that the 1946 purse of $115,679 was the largest ever paid.

ASPAR was not satisfied. The attitude became even more confrontational when the power base switched from Los Angeles to Chicago. Mays began to distance himself from the group, and the equally mild-mannered Hepburn, who had

moved to Chicago to become an integral part of Preston Tucker's new automotive venture, became ASPAR's president. To the dismay of many, a feisty, cantankerous, and outspoken Chicago-based car owner/mechanic named Joe Lencki became the spokesman.

While many probably were satisfied with the $75,000 guarantee, Lencki, who claimed to have "everybody" in his corner, stated that unless the track guaranteed $150,000 against 40 percent of the gate, they weren't coming.

A number of meetings took place between Wilbur Shaw and ASPAR representatives, some amused and others irritated by Shaw's apparent switch in allegiance. Whereas he had always been right at the head of the line in any dispute as a driver, he was now playing the executive, sitting behind the big desk and pretending not to understand quite what "the boys" could possibly be unhappy about.

As it turned out, Lencki did not quite have "everybody." Cotton Henning entered the Maserati for Ted Horn; Lew Welch registered two Novis (a second one having been built during the winter); and Lou Moore entered a pair of brand-new, low-sitting, Offenhauser-powered Novi-looking front-drives he had commissioned from Emil Deidt. Backed by the Blue Crown Spark Plug Company, Moore's lead driver was Mauri Rose.

On the closing date of April 15, only 19 entries had been received in the office, but several reportedly were in the mail. With ASPAR still holding out, the final count, days later, was 35. The quality varied greatly.

The AAA Contest Board typically held a one- or two-day meeting during the early part of May at the Indianapolis Athletic Club, and on May 7, 1947, five hours were devoted to ASPAR pleading its case. Behind the scenes, Hepburn had been discreetly negotiating with Shaw, the latter assuring Hepburn that Tony Hulman had every intention of building the purse on an annual basis. But every time the two old friends seemed to have something worked out, Lencki would shout it down or make some other outlandish statement. He had arrived with a Chicago lawyer, retained just hours earlier, who,

as always seemed typical in such situations, knew absolutely nothing about automobile racing.

Hulman offered to post special cash awards for each qualification day, something never before offered, and it was finally decided that post entries from ASPAR members would be accepted, providing a waiver could be obtained by everyone who had filed an entry before the deadline.

A clause that no pre-entered car could be "bumped" by an ASPAR car was agreed upon, but a hurriedly written bulletin stating that ASPAR qualifiers would have to start at the back and not be eligible for qualifying prize money threw everything up in the air again.

The first weekend of time trials came and went, and only seven cars qualified. With just hours remaining before what was supposed to have been the final weekend, Hulman offered to post duplicate qualifying awards for the ASPAR cars. That, apparently, was the deal-breaker.

The next order of business was to get the waivers signed. It was agreed that this should be carried out by a neutral party, who would turn a blind eye to all of the unpleasantness and perform the duty for the good of the event. The universally respected William F. Fox, a fatherly, silver-haired sports editor for *The Indianapolis News*, agreed to take on the task, and miraculously, everybody signed.

Not unexpectedly, the ASPAR people had spent so much time involved in the dispute that they had nearly run out of time for getting their cars to the track. Qualifying was extended to Monday and Tuesday, but when the track closed on Tuesday, there were still only 17 cars in the field.

Yet another extension – emphasized as being positively the last one - was held on Wednesday, May 28. Eleven more cars were able to beat the four-lap minimum speed of 115 mph, several of them being allowed on the track at the same time in the final hour. The day ended with 28 qualifiers.

It still wasn't over. At the drivers' meeting, held in a tent at 4:00 P.M. on the eve of the race, Lencki made an impassioned plea for more time, one of his two cars not yet having made it. He pointed out, quite accurately, that in the 1920s there had been several instances in which the issue of short fields had been partially addressed by allowing cars to qualify on race morning. He drew a huge laugh when he recalled that in 1928, none other than Wilbur Shaw had been one of the drivers involved, as indeed he had.

Following a quick huddle, it was agreed that a further hour would be granted, starting in less than two hours' time, at 6:00 P.M. With several cars on the track at the same time, four went the distance, two beating the 115-mph minimum (increasing the field to 30) and two failing. No individual lap speeds were announced, due to the fact that the timing-and-scoring crew was not on the grounds. In their absence, hand-held stopwatches were used to record the times, the elapsed time for four laps being the only item of immediate concern.

Rather than "24 to 30 of the top cars," as Lencki had claimed, ASPAR sought waivers for just 16 cars, only 10 of which made the lineup. The sixth-placed finisher of Rex Mays was the only one which cracked the top nine.

A few weeks after the race, Hulman mailed out an additional $15,000 in prize money, including an extra $4,000 for first, with promises of more in the future.

ASPAR was never heard from again.

One of the non-ASPAR entries which had drawn a considerable amount of interest was a car entered as the Don Lee Special. Referred to by the press as "the mystery car," it was, in fact, a 1938 V-12 Mercedes–Benz type-154 Grand Prix car which had spent part of the war in Czechoslovakia and then had been spirited over to England.

Quite apart from the car, European racing itself was a "mystery" to the average Indianapolis fan. The interpretation by many, upon learning that, as chancellor of Germany, the late Adolf Hitler had annually authorized vast sums of government money for underwriting the Grand Prix teams of Mercedes–Benz and Auto Union, was that Hitler had *owned* racing cars! The classic and most preposterous rumor of all was that Hitler had commissioned this particular car solely for the purpose of escaping from Germany! One can only ponder the looks on the faces of the guards at the border (had this

really happened) upon seeing a GP Mercedes roaring towards them on the Autobahn at high speed with Der Führer at the wheel!

Certainly the *loudest* car most people had ever heard, the Mercedes was fast while it ran, but working on it presented quite a challenge for the mechanics because everything within the engine compartment was so tightly packed. When Duke Nalon qualified it on May 28, his speed of 128.082 mph was the second-fastest of the year, but he was out with piston failure after 119 laps.

Cliff Bergere, driving the Hepburn Novi of the year before, started second and led the first 23 laps. He fell out after 63 laps, took over the second and newer car (driven by returning veteran Herb Ardinger), and finished fourth, bringing joy to the growing legion of Novi fans.

There was a great tragedy just past the 100-mile mark

Left: Changed quite a bit in appearance since its debut almost ten years earlier, one of the Harry Miller-designed rear-engined cars qualifies for the 1947 race. Driven by Al Miller, who is not related to Harry, it is knocked out by magneto failure after only 33 laps.

Below: The Don Lee Special, the second-fastest qualifier overall in the hands of Duke Nalon, is in reality a V-12 1938 Mercedes–Benz W154 Grand Prix car. **Photograph: IMS**

Above: Popular Shorty Cantlon, the 1930 runner-up, and recently a local tavern owner, is fatally injured during the 1947 event. Photograph: IMS

when the very popular Shorty Cantlon, until recently a local tavern owner, crashed in the first turn and was fatally injured. Because considerable difficulty was experienced in trying to remove the car from the track, it was decided to place it as close as possible to the outer wall and simply leave it there. For the next several hours, participants were continuously reminded of the dangers of the sport, the wrecked orange car sitting about halfway through the turn, in the ever-lengthening shadows of the tall trees which now towered over the south end of the track.

Following the lap-23 pit stop to change tires by Bergere, the remainder of the race was led by Lou Moore's pair of new front-drives, a late-race lead change sparking off yet another controversy. Much of the race, 143 laps in fact, was led by Bill Holland, who at 39 was making his first Indianapolis start. The son of a turn-of-the-century Major-League Baseball player and himself a former champion roller skater who had also been an ice skater of Olympic quality, Holland had been the fastest qualifier. In spite of making two pit stops to the one of

teammate Mauri Rose, Holland was ahead by about half a minute in the late stages, when Moore began to hang out pit boards on which were chalked the letters "EZY," meaning "slow down and take it easy."

Holland nodded and backed off. Rose nodded and did not. Rose began catching Holland at the rate of three and four seconds per lap until the 193rd lap, when he drew alongside. Seeing him there, Holland believed Rose was merely unlapping himself, and he waved Rose by. Rose roared off into the distance, took the white and the checker, and won the race.

Holland, still unaware of the situation, did the same, and, as was the normal practice in those days, stayed out and ran a couple more laps just to make certain that there had been no scoring errors. When he came into the pit area, shut off the engine, and then heard Rose being proclaimed over the public address system as the winner, he was understandably upset. He demanded to know why his crew had not informed him that Rose was catching up, and he was told that Moore had told them not to. It appeared to the media and to the

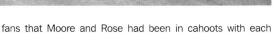

his relationship with Moore. A good businessman – he owned several roller-skating rinks – he apparently consoled himself with the fact that he did, after all, have one of the best cars at the track, and that it could well be at his disposal the following year, as indeed it was.

Ironically, Holland was not the driver originally assigned to this car. Rose's teammate was to have been Chicago midget car graduate Tony Bettenhausen, whose first name was really Melvin. "Tony" had evolved from his boyhood nickname of "Tunney" (for heavyweight champion Gene Tunney), earned as a result of his tendency to become involved in fistfights.

Knowing that Tony strongly supported the ASPAR cause, Moore made it clear that if things were not resolved by the time he was ready to start running the cars in practice, and Tony was still standing firm, he (Moore) would have to hire another driver. It is conceivable that had it not been for Bettenhausen's stand, Holland, who became one of the great Indianapolis 500 drivers of the post-war years, might not ever have turned a lap at the Speedway. By the same token, Bettenhausen's friends shook their heads over the fact that he effectively cost himself the win. While Holland dutifully slowed down when shown the board, it is highly unlikely the stubborn Tony would have allowed the win to get away from him.

Greeting Rose in Victory Lane was actress Carole Landis, who had been flown in especially for the occasion by Borg–Warner Corporation. The company was to make similar arrangements for the next twelve years, those following Miss Landis being Barbara Britton, Linda Darnell, Barbara Stanwyck, Loretta Young, Arlene Dahl, Jane Greer, Marie Wilson, Dinah Shore, Cyd Charisse, Shirley MacLaine, and Erin O'Brien.

Below: James Melton of the New York Metropolitan Opera Company exchanges pleasantries with Tony Hulman and actress Carole Landis. Miss Landis is the first of the Hollywood actresses to be flown in for the festivities by Borg–Warner Corp., a tradition which will continue through 1959.

Bottom: So popular was his rendition of "Back Home Again in Indiana" on race morning, 1946, that James Melton of the New York "Met" is invited to return and perform it again. Ironically, having just left "The Met" after several seasons as a colleague of Melton's, playing lesser roles, is John Gurney, the father of future driver Dan.
Photographs: IMS

fans that Moore and Rose had been in cahoots with each other and that they had ganged up on the new boy.

Moore and Rose both denied that there had been any "deal." Moore stated it made no difference to him in which order the drivers finished, and since everything he owned was tied up in the two cars, it would have been foolish for either or both to have dropped out due to overexertion of equipment or an accident. Rose contended that as a professional driver, it was up to him to try to win at all reasonable costs, and, as he confided years later, it *did* make a difference to Moore. Because Rose was guaranteed 40 percent of the car's prize money and Holland had agreed to drive for 30 percent, it would have been financially more rewarding for Moore to have had Holland win instead.

It was of extreme interest to friends of Holland to see just how he would react to it all. He was known to have a rather cynical outlook on life, and always seemed to be under the impression that "everyone was out to get him." Even his wife was in fear that he would "blow his top," but while he was far from happy, no statement he made was bitter enough to end

Above: Although the rule requiring that the driver climb out of his car during a pit stop is no longer mandatory after 1946, veterans like Mauri Rose continue to do it anyway.

Right: The pairing of Mauri Rose with Lou Moore results in a third win.

Photographs: IMS

Official PROGRAM
32nd 500 Mile Race
MAY 31 1948

INDIANAPOLIS MOTOR SPEEDWAY CORPORATION

1948: A Novi almost wins, but a Rose is a Rose is a Rose

The big story of 1948 centered around the Novi cars. Were they safe? Cliff Bergere, after a couple of spins during practice, told members of the press that he didn't think they were. He left the team, and who should be invited to replace him but Ralph Hepburn. The veteran driver, with thoughts of unfinished business in 1946 still vivid in his mind, was now 52 years old. On Sunday, May 16, the second day of time trials, Hepburn took the Novi out for a practice run and had just turned a lap at 128 when it got away from him in turn three, veering down into the infield grass. He turned the wheel to the right and applied the throttle in an attempt to get it back to the track, but when the spinning front wheels caught the blacktop, the car shot forward and he was propelled into the outer wall.

Hepburn's passing was one of the Speedway's darkest hours.

Chet Miller, a longtime friend of Bergere, had already resigned from the second car, and not every driver at the track was jumping at the opportunity to replace him.

One driver who was willing to take a few laps was Duke Nalon.

In just a matter of minutes, one of the Speedway's great relationships was solidified. Duke Nalon and the Novi seemed to be made for each other, and one would forever associated with the other. Duke qualified at 131.603 mph, which was slower than Hepburn's two-year-old record but faster than Rex Mays, who earlier had won the pole for a record fourth time. Duke's first lap was just over 134.

In twenty years of trying, a Novi never would win the Indianapolis 500. But in 1948, one came awfully close. Since the car Nalon drove could carry a hefty 112 gallons of fuel, the plan was to make one pit stop right at half-distance. Duke pitted while leading at lap 101 and in went the fuel. One minute and 48 seconds later, he was on his way, now running third behind Mauri Rose and Ted Horn. Rose and Holland, driving the same Lou Moore Blue Crown cars with which they had finished one–two in 1947, were trying to get by on one stop, but Horn was going to have to make two. When Horn stopped at lap 143, Nalon went to second.

The separation between Rose and Nalon varied only slightly for the next 100 miles, Duke normally being about half a minute behind. Whether or not he had anything in reserve will never be known, because on his 186th lap, he had to come back in.

He had been on the verge of running out of fuel.

But how could this be? He had run 101 laps on the first tank. The answer was that he did not get a full load at the halfway stop. Pressurized refueling, soon to be ruled out, was still permissible at the time, and the Novi team was using it. When crewman James "Radio" Gardner saw fuel rapidly coming to the top of the tank and momentarily spilling over, down went the cap and away went Duke. But what the crew had not considered was aeration in the fuel. Once Duke had returned to action and things had settled down, the trapped bubbles rose to the surface and down went the level.

In he came at lap 186, and in went some fuel.

Then he STALLED!

It was over two minutes before the Novi could be refired, and by the time it returned to action, Holland had taken over second. The Novi was lucky to salvage third ahead of the Maserati of Horn, and it would never finish that high again.

Rose joined Louis Meyer and Wilbur Shaw as a three-time winner, and in spite of having transferred to Studebaker up in South Bend, he was still able to practice for the race, qualify, and win without having taken any time off from work.

Among the more impressive performances in this race was that by a 37-year-old "rookie," as the first-time starters were now being called. He was Lee Wallard, a good-natured East Coast sprint car driver who had been through the school of hard knocks, having raced since 1932, and not always in the best of cars. In fact, the Iddings Special he was driving on this day was a high-sitting sprint car which had been "stretched out" in order to meet the wheelbase requirements for Indianapolis. The fifth-fastest qualifier in the field, he ended

up seventh. He would have finished even higher had it not been for four pit stops for fouled plugs, which used up over 12 minutes.

The really noteworthy point concerns Wallard's pattern for driving the track. It had always been the custom to drive down the middle of the straights and then hug the turns, drifting out a little in the north and south chutes, but typically staying fairly close to the inside line. Wallard's technique was to keep up the revs by veering all the way out to the wall after exiting turns one and three, barely lifting, and then diving back down to the apex of the next turn. He was covering a greater distance, but stopwatches were proving that the shortest way around was not necessarily the fastest. In no time at all, this became the accepted "groove."

Powerboat racer Bill Cantrell dropped out late in the race, after having run sixth for a considerable distance driving a car powered by a six-cylinder Fageol bus engine. Former dirt-track driver-turned-truck line owner, Pat Clancy, arrived with a car which caused plenty of double takes. Based on a suggestion for superior traction by one of Clancy's route drivers, the car had *six wheels*. It was basically a dirt track-style car with tandem rear axles. While numerous cars were unsuccessful in trying to earn a starting position, Billy Devore qualified the six-wheeler, ran all day, and finished twelfth.

Nineteen forty-eight is also the year in which another tradition was introduced, that of the release, shortly before the start, of hundreds of brightly-colored balloons. It is believed to have been the idea of Mary Fendrich Hulman, Tony's wife.

Below: The media starts referring to Duke Nalon as "The Man Who Tamed the Novi."
Photograph: IMS

Above: Former dirt-track driver Paul "Pat" Clancy, now owner of a small trucking company, builds a car for 1948 which has six wheels. Not only will second-generation driver Billy Devore qualify it, but he will finish in 12th place. The car will qualify again in 1949 (driven by Jackie Holmes) but will be converted to a "four-wheeler" by 1950.
Photograph: IMS

Left: Locally based radio announcer Tom Carnegie (left) embarks on his third year on the public address system. He will step down in 2006, shortly after having called the race for an incredible sixty-first consecutive time.
Photograph: IMS

1949: One more for Moore

While the IMS headquarters were still downtown on North Capitol Avenue, they were no longer at 444, which had been "home" since 1919. As the result of a move on February 19, 1949, the new location was three blocks further to the north, at 729 North Capitol.

Going into the month of May, it was hard to bet against the Novi team. The car Bergere had vacated (in which Hepburn had lost his life) had been rebuilt, with no less a man than Rex Mays agreeing to drive it. Mays was going for an unprecedented fifth pole, but he couldn't beat Nalon, a man who had idolized Mays for years. A pair of Novis lining up one–two on race morning was a formidable sight.

It was even more formidable when they came down for the start, Duke leaping ahead and building a huge lead by the end of the first lap. Rex was second, and it was quite an interval before Duane Carter came by in third.

For 23 laps, Nalon ran away with it, lapping cars at will. At

20 laps, he was averaging 125.111 mph and already lapping up to eighth place. As he entered turn three of the next lap, the rear axle evidently snapped and the right rear wheel came off, sending the Novi spinning into the outer wall. He hit hard with the left side of the car and the fuel tank erupted. In an accident which was captured on film and was to be used in countless Hollywood racing epics, the car slid backwards for about a hundred yards, trailing flaming fuel. As the car began to grind to a halt, the fuel then began flowing down the banking, car after car being forced to drive through the flames.

Nalon, who climbed out and rolled over the wall, was hospitalized for many weeks with burns about his cheeks and upper body. He returned to racing the following year, and Dennis Nalon became "The Iron Duke."

Car owner Lew Welch always contended Nalon hit the wall before the wheel came off, but photographs clearly show the wheel and part of the axle flying through the air before the car touched a thing.

Into the lead went Mays with the other Novi, but by lap 48, he had been sidelined with engine failure.

The leader became Lee Wallard, now graduated from the Iddings Brothers' stretched sprint car and into the ex-Shaw Maserati. Motor racing had an ever-present danger in those days which threatened more than merely damaging a car. Every driver faced the danger of being injured, and worse. No one was exempt, and stunningly, Ted Horn, having just won the AAA National Championship for the third year in a row, had been cut down in the last race of 1948, a 100-mile dirt-track event at DuQuoin, Illinois.

Not only was Horn gone now, but so was the beloved Cotton Henning, the four-time winning chief mechanic who had masterminded the multi-car Boyle team through its glory years. Cotton had fallen into ill health a year earlier and had passed away in December, just two months after Horn. Originally from Independence, Missouri, Henning had, as a teenager, worked in the service department of an automobile dealership. He became friends with one particular customer, who was about to be married to a lady named Bess, and Cotton worked out a secret arrangement whereby he would quietly service the car at his home, thereby saving the customer much expense. They kept in touch over the years, even after his friend, Harry Truman, became President of the United States.

Another point of interest is that Cotton was the older brother of Paul Henning, the creator of such television shows as "The Beverly Hillbillies," "Green Acres," and "Petticoat Junction." Over the years, quite an assortment of West Coast-based drivers and mechanics were to be employed (between races) as carpenters and electricians on Paul Henning lots.

Lee Wallard had to pull out with a gear problem in the Maserati after 55 laps, and into the lead, for good, went Bill Holland. There was an ironic situation late in the race when Mauri Rose was running second, about 45 seconds behind. Out came the "EZY" signal again, and this time Holland was a little more protective. He eased off somewhat, but Rose kept charging. With less than eight laps to go, Rose slowed and pulled to the infield grass, a magneto strap having broken, causing an electrical failure.

Into second place went handsome and dapper Johnnie Parsons, a West Coast driver who was making his first "500" start. Finishing third was a driver Parsons had seen race at Legion Ascot Speedway 15 years earlier. A teammate of Holland and Rose on this occasion, George Connor, was at the wheel of a rear-drive Blue Crown Special which Moore had commissioned the year before for Holland to drive on the dirt tracks.

The marriage between Rose and Moore was over. A shouting match developed back in the garage, Rose appalled that the magneto strap would break within sight of the finish, and Moore contending that a more conservative approach by Rose easily could have resulted in second.

Holland said nothing.

A famous racing car came to a sad end in 1949. Wilbur Shaw's streamliner, which he affectionately called "The Pay Car," had been re-bodied for 1948 and it no longer appeared as it once had. Two days before the 1949 race, "rookie" George Metzler crashed it while trying to build up to qualifying speed and became another Speedway casualty.

Another historical moment had taken place on race day. The "500" had, for the first time, been televised. The city's first television station, WFBM Channel 6, had been experimenting with test patterns over the previous several days and even aired about 40 minutes of the final day of qualifications, unadvertised, although the shots were mostly of the crowd. The station officially went on the air on race morning. After opening with a 1946 Firestone documentary about the "500" entitled "The Crucible Of Speed," viewers were treated to several hours of flag-to-flag coverage of the 500-Mile Race – using *three* cameras. Very few people

Above: After finishing second to teammate Mauri Rose in 1947 and 1948, Bill Holland finally wins.
Photographs: IMS

Inset below: Because Lew Welch withheld his entry for the two Novis until the very last minute (in a dispute over prize money), all of the available garage space had been taken. He had to make an arrangement to house his cars at a downtown automobile dealership, transporting them back and forth by truck whenever the cars were to practice. They finally move into the garage area, but to everyone's amazement, mechanical problems prevent both cars from qualifying.

Inset bottom: Diminutive Walt Faulkner, nicknamed "The Little Dynamo," breaks the qualifying records as a "rookie" in 1950, then will break them again in 1951.
Photographs: IMS

actually owned a television set at this time, the majority of viewers peering, transfixed, through central-Indiana appliance-store windows. With regular programming in place by 1950, viewers had to be satisfied with just an occasional update, while in 1951, there was no live coverage at all. Management had determined that live TV just might be hurting the "gate."

1950: The cracked block that wasn't

For 1950, Lou Moore expanded his stable to four cars, a second rear-drive combination dirt-track car coming into the fold. Holland and Connor kept the same cars they had driven in 1949, Wallard was given the new one and Tony Bettenhausen took over the ex-Rose car.

Rose moved into a virtual look-alike, a car Emil Deidt had built in 1948 for the reclusive Superior Oil magnate Howard Keck, and which Jimmy Jackson had driven to a pair of top-ten finishes.

Duke Nalon was out of the hospital and back driving a Novi, joined by Chet Miller, who had left the team just before

the demise of Ralph Hepburn.

Stunningly, considering their one–two start in 1949, qualifications ended with neither Novi in the race. The problems began with Lew Welch's dissatisfaction with the purse, his feeling being that both qualifying (considering the Novi participation) and the race should be worth more. He stated that unless management increased the minimum by another $25,000, his cars would not be coming. There was, of course, no other track on which the Novis could reasonably run at that time, and certainly no other track paying anywhere near the purse.

At the very last minute, Welch entered anyway, by which time all of the garage space at the track had been filled. An arrangement had to be made with a downtown dealership until space could be made available, resulting in the encumbrance of having to truck the cars back and forth anytime they wanted to run. There seemed to be mechanical problems just about every time they went out, the final blow coming when both cars had to call off their last-shot qualifying runs.

There is not a single person at the track who would have guessed the pole sitter in advance.

With the final seconds ticking away before 6:00 P.M. on Saturday, May 13, it appeared that the teammate of Johnnie Parsons, articulate Fred Agabashian, had the pole won. Onto the track went a dirt-track car driven by a "rookie" who had passed his test only two days before. Standing only five-foot-four and weighing 122 pounds, Walt Faulkner was about to make history. The late Hepburn's now four-year-old single-lap mark with the Novi was 134.449 mph. Many were surprised when Faulkner's first lap was 132.743, because that was quite a bit faster than anyone had expected that combination to go.

"Surprise" wasn't the word to describe the reaction to lap two. "Pandemonium" would have been closer.

The lap was turned at 136.013 mph.

The Novi record had been broken.

The four-lap record went as well, Faulkner raising the standard to 134.343 mph. J. C. Agajanian, the car's flamboyant owner, was leaping around and waving the cowboy hat which was instantly to become his trademark, while the most nonchalant person at the track was Faulkner.

As a further illustration of just how different things were in those days, it was learned that Faulkner's coach had been

OFFICIAL **PROGRAM** 34th 500 MILE RACE MAY 30, 1950

50¢
INDIANAPOLIS MOTOR SPEEDWAY CORPORATION PAY NO MORE

Main photograph: Rookie Faulkner leads from the pole but will be overhauled by Mauri Rose (to the left) before the end of the backstretch.
Photograph: IMS

none other than Agabashian. In fact, Freddie had even taken the car out for a practice run after his own qualification run and had suggested some changes to the setup. He then stood next to Agajanian, holding a stopwatch while Faulkner was trying out the changes, and it was Fred who suggested the run be made. Winning the pole was of very little financial benefit at the time, and Agabashian was just as happy for Faulkner and Agajanian as anyone.

No fewer than 20 drivers passed a "rookie" test that year, three of the four fastest qualifiers (Faulkner, Cecil Green, and Bill Schindler) being first-time starters. There had been an attempt in 1949 to help the veterans be aware of a "rookie" taking a test, by having the newcomers attach streamers to their goggles. The 1950 procedure, which was much more successful and which was to remain in effect for the next several decades, was to place three adhesive stripes of colored tape across the tail, these being removed as soon as the driver had been "passed" by the committee.

A number of films with racing backgrounds had been made over the years, the latest being 1949's "The Big Wheel," starring Mickey Rooney. It was shot in a hurry, during the period in which Rooney was trying to get out of his contract with MGM, and while a few cars and drivers were hired to stage some "mock" action, none of the principals ever came to the track.

In 1950, there was a much more serious attempt. Clark Gable had been a longtime racing enthusiast and had frequently attended midget car races at a variety of southern-California tracks. He had been a regular at Legion Ascot Speedway prior to its closing in 1936. He had also been a longtime friend of Wilbur Shaw, and it is possible that Shaw might have had Gable as a student during Shaw's flight-instruction days in Los Angeles.

In 1947, Gable came to the "500" as a guest of Tony Hulman, and the seeds for a motion picture might well have been planted at that time. Arriving in 1950 to shoot "To Please A Lady," Gable had landed Barbara Stanwyck as his leading lady, and his friend Clarence Brown, who had made two films with Greta Garbo, as the movie's director. Many of the crew were old hunting, fishing, and drinking buddies, and everybody had a great time. In contrast with the "tough" roles Stanwyck and Gable typically played, both were exceedingly easygoing, mingled with the race crowd, and regularly played cards with the film crew between shots.

Doubling for "Mike Brannan," Gable's character in the film, was Bud Rose, a West Coast racer whose real name was Harry Eisele and who bore an uncanny resemblance to Gable. The double for Gable during actual race footage was seven-time participant George "Joie" Chitwood, who finished fifth in the "500" three times and who was well on his way to becoming legendary in the auto thrill-show business.

Making a brief appearance as a safety patrolman near the end of the film was Cliff Bergere, who earlier in the month had announced his retirement as a driver. Bergere, whose 16 starts in the "500" were more than by any other driver at that time, had been a Hollywood stuntman for well over 20 years. He estimated that he had performed stunts in something like 400 films, having doubled for some of the greatest names in the business, including Katherine Hepburn! His fascinating-sounding assignment for D. W. Griffith's 1923 "The Ten Commandments" had been that of "chief chariot wrecker."

The Indianapolis 500 took on added stature this year due to the fact that it was to be included in the recently announced World Championship of Drivers. In spite of major international motor racing having been in existence for more

Inset above: Wilbur Shaw and Tony Hulman are joined on a practice day by Tony's monthlong guest, Clark Gable (at the track to shoot "To Please A Lady" with Barbara Stanwyck), and comedian Jack Benny, in town with his troupe for an appearance at the Indiana State Fairgrounds. Over the shoulder of Shaw is a very young Bob Collins, later sports editor of *The Indianapolis Star*.

Below: Johnnie Parsons qualifies for the 1950 race, which he will win. Photographs: IMS

than half a century, there had never before been any such thing except for a world championship for manufacturers between 1925 and 1927, the "500" having been one of the events which counted. When the Federation de L'Automobile held its annual meetings in Paris during the winter of 1949/50 and announced the plans to proclaim a world champion driver, Pop Myers, who was in attendance, suggested that in lieu of a United States Grand Prix, the "500" should be included as one of the events.

The term "Formula One" had first come into use in 1947 for the purpose of identifying the set of specifications under which all Grand Prix events would be conducted. The latest specs called for unsupercharged engines to be limited to 4½ liters, just as they had since 1938, but that supercharged engines would be allowed only 1½ liters. As much as Indianapolis had wanted to remain in step with European formulae, it was decided that 1½ liters was a little too restrictive and that supercharged engines in the "500" would still be permitted up to three liters.

In spite of this, the FIA agreed to include the "500" anyway, and while there would be still more changes in specifications in the future, it was to remain as a World Championship event until 1960. It was to cause quite a bit of confusion over the years and continues to do so to this day, because while it is frequently stated otherwise, it never at any time was a *Formula One* race. The "500," however, did award World Championship driver points, although very few of those who finished in the first five between 1950 and 1959, or the first

six in 1960, were probably ever aware of that.

For the first time since 1926, and for only the second time in history, the race was ended prematurely by rain, 345 miles having been covered when darkened skies opened. Two-time winner Tommy Milton was the chief steward by this time, and he wisely recognized that there would be little chance of drying out the track for any restart. At his signal, Starter Seth Klein displayed both the red and the checker.

The one–two finish was a reversal of 1949, Bill Holland edging Mauri Rose for second and extending his extraordinary record for his first four Indianapolis 500-Mile Races to second, second, first, and second.

Into Victory Lane went Johnnie Parsons, the "500" runner-up and AAA national champion of the year before, whose background was extremely colorful. Born into a show-business family, he had been a tuxedo-and-top hat-wearing member of his parents' song-and-dance vaudeville act by the time he was four. He was interested in racing from his earliest recollection, his uncle having rented space to several dirt-track racers including Frank Lockhart, whom Johnnie met as a youngster. He continued hanging around race shops and "stooged" on the car being built for eventual winner Kelly Petillo in 1935, and, more recently, on the Lou Moore Blue Crowns now running.

Of all the perpetual myths of the Speedway which refuse to die, as famous as any is one concerning the Parsons win.

The myth is that on race morning, a crack was discovered in the engine block of the Parsons car, and that the engine was doomed to fail at some point during the race. The race strategy allegedly became that Parsons would grab the lead as quickly as he could and then rack up as much lap prize money as possible before the inevitable breakdown.

He was, according to the myth, saved by the rain.

The reality is that a crew member had noted some moisture on the top of the block, and a few minutes after it had been wiped dry, more materialized. After the process had been repeated a couple of times, rags were placed around the block and a couple of the mechanics began to gently peen with hammers. Their conclusion was that porosity in the metal was allowing the moisture to seep to the surface and that peening would help seal it.

In spite of Chief Mechanic Harry Stephens gathering the crew together and requesting that this be kept under wraps, word filtered out. It had long been accepted that a rumor in the garage area at the Indianapolis Motor Speedway could spread more quickly than at any other location in the world.

The night before the race, car owners Ed Walsh and Frank Kurtis had agreed to sell the car to Jim Robbins as soon as the event was over, and it returned to finish second, with Mike Nazaruk driving, the following year. According to the late Frankie Del Roy, who became the car's chief mechanic, Robbins would never put up the money to replace the offending part, and when Nazaruk finished second in 1951, completing the entire 500 miles, the supposed "cracked" block was still in the car.

1951: Cinderella Man

The driver to whom Mike Nazaruk finished second in the 1951 "500" was his fellow East Coast sprint car rival, Lee Wallard, the man who three years earlier had discovered the now generally accepted "groove" at the Speedway.

Wallard, who averaged 126.244 mph and was the first ever to complete the 500 miles in under four hours, was one of the most popular winners ever. Now 40 years old, he was dubbed by the press "The Cinderella Man." A WWII Navy veteran, he had once operated a bulldozer to help support his family. The car, based by Frank Kurtis on his Kurtis–Kraft midget car, had been commissioned in 1949 by Louis Meyer and Dale Drake as an experimental venture, powered by a supercharged "Offy." Eventually they switched to a nonsupercharged Offy, and because their customers were less than pleased that the engine's builder was racing against them, Meyer and Drake sold the car to Murrell Belanger of Crown Point, Indiana. Tony Bettenhausen, their driver, went with the deal.

The third person to win the Indianapolis "500" three times, joining Louis Meyer and Wilbur Shaw, was Mauri Rose (May 26, 1906–Jan 1, 1981), who took the checkered flag in 1941, 1947, and 1948. The first of these was actually considered to be a co-win, Rose having been in the interesting position of starting on the pole and winning the race in two different cars.

When his Lou Moore-owned Maserati fell out after 60 laps, Moore elected to call in Floyd Davis, who was running 12th with the car Rose had driven to third the year before, and make a driver switch. By the time Rose returned to action after the lap-72 stop, the car had dropped to 14th. Literally hanging out of the side of the cockpit in order to see properly, the tiny but muscular Rose advanced to eighth by lap 100 and fourth by lap 120. On the 162nd lap he moved around leader Cliff Bergere and sailed on to the win. The 1947 and 1948 victories were also for Moore, both coming in one of the famous front-drive Blue Crown Spark Plug Specials.

The Columbus, Ohio-born Rose had a total of 15 starts in the "500," the first coming in 1933 when Howdy Wilcox II, the previous year's runner-up, was ruled out at the last minute for medical reasons. After a near strike was averted on race morning, delaying the start by about 15 minutes, many competitors objected to the hastily substituted Rose being allowed to start from the sixth position Wilcox had earned. This latest dispute was settled by moving Rose all the way back to last position, which in 1933 happened to be 42nd. Rose dropped out after only 48 laps, but not before he had climbed all the way to

fourth. He finished second to Bill Cummings in 1934, was fourth in 1936 (the year he won the AAA National Championship), and was third in 1940.

Faced with the opportunity of winning for a third consecutive year in 1949, he dropped out with eight laps remaining while running second, then switched teams for 1950 and finished third when rain halted the contest prematurely at 138 laps. He was running third again in 1951 when a wire wheel collapsed at 126 laps, causing him to spin down to the muddy infield and flip. He escaped uninjured, and, at 45, soon announced his retirement.

While Rose had a reputation for being snappy – and it is certainly true he did not suffer fools, or care for small talk – he was, in fact, very witty, a needler, and given to pulling faces for the cameras. Wiry and energetic, he was never still. A professional engineer for much of his life, for such companies as Allison's, Studebaker, General Motors, and Lockheed, he took delight in being able to practice briefly, return to the track to qualify, and then stay away until race day, thus never having to take time from work.

The fact that this bothered his rivals pleased him to no end. Rose raised his two polio-afflicted children by himself for several years, as a loving and attentive father who even devised his own exercise equipment to help them through those difficult times. One of his proudest accomplishments came during his days at Studebaker, when he developed a hand-operated throttle and braking system which would enable a physically challenged person to be able to drive an automobile.

Left: The tradition of the driver's meeting dates back to the very beginning, the drivers during the 1920s and 1930s being required to sit on the grass. By 1951, they would sit in the grandstands, lined up according to their starting positions. The front rank here comprises Jack McGrath, Lee Wallard, and pole winner Duke Nalon. In the second row are Troy Ruttman, Mauri Rose, and Duane Carter.
Photograph: IMS

Left: The front row poses after the first day of time trials: Eventual third-place-finisher Jack McGrath on the outside, winner Lee Wallard in the middle, and Duke Nalon on the pole.
Photograph: IMS

Above: A look at the V-8 supercharged Novi engine.

Top: Mike Nazaruk finishes second in the 1951 "500," the engine in his car still outfitted with the same "cracked" block (a perennial Speedway myth) from last year when Johnnie Parsons was supposedly "saved" by the rain.

Main photograph: Duane Carter, driving one of the ex-Lou Moore Blue Crowns, is lapped by Lee Wallard.
Photographs: IMS

Bettenhausen, who was still smarting over the fact that he had given up the Lou Moore "ride" in 1947 because of his allegiance to ASPAR, still believed that "front-drive" potentially held the advantage at Indianapolis. He told Belanger in both 1950 and 1951 that while he still wished to drive the ex-Meyer & Drake car on the dirt tracks for the remainder of the year, he wanted to drive for Lou Moore at Indianapolis. Belanger, of course, needed a driver for the "500," and for 1951, Bettenhausen recommended Wallard.

Tony's front-drive car spun out late in the race while running fifth, and the car he *could* have driven went on to win.

The win did not come easily for Wallard in spite of the fact that he led for a total of 159 laps. At some point, the right rear shock mounting broke and Wallard began to take a terrible pounding, especially over the bricks on the main straight. Next, the exhaust pipe broke, and while it did remain in place, the noise level increased dramatically. With 12 laps still to go, the brakes gave out, but still Wallard didn't quit.

He took the checkered flag with three minutes to spare over Nazaruk, with third being the combination of ex-hot-rodders Jack McGrath and Manny Ayulo (the latter two having been friends since high school). After a couple of "insurance" laps, Wallard shut off the engine as he came through turn four, climbed up onto the tail of the car, and then drifted, brakeless, down past the pits, jockey-style, waving to the crowd on either side. Somebody threw him a rag and for several seconds, using both hands, he buried his face in the rag, still rolling slowly on down towards Victory Lane.

He was in quite a bit of discomfort. Although fire-retardant uniforms were not mandatory in those days, Wallard had chosen to wear one anyway. In fact, the uniforms were not even produced with fire-retardant properties, but rather had to be treated, and in a most archaic fashion. The recommendation was that eight ounces of boric acid and four ounces of Borax should be mixed in with two quarts of warm water. Before long, friends would team up and share a 55-gallon drum, in which several uniforms would be soaked in the solution, stirred with a stick, and then hung up to dry on coat hangers. It was virtually impossible for the solution to be distributed evenly, and it would tend to dry in abrasive blotches.

The constant pounding on the bricks, coupled with the fact that Wallard had decided not to wear an undershirt, caused his skin to be severely chafed. After the victory ceremonies were concluded, he went over to the infield hospital, where he was rubbed down with liniment. He then climbed onto the scales and discovered that since breakfast, he had lost 15 pounds. Earlier, he had quipped that due to having carried block after block while building his own house over the last few months, he estimated he was one inch shorter than he had been in 1950.

The rate of attrition had been exceptionally high during the race, and only eight cars were running at the end. All but two of the retirements were the result of mechanical failures, the only accident involving Mauri Rose, who was running third at

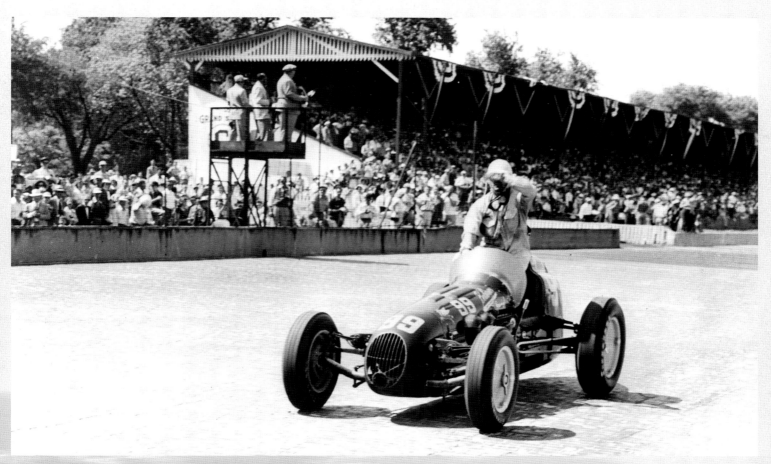

126 laps. A wire wheel collapsed and sent the car veering through the infield grass, where it dug into standing water from a rainstorm a couple of days before and flipped upside down. The three-time winner climbed out, jammed his pipe in his mouth and, covered in mud, growled, "Some days you just can't make a nickel."

The following January, he announced his retirement.

There had been plenty of dramatic moments during qualifying, led off by Duke Nalon winning the pole with a Novi. In so doing, he broke Walt Faulkner's 1950 records, but Faulkner wasn't even on the grounds with a chance to retaliate. Walt and chief mechanic Clay Smith had left California, towing a brand-new car Eddie Kuzma had built for J. C. Agajanian, and they had run into several delays along the way, including being detained by a snowstorm. It was not until they were able to find a newspaper (in a diner near the Indiana border) that they finally learned that Nalon had broken their records.

Duke didn't hold the records for long. Just a couple of days after arriving at the track, Faulkner, Smith, and Agajanian had their records back, this time upping the four-lap mark to 136.872 mph and the single-lap to 138.122.

Not only had Bill Holland's extraordinary streak (second, second, first, and second in his first four starts) come to an end, but he wasn't even in the lineup. AAA had continued to rule with an iron hand, and it did not take kindly to drivers straying from the fold, no matter how slightly. Holland, who had now moved to Miami, made the mistake of appearing at a local track and taking part in a match race. Even something as seemingly minor as driving a pace car was not acceptable, and Holland received notice that he had been suspended. This he did not take lightly, expressing his displeasure to the media in no uncertain terms. Not surprisingly, at the annual wintertime meetings, his application for reinstatement was denied, and in spite of his stature within the sport, he was not permitted to compete in any AAA races in 1951.

Holland's criticism of AAA continued, and when he applied for reinstatement the following year, the sanctioning body made certain he realized just who held the upper hand. He was turned down *again*, and it was 1953 before he was welcomed back into the fold. By the time that happened, the cars at Indianapolis had begun to take on a completely different look.

Above: One of the most crowd-pleasing moments in the history of the "500" comes when the 40-year-old graduate of the school of hard knocks, "Cinderella Man," Lee Wallard, rides the tail of his brakeless car down to Victory Lane.

Left: Wallard, who will soon learn that he has lost 15 pounds since breakfast, celebrates his win with actress Loretta Young.
Photographs: IMS

THE COMING OF THE "ROADSTER"

1952: Youth is served

During the winter of 1951/52, the Glendale, California, shops of Frank Kurtis produced two chassis which would have a major impact on the design of the Indianapolis car over the next several years.

Car owner Howard Keck's co-chief mechanics, Frank Coon and Jim Travers, were innovators. Later the founders of the famed Traco Engineering, they were among the first to use both Halibrand magnesium wheels and disc brakes at Indianapolis, and through another friend, Stu Hilborn, they were the first to use fuel injection, all circa 1948/49. The Keck Kids, as they were known, designed a car which used some of the Art Sparks theories of placing as much weight as reasonable over to the left for the Speedway's constant left turns. Where their design differed was in placing the cockpit over to the right. With the engine mounted on the left, and the driveshaft running along the left side back to the rear axle, the driver sat down next to it, thereby achieving a lower center of gravity. They also tilted their upright Offy slightly over to the left.

With Mauri Rose retired, standout West Coast midget car performer Bill Vukovich became the Keck driver. When Vukovich first saw the nearly completed car, he looked at the shape, then at the grille, and said something along the lines of, "That looks just like a roadster." The crew started to refer to the car as "the roadster," and not only did the nickname catch on, it was soon being applied to any low-sitting race car at the track. It wasn't long before, in print, the quotation marks around "roadster" were dropped and it began to be spelled with a capital "R." The term created even more confusion in an already confusing sport, since the true meaning of "roadster" was a road-going vehicle, whereas these were pure racing cars designed basically for one specific oval track featuring all left turns.

In the meantime, Cummins Engine Company was going to try it again. Having been absent since 1934, they had entered a car in 1950, driven by Jimmy Jackson. There was no longer a special qualifying-speed dispensation for diesels, but they certainly had the specifications in their favor. The six-cylinder Cummins engine was boosted by a supercharger, and whereas the other supercharged racing engines were restricted to 183 cubic inches, the diesel was allowed a whopping 401. Jackson had qualified, but only just, scraping in with the 33rd-fastest speed and then dropping out with supercharger trouble after 52 laps.

For 1952, Kurtis built an extremely low-sitting chassis into which the diesel engine was not just tilted, but laid completely over on its side. The respected Freddie Agabashian (now

more and more in demand for "test-hopping" cars during practice, for his analysis) was the driver. The right-hand-mounted driver's seat was placed so low in the frame that from the left side, Agabashian was described as looking like someone sitting in a bathtub. Not only that, but the car's body sat so low that the tops of the front wheels were higher than the bodywork, as would have been the rear wheels if not for the headrest. Although he emphasized he had no intention of doing so, Agabashian pointed out that if it weren't for the headrest, the car could have been driven upside down.

There was one other technical innovation on the diesel. It was boosted by what was variously described as a super-charger or a turbo-supercharger. It was, in fact, by a full 14 years, the Speedway's first-ever *turbocharger*. As it turned out, it was the location of this very implement which led to the car's eventual retirement.

During early testing, Agabashian told the crew that the car possessed extraordinary power and that because of the huge advantage in cubic-inch displacement, plus the strong likelihood that complaints would be lodged by the other teams, they might be wise to not show all of it off. As the first qualifying day drew closer and closer, Agabashian and the Cummins crew were accused of "sandbagging," meaning that they were not lapping as rapidly as they could have. When it came time to qualify, there was no point in keeping the secret any longer. Agabashian's first lap was a blazing 139.104 mph, the fastest ever turned at the track. Each succeeding lap was a tick slower, but the four-lap average of 138.010 also was the fastest ever turned. Nobody was able to top it by the end of the day, and in one of the Speedway's biggest-ever upsets, the Cummins Diesel was on the pole.

While the pole was set, the Cummins's track records did not last for long. On the following Saturday, Vukovich came along with the Keck "roadster" and turned his second lap at 139.427 mph, his four-lap speed also marginally faster than Agabashian's, at 138.212.

The run everybody was waiting for was that of Chet Miller with a Novi.

Because the public address system was not used on practice days until 1967, the only indication of a good lap for fans sitting in the bleachers prior to that (unless they happened to catch a glimpse of the speed written on the pit board) would be signs of excitement by crew members holding stopwatches. Just before closing time on Wednesday, May 21, there was considerably more than that. Huge whoops of delight and sounds of disbelief were accompanied by people staring at their watches and at each other. Several people had caught Chet Miller at slightly *over* 140 mph.

Interestingly, Miller's own crew downplayed it and said it

Inset top: In one of the greatest upsets ever, Freddie Agabashian wins the 1952 pole position with a low-sitting Kurtis-Kraft, powered by a 401-cubic-inch Cummins Diesel.

Photograph: IMS

122

was "only" a high 139, but everyone was paying attention three days later when Chet went to make an official run. Waiting until late in the day, he didn't miss it by much. His first lap was 139.600, the "magic 140" now being just a blink away. Lap two dropped off just slightly but was still above 139, after which (not surprisingly, because Novi fans were becoming used to such things) came a letdown. The Novi had to return to the pits with a fused piston.

Masterminding the Novi cars now was Jean Marcenac, the colorful little Frenchman who had come over with the Ballot team in 1919, been befriended by Ralph de Palma, and became so enamored with American racing that he had decided to stay. In addition to winning with Lockhart, Keech, Arnold, and Frame, he had been one of several notables who worked under Art Klein at the Warner Brothers transportation department. He was still there, and upon the death of Bud Winfield in an automobile accident in 1950, Lew Welch had put him in charge of the Novis.

For the first time this year, the intent was that there would be only four qualifying days, to be conducted on two consecutive Saturdays and Sundays. Unfortunately, the final Sunday was completely rained out and a weekday had to be used after all, Monday, May 26, becoming the final qualifying day. Late in the afternoon, Chet Miller came back and ran four laps. His fastest, at 139.513 mph, just missed his record of two days earlier, but his four-lap average of 139.034 was the fastest ever turned. Although there were several more qualifying attempts made after the 48-year-old Miller had made his run, no one else was fast enough to qualify. So in addition to this being one of the rare occasions on which the one-lap and four-lap records were set on different attempts, it was (and remains) the only time ever that the fastest qualifying speed of the year, not to mention the all-time track record, was established by the last person to successfully make the field.

There was much interest and excitement among sports-car and road-racing enthusiasts this year over the entry of five Ferraris. Reported as having been built especially for the "500," they were in fact all 4½-liter 1951 Grand Prix cars which had been refurbished. Two of them were to be driven by Dr. Giuseppe Farina, the inaugural 1950 world champion, and Alberto Ascari, who was destined to win the world title in 1952 and 1953. The other three cars had been sold to Americans. Howard Keck purchased one; owner/driver Johnny Mauro took delivery of another, and John Bartlett and Gerry Grant of the Grant Piston Ring Company obtained one for Johnnie Parsons. In fact, Ferrari was interested in having Parsons compete in some Grand Prix events, and the 1950 winner even traveled to Italy for the purpose of meeting with Enzo Ferrari. They could not come to terms.

Farina crashed his car at the Valentino Grand Prix in Turin in early April and had to withdraw; Parsons never really felt comfortable in his and voluntarily stepped out; Travers and Coon had little interest in the Keck Ferrari and preferred instead to concentrate on their "roadster"; and Mauro never could really get going.

The only qualifier was Ascari, a delightful man who reportedly spoke no English but endeared himself to the others with his sportsmanship and his willingness, in spite of being one of the world's great drivers, to go through the formality of the "rookie" test. He started 19th and had moved up to eighth when the right rear wire wheel collapsed after 40 laps, sending him spinning into the north-end infield. He ended up only 31st, but he attended the victory banquet regardless, dressed in a suit and tie, smiling, posing for pictures, and generally eager to please.

In fact, Ascari understood a lot more than he was letting on. He came in from a practice run one day, and climbed from the car not overly pleased with his speeds. "Well, Alberto," muttered one brash young driver (a future winner) sitting on the pit wall and to no one in particular, "I guess you're just going to have to stand on it a little harder." Whereupon Ascari smiled, dropped his goggles and gloves into his upturned helmet and, bowing, offered them to the driver.

Main photograph: The stricken mount of Vukovich rests against the wall nine laps short of victory, its still-helmeted driver standing on the wall second from left.

Inset top right: To the victor go the spoils: Ruttman embraces film actress Arlene Dahl, later famous for her line of cosmetics, her expertise in astrology, and for being the mother of actor Lorenzo Lamas.

Inset below: Winner-to-be Troy Ruttman makes a pit stop.
Photographs: IMS

Both Novis (Miller and Nalon) were eliminated before half-distance because of supercharger difficulties, while Agabashian's diesel, which ran fourth for many laps, was obliged to retire after 71 laps due to an oversight concerning its revolutionary turbocharger. The crew had not considered that by installing it down in front of the engine, just inside the grille, the inlet could eventually become blocked by rubber particles sucked up from the track. This is precisely what occurred.

Cummins never returned with a diesel after that, and with good reason. Management was well aware that complaints by other participants would surely lead to AAA reducing the cubic-inch displacement and that, rather than try to campaign in the future with a less powerful engine, the company should

rest on its laurels. The mission, in the first place, had been to try to showcase the potential of the diesel engine for commercial use; and with Cummins truck engine sales having increased dramatically, that mission had certainly been accomplished.

The majority of the race was a struggle between the "road-ster" of Vukovich and a dirt-track car (actually the Faulkner record car of the year before) driven by Oklahoma-born Troy Ruttman. After starting eighth, Vukovich had needed only seven laps to get to the front, and he eventually was to lead a total of 150 laps. Ruttman, who led 35 laps in three different segments, was approximately 30 seconds behind for much of the last 100 miles, but it became apparent that Vukovich was beginning to slow down. The steering was tightening up and Ruttman, lapping at 131, was reeling him in. By the 190th circuit, the margin had been whittled down to 22 seconds.

Just as Vukovich was negotiating turn three of his 192nd lap, the steering arm came adrift and the race leader had no choice but to drift wide and then grind along the north-chute wall until the car was stopped.

Ruttman was where he needed to be, and he cruised the final eight laps to become, at 22, the youngest "500" winner ever, a record still unbroken in 2006. A giant of a man, in spite of being quite boyish in demeanor, he was also the tallest at six-foot-three and the heaviest at 265 pounds. The fact that AAA had a long-standing rule that drivers had to be at least 21 years old, and Ruttman was now in his fourth "500" at 22, required some explanation, considering that he was *supposed* to have been 23 when he made his "500" debut in 1949. He actually started racing at 15 and was one of the leading drivers on the West Coast by the age of 18, his mother having skillfully altered his birth certificate when his talent became apparent at an early age. He had begun driving her around in a passenger car when he was nine.

In second place was another driver who had employed some ingenuity in hiding his true age. Because Richard Rath-

mann had wanted to start racing hot rods at 16, he had swapped identities with his brother, who was two and a half years older. His name was James. They eventually went back to using their correct dates of birth, but for the remainder of their professional careers, 1960 "500" winner Jim Rathmann was really Richard, and 1950 pole winner Dick Rathmann was really James.

Ruttman and Rathmann were among a growing number of drivers at the track who had known each other virtually since adolescence, having been members of the same hot rod club as teenagers. It is estimated that nine of the 33 drivers from the 1953 lineup fell into this category, and probably better than two dozen of them would be competing over the next few years.

The 1952 race was further notable for the fact that for the first time ever, there had been not a single use of a relief driver. In addition, after World War II Purple Heart veteran Art Cross finished fifth in his first "500" start, he was honored with the inaugural Stark & Wetzel Rookie of the Year award. While recognition for the most outstanding newcomer in a motor racing event or series is now extremely commonplace, it is believed that the 1952 "500" marked the very first occasion on which there was such recognition in motorsports.

Stark & Wetzel was a local meat-packing company, and the prize, in addition to a check for $500, consisted of what was described as a year's supply of meat. Indeed, the winners were invited to visit the headquarters on a regular basis throughout the year and help themselves to product. It was a most appreciated prize at the time. The majority of the drivers still came from less-than-well-heeled upbringings, had served on active duty during WWII, and now generally derived their income strictly from a percentage of the prize money won by the race cars they drove. It has been suggested that while several of the drivers in the 1953 lineup may have started small businesses in the interim, every single one of them basically made his living driving racing cars.

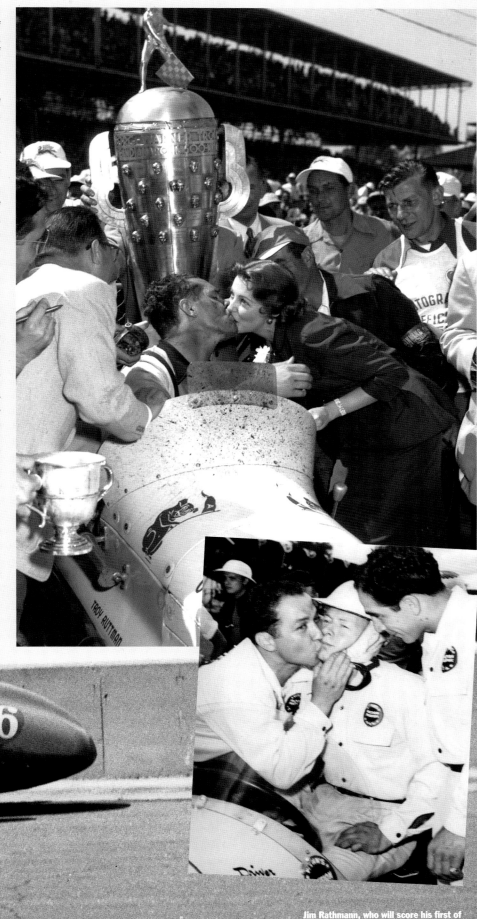

Jim Rathmann, who will score his first of three runner-up finishes this year, is enthusiastically greeted after qualifying by a very young Andy Granatelli. Brother Joe Granatelli is at right.
Photograph: IMS

1953: The Hottest "500"

The 1953 "500" was "all Vukovich." There was no steering-arm failure *this* year. He started on the pole, and other than for five laps of shuffling while he made his first pit stop, he led the entire distance. It was a blazingly hot day, climbing all the way into the low 90s, and unlike the previous year, relief driving was in abundance. Vukovich and Art Cross, who drove a dirt car to second place, both went it alone; but several cars, some of which didn't even finish, used three drivers. Chuck Stevenson and Andy Linden drove three cars each, and Gene Hartley had the distinction of crashing a car, being released from the infield hospital, and then going back out to crash another.

Vukovich, the son of a Slavic immigrant who had died during the Great Depression, normally was a man of few words except when around friends. He was, however, extremely quotable, and many of his snappy retorts became legendary. When asked in Victory Lane about the oppressive heat, he fired back with, "Hot? You think this is *hot*? You ought to try driving a tractor in Fresno in July!"

For someone from such meager beginnings, this was a most rewarding day. The lap prize fund had been increased for the first time since its inception in 1920, the leader on each lap now earning $150 instead of $100. Vukovich piled up $29,250 in lap prizes alone, his total take being a record $89,497.

But the heat did take its toll in a serious way. Carl Scarborough, a 37-year-old who looked considerably older, climbed out of his car during a pit stop and collapsed. He was taken to the infield hospital, and while another driver, Bob Scott, went on to finish the race for him, the stricken Scarborough could not be saved.

Sadly, Scarborough was not the only driver who lost his life. After three consecutive years (1950–52) had passed without a serious injury, there was a major loss on the day before the first qualifying day, when Novi driver Chet Miller had an accident which was eerily similar to that of Ralph Hepburn's in 1948. Miller was trying for an unofficial 140-mph lap when he veered into the first-turn grass, continued applying the throttle, and then careened, fatally, into the first-turn wall as soon as the spinning front-drive wheels met the track's surface.

In qualifying for the 1952 event, Miller had tied Cliff Bergere for the record of having the most "500" starts ever, at 16. This jointly held record would remain unbroken for almost a quarter of a century, until A. J. Foyt qualified for a 17th "500" in 1974.

Bill Holland, the 1949 winner was finally back, and certainly made his presence known late on the final qualifying day. After having qualified another car and been "bumped," he stepped into a new "roadster" entered by "500" hopeful, and eventual three-time starter, Ray Crawford. With very little practice, Holland posted the second-fastest qualifying speed of the year, the average of his first three laps actually being faster than those of Vukovich's pole speed.

In spite of reports to the contrary, *this* and *not* 1952 was the first year in which the race was broadcast in its entirety by the recently formed Indianapolis Motor Speedway Radio Network. Since the mid-1930s, the prime source for race-day radio coverage had been the Mutual Radio Network. Up until WWII, Mutual's "flagship" station for the "500" was the famed Powel Crosley, Jr.'s Cincinnati, Ohio-based power-house, WLW. By 1946, however, that duty had been transferred to a fledgling Indianapolis station, WIBC, and other than for the anchor, Bill Slater, who flew in from New York for just a couple of days, all of the technical people and "on-air" voices were employees of the local station. When Mutual decided, at the last minute, not to broadcast the race at all in 1951, WIBC did it on its own and offered it to any other Mutual station which wished to pick it up.

During the winter of 1951/52, the sales staff arranged with Tony Hulman and Wilbur Shaw to create the Indianapolis Motor Speedway Radio Network. A total of 26 stations were signed up, and the format was virtually as it always had been: thirty minutes at the beginning, thirty minutes at the end, and

Opposite: The smoke pouring from the chimney stack at Carl Fisher and Jim Allison's old Prest-O-Lite factory to the south indicates to cagey veterans on this qualifying day that there is a moderate wind blowing from east to west.

Below: Covered from head to foot in grime, perspiration, and splashes of oil after the murderously hot race of 1953, the triumphant Vukovich manages a grin. At left is Wilbur Shaw, the actress is Jane Greer, and next to her is Raymond Firestone.
Photographs: IMS

OFFICIAL
Program

37th 500-MILE RACE . . . MAY 30, 1953
INDIANAPOLIS ★ MOTOR ★ SPEEDWAY ★ CORPORATION

a trio of 15-minute updates in between.

There were only four other radio stations in the city at that time, and it quickly came to light that the staffs at all of them had been planning to make a similar proposal and were less than happy at having been upstaged. As a way of consoling them, Hulman and Shaw devised a plan for involving everybody. The history-making result was that the "500" was covered from the pre-race ceremonies until after the race was over, with at least one "voice" from each local station being heard on those of all of its competitors. With WIBC's Sid Collins as the chief announcer, the station count ballooned from 26 to 135 (it eventually would exceed 1,000 stations), and the race was broadcast on a delayed basis to the Armed Forces Radio Network in Europe and the Armed Forces Radio Service in the Far East. The impact was phenomenal.

As further evidence of the seemingly endless phenomenon of so many famous names having been intertwined with the lives of others throughout the history of the track, even WLW's Powel Crosley had had an early connection. Long before he became the prolific manufacturer of radios, refrigerators, and the Crosley automobile, and long before he owned the Cincinnati Reds baseball team, Crosley had worked at an automobile showroom in Indianapolis. It was no ordinary establishment, either: Its owner was none other than Carl Fisher. Saving on expenses by rooming at the YMCA, young Crosley was a Fisher salesman for a short time, until moving over to the National Motor Vehicle Company as assistant sales and advertising manager. When the inaugural meet was held at the Speedway in August 1909, all of the publicity for Howdy Wilcox, Johnny Aitken, Charlie Merz, and National's other drivers was handled by Crosley.

1954: Can anybody beat Vukovich?

No driver ever before had been able to turn an official lap in under one minute and four seconds, but in 1954, genial Jack McGrath managed it on all four of his qualifying laps. Not only was he the first to exceed 140 mph, but his opening lap was 141.287. Effectively his own chief mechanic, McGrath was on the pole at 141.033 mph. The rather surprising second-fastest qualifier, starting back in 13th, was underrated Cal Niday, a professional barber who at the age of 17 had lost a leg in a motorcycle accident.

Although Carl Fisher and Jim Allison were long gone by this time, they had left behind a legacy which had been of great benefit to the drivers for many years, but was purely unintentional, and was now coming to an end. As the speeds had picked up, the direction of the wind had been of growing importance, particularly on a gusty day. For some time, the more wily of the veteran drivers had been using a secret indicator, the smoke flowing from Fisher and Allison's old Prest-O-Lite smokestack just to the south telling them what they wanted to know. The problem now was that Tony Hulman had begun to erect double-decker stands through turn one, thus severely hampering the view!

The two biggest surprises of qualifying were the difficulties encountered by defending winner Vukovich and two-time pole sitter Duke Nalon. Driving the only Novi at the track – the wrecked Chet Miller car had not been rebuilt – Duke qualified, due to a misunderstanding, at 136.395 mph, a speed which did not hold up. The result was that the entire 33-car starting field was powered by Offenhausers, the first time ever that one engine manufacturer had been able to claim every spot.

Vukovich finally made it in, but not until the third day, burying him back in 19th starting position. It didn't seem to make much difference once the race began; by lap 10 he was up to seventh. McGrath led the first 44 laps, but had to stop early for tires because of his torrid pace. The lead then became a battle between defending Rookie of the Year Jimmy Daywalt, from Wabash, Indiana, and Art Cross, who had been "bumped" in his 1953 second-place-finishing car, qualified another dirt track car in 27th place, and then come all the way to the front by lap 51. Daywalt and Cross swapped the lead four times in ten laps before both stopped at lap 61. Vukovich and Sam Hanks led one lap apiece before rising star Jimmy Bryan went to the front.

Bryan, who hailed from Phoenix, Arizona, and was built like an ox, was manhandling a dirt-track car owned by self-made moving company magnate Al Dean. The second half of the race became a two-man struggle between Vukovich and Bryan, who were two of the toughest human beings the track had ever seen. Although this was mostly an overcast day, the heat and humidity were considerable, and the call on relief drivers was even greater than it had been the year before, with 28 changes taking place involving 15 different cars.

Bryan had to make three stops to Vukovich's two, and when Bryan came in for fuel and tires at lap 149, Vukovich was in front to stay. Bryan was having a struggle. The right rear shock mounting had broken and he was taking a dreadful pounding, especially on the 600-plus yards of bricks and mortar on the main straight. He started falling back, and in spite of attempts by Vukovich's crew to slow their man down, "Vuky" didn't want to break his rhythm. He just kept on charging.

There was a new flagman this year, veteran Seth Klein having retired. The nattily dressed Bill Vandewater, who had been flagging midget car races for years, greatly impressed those watching with his skills in the final lap. Vukovich had been within a few yards of lapping the never-say-die Bryan when Vukovich started his final lap, and on the next circuit, as Vukovich was coming down to win, he was on the verge of drawing alongside. The heads-up Vandewater, who liked to work standing on the track's surface, dipped to one knee as he gracefully waved both the white for Bryan and the checker for Vukovich at the same time.

McGrath, driving a "roadster," was closing in on Bryan, but the "Arizona Cowboy" reached the checker with a scant seven seconds to spare. Instead of stopping at his pit after the

Left: The grand old pagoda, which has stood since 1926, is down to its final months. It will be razed on June 20, 1956.

Bottom: The field is pushed off for 1954, the car ahead being that of the second-starting Sumar Special, driven by Jimmy Daywalt from nearby Wabash, Indiana, the previous year's rookie of the year. Jimmy Bryan is on the outside of the front row, Jack McGrath on the pole.
Photographs: IMS

OFFICIAL PROGRAM

May 31   1954

Indianapolis
Motor Speedway
Corporation   50¢

38th 500 MILE RACE

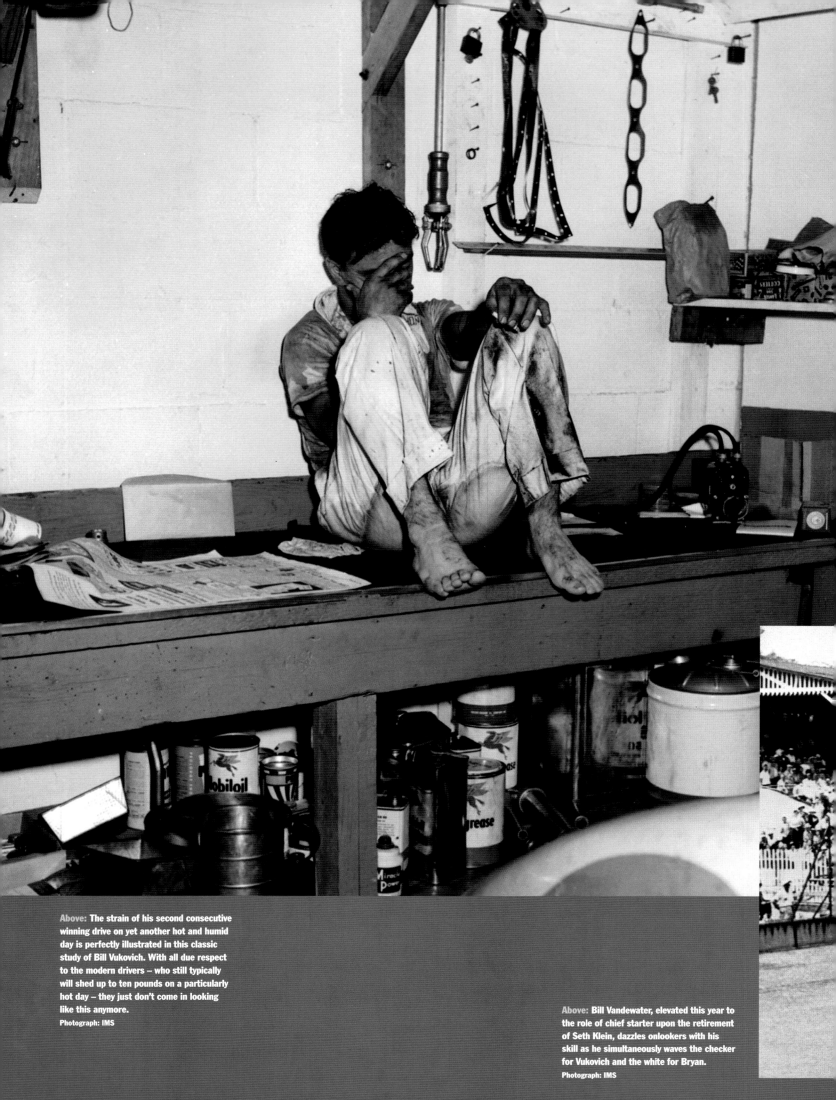

Above: The strain of his second consecutive winning drive on yet another hot and humid day is perfectly illustrated in this classic study of Bill Vukovich. With all due respect to the modern drivers – who still typically will shed up to ten pounds on a particularly hot day – they just don't come in looking like this anymore.
Photograph: IMS

Above: Bill Vandewater, elevated this year to the role of chief starter upon the retirement of Seth Klein, dazzles onlookers with his skill as he simultaneously waves the checker for Vukovich and the white for Bryan.
Photograph: IMS

"cool-off" lap, Bryan drove straight back to his garage, something he later said he had no memory of. A crew member arrived to unlock the door and Bryan walked in, then promptly collapsed on the floor. A call went to the infield hospital and a nurse arrived within moments. She placed a hand under his neck, and he is said to have barely opened his eyes and muttered, "Well, he beat me."

"How are you feeling?" asked the nurse, whereupon the larger-than-life he-man is reported to have drawled, "Well, I'm feeling just fine, baby. And how are *you* feeling?"

Bryan was so badly beaten up that he was in no condition to drive the Dean Van Lines dirt car at Milwaukee a week later. It qualified for the pole anyway, in the hands of a one-race substitute, Bill Vukovich.

There was another record broken in the relief-driving department this year. Tough Art Cross, the former U.S. Army tank driver who was wounded in Belgium in WWII, was unable to duplicate his 1953 feat of driving a dirt car to second place. The effort of driving from 27th to the lead and then battling with an overheated cockpit was too much for him. Johnnie Parsons took the wheel, but 79 previous laps in his own car, coupled with the lasting effects of a midget car crash injury in February, forced him back in after only 22 laps. Defending National Champion and former Air Force Lieutenant Sam Hanks took over, but the cockpit heat was too much for Sam. Muscular Andy Linden, who had boxed in the Navy, stuck with it for 17 grueling laps before he came in to hand over to Jimmy Davies, a Hanks protégé who had objected to being beaten by his stepfather at the age of 12 and had run away to make his own way in the world ever since. Davies hung with it for the final 23 laps, and finished the 500 miles in 11th place as the fifth different driver in the car.

Davies, by the way, was one of several drivers whose careers had been interrupted by military duty, Jerry Hoyt having been stationed in Germany and Davies in Korea during the time the 1952 race was taking place. Davies had led 25 laps of the 1951 race as "Private" Jimmy Davies, on furlough from Camp Roberts, California.

In the meantime, Bill Vukovich, who had averaged a record 130.840 mph, was by this time clearly "The Man." Only Wilbur Shaw and Mauri Rose before him had won the "500" twice in succession.

A major news story sent shock waves through the racing community on the evening of October 30, 1954. Wilbur Shaw, as important a person as any in the entire history of the track, had flown with a couple of friends in a private plane to Detroit for the purpose of testing an automobile and then writing his impressions for a magazine story. The weather was not good but Shaw was anxious to get home to Indianapolis because the following day, Halloween, was to be his 52nd birthday. The phone rang in the Shaw household in the early evening, and ten-year-old Billy Shaw took the call. The plane had gone down near Decatur, just southwest of Fort Wayne. There were no survivors.

There was all manner of speculation during the next few weeks over who would become Shaw's successor as the Speedway's president and general manager. There were certainly quite a number of applicants.

1955: The demise of a legend

One of the more public duties of the track president in recent years had been the announcing of the command to start the engines. The beginnings of this ritual are clouded, and as with several other traditions, it appears to have evolved rather than been created. All the way from the early days, the signal to start had been the latest in a morning-long succession of aerial bombs exploding at various intervals. The sound of the "starting" bomb had been accompanied in more recent years by Seth Klein holding up a green flag and then twirling it, still furled, above his head.

In 1948, a friend of Wilbur Shaw's came onto the public address system staff. A longtime showman who had once been a circus barker, and recently had formed a traveling auto "thrill" show, his name was John "Irish" Horan. A number of participants had been feeling for quite some time that this most dramatic of moments at which the engines were fired really "needed something." Irish Horan agreed. He is credited for the first time, in Floyd Clymer's *Indianapolis 500 Yearbook* in 1951, with having made an announcement over the public address, believed to have been little more than "opening the mike" upon the sounding of the bomb, and uttering, quietly and almost as an afterthought, "Gentlemen, start your *motors.*" Whether or not he actually said "motors," or was misquoted and really said "engines," he definitely said something. He may also have said it the year before, while the late Bob Russo, one of oval track racing's greatest historians, claimed he heard Horan make the announcement as early as 1948. W. F. Fox, sports editor of *The Indianapolis News*, stated in the early 1950s that Seth Klein made the announcement, not over the public address, but rather strictly for the benefit of the participants, by using a megaphone. In 1952, a command definitely was delivered, but it was clearly not yet an established tradition, because one version states the final word as being "engines" while another records it as "motors." It is unclear who said it, although it most likely was Horan, with Wilbur Shaw finally assuming the duty for certain by 1953. An insider once suggested that Shaw, Horan, and longtime track publicist Al Bloemker used to play cards regularly throughout the winter and that they probably agreed among themselves at some point that Shaw should take it over.

Regardless, someone else would be doing it in 1955, and the weeks of speculation came to an end with Tony Hulman quietly deciding to do it himself; just as he would, with increasing flair each year, all the way until 1977, the final year of his life.

One other famous phrase, which *does* have a clearly documented beginning, was heard for the first time in 1955. The IMS Radio Network had grown by leaps and bounds, and the most common request by station managers was that some sort of standard "out cue" could be developed so that "board operators" on duty at the various stations around the world would be aware that a commercial break was imminent. The challenge was given to the WIBC sales staff, and 22-year-old Miss Alice Greene made the suggestion everyone else

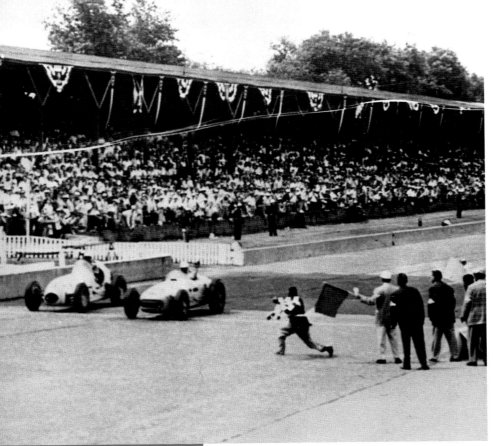

liked the best. On race day, whenever it was time for a commercial break, anchor Sid Collins would deliver the eight-word phrase still very much in use today: "Stay tuned to the greatest spectacle in racing."

During the winter, Vukovich had found it necessary to start looking around for a car to drive. The decision had been to "park" Keck's two-time winning car and compete instead with a revolutionary streamlined car with its wheels enclosed, as influenced by the W196 Mercedes–Benz Formula One car which had taken Grand Prix racing by storm in 1954. Keck had wanted to power it with a Novi engine, but with Lew Welch not wanting to sell him one, Keck retained Leo Goosen to design a V-8 supercharged version of the "Offy."

The program came to a screeching halt when Keck was informed by the Internal Revenue Service that his racing could not be written off as a business expense.

At liberty for the time being, Vukovich called his friend Henry Banks, the now-retired 1950 AAA national champion, to find out what sportsman car owner Lindsey Hopkins might be doing for 1955. Banks called Lindsey to ask how he would like to have Vukovich for a driver. *Would* he?! Oh, and by the way, there was one other thing that hopefully wouldn't be a problem: Travers and Coon went with the deal. This was *not* a problem.

The very wealthy Hopkins, who was a "500" car entrant every year from 1951 until 1982, divided his time between Atlanta, Georgia, and Miami. A true southern gentleman and an accomplished magician (hence his rabbit-out-of-the-hat logo) he, too, had an indirect connection with the track from its earliest days. Not only was he president of the Montauk (New York) Beach Company, but he was director of a real estate company his late father had purchased many years

before. It was, of all things, the Carl G. Fisher Corporation. Lindsey, as a young man, had known Fisher.

Vukovich, who raced very little during the balance of the last two seasons (his current tax bracket made it pointless), was anxious to get going. He couldn't take two steps without someone asking him about his chances of being the first driver ever to win "three in a row." He just wanted to get it over with. "Test-hopping" was a very common practice in those days, and it seemed as if everyone would drive everybody else's car at some point. With the Hopkins car not yet having arrived and Vukovich anxious to turn laps, Jack McGrath, perhaps his greatest on-track rival, let Vuky take the Jack Hinkle-owned Kurtis "roadster" out for a few laps.

Two cars which received quite a bit of attention during practice were the streamliners of Jim Rathmann and Jimmy Daywalt, the Sumar Special of Daywalt having been greatly influenced by the 1954 Mercedes–Benz W196 Grand Prix car. Its wheels were completely enclosed by bodywork. As aerodynamic as the car looked, Daywalt's lap speeds were not that spectacular. Several experiments were made, and the result was that the more the streamlining was removed, the faster he would go. One theory was that he was unnerved by not being able to see the left front wheel through the turns. He eventually finished ninth, with most of the streamlining removed and the wheels exposed.

Qualifying records were fully expected to fall by the wayside on the first day of time trials, but instead it turned out to be a very strange day. Drivers returned from the early practice sessions complaining that the blustery winds were actually moving the cars around on the straightaways. One thing led to another,

Below left: Unaware that all of the other drivers have made a "pact" not to qualify because of the windy conditions on the opening day of qualifying, Jerry Hoyt goes out with minutes to spare and snags the pole.
Photographs: IMS

the 39th **500**

OFFICIAL PROGRAM · 50¢
MAY 30, 1955

BILL VUKOVICH

He was undeniably the most outstanding Indianapolis 500 driver of the early 1950s, and many believe that Bill Vukovich adapted to the 2¹/₂-mile track better than any other driver ever. Born in Alameda, California, on December 13, 1918, to a struggling Slavic immigrant grape farmer who left behind a sizable family when he died during the Great Depression, Vukovich completely dominated the Speedway between 1952 and 1955.

Perhaps it was aggression over his less-than-privileged upbringing which made him the way he was, but Vukovich seemed obsessed with trying to lead every lap of every race. Starting in midget race cars in 1938, he raced them as hard as anyone, and he emerged as the most successful driver on the West Coast in 1946 and 1947.

After turning down opportunities to race at Indianapolis as early as 1948, he took and passed a "rookie" test in 1950 and made his first start in 1951. He moved from 20th to 10th in 20 laps, but soon dropped out. In 1952, driving the first of the so-called "roadsters," a nickname Vukovich himself is believed to have coined, he broke the one-and-four lap qualifying records and then vaulted from eighth to the lead in seven laps.

He led a total of 150 circuits and was within nine laps of the win when the steering arm came adrift, rendering the car unsteerable. In 1953, he started from the pole and effectively led the entire race, giving up the lead only for five laps while he was making his first pit stop. He had difficulty in qualifying in 1954 and was forced to start back in 19th, but not

surprisingly, he quickly charged into the first ten and led for the first time at lap 61. He was free and clear from the 150th lap on as he became the only driver other than Wilbur Shaw and Mauri Rose to have won in consecutive years.

In 1955, the eyes of the world were on him. Could he become the first ever to win three in a row? He battled back and forth with his great friendly nemesis, Jack Mc-Grath, and when McGrath fell by the wayside after 54 laps, Vukovich seemingly had the situation in hand. Only moments later, however, he became entangled in a multi-car accident on the backstretch, and in one of the most stunning developments in the entire history of the track, the great Vukovich perished in the accident.

Of the 647 laps he had completed between 1952 and 1955, he had led 485, including, appropriately, the last one he ever completed. In spite of his reputation for being standoffish and uncooperative with the press, he was basically a very shy person. He enjoyed a good laugh and was a chronic needler – just as long as he was around friends.

He could be laughing and joking with a group for minutes on end, only to clam up completely upon the arrival of someone with whom he was not entirely comfortable. Whether it was his relentless runs at the front, the occasional reports of a snappy and witty comeback to a reporter, his almost alarming Russian-sounding surname, or simply that so little was known about him – or even just a combination of *all* of these – Bill Vukovich was clearly the most fascinating and feared competitor of his time.

and a pact apparently was made whereby nobody would make a qualifying attempt. That way, the pole still could be contested for under more favorable conditions on a later day.

The day wore on and people began heading for home, disappointed that, while there had been plenty of practice, not a single qualifying attempt had been made. Suddenly, at about twenty minutes until six, there was some excitement at the start/finish line. It appeared that young Jerry Hoyt was going to go out. A large crowd of participants gathered round to remind his crew of "the deal," only to learn that because they had been working back in the garage area behind closed doors for much of the day, they had been overlooked. The crew had just made a change which had helped Hoyt's practice speeds considerably, and he wasn't about to stop now. Out he went, and the others went scurrying in every direction, many already having taken their cars back to the garages for the day. One who had covered himself was cagey Tony Bettenhausen. His car had been discreetly placed within the vicinity "just in case," and it was quickly pushed into line.

Hoyt took the green flag and then ran off four laps at a very respectable 140.045 mph. With just minutes remaining, Bettenhausen took off in his turquoise "roadster." Lap one was faster than any of Hoyt's, at 141.8, and while he did slow a little, his three-lap average was still good enough for the pole. The final lap, however, was barely over 139, dragging his four-lap average down to 139.985. He had been caught by a gust of wind. Pat O'Connor came in after three laps at just under 138, and the day was over. Hoyt was on the pole and Bettenhausen was not at all happy.

The following day, Vukovich raised the single-lap record to 141.309 mph, but it didn't hold up for long. In the middle of the afternoon, McGrath came along and raised it by an amazing two and a half miles per hour, to 143.793. He wound up with a four-lap average of 142.580, but he would be starting on the outside of the front row, not the pole.

Later that day, just minutes before the track closed, McGrath's longtime friend and partner, Manny Ayulo, was making a practice run when he ran headlong into the first turn wall. Runner-up to Jimmy Bryan for the 1954 AAA championship, and the son of a Peruvian diplomat, Ayulo died the following day.

It was no surprise when McGrath jumped to the lead at the start, and not much less of a surprise when Vukovich came up from fifth starting position to challenge him. For the next many laps these two engaged in a tremendous duel, the lead changing hands five times in the first 27 laps. McGrath, against the advice of his colleagues, had mixed a little nitromethane in with his methanol, and while this was a common practice for qualifying, it was considered inadvisable for the race. A light-colored smoke began to flow from his exhaust, although it did not appear to be affecting his speed.

Vukovich was relentless, on one occasion taking the lead in turn one by running the entire car below the inside line, the left-hand wheels actually being completely down in the grass.

It all happened in a hurry.

At the end of the 54th lap, McGrath came rolling slowly into the pits. He climbed from the car, raised the hood, and began removing the sparkplugs.

The booming voice of the legendary announcer, Tom Carnegie, was then heard over the public address system drawing attention to the fact that the yellow light had just come on.

McGrath put down the sparkplug wrench, turned around, and began counting off the passing cars, trying to determine who was missing. In fact, there were five who did not come around. One of them was Vukovich.

Rodger Ward, driving Troy Ruttman's 1952 winning car, had hit the outside wall coming out of the second turn and turned upside down. "Rookie" Al Keller, driving a dirt-track car, had veered over to the grass verge on the left and then attempted to come back onto the track's surface, banging wheels with a car driven by Johnny Boyd, another "rookie." Boyd's car was deflected to the right and directly into the path of Vukovich who was coming up to lap all of these cars for the second time. Vukovich hit the car of Boyd (which had been headed

for the outer fence) and with his front wheels now slightly off the ground, the car was turned marginally to the right, causing the right front wheel to ride up over the low-sitting wooden barrier. Boyd was turned upside down but remained on the track. Vukovich vaulted over the fence, right at the foot of the "golf" bridge, and then began cartwheeling parallel with the track, coming to rest upside down.

Ed Elisian, a driver from northern California who idolized Vukovich, stopped his car and ran across the track to try to help his mentor – but Vukovich was beyond help. Although his car was burning gently, he had died of a basal skull fracture.

The repercussions of the two-time defending winner losing his life in his attempt to become the first to win for an unprecedented third consecutive time would be felt and heard around the world.

The Vukovich accident almost completely overshadowed the excellent victory by the dynamic and intense Bob Sweikert, who many have rated as one of the great American drivers ever.

Broadcaster Charlie Brockman, who was conducting the Victory Lane interviews for the IMS Radio Network, was placed in a most challenging position when Sweikert, a friend of his, was pressing for details of the accident over the public address system and the worldwide radio broadcast. Brockman handled the situation with great diplomacy, and Sweikert did not know that Vukovich even was involved until after the interview was completed. The tipoff came a few minutes later when, for the second year, The Indianapolis News scored a major coup by having a helicopter land just yards from Victory Lane and then having a newspaper delivered to Sweikert, bearing a headline proclaiming his victory. The front page also carried details of Vukovich's fatal accident.

Not only was Sweikert leading the AAA National Championship point standings as a driver, but he was also in a virtual point deadlock with Jerry Hoyt for the lead in the Midwest Sprint Car Championship. There was more. Not only did Sweikert own his own sprint car and perform all of his own mechanical work, but he was maintaining Hoyt's car as well.

An amazing story came to light at the victory banquet. The winning chief mechanic, for his first of four, was the boyish-looking A. J. Watson, who within a very short period would become one of the most prolific and respected car builders in the history of the sport. The Ohio-born Watson had been living for many years in Burbank, California, but would spend his summers in Indianapolis. This spring, however, his pregnant wife had stayed behind, and approximately at the time of the final qualifying weekend, she had lost the child. Watson flew home.

At the victory banquet, Watson made it known that in his absence, the Offenhauser engine in the winning car had been completely torn down after qualifying and painstakingly reassembled for the race, entirely by none other than Sweikert himself.

There was one other extreme example of giving credit where credit is due. With veteran driver Paul Russo having failed to qualify, his longtime friend, Tony Bettenhausen, had theorized that since two pit stops were going to have to be made anyway, it would make sense to change drivers during the stops so that a fresh Russo would be able to drive while Tony took a break. Tony would get back in to finish. The plan almost paid off. Art Cross and Don Freeland each dropped out in the late stages while running second, and when a blocked fuel line forced Pat O'Connor to the pits only eight laps from the end, the runner-up position went to Bettenhausen. When he went up to accept the check for second place at the dinner, he insisted on taking Russo with him, unselfishly explaining to the audience that Russo had not been his relief driver, but rather his prearranged co-driver.

Another fine performance had been that of Jimmy Bryan, now in an Eddie Kuzma-built "roadster." He led for 31 laps until the fuel pump went out just before the halfway mark, upon which he endeared himself even further to the adoring crowd. While the car was still rolling at speed across the north end of the track, the macho, T-shirted Bryan hoisted himself up on to the tail, removed his helmet, shrugged his shoulders

Below: Although Sweikert's car is affectionately referred to as "The Pink Zink," the color is, in fact, "tropical rose."
Photograph: IMS

Main photograph: It's the spring of 1956, and after almost half a century, the Speedway finally has year-round offices at the track. On the left of the main entrance is the ticket office, publicity department, and accounting department, and on the right, the first-ever Museum.

Inset right: The De Soto pace car leads the field under the "golf" bridge on the backstretch. Sadly, the landmark bridge will be taken out very shortly and replaced for the following May by a tunnel.

Photograph: IMS

in exaggerated fashion, and steered with his feet! He pulled up at his pit, climbed out, jammed a cigar in his mouth, and walked around to the back of the car where he angrily delivered a swift kick to the tail with the heel of his cowboy boot. Ace fabricator Don Edmunds, who two years later, as a driver would win the "rookie of the year" award, later recalled with pride that his first duty upon being hired by Kuzma, had been to straighten out the dent inflicted by Bryan.

This was a perfectly dreadful time for world motorsports and there was probably never a time in history when it would come under so much universal criticism. Vukovich and Ayulo were not the only drivers to lose their lives. Larry Crockett, the 1954 Rookie of the Year, and Mike Nazaruk, the 1951 runner-up, both lost their lives during the spring, and before the season was out, McGrath and Hoyt would be gone as well.

On May 26, just four days before the demise of Vukovich, the great Ascari had crashed to his death while testing a Ferrari sports car at Monza, thus the world was robbed of two of its greatest drivers in less than one week.

Then, on June 11, there was the major disaster during the 24-Hours of Le Mans enduro in which more than 80 spectators were killed.

On August 3 came the bombshell that the AAA Contest Board had had enough, and that while honoring all sanctions for the balance of the season, it would accept no new dates and no longer would be involved in motorsports at all after the first of the year.

The number-one question on everyone's minds immediately concerned who would be sanctioning the Indianapolis 500, if indeed Tony Hulman even *needed* a sanctioning body.

As it turned out, Hulman believed that he did, and that it was essential for a sporting organization to oversee a "farm system" of sprint cars, midgets, and stock cars, not to mention championship events. Plans were immediately put into effect for the formation of the United States Auto Club. The group, forever after referred to by the pronunciation of its four initial letters as "yew-sack," took over on January 1, 1956. Since many of the old AAA officials continued to perform their same functions, the only notable difference in the appearance of everyone in the pits and the garage area during May 1956 was that the officials would be wearing different armbands.

1956: "Hey, we only build 'em to run 200 laps"

As early as 1947, Hulman had stated that he eventually would like to build a museum as a shrine to the Indianapolis 500 and its participants. In July 1955, ground was broken next to the track's main entrance at the corner of West 16th Street and Georgetown Road, where a single-story brick building would be erected. To the right of the building's entrance was to be the museum, and on the left, the ticket department, publicity and accounting departments, and a boardroom. The days of North Capitol Avenue were over, and after 45 years, the Speedway *finally* had year-round offices on the grounds themselves. It opened for business on March 19, and on the first weekend of qualifications, the museum was ready to accommodate the public – at no charge and with precisely six cars on display.

The decision had been to repave the entire track with asphalt (with the exception, of course, of the greater part of the main straight), and not unexpectedly, the speeds went up. Lew Welch had finally given up on the now ten-year-old front-drive Novis and had commissioned Frank Kurtis to build two rear-drive versions, both featuring a distinguishing and menacing looking tail fin. Even when standing perfectly still, they *looked* fast. With one of them, Paul Russo did an unofficial lap at 146.6 mph.

A. J. Watson had constructed a "roadster" of his own, based on that of Frank Kurtis but with a number of refinements, including the use of magnesium for some of the parts. It had been intended for Sweikert, but the 1955 champion had fallen out with car owner John Zink and had left for another team. His replacement was an ex-hot rod colleague of Watson, the Rathmann brothers, and numerous others: George Francis Flaherty, Jr., who went by the nickname "Pat."

Flaherty surprised many by winning the pole with a four-lap average speed of 145.596 mph and a single lap of 146.056, both new records. He surprised even more people by winning the race, never having been headed after lap 76. The race average speed of 128.490 mph was not a track record, but quite remarkable considering the large number of accidents which slowed it down, happily with no serious injury. Between caution periods, Flaherty routinely would lap at well above

140, and would delight the fans by dirt-tracking the lightweight car through the turns with such verve that the front left wheel would lift several inches from the track surface.

It was a truly virtuoso performance.

Flaherty, whose trademarks were his shock of red hair and a green shamrock painted on his helmet, failed to take the traditional precautionary extra couple of laps for the simple reason that the throttle linkage had broken just moments later, causing Watson to quip, "Hey, we only build these things to run 200 laps."

Flaherty stood up in the cockpit, blackened with grime from the track, and wearing only a pair of light blue slacks, no belt, and a sleeveless T-shirt. The mandatory wearing of fire-retardant uniforms was still another three years away, but Flaherty was the last person to drive into Victory Lane not wearing one.

As a further indication of the passing of time, the cars finishing 14th, 15th, and 16th were all of the dirt-track variety, the last three such cars ever to appear in the race. The tenth-placing finisher of Cliff Griffith also was registering a "last" in that it was the last time a car outfitted with wire wheels would compete in a "500."

European fans were disappointed when Giuseppe Farina, the 1950 world champion who was soon to retire, was unable to qualify. A six-cylinder Ferrari engine had been placed into a Kurtis chassis, but the car lacked enough speed to get in.

That the race could even be held at all was of amazement to many considering that it had rained constantly for several days. Clarence Cagle, the hard-working grounds superintendent, did not see a bed for 48 hours while he supervised the pumping of several hundred thousand gallons of rainwater from the tunnels running beneath the track, and the fact that the race was able to start on time, albeit under threatening skies, was referred to as "Cagle's Miracle."

The first three laps were led by Jim Rathmann, driving the very car in which Vukovich had lost his life in 1955. It was most ironic that the last time the crowd had seen the car in competition, it had been leading. Now, one year later, it had been rebuilt and was leading again with another driver. The early stages of the race featured breathtaking racing with Rathmann, O'Connor, Flaherty and Bettenhausen all racing within inches of each other and constantly swapping positions. The crowd gasped in unison on lap 10 when the roaring red Novi of Russo came up behind O'Connor and Flaherty on the main straight and then blasted past both of them to take the lead. O'Connor tucked in behind the Novi going into turn one and the nose of Flaherty was so close to the tail of O'Connor, it was as if they were three beads on a necklace.

Sam Hanks, who finished just 21 seconds behind Flaherty, owed a great deal of gratitude to the team which finished third. Paul Russo had jumped from eighth starting position to the lead in ten laps with the Novi, and he was running away with the race when his right rear tire exploded as he was ne-gotiating turn one of his 22nd lap. He escaped uninjured, but a minute or so later, there was a jam-up of several cars, including that of Hanks, whose left front tire was flattened.

Sam was able to keep the car under control, and he then limped, although at considerable speed, around to his pit, his acceleration helping to lift the left front wheel from the ground. When he arrived at his pit, his crew was nowhere to be found. They had seen Sam spin down through turn one and had run down there to help. The Hanks car was pitted next to that of Don Freeland's Bob Estes Special, headed up by Chief Mechanic Jud Phillips. The Phillips crew instinctively ran over and changed Sam's wheel, the irony being that Sam was able to come home second, while Freeland was third.

By the time everyone would return for May 1957, the entire facility would have taken on a completely different look, and there also would be a car of revolutionary design. George Salih, the winning chief mechanic for Lee Wallard in 1951 and the crew chief for Hanks these last two years, had been mulling over a design in his mind for four years.

Towing the second-placed Jones & Maley Special home to California after the race, Salih made a decision.

He would build that car.

Chapter 10:
"UPRIGHT" OR "LAYDOWN"?

Main photograph: Pat O'Connor leads at the start, with Fred Agabashian coming from the inside of row two to take second away from "rookie" Eddie Sachs.

Below: George Salih's revolutionary concept is to lay the Offenhauser engine virtually on its side.
Photograph: IMS

1957: Salih's dream

WHEN Freddie Agabashian scored his major upset by qualifying the "lay-down" Cummins Diesel for the pole in 1952, nobody had been more fascinated by the car's design than George Salih. The Keck/Kurtis "roadster" also had been of interest to him, and he began to consider the potential of laying an "Offy" over on its side. He discussed it with several friends, but most felt that while it certainly would achieve an even lower center of gravity, lubrication of the engine would pose too many problems.

The years rolled by, and Salih could not get the idea out of his mind. Chief mechanic for car owner Murrell Belanger for all of the AAA championship races between 1950 and 1953 (in addition to being a plant foreman at Meyer & Drake), George had cut back to competing in the "500" only in 1954, serving as chief mechanic for the Jones & Maley Kurtis "roadster," driven in 1955 and 1956 by Sam Hanks. Salih towed the car back to his home in Whittier, California, as soon as the race was over and immediately "prepped" it for the 1957 "500." He then turned his attention to some tubing he had

acquired and began to weld up a frame. During the next few weeks, he would invite people over to the house to show them what he was building, hoping that someone would become enthusiastic enough to want to be the car's owner. None did, but Salih couldn't stop.

Aided by his friend Howard Gilbert (later A. J. Foyt's engine man), Salih finished up the frame and then retained fabricator Quin Epperly to craft the bodywork. Still no buyer. There was, however, a prominent high-performance muffler specialist named Sandy Belond, who, while declining ownership, did agree to be the car's sponsor, for an amount believed to be quite a bit in excess of the typical amount for such an arrangement in those days. Hanks, who seriously had contemplated retiring after failing to win by such a narrow margin in 1956, changed his mind when he saw what Salih was building. Working at night after a full day at Meyer & Drake, and begging and borrowing whatever he could, George finished up the car. He had mortgaged his home, dipped into his teenage daughter's college fund, and fallen about $18,000 into debt. He entered the car himself and set off for Indianapolis, hoping against hope that he would be able to sell the car after he got there.

When Salih pulled into the racetrack in early May 1957, the front straight looked nothing like it had the last time he had seen it. Everything had been completely revamped. Gone was the Japanese-style pagoda, and in its place was a squared-off, glass-and-steel construction called the Master Control Tower. Either side of this were rows and rows of permanent seating. The old 1926 pagoda, so rickety in recent years that it would bend and sway in a high wind (and even a portly gentleman climbing the stairs would telegraph his impending arrival), had been demolished on June 20, 1956. The fire marshal finally breathed a sigh of relief, having wanted to condemn it in 1952 but allowed it to remain with only limited access.

The pit area had been completely modernized, now consisting of a pit lane which was separated from the racetrack itself. No longer would contestants come down the main straight during the race and simply pull over to make a pit stop at the side of the track. And no longer was the pit area merely to the south of where the pagoda had been located. Now, drivers making stops would drive just a short distance down the main straight after clearing turn four, and then jog left through a pit lane entrance which was several hundred yards north of the Master Control Tower. The pit lane was separated from the track itself by a grass verge and a low-sitting wall, so that crews working on cars in the pits would no longer

have to worry about race cars speeding past them on the track.

For over 40 years, the standard procedure during practice had been to fire up a car's engine outside of its individual garage, and then drive the car out through the pit gate, turn left, and head out onto the track. At the conclusion of the run, the driver would then either stop in the pit area or else drive straight back to the garage. Not anymore. From this point on, any car making a practice run would be required to depart from the pit lane, making it necessary to either push it back and forth between one and the other or else tow it. In no time at all, miniature tractors became part of a team's inventory.

The famous bridge across the backstretch, just north of turn two, also was gone, a three-lane tunnel now serving as the link between the inside nine holes of the golf course and the outside nine.

There was another rumor which turned out to be accurate, although a little premature. The little racetrack across the street was going to be razed to make way for a shopping center. The West Sixteenth Street Midget Speedway, as it was generally known, was a quarter-mile paved oval which had opened in May 1946. Midgets and various types of stock cars had raced there throughout each succeeding summer, but by far the biggest attraction was the annual Night Before the "500" Midget Races. Although there had long since been extreme cases of "early-bird" arrivals for the "500" (an ex-auto mechanic named Larry Bisceglia making a career out of it by parking outside the front gate up to *six weeks* in advance), the bulk of the traffic would begin assembling two or three days before the race. By the eve of May 29, the traffic on West 16th Street would be backed up for several miles towards downtown, those in line hoping for as advantageous a view of the track as possible from somewhere on the infield. Some of the locals felt as if they were prisoners in their own homes, peeking through their front curtains at the boisterous and partying out-of-towners camped along the sidewalk, in their front yards, and even on their porches. Others made the best of the situation by selling food and drinks, some locals turning their homes into veritable restaurants. For many years, a midway would be set up across the street from the track, complete with a Ferris wheel, roundabouts, sideshows, novelty acts, circus barkers, and just about every con game imaginable.

A quarter-mile racetrack, therefore, could hardly fail.

The "Night Before" promotion became a real extravaganza, eventually expanding to *three separate programs,* the first of

Inset above: The old pagoda has been replaced by the Master Control Tower, plus there is a brand-new pit lane, separated from the main straight by a wall. No longer is it permissible for drivers to fire up the engines in the garage area and then motor out through the gate. The cars must now be pushed to the pit lane and started from there.

Pat O'Connor, on the pole with chief mechanic Ray Nichels.
Photographs: IMS

which would start in the afternoon. There would be a full complement of "hot laps," qualifying, heats, semi-feature, and a main event, after which the spectators would be required to file out through the exits. Even while workers were scurrying through the bleachers to clean up the trash, the fans already would be standing in line at the ticket window and ready to purchase their tickets for the next program. About three hours later, they would go through the same procedure yet a third time, the checkered flag for "The Late Night Final" normally falling at about 2:30 A.M. There would then be just enough time to try to catch a couple of hours of slumber in one's automobile before an aerial bomb would signal the opening of the gates across the street. Perhaps the most remarkable performance ever witnessed at the little track was that by Clark "Shorty" Templeman in 1956. Having failed to qualify for the "500" that year, Templemen proceeded to pull off the virtually impossible feat of winning all three features: a 100-lapper, followed by a "150," followed by another "100." Also of note was that failing to qualify for the first two features, but placing 13th in the Late Night Final, was a 21-year-old from Houston, Texas, named A. J. Foyt, Jr.

The sad news that the track was going to be pulled down was indeed true, although it did get a brief stay of execution. The "Night Before the 500" was held again in 1958, even

though there was no midway this time, all permits having been denied. The track did, in fact, remain in place for another couple of years, but the bleachers were dismantled within weeks and there was no further racing activity.

The face of the area had changed quite a bit over the years, and West 16th Street was no longer a country road. There was still an abundance of trees, but many of them would start to disappear in the early 1960s. Even the race-day transportation by rail between the track and downtown was coming to an end, and while trains still would be rumbling through the neighborhood on into the 1970s, the race-day specials would cease after 1963.

It was around this time that law enforcement began to prohibit parking on the street for days in advance. They would keep the traffic moving until at some point on the eve of the race (normally anywhere between 7:00 P.M. and 10:00 P.M.), they would put up the first barricades and permit the line to form. The motorists would keep "cruising" and playing a game of "musical chairs," hoping they would be somewhere in the vicinity of the golf course when the decision was made to start the line.

On the other hand, there were new beginnings. Influenced by all of the pageantry leading up to the Kentucky Derby each year, the Five Hundred Festival Committee was formed in

spun out of turn four and hit the inside rail, caving in the tail and snuffing out his life. Heartbroken, Farina never drove again.

Sam Hanks qualified the Salih "lay-down" at a respectable 142.812 mph for 13th starting position, but Salih still was unable to land a buyer. Several people came awfully close, one car owner, Peter Schmidt, even writing out a check, but never handing it over. He would come to regret that.

No sooner had the race started than Hanks and Russo began moving to the front, Russo running second by lap 10, with Hanks fifth. Troy Ruttman and Pat O'Connor swapped the lead four times in 12 laps, at which point Ruttman had to drop out, while Russo blasted into the lead.

Hanks ran second for about 20 laps, but then a real battle began to shape up. Russo would have the advantage on the straights, but the little Salih car was demonstrating superior handling through the turns. Its engine was laid over 18 degrees from the horizontal, the hood (at a point just behind the front wheels) being only 22 inches from the ground. Hanks would close up through a turn, but then lose some distance on the next straight. It then got to the point where Hanks could even pass Russo through a turn, but he would be repassed soon after leaving it. The "repasses" kept occurring later and later until finally, Hanks was gaining enough through a turn that he was able to reach the next one before the Novi could catch him. The smallest car in the race was beating the most feared monster.

Russo began to fade, but kept going, eventually to finish fourth. It later transpired that there was a crack in the frame,

Below: Former winners at the Champion 100-Mile Per Hour dinner include Lee Wallard (1951), Johnnie Parsons (1950), Bill Holland (1949), Fred Frame (1932), Peter de Paolo (1925), and Tommy Milton (1921 and 1923).

Bottom: Almost 50 years after the construction of the track, a creek still flows into the grounds beneath the main straight and departs under the south short straight.
Photographs: IMS

1957, and a variety of celebrations and events were capped by a huge parade of floats and celebrities winding its way through downtown a couple of nights before the race. The parade continued to be an evening affair until 1973, when, following the 1971 decision by the United States Congress to change the recognition of Memorial Day to the last Monday in May, the parade was moved to Saturday afternoon, with the race, beginning in 1974, forever after to be scheduled on Sunday.

In an attempt to slow the speeds down somewhat, the engine sizes had been reduced slightly for 1957, unsupercharged engines being reduced from 4.5 liters to 4.2 (274 cubic inches to 256) and supercharged engines from 3 liters to 2.8 (183 cubic inches down to 170). As it turned out, it didn't make a lot of difference. Pat O'Connor won the pole at 143.948 mph, and Paul Russo was the fastest qualifier (on a later day) with a Novi at 144.817, two of his laps being over 145.

Giuseppe Farina, intent on having at least one "500" start before his career was over, had given up on the six-cylinder Ferrari and had gone ahead and ordered his own Kurtis–Offy. Keith Andrews, the 1954 Pikes Peak Hill Climb winner who had competed in the previous two Indianapolis races, was out in the car and trying to build it to speed for Farina when he

making the car harder and harder to handle. Hanks led for most of the rest of the way, his longtime friend Jim Rathmann being his chief opponent during the second half. The 1952 runner-up made a go of it in the late stages, until chief mechanic Jack Beckley gave him the signal to play it safe and protect second.

In one of the greatest upsets ever, Hanks won the race, knocking eight minutes from Bill Vukovich's record elapsed time from 1954, and raising the race average speed from 130.840 mph to 135.601.

So much for slowing down the cars.

The winner's share of the purse was a record-breaking $103,844, and Salih had people lining up to purchase the car. It was no longer for sale. Peter Schmidt, still with his filled-out check in his pocket, took it home, framed it, and placed it above his mantel.

Hanks, one of the most popular winners ever, was warmly greeted (even hugged) both by Rathmann and by third-placed Jimmy Bryan. In fact, Rathmann walked back to the garage with Sam and his wife, Alice, practically arm in arm. Because the door was still locked when Sam arrived there – Salih and the rest of the crew were caught up with well-wishers – Sam did a number of his post race interviews from Bryan's garage.

Hanks became the first person since Ray Harroun in 1911 to announce his retirement in Victory Lane, and he made it stick. He met a contractual obligation by finishing out the season driving USAC stock cars (finishing third in points) and then never raced again. By the following year, Sam had been named by Tony Hulman as director of racing, which was pretty much a month-of-May-only public-relations position. For the next six "500s," Sam would be driving the pace car.

George Salih needed a driver, and there was a good one already standing in the wings. Jimmy Bryan, who had won the National Championship in three out of the last four years (and been runner-up in the other, 1955), decided that he no longer wanted to race on the dirt tracks. He parted with Al Dean after four phenomenal seasons and signed with Salih, Dean replacing Bryan with 23-year-old "rookie" A. J. Foyt, Jr.

1958: The huge build up, and then....

Much pre-race attention in 1958 was centered upon the entry of the great five-time world champion, Juan Manuel Fangio. The Argentinian had witnessed the "500" in 1948 as a virtual unknown while on his way to competing in Europe for the first time. He had been fascinated by the "500" ever since and often expressed his interest in competing. Certain car owners sought his services, and there would be annual rumors as to what he might be driving. In March 1954, while in America to compete in the Sebring 12-Hours sports-car race in Florida, he had visited Kurtis–Kraft, and Meyer & Drake in Los Angeles. He had then flown to Indianapolis to meet with Wilbur Shaw, the two of them driving around the

track in a sports car. When Bob Sweikert took part in the 1956 Sebring event (sharing Jack Ensley's D-type Jaguar, which finished third), the shy and rather private Fangio, who spoke no English, sought him out. The two bonded, and through an interpreter, Fangio passed on numerous road-racing tips.

It was now 1958 and he was finally here, but things were not going well. Through the acquaintance of an engineer he had known at Alfa Romeo, Fangio had agreed to drive a Kurtis–Offy for a Dayton, Ohio, car owner, George Walther. He arrived early for practice, but it quickly became apparent that the world champion was having a struggle. There had been an inexplicable change of the team's chief mechanic since the previous year and, above all, the language barrier was a problem. Several of the car owners certainly knew who Fangio was, as did many of the drivers, although he was treated somewhat as a curiosity. With upwards of two dozen people crowding around the car at times and trying to offer advice, poor Fangio would sit in the cockpit, stare at the floor, and project the unmistakable impression that he would just as soon be somewhere else. One day, during such a scene, he looked up, and to his delight, saw Mauri Rose standing there. Recognizing the man he had seen win in 1948, he grinned and held out both hands. Before long, Rose was down on his knees and drawing diagrams of the track in chalk on the pit lane, Fangio looking over the side of the cockpit and nodding in understanding as Mauri traced in "the groove."

Fangio finally reached a respectable 142 mph, although his speeds would vary from one day to the next. He made a couple of side trips, during which time the rumor would be that he wasn't coming back. One day, an interpreter went into the Novi garage, telling Jean Marcenac that Fangio, who had been fascinated by the front-drive Novi in 1948, would like to take one of the cars out for a few laps. No driver was assigned to Paul Russo's sister car, and Marcenac, who had met Fangio at the French Grand Prix the year before, nearly fell over himself in the scramble to accommodate. Fangio took a few laps, got up to 135, and returned with a big grin on his face. Lew Welch, who had tried to hire him two years earlier, promptly offered him a staggering $20,000 to qualify the car, but Fangio, regrettably, *couldn't* do it. George Walther had been only too happy to let him go, but it came to light that Fangio had signed a lucrative and exclusive contract with British Petroleum, a company which had no involvement at Indianapolis. They paid him well and were not about to let him run anyone else's product. By the time the first qualifying day arrived, Fangio had already left for good.

Most of the headlines during the previous week had been grabbed by the daily speed battle between two unlikely contenders. During the winter, A. J. Watson had built two new cars for car owner John Zink, plus another which Watson had entered himself, strictly for the purpose of selling it in May. The building of this extra car did not go down at all well with Zink, who felt that Watson should have been working solely for him. The extra car was purchased by trucking magnate Lee Elkins, who turned it over for "test-hopping" to Jim Rathmann's older brother, Dick, who was already entered in another car but not lapping as fast as he would like to be. Mechanic Floyd Trevis took the Offy engine from the team's dirt-track car, placed it in the Watson "roadster," and in something like half a dozen laps, Dick Rathmann was running up near the track record.

Going equally fast in one of Zink's cars was the mysterious Ed Elisian, a fellow most people held at arm's length. Hardly the finest role model the sport ever had, he was a compulsive gambler who was heavily in debt and holding a fistful of citations for various traffic violations. He had both good days and bad days on racetracks, was completely unpredictable, and was in the unfortunate position of having been blamed (for the most part unfairly) for several high-profile accidents. He had idolized Bill Vukovich, and always had tried to duplicate the driving style of the late two-time "500" winner. Now, with one of the finest cars at the track at his disposal, perhaps he could emulate his idol, win the race, and then be able to pay off all of his numerous debts.

Every day for a solid week, between the hours of 5:00 P.M.

Far left: After several years of rumored participation, the soon-to-retire five-time world champion Juan Manuel Fangio finally arrives as an entered driver. Binding contractual problems will prevent him from making a qualifying attempt.

Below left: Of all the Hollywood actresses who participated in the race festivities on behalf of Borg–Warner between 1947 and 1959, insiders seem to have been most impressed by the "homespun girl next door" qualities of Miss Shirley MacLaine, then merely a starlet.

Below center: Four legendary chief mechanics: A. J. Watson, Ray Nichels, George Bignotti, and George Salih.

Bottom: "Steady" Johnny Boyd has to make a late stop for a right rear tire, which drops him from second to third after having led 18 laps during the second half. He will eventually drive in 12 "500s" and place sixth or better in four of them.
Photographs: IMS

and 6:00 P.M., when the sun-baked track was beginning to cool, mechanics on other teams would lay down their tools and then turn their attention to Rathmann and Elisian going out alternately to engage in a classic display of one-upmanship. Elisian had the best lap of all, an unofficial 148.148 mph.

The second person to go out on the opening day of qualifications, Elisian broke the track record the first time around with 146.341 mph. He broke it again on the third lap, upping his speed to 146.508. Laps two and four, however, both were at 145, the final lap being "only" 145.114. Even so, his four-lap average of 145.926 mph broke Pat Flaherty's 1956 record. About three quarters of an hour later, it was the turn of Dick Rathmann in the car Watson had sold to Lee Elkins. Rathmann was much smoother, and while none of his laps came within half a mile per hour of Elisian's single-lap mark, his four-lap average of 145.974 mph was good enough to break the record. The day ended with Rathmann on the pole and Zink teammates Elisian and Jimmy Reece starting next to him. Zink was not at all happy about being knocked off the pole by a car his "employee" had built during his spare time.

This was the second year for the new pit area, and in spite of some problems in 1957, the starting procedure used then remained unchanged. Instead of lining up the cars on the main straight and then having them depart behind the pace car, it had been decided instead to line them up next to their individual pits. The engines would be fired and then the pace car, on the track, would come down the main straight. As it passed by the pit lane's exit, virtually at the entrance to turn one, the field would be pushed off in single file and then, once underway, would form into the rows of three. Dating all the way back to 1911, the pace car had always pulled off to release the field to the flagman at the end of the very first lap. Starting in 1957, a second lap had been added, the first now referred to as the "parade lap," with the second being the pace lap proper.

Just as there had been a problem in 1957, so there was again. That time, "rookie" Elmer George, who was to have started ninth, left a little later than some of the others and was trying to get to his position when he hit the tail of the car driven by Eddie Russo, Paul's nephew. Both cars were eliminated before the race had even started. The 1958 problem began when, due to a miscue, the cars of Rathmann, Elisian, and Reece were dispatched before the pace car came by. The

What is fully expected to be an outstanding race is all but ruined on the very first lap by a huge accident which develops in turn three. It eliminates eight cars, causing the delay of several more, and taking the life of Pat O'Connor. In two of the shots, Jerry Unser, who was lucky to escape with a dislocated shoulder, can be seen vaulting the outer wall. The accident began when Ed Elisian (number 5) spun and was hit by Dick Rathmann (number 73). In just one month's time, the Elisian car will have been repaired and will win all three heats of the Monza (Italy) 500 in the hands of Rathmann's brother, Jim.

Photographs: IMS

three drivers went as slowly as they could, hoping the pace car would catch up. Once on the backstretch, the three drivers then, through hand signals, agreed among themselves that they would race around and approach the field from the rear. When the pace car came through turn four for what should have been the start, the front row still was not in place. The pack picked up speed – led by row two – and at the last minute, the three members of the front row sprinted past on either side in an attempt to take their positions. It was decided, at the very last second, to call off the start and send the field around for another lap. This was the very first race "call" for a new chief steward this year, former driver and car builder Harlan Fengler having taken over from another former driver, Harry McQuinn, who had held the post since 1953.

At the end of the next lap, the green finally was waved, with Dick Rathmann already accelerating away from the field. Just as he enjoyed a lead of many car-lengths going into turn one, so Elisian was far ahead of Reece. On the backstretch, Elisian charged after Rathmann and, to the surprise of many, caught and passed him before the entrance to turn three. As he led into the turn, the tail of Elisian's car came around and the car slid sideways for a second or two, giving the impression he might be able to save it. Instead, it came around anyway. Rathmann aimed straight for the car, since the old rule of the racetrack was, "Aim for the spinning car, because when

you get there, it won't be." That didn't work every time. Rathmann, believing Elisian would spin down into the infield, tried for the outside. Instead, Elisian's car slid tailfirst for the outer wall, collecting Rathmann in the process. The cars locked together and hit the outer wall in unison. In the meantime, Jimmy Reece tapped his brake and was hit from behind by Bob Veith, who in turn was hit by fifth-place-starting Pat O'Connor.

A huge accident developed behind them, involving up to fifteen cars in varying degrees. Even cars not directly involved had to take evasive action by driving through the infield, thereby making the accident appear even larger than it already was. Completely over the third-turn wall went "rookie" Jerry Unser, who, amazingly, escaped with only a dislocated shoulder. He was released from the infield hospital not long after, with his arm in a sling.

Pat O'Connor was not so fortunate. His car landed upside down after running over the cars of Veith and Reece and then bounced back onto its wheels. The very popular O'Connor— perhaps as highly regarded as any driver at the track at that time – did not survive the accident, leading many hundreds of fans to leave early when they learned the sad news over the public address system.

It took 25 minutes to clean up the aftermath, after which an excellent race took place. Few, however, really enjoyed it. The battle was mainly between Jimmy Bryan in George Salih's

Inset bottom left: A spinout on lap 148 ends the run of "rookie" Anthony Joseph Foyt, Jr., but he will return, eventually to extend his record of "500" starts to an incredible 35 in a row. He will also become the first to win the "500" four times.
Photograph: IMS

"sidewinder" and two similar cars Quin Epperly had built over the winter, driven by veteran Tony Bettenhausen and a very impressive rookie named George Amick. The new Epperly cars varied slightly, in that whereas Salih's engine was 18 degrees from the horizontal, Quin's engines were laid completely flat. Surprisingly, when Bettenhausen came around at the head of the pack on lap 19, it was the first time he had ever led, in spite of having come literally within inches in 1956.

During the second half of the race, Johnny Boyd came into the mix and ran second for well over 100 miles, trying to get by on two stops to the three of Bryan and Amick. He had to duck in to change the right rear wheel only 18 laps from the finish, ending up third. Bryan held on to win by less than 28 seconds over Amick, who was unanimously voted "rookie of the year." Bryan rolled into Victory Lane, having backed up his three national titles in four years with a win in the "500." He should have been on top of the world, but he wasn't. Pat O'Connor had been one of his closest friends.

There was much furor and controversy during the next few days. Elisian had been suspended by USAC, temporarily reinstated, and then suspended again. He was charged with poor judgment, and indeed, the theory was that he had been trying to emulate Vukovich and was seizing upon this incredible opportunity to try to turn his troubled life around. He had entered turn three just as hard as he had throughout much of the month, but evidently without taking into consideration a very important fact. Whereas before he had been doing so with a light load of fuel, he was now carrying a full tank of 75-plus gallons, and it is believed that the effects of the extra weight must have taken him by surprise. Rathmann was most critical of Elisian, even to the point of saying he would never forgive him. That didn't last long. They had been friends for several years, and what was not generally known was that in spite of the great rivalry built up by the press over the daily "speed battle" earlier in the month, Rathmann and Elisian were actually sharing the same digs. They had been traveling to races together for some time, and this would continue as soon as Rathmann calmed down.

The new United States Auto Club, a very democratic organization in which every phase of the sport had at least one "voice" on the board of directors, had already taken on the issue of safety, and during the next few years, extraordinary advancements were to be made. Even before the O'Connor accident, roll bars behind the drivers' heads had been announced as becoming mandatory for 1959.

1959: The birth of the flying W's

No sooner had 1959 practice begun than another accident took place. Jerry Unser, who had survived going over the wall in 1958, was out practicing on May 2 when he hit the wall after spinning through turn four and his car took fire. Although he did not appear to be that badly injured at first, he had received burns on his arms. Rather than wearing a uniform, he had been dressed only in slacks and a short-sleeved shirt, which was still driver's choice at that time. Complications set in, his condition worsened, and two weeks later, on May 17, Unser passed away. The use of fire-treated uniforms became

mandatory at that point.

On May 19, there was another accident, this time involving a "rookie" named Bob Cortner. He, too, succumbed to his injuries.

On the pole was Johnny Thomson, driving a Lujie Lesovsky creation which employed the "lay-down" concept, but with the engine laid over on its right side and the cockpit on the left. Thomson's four-lap speed of 145.908 mph was just under Dick Rathmann's record from 1958, but his third lap of 146.532 broke Elisian's single-lap mark.

Thomson led only the first four laps before Rodger Ward, who had made a blazing start from sixth, came through to take over.

Ward was driving for a brand-new team. Robert Wilke, a racing enthusiast from Milwaukee, Wisconsin, had sponsored a number of cars over the years through Leader Cards, Inc., a very successful company owned by his family. Wilke, a collector of classic sports cars and a onetime distributor for Kurtis–Kraft midgets, wanted to start his own team and make

Far left: Winner Jimmy Bryan is hounded – and even briefly headed – for much of the race by the very impressive "rookie" George Amick. While the engine in Bryan's George Salih-built car is tilted 18 degrees from the horizontal, constructor Quin Epperly has taken the concept a stage further for Amick's 1958 car and has laid the engine completely flat.

Bottom left: No, a Hollywood press agent has not "created" the macho Jimmy Bryan. The three-time national champion and 1958 "500" winner – a great practical joker, and a boy at heart – is the real thing. Casual spectators are astonished and longtime fans delighted when Bryan comes down for the checkered flag in 1958. Just as has been his habit in other events for years, he jams one knee under the steering wheel and acknowledges by raising *both* arms in the air.

Inset below left: Johnny Thomson, the bashful 1959 pole winner, chats with track owner Tony Hulman.

Inset below near left: Jim Rathmann, three times a bridesmaid and not yet a bride.

Bottom: The perfectly aligned 1959 field comes down for one of the most beautiful starts ever.
Photographs: IMS

Right: Joyful Rodger Ward is greeted by his wife, Jo (left), and by Erin O'Brien, who will be the last of the Hollywood actresses to be imported by Borg–Warner Corporation.

Below: This fine aerial view from 1959 clearly shows the West 16th Street Midget Speedway across from IMS's turn two in the bottom right-hand corner. The already shut-down quarter-mile track is being used for parking cars, and will soon be razed to make way for a shopping center.

Below right: Another unique Speedway tradition – from the early 1950s until 1961 – would take place a day or two before the race when representatives of the Filter Queen Company would actually vacuum the bricks on the main straight.

In a preview of their classic 1960 battle, Rodger Ward and Jim Rathmann spend numerous laps racing within feet of each other.
Photographs: IMS

it a winner. He contacted A. J. Watson, well aware that John Zink, by whom Watson was still employed, was not happy about Watson having built the extra car which had ended up on the pole. The choice of driver took several different turns, and at one point, Leader Card Racers was going to field a two-car team with Jim Rathmann and Rodger Ward. Because Rathmann still felt an allegiance to Lindsey Hopkins, for whom he had driven since 1956, it was decided to sell the second car to Hopkins and run Ward only.

No sooner was the race underway than it became a spirited contest between Thomson and these two. There were

eleven lead changes before one-quarter distance, a fourth driver having thrown his hat into the ring: Pat Flaherty, the 1956 winner who had suffered a serious arm injury later that season and been out of action for two years. This was his first "500" appearance since his win. He led three times for a total of eleven laps, and was soldiering along in fourth position when he spun and hit the wall on the main straight with 38 laps still to go. Several friends felt that he had simply run out of "personal horsepower" and perhaps should have taken a relief driver.

Rodger Ward did not give up the lead after lap 85 and held Jim Rathmann at bay by just over 23 seconds at the finish. It was the third time Rathmann had finished as a runner-up, and the second time in the last three races. Johnny Thomson was not that far behind, in third.

Ward and Rathmann had made three stops apiece, each of which were completed in less than 30 seconds, a 22-second stop by Ward being the quickest. One contributing factor was the incorporation by Watson of a device car builder Eddie Kuzma had pioneered the year before on a new J.C. Agajanian-owned creation which Troy Ruttman had been unable to qualify. The moment the new Watson cars (and a few others) came to a halt, a crew member would insert the nozzle of a pressurized air hose into a port in the side of the car and the prongs of a pneumatic onboard jack would be pushed down, raising the car into the air. Upon completion of a wheel change, the crew member merely needed to remove the nozzle in order for the car to "drop."

The 1959 win was very much "a turning of the corner" for Ward, who was competing in the "500" for the ninth consecutive time. Eighth in 1956 had been his only previous finish. He had arrived as a rather brash and cocky "rookie" in 1951, and soon gained a reputation for enjoying the nightlife. He would win races, but he was involved in a couple of high-profile accidents for which he was unfairly blamed. On the night of the 1955 "500," a few hours after the fatal accident involving Bill Vukovich, Ward sat alone in the darkened grandstands and pledged to change his approach to life. He remarried, sharpened up his wardrobe, started going to church, and, in spite of already being better than most of his colleagues at addressing an audience, took a course in public speaking. He won three USAC national championship races in 1957 and two more in 1958, including the prestigious Milwaukee 200, the latter grabbing the attention of Bob Wilke. Ward never did lose his swagger, but at 38, he was beginning to be looked upon as an elder statesman and a spokesman. He was also on the cusp of compiling an amazing record at Indianapolis and in USAC championship racing.

RODGER WARD

The transformation was amazing. Rodger Ward (January 10, 1921 – July 5, 2004), once a hell-raising, ragged-edge, leather jacket-wearing hot-rodder, who blew up cars left, right, and center, had evolved into a well-dressed, well-spoken, cagey "bring 'em home" elder statesman, who attended black-tie social functions and represented his colleagues at committee meetings. Between 1951 and 1955, Ward had no finishes at all in the "500," and by 1958 had registered only one eighth-place showing. In the six-race run with A. J. Watson-wrenched Leader Card Specials between 1959 and 1964, however, he was never lower than fourth, as he placed first, second, third, first, fourth and second in consecutive years.

Even with that, it doesn't require much stretch of the imagination to see him as a possible FIVE-time winner, the events of 1960, 1964, and 1966 all potentially having been within his reach. Placing second in 1960's all-time classic, he had been forced to slow down in the final couple of laps because of tire wear after an incredible two-man struggle for 250 miles with Jim Rathmann. Had he not stalled on his first pit stop and lost valuable time, he would not have been in the position of abusing his tires in the effort to claw back to the front.

Had he not been confused in 1964 by a last-minute altered installation of a lean-rich fuel lever in his cockpit, he might have been able to get by on two or three stops instead of being forced to make *five* and ultimately fall too far behind twice-stopping winner A. J. Foyt. And had he not become dis-

gusted during the 1966 race and pulled in with "handling problems" (which were later questioned), he could well have benefitted from the numerous difficulties encountered by the leaders and come home first. To Ward should go the credit for convincing Jack Brabham and John Cooper they should try a rear-engined Cooper at Indianapolis.

That came out of a friendship born at Sebring in 1959, when Ward tried to take on the Formula One set with a USAC midget car at the season-closing Grand Prix of the United States. To Ward should go the credit for the design of the road course and the five-eighths-mile oval at Indianapolis Raceway Park in 1961. He even rode the grader while the oval was being laid down.

He famously won a Formula Libre race at Lime Rock, Connecticut, in 1959, beating a field of sports cars and single-seaters with a standard upright front-engined midget, but he also drove a BRM in the 1963 U.S. Grand Prix at Watkins Glen.

If there is a statistic about Ward which is even more impressive than that of his "500" record between 1959 and 1964, it would be his USAC National Championship rankings. After placing fifth in 1958, he won the title in 1959, lost out to a young A. J. Foyt in the last race of 1960, was barely nudged out of second by Eddie Sachs (and behind Foyt) in 1961, returned to win the title (beating Foyt) in 1962, and then was runner-up to the Texan in 1963 and 1964. "You know what?" chuckled Rodger after having been introduced at a function with this summary, "If it hadn't been for Foyt, I would have had a hell of a record."

Above: Jim Hurtubise, the sensational rookie of 1960, turns out to be quite the prognosticator. After almost breaking the 150-mph "barrier" in qualifying, he tells the fans to wait until next year when his friend Parnelli Jones will be here. In fact, Parnelli is already here, tagging along with "Herk" and checking things out. That's the legendary future winner and record breaker over on the left, in the blue sweater.
Photograph: IMS

1960: It's Rathmann and Ward! Rathmann and Ward!

Onto the scene in 1960 rocketed a sensational "rookie" named Jim Hurtubise. The popular Eddie Sachs, who had qualified in the middle of the front row in both 1957 and 1959, had just replaced young A. J. Foyt on the Dean Van Lines team and captured the pole position with new records. His four-lap average of 146.592 mph was topped by a single lap of 147.251.

During the week which followed, young Hurtubise began turning some very impressive times, and on the morning of the final qualifying day (the third day had been completely rained out) several crew members caught him on their stopwatches at over 148. Surely they had made a mistake. They had not! Hurtubise, who had just come off of several summers of dirt-track sprint car racing, had been experimenting with broad-sliding techniques around the Speedway, and they were working. First off the line when the track was open for qualifications, his first lap was 148.002 mph, a new track record. It held up for just over one minute. He knocked off a full half a second on the second trip around for over *one hundred and forty-nine*. Even *that* wasn't it. Lap three was 149.601, and those on hand came to the realization that the next lap could well exceed the "magic" 150. He didn't quite make it. He bobbled, gathered it up, and *still* recorded the third-fastest lap in history at 149.402. His four-lap average of 149.056 mph beat the Sachs record by four seconds and two and a half miles per hour.

"You think *that* was something," laughed a most prophetic Hurtubise, in reference to his close friend and rival who was standing discreetly in the background, "Wait until next year when my friend Parnelli Jones gets here."

Hurtubise, who had to start back in 23rd, did make it up to fifth at one point during the race and was running eighth when an oil leak forced him out with 15 laps remaining. He was the clear winner of the Stark & Wetzel Rookie of the Year award.

Up ahead of Hurtubise had been the greatest sustained two-man battle in the history of the event. For the entire second half of the race, Ward and Jim Rathmann, the one–two finishers of the previous year, were never any more than a few feet apart from each other in a purely classic contest. There were a record 29 lead changes (still unbroken through 2006), of which the last 14 were strictly between these two.

Inset right: The team of driver Eddie Sachs, Chief Mechanic Clint Brawner, and car owner Al Dean (not to mention the Offenhauser engine) makes a formidable combination.
Photograph: IMS

There had been a massive traffic jam on race morning, and the entire front row was delayed in getting to the track. In brief summary, pole sitter Sachs was given a lift by a motorcycle policeman, Sachs sitting in the sidecar with his wife on his lap; number-two starter Jim Rathmann, realizing he had loaned all of the vehicles to which he had access to friends, *walked* over from his hotel; and Ward, outside front row, became ensnarled in traffic north of the track, left his car in charge of his wife, and trotted down Georgetown Road to the "credentials" gate until being picked up shortly thereafter by friend John Conkle, who delivered Rodger to the garage area in the Conkle Funeral Home ambulance.

Minutes later, Ward and Sachs were fighting for the lead in the race, Rathmann right behind them. Troy Ruttman edged ahead a couple of times, and Johnny Thomson led for ten laps. A key moment came when Ward stalled at the completion of his first pit stop. He was stationary for one minute, which by current standards was interminable. During the late 1930s and through to the early 1950s, cars using nonsupercharged engines typically could get by on one pit stop, with one minute in duration being excellent. As the speeds picked up and tire wear began necessitating a second and even a third stop (coupled with the fact that the elapsed time between first- and second-place finishers was now typically in the range of 20 seconds), strategists realized they needed to devise ways of saving time *while* they were stopping. The result of much preplanning and plenty of practice was a beautifully choreographed virtual ballet, in which a crew would have their man away in less than 20 seconds.

The stall by Ward put him half a minute behind the leaders, and he spent the next hour catching up. He took the lead again at lap 123, realizing, of course, that he had put undue stress on his tires. But the cagey veteran had a plan. There

were no two-way radios being used in those days, and no spotters, the only source of communication being a pit board informing the driver of his position, what lap he was on, when to pit, and so forth. When Ward caught up with Rathmann, he put his plan into play. He knew that Jim liked to race for the

Below: The famed Gasoline Alley as it appears in 1960.
Photograph: IMS

Center left: The Purdue University Band marches on the still-bricked main straight on race morning. In less than 18 months' time, the bricks will be covered over with asphalt.

Near left: The strip of grass next to the pit wall is considered "off limits" except to participants, and Eddie Sachs uses the privacy during a lull to take a nap.
Photographs: IMS

lead, but once there would tend to slow down very slightly. Rodger would trade back and forth, always aware that the pace could be reduced slightly by allowing Jim to lead. Years later, he would confide, "Although I was running second, I felt as if I was controlling the race." Everything was going along fine until his pit board apprised him that Johnny Thomson (third behind the two of them the year before) was beginning to catch up. It became necessary to increase the speed, and Rodger later stated that he believed this cost him the race. Thomson was forced to back off in the closing laps as he nursed home a sick engine and dropped to fifth. But the damage had been done. Ward was leading with only four laps to go when the white cord began to show through his right front tire. He could have stopped for a change, but thousands of miles on the Speedway in recent years as Firestone's number one test driver told him he could slow down and nurse it home. This he did as Rathmann, who but for this development might well have been the Speedway's only four-time runner-up, sailed home to win. Ward, running against the inside wall at a reduced rate, rolled home just over 12 seconds later. (While there were eventually to be three drivers who would win the "500" four times, through 2006 there had never been a driver who finished second four times).

At the victory banquet the following night, retired driver Fred Agabashian, serving as master of ceremonies, jokingly suggested Rathmann and Ward be named co-winners.

Rathmann was greeted in Victory Lane, not by a Hollywood actress, but rather by Miss Julie Pratt, an Indiana University college student from Indianapolis. Starting in 1959, the Five Hundred Festival Committee had decided to choose a queen and court from 33 finalists, all of whom would have to be college students from within the state and attending Indiana colleges. In 1960, it was decided that the queen should participate in the victory ceremonies, and thus it has been ever since. Another tradition began when an Olympic-style wreath was draped around Rathmann's shoulders.

Earlier in the day there had been a tragedy, one which finally brought to an end a famous (but dangerous) race track tradition management had been trying to do away with for years. Some time around the late 1930s, a few of the more imaginative infield spectators had begun arriving with scaffolding for the purpose of erecting their own personal grandstands. A straightforward platform on top of, or next to, a vehicle, sufficed to begin with but it wasn't long before more elaborate constructions would spring up, boasting two, three and four floors and more. Everybody would try to outdo everybody else. Within an hour or two of the gates having opened on race morning, a veritable city of multi-story constructions would have materialized. With liability having become more of an issue by the early 1950s, there was an effort to stop this practice, but fans still found ways to sneak in the materials they needed.

In 1960, a few enterprising individuals erected a five-story job on the back of a pick up truck stationed right next to the fence approximately at the exit of the third turn. By the time the 33 starters rolled away for the parade lap, an estimated 60 people were on it, everything being fine until they leaned forward to watch the cars come through the turn. The stand, which had not been mired properly, began to lean and then topple. It went over completely, crushing the wire fence and sending the tangled mass of occupants over on to the infield grass near the edge of the track's surface. Many of them were injured, two being fatalities and the irony being that both were members of the enterprising team which had built it.

That was the end of the homebuilt scaffolding on the infield.

Because neither of the Novis had qualified (for the second year in a row), the entire field had been powered by Offenhauser engines. The "roadster," for the moment, was still the car to beat and the Offenhauser engine was still "king," but growing opposition was just around the corner.

This was the very last year in which every single car in the lineup had its engine mounted in *front* of the driver.

The entire look of the Indianapolis 500-Mile Race was about to undergo major changes.

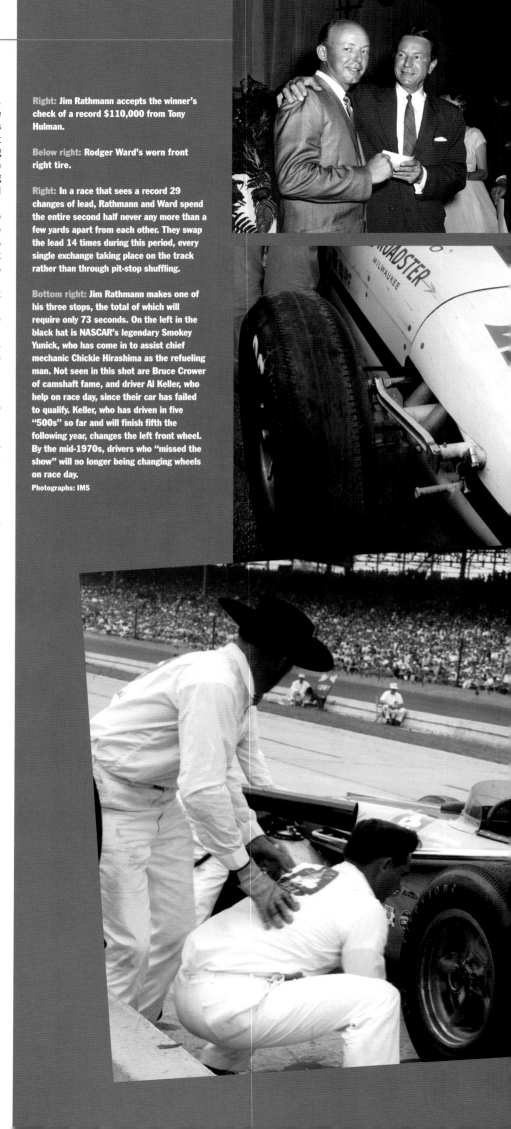

Right: Jim Rathmann accepts the winner's check of a record $110,000 from Tony Hulman.

Below right: Rodger Ward's worn front right tire.

Right: In a race that sees a record 29 changes of lead, Rathmann and Ward spend the entire second half never any more than a few yards apart from each other. They swap the lead 14 times during this period, every single exchange taking place on the track rather than through pit-stop shuffling.

Bottom right: Jim Rathmann makes one of his three stops, the total of which will require only 73 seconds. On the left in the black hat is NASCAR's legendary Smokey Yunick, who has come in to assist chief mechanic Chickie Hirashima as the refueling man. Not seen in this shot are Bruce Crower of camshaft fame, and driver Al Keller, who help on race day, since their car has failed to qualify. Keller, who has driven in five "500s" so far and will finish fifth the following year, changes the left front wheel. By the mid-1970s, drivers who "missed the show" will no longer being changing wheels on race day.
Photographs: IMS

JIM RATHMANN

Jim Rathmann must have breathed a huge sigh of relief during the final two laps of the classic 1960 Indianapolis 500. Had not a worn right front tire forced Rodger Ward to back off after almost two solid hours of back-and-forth, wheel-to-wheel racing, he might have been able to edge Rathmann and repeat his 1959 victory.

Had that happened, Rathmann would have been in the unenviable position of having finished second for the *fourth* time. He had already been runner-up to Troy Ruttman in 1952, to Sam Hanks in 1957, and to Ward in 1959. Instead, he was finally able to realize an ambition cherished since boyhood. Born in Los Angeles on July 16, 1928, young Richard Rathmann "fudged" his age in order to start racing hot rods at age 16, doing so by swapping identities with his older brother, James, who, as "Dick" Rathmann, would win the "500" pole in 1958.

Thus, Richard Rathmann became "Jim," an identity he retains to this day. An entrepreneur from his earliest days, he graduated from an ever-expanding paper route to being the proprietor of his own hot rod shop at a very early age. Claiming to be 24 when, in fact, he had not yet turned 21, "Jim" made his Indianapolis 500 debut in 1949 and finished 11th. He developed into an outstanding driver on paved tracks, winning the Milwaukee 200 in 1957.

In 1958, he won all three legs of the triple-stage 500-mile race at Monza, Italy, averaging a startling 166.722 mph.

In April 1959, he was victorious in the first and only USAC National Championship car race ever held at the then brand-new Daytona International Speedway, where the speeds were even faster. He completed the 100 miles in just a little over 35 minutes, his average speed being an astonishing 170.261 mph. Photographs and film footage of Rathmann having just won a race do not accurately portray his character.

Standing in the winner's enclosure, he appears to be almost bored with the situation, gently waving a hand at waist level, but either barely smiling or looking virtually expressionless.

He was (and is), in fact, easy-going, friendly, and a major-league practical joker. Owner of a huge Cadillac and Oldsmobile dealership in Melbourne, Florida, Rathmann became very close friends with Gus Grissom, Alan Shepherd, Gordon Cooper, Pete Conrad, and others among the pioneer astronauts.

At the time of his retirement from racing in 1964, he had completed 2,295 laps in "500" competition, and was within less than one full race of taking over the lead in that category. Only Cliff Bergere (2,452) and Mauri Rose (2,420) had completed more laps.

PART 2
FRONT TO BACK
1961
2006
BY RICK SHAFFER

Chapter 11
THERE WAS CLEARLY CHANGE IN THE WIND

---1961: Roadster's Last Great Epic Duel?

FEW may have considered it at the time, but as pre-race ceremonies unfolded for the 45th Indianapolis 500, everyone was getting a view of the past, the present and the future.

The past was represented by the ceremonial lap taken by Ray Harroun and the Marmon Wasp on the 50th anniversary of his victory in the inaugural Indianapolis 500 of 1911. Joining him were former track owner and 500-mile race starter Eddie Rickenbacker, who drove a 1914 Duesenberg, and 1924 runner-up Earl Cooper, who drove the Stutz he had raced at Indianapolis in 1919.

As the 33 cars were being rolled onto the front straightaway, 32 front-engined roadsters that had been the mainstay of Indianapolis car racing since 1953 represented the present. One was totally different – it was a rear-engine design that was based on a European Formula One car. Its driver was Jack Brabham, who had qualified it a respectable 13th on the grid.

No one was giving this entry a serious chance and if nothing else, the car was something of an oddity. However, it was clearly representing the future of the sport.

As had been the case throughout the history of the race, getting to the Race Day was a month-long process of practice and qualifying.

On the heels of two straight Rodger Ward-Jim Rathmann epics, the 1961 Indianapolis 500 was hopefully going to provide more of the same. It certainly had the ingredients for another epic race.

Rathmann and Ward were back. So were national champion A.J. Foyt and defending 500 pole position winner Eddie Sachs. Rathmann would be piloting a Watson-Offenhauser prepared by Smokey Yunick. Ward, the winner in 1959, was returning with the Leader Card Racers team and a car pre-pared by A.J. Watson.

Foyt was wheeling a George Bignotti-prepared, Floyd Trevis-built Watson copy, beautifully turned out in Bowes Seal Fast's red, black and mother-of-pearl white livery. Sachs' mount was a Wayne Ewing-built Watson copy prepared by Clint Brawner and owned by moving van magnate Al Dean. Neither driver, chief mechanic or team had ever won racing's biggest prize, but both operations were more than capable of a break-through victory.

Two-time national champion Tony Bettenhausen figured to be a force in Lindsey Hopkins' Epperly-Offenhauser. Another Epperly driver of note was Jim Hurtubise, who smashed the track record as a rookie the previous year (149.056 mph). Norm Demler, whose car had finished second in 1958 and third in 1960, was hoping Hurtubise could give him his first victory at Indianapolis.

J.C. Agajanian, the winning owner in 1952, was seeking his second 500 victory with promising rookie Parnelli Jones. The Hoover Motor Express team pinned its hopes on a two-pronged effort with Epperly-Offenhausers for veteran Don Branson and rookie Bobby Marshman.

And there was that other rookie named Brabham.

Brabham was at the wheel of the Kimberly's Cooper-Climax Special. Based on the "lowline" Cooper Formula One car that had dominated the Grand Prix scene in 1960, Brabham was driving the Cooper T-54 built exclusively for the 500 and complete with a slightly offset suspension for the Speedway's left-hand turns. The car had a longer wheelbase than its F1 counterpart and its 2.5-liter Coventry Climax had been bored to 2.7 liters for Indianapolis and the engine was slightly canted to help in weight distribution. It also featured two items unheard of in F1 – a rear nerf bar and rollbar behind the cockpit. Rollbars had been mandatory at Indianapolis since 1959. However, it was two other aspects that made Brabham's car stand out.

The first was that the car was painted British racing green despite the long-held superstition against the color green in American racing. More importantly, the Climax engine in Brabham's Cooper was behind the driver. Although rear-engined (or mid-engined) cars had competed at the Speedway between 1939 and 1947, none of the cars had gone beyond 47 laps and none had been entered since 1951. While the placement of the Cooper-Climax's engine made it unique in 1961, it was not the first, but as history would show, it would not be the last.

In fact, it wasn't the only rear-engined car in the 1961 entry. John Zink, owner of the cars that won the 500 in 1955 and '56, entered a rear-engined design that was to be powered by a turbine! The chassis was at the track, but the engine never arrived and the car never turned a wheel.

In one of the sport's ironies, it was Ward who suggested the idea of running at Indianapolis to Brabham and team owner John Cooper. Fresh from winning the 500 and USAC's National Championship, Ward showed a degree of versatility by capturing a Formula Libre race at Lime Rock, Connecticut, in the most unlikely mount – a Kurtis-Offenhauser designed for USAC's Midget Division.

With the victory in hand, Ward headed to Sebring, Florida, to run in the inaugural United States Grand Prix, the final event on the 1959 Formula One World Championship calendar. Ward was confident he could win. He reasoned that the car's cornering speed would more than compensate for the horsepower advantage that the F1 cars possessed on the straightaways. Ward quickly learned he was wrong and qualified more than 43 seconds slower than the pole position winner Stirling Moss. Impressed with the cornering speed of the F1 cars, Ward befriended Brabham and Cooper and urged them to try Indianapolis.

A year later they took him up on the offer and headed to the Speedway, where Brabham tested his 1960 title-winning

Cooper T-53 prior to the season-ending USGP in Riverside, Cal. A number of 500 drivers, including Ward, gathered to watch the proceedings and Brabham left them impressed with several laps topping 144 mph. Such an average for four qualifying laps at Indianapolis would have landed him in the third or fourth row for the 1960 race. Ward was permitted to test the car as well and came into the pits impressed with the handling characteristics but aware of the shortcomings in the horsepower department. During the visit, Cooper and Brabham were also introduced to wealthy businessman Jim Kimberly who offered to underwrite the project.

Interestingly, Brabham began his racing career driving American-style midgets on dirt tracks in his native Australia, before moving to Europe and ultimately capturing two World Championships in Formula One Grand Prix racing. Regardless of his titles and previous experience, he was still considered a rookie by Indianapolis Motor Speedway standards.

The month of May at Indianapolis proved to be a learning experience for Brabham and the Cooper team when they returned for the 1961 race and became acclimated to the Speedway's manner of doing things. Practice was uneventful and Brabham qualified comfortably on the inside of the fifth

Below: Sitting in the cockpit of the attention-grabbing rear-engined Cooper is none other than team principal John Cooper. To the right, wearing the striped shirt is Harry Stephens, former chief mechanic for Johnnie Parsons (winning in 1950), Sam Hanks, Rodger Ward, Fred Agabashian, Johnny Thomson and Art Cross. A friend of sponsor Jim Kimberly, he "un-retires" after four years to help oversee the Cooper effort.

Bottom: The strong mutual admiration between Rodger Ward and Jack Brabham is clearly illustrated here as the 1959 winner congratulates the two-time defending world champion upon having qualified. It was Ward's urging 18 months earlier that led to John Cooper and Jack Brabham giving the Speedway a try. It would have far-reaching affects.
Photographs: IMS

159

row with a 145.144 mph average. Brabham managed to squeeze his qualifying time at Indianapolis in between qualifying for the Monaco Grand Prix back in Europe.

Prior to qualifying, practice had pretty much been dominated by one man – Bettenhausen. In his spectacular career, the popular Bettenhausen had done everything but win the Indianapolis 500 and was hoping to snare that elusive prize before retiring to his farm in the Chicago suburb of Tinley Park, Illinois.

Above: The infield is still one huge picnic ground.

Top right: An outstanding study of the normally jovial Sachs as he sits in the garage area contemplating what might have been.

Bottom right: A. J. Foyt wins his first of four Indianapolis 500s.

Main photograph: Eddie Sachs (12) and A. J. Foyt (1) are just about evenly matched until the refueling mechanism fails on what should have been Foyt's last stop, thereafter allowing Foyt to be able to pull away by "running light."

Below: Tony Hulman enjoys a moment with his grandson, Tony Hulman George, who in January 1990 will be named IMS president.

Photographs: IMS

As Hurtubise had done during qualifying the previous year, Bettenhausen flirted with the magical 150-mile-per-hour barrier. With the exception of Hurtubise, no one had ever averaged more than 149 mph during a qualifying run at the Speedway. During practice, Bettenhausen turned a number of laps in the high 149 range and appeared poised to be the first man to crack 150 as qualifying weekend drew near.

His closest competition came from Dick Rathmann, the 1958 pole winner who was entered to drive the Jim Robbins Special, but posted a top lap of 148.2 in a Kurtis-Novi entered by the Chicago-based Granatelli brothers. After Lew Welch suffered a reversal of fortune, the Granatellis purchased the cars in March and entered one car for the 500. Rathmann believed he had a better chance to win the race in the Novi and team patriarch Andy Granatelli was prepared to announce that Rathmann was changing teams. His contractual obligations to Robbins prevented that move and three other drivers (Ralph Liguori, Russ Congdon and Paul Russo) were unable to put the Novi in the field.

Sadly, a ride in another car proved to be the undoing of Bettenhausen.

While testing the car of longtime friend Paul Russo, Bettenhausen crashed to his death on the front straightaway. A suspension bolt had fallen off, causing the car to turn right and begin a series of barrel-roll flips along the top of the wall, tearing out fence posts as it flipped. The front part of the car ended up in the front-row box seats, on fire and wrapped in fence. The man they called "the Tinley Park Express" had died from a basal skull fracture.

Ironically, it marked the second time in less than a year that a former USAC national champion had met his demise. The previous June, three-time champ and 1958 500 winner Jimmy Bryan had lost his life at Langhorne, Pa.

Bettenhausen's accident resulted in at least two significant changes. Because the cause of the accident was blamed on an error by a crew member, the United States Auto Club took steps to make sure that mechanics were certified before being allowed to work on a champ car. And because Bettenhausen's car had ended up in a spectator area, the Speedway strengthened its fence with steel cables to further protect the fans, especially those in seats located right next to the wall. Bettenhausen's accident occurred on the Friday before qualifying opened, when the outside stands were

closed to the public. The day after the accident, fans were seated in the area where Bettenhausen's car had crashed. In fact, Clarence Cagle's crew had done such an incredible job of fixing the fence, it was virtually impossible to detect there had been an accident at the site.

While Bettenhausen's family began preparations for his funeral, the show, as it were, went on.

Sachs took his second straight 500 pole position with an average of 147.481 mph. Filling out the front row would be Branson and Hurtubise. The likable second-year driver from North Tonawanda, New York, qualified at a much slower average than he had the previous year when he established a track record of 149.056 mph. Still, his 1961 average of 146.306 mph was good enough for third on the starting grid. Ward, Jones and Rathmann filled the second row and Foyt wound up seventh.

It was now time to go racing.

Veteran starter Bill Vandewater dropped the green flag and Hurtubise promptly jumped into the lead where he would stay for the first 35 laps. Jim Rathmann, who started 11th, took over the lead for six laps and on Lap 42, the impressive Jones took over the point. Before the day was out, Jones would lead a total of 27 laps. He definitely would have been a factor in the latter stages of the race had his engine not lost a cylinder. A lengthy pit stop to change spark plugs took him out of contention.

Fans on the front straightaway witnessed one of the more thrilling moments of the day when Don Davis crashed on Lap 49. The dazed rookie got out of his car and crossed the track to get into the pit area. Unfortunately, it set off a chain-reaction accident that involved Jack Turner, A.J. Shepherd, Roger McCluskey and Bill Cheesbourg. Turner's car did a spectacular flip, but miraculously, no one was injured.

Well, almost no one. Jones was apparently struck by debris from the accident and suffered a cut over his eye. He pressed on, despite having to occasionally tilt his goggles once they started to fill with blood!

With the exception of six laps led by Ward (Laps 161-167), the second half of the race was purely a Foyt-Sachs affair.

Foyt led Laps 95-124 when Sachs took over for the next 13. Foyt led for a lap and then Sachs took the lead from Laps 139-141. Foyt led the next five laps followed by four laps with Sachs in the lead. Foyt then led Laps 152-160 when Ward took over until Lap 167 before pitting and handing the lead back to Foyt.

While they were doing battle, Brabham ran as high as sixth place, but tire wear proved to be a problem and lengthy pit stops prevented him from being a contender. Despite the time lost in the pits and a decreased pace designed to conserve his Dunlop tires, Brabham would ultimately finish in ninth place.

Foyt seemingly had the upper hand on Sachs, but his fueling apparatus malfunctioned on what was supposed to be his final stop. Ironically, it would affect both of the leading cars. Foyt's crew was forced to borrow the fueling rig from Len

Sutton's pit, which adjoined the Foyt pit.

In William Libby's biography "A.J.," Foyt explained what happened when he rejoined the race.

"I could see Sachs go past, down the front straightaway and into the first turn," Foyt said. "For some reason, I was suddenly faster than Sachs, even in the straightaway. I don't why… and I sailed right past him. I had that race won. Sachs was right on my tail. He just couldn't muster up quite enough horses to get by, but he didn't drop back.

"Then I saw the pit sign. It said: 'A.J. Fuel low.' What had happened? I stayed out there, hoping they would take the sign away, but they didn't. Something must have happened in the pits on my last stop. They put up a sign: 'Stay there,' and I knew they must be working on whatever it was that went wrong. I knew I was running out of fuel. That was why my car was faster than Eddie's all of the sudden. I was lighter because he had a full fuel tank – enough to go the distance.

"The sign I feared went up: 'Pit A.J. 1.' They put in just enough fuel to finish the race. Eight seconds later, I was moving again. There were 15 laps to go. I got within sight of Eddie and drove deeper and deeper with each lap. I was right on the edge. Eddie was, too, so it didn't look like I was going to catch him."

Sachs now appeared to be the likely winner, but with three laps left, he dashed into the pits for a tire change as the right rear clearing showing the wear.

Foyt continued: "I felt the vibration. It wasn't the car. It was the crowd. There were 300,000 people screaming. I knew something had happened to Sachs. When I came around, I saw Sachs' car in the pits. Race tires have a layer of white rubber beneath the tread rubber as a warning to let drivers know they have run the tire into the danger area. At the

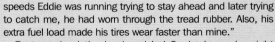

speeds Eddie was running trying to stay ahead and later trying to catch me, he had worn through the tread rubber. Also, his extra fuel load made his tires wear faster than mine."

Foyt regained the lead and led Sachs home by eight seconds to capture his first 500. Ward finished third to complete a hat trick of sorts. In the past three 500s, Ward had placed first, second and third. Rounding out the top 10 were Shorty Templeman, Al Keller, Chuck Stevenson, Marshman (who had started 33rd), Lloyd Ruby (who wound up qualifying Bettenhausen's car), Brabham and Norm Hall. Gene Hartley was 11th and Jones eventually struggled home to a 12th-place finish.

The extra Foyt pit stop resulted in a rule change. In future Indianapolis 500s, competitors would not be allowed to use another's fuel apparatus during the race.

The Foyt-Sachs battle was worthy of comparison to the previous Ward-Rathmann encounters, but the race would clearly be the forerunner of things to come. Brabham's Cooper was the first rear-engined car to compete with success at Indianapolis and the best was yet to come from Foyt and Jones.

1962: 'Brakes' Of The Game For Parnelli

If the previous May at the Indianapolis Motor Speedway had been the "coming out party" for Parnelli Jones, then May 1962 should have been his coronation. After all, Jones would be the talk of the town throughout the month. Jones arrived at Indianapolis after capturing USAC's Sprint Car title in 1961 and winning the '61 Championship Division finale on the dirt mile at Phoenix, Ariz. He opened the '62 season by following A.J. Foyt home in the 100-miler at Trenton.

Jones led an entry list that featured most of the top names from previous Indianapolis 500s. His chief competition figured to be people like defending race winner Foyt, his nemesis Eddie Sachs, two-time winner Rodger Ward, 1960 winner Jim Rathmann, track record holder Jim Hurtubise, Bobby Marshman, Don Branson and a couple of promising rookies.

True to form, Jones set the pace in practice.

Topping the rookie class of 1962 were Jim McElreath, a soft-spoken, fast-driving sprint-car driver from Arlington, Texas, and a Formula One driver by the name of Daniel Sexton Gurney.

McElreath was piloting a Kurtis KK500G-Offenhauser entered by C.O. Prather. Gurney, by contrast, drove a most interesting collection of cars in his first month of May at the Speedway. Entered by John Zink, whose cars had won the race in the 1955 and '56, Gurney was assigned to a rear-engined car powered by a Boeing turbine engine. Because

the car was not ready when the track opened, Gurney familiarized himself with the Indianapolis oval by taking his rookie test in one of Zink's front-engined Watson-Offenhauser roadsters.

When Gurney was unable to get the turbine car up to qualifying speed, he stepped out it and into the Buick-powered, rear-engine car built by Englishman John Crosthwaite and entered by drag racing innovator Mickey Thompson. Gurney probably wasn't all that unhappy to leave the Zink team. The turbine car had arrived late because Zink himself had flipped it during a test session in Oklahoma.

Once in Thompson's car, Gurney quickly found speed and qualified an impressive eighth. Although McElreath started seventh, it was only Gurney's second time on an oval (he had run in that year's Daytona 500) and for the second straight year, a rear-engined car would start in the 500.

Qualifying, of course, became the domain of Parnelli Jones.

With his trusty Watson-Offenhauser, nicknamed "Calhoun," Jones captured the pole position with one- and four-lap records (150.729 and 150.370). He became the first man to crack the 150-mile-per-hour barrier during his qualifying run. Jones was the only man in the 1962 Indianapolis 500 field to record a 150-mph lap. To commemorate his accomplishment, longtime Bryant distributor Phil Hedback dumped 150 silver dollars into Jones' helmet. The gauntlet had been laid down; all that was left was the race.

One factor for Jones' speed could be tied to a change in

the Speedway – it was noticeably smoother. The previous October, they had paved the balance of the exposed bricks with asphalt except for a one-yard-wide strip at the start-finish line.

When the first-year starter Pat Vidan dropped the green flag, Jones left Rodger Ward, Bobby Marshman and 30 other cars and drivers in his wake and built a seemingly unassailable lead of more than a lap before the halfway point. It appeared that the Agajanian stable, that had scored its first Indianapolis 500 victory 10 years earlier, was about to take racing's top prize for the second time.

But it is a 500-mile race and things happen. Jones could already attest to that from his eventful first 500 the year before.

In Bill Libby's biography *"Parnelli,"* Jones recalled: "I always wanted to be impressive at Indy. Later, I realized I was. Later, I realized I'd led, so I could win (the race). Later, I realized these things happen in racing, especially in this race, and I just had to wait my turn."

Judging by his performance leading up to the mid-point of the race, it should have been his turn in 1962. However, in an effort to make Jones' car lighter, Pouelsen had opted against installing an auxiliary brake system. That miscalculation reared its ugly head when Jones swerved to avoid Foyt on Lap 70 after the latter lost the rear wheel from his Bowes Seal Fast Special.

To Jones' horror, the brake pedal went to the floor – the

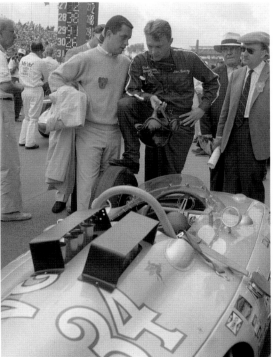

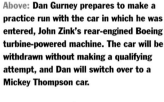

Above: Dan Gurney prepares to make a practice run with the car in which he was entered, John Zink's rear-engined Boeing turbine-powered machine. The car will be withdrawn without making a qualifying attempt, and Dan will switch over to a Mickey Thompson car.

Left: Paying Dan Gurney a visit shortly before the start of the 1962 race is none other than ace sports car driver Roger Penske.

Bottom: Shortly after asphalt has covered over the bricks, a trough is cut into which a three-foot-by-50-foot strip of paving bricks and mortar is laid to mark the start/finish line. Assisting Tony Hulman with the dedication is 1911 "500" winner Ray Harroun.
Photographs: IMS

Main photograph: In his first year as chief starter, Pat Vidan waves the checkered flag for Rodger Ward.

Bottom: A mechanic's work is never done.
Photographs: IMS

Agajanian Willard Battery Special was running without brakes! In his biography, Jones recounted how he had tried to convince himself to run at Indy without ever braking.

"I'd been told the fastest way to get around the track was not to use my brakes at all," Jones said. "So I tried not to. But I couldn't resist hitting the brake a little. I tried like hell not to the first and the second time and the third time. I'd be screaming into a corner and I'd be telling myself: 'you can do it. You can get around without that brake. You got more guts than anyone. You don't have to hit the brakes.'

"But then I'd be in the corner and my left foot would move out just like I didn't have any control over it, and I'd tap the brake. Just a little maybe, but I'd have to tap it and I'd slow down a little and I'd feel a little better for it, you know, like I could breathe again."

Lapping at the Speedway without brakes is one thing, but there was the matter of having to come into the pits for fuel and tires. By Lap 75, Jones made a surprise visit to the pits. He slowed as best he could and drove past his pit – shouting and gesturing – and then returning to the track without stopping. The culprit had been the exhaust pipe burning a hole in the brake line.

Although still in the lead, Jones was in trouble and everyone on pit row knew it. What type of trouble became evident when he rolled into the pits for this second stop. On Lap 126, Jones pitted but overshot his pit. With a member of his crew dragging his car back, Jones' car got new tires and a full tank of fuel, but the whole procedure had taken 37 seconds. While he pitted, Ward, who had cut the lead to 12 seconds prior to the stop, now was firmly in command.

For Jones, the race was lost and he was forced to run over spare wheels to get slowed down on his final stop. The man who should have won the 1962 500 wound up a disappointing seventh.

With Jones' brake problems taking him out of contention and Foyt sidelined early in the race, Ward had only his Leader Card teammate, Len Sutton, to worry about. Ward's crew gave him slightly quicker pit stops and that made the difference for the 11-second gap that separated Ward and

Sutton at the checker.

Ward even allowed that his victory had come courtesy of Jones' misfortune.

"If nothing had happened, I wouldn't have caught Parnelli," Ward said afterward. "But I ran smart and he was unlucky."

The race marked a 1-2 finish for Milwaukee greeting card magnate Bob Wilke and a continuation of Ward's string of impressive runs at Indianapolis. It also marked the first 1-2 finish for a team since 1948 when Mauri Rose and Bill Holland took the top two spots for Lou Moore.

Eddie Sachs, whose trouble-plagued month relegated him to 27th starting position after winning back-to-back poles, charged through the field to finish third. Second-year drivers Don Davis and Marshman were fourth and fifth, respectively, and McElreath finished sixth to take top rookie honors. Rounding out the top 10 were Jones, Lloyd Ruby, Jim Rathmann and Johnny Boyd.

Although Gurney finished in 20th position after retiring with transmission problems on Lap 92, it seems that he intended for the rear-engine trend to continue for years to come. Based on what Brabham and Cooper had done the previous year, Gurney invited Colin Chapman of Lotus to the 1962 race with the intention of enticing Chapman to enter cars in the future.

One other racing personality was part of the Speedway crowd witnessing the 1962 500. A young sports-car racer named Roger Penske dropped by to wish Gurney well prior to the race. Both Chapman and Penske would leave lasting impressions on the Speedway. And Gurney would also wind up becoming a key player in more ways than one.

Above: Dirt-track specialist Don Branson, later mentor to Mario Andretti, Johnny Rutherford, and others, makes a stop.

Bottom: Ward celebrates with his two sons, Rodger, Jr. (left) and David (foreground).
Photographs: IMS

Below: Jim Clark qualifies for his first "500." Left to right behind the car, team principal Colin Chapman, lead mechanics Jim Endruweit and Dave Lazenby, and Colin Riley.
Photograph: IMS

1963: An Oily Grail And A Second British Invasion

To put the Indianapolis 500 of 1963 in a nutshell, the end result was that Parnelli Jones and the Agajanian team overcame the type of misfortunes that had hampered their races in 1961 and '62 and did what everyone expected them to do: break the track record, capture the pole position and dominate the race. And that's exactly what they did.

However, there were at least two factors that stand out that made May of 1963 more than the crowning achievement of Jones and Agajanian.

First, the 1963 Indianapolis 500 would mark a milestone in that four of the 33 starters were driving rear-engined cars. A look at the record books reveals that on only one occasion did two cars start the race with the engines behind the drivers. That would have been the 1946 500 with the cars of Paul Russo and George Barringer. Russo's Fageol Twin Coach Special would require an asterisk as it had a pair of Offenhauser midget engines supplying power. One engine was located behind the driver and the other was located in front, making it the only twin-engined car to make the race. In 1941, a pair of the Miller-Gulf cars qualified for the race, but one was destroyed in the garage fire that occurred on Race Day morning.

The second factor to stand out is that the performance of two of the rear-engined cars exceeded that of Brabham and one nearly won the race.

Thanks to Dan Gurney's invitation to Colin Chapman to make a reconnaissance trip to the Speedway in 1962, Chapman, Gurney and top Lotus driver Jim Clark returned with three new Lotus 29 chassis powered by Ford's small-block Fairlane V-8.

Gurney's impressive qualifying run and race convinced Mickey Thompson to come back with two cars from his 1962

effort (with Chevrolet V-8s replacing the Buick powerplants), plus three of the most radical vehicles to ever grace the 2½-mile oval. Thompson's new concept for 1963 was dubbed the "Skateboard" because of its extremely low profile. It was so low, the base of the front windscreen was only 21½ inches tall. Even more noteworthy were the low, wide Firestone tires that had been specially made for the cars. According to Thompson, the tire's "bead diameter was just 12 inches, the rim width was nine inches and its cross section was 11 inches at the widest point and terrifically low and squatty. It smacked of drag slicks and the (land speed record) tire."

Although Thompson lost Gurney to Lotus, he more than compensated by signing reigning F1 World Champion Graham Hill to lead his team.

Jim Kimberly, who had sponsored the Cooper effort in 1961, returned with two Buick-powered chassis designed by John Crosthwaite (one was new; the other failed to make the 1962 starting field). The Cooper that Jack Brabham had piloted to ninth in 1961 was also entered although now powered by an Aston Martin engine. The driver was Mexican sports-car ace and future F1 winner Pedro Rodriguez and the car now featured a longer wheelbase as mandated by the United States Auto Club. The enforcement of the wheelbase rule seemed to be all that a group of roadster owners had gotten in their move to have the rear-engined cars banned from the Speedway and USAC competition.

Thanks to financial support from Ford Motor Company, Chapman's Lotus 29 was based on his successful Lotus 25 Grand Prix car that featured a monocoque tub and nearly carried Clark to the World Championship in 1962. Borrowing from what was learned from the Cooper effort of 1961, Chapman also chose to offset the chassis of his Indianapolis Lotus. Ford's 260-cubic-inch V-8 produced enough horsepower to compete against the venerable 4-cylinder Offenhauser. Coupled with the car's lighter weight, it also

promised to get better mileage and allow the drivers to go the distance on two fuel stops. The Lotus-Fords would also be the last cars to race at Indianapolis using carburetors.

The Lotus team suffered a setback during the practice session on the opening day of qualifying. While trying to adapt to hard compound tires, Gurney lost control of his car and clouted the Turn 1 wall. Gurney was unhurt and the team prepared the backup entry. Dubbed "the Mule," this car was chassis No. 29/1, the original Lotus built for Indianapolis and the one that got all of the test mileage. Although painted in the familiar British racing green with yellow trim, the plan was to have Gurney qualify it and repaint in America's national racing colors of white with two blue stripes.

As expected, Jones, who had set the pace in practice, did likewise in qualifying.

Still driving "Calhoun," the same Watson-Offenhauser he drove in for the past two years, Jones established a new four-lap average of 151.153 mph and a top lap of 151.844 mph, also a record. Joining Jones on the front row were Jim Hurtubise, who put one of the famed Novis back in the 500 field for the first time since 1958. Driving a bright orange Kurtis-Novi owned by Andy, Joe and Vince Granatelli, Hurtubise was a people's choice driver in the people's choice car. Ever since its first appearance at Indianapolis in 1941, the loud Novi V-8 engine was a favorite of the fans. It also had something of a jinx image (two drivers had died in Novis and a third was seriously burned), but in 1963, it seemed that Hurtubise was just the man to break that jinx. Rounding out the front row was Don Branson in one of the Leader Card Watson-Offenhausers.

Branson's teammate, Rodger Ward, wound up fourth, and Clark completed his successful four-lap qualifying run with a 149.750 mph average that put him in the middle of the second row. Gurney tried to qualify at the end of the day, but was forced to abort the run when his foot got tangled in the pedal safety strap. The following day, he joined Clark in the field with an average of 149.019 mph, good for 12th starting position.

Thompson's month was a mixed bag as Hill decided to step out of the car after hitting the wall. Teammate and fellow rookie Billy Krause was in involved in an accident and Masten Gregory was unable to get up to speed. Gregory would be bumped in another of the "skateboard" cars. Veteran Duane Carter, who celebrated his 50th birthday during the month of May, was the only driver able to successfully qualify one the new Thompson "skateboards." Carter qualified for his 11th Indianapolis 500 in 15th position.

The Granatellis had given Indianapolis a record of three Novis in a starting field with rookies Bobby Unser and Art Malone joining Hurtubise.

One driver who would not be starting was veteran Jack Turner. Turner, who got caught up in someone else's accidents and flipped on the front straightaway in the 1961 and '62 races, lost control by himself during practice for the 1963 race and barrel-rolled down the front straightaway. He retired from his hospital bed and would later receive a trophy with an upside-down racing car during the victory banquet. It's unfortunate that Turner, a two-time national midget champion who had a distinguished career as a racer, would generally be remembered for his flips at Indianapolis.

Another driver who failed to qualify was Len Sutton, who had finished a close second to Rodger Ward a year earlier.

Out of the 33 starting cars, four were rear-engined designs. The other 29 were front-engined cars with three powered by the supercharged Novi V-8 and the remainder powered by the 4-cylinder Offenhauser that had been the mainstay at Indianapolis since the mid-1930s. The 1963 Indianapolis 500 may have not been the last stand for the front-engine roadster, but it was clearly the beginning of the end.

While one era was beginning, another was ending. Throughout the month, a number of drivers tried unsuccessfully to get John Chalik's car up to speed and into the starting field. The Chalik entry was a Kurtis KK500L, the last Indianapolis car built by the legendary Frank Kurtis and first in Indianapolis to feature a roll cage. Kurtis-designed cars had won at Indianapolis in 1950, '51, '53, '54 and '55.

When Pat Vidan dropped the green flag to start the 47th Indianapolis 500, Jones jumped into the lead as expected, but unlike 1962, it was short-lived. Hurtubise dropped to seventh as the Novi worked up to speed, and by the time the

field entered Turn 4, he was back in second. He then relied on the Novi's horsepower and nudged in front as he crossed the start-finish line to lead the first lap.

Now it was Jones' turn to return the compliment, which he did as the pair headed down the backstretch on the second lap. Once again, Hurtubise dropped to the inside on the front straightaway and passed Jones – after the pair had crossed the start-finish line.

That would be the high point for the Novi team as Malone was already in the pits and Unser brought out the first yellow after hitting the wall in Turn 1. But the Novi would be the least of Jones' worries that day.

As he had done a year before, Jones would build a lead and surrender it when he made his first of three pit stops on Lap 64. Roger McCluskey, who had started 14th in the Konstant Hot Watson-Offenhauser, led the next four laps before pitting and handing the lead over to Clark, whose Lotus was now the first rear-engined machine to ever lead the Indianapolis 500. And if that wasn't enough, Gurney had moved up to second, giving Team Lotus and the rear-engine advocates a 1-2 until pitting on Lap 92.

Because of superior fuel mileage and tire wear, Clark was

able to go until Lap 95 until his first and only stop. Like the Cooper team of 1961, Team Lotus found itself in another league when it came to making Indianapolis 500 pit stops. Gurney had required 38 seconds for his stop while Clark's was even longer at 42 seconds. To put it in perspective, a normal Indianapolis stop would take anywhere from 15 to 20 seconds.

Clark's first stop gave the lead back to Jones, who would stay there for the remainder of the race. However, those 105 laps were not without drama for the race leader, who would lead by as many as 48 seconds with 50 laps to go.

On Lap 160, Jones pitted during a caution for Eddie Sachs' spin. Sachs managed to keep the Bryant Watson-Offenhauser off the wall, but maintained he had spun in oil – specifically oil left by Jones' car. Oil streaks could be seen on the underside of the lead car's tail section and there appeared to be a slight crack in an oil reserve tank mounted on the outside of the car. The leaking oil was leaving a blue stream of smoke as it sprayed onto the exhaust pipe.

On Lap 170, the drama truly kicked into high gear as Chief Steward Harlan Fengler appeared ready to have Vidan wave the black flag at Jones. Before that could happen, Agajanian argued his case, which was the fact that most of the cars were leaking some fluids and that Jones' car was no longer leaking. At the time, the chief steward watched the race from the starter's stand (a platform on the grass verge by the wall), making him accessible to anyone in the pits. After a brief consultation, Fengler agreed with Agajanian and the black flag was withheld.

With two laps to go, McCluskey spun while running third and shortly afterward, Jones crossed the finish line. Two years earlier, Jones had led, bled and then struggled home with a sick engine. A year ago, the only thing that could stop him was a brake line. This time, even the oil controversy couldn't stop him from winning racing's biggest prize – a whopping

$148,000 and a brand new Chrysler 300 convertible pace car.

But Jones had a hard time celebrating, thanks to a lot of bickering from those he had vanquished. In addition to the oil situation, it was suggested he might have increased his lead over Clark during the caution periods where the rule states a driver must maintain his position. Jones bristled at both criticisms.

The following day at the Speedway Motel, Sachs confronted Jones, accusing him of being a cheater. One punch later, a stunned Sachs was on the floor and Jones continued on his way.

In *"Parnelli,"* he explained: "Sure I dropped oil, but so did a lot of guys. But how much is too much? Where do you draw the line? The officials have to decide, and they can't always call you in to check. When... was the last time a leader was black-flagged out near the end of the race? I can tell you when. Never."

As for Clark's interpretation of the yellow flag rule, Jones said: "Did I run too hard under the yellow? I don't think so. What am I supposed to do, park it? It was up to the others to keep up. If Clark didn't understand this, it was his tough luck."

Clark, who finished second and earned Indy's top rookie award, did not dwell on either controversy and graciously congratulated Jones. He had learned in his first Indianapolis 500 and so had Team Lotus, which had two top-10 cars that day with Gurney winding up seventh. They would be back. In fact, they would remind everyone what was ahead in the future by running in select USAC Championship Division events and thoroughly dominating the 200-miler at Milwaukee. Dominance was becoming almost commonplace to Clark, who also won the 1963 F1 World Championship by winning a record seven races in 10 starts.

The next Indianapolis 500 was going to be very interesting.

Main photograph: A Watson "roadster" partially stripped, but no "ordinary" Watson. This one is Foyt's 1964 winner.

Inset right: The greatest showman the track has ever seen: Innovator, entrepreneur, impresario, and a tireless marketing genius, Andy Granatelli had as high a profile as anyone at the track for years. After several years of fielding Ford (Mercury)-powered cars outfitted with his company's Grancor heads, Granatelli turned to Offy power and finished second with Jim Rathmann in 1952. He purchased the hugely popular Novi team from Lew Welch in 1961, and later grabbed headlines transcending motorsports by campaigning turbine-powered cars. The winning sponsor/entrant in 1969 (with Mario Andretti) and 1973 (Gordon Johncock), he began to fade from the limelight after that. But not by much.

Photographs: IMS

1964: A Meeting Of Triumph And Disaster

For obvious reasons, the 1964 Indianapolis 500 will always be remembered as a race marred by fire and tragedy. It should have been remembered as much for some incredible innovation, a major jump in speed, racing's first major tire war and one last hurrah before the changing of the guard.

On the engineering front, more teams went the rear-engine route with new designs from Jack Brabham, Mickey Thompson, Rolla Vollstedt, Joe Huffaker, Troutman-Barnes, Ted Halibrand, Fred Gerhardt, Smokey Yunick and, to the surprise of many people, A.J. Watson.

Brabham made history with his successful run in the Cooper-Climax in 1961. However, the two-time world champion had always talked about building his own car. He formed a partnership with designer Ron Tauranac and their Motor Racing Developments team turned out the first Brabham F1 car in time for the 1962 German Grand Prix. For Indianapolis, Brabham returned with John Zink as entrant and veteran mechanic Denny Moore. Interestingly, Brabham and Tauranac shunned the idea of using an offset suspension on the first Indianapolis Brabham. They also chose the Offenhauser engine as the powerplant.

Thompson, whose radical "skateboard" cars turned heads in 1963, returned to Indianapolis with even more radical cars and a hefty sponsorship package from Sears. Like its predecessor, the new Thompson was low and wide with the first fully streamlined body since the Sumar and Belond cars from 1955.

The chassis was a space-frame design with enough fuel tanks Thompson hoped would allow the car to need only one pit stop for the 500 miles. Power was from the new dual-overhead camshaft Ford V-8 while General manufactured the low profile, Thompson-designed tires that were rebadged with the Sears name. Driving the cars would be a pair of sports-car drivers and 500 rookies – Masten Gregory and Dave MacDonald. In its original configuration, fenders covered the front wheels of the cars. Thompson ultimately cut the tops off the fenders.

With or without them, they proved to be a handful in the handling department as Gregory heavily damaged one in a practice accident and MacDonald complained to various people about the car's propensity to float in the corners. MacDonald would qualify a respectable 14th and veteran Eddie Johnson would place a second car in the field in 24th spot. For the second year in a row, Gregory was unable to make the field.

By contrast, Vollstedt's car was taller and more bulbous in appearance. It was powered by the 4-cylinder Offenhauser and driven by veteran Len Sutton.

Like the Vollstedt chassis, Offenhausers powered Joe Huffaker's MG Liquid Suspension Specials that employed the hydrostatic suspension system used on BMC domestic vehicles. West Coast import car dealer Kjell Qvale was the entrant with rookies Pedro Rodriguez and Walt Hansgen assigned as drivers. A.J. Foyt briefly tested a Huffaker entry bearing the No. 1, but decided to stay with his front-engined Watson-Offenhauser. Veteran Bob Veith would end up qualifying the car. Rodriquez crashed his car in practice and was hospitalized with burns. Hansgen had a smoother month and qualified an impressive 10th.

Parnelli Jones, the defending winner, also had a rear-engined car at his disposal. Commissioned by team owner J.C. Agajanian, the car was built by sports-car specialists Troutman-Barnes and powered by an Offenhauser. Jones came to the same conclusion as Foyt and opted to go with his trusty "Calhoun," now in its fifth year at Indianapolis.

Halibrand, a provider of such racing staples as wheels and rear ends, tried his hand at race-car design with the Shrike. Low and sleek like a Lotus, the Shrike was powered by the new DOHC Ford V-8 and entered for Eddie Sachs.

Gerhardt's car was powered by an Offenhauser and entrusted to yet another rookie from the sports car ranks – Jerry Grant.

Watson basically copied Vollstedt's design and had a Ford-powered entry for Rodger Ward and an Offenhauser-powered entry for Don Branson.

But the most radical design of the 1964 entries came from Yunick. His Hurst Floor Shift Special featured a tubular-shaped chassis powered by an Offenhauser engine. In order to carry an adequate fuel load, Yunick's chassis had no cockpit! The driver controlled the car from a cockpit mounted on the left side of the chassis. Veteran Duane Carter practiced at speeds fast enough to have made that year's race. Unfortunately for Yunick and Carter, Yunick's contractual obligation to Autolite Spark Plugs clashed with Carter's contractual obligation to Champion. Carter was forced to vacate the car and Yunick summoned NASCAR driver Bobby Johns, who crashed during his qualifying run. One of the most unique cars in racing history became a permanent footnote.

Innovation was not restricted to the rear-engine contingent.

Returning with the powerful Novis were the Granatelli brothers with three cars for Jim McElreath, Art Malone and Bobby Unser. McElreath would wind up qualifying the Kurtis-Novi driven by Unser the previous year while Malone took over the car that Jim Hurtubise had qualified on the front row in '63. However, it was Unser's car that was unique. Based on the Ferguson P99 F1 car and built by Ferguson, the new Novi employed a four-wheel-drive system that the Granatellis reasoned would make better use of the Novi's incredible horsepower.

Thanks to its sound and its reputation as a fan favorite, the Novi team needed to do very little to attract attention. But 1964 was also a time in which Andy Granatelli decided to go all out to promote a product called STP, which stood for "scientifically treated pretroleum." The Granatelli marketing machine began to come up with a number of clever promotional ideas that ultimately made it a household name. For 1964, the Novi crew members unveiled the STP coveralls, which resembled pajamas covered in STP logos. Andy Granatelli even had a tailored suit made that was likewise covered in STP logos. Like the cars, they were loud and colorful.

Meanwhile, there were the Lotus-Fords with Jim Clark and Dan Gurney using the latest Lotus 34 chassis and Ford's new DOHC V-8 and Bobby Marshman in Lindsey Hopkins' Lotus 29, also powered by one of the new Ford DOHC V-8s.

Ford Motor Company once again served as the principal backer of the Team Lotus effort and because they owned the Lotus 29s from 1963, they made one of the chassis available

to Hopkins, who procured sponsorship from Pure Oil. The car was called the Pure Firebird Special and Marshman used it to do the brunt of the development work on the new Ford engine. In addition to making the transition from front-engine roadster to rear-engine "funny car," the likable Marshman looked to be the only man capable of competing with Team Lotus.

In the midst of all this, the tire war between Firestone and Goodyear was beginning in earnest. Firestone could boast to having provided the winning tire at Indianapolis for the past 40 races. Goodyear, anxious to cash in on the growing

Left: Larry Bisceglia, a race fan who had attended the "500" as far back as 1926, showed up several days early with his 1933 De Soto in 1948 and was surprised to find two cars already parked in line. The following year he came a little earlier, fully believing he would be first. He was second. Arriving in 1950 on May 11, he finally achieved his goal, thereafter making quite a career out of it and becoming somewhat of a celebrity. By 1955, he had acquired a 1951 Chevrolet panel truck which served not only as his transportation but also his "hotel room." His "streak" lasted all the way until 1984, when he had to give up due to ill health.

Inset left: NASCAR's Henry "Smokey" Yunick loved competing at Indianapolis and entered a number of cars between 1958 and 1975. By far his most unusual was the Hurst Floor Shift "side car" in 1964. Powered by an "Offy," veteran Duane Carter worked it up to 150 mph in a practice run, and NASCAR driver Bobby Johns went out to make a qualifying attempt but spun and hit the wall before taking the green flag. Johns, who had wanted to compete at Indianapolis ever since boyhood, finished seventh the following year with the rather surprising assignment as teammate to Jim Clark on the Lotus team.

Photographs: IMS

Main photograph: Perhaps the highlight of the tragic 1964 race is the brief battle at the front between laps 48 and 54, featuring the front-engined cars of Foyt and Jones. Although Parnelli leads past the start/finish line every time, the two are frequently side by side.

Insets bottom right: Eddie Sachs (left) and Dave MacDonald, both lost in the accident.

Far right: Bobby Marshman prepares to make a low pass around leader Jim Clark. Marshman was very highly regarded by the Lotus team members.

Bottom far right: Tragedy at the Indianapolis Motor Speedway. The 500-Mile Race is about to be stopped for the first time ever due to an accident.

Photographs: IMS

interest in auto racing, produced tires for the Speedway as early as 1963 and had Foyt as its chief test driver.

While practicing with both tires, Foyt determined the Goodyear to be good enough to win. Goodyear's engineering team wasn't convinced and ultimately withdrew, releasing its contract drivers to run with Firestones. Goodyear's all-out assault on Indianapolis would have to wait another year.

On the opening day of qualifying, Marshman wowed what was determined to be a record crowd with a practice lap at 160 miles per hour. All during the first week of practice, Marshman and Clark had pushed each other for top speed honors. It was hard to believe that only two years earlier, the previously unthinkable 150 mph mark had fallen. And now the Speedway was witnessing a driver flirting with 160. Of course, Marshman's lap was unofficial. Only laps during qualifying runs are considered official records.

Marshman qualified early, but could only muster an average of 157.867 mph. It was a new track record and he was temporarily on the pole, but he wasn't happy. He felt he could have gone faster and Clark was yet to qualify.

It certainly gave Clark something to think about as he began his run. With his typical coolness, Clark qualified with a one-lap record of 159.377 mph and a four-lap mark of 158.828 mph – more than seven mph faster than Parnelli Jones' record pole average from 1963. Clark's record run couldn't have come at a more opportune time. With the musical invasion staged by the Beatles earlier in the year, Clark found a following eager to embrace anything or anyone from the British Isles. It mattered not that he shunned any form of adulation, Indianapolis fell in love with the sheep farmer-turned racing car driver.

Rodger Ward completed the all-Ford-powered front row with a 156.406 mph average.

Jones and Foyt posted speeds good enough for fourth and fifth positions, respectively to spearhead the front-engine charge and Gurney filled out the second row in his Lotus. Gurney, who was suffering from burns caused by fuel dripping on his legs in his F1 car, was more than four mph slower than Clark in an identical car.

One notable qualifying attempt came courtesy of four-time 500 starter Cliff Griffith. Driving Pete Salemi's Central Excavating Special, Griffith's effort might have gone unnoticed had it not been for the fact his car was an Offenhauser-powered dirt

car. Dirt cars had last started in the 1956 500 and it marked the final time someone would attempt to qualify one although dirt cars would be seen at pavement champ car races through 1969.

When qualifying ended a week later, the starting field was composed of 12 rear-engined cars and 21 front-engined machines, including three powered by Novis. Of the rear-engined cars, Ford powered seven cars with five powered by Offenhauser. Ford had its biggest presence at Indianapolis since 1935 when four cars (out of 10) designed by Harry Miller and powered by Ford's V-8 made the starting field. Ford also used its opportunity as pace car supplier to showcase its new Mustang that had just become available in March. The Speedway offered many their first glimpse of the car.

With Benson Ford wheeling the pace car, the field took the green from Pat Vidan and roared into what would be a historic and tragic Indianapolis 500. Clark sped into the lead with Marshman in hot pursuit while Jones and Foyt dispatched Ward and took over third and fourth.

Also moving up early were rookies MacDonald and Hansgen. MacDonald started 14th and Hansgen 10th and as the pair exited Turn 4 to complete Lap 2, they were battling for seventh place. While attempting to pass Hansgen, MacDonald lost control and slammed into the inside wall. Driving a car laden with fuel, the car exploded on impact and shot to the outside of the track. MacDonald's car was T-boned by Sachs and then hit and/or run over by a group that included Bobby Unser, Johnny Rutherford, Ronnie Duman and Chuck Stevenson. Norm Hall would also spin to avoid the fracas and backed into the wall.

The north end of the track appeared to be blocked with wreckage and consumed in flame as a black mushroom cloud shot skyward several hundred feet in the air. Clark instinctively raised his hand as he led the pack down the backstretch. By now, the drivers could see the smoke and ascertain that a major accident had occurred. Vidan brought out the red flag and for the first time in race history, the Indianapolis 500 was stopped due to an accident.

Sachs, who had nowhere to go, was killed instantly, crushed by the impact into MacDonald's car. MacDonald, who sat in his burning cockpit for the duration of the fire, somehow managed to live through the carnage but died two hours later. Duman's car caught fire when it backed into the

Turn 4 wall and he received burns. Unser, who had crashed on Lap 2 the previous year, failed to make it to Lap 2 as his Ferguson-Novi was damaged in the melee. Rutherford, Stevenson and Hall also were out of the race due to damage.

The race was halted for nearly two hours and when the field came down to restart the race, the crowd shuddered again. This time it was a white cloud of dust from the chemicals used to put out the fire. Fortunately, there was no accident and Clark resumed in the lead. But Marshman got faster and braver and dove underneath Clark to lead on Lap 7. Gurney made 1-2-3 for the Lotus-Fords by passing for third. Marshman left Clark and continued to build a lead, passing backmarkers everywhere he could. With Chief Mechanic Jack Beckley signaling Marshman to take it easy, the Pennsylvania driver almost seemed determined to put a lap on Clark. His tactics proved to be his undoing. While dropping down to the warmup apron to lap a car, Marshman's Lotus bottomed out and ripped out the oil plug, allowing the oil to spill. By Lap 39, the marvelous run of Bobby Marshman was over.

Clark took the lead back but felt a vibration as he prepared to complete Lap 47. Lotus boss Colin Chapman had chosen to go with Dunlop tires, whose softer, stickier compound made Clark the fastest man in qualifying. Unfortunately, the compound was too soft for prolonged race speeds and began to chunk. The vibration Clark felt was the suspension beginning to collapse as a result of the chunking tire. As he crossed the start-finish line, the left rear suspension collapsed and Clark brought the car safely to a halt on the inside of Turn 1. His day was done and later on, Gurney's car was withdrawn from the race.

That left Jones and Foyt to duel for the lead and duel they did — from Lap 48 until Lap 55 when Jones made his first stop. As he got ready to leave his pit, the fuel tank on "Calhoun" exploded (apparently due to static electricity) and Jones drove away with the car on fire. Jones' car was using methanol, which burned with an invisible flame. In no time at all, Jones realized the car was burning and jumped out. He was unhurt, but the defense of his 500 win was over.

Foyt was firmly in command and the only driver capable of a challenge was Ward. Unfortunately for Ward, he was continually forced to come into the pits for fuel. Advised to use only gasoline, the Leader Card team thought they might have a hidden advantage with methanol. What they got instead was horrible mileage and Ward was forced to pit for fuel five times while Foyt pitted only twice.

Actually, methanol was not the problem. A lever had been installed to help Ward control the fuel mixture from the cockpit. During Carb Day testing, he found the lever was poking him in the leg. The lever was turned around. During the race, Ward inadvertently was enriching the fuel mixture while thinking he was leaning it out. That caused the poor mileage.

In "A.J.," Foyt recalled: "It was Parnelli and me — in the dinosaurs. We were both running as hard as our Offys would go, and we were pulling away from the Fords that were left in the race. Nobody seemed to be able to run with us. When Parnelli's car caught fire in the pits, I no longer had any competition. I sailed on to win my second Indianapolis 500."

Ward finished a distant second and the slow-talking Texan, Lloyd Ruby, was third. Johnny White took fourth to earn the top rookie honor.

Unlike the 1961 victory, however, this was a somber affair as two drivers had perished in the race. Foyt, who was defiantly wearing a Goodyear suit, made what appeared to be a mockery of some of the innovations that were trying to change Indianapolis.

"We're thinking of coming back next with an enclosed cockpit car," Foyt told the public address announcer in Victory Lane.

Even in jest, Foyt had to know the roadster's days were numbered although he would go on to win several USAC events in the roadster. However, Foyt's 1964 victory would be its last at Indianapolis. Ward's runner-up car was the only rear-engined machine in the top 10. Reliability was still the Achilles' heel of the rear-engine, but development would make them stronger.

Foyt would certainly give the roadster a victorious farewell tour. En route to his fourth national championship in five years, Foyt won 10 of 13 races and drove his Watson roadster to victory five times.

Sadly, fiery accidents continued to plague the sport throughout the remainder of the year. A week after Indianapolis, fan favorite Jim Hurtubise received serious burns to the hands and face at Milwaukee. And Bobby Marshman, the first of the roadster set to master the rear-engine car, died after suffering burns over most of this body following a test accident at Phoenix in late November. A few months earlier, the popular Marshman had tested at Indianapolis and run a lap at 162.3, at the time the fastest unofficial lap in track history.

By changing the rules requiring two mandatory two pit stops in future 500s, the United States Auto Club made the use of methanol-based fuel preferable over gasoline for its Championship Division cars. The rule to stop twice effectively negated the advantage of using gasoline for better mileage. Through 2006, the cars that participated at Indianapolis ran on methanol.

Below: Bobby Marshman: a superstar in the making whose potential was never realized, injuries in a testing accident at the end of the 1964 season taking his life. When the Lotus team returned to England after the 1964 race, mechanics who had not made the trip inquired, "So who is this Bobby Marshman?" "Well," was the reply, "he is sort of an American Jimmy." High praise indeed.
Photograph: IMS

1965: Fait Accompli For Clark And Lotus

In many ways, May of 1965 at Indianapolis was as pleasant as May of 1964 had been tragic.

Not only did changes in the rules mandate a safer fuel in methanol, Firestone and Goodyear temporarily forgot their tire war and for the good of the sport, each devised rubberized fuel cells that would be less prone to tearing upon impact and therefore less prone to catch fire.

Drivers also began wearing suits employing fireproof materials like Nomex while Parnelli Jones even tried out a flameproof cream used by movie stuntmen.

The season opened on the Phoenix tri-oval with Don Branson giving the roadster its last-ever victory in USAC competition. A newcomer named Mario Andretti led a good portion of the race. Driving the Watson-based Blum roadster for the Dean Van Lines team, Andretti showed his true potential as a future champion.

After a major jump in speed the previous year, 1965's gains were mild despite advances in car design and tire construction. The British invasion took another step as firms like Lola and BRP produced chassis for Indianapolis. Ford wound up selling the Lotus 34 chassis to Foyt's Sheraton-Thompson team and J.C. Agajanian, who lined up Hurst sponsorship for Jones. Lola produced the T-80, which served as a backup car for Foyt and Jones and became the primary car for Lindsey Hopkins and driver Bud Tingelstad. The BRPs were built at the behest of George S. Bryant, whose former stepson Masten Gregory persuaded him to back his attempt to run at Indianapolis. Veteran Johnny Boyd was signed as his teammate and 500-winning mechanics George Salih and Howard Gilbert handled the mechanical duties.

Naturally, Team Lotus returned with one of the sleekest looking machines in racing car history. Penned by Len Terry, the Lotus 38, the car was literally shaped like a cigar, with a low, narrow nose and nicely rounded tail section. Team Lotus entered two of the cars while Dan Gurney's new All American Racers team entered a third Lotus 38.

Local car dealer Jerry Alderman entered a fourth Lotus-Ford – one of the original Lotus 29 chassis – for Al Miller. Miller's car was thought to be chassis 29/2, the car crashed in practice in 1963 by Gurney.

Although Andretti raced the Dean Van Lines roadster at Phoenix and Trenton (where he finished second), he had a new car for Indianapolis. Literally copying the Brabham chassis owned by the Zink team, Clint Brawner and Jim McGee built the Hawk. Unlike the Brabham, this car would be powered by Ford.

Updated rear-engine chassis were not restricted to British manufacturers. In addition to cars that had run in 1964, new designs emerged from A.J. Watson, Ted Halibrand and Fred Gerhardt.

Watson, whose 1964 rear-engine design maintained a round, roadster-like look, unveiled his new chassis for 1965,

Above: **Jim Clark: shy, polite, driven, and adored by the American public.**
Photograph: IMS

one of the sleekest looking machines to ever grace the Speedway. As low as any car entered that year, Watson's cars were powered by Ford and entered for veteran drivers Rodger Ward and Branson. The Watson-Offenhauser driven by Branson the previous year was assigned to Jud Larson and for fun, Watson also stuffed a DOHC Ford V-8 in one of his roadsters. Branson, never happy with any cockpit in which the driver did not sit upright, spent considerable time in the Ford-powered roadster, even after qualifying his car safely in the field.

Gurney's team also entered two of the new Halibrand chassis for Roger McCluskey and motorcycle champion Joe Leonard. Jim Hurtubise, Johnny Rutherford and Lloyd Ruby had Ford-powered Halibrands while Chuck Rodee piloted an Offenhauser-powered model. And no less than four drivers would make the field in Offenhauser-powered Gerhardts. Rolla Vollstedt also produced a new Ford-powered car for Len Sutton and brought back his Offenhauser-powered '64 model for Canadian rookie Billy Foster.

Another American design was the Chevrolet-powered Harrison Special built by Jerry Eisert. Enhanced by an eye-catching, coppertone paint scheme, the Eisert had a sleek, beautiful look that rivaled the Lotus 38 and the latest Watson.

One other car of note was the entry by Mickey Thompson. Still looking for something unique, Thompson showed up with the first front-wheel-drive car at Indianapolis since the early 1950s. Powered by a Chevrolet stock-block engine and piloted by second-year driver Bob Mathouser, the car showed some promise, but was unable to qualify.

The Granatellis, who would make future history by trying something unique, returned with their Novis. For 1965, the team built its own lightweight version of the four-wheel-drive Ferguson for Bobby Unser. The 1964 Ferguson chassis was also entered along with the Kurtis-Novi driven in the previous 500 by Art Malone.

For the first time, qualifying featured a new procedure – a draw for the order. It was not mandatory, but it provided a more sensible and sportsmanlike manner to determine when someone would qualify. In the past, teams would present their cars in a line that began in the garage area to determine the qualifying order. In order to get a desirable position for a qualifying attempt, some teams would resort to presenting their cars the night before and having crew members sleep with the cars.

Qualifying would be a Ford affair with Ford-powered cars taking the first five spots and seven of the first 10 starting positions.

Nearly two hours after qualifying began, the track record was broken. In fact, it would be broken a number of times in the next few minutes. First to do so was Andretti, whose average of 158.849 eclipsed Clark's year-old mark. Clark was next and reclaimed the record with an average speed of 160.729. Following Rutherford's unsuccessful attempt (he spun), Foyt took his turn. He emerged with a one-lap record of 161.958 (his first lap) and a four-lap mark of 161.233.

The front row was all-Lotus, although Foyt edged out Clark with his year-old Lotus 34 to capture his first pole position at Indianapolis. Gurney immediately followed by qualifying third fastest at 158.898.

"I just wanted to bring the record back to the United States," Foyt said to the cheering crowd. Clark and Team Lotus certainly had a following, but there was also an "us against them" mood regarding the foreign delegation.

There was also a tire war going on and Round 1 went to Goodyear as they provided tires for Foyt and Gurney. After the problems with Dunlop in 1964, Team Lotus was taking no chances and shod its cars with Firestones, whose tires were also on the fourth and fifth fastest qualifiers – Andretti and Jones.

When the field was filled a week later, the makeup of the starters was a clear indication the future had arrived. Twenty-seven of the 33 were rear-engine designs with Ford powering

Above: **Another superstar in the making, 25-year-old Italian immigrant Mario Andretti, a "rookie," drives a rear-engined car for the very first time and finishes third.**
Photographs: IMS

17 of the cars. Only five years earlier, all 33 starters had Offenhauser power – in front-engined roadsters.

Interestingly, the distributor for the Ford racing was now three-time 500 winner Louie Meyer, who was still partner to Dale Drake, the manufacturer of the Offenhauser engine. Meyer ultimately sold his interest and the company became known as Drake Engineering.

In the chassis department, the field included five Halibrands, four Lotuses, four Gerhardts, three Watsons, three Huffakers, two Lolas, two BRPs, two Vollstedts and two by Kurtis. Jim McElreath qualified the year-old Brabham which served as the template for the Brawner Hawk driven by Andretti. The tire war was more like a split with Firestone on 17 cars and Goodyear on the other 16. Earlier in the month, Goodyear had overcome a chunking problem on one of the

PARNELLI JONES

Curiously, the Indy-car racing career of Parnelli Jones is very short when compared to those of Foyt and Andretti. But Jones possessed such an extraordinary amount of talent that makes it easy to overlook the fact that he scored only six Indy-car victories over a span of five seasons. Born Rufus Parnell Jones, a childhood nickname left him with one of the catchiest racing names in history. Parnelli, like A.J. and Mario, would signify the top rung of the auto-racing ladder and his first name would be synonymous with the sport.

Jones figuratively and literally cut his teeth in jalopies on the short tracks in the Los Angeles area. It was an era in which contests that got out of hand on the track would invariably be decided with fists in the pits. Despite the tough image, he was smooth enough to graduate to midgets and then sprint cars where he drew national attention.

That allowed him a shot at Indianapolis in 1961 where he led in his first 500. Hit in the face with a piece of metal, Jones continued to race – and bleed. Only a sick engine could slow him down that day and everyone knew it was only a matter of time before this guy won at the Speedway.

With the perpetual look of a gunfighter, Jones' legend took off the following May when he became the first man to break through the elusive 150-mile-per-hour barrier. Jones had done the impossible and

even though brake problems robbed him of victory, he was suddenly The Man at Indy. A year later, he overcame an oil leak to win his first and only 500. Colin Chapman was impressed enough to ask Jones to drive for his Lotus team in Formula One.

Interestingly, he began to look at retirement instead of expanding his horizons and 1964 would be his last full season. By 1967, his only Indy-car start was at Indianapolis, where he nearly captured a second 500 at the wheel of Andy Granatelli's radical turbine. Jones would retire from Indy cars – but not from racing, turning his attention to off-road events and the SCCA Trans-Am series. Jones won in both disciplines, but did not turn away from Indy cars entirely.

Joining forces with long-time sponsor Vel Miletich, Jones became an Indy-car team owner and in a short time, became part of one of the most successful operations in history. With top mechanic George Bignotti and rising star Al Unser, the Vel's Parnelli Jones team captured an incredible 22 victories in a 41-race stretch.

The team would win three straight Indy-car titles and even try its hand at Formula One before closing its doors in 1978. During the same period, Jones had built a massive business empire with real estate investments and more than 40 Firestone stores at one time. The winning, it seems, was not restricted to the racetrack.

One sign of the tire situation was the location of each company's on-track warehouse. At the entrance to Gasoline Alley between a gap in the Tower Terrace grandstands, Firestone and Goodyear stored tires and fit them on wheels. Firestone was on the south side of the gap and Goodyear was on the north side. It was almost as if there was an imaginary line of demarcation. Goodyear's facility was also adorned with various racing car paintings done by Johnny Rutherford.

The Novi V-8 powered two of the starters. After crashing the new lightweight car in practice, Unser rebounded to place the year-old Ferguson-Novi on the middle of Row 3. Hurtubise qualified the Kurtis-Novi after destroying his Halibrand-Ford in practice. Hurtubise's return to the Speedway was certainly welcomed by the fans. Bearing the heavy scars from his fiery accident a year ago, Hurtubise had his fingers curled so that he could grip a steering wheel. Once again the "people's choice" driver had made the race in the "people's choice" car.

Another aspect of interest in the starting field was the number of rookies. The 1965 race featured a bumper crop of 11 newcomers led by Andretti. Their ranks also included Leonard, Foster, Al Unser, Gordon Johncock, Mickey Rupp, Bobby Johns (who found the Team Lotus entry more to his liking), Arnie Knepper, George Snider, Jerry Grant and Masten Gregory, who finally scraped into the field. Johncock and Knepper drove front-engined roadsters while Johns was making his first Indy-car start ever.

The most noteworthy driver to not qualify was Ward, who could never seem to come to grips with the new Watson. Ward failed to reach speed during the opening weekend of qualifying, crashed on the third day and was unable to bump his way into the field on the final day. After recording finishes of first, second, third, first, fourth and second in the past six 500s, Ward now found himself an unlikely spectator on Race Day.

With the Goodyear Blimp hovering over the track for the first time since before World War II, a standing-room-only crowd at the Indianapolis Motor Speedway watched the 33 starters take off at the drop of the green flag. From the middle of the front row, Clark took the lead on Lap 1, only to be passed by Foyt, who led Lap 2. Hurtubise, the sentimental favorite, was already out of the race with a broken transmission.

In Graham Gauld's biography entitled, *"Jim Clark,"* Clark said: "I held the lead through the first lap and on the second, Foyt was right behind me and when I saw him pull out, I backed off. I thought that if he wanted to run quicker than I did, let him get on with it, remembering that he had tire trouble in practice and he was with a full fuel load in the opening laps, really powering it on.

"If he was ever going to have trouble, it was going to be driving like that. However, I found that he was slowing me down so I repassed him in effort to make him come after me."

Clark passed Foyt to lead Lap 3 and for all practical purposes, the race was over.

Keeping Foyt at bay, Clark would only surrender the lead when he made his first pit stop on Lap 66. Foyt took over the lead and built a margin of 34 seconds. But thanks to the foresight of having the Wood Brothers NASCAR crew handle Clark's stops, Foyt's lead looked shaky as he headed into the pits for his first stop on Lap 75. Clark's first stop was 19.8 seconds; Foyt's stop exceeded 44 seconds.

Clark continued: "I realized things were going well just after the first pit stop. I went back out on the track to find Parnelli Jones in front of me and I wasn't sure if he had had his pit stop or if he hadn't so I passed him. The pit gave me the sign 'plus 58 Parnelli' so that was me a full lap ahead of him.

"A few laps later, we both shot past another car and I looked, only to find it was Foyt who was lumbering away from his pit stop, but he soon came charging up again so I let him past. The pit gave me the sign 'plus 58 plus 58' which meant I was a lap ahead of both Parnelli and Foyt. After that, I knew we had won."

Clark was also setting a record pace, thanks to his on-track

speed, the superior pit work and one short caution period when Tingelstad's Lola shed its right rear wheel on Lap 115. By that time, Foyt's car was out with transmission trouble. Clark's closest competitor was Jones and by the end of the race, the Scotsman was nearly two laps ahead of the 1963 winner.

As the Lotus-Ford took the checkered flag, Clark scored a victory of historic proportions. For the 500 miles, he averaged a record 150.633 mph. His car was the first rear-engined machine to win the Indianapolis 500. His car was the first Indianapolis 500 winner to be painted green since 1920. And Clark was the first foreign driver to win the 500 since Dario Resta in 1916.

Jones made it a Lotus-Ford 1-2 by finishing in second place. Andretti finished third to lead an impressive group of rookies, four of whom joined him in the top 10. Miller was fourth in the two-year-old Lotus 29 and Johncock was fifth in what would be the final strong performance in a roadster. Fellow rookies Rupp and Johns were sixth and seventh, respectively, while an unhappy Branson brought his new Watson home in eighth. Al Unser, who qualified Foyt's backup Lola on the final day, ran as high as fifth after starting 32nd and wound up ninth. Journeyman driver Eddie Johnson rounded out the top 10 in another roadster.

Indianapolis was only the beginning of things to come that season for a number of the drivers in the 1965 field. Clark would return to Europe and win five straight F1 World Championship races to clinch his second crown. Andretti would win USAC's first road-course event (held at Indianapolis Raceway Park) and amass enough points to win the national championship. Al Unser would win the Pike's Peak Auto Hill Climb (part of that year's USAC Championship) for a second straight year. Joe Leonard would capture the 150-miler at Milwaukee in the same AAR Halibrand-Ford he had raced at Indianapolis. Johncock's team would put him in a rear-engine Gerhardt after a number of strong performances in the roadster (including a pole and a third-place finish at Langhorne). He would respond by winning the 200-miler at Milwaukee.

And then there was Rodger Ward. After parting company with the Leader Card team, he joined Texas oilman John Mecom and master mechanic George Bignotti to run a number of USAC events as a factory effort for Lola Cars Ltd. The battle for the 1966 Indianapolis 500 was already shaping up.

OFFICIAL PROGRAM · 75¢

MAY 31 1965

Top: In as dominant a performance as ever seen at the Speedway, Clark leads 190 of the 200 laps on his way to the win.

Above: The rear-engined car, once an oddity, is now a winner at Indianapolis, and a visiting foreign driver is in Victory Lane for the first time since 1916.

Photographs: IMS

Main photograph: For the second time in three years, an accident stops the race.

Right: Substituting for Walt Hansgen, who lost his life in spring testing at Le Mans, Englishman Graham Hill wins in his first start.
Photograph: IMS

THE FIFTIETH INDIANAPOLIS 500
OFFICIAL PROGRAM
INDIANAPOLIS MOTOR SPEEDWAY
MAY 30, 1966
ONE DOLL

1966: Whatever Lola Wants

In many ways, innovation was alive and well when contestants gathered on opening day for practice for the 1966 Indianapolis 500.

There were all sorts of new cars and many were capable of being contenders. There were a number of unusual cars. The tire war between Firestone and Goodyear was in full swing. And there were a number of new drivers to follow the highly successful rookie class of 1965.

Leading the way among the new cars and teams was All American Racers, which unveiled the new Eagle designed by ex-Lotus man, Len Terry. Using his successful Lotus 38 design as a guide, Terry basically copied the sleek lines of the Lotus 38, but gave the Eagle an extra-wide fuel tank and a nosecone that resembled an eagle's beak. Gurney entered cars for himself, Joe Leonard, Jerry Grant and Lloyd Ruby. A fifth car was sold to Lindsey Hopkins for Roger McCluskey.

Eric Broadley returned with a new, improved Lola T90 for the Mecom Racing Team that originally entered cars for Rodger Ward, Jackie Stewart and Walt Hansgen. When Hansgen was killed during the April trials for the 24 Hours of Le Mans, Graham Hill was signed in his place. Stewart and Hill would be driving Ford-powered cars while Ward's car featured a supercharged Offenhauser. George Bignotti, the winning chief mechanic with A.J. Foyt's two 500 victories, was in charge of the new Mecom team, which was already showing the racing world they would be a contender. Ward got them off to a good start by finishing second to Jim McElreath at Phoenix and winning a rain-shortened event at Trenton to lead the championship.

Foyt unveiled the new Coyote-Ford, which bore strong re-

semblance to the Lotus 38. Two of the Coyotes were entered for Foyt and George Snider with a conventional Lotus 38 as a backup. However, Snider's car had an interesting history. In 1965, it was the car that Bobby Johns drove to seventh place in the 500. Afterward, Clark's winning car went straight to Ford Motor Company where it would ultimately reside in the Henry Ford Museum and Johns' car was sent to various shows with Clark's number 82 painted over Johns' number 83. At the end of 1965, Ansted Thompson Racing purchased the car and veteran fabricator Eddie Kuzma modified it to become a Coyote.

Team Lotus also returned, but with a new partnership with the Granatelli brothers. British racing green became a thing of the past as the STP sponsorship dictated the cars be painted in bright orange (or as someone joked: "Granatelli green"). The Granatellis had not given up on the Novi. In addition to the involvement with Team Lotus, they entered a revised version of the Paxton 4WD Novi that had been damaged in a 1965 practice crash. The main revision centered on moving the water radiator to the back of the tail section and closing off the nose of the car. It was to be driven by rookie Greg Weld.

Thanks to the new 3-liter rule in Formula One, Lotus had entered into an arrangement with BRM to use its complicated H-16 engine. In anticipation of using the BRM engine at Indianapolis as well, Lotus designed the Type 42 chassis to house the unique powerplant. However, BRM got behind on development and for Indianapolis, drivers Jim Clark and teammate Al Unser were given the more conventional Lotus 38 powered by the Ford DOHC V-8.

Rolla Vollstedt also unveiled his third-generation design – a pair of Lotus 38 look-alikes powered by Ford and entered for Billy Foster and Ronnie Duman. Also trying to make their cars

Inset above left: A. J. Foyt walks back from
the accident with Chief Mechanic Johnny
Pouelsen. An excellent dirt-track driver in
the 1950s, Pouelsen was chief mechanic for
Parnelli Jones between 1961 and 1965.

Inset above: Mechanics rush to the aid of
their drivers.
Photographs: IMS

look more like the Lotus 38 was the George Bryant team
with body revisions on its BRP-Fords for Johnny Boyd
and Bobby Johns.

Ted Halibrand collaborated with the Agajanian team to
design a sleek new Shrike. It was powered by a supercharged
Offenhauser and entered for Parnelli Jones and rookie
Dick Atkins.

Aerodynamic considerations were also becoming prevalent
as a number of cars featured tail sections with "ducktail"
spoilers. Chief among the spoiler set was the Hawk-Ford of
Mario Andretti. McElreath's newly built John Zink Special,
based on the team's 1964 Brabham, likewise had a rear
spoiler tail, as did the Ford-powered Watson entered for
Chuck Hulse. However, the award for the largest spoiler went
to the Jerry Eisert's latest Harrison Special.

Joe Huffaker gave his new MG Liquid Suspension cars a
slight wedge shape but the new chassis still featured the
hydrostatic suspension system.

Dick Cecil also unveiled an innovative chassis for the DVS
Team and driver Arnie Knepper. The Cecil-Ford featured a
monocoque tub that had no rivets.

One other entry merited attention if only because of the
entrants. NASCAR rookie Lee Roy Yarbrough was assigned
to a Gerhardt-Offenhauser sponsored by Union 76 fuel and
entered by GCR Racers. The "R" stood for 1960 winner
Jim Rathmann while the "G" and the "C" stood for Virgil
"Gus" Grissom and Gordon Cooper. Grissom and Cooper were
among the original seven chosen by NASA for its
astronaut program.

And while much attention was being paid to chassis
design, the Offenhauser engine was getting some help in an
effort to compete with the high-horsepower Ford DOHC V-8.
Superchargers were used to boost the horsepower on the
Offenhauser-powered cars driven by Jones, Atkins, Ward and
Bud Tingelstad while turbochargers appeared on a number of
cars including those driven by Bobby Unser, Jim Hurtubise and
Bobby Grim.

A pair of oddities also made up the 1966 entry list. One
was the Jack Adams Aircraft Special, an Epperly laydown
chassis now powered by a gas turbine engine. The other was
the Stein Twin Porsche Special that featured Porsche 4-cylin-
der engines in front of and behind the driver. Bill Cheesbourg,
the slowest qualifier in the last two 500s, spent the month
driving both cars. The Stein entry was the first twin-engined
car at Indianapolis since the Fageol Twin Coach Special that
Paul Russo qualified in second position in 1946.
Unfortunately for Cheesbourg, neither car would go fast
enough to merit a qualification attempt.

Although the Team Lotus and the numerous Lotus copies
were the cars to beat, qualifying was once again the domain
of the Dean Van Lines team and second-year driver Mario
Andretti. Driving the Hawk-Ford built by Clint Brawner,
Andretti, who set a track record when he qualified a year earlier, did it again to the tune of a one-lap mark of 166.328
mph and a record four-lap average of 165.899 mph.

For the second straight year, Clark qualified second fastest
– this time with a 164.144 mph average. Later on, George
Snider posted at 162.521 mph in Foyt's (Lotus-based)
Coyote-Ford to fill out the front row. Jones gave the Offen-
hauser faithful some hope by qualifying fourth in the
Agajanian Shrike. Ruby led the Gurney's squadron of Eagles
by qualifying fifth. And Gordon Johncock, like Andretti and
Snider a member of the class of '65, qualified his Gerhardt-
Ford sixth fastest.

The entire Mecom Racing Team also qualified on opening
day. Stewart led the way with the 11th-best time in the

Above: Lloyd Ruby, slow-talking Texan and underrated road racer who probably should have won the 500 several times. Third-placed finisher in 1964, he led in five out of six "500s" between 1966 and 1971, and appeared headed for victory in 1966, 1968, and 1969.

Main photograph: Jim Clark, caught at the beginning of one of two very elaborate spins on his way to finishing second, draws rave reviews for his ability to "save" the car.

Photographs: IMS

Bowes Seal Fast Lola-Ford, followed by Ward in the Bryant Lola-Offenhauser in 13th and Hill in the American Red Ball Lola-Ford in 15th. BRM teammates Hill and Stewart were in their first Indianapolis 500 while a tearful Ward made his 15th 500 after missing the 1965 race.

Slowest of the 17 first-day qualifiers was midget star Mel Kenyon. Kenyon lost the fingers on his left hand in a fiery crash at Langhorne the previous summer, but embarked on a comeback that earned him the nickname "Miraculous Mel." Using a special driving glove that fit over a peg on the steering wheel, Kenyon was able to race despite the handicap.

After the exceptionally safe month of May in 1965, the fatal accident of Chuck Rodee in May of '66 served to remind everyone that racing was still a dangerous business. Driving the Watson that Ward had failed to qualify a year earlier now fitted with an Offenhauser, Rodee posted impressive speeds in practice. It all went sour when he spun in Turn 1 during warmup for a qualifying attempt and backed into the wall – hard. In the impact, Rodee suffered a ruptured aorta. A shocked Speedway crowd learned of his passing two hours later.

Among those unable to qualify on the first day were Foyt, who crashed during practice, and Gurney, who had to abort his run. Both made the show the following day, although Foyt's qualification was accompanied by drama as his crew worked overnight to assemble a new Lotus 38 in time for his run.

The 1966 starting field was reasonably diverse with a number of new chassis designs, some interesting engine variations and drivers from a variety of backgrounds. There were six Gerhardts, five Eagles, four Lolas, four Lotuses, three Huffakers, two Vollstedts and two Watsons as well as a Hawk, a Brabham, a Coyote (formerly a Lotus 38), a BRP, a Shrike, a Cecil and an Eisert. Ford powered 25 of the cars with Offenhauser powering the remaining eight. Pitted against USAC's best from the past, present and future were four F1 stars (Gurney, Clark, Hill and Stewart), a NASCAR standout (Cale Yarborough) and a sports-car ace (Grant).

For the nostalgia buffs, there was a solitary Watson roadster that veteran Bobby Grim qualified on the final day of time trials. But even this relic from the past needed a new technological boost. The 4-cylinder Offenhauser in Grim's car was one of three starters in the '66 lineup to have a turbocharger. Missing from the field was the Novi, which failed to reach qualifying speed and wound up crushed against the Turn 4 wall.

With so many strong car-and-driver combinations, the 1966 Indianapolis 500 was anybody's race. And what happened at the start truly made it a race that was up for grabs.

Andretti led the field down for the start, but Snider appeared to get the jump on the polesitter as they headed into Turn 1. Behind them was melee. Starting on the outside of Row 4, Billy Foster, who later claimed he was bumped, clouted the outside wall along the main straightaway as he tried to squeeze by Johncock, who started on the outside of Row 2. Foster had the advantage of a five-speed gearbox, while Johncock's car had a two-speed gearbox. It might have been a one-car accident had one of his right-side wheels and his nosecone not bounced in front of the oncoming pack of cars.

With nowhere to go, Kenyon slid sideways, nearly blocking the straightaway. Johncock hit debris, but continued on. Foyt hit the outside wall and Gurney had his left-side wheels sheared off. Branson slid into the inside wall and launched Gary Congdon. Cale Yarborough, Tingelstad and Knepper got caught up in their accident. In the meantime, Larry Dickson, Al Miller, Ronnie Duman and Grim either hit the wall or some other car. In the middle of the accident, no less than 10 wheels went airborne.

Other cars managed to snake through the wreckage, chief among them Hill and Al Unser. As the field came around to complete the first lap, Pat Vidan already had the red flag out. For the second time in three races, the Indianapolis 500 was halted because of an accident. All told, 11 cars were too badly damaged to continue. Tingelstad's suffered radiator damage while Johncock's car appeared with only damage to the nosecone. Miraculously, Foyt incurred the only injury, cutting his finger while climbing over the fence.

Relief turned to anger and in at least one case, humor.

"You have 33 of the best drivers in the world here and you'd think they could go down a straightaway without running into each other," fumed Gurney.

"It looked like worms going through spaghetti," added Knepper.

The race restarted some 100 minutes later and it was apparent this would be one of the wilder 500s on record.

On Lap 5, Boyd spun and hit the Turn 1 wall. He blamed the accident on leaking fluid from Hurtubise's car. Eleven laps later, Tingelstad retired with radiator problems, another victim of the opening-lap accident. On Lap 22, Snider and Chuck Hulse tangled on the backstretch, putting both cars into the wall and out of the race.

Next, it was Andretti's turn. His pole-winning Hawk-Ford led

the first 16 laps, but blue smoke began to trail from the pipes and by Lap 27 he was out. The defending race winner, Clark, took the lead on Lap 17 and led until Lap 64, when he spun in Turn 4. Clark's save drew a standing ovation. He made it into the pits where it was determined he had suffered no damage to his tires.

He rejoined the race in second place behind Ruby, who led the Indianapolis 500 for the first time in his career. Ruby pitted on Lap 75 and Clark took over the lead for the next 11 laps, only to spin again. Ruby clearly had the upper hand on Clark and built a lead of 50 seconds. It's important to note that Clark was not driving the car he had used to win the 1965 race. That car went straight to the Henry Ford Museum in Dearborn, Mich., where it sits to this day.

Moving up quietly was Stewart, already considered heir apparent to Clark in F1 circles. Although Indianapolis was his first race on an oval, he drove like a veteran, engaging McCluskey in a long duel for third place and then battling Clark for second.

A stall on his final pit stop dropped him behind Ruby and Clark, but his challenge was far from being over.

Ruby caught and passed Clark for the lead on Lap 140 and shortly after, Clark ducked into the pits. But Ruby was now in trouble as oil could be seen streaking on the Eagle's tail section. By Lap 150, the Texan was out and Stewart was now in the lead.

The rookie from Scotland would stay there for the next 40 laps. Stewart was 10 laps away from his greatest payday, but unbeknownst to everyone except the Mecom driver, there was trouble. Stewart's engine had been losing oil pressure. On Lap 192, he coasted to a halt in Turn 4 and walked to his pit, shrugging and waving to the crowd while receiving a tumultuous ovation. Stewart would be asked why he purposely shut off the engine instead of trying to go for broke. He replied that as a Scotsman, he was trying to protect his owner's investment!

Hill was now in the lead. Or was he?

Eight laps later, the 1962 world champion took the checker and headed for Victory Lane. Shortly after he arrived, Clark, thinking he had won, also drove to Victory Lane, only to find it occupied by Hill & Co. Clark was apparently second for the second time in four years and McElreath came home third in his Brabham. Johncock wound up fourth, but actually had a quicker time for the 500 miles than the race winner. But because of the damage to his car, he spent significantly more time in the pits.

Despite his opening-lap spin, Kenyon ended up fifth and Stewart recorded enough laps to be credited with sixth. Although a fellow rookie won the race, Stewart garnered the top rookie honor for his impressive drive. Hill became the first rookie to win the 500 since George Souders in 1927.

In the wake of the race's dramatic finish, there was considerable question about Clark's actual finishing position. It came down to the confusion over the identical paint scheme on the two STP Lotuses. A lap by teammate Al Unser had been erroneously credited to Clark. The discrepancy showed up in the official timing and scoring tapes and no protest was filed.

Hill's victory stood and the Englishman won over the Speedway crowd with a hilarious speech at the victory banquet. Before Hill collected his winner's check, his teammate Rodger Ward made a tearful announcement that he was retiring from racing.

"I always said that when it wasn't fun anymore, I would retire," Ward told the audience. "Well yesterday, it just wasn't fun."

The two-time 500 winner and national champion later told friends he could visualize his children as he drove in the race. He pulled into the pits on Lap 74 and got out of the car, complaining of "handling problems."

The ramifications of the win did not go unnoticed and Hill took the occasion to have some fun. "Jimmy and I are thinking of sponsoring an award for the top-finishing American next year."

Ah, next year. Could it be any more exciting?

The British Invasion, motor racing version. Top to bottom, Jackie Stewart, Jim Clark, and Graham Hill. Between them, this trio will eventually earn the World Championship seven times.
Photographs: IMS

Top right: On his way to winning his third "500," Foyt races with New Zealand's Denis Hulme, who is making his debut at Indianapolis. He will finish fourth. In two weeks' time, Foyt will share the winning Ford Mark V11 at Le Mans with Dan Gurney, while Hulme, a Foyt teammate there, will "dnf," sharing a car with Lloyd Ruby. Hulme will win the 1967 World Championship.

Above near right: In recognition of a balloon race being the first competitive event ever held at the Speedway, on June 5, 1909, several balloonists were to take part in ascents on qualifying days in the late 1960s.

Above right: The Master Control Tower in all its glory. For over 40 years, this was the "home" of timing and scoring, traffic control, and the Indianapolis Motor Speedway Radio Network.

Photographs: IMS

1967: Not With A Bang, But A Whimper

If there was any doubt that the 1967 Indianapolis 500 would be able to match the previous year's race in action, it was dispelled the moment the track opened for practice.

As had been the tradition, there was a certain amount of bragging rights for the driver and team who could make it out onto the track first. A year earlier, there had been a small traffic jam with the G.C. Murphy Special of Roger McCluskey and the Harrison Specials of Ronnie Duman and Bob Mathouser parked at the entrance to Gasoline Alley.

For 1967, the combatants for "first on the track" honors were Cale Yarborough and George Snider. As the crews pushed their respective cars toward the pit lane, there was a collision and Yarborough's car lost its nosecone. And it was only the first day of what would be one of the more interesting Mays at the Indianapolis Motor Speedway.

If USAC regulars believed Graham Hill had been kidding them about sponsoring a prize for the top-finishing American, they might have had some second thoughts after seeing the makeup of the entry list.

For years, the Indianapolis 500 had been billed as the "International Sweepstakes." In 1967, the international aspect came to the forefront.

Rivals in 1966, Hill and Clark returned as teammates, as Hill had joined Team Lotus for the '67 season. Jackie Stewart was back with Mecom Racing Team. For 1967, they would be joined by a number of cohorts from the world of grand prix racing. New Zealand's Denis Hulme was entered to drive an Eagle-Ford for Smokey Yunick. Fellow Kiwi Chris Amon was entered to drive one of the BRP-Fords. Mexico's Pedro Rodriguez, who failed to make the race on his previous two attempts, was entered in a new Watson-Ford. Belgium's Lucien Bianchi was entered in Jim Robbins' Vollstedt-Ford. Friedkin Enterprises entered Austria's Jochen Rindt in an Eagle-Ford. And had he not perished in a fiery accident at Monaco, Italian star Lorenzo Bandini would have driven a Gerhardt-Ford for Wally Weir.

There were three other American rookies with F1 backgrounds. All American Racers entered Richie Ginther. Ginther's former Honda teammate, Ronnie Bucknum, wound up in the Vita-Fresh Gerhardt-Ford, while Bob Bondurant hoped to make his first 500 in the Walther Lola-Offenhauser.

The favorites were pretty much the drivers and teams one would have expected.

Leading the way in his three-year-old Hawk Ford was defending national champion and track record holder, Mario Andretti. Chief mechanic Clint Brawner added a pair of fins to the nosecone for aerodynamic effect and Andretti was poised to be the first man to crack the 170 mph barrier.

Mecom Racing Team, which surprised everyone with its winning performance in 1966, was back with Eric Broadley's latest Lola-Ford for Stewart and Al Unser.

A.J. Foyt returned with a pair of new Coyote-Fords for himself and Joe Leonard. After years of running red, white and blue paint schemes, Foyt's cars were now painted in what would become his trademark poppy red color.

Dan Gurney spearheaded the All American Racers effort with the latest Eagle-Ford and several using customer Eagles. Among those drivers were Roger McCluskey, Bobby Unser and Johnny Rutherford.

McCluskey was back with Lindsey Hopkins while Unser was in his first full season with Leader Card Racers. Towards the end of the 1966 season, Unser had been signed to replace the late Don Branson, the victim of a sprint car accident at Ascot. Rutherford, who had missed the 1966 race after breaking his arms in a sprint car accident, was making a comeback in the Weinberger Homes entry. Leader Card also had a pair of new Watson-Fords for Rodriguez and fellow rookie Mike Mosley.

Turbocharging gave the 4-cylinder Offenhauser its best chance to run with the Ford V-8s and the strongest teams using these engines was Gene White Racing and Fred Gerhardt. Veteran Lloyd Ruby and NASCAR rookie Lee Roy Yarbrough were assigned to a pair of White's new Mongoose chassis, while Gerhardt entered Mel Kenyon and rookie Art

Pollard in a pair of new Gerhardt chassis, featuring an elongated nosecone and "ducktail" spoiler. (Yarbrough would ultimately qualify one of the Jim Robbins Vollstedt-Fords.)

Gordon Johncock was now running his own team, using the Ford V-8 to power his new Gerhardt chassis.

In reality, though, there was one car that captured virtually all of the attention and it nearly changed the face of Indy-car racing forever.

Always looking for an innovation, the Granatelli brothers struck the mother lode when they unveiled their STP Paxton Turbocar for 1963 winner Parnelli Jones.

Designed by Ken Wallis, the car featured an aluminum box-shaped frame that went down the middle of the chassis. Hanging on the right side was the cockpit; hanging on the left side was a Pratt-Whitney ST6 turbine normally used in helicopters. The car also used a Ferguson-style four-wheel-drive system and if that wasn't enough, a moveable spoiler behind the cockpit served as an air brake. Mercedes-Benz tried a similar system on its 300SLR endurance racer in 1955, but the Granatelli car's air brake was closer to the moveable flipper spoiler used on various Chaparral sports cars in 1965 and '66.

The car could run on kerosene and reportedly had 550 horsepower, comparable to the Fords and Offys. Granatelli tried to reason with the critics that the engine would be a cost-saver. Priced in the same range as the Ford, the turbine engine needed overhauls one-tenth of the time.

Although USAC had previously avoided restrictions on turbine engines, for 1967 they attempted to curb the horsepower by limiting the annulus intake area to 23.999 inches.

But it was the sound of the turbine, or lack thereof, that got everyone's attention. Nicknamed "Silent Sam" and the "Whooshmobile," the STP Turbocar sounded like a vacuum cleaner. Pre-season testing showed it was going to be competitive and envious car owners sought to have it banned before it turned a wheel at the Speedway.

For the time being, the United States Auto Club allowed

the car to run and Jones practiced at speeds slightly slower than the favorites for the pole. Whether he was showing his hand or not (nearly 40 years later, Jones still insists he was), the car's real strength was going to be in its race setup, thanks to the four-wheel-drive system.

Granatellis weren't the only ones with innovations in 1967. Back at the Speedway for the first time in two years was Mickey Thompson, who entered a rear-engined car for Gary Congdon and a front-engined car for Sam Sessions. Both were Chevrolet-powered, and Sessions' car would be the last front-wheel-drive car to run at Indianapolis. Needless to say, neither car went quick enough.

The first day of qualifying clearly belonged to Andretti, who seemed to have his own groove at the track. Running closer to the wall than anyone else (rooster tails of dust would fly up whenever he neared the short chute walls), Andretti set one- and four-laps marks for the second straight year. Andretti av-

Below: Parnelli makes a pit stop. The large cylindrical object (held by Ken Wallis) is for deflecting the considerable heat from the turbine's exhaust while the car is stationary. Note that all three Granatelli brothers are actively involved in the servicing. Joe and Vince are refueling, while Andy is tending to something behind the left front wheel, still holding the drinking cup he has just retrieved from Parnelli. Holding the hose are famed engineers Ron Falk and Vince Conze, while note also that, with his Lotus already done for the day, discretely watching the proceedings with great interest is Jim Clark.
Photograph: IMS

eraged 168.892 with a top lap of 169.888 mph. The 170-mph lap would have to wait for another year.

Joining him on the front row were Gurney and Johncock while Foyt and Leonard qualified fourth and fifth, respectively. And sitting on the outside of Row 2 was Jones and the STP Turbocar. The cry of "sandbagging" could be heard throughout the paddock.

Although F1 drivers had dominated the proceedings the previous year, their contingent found the going a bit more difficult in 1967. Clark qualified a disappointing 16th and Stewart found himself hopping into the Mecom team's backup Lola-Ford and qualifying 29th after being bumped.

Hulme qualified 24th while Hill struggled in the Lotus 42 chassis to start 31st. Hill's car was originally designed in 1966 to house the BRM H-16 engine and modified to accept the Ford V-8. Rindt survived a fiery practice accident, went too slow in his team's backup Eagle-Ford and then qualified the AAR Eagle-Weslake in 32nd position.

However, they made the race. Bianchi, Rodriguez and Bucknum all qualified at speeds too slow to make the field. Bondurant failed to find enough speed to make a qualifying attempt while Amon crashed twice during the month and likewise failed to make an attempt. Ginther made an incomplete qualifying attempt, but shortly afterward, he decided to retire from racing.

Also failing to make the race were the new Mallard-Offenhausers entered for Jim Hurtubise and Ebb Rose. For the first time in the history of the 500, no front-engined cars would be in the starting field.

Almost overlooked, thanks to the turbine controversy, was the tire war, now in its third full year. Firestone got the initial bragging rights with Andretti's pole position, but the next four spots on the starting grid belonged to Goodyear-shod drivers. Of course, the STP Turbocar had Firestones.

The so-called war even took on a humorous note as the parents of Al and Bobby Unser found their sons on opposing sides. To avoid showing favoritism, someone presented Jerry and Mary Unser with special jackets. By cutting a blue Goodyear jacket and a red Firestone jacket in half and sewing the opposite sides together, Dad Unser's jacket read "Goodstone," Mom Unser's "Fireyear."

When field came down to take the green flag on Memorial Day, it was under an overcast sky. Rain was in the forecast, although it had not rained on the Indianapolis 500 since 1950. This year would be different.

As Pat Vidan dropped the flag to start the race, Andretti jumped out in front. As the field headed into Turn 1, Jones simply drove around the outside of Leonard, Foyt, Johncock and Gurney to take second place as they headed into the short chute. Ducking behind Andretti as they exited Turn 2, Jones shot past on the inside to take the lead. It was that simple.

It's important to note that regardless of the sandbagging issue, Jones pretty much qualified in his race setup. His chief rivals had set their fastest practice and qualifying speeds with a mixture of nitro in their fuel to give them added horsepower. Nitro was impractical for a race because it was hard on engines and adversely affected fuel mileage.

For 18 laps, Jones drove off and left the opposition. But on this day, the only thing that was going to stop him and the STP Turbocar was the weather. For the third time in four years, the red flag came out, only this time it was for rain. It would be a historical rain, however, as the race officials were forced to postpone the race until the following day. For the first time in 500 history, the race would take two days to run.

One man who was expected to give Jones a run was already in trouble. Early on, Andretti's car began to slow and on Lap 12 he dashed into the pits. It looked like 1966 repeating itself, but unlike the previous year, the problem did not sideline the polesitter. This year's problem was a slipping clutch, which would have necessitated a lengthy pit stop. However, a change to the rules allowed repairs to made during a red flag period and Andretti's clutch was repaired overnight. Nevertheless, Andretti found himself restarting the race the following day, six laps behind the leader.

Race Day Part II was cool, but sunny and dry enough for the race. Jones continued to dominate, primarily surrendering the lead when he came in for pit stops. The 1963 winner had only one close call and that came when he and Lee Roy

Yarbrough made contact on Lap 52. Both cars spun into the infield, straightened up and rejoined the race. In the meantime, Gurney sailed past into the lead giving him the distinction of being the only driver to have passed Jones in the race. However, it took Jones only two laps to retake the lead.

Prior to the Jones-Yarbrough caution, a pair of 500 winners made early exits. Graham Hill, the 1966 winner who barely scraped into the 1967 starting field, retired with a burned piston on Lap 23. His teammate, 1965 winner Jim Clark, joined him on the sidelines 12 laps later. Although no one knew it at the time, it would be Clark's last 500.

Andretti's frustrating race came to an end on Lap 58 in Turn 1. Six laps down, thanks to the clutch problem the previous day, the Brawner Hawk shed its right front wheel to put the polesitter out of the 500 for a second straight year.

Jones continued to build his lead, but the 1967 Indianapolis 500 would be a race filled with caution periods for accidents. On Lap 73, rookie Wally Dallenbach crashed the Vatis Huffaker-Offenhauser on the main straightaway. On Lap 99, Yarbrough and Lloyd Ruby, who took over George Snider's car, crashed in Turn 4. Both drivers were trying to avoid the spinning car of Cale Yarborough.

Jackie Stewart, who nearly won the 1966 race, was making a major charge to the front. After starting 29th, Stewart got as high as third and might have been able to catch second-place man Foyt had his car lasted. Unfortunately for the Scotsman, the Bowes Seal Fast Lola-Ford lost its oil pressure for the second straight year and Stewart coasted to a halt in Turn 4 on Lap 168.

Stewart's demise was followed by a Turn 3 accident on Lap 177 following a tangle between Yarborough and Kenyon. Both cars ended up in the infield, but a second accident unfolded in the same turn involving Carl Williams, Bob Veith and Bud Tingelstad. Williams and Veith each suffered damage to the nosecones of their respective cars while Tingelstad was able to continue unscathed after spinning into the infield.

As the race neared the end, it appeared that Jones had locked up his second 500 victory with Foyt running a safe second and Al Unser now third.

Next came drama in the form of Jones' Turbocar drastically slowing down on Lap 197. He coasted into the pits with a broken transmission. The culprit was a $6 ball bearing.

Foyt was now in the lead, but by no means was he safely home. As he headed down the main straightaway to take the checkered flag, Bobby Grim's Gerhardt-Offenhauser broke a half-shaft and spun. Caught up in his spin were Williams and Chuck Hulse, whose Lola chassis had won the '66 500. All three cars hit the wall while Tingelstad and Larry Dickson spun to avoid the accident. Foyt zigzagged through the accident to capture his third Indianapolis 500.

Foyt's victory came at the expense of Jones' retirement and gave Goodyear its first 500 win since 1919.

Al Unser, who cut a tire earlier in the race, finished second and Leonard came home third in Foyt's sister car. Hulme finished a respectable fourth and would garner Indy's top rookie honor. Jim McElreath wound up fifth in the Zink Brabham-Ford and Jones managed to finish a very disappointed sixth place.

The STP Turbocar had made its mark at Indianapolis. The question facing the United States Auto Club and the Indy-car racing community was whether or not it would be allowed to compete in the future.

There's an incredible footnote to this chapter. Foyt's victory occurred on Tuesday, May 31. Less than two weeks later, he and Dan Gurney captured the 24 Hours of Le Mans in a Ford GT-40 Mark IV. The following Sunday, Gurney made history by capturing the Belgian Grand Prix in his Eagle-Weslake. Gurney's victory marked the first time since 1921 that an American car had captured a European Grand Prix. His feat harkened back to Jimmy Murphy's upset win in the French GP. Murphy drove the same Duesenberg chassis he would pilot to victory in the 1922 Indianapolis 500.

Top left: Waiting for the infield gates to open.

Above left: The timing and scoring level in the Master Control Tower.

Above: The garage area is a hive of industry in anticipation of a heavy practice session.
Photographs: IMS

Above: The huge haulers are still several years away, as even the car of defending winner and USAC National Champion Foyt arrives on an open trailer.

Opposite: Pole sitter Joe Leonard racing Johnny Rutherford. For several years, Granatelli cars on race day would be enhanced with fluorescent paint of varying colors for identification purposes.

Main photograph: Joe Leonard, on the pole with the Lotus turbine. Three times the AMA (American Motorcyclist Association) national champion (1954, 1956 and 1957), Leonard has already finished third in the "500" for A. J. Foyt in 1967, and will finish third again (for Vel's Parnelli Jones) in 1972.

Photograph: IMS

1968: Sounds Of Silence, Part II

To the surprise of no one, the United States Auto Club began to look at rule changes governing turbine engines. The Granatelli STP Turbocar had been built within the guidelines of the rules, but the chorus of complaints from team owners now faced with the prospect of having to buy turbine engines spurred USAC's rules committee to take action.

Team owners weren't the only ones to complain. Motorsports purists did not like the prospect of auto racing without sound. Someone even suggested that if the turbines were allowed to stay and grew in number, perhaps they could pipe in some kind of piston-engine sound.

Despite the threat of lawsuits by the Granatellis, USAC came up with a formula that would limit the horsepower on the turbine, but keep it competitive with the Offenhausers and Fords. The term "annulus intake area" became commonplace as a result of the new rule, which now limited the amount of air that could be forced into the engine from 23.999 inches to 15.999 inches.

The new rules may have made the STP Turbocar obsolete, but it would transpire that the Granatellis had something else up their creative sleeves.

They turned to Colin Chapman of Lotus, whose Indy-car operation had been sponsored by STP since 1966. Chapman, the top innovator in F1 racing at the time, turned his design team loose and came up with the Lotus 56. The new Lotus was as radical as its STP Turbocar predecessor. Its wedge shape was not unlike a doorstop and the car also featured four-wheel drive.

March testing at Indianapolis left everyone encouraged at Lotus. One of those people was Jim Clark, who returned to Europe and told folks he had just "tested the car that was going to win the Indianapolis 500." Sadly, that would be Clark's last visit to Indianapolis as he was killed in a Formula 2 race at Hockenheim, Germany, only a few days later.

Despite the loss, the STP team came to Indianapolis with four of the new Lotus 56s and a renovated version of the STP Turbocar. Slated to drive the cars were Graham Hill, Jackie Stewart and rookies Mike Spence and Greg Weld. Joe Leonard was assigned to drive the older car. However, Stewart was a question mark, having injured his wrist in a Formula 2 test in Jarama, Spain. Stewart had been signed to take Clark's place and there was still hope the Scottish driver would be able to compete.

Gene White returned with its 1967 Mongoose-Offenhauser for driver Lloyd Ruby. Bobby Grim would eventually qualify the team's second car. Another 1967 Mongoose was entered for George Snider but powered by a normally aspirated Ford. It marked the first 500 entry of Vel's Parnelli Jones Racing, a partnership formed by '63 winner Parnelli Jones and Vel Miletich.

When the track opened on May 4, there was an air of international harmony as the Indianapolis Motor Speedway took time to welcome the foreign drivers. Along with the Lotus lineup, other F1 drivers entered were Bruce McLaren, Denis Hulme, Jochen Rindt, Ronnie Bucknum and Masten Gregory. During opening day festivities, the international drivers were recognized and presented with gifts. A kilt was to be presented to Stewart, but because he was absent during the ceremony (he was the keynote speaker at the 500 Mayor's Breakfast that year), Spence accepted on his behalf, telling the crowd: "I'm sure Jackie will know what to do with this."

The STP team was not the only team arriving at Indianapolis with turbine-powered cars. Ken Wallis, who designed the original STP Turbocar, made some revisions and penned a pair for McLaren and Hulme. Heavily funded by Goodyear, the team was run by Carroll Shelby and sponsored by Botany 500 menswear.

Defending winner A.J. Foyt was back with slightly modified Coyote-Fords for himself and Jim McElreath. The normally aspirated Ford DOHC V-8 powered both cars, but before the month was out, Foyt would try a turbocharged version of the engine and an automatic transmission. He stuck with the conventional engine and transmission for the race.

Dan Gurney unveiled the second generation Eagle. Designed by Englishman Tony Southgate, the new cars were entered for Gurney's AAR team, the Leader Card team for Bobby Unser, the Lindsey Hopkins team for Roger McCluskey and the Friedkin team for Jerry Grant.

The Mecom team was no more, as '67 sponsor Al Retzloff purchased the operation. Retzloff returned to Indianapolis with Al Unser, George Bignotti and a pair of new Lola chassis. The car Unser would ultimately qualify had four-wheel drive and was powered by a turbocharged version of the Ford DOHC V-8. The sister car was standard rear-wheel-drive and powered by a normally aspirated Ford DOHC V-8. Both cars were turned out in a beautiful candy-apple red paint scheme with polished chrome wheels.

Mario Andretti, the pole position winner the last two years, returned with a new Brawner Hawk and a new role – team owner. During the off-season, longtime owner Al Dean had succumbed to cancer and the team was disbanded. Andretti was able to find a sponsor in Overseas National Airways and kept the operation alive. Andretti's new car was another to employ the turbocharged Ford.

The 1968 entry list also featured the offspring of two of Indy's greatest legends. Bill Vukovich Jr., whose father won the 500 in 1953 and '54, was entered in J.C. Agajanian's Shrike now powered by a turbocharged Offenhauser. The Bettenhausen name also made its Speedway return with the entry of Gary Bettenhausen.

Joe Hunt actually entered the eldest son of the late Tony Bettenhausen in Hunt's dirt car. Bettenhausen had run the car in USAC Champ Car events at Hanford (where he finished 10th) and Phoenix. He hoped to take his rookie test and then install a turbocharged Offenhauser as it was soon apparent the conventional 4-cylinder version lacked the necessary horsepower. Bettenhausen would eventually complete his test in one of J.C. Agajanian's cars and later hop into one of Fred Gerhardt's rear-engined cars.

The STP team got some bad news as Stewart was unable to pass his physical. It was determined he had a hairline fracture of the scaphoid bone and would be forced to wear a cast a minimum of 20 weeks. Although he would return to racing in the middle of June, he missed the Indianapolis 500 as well as grand prix races in Spain and Monaco.

When practice began, attention was naturally focused on the turbine cars. On Tuesday, May 7, Spence got everyone's attention by turning a lap in excess of 169 miles per hour. The likable Englishman had never driven on an oval before. He seemed to be able to adapt although there was concern about the low lines he took in the turns.

Late in the day, he took out Weld's car and began to work up to speed. Once again taking an unusually low line in Turn 1, Spence drifted up into the wall. The impact knocked the right front wheel into the cockpit, knocking Spence's helmet off and seriously injuring the driver. He died a few hours later and a shaken Colin Chapman, who had lost his second driver in a month, returned to England.

The following week, the STP team also lost its '67-spec Turbocar when Leonard backed it into the wall. The car that nearly won in 1967 never raced again.

The Shelby-Wallis cars also had their problems finding speed and what transpired turned out to be one of the great-

Above: Only days before his fatal accident at Hockenheim, Germany, Jim Clark tests the wedge-shaped Lotus turbine at IMS. Left to right: Andy Granatelli, Clark, Parnelli Jones, Firestone Racing Director Bill McCrary, and Lotus principal Colin Chapman.

Left: Andy Granatelli confers with his drivers, Joe Leonard and Art Pollard, on the first day of time trials. On the right are Andy's younger brother, Vince Granatelli, and (far right) Andy's son, also named Vince.
Photographs: IMS

Top right: Mel Kenyon, USAC's most successful midget car driver with 111 wins, seven national titles, and eight second-place point rankings, also drove in eight consecutive "500s" between 1966 and 1973. He scored a third, two fourths, and a fifth. What is truly remarkable is that as the result of a fiery accident at Langhorne, Pennsylvania, in June 1965, he was doing so with no fingers on his left hand. He, his father, and his brother designed a special glove, outfitted with a rubber grommet sewn into the palm so that it could fit over a stud on the steering wheel. Even more remarkable is that when the deeply religious Kenyon finished third in 1968 (behind Bobby Unser and Dan Gurney), he also served as his own engine man, tearing down and reassembling his Offy engine, quite literally "single-handedly."

Center right: Lou Palmer of the Indianapolis Motor Speedway Radio Network interviews Chief Mechanic Jud Phillips as Bobby Unser celebrates his first "500" victory.

Lower center right: Eventual winner Bobby Unser qualifies on the outside of the front row.

Bottom right: At the track during the summer of 1968 to shoot the motion picture "Winning," actor Paul Newman portrays the fictitious driver Frank Capua. Although the car is a year-old Eagle rather than a current model, it is painted up in such a way as to resemble (from a distance) the Rislone Special with which Bobby Unser won the "500." It is understood that Newman had no particular interest in motor racing prior to making this film.

Photographs: IMS

est mysteries in Speedway history. One day, the cars and drivers were on the track practicing; the next day, the cars had vanished and the garage was padlocked. The cars had passed tech, but apparently had some sort of illegal device that affected the annulus intake. Once this device was made known to USAC, another inspection was forthcoming, but by that time, the cars had already been withdrawn. Without specifying what they were, a press release from the team stated that the cars had been withdrawn for "safety reasons." McLaren decided to return to Europe while Hulme found a ride with Gurney.

As qualifying drew near, it became apparent that the run for the pole was going to be between the Lotus-Pratt & Whitney turbines of Hill and Leonard (who hopped into what would have been Stewart's car) and Bobby Unser's new Eagle-Offenhauser. Unser threw down the gauntlet by posting the first 170-mph lap during practice.

Hill became the first qualifier of the day and wound up with a whopping 171.208 mph average, a new track record. A tearful Chapman greeted Hill as he returned to the pits. Without the benefit of four-wheel drive, an oily track held Bobby Unser to an average of 169.507. In mid-afternoon, it was Leonard's turn and he eclipsed Hill with one- and four-lap records of 171.953 and 171.559 mph, respectively, to capture the pole.

Andretti was fourth fastest and one row back from where he started the previous two years. Lloyd Ruby and Al Unser, who opted to stay with the 4WD Lola, filled out the second row. Gurney qualified his stock-block-powered Eagle 10th and second-year driver Art Pollard jumped into a third Lotus and qualified it 11th. If nothing else, the turbine advocates had three contenders in the field, despite the rule changes.

One problem that plagued the month of May in 1968 was rain and when the gun went off to close the fourth day of qualifying, the 33-car field had not been filled. Because rain had affected qualifying, only 25 cars were in the field when the 6 p.m. deadline elapsed on the final day.

The decision was made to continue qualifying until it became too dark to run. Cars were lined up and each would be given one opportunity to make an attempt. The previous 25 qualifiers were locked in the field and only the extra session qualifiers could be bumped. After a short practice, qualifying resumed and continued until 7:40 p.m. By that time, only Bill Cheesbourg and Bill Puterbaugh had qualified, each with a 157 mph average.

As a result, an extra day was needed and for the first time, since 1952 qualifying was held on Monday and the field was finally filled. Cheesbourg and Puterbaugh were bumped while Ronnie Duman, Mike Mosley, Carl Williams, George Snider, Jim Hurtubise, Sam Sessions, Arnie Knepper and Larry Dickson all qualified.

Once the starting grid was established, the engine breakdown provided a bit of diversity. There were three turbines, eight normally aspirated Ford DOHC V-8s, one normally aspirated Weslake V-8 and one normally aspirated Repco-Brabham V-8. The remaining 20 engines were turbocharged (15 Offenhausers and five Fords). Turbocharging was clearly the wave of the future and while the Fords were still suffering from developmental woes, the Offenhauser was stronger than ever.

In the chassis department, the past and the future were in stark contrast with the swoopy, wedge-shaped Lotus up against Hurtubise's bulky looking Mallard, the last front-engined car to ever qualify at Indianapolis.

In addition to Hurtubise's car (and Herk himself), nostalgia buffs also had a Vukovich and a Bettenhausen to cheer for. It marked the first time since 1955 that both famous family names had graced the 500 starting lineup.

The race would turn out to be a thrilling affair, although a glimpse at the laps-led category indicates otherwise.

At the drop of the green flag, Leonard shot into the lead with Bobby Unser in hot pursuit, while Hill quickly lost positions. Ruby and Al Unser also moved up, but Andretti was already in trouble with blue smoke indicating a burned piston.

Al Unser brought out the first caution of the day when he hit the wall in Turn 1. The right front wheel had come off the new Lola and Unser slammed into the wall hard. Fortunately he was unhurt.

Bobby Unser took over the lead on Lap 8 and stayed there until pitting on Lap 56. In his six Indianapolis starts, these were the first laps he ever led. Furthermore, that Unser was ahead of the mighty Lotus-Turbine was a complete surprise. Unser's stop put Ruby in the lead and he stayed there until Lap 89 when Unser took over for the 22 laps. He pitted a second time, giving the lead to Leonard who gave it back to Unser on Lap 120.

The turbine team was down to two cars as Hill was sidelined on Lap 110 after suspension failure put him into the Turn 2 wall.

Although he easily led the most laps up to that point, Unser was having problems with his gearbox. The problem (he lost all but the top gear) forced him to leave the pit lane very slowly and it cost him valuable time on the track, especially following his last two pit stops. Amazingly, Unser was able to get the car out of the pits without stalling, a testament to his ability as a driver. In fact, it made the race closer than it might have been.

Unser led until his final stop on Lap 165. Ruby took over the lead and with Unser's clutch problem, it appeared the Texan might get the race he nearly won two years earlier. Eight laps later, Ruby was in for an unscheduled stop. A magneto coil needed to be replaced and even though he rejoined the race, he was now out of contention to win.

The race was down to Leonard and Unser, but that battle had to be postponed when the caution came out for Carl Williams' accident on the backstretch. Because the safety crew had difficulty extinguishing the fire, the caution period was longer than normal and allowed Andy Granatelli to try some "strategy." Between Leonard and Unser were several lapped cars, including the Lotus of Pollard.

Speedway rules mandated that a driver could not improve on his position during a caution period. There was no pack-up rule at that time – drivers were to maintain their interval to the car ahead. Leonard did not increase his lead as such, but Pollard was given the "Slow Down" sign by his crew to put Unser further behind. Unser's crew was onto the tactic and so was the crowd which began to boo loudly. Crew Chief Jud Phillips complained to Chief Steward Harlan Fengler, who ordered Granatelli to make Pollard go faster.

That restored the gap between Leonard and Unser, but Unser was still faced with the prospect of having to pass several cars to catch up to Leonard. On Lap 191, the green came back out, but to everyone's surprise, Leonard quickly shot up his hand and pulled down to the inside of the track. The turbine engine had suffered a broken fuel shaft. Ironically, Pollard's car was slowing at approximately the same time with the same problem!

Unser was now in the lead and stayed there to earn a popular victory. Brother Al was one of the first to greet him as he entered Victory Lane.

Gurney finished second in the Eagle-Weslake, but fans noticed something different. For the race, Gurney had been wearing one of the Bell Star full-face helmets originally developed for motorcycle racers. It would establish a new trend in headgear at the Speedway.

Third place went to "Miraculous" Mel Kenyon, the man who lost all the fingers on his left hand in a 1965 accident. Hulme repeated his fourth-place finish for the second straight year and the hard-luck Ruby wound up fifth. Ronnie Duman, who had been injured in the fiery accident of 1964, finished sixth to score his first top-10 finish in the 500.

And despite an earlier spin, Vukovich came home seventh and was awarded the top rookie honor.

Unlike 1967, the turbine had failed to dominate the 1968 Indianapolis 500. There was still concern and by the time the teams returned to the track for the '69 race, there would be more rule changes made. Shortly after the race, USAC reduced the annulus intake from 15.999 inches to 11.999 inches.

Hollywood would pay a visit to the Speedway following the 1968 race. With matinee idol Paul Newman heading the cast, work began on the film "Winning" that used the 500 as a backdrop. Newman's character Frank Capua drove a car similar to '68 race winner Bobby Unser and naturally, Newman's Capua would win the race.

Above: Turn one action with Joe Leonard, who ran second for several laps, at the head of this group with a Smokey Yunick-prepared 1969 Eagle.

Main photograph: The aftermath of Andretti's horrendous accident which destroys the four-wheel-drive Lotus.
Photographs: IMS

1969: At Long Last – A Victory

By 1969, Andy Granatelli and his brothers, Joe and Vince, must have wondered what it was going to take to win at Indianapolis.

They had failed to win with conventional cars during the 1950s, although Jim Rathmann had given them a second-place finish in 1952 and Fred Agabashian had qualified second and finished fourth in 1953. After a hiatus of several years, they returned with the Novi in 1961 but would not make the race until 1963. The cars were fast and noisy, but only one of the Granatelli Novis finished (Art Malone in 11th in 1964). A rear-engined Novi was considered but never materialized and by 1966, Indianapolis had seen the Novi on track for the last time.

Jim Clark and Team Lotus nearly gave the Granatellis a victory in 1966, but a scoring misunderstanding relegated him to second. Then came the back-to-back near misses with the turbine cars of 1967 and '68. One thing was certain: the Granatellis would not be going the turbine route, but they still had some ideas. For 1969, they arrived with a wedge-shaped chassis powered by a stock-block Plymouth V-8 engine as well as a new Lotus 56-look-alike powered by a turbocharged Offenhauser. Also entered was a new wedge-shaped Gerhardt-Offenhauser. Art Pollard was back to drive for the team. And that was only part of their entry.

Still sponsored by STP, Colin Chapman returned to Indianapolis with an idea of his own for the 1969 effort. His design team produced the Lotus 64. Wedge-shaped like its predecessor, the Lotus 64 had four-wheel drive, a turbocharged Ford and aerodynamic tabs fore and aft. The tabs were attached to the nosecone and the spoiler on the tail of the car. Rules stated that any aerodynamic device had to be an integral part of the body. Slated to drive these cars were a most impressive lineup featuring Mario Andretti, Graham Hill and Jochen Rindt. And just in case Andretti needed it, Clint Brawner had an updated version of the Brawner Hawk, now owned by the Granatellis.

The Granatellis, Gerhardts and Lotuses weren't the only new designs as aerodyamic aids appeared to be the shape of things to come on Indy cars.

Gurney returned with the latest Southgate-designed Eagle, dubbed the "Santa Ana." This car was wedge-shaped with the sides of the tub slanted inward. Gurney would have a Weslake-powered version for himself and a turbocharged Ford version for Denis Hulme. Gurney's car would undergo a number of changes during the month but would wind up resembling Hulme's car. A customer version of the new car was sold to Smokey Yunick for Joe Leonard.

The Gene White team also had a new wedge-shaped Mongoose built by Dave Laycock. However, the decision was made to stick with the more conventional 1967 chassis powered by a turbocharged Offenhauser and driven by veteran Lloyd Ruby.

George Morris unveiled a new wedge-shaped car for the MVS team while a number of other teams experimented with spoilers and wedge-influenced bodywork. Jim McElreath was back in similar surroundings. The Hawk chassis he drove was a copy of the Brabham he had raced from 1965 through '67. His mount for '69 was a Brabham-based Hawk powered by a turbocharged Offy and featuring a wedge-shaped body.

A.J. Foyt did not go the wedge route on his new Coyote, but the '69 version had a bulked-up appearance to accommodate the turbocharged Ford. Foyt had cars for himself, Roger McCluskey and George Snider. All three cars featured oil radiators mounted on either side of the cockpit while Foyt's car had a pair of small wings and a spoiler over the engine.

Lola provided four-wheel drive cars for Leader Card Racers and the new kid on the block, Penske Racing. turbocharged Offenhausers powered both teams' cars.

Another prominent Lola in the entry belonged to Vel's Parnelli Jones Racing that had purchased the assets of Al Retzloff's team at the end of 1968. Al Unser was again the driver and George Bignotti was chief mechanic. The car was the '68 Lola Unser had crashed in practice and now converted to four-wheel drive with turbocharged Ford power. The team also added a turbocharged Ford to a heavily modified Lotus 56 – the same chassis that Joe Leonard used to capture the 500 pole the previous year with turbine power.

Jack Brabham, who started the rear-engine revolution with

Cooper in 1961, was back as a driver for the first time since 1964. He and rookie Peter Revson were slated to drive a pair of Brabhams powered by the Repco-Brabham V-8.

A turbine-powered car was also back at the Speedway although reductions to the annulus intake all but rendered it obsolete before it turned a wheel. Designed in a wind tunnel by a college professor named Glenn Bryant, the front-engined Jack Adams Special resembled an airplane minus its wings. Unlike the STP cars that used Pratt & Whitney turbines, the Adams car used an Allison turbine.

Jim Hurtubise returned with an updated Mallard-Offenhauser roadster and Quin Epperly produced the Maxson, a radical design based on the '67 STP Turbocar and powered by a turbocharged Offenhauser. West Coast midget driver George Benson was originally assigned to the car, but Les Scott wound up driving it and even made an unsuccessful qualifying attempt.

There was another car of note, although it was not actually entered. Lear Jet's Bill Lear was hoping to produce a race car featuring a steam-powered engine, and even signed Jackie Stewart to drive it. But the engine reportedly suffered a number of failures during dyno testing and the car never raced.

Once practice began in earnest, the battle for the pole appeared to be a battle between Andretti and Foyt, with Al Unser occasionally joining in the fray for top-speed honors. As Pole Day neared, the so-called "Happy Hour" at the Speedway (the final hour of practice) turned into an Andretti-versus-Foyt contest.

With one day to go, Andretti had the upper hand, with the month's fastest (unofficial) speed of 171.494 mph. Andretti seemed to have the only new Lotus that worked properly. Andretti & Co. had tested his car at Hanford earlier in the year and found it in need of several modifications. When Andretti drove it the next time – in practice for the 500 – it was vastly improved. Apparently, the same modifications had not been made to the Hill or Rindt cars.

First, Hill spun his car without hitting anything and then it was Rindt's turn to spin. The Austrian driver had suffered a fractured skull in an accident in Spain and may have been suffering after-effects of the injury.

Rain all but washed out Pole Day, but crews got the track dried in time for a couple of attempts. The first one would make history and people today are still scratching their heads over it.

A rookie named Jigger Sirois was first to go out to qualify once the track was sufficiently dried. He averaged 161-plus for the first three laps before his crew threw the yellow flag, aborting the run. Fearful a 161 average would be too slow, the run brought forth considerable discussion as to what might have happened. Arnie Knepper also went out and promptly returned to the pits when the skies opened up again. There would be no more qualifying attempts that day and rain would wash out qualifying the following day.

Had Sirois completed the run and been the only first-day qualifier, he would have won the pole position as Speedway

rules allow for the fastest on the first day only to be the pole winner. It would not have mattered if Sirois had been the slowest of 33 starters that year – he still would have had the pole position by virtue of the rule. There was also discussion as to whether or not he would have been bumped. Crews generally time their driver as he emerges from the fourth turn. That allows them time to determine if the time will be quick enough. It is believed that Sirois had slowed somewhat on his fourth lap, hence the aborted run.

But the slowest man in the 1969 race would be Revson, who averaged 160.851 mph, even though a number of drivers had waived off runs, some averaging as high as 163. If Sirois had completed his run and been slower than Revson, then he would have been the first and only man to be bumped from the pole at Indy because of the rule which states the fastest 33 cars qualify for the starting field. Of course, we'll never know if that would have happened and Sirois, one of the nicest men to attempt to race at Indianapolis, would never make the field in subsequent attempts.

Later on Saturday, a pre-race favorite would be eliminated. Al Unser, the third fastest driver in practice, decided to go motorcycle riding in the Speedway infield with team owner Par-

Above: Dan Gurney, an introspective, incurable romantic and hero to millions, contemplates another qualifying run. Runner-up (with a stock-block engine) in 1968 and 1969, it was Dan who paired Colin Chapman with the Ford Motor Company in 1962. Retiring as a driver after finishing third in the 1970 "500," he was the winning constructor in 1968, 1973, and 1975.
Photograph: IMS

Left: Co-Chief Mechanics Clint Brawner (in the straw hat) and Jim McGee prepare to start the Brawner Hawk prior to a qualification attempt by Mario Andretti. Note the flash burns on the cheeks of Mario, the result of crashing the four-wheel-drive Lotus three days earlier.
Photograph: IMS

Below: The kiss: After trying almost annually since 1946, Andy Granatelli finally has a winner. Mario Andretti is the only "500" winner in history to have been joined in Victory Lane by his own twin brother. Aldo, father of John Andretti, can be seen at left, in the orange shirt.

Bottom: The Brawner Hawk, pressed into service after the four-wheel-drive Lotus was destroyed, originally was entered only for the garage space. It ended up qualifying second and finishing first. This shot was evidently taken during "carburetion" runs since the car is sporting a huge radiator mounted behind Mario's head. Added by Clint Brawner in anticipation of a very hot race day, others complained that it "altered the configuration of the car as qualified." Clint was obliged to remove it.
Photographs: IMS

nelli Jones. While trying to cross a ditch, Unser fell and broke his ankle. The four-time Indy starter was out.

The rain-plagued qualifying weekend allowed Andretti to continue his battle with Foyt, who now had the fastest unofficial speed at 172.315 mph. Late on Wednesday afternoon, Andretti went out to try to beat Foyt's speed, but as he exited Turn 4, the right rear hub collapsed and the Lotus backed into the wall. Pollard, following in the STP team's Gerhardt, spun to avoid Andretti's car as it careened across the track.

Andretti suffered slight flash burns on his upper lip, but was otherwise unhurt. The Lotus was totaled and there was fear that the other cars would suffer similar failures. Ultimately, Team Lotus withdrew the cars and never returned to the Speedway. For Andretti, the only recourse was to haul out the backup Hawk and get it ready for qualifying.

Despite his practice pace, Foyt failed to break Leonard's track record and settled for a 170.568 average. Now it was Andretti's turn, but not much was expected from his backup

car. Although he didn't win the pole that year, he showed why he had been the fastest around the Speedway so many times. He turned in an average speed of 169.851 to sit second on the grid next to Foyt.

Bobby Unser, who had struggled all month with his new 4WD Lola, duplicated his 1968 effort by posting third fastest time. Rookie Mark Donohue showed that he and the Penske team would be a force by qualifying fourth fastest. Gordon Johncock was fifth fastest in his Gerhardt-Offenhauser and McCluskey put Foyt's team car on the outside of Row 2. Pollard, unable to find speed in the Plymouth-powered entry, test-hopped the Gerhardt and then posted the 12th best speed in the Granatelli-Offenhauser based on the Lotus 56.

With qualifying restricted to only two days because of the weather, there was a major scramble to get into the race. Some teams went with times that might have held, had time been on their side. One was the Jack Adams team, which put veteran Al Miller in its turbine car for a qualifying run. Miller averaged 156.440 mph and for a time was in the field. He would be bumped and would be second alternate until the car was disqualified for a rules infraction.

Andretti also figured to be Foyt's biggest rival, but the cooling system on the Hawk was a concern. To combat rising engine temperatures, Brawner rigged a special radiator and placed it over the engine cover. The car appeared in its new configuration for Carburetion Day and Brawner was informed the new radiator would have to go.

Rules dictated that there could be no significant change in a car's bodywork once it had qualified for the race. For Andretti, Brawner and the Granatellis, it was another hurdle to overcome and the mood was less than optimistic for Race Day.

But the once the green flag dropped, Andretti forgot the cooling problem and jumped into the lead. He stayed there for five laps but dropped back to second when the water temperatures predictably went up. Foyt took over for the next 45 laps before pitting. Wally Dallenbach would lead his first 500 and stay out in front from Lap 52 to 58. Foyt regained the lead, but on Lap 79, he dashed into the pits with turbocharger trouble. It would take 22 minutes before Foyt could rejoin the race.

In the meantime, it turned into a battle between Andretti and Ruby, who led until Lap 86. Andretti passed for the lead until pitting on Lap 102. Ruby led for the next three laps and then made his second stop. The hard-luck Texan was bitten again. Ruby's Mongoose had tanks on both sides, but for efficiency, both were fueled on the left side, thanks to the location of the couplers. One side was filled, but Ruby began to edge forward with the fuel hose still connected to the car. As the fuel hose grew taut, the slight movement of the car tore a hole in the fuel tank and methanol gushed out.

Ruby's misfortune couldn't have come at a better time for Andretti. Both drivers were way ahead of the third-place car of Mike Mosley, and with a commanding lead and Ruby out of the race, Andretti only needed to keep his car on the track and cool enough to finish.

For the next 95 laps, Andretti went unchallenged and crossed to finish at a new race record of 156.867 mph. Andretti and Brawner finally won their first Indianapolis 500. And so had the jubilant Granatellis, who appeared to have the race locked up the previous three years and seemed less

MARIO ANDRETTI

Someone once suggested that if there were no such thing as auto racing, Mario Andretti would have probably been an acrobat in a circus. And there may be some truth in that observation. Actually, Andretti maintains he would have raced motorcycles if he had not gotten involved in auto racing and the sight of him turning laps at speed on one of Kenny Roberts' superbikes at Nazareth and Laguna Seca in 1992 was awe-inspiring for those lucky enough to be there to bear witness. There was always a daredevil aspect in Mario Andretti's approach to racing. In the 1960s, he drove his car closer to Indy's wall than any other driver – the dust raised by his tires being testament to his razor-edge style.

On top of that, he was always fast. He led laps. And he either brought his car home for a win or high placing or he didn't finish at all. Like Stirling Moss, Andretti was often criticized being too hard on his cars. And yet, it's hard to believe someone so hard on equipment would be capable of winning four national titles, a Formula One World Championship and dozens and dozens of races throughout his illustrious career in a number of different disciplines.

Like A.J. Foyt and Parnelli Jones, he achieved such a lofty status in the 1960s that the mention of his first name generally turns ones' attention to the sport of auto racing. From his rookie year at Indianapolis, where he broke the track record in qualifying and then followed Jim Clark and Jones home to finish an impressive third, Andretti was always a favorite at the fabled track. Never mind that he only won one Indianapolis 500. One could fill a book on some great drivers who never won there, but on the Borg-Warner Trophy is his likeness for his victory in 1969.

What Andretti added to his status, however, was the element of professionalism that stood him head above shoulders over his peers. Multi-lingual, Andretti could converse with the world's racing journalists in their own language. It certainly didn't hurt him to be fluent in Italian (his native tongue) when he drove for Ferrari and yet his biggest days came with the British Lotus team and various American Indy-car operations. He also possessed flair in and out of the racing car. With the air of celebrity and sometimes even appearing to be aloof, in actuality he was deep in thought. There would always be time for the fans, photographers and journalists who sought his words of wisdom – as long as his car was performing properly. As the years passed, Andretti found himself more and more becoming ambassador to the sport. It is a mantle he continues to wear proudly today as he witnesses a third generation of his family racing, and, not unsurprisingly, winning.

likely to win this particular year.

Runner-up for the second year in a row was Gurney, followed by Bobby Unser and Mel Kenyon, who scored his third top-five finish in four years. Soldiering home from 33rd to fifth was Peter Revson, followed by Leonard and Donohue, whose lengthy stop to replace a magneto dropped him out of contention. Because he had been so competitive all month, Donohue was given the nod over Revson for top Indy rookie.

Andretti's win closed out one of the most interesting decades in Indianapolis 500 history.

The decade began with 33 starters in front-engined, Offenhauser-powered roadsters that raced on a track whose main straightaway was still paved in brick. It finished with 33 rear-engined cars that raced at speeds 25 mph faster and the potential to go much quicker. In between, there had been foreign invasions, turbines, fiery accidents and advances in safety. It promised an even more exciting decade to come.

Main photograph: Mario Andretti poses on the day after the race with wife DeeAnn and sons Michael and Jeff, both of whom will grow up to drive in the "500."
Photograph: IMS

Chapter 12
WINGS AND THINGS AND RECORD FLINGS

1970: (Johnny) Lightning Strikes

IF anyone had any question about who the favorite might be for the 1970 Indianapolis, they only needed to go back to the middle of the 1969 season and then look forward. The answer would be obvious.

The 1969 season will clearly be remembered for Mario Andretti's break-through victory in the Indianapolis 500 and a subsequent third USAC national title. However, it was a driver who didn't even race in that year's Indianapolis 500 who got everyone's attention during the second half of the season.

While riding a motorcycle following a rained-out Pole Day at the Speedway in 1969, Al Unser suffered a broken ankle after a fall. Unser missed the 500 and the next two races before rejoining the Championship trail at Castle Rock, Colorado. Unser ultimately finished a career-high second in the standings. He was clearly the hottest driver in the series the second half of the season, winning five races.

And he didn't stop there. Driving the new PJ Colt-Ford, Unser and the Vel's Parnelli Jones team had a new sponsor in Johnny Lightning. George Bignotti built the beautiful blue car that was inspired by the Lola. Like its predecessor, it was fast. Unser opened the 1970 season at Phoenix with a victory and followed up with a third at Sonoma and a third at Trenton,

where he won the pole.

As practice began for the Indianapolis 500, it was clear that the man in the Johnny Lightning 500 Special was going to be the man to beat. Unser would also have a teammate in 1968 pole winner Joe Leonard.

There would be competitors and several had new equipment. Andretti and the STP team were back with a new chassis produced by American expatriate Francis McNamara, whose firm was located in Germany. Designed by ex-Lola man Joe Karasek, it would be a major undertaking for a company known for its Formula Vee, F3 and F2 cars. As a backup entry, Andretti also had the same Hawk-Ford he had used to win Indianapolis and the 1969 championship.

Lotus may have departed from the Indianapolis, but there was a suitable replacement from overseas.

Team McLaren made its Indianapolis debut with new Offenhauser-powered cars for Chris Amon and Denis Hulme. On opening day, Bruce McLaren was on hand in a third car and led his minions in formation onto the track. For the tradition-minded Indy 500 set, the trio of cars heading out together was unprecedented. McLaren (the driver) was strictly there for test purposes – he had no intention of running in the race.

With the Vel's Parnelli Jones Team building its own car, Lola's factory effort centered on Penske Racing with its latest Lola-Ford for Mark Donohue and turned out in typically immaculate fashion.

Jack Brabham, in his final season of racing, returned to the Speedway with the first monocoque Brabham chassis for Indianapolis. A longtime advocate of space-frame chassis, Brabham was also using a monocoque chassis in F1 for the first time. A turbocharged Offenhauser would power the new Brabham Indy car.

A.J. Foyt was back with several updated versions of the Coyote he used to capture the pole position at Indy the previous year. He strongly believed 1970 was going to be his year. Numerically speaking, he had a point having won in 1961, 1964 and 1967. With victories every three years, Foyt felt it was his turn again.

Dan Gurney also returned with a new car from Len Terry, the man who had designed the original Eagle chassis. For the first time in Gurney's history, he would run the 500 in an Offenhauser-powered car. In addition to Gurney's car, Gordon Johncock and Bobby Unser each had Ford-powered '70 Eagles at their disposal although neither driver would end up qualifying the cars. Jim Robbins also purchased one of the new cars and it would be heavily modified by Chief Mechanic Bill Spangler and driven by Sam Sessions.

Curiously no one would make the 1970 race in the 1969 wedge-shaped model. Several drivers used modified versions of the 1968 chassis while Bobby Unser and rookie Donnie Allison drove 1967 models.

Clint Brawner and Jim McGee left the STP team at the end of 1969 and built the new Scorpion-Ford for Jim Hayhoe and driver Roger McCluskey.

Aerodynamic ideas were still getting consideration and a number of the cars either featured wedge-shaped bodies or spoilers mounted over the engine compartments. The new McLarens sported small winglets on each side of the engine cover.

For the nostalgia-minded, Jim Hurtubise was back with his front-engined, Offenhauser-power Mallard. There was also one turbine-powered Gerhardt from the Jack Adams team, which signed Jigger Sirois, the rookie who almost won the pole the previous year. This car was rear-engine design, but it was the same engine that had been in the Adams front-engined entry in 1969.

Practice, for the most part, was uneventful, but things began to go wrong for the McLaren team during the second week. After posting one of the top practice times the previous day, Hulme went out for a run, only to discover the car was on fire. The fuel cap somehow worked loose and burning methanol was spraying back into the cockpit. Hulme managed to stop the car and began rolling himself on the track. For some reason, fire crews went straight to the car and ignored the driver, who sustained burns on both hands.

Hulme would not race at Indy in 1970 and Peter Revson would take his place. Amon managed to avoid any incidents, but never found the necessary speed and stepped out of the car. Veteran Carl Williams took his place.

When Pole Day arrived, Al Unser continued to be the man to beat. The Johnny Lightning car had the fastest practice speed of 171.233 and Foyt was next at 170.154. Unser would be one of the first men to qualify and his four-lap average was 170.221. A morning rain had delayed activities and washed a lot of rubber off the track, resulting in slower speeds.

One person who wasn't slowed by the track conditions was Johnny Rutherford. Driving an Eagle-Offenhauser heavily modified by Mike Devin and entered by oilman U.E. "Pat" Patrick, the Texan nearly stole the show. When his run completed, he was a close second to Unser. Rutherford had missed supplanting Unser by three thousandths of a second. Foyt, who qualified before Unser, filled the front row.

A total of 17 cars qualified, but had it not been for an error, there would have been 18. In one of the strangest occurrences in qualifying history, rookie Tony Adamowicz took the green flag to begin his run, but then watched the caution light come on and instinctively slowed. Then the green light came right back on and Adamowicz finished his run. Because of the hesitation, Adamowicz's first lap was considerably slower than the last three laps. Based on the last three laps, the sportscar ace would have easily qualified for the race. Unfortunately, the run stood and Adamowicz was ultimately bumped.

Lloyd Ruby continued his hard-luck saga at Indianapolis by blowing a number of Offenhauser engines in his Gene White wedge-shaped Mongoose. Ruby had six engine failures during practice and qualifying but finally made the field on the third day.

When the field was filled, the 33 starters provided a "first" for the 500. For the first time in history, the engine of each car was turbocharged with Ford powering 17 cars and Offenhauser powering 16. Sirois completed a four-lap run in the turbine-powered car, but his average of 157.487 mph was too slow. It would be the last turbine car at Indy.

One other starter merits mention. Bruce Walkup qualified J.C. Agajanian's Mongoose-Offenhauser. It would be the first and only car to run in the Indianapolis 500 with a full roll cage.

Rain delayed the start of the race and as the field came down to for the start, the yellow came out instead. Jim Malloy, who had qualified ninth in the Federal Automotive Gerhardt-Offenhauser, had a half-shaft fail and spun across

Top: Turning from stock-block Ford power to Offenhauser, Dan Gurney will finish third.

Insets above: A moment of relaxation for A. J. Foyt... and Mario Andretti.

Main photograph: Fellow participants are somewhat alarmed at the preparedness of Team McLaren, which has never participated at Indianapolis before. Whereas the early days of practice are normally quite leisurely affairs, McLaren has three cars lined up diagonally in the pits, all ready to go, on the opening day. At the appropriate signal, all three roll onto the track nose-to-tail, driven by Denis Hulme, Chris Amon, and team principal Bruce McLaren. It looks like it's going to be a long month.

Photographs: IMS

the track into the Turn 4 wall. Somehow, everyone in the eight rows behind managed to miss Malloy, who was out of the race before it started.

The race was also red-flagged briefly to allow the cleanup of the accident. Shortly after, the cars restarted and came down for the green.

Rutherford, who came so close to winning the pole, won the race into Turn 1 with Unser closely behind. Exiting Turn 2, the Johnny Lightning 500 Special flashed past for the lead. By the time they came past to complete Lap 1, Unser was way out in front. For all practical purposes, that was the race.

Unser would lead 191 of the race's 200 laps and only surrendered the lead when he pitted. Rutherford had been the only man to pass him on the track that day.

One other driver who might have challenged Unser was Ruby, who led when Unser made his first stop. On Lap 54, a blown engine halted Ruby's charge from 25th to first. It had been the seventh major engine failure for Ruby that month.

Finishing second and showing he and his team would be a force to deal with was Donohue. Gurney, who would retire from driving at the year's end, placed third in his new Eagle while Allison was an impressive fourth in Foyt's '67 Eagle. He earned the top rookie honor. Jim McElreath, who started last, gave the Foyt team another good finish by placing fifth.

Some of the new designs produced respectable results. Andretti was sixth in the new McNamara and Williams gave the McLaren team something to smile about by placing ninth.

Foyt suffered gearbox troubles late in the race after running second to Unser most of the afternoon. He retired in a somewhat spectacular fashion. After crossing the start-finish line to complete Lap 195, Foyt slowed as he approached the pit exit and made Indy's first hairpin turn by going the wrong way up the pit lane.

The McLaren team would need a bigger lift in the ensuing week. While testing his Can-Am car at Goodwood, McLaren crashed to his death after the rear bodywork came off the car.

Unser had recorded the most dominant Indianapolis 500 victory since Jim Clark in 1965. It also established a precedent. In joining his brother Bobby as a 500 victor, they became the first (and thus far only) siblings to have won at Indianapolis. There would be more wins for Unser that season and more wins for the family at Indianapolis in the future.

1971: A Case of Lightning striking twice

After winning the 1970 Indianapolis 500, Al Unser and the Vel's Parnelli Jones team did not rest on their laurels. They kept on winning. At Milwaukee the week after the 500, Joe Leonard gave the team its third victory of the season. Unser followed up with victories at Indianapolis Raceway Park, Springfield and Milwaukee, where he won by a whopping four-lap margin over Roger McCluskey.

Unser then dominated the inaugural Ontario 500, only to retire in the lead with turbo problems on Lap 186 with a lap lead on the field. But that was only a minor hiccup as Unser won the next five races and finished second in the finale at Phoenix. For the year, Unser led 1,527 laps with his nearest rival (brother Bobby) leading 130. In 18 USAC championship races that season, the Vel's Parnelli Jones team won 11 and Unser was a perfect five-for-five on dirt.

However, 1970 would be the final season of diversity as USAC established a separate division for dirt cars and attempted to promote a Formula 5000-style road-course series.

Unser may have won on all types of tracks in capturing his first championship, but he still figured to be the man to beat on the all-oval series for 1971 that now had a full-time sponsor – Marlboro.

Picking up where he left off, Unser won both races at Rafaela, Argentina, and captured the subsequent 150-miler at Phoenix. Even with a DNF at Trenton, Unser arrived at the Speedway with a healthy lead in the championship. For Indianapolis, Bignotti built a new PJ Colt with a number of revisions, but outwardly similar to the 1970 car. One noticeable change was the appearance of small nose wings. The Johnny Lightning car still retained the spoiler over the engine compartment and a slightly upturned tail section. A second car was entered with Samsonite sponsorship for Leonard.

That was an attempt to bridge the past with the future. And for Indianapolis 500 competitors in 1971, the future presented itself in the form of the McLaren M16-Offenhauser.

Designed by Gordon Coppuck, the car borrowed many of the innovations of the Lotus 72 F1 car Colin Chapman had unveiled the previous year. The new McLaren featured a wedge-shaped nose section with wings on each side. Water radiators were moved back in line with the driver and neatly concealed by bodywork. The turbocharged Offenhauser featured an engine cover that swept into a large wing behind the rear axle line. Although wings were not yet allowed at Indianapolis, the McLaren team successfully argued the wing was part of the engine cover and therefore not a true wing. The USAC technical committee allowed the "engine cover" to remain on the car.

Along with Team McLaren's entries for Denis Hulme and Peter Revson, Penske Racing entered a new McLaren for Mark Donohue. Penske also entered the team's 1970 Lola-Ford for rookie David Hobbs.

A.J. Foyt, the STP team and Lindsey Hopkins also had new cars for their drivers.

Foyt's latest Coyote-Ford went the wedge route and Donnie Allison was assigned one of the team's older cars. By qualifying, the new Coyote would sprout a rear wing – appropriately (and legally) attached to the engine cover. STP returned with the second-generation McNamara-Ford for Mario Andretti and rookie Steve Krisiloff with more of a wedge shape over its predecessor.

Hopkins entered a trio of smart new chassis built by long-time Indy mechanic Eddie Kuzma. Wally Dallenbach, Mel Kenyon and Roger McCluskey drove the cars, sponsored by Sprite and painted in a (now acceptable) bright green color.

All American Racers had new Eagle-Offenhausers for Bobby Unser (who replaced the retired Dan Gurney) and NASCAR ace Lee Roy Yarbrough. The car resembled the 1970 model, but featured small winglets behind the front wheels and a small wing-shaped spoiler located immediately behind the cockpit.

By the third day of practice, it was clear that the new McLaren was going to be fast. Donohue, in the dark blue, Sunoco-liveried entry, had a top lap of 174.757 mph. That was nearly three miles an hour faster than the track record. Two days later he duplicated that speed and the following day, he upped the ante to 177.901.

For the week leading up to Pole Day, Donohue continued to set the pace. On Monday, he was quickest with a lap of 177.340 mph. On Tuesday, he was quickest at 176.125. On Wednesday, he nearly broke through the 180 barrier with a lap at 179.6. On Thursday, he made it with a top lap of 180.977.

Donohue's performance resulted in an extraordinary display of sportsmanship from Al Unser, the man who got most of the headlines the previous year.

In his autobiography, *"The Unfair Advantage,"* Donohue recalled: "He (Unser) knocked and asked permission to come in, because it's an unwritten rule there that no one ever goes into anyone else's garage without asking. Al said, 'Look, we've been competitors for a long time and you have your way of doing things and I have mine, but when you can come here and run six miles per hour faster than anyone else – I gotta shake your hand.' I was really impressed. I don't know if I would have been that big a guy to have the courage or sportsmanship to do that."

On Friday, Donohue rested, but McLaren still led the way. Revson took top honors with a lap of 175.610. Foyt was fastest of the non-McLaren runners with a 175.370 lap.

The pole position appeared to be a foregone conclusion for Donohue. But as he later admitted in his autobiography, he "wasn't Superman."

There would be a slight change in the qualifying draw pro-

Above: Having carefully analyzed the rule which states that "any aerodynamic device must be an integral part of the body," Team McLaren engineers have figured out how to slip one in anyway. When the technical inspectors inform the crew that the wing will have to be removed, they protest, "But it is an integral part of the body!" The wing isn't even molded in, but rather is bolted onto a plate which they claim to be, ahem, "the engine cover." Score one for McLaren. Mark Donohue in a Penske-entered version builds during practice to almost 181, which is TEN mph faster than the official track record. The rules are changed for 1972 and massive bolt-on rear wings will be permitted, allowing speeds to skyrocket a stunning 15 mph beyond that. Scary times.

Top: Although Peter Revson has won the pole, nobody is really surprised when Mark Donohue leads at the start, although Bobby Unser is not allowing him to go without a contest.
Photographs: IMS

Above: Al Unser stops for replenishments en route to his second consecutive victory.
Photograph: IMS

cedure. For 1971, any car that had drawn a number and was properly presented in the qualifying line would be entitled to make an attempt as a first-day qualifier. The previous year, one of the pole position contenders – Lloyd Ruby – had to qualify on the second day because he had drawn a high number and a rain-shortened schedule prevented him from qualifying on the first day.

Following the record run by Foyt, who temporarily occupied the pole with an average speed of 174.317, Donohue went out for his run. He returned to the pits on the pole and with new one- and four-lap records. However, they were significantly slower than his practice runs. Donohue opened with a 178.607, but went slower each lap to average 177.087. Even with new track records, Donohue's run was something of a shock – everyone expected him to top 180.

Donohue reportedly wanted a different setup and following his run, unthinkingly shared it with Revson, who quickly had it installed on his car as soon as Donohue had left. Revson then went out and returned with the pole and more track records, averaging 178.696 mph with a top lap of 179.354 mph. It was the second shock of the day as everyone expected Donohue to win the pole. Revson received a tumultuous round of applause from the crowd.

Donohue would have to settle for second and Bobby Unser filled out the front row with an average of 175.816 – noticeably slower than the McLarens.

Hulme qualified at 174.910 to take fourth spot and Al Unser joined him in the middle of Row 2 with an average of 174.622. Foyt was bumped to the outside of the second row.

Jim Malloy, whose strong qualifying effort of 1970 was negated at the start of the race, rebounded to qualify 10th. Malloy was driving for All American Racers in a year-old Eagle-Offenhauser. The affable Colorado driver replaced Yarbrough after the NASCAR driver demolished his car in a practice accident.

Qualifying also produced a pair of somewhat bizarre stories.

On the third day, George Snider made his sixth Indianapolis 500 by qualifying the Leader Card Racers Eagle-Offenhauser

at an average speed of 171.600. What made Snider's run so unusual was the fact that three of his laps were an identical 52.45 seconds. The other lap (the third on the four-lap run) was at 52.44. It was undoubtedly the most consistent run in the history of 500 qualifying.

Another third-day qualifier was a rookie named John Mahler, entered in a Vollstedt-Ford by Dick Simon. Mahler easily qualified with an average of 170.164, making him the fastest rookie qualifier as well. Unfortunately for Mahler, when team owner Simon failed to qualify his mount, he put himself in Mahler's car, citing a contractual arrangement with the sponsor.

And still trying to give the front-engined roadster its last hurrah, Jim Hurtubise practiced in the 167 mph range, but crashed on his qualifying attempt. Despite the setback, Hurtubise and his beloved Mallard would be back for other tries.

With McLarens in three of the top four qualifying positions, it didn't take much guessing on who was favored to win. However, a lot of things can happen in a 500-mile race. The 1971 edition would be no different.

There was something different where the date of the race was concerned. Throughout its history, the Indianapolis 500 had always been scheduled for Memorial Day, May 30, except for the years when May 30 fell on a Sunday. On those occasions, the race would be held on Monday, May 31. For 1971, Congress changed the recognition for Memorial Day to the last Monday of the month. In 1970, the race had been held on Saturday, May 30. For 1971, instead of holding it on Monday, May 31, the race would be held on Saturday, May 29.

When Pat Vidan dropped the green flag to start the 55th Indianapolis 500, a McLaren-Offenhauser jumped into the lead – Donohue, who was closely pursued by Bobby Unser. By the time the field came by to complete the first lap, the blue Sunoco car was way ahead of the field. His opening lap was four miles an hour faster than the existing record.

In the meantime, there was drama at the exit to the pit lane. Local car dealer Eldon Palmer had been selected to drive the 1971 Dodge Challenger Pace Car. Palmer brought the field down for the start fast enough, but lost control at the end of the pit lane and swerved into a photography stand. Three people were injured in the incident, but the race continued without the caution coming out.

The caution did come out following a pileup in Turn 3 on Lap 11. The engine blew in Krisiloff's STP McNamara, sending the car into the wall. Kenyon spun in Krisiloff's oil and also hit the wall. As Kenyon began to emerge from the cockpit, he quickly ducked back in as the McLaren-Offenhauser of Gordon Johncock slammed into his car. Andretti also got caught up in the accident, which eliminated both STP cars.

When the green flag came out, Donohue continued his romp and drove off from the field. Al Unser was now second as the leaders made their first pit stops on Lap 51. Joe Leonard led and pitted, putting Bobby Unser into the lead. Donohue caught and passed Unser on Lap 65 and set the fastest lap of the race at 174.961. He then coasted to a halt inside of Turn 4 with a broken transmission.

For several laps, the Vel's Parnelli Jones teammates – Unser and Leonard – battled for the lead. The two drivers continued to pass and repass on the front straightaway, much to the delight of the fans in the stands.

Leonard recalled the battle.

"I'd get by him on one lap and he'd get by me on the next one," Leonard said. "We did that for several laps, but then a pebble got into my turbocharger and that put me out of the race."

For the second straight year, Unser was home free. There was some drama, however.

On Lap 167, Mike Mosley spun his Leader Card Racers Eagle-Ford into the Turn 4 wall. Bobby Unser was unable to avoid the accident and also struck the Turn 4 wall. Both spun into the inside of the track, hitting Donohue's long-since abandoned McLaren as well as the abandoned cars of Steve Krisiloff and Bentley Warren. Mosley suffered a broken leg and elbow and the cleanup was lengthy.

With 11 laps to go, the green came on and Unser continued on to capture his second straight Indy 500. In doing so, he became the first man since Bill Vukovich (1953-54) to win back-to-back 500s. He also joined an exclusive club of Vukovich, Wilbur Shaw and Mauri Rose as the only men to win consecutive races at Indianapolis. And if that wasn't enough, it was also Unser's 32nd birthday.

For Unser, there was a new place to celebrate. After having the victor drive to the south end of the pit lane for decades, for 1971, the victory enclosure was relocated to the horseshoe-shaped area at the foot of the Master Control Tower. Unser turned left and drove up a wooden ramp covered in black and white checkered carpet.

Unser's team also took advantage of technology. Throughout the race, they were able to communicate with him thanks to a radio in his helmet. Although it has become commonplace today and had been attempted a number of times, Unser was the first 500 winner to use a helmet radio.

Revson finished second, but never led a lap. Foyt finished third and Malloy was fourth. Billy Vukovich scored his best Indy 500 finish with a fifth and Donnie Allison scored another top-10 for Foyt at Indy by placing sixth. Bud Tingelstad was seventh in a sister car to Vukovich and Denny Zimmerman placed eighth to take top rookie honors.

Zimmerman's effort was especially noteworthy considering the investment put up by team owner Frank Fiore. Using a five-year-old Vollstedt (the car driven by Billy Foster that set off the 1966 starting line accident), the Fiore Racing Enterprises team truly operated on a "shoestring budget." At the end of the month, Fiore reportedly had spent slightly more than $18,000! For finishing eighth, Zimmerman earned $27,658 – clearly a profit.

On the other end of the scope, one still had to feel for Donohue, who dominated practice, appeared to have the pole in hand and was untouchable in the race, only to come away with nothing.

Well, almost nothing. Donohue did receive $26,697 for finishing 25th (a figure buoyed by lap prize money for leading 50 laps). As the winner, Unser received $238,454. He received $33,000 more for winning the 1970, but he had also led nearly 80 laps more. More significantly, the Speedway's total purse exceeded $1 million for the first time.

It was a wild month of May, but with the new technology, the future looked to be even wilder.

1972: A new track record – and then some

It can be said that the McLaren M16 of 1971 clearly shaped the future of racing car design at Indianapolis. But it should also be noted that the introduction of slick racing tires by Goodyear and Firestone definitely enhanced it.

By the time the 1971 season was winding to a close, everyone was trying to copy the McLaren design. A prime example was the Vel's Parnelli Jones team. Using the PJ Colt, Chief Mechanic George Bignotti closed off the nosecone and moved the water radiators to the sides. He added a rear wing (bolt-on wings were now legalized by USAC) and changed the engine on Al Unser's car from a Ford to an Offenhauser.

For the second straight year, Unser appeared to have the Ontario 500 locked up, but engine trouble sidelined him. The race winner was teammate Joe Leonard, whose PJ Colt still used Ford power and did not have such amenities as side-mounted radiators.

Leonard also captured the national championship and for 1972, Vel's Parnelli Jones Racing embarked on an all-out effort to top the speedy McLarens. Signed in the off-season was Mario Andretti to make it a three-car team and former Lotus designer Maurice Phillipe, the man who designed the Lotus 72 F1 car and the Lotus 56 wedge-shaped turbine car for Indianapolis. The team was also bolstered by a major sponsorship package from Viceroy cigarettes. Someone began calling them "Super Team" and the name stuck.

For Indianapolis, Phillipe created the Parnelli VPJ-1, one of the most radical cars to run at the Speedway. The tub was triangular (a style that would soon be adopted by the Brabham, BRM and Surtees F1 teams). The nose was wide and flat with aerodynamic flaps over the suspension mounts. Mounted on the engine cover behind the cockpit were racing's first dihedral wings. A conventional rear wing finished off the car, which also had Indy-car racing's first rising-rate suspension.

McLaren was back with revised M16s that now sported much larger rear wings (no longer part of the engine cover). Revson was back and joining him on the Indianapolis project was Gordon Johncock. Penske Racing also had two of the later M16s for Mark Donohue and Gary Bettenhausen.

Two former McLaren fabricators – Graham Bartels and Eamon Fullalove – introduced the Atlanta chassis, a McLaren M16 look-alike designed to house the turbocharged Foyt V-8. (The engine was the same Ford V-8, but renamed after Foyt purchased the rights to the engine.) Grant King's new King-fish-Offenhauser entered for Steve Krisiloff copied the McLaren's lines even more than the Atlanta.

But the car that would capture the most attention was the new Eagle designed by Roman Slobodynskj. Slobodynskj took a long look at the McLaren and proceeded to build a

better mousetrap. Incorporating a wedge nose adorned with wings and a wider body that concealed the side-mounted radiators, the new Eagle was entered for Bobby Unser, Jerry Grant, Bill Vukovich, Jim Malloy and rookie sports-car racer Sam Posey.

A.J. Foyt had a new Coyote-Ford that bore a strong resemblance to the new Eagle. George Snider was entered in one of Foyt's '71 wedge Coyotes and Jim Hurtubise entered his own '71 Coyote. It would be Hurtubise's first ride in a rear-engined car since 1967.

STP Racing entered the first new Lola design in four years for Art Pollard. The car featured a wide, wing-shaped nose section and side-mounted radiators.

One other new design of note was the Manta, although it was commonly referred to as the Antares, the name of the engineering company that produced it. Deemed one of the most ungainly looking cars, Antares chassis were entered by Michner Racing and Lindsey Hopkins. Powered by turbocharged Offenhausers, the car resembled an upside-down boat with a prow-shaped nose.

The Speedway track also featured a new innovation – the pacer light system. In previous races during a caution period, drivers were expected to maintain their position. In short, it was an honor system. The new system employed a series of electronic displays giving drivers a number as they passed. The driver was to maintain that number throughout the lap, thereby holding his position. If the driver saw a higher number at a different station, it meant he was going too fast; a lower number meant he could speed up to get back to his original number.

On opening day, Malloy gave everyone a brief glimpse at the potential of the new Eagle. On a green track, Malloy's Thermo-King Special was clocked at 179.4 for the day's fastest time. And that was only the beginning.

Two days later, Malloy had an unofficial track record at 181.415. Of course, everyone knew there was more to come. Malloy had run laps nearing 190 during spring testing at the track.

One notable change was the braking points. In previous years, drivers would rely on 3-2-1 signs mounted along the end of both long straightaways for braking reference points. With the new large wings and slick tires, drivers were now braking well beyond the No. 1 sign. The aerodynamic aids and improved tires were allowing them to corner at speeds previously unheard of.

All through practice, drivers continued to creep up on the 190 mark. On the seventh day, Bettenhausen got there with a lap of 190.285. Two days later he topped the 191 mark and the day after that, Bobby Unser went 194.721 in the new Eagle.

Top contenders for the pole were going to be the new Eagles and the improved McLarens. The battle lines were drawn, but no one realized how fast they would be going in qualifying.

Rain hampered most of the opening qualifying day and part of the second qualifying day, but the track was eventually dried and practice began. The track quickly got quiet as the caution came out for Jim Malloy's accident. Heading into Turn 3, Malloy inexplicably lost control and slammed into the wall nearly head-on. The car was bent like a pretzel and the unconscious Malloy was taken to nearby Methodist Hospital. He never regained consciousness and succumbed after being taken off of life support four days later.

Despite a lengthy cleanup for the accident, qualifying commenced and three cars qualified, with each driver breaking Revson's track record. Leonard was first with an average of 185.223 in the Samsonite Parnelli, followed by teammate Andretti who topped his mark with a 187.617 in the Viceroy Parnelli. Both cars ran without the dihedral wings after numerous complaints from the teams' drivers.

Bettenhausen was next and he emerged with a record run of 188.877. Now it was Bobby Unser's turn.

Lap 1 produced an average speed of 194.932. Lap 2 produced an average of 196.036. Lap 3 was 196.678 and Unser finished the run with a 196.121 for a new track record of 195.940—a jump of more than 17 miles an hour over Revson's record. Never in the history of the Indianapolis 500 had a qualifying record been smashed by as big a margin.

(When the field was filled, the average would also be a record 183.655 – up from the 1971 record of 171.665.)

Because of the rain-shortened day, first-day qualifying would continue the following weekend with five drivers still in line to make a run for the pole position. Krisiloff, Mel Kenyon and rookie Jerry Karl did not figure to be pole contenders, but Donohue and Revson certainly did.

When qualifying resumed the following Saturday, the two road-racing specialists failed to surpass Unser, but did manage to post speeds that put them on the front row for the second straight year. Revson was second fastest with a 192.885 average while Donohue posted an average of 191.408.

It was easily the fastest front row in the history of the 500, but starting behind them were a trio of chargers in Bettenhausen, Andretti and Leonard. Further back were Jerry Grant in Unser's AAR team car (now dubbed the "Mystery Eagle"), Art Pollard and Sam Sessions in the new Lola-Fords and Al Unser, who overcame numerous engine problems to qualify 19th.

One driver whose successful qualification run seemed to make a lot of folks happy was John Mahler. Driving a two-year-old McLaren-Offenhauser, Mahler made sure he would not be ousted from his ride. He owned the team and the car this time!

Making his first 500 in four years was Hurtubise, the fan favorite who couldn't resist pulling a fast one on the paddock. Safely in the field with an average speed of 181.050, Hurtubise surprised everyone by putting his front-engined Mallard in the qualifying line on the final day. "Herk" hinted he might withdraw the Coyote and try to qualify his trusty Mallard, but every time he neared the tech area, he moved the Mallard to the rear of the line.

When the gun went off to close qualifying for good, Hurtubise opened up the engine compartment of Miller-sponsored Mallard, which had been converted to the world's fastest "beer chest" – complete with the sponsor's product.

The 1972 Indianapolis 500 can best be described as a race divided into three unequal parts and a somewhat confusing start.

When Tony Hulman delivered his traditional command to start engines, everyone but Foyt was able to get their cars started. Foyt's crew hoped to take a shortcut through the opening to the pit lane where the starter's platform was located. They were ordered by Chief Steward Harlan Fengler to move to the pit exit. With the field coming around for the parade, Fengler grabbed the P.A. system microphone and shouted: "Get that car out off the track."

Foyt's crew pushed his disabled car to the pit exit and continued to attempt to get it to start. It was hoped they would take an extra pace lap so that Foyt could rejoin the field in his starting position of 17th before the race started. However, the green flag was unfurled and the race was on. Foyt finally got started, but was already down a lap to the leaders.

Polesitter Bobby Unser took off and left everyone in his wake, much like Donohue had the previous year. Andretti, starting sixth, made an incredible start and was second by the time they reached Turn 2. And like Donohue, Unser was soon out of the race after setting a torrid pace. A broken distributor rotor sidelined the Olsonite Eagle on Lap 31.

For the next 150 laps, Bettenhausen dominated the race in the Sunoco McLaren. Like Hurtubise, Bettenhausen was a fan favorite as many fans held fond memories for his late father. Tony Bettenhausen won virtually everywhere he raced and had died trying to win an elusive Indianapolis 500. With challenges from Donohue and Grant, Bettenhausen stayed in front for 138 laps.

With 20 laps to go, something was apparently wrong with Bettenhausen's car. The Offenhauser was clearly off-song and by 182, he slowed to a crawl – the victim of apparent ignition failure.

Now Grant was in the lead, but he was struggling. The higher speeds created higher G-forces for the drivers and Grant's head began to lean to the right as he went around the Speedway's left-hand corners. At the time, drivers did not wear shoulder straps or HANS devices and the G-force was affecting Grant's neck muscles.

On Lap 188, he came in for his final pit stop to replace a

deflating front tire. Unfortunately for Grant, he had stopped in the pit of his teammate and Unser's crew serviced the car and sent him back into the race in second place. It transpired that the stop violated a rule and each subsequent lap he completed would ultimately be disallowed. The violation was that Grant's car had taken fuel from another competitor's tank. The crew maintained that although the fueling rig was hooked up, they only changed the tire. It was to no avail.

Donohue was now in the lead and went on to capture his and Roger Penske's first Indianapolis 500. He had been expected to win last year and now when least expected, he won the race.

Al Unser crossed the line in third, but benefited from Grant's demise to move up to second. Had he won, he would have been first to win three in a row at Indy. But even the two-time defending winner knew his car had been no match for the new Eagles or McLaren.

Following Unser home were Leonard, Sessions, rookie Sam Posey in an Eagle-Offenhauser, Lloyd Ruby in one of the new Atlanta-Foyts and Mike Hiss, who garnered top rookie honors. Andretti, who might have finished fourth behind his new Vel's Parnelli Jones teammates, ran out of fuel and finished eighth.

The 1972 race was history in the making and 1973 promised a serious attempt at the 200-mile-an-hour barrier.

Above: The classically educated Sam Posey, a thoroughly entertaining storyteller who later will serve as a television commentator, finishes fifth with a 1972 Gurney Eagle. In typical self-effacing fashion, Posey will chuckle, "We made a lucky choice of car. Just about anybody else could have won with this."
Photograph: IMS

1973: Entirely too much fire and rain

Once upon a time, there were people who believed the earth was flat. Since technology was non-existent, they could be excused for that belief. Where the Indianapolis Motor Speedway is concerned, the closest thing to a "flat-earth society" would have been the folks who clung to the belief that it was impossible to run a lap at 150 miles per hour around the track.

Of course, Parnelli Jones proved them wrong by doing just that in 1962 and three years later, they had burst through the 160-mph barrier. In three more years, the 170-mph barrier fell and by 1972, the 190-mph barrier had been surpassed.

Now with 1,000-horsepower, winged Indy cars descending on the track, it was apparent that the 200-mph barrier would be cracked. Jerry Grant had already achieved it the previous September at the Ontario Motor Speedway, a slightly faster copy of IMS. In May of 1973, the only question was whether it would be a McLaren or an Eagle making the breakthrough at Indy.

The 200-mph barrier would indeed be broken at Indianapolis – but not for four more years and the pursuit of that speed would be costly to the sport in general and the Speedway in particular.

The 1973 entry list produced an array of racy equipment.

First, there were the McLaren M16Cs, which now featured a headrest-style engine cover that swooped back to the gigantic rear wing. There were new cars for Team McLaren, which now employed Peter Revson and Johnny Rutherford, and Penske Racing, which had entries for Gary Bettenhausen and rookie Bobby Allison. Second-year driver Salt Walther also had a 1972 McLaren for his father's Dayton-Walther team and John Martin entered a '72 version for himself. Roger McCluskey figured to have a more competitive month of May in a 1971 McLaren entered by Lindsey Hopkins. McCluskey had been the only driver to make the 1972 500 in one of the ungainly Antares, but switched to a McLaren shortly after and ended up winning the Ontario 500.

All American Racers returned with the latest updated Eagle for Bobby Unser, Jerry Grant and Wally Dallenbach. They figured to have strong competition from Penske Racing, which purchased one for defending winner Mark Donohue.

The entry list was also swelled by a number of teams and drivers using customer Eagles. They included Patrick Racing for Gordon Johncock and Swede Savage, O'Connell Racing for Billy Vukovich, Fletcher Racing for Art Pollard and Jimmy Caruthers, Thermo-King Racing for Mike Hiss, Leader Card Racers for Mike Mosley, Champ-Carr Enterprises for Sam Posey, Lindsey Hopkins for Lee Kunzman, Commander Motor Homes for Lloyd Ruby and Roy Woods Racing for David Hobbs. All were powered by turbocharged Offenhausers.

Foyt-powered Eagles were also entered for Dick Simon, M.V.S. Racing for Sam Sessions and Hopkins Racing for Mel Kenyon. Smokey Yunick entered a Chevrolet-powered Eagle for rookie Jerry Karl (featuring dual turbochargers) and Bob Harkey had an older Ford-powered Eagle owned by Hopkins at his disposal.

After copying McLaren in 1972, Grant King produced an Eagle look-alike called the Kingfish with Steve Krisiloff listed as driver.

The main competition against the McLarens and Eagles came from A.J. Foyt and Vel's Parnelli Jones Racing. Foyt contracted engineer Bob Riley to design the latest Coyote and Riley responded with one of the lowest, sleekest looking machines to ever run at the track. Two of the new Foyt-powered cars were entered for Foyt and George Snider.

Despite winning the 1972 national championship, the Vel's Parnelli Jones team scrapped their radical car and had Maurice Phillipe come up with something more conventional. The Parnelli VPJ-2-Offenhauser was unique, borrowing some traits from Eagle and some from McLaren. As had been the case in '72, Viceroy cars were entered for Al Unser and Mario Andretti and two-time champion Joe Leonard returned in the Samsonite special.

"Super Team" would be affected by a major change in personnel. That was the departure of Chief Mechanic George Bignotti, who guided the Vel's Parnelli team as it captured three straight national championships, back-to-back Indianapolis 500s and 20 other Indy-car victories. Bignotti assumed the same role with Pat Patrick's new, improved team now sponsored by STP. In fact, Patrick basically cleaned house and formed something of a "super team" himself.

After nearly 25 years of trying to win the 500 and scoring

their only victory at Indy in 1969, the Granatelli brothers were winding down their participation. In addition to sponsoring Patrick Racing, they entered their 1972 Lola-Ford for rookie Graham MacRae, but when the New Zealander was unable to go fast enough, they put him in one of Patrick's Eagle-Offenhausers.

The Speedway also had a new look with the main entrance being moved further to the east on 16th Street between Turns 1 and 2. The new entrance featured a four-lane tunnel that obviously aided incoming traffic on the busier days of the month. With teams beginning to use moving-van-style transporters to haul their cars and equipment, the spacious confines of the tunnel made it a welcome and far-sighted addition.

May of 1973 was wet and miserable and as a result, it took a week for drivers to near the 200-mph mark. The first man to get close was Savage, whose top speed on Day 8 was 197.802. With a rainy second week of practice, Savage's speed would clearly be the fastest prior to the first day of qualifying.

During the morning practice session, tragedy struck.

Pollard, who had posted one of the best speeds of the month, slammed into the wall exiting Turn 1. The car burst into flame and then slowly rolled over as it slid into Turn 2. The car then landed in an upright position. Pollard died an hour later.

Once qualifying commenced, the marks began to fall. Savage opened his run with a record lap of 197.152 and finished with a four-lap record of 196.582.

Several drivers made the field and it was time for Rutherford to make his run. It would be a memorable one. His first lap was 198.676 – a new track record. The next lap was slower at 197.846. Lap 3 was his fastest at 199.071, only 21/100ths of a second away from the magic 200 mph mark! He finished his run with a 198.063 for an average of 198.413, another new track record. He then dedicated the run to Pollard, who had been a close friend.

Driver after driver failed to dislodge the Texan from the pole and that would be as close as anyone would get to going 200.

Bobby Unser, the fastest man at the Speedway in 1972, nearly took his second straight pole with an average of 198.183. He was 21/100ths off Rutherford's time. Donohue showed he liked the new Eagle by qualifying third fastest at 197.412. Savage, the fastest man in practice, qualified fourth and was joined in Row 2 by Bettenhausen and Andretti, the quickest of the "Super Team."

By the time qualifying ended the following weekend, the chassis breakdown was reminiscent of the late 1950s with Watsons, Watson copies and Kurtis chassis making up the field. The 1973 Indianapolis 500 was going to have 20 Eagles, seven McLarens, three Parnellis, two Coyotes and one Kingfish. Offenhausers powered 26 cars with Fords in six chassis and one lone Chevrolet. All 33 engines were turbocharged.

For the first time in years, it looked like there was a significant degree of parity. However, what would transpire would be one of the more infamous Indianapolis 500s on record.

Once again, there was a change in the calendar. With a request by the 500 Festival Committee to schedule the parade on Saturday and the desire to avoid running the race on Sunday, the race was to be held on Monday, May 28, which coincidentally was Memorial Day.

The race began under extremely overcast skies. Early morning rains dampened the track, but it provided something of a sustained last hurrah for its oldest living 500 winner. René Thomas, the Frenchman who won in 1914 and was making his first appearance at the track since 1921, arrived in Indianapolis unexpectedly and was soon given the VIP treatment. Normally, a dignitary would be given a lap of honor, but because the effort to dry the track was ongoing, a delighted Thomas got a number of laps in his race-winning Delage, waving his checkered cap to the fans.

Finally, it was time to race, but as Pat Vidan dropped the green from his platform inside the track, trouble began almost instantly.

Walther's car swerved right and climbed into the catch fence on top of the wall. The impact with the fence and the steel safety cables tore the front end off of the McLaren. As the car gyrated through the air, it sprayed burning fuel over a number of fans sitting right along the track.

Twelve years earlier, Tony Bettenhausen's car had hurdled the wall at nearly the same spot and partially landed in the seats. Although Walther's car did not penetrate the fence, it was certainly a close call and several spectators required treatment for burns.

In the meantime, Walther's car landed on the straightaway upside down. As numerous cars hit it, the car spun like a top. Walther did not have a six-point shoulder harness and did what they call "submarining" or sliding down in the cockpit. It undoubtedly saved his life as the rollbar was bent back. With the front bulkhead ripped off, Walther's feet protruded from the wreckage.

Dallenbach, who got caught up in the accident, immediately got out of his car and tried to help Walther. The accident also involved Mosley, Kunzman, Hiss, Jim McElreath, Hobbs, Martin, Simon and Karl. The red flag came out immediately and for the third time since 1964, the race was stopped due to an accident.

Hobbs' view of the proceedings was a case of déjà vu.

"You'd think the best drivers in the world could come down the straightaway without hitting each other," said Hobbs in a remark very reminiscent of Dan Gurney's observation of the 1966 pileup.

And then it rained. In fact, the rain came on so quickly, it was almost as if nature was trying to extinguish the various fires on the front straightaway. It also continued and the race was postponed until the following day.

Walther miraculously lived through the accident and was taken to Methodist Hospital. He suffered burns to his hand

and face as well as internal injuries, but somehow he received no fractures.

Other drivers received flash burns, but all were able to run and Walther was the only driver missing from the lineup when they attempted to start the race the next day. After off-and-on rain, Speedway crews were finally able to get the track dry and the 32 remaining cars set out on the pace lap. They got no farther than the pace lap as the skies once again opened up and the race was postponed a record third day.

Once under cloudy skies, Speedway crews labored to dry the wet track. At this point, no one knew when the race would actually start. Thousands of fans made a dash to the track

after the Speedway Radio Network announced the race would be starting in less than an hour.

For the record, the green flag dropped at 2:10 p.m. (normally the starting time would have been 11 a.m.). Bobby Unser got the drop on polesitter Rutherford and the race was on. Unlike last year, there would be a closer spectacle.

Revson was an early departure after hitting the wall in Turn 4. Damage was light, but the McLaren suffered more damage when the wrecker crew dropped it on the wall while removing it.

For 20 laps, Donohue followed Unser, who stayed out in front until pitting on Lap 39. Johncock took the lead and then turned it over to his teammate, Savage. Al Unser had been quietly moving up from the third row. On Lap 55, he passed Savage for the lead.

Three laps later, Savage crashed in Turn 4. In one of the most grisly accidents at the track, Savage's Eagle slammed head-on into the inside wall. The car disintegrated spewing parts, wheels and burning fuel everywhere. The engine went tumbling down the track while Savage ended up still strapped to his seat. There was nothing else left of the car around him.

Suddenly, the entire track seemed to erupt in flame as one portion of the wreckage burned inside the track and another portion was on fire near the outside wall. The fuel that spilled onto the track ignited. Seeing his driver's car crash, Armando Teran dashed up the pit lane towards the accident. The board man who signaled Savage, he had failed to see an oncoming safety truck and was struck. He died instantly.

Like Walther, Savage somehow managed to survive the accident. He was hospitalized with severely broken legs, a broken arm, internal injuries and numerous burns.

For the second time, the race was stopped due to a major accident.

Following an hour of cleanup, the race was restarted and Al Unser continued to lead the next 15 laps. Then his car broke a piston and his bid for a third victory at Indy was over.

Johncock now led with Vukovich in second. McCluskey, who had started 14th, also moved up and as the skies began to darken once more, he was third.

On Lap 133, it rained again. This time due to the lateness of the day, Vidan waved the red and the checker. The race was over and the 332.5 miles completed made it the shortest 500 in history. (The rain-shortened 1950 race was 345 miles long.)

Vukovich and McCluskey each scored career-high finishes at the Speedway. Lindsey Hopkins wound up having a very successful day. In addition to McCluskey, his cars finished fourth with Kenyon and seventh with Kunzman. Bettenhausen, who dominated the year before, finished fifth. Krisiloff scored a career-best sixth and Rutherford, who never led a lap, wound up ninth behind the unsponsored McLaren of Martin.

For Johncock, it was justice after his near-miss of 1966. For Bignotti, it marked his sixth victory at Indianapolis as chief mechanic.

However, the mood was less than celebratory. The victory banquet had been cancelled due to the continual postponement of the race, Johncock's teammate Swede Savage was in Methodist Hospital with critical injuries and it was still raining. Johncock, Patrick and their entourage had dinner at a local fast-food restaurant after visiting the hospital to check on Savage.

The month of May had been costly in terms of human life. A month after the race, poor Savage would succumb to his injuries.

However, the United States Auto Club immediately took action to cut back on the fiery accidents and to slow down the cars.

New rules would go into effect for the Pocono 500. They included a reduction in the rear wing size from 64 inches to 55 inches in width, all fuel would be carried on the left-side tanks, total fuel would be reduced from 75 to 40 gallons on board, and right-side fuel tanks would be filled with energy-absorbing material. Any new car would be required to have tanks only on the left side. Turbocharger boost would now be restricted to 80 inches and governed by a popoff valve. Another change required the signalman (the pit board holder) to be stationed near the pit wall for each team to remain at his post throughout the race.

Below: The intense David Earl "Swede" Savage, a protégé of Dan Gurney, is tipped by many to be the 1973 victor. He will lose his life in the attempt.

Bottom: Eventual winner Gordon Johncock lines up in row four between Peter Revson and Bobby Allison. Photographs: IMS

1974: Two 'Tall' Texans wage a Duel

The real story of the 1974 Indianapolis 500 centers on a pair of "tall" Texans. OK, perhaps the headline is a little misleading, but people do tend to describe certain 500 drivers as "gunfighters." That term would fit both men, although neither could be considered tall and one of them was actually a native of Kansas, who ultimately wound up in Texas.

However, the 500-mile race of 1974 could be considered something of a classic with the main combatants providing a Southwestern flair to the outcome. Yes, there were 31 other drivers in the starting field besides the pole position winner A.J. Foyt and Johnny Rutherford. And yes, other drivers led that year's race.

In the end, though, it was the Foyt-Rutherford version of "hound and hare" that captured everyone's attention.

The two drivers offered something of a contrast. Foyt's father was a mechanic who was heavily involved in the sport of auto racing and owned racing cars. He even built a miniature version of a midget for his six-year-old son. As a teen, Foyt spent some time in drag racing and then went into midgets. He graduated to sprint cars and by the time he made it to Indianapolis in 1958, he was the beneficiary of a well-rounded racing education.

Rutherford's father was also a mechanic, but a member of the United States Army. At age nine, Rutherford's father took him to his first auto race – a midget event in Tulsa, Oklahoma. Because of the father's involvement in the military, he lived in a number of cities while serving at a number of bases. Ultimately, the family settled in Fort Worth, Texas, and the younger Rutherford became an adopted Texan, even though he was born in Coffeyville, Kansas.

When the younger Rutherford became a teenager, his father bought him an old car and encouraged him to build it into a hot rod. Somewhere along the way, the elder Rutherford owned a midget. After racing hot rods, Rutherford turned to midgets and sprints and by 1963, he was ready for Indianapolis.

Foyt tasted success much earlier, winning USAC national titles in 1960 and 1961 and capturing his first victory at Indianapolis, also in 1961. He added two more national titles in 1963 and '64, scoring a record 10 victories the latter year including his second win at Indianapolis.

Rutherford had to wait until 1965 to win his first Indy car race (at Atlanta, where he won in the Watson-Ford that Rodger Ward had failed to qualify at Indianapolis) and then nine more years to win his first Indy 500. His first champ-car title would not come until 1980.

In fairness, Rutherford's career suffered a major setback when he broke both arms in a sprint-car accident early in 1966. He was beginning to make an impact, but the injuries delayed that phase of career until 1973 when he joined Team McLaren. For 1974, he was truly coming into his own and capable of giving Foyt a run for his money.

But to get to the race, there were several days of practice and qualifying. Here's what happened.

The tire war was about to end with Firestone deciding to pull out of major competition at the end of the season. After 1974, every Indy car would be shod on Goodyear tires for the next 20 years.

Replacing that "war" was the battle of chassis with most top drivers entered in an Eagle or McLaren or cars that strongly resembled those makes. However, it is important to note that the Eagles clearly outnumbered the McLarens.

Since 1972, the Eagle became the most popular chassis at Indianapolis. All American Racers entered their latest car for Bobby Unser with customer cars entered by Patrick Racing, Fletcher Racing, O'Connell Racing, Gerhardt Racing, Leader Card Racers, Dick Simon Racing, Lindsey Hopkins, Richard Beith and a pair for Vel's Parnelli Jones Racing for star drivers Al Unser and Mario Andretti.

The latter team was using a customer car for the first time since 1969, but would wind up putting sprint-car sensation Jan Opperman in one of its year-old Parnelli VPJ-2 chassis. Opperman was a last-minute replacement for Joe Leonard, who received what would ultimately be a career-ending leg

injury. The popular Leonard crashed after suffering a tire puncture during the Ontario 500 in March.

A promising rookie named Tom Sneva was entered in the Grant King's Kingfish, an Eagle look-alike, while fellow rookie Johnny Parsons was entered in Tassi Vatis' Finley-Offenhauser, dubbed the Fleagle for obvious reasons. Rick Muther was entered in a two-year Coyote that bore a strong resemblance to the Eagle and Bob Harkey's Kenyon started life as a 1967 Coyote that now looked more like an Eagle, circa 1972.

In addition to two Team McLaren chassis for Rutherford and David Hobbs, there were customer McLarens for Team Penske and drivers Gary Bettenhausen and Mike Hiss; Dayton Walther for Salt Walther; one for crowd favorite Jim Hurtubise, who also entered his front-engined Mallard; and for John Martin, who ended up with one of the most unusual sponsorship deals in the history of the 500. Martin's McLaren-Offenhauser was Peter Revson's car from 1972 and dubbed the "Sea Snack Shrimp Cocktail Special."

Mark Donohue, the 1972 winner, had retired at the end of 1973 and was now in a less-than-enthusiastic role of team manager. Donohue was to have been replaced by Revson, but sadly the 1971 500 pole winner had been killed during a test session for the South African Grand Prix in March. Hiss got the nod, having previously subbed for Donohue and finishing second in the 1972 Ontario 500.

Foyt was back in an updated version of his Coyote-Foyt from 1973. Bob Riley, the man who designed that car, penned a similar version with Offenhauser power for Lindsey Hopkins and driver Roger McCluskey, who captured the 1973 USAC national championship in Hopkins' McLaren. McCluskey's car originally appeared with a low tail section that was supposed to serve as a rear wing. The idea did not work and the new Riley sprouted a conventional rear wing by qualifying.

There was also a new "sheriff" in town, so to speak. Following the disastrous 1973 race, longtime USAC official Tom Binford replaced Harlan Fengler as chief steward. Fengler, who raced at Indianapolis in 1923, remained as a consultant to Binford.

There were other major changes at the Speedway that year. Due to the accidents involving Walther and Swede Savage, the Indianapolis Motor Speedway made a number of revisions. The wall, originally 36 inches tall, was raised to 54 inches. Spectators in the lower rows along the front straightaway could only see the tops of the cars' wings and the drivers' helmets. That may have been a disappointment, but it was safer.

Box seats once located right by the wall along the main straightaway were totally removed. And the inner-retaining wall in Turn 4 was no longer angled. The inside wall was now parallel to the track and drivers could actually enter the pit lane immediately after Turn 4.

Starter Pat Vidan would also have a better view of the action. Gone was the small platform on the inside of the front straightaway. A small starter tower was erected on the outside of the track with a platform 15 feet high for Vidan and a second platform for Binford 22 feet high. Interestingly, Vidan would have preferred the old location where he could actually leap onto the track at the end of the race and perform his unique style of acrobatic flag-waving.

That was the Indianapolis Motor Speedway. There were also changes for the cars.

With new rules in place governing rear wing size, fuel loads and turbocharger boost (for the first time, engines now employed a turbo popoff valve to limit the boost), speeds were predictably down during practice. Well, the speeds were slower than 1973, but the drivers and cars were still traveling very quickly. Despite a number of practices cut short or washed out by spring rainstorms, Bobby Unser turned in the month's fastest speed at 192.513.

When qualifying was finished, only two drivers would make the field with an average speed in excess of 190.

There was a significant change in the qualifying procedure. In the past, drivers had signaled the starter to indicate if they wanted to take the green flag and begin their qualifying attempt. Under the new rule, a team representative (usually the crew chief) would now be responsible for signaling the

JOHNNY RUTHERFORD

Look at most pictures of Johnny Rutherford and you're bound to see him smiling. Perhaps that's what has drawn so many fans to the man known as "Lone Star J.R." In his star-studded career, Rutherford has made a number of comebacks and perhaps three major transitions. Bred on the tough sprint-car tracks of the southwest, he emerged on the scene of big-time racing in 1963 at two of the sport's biggest venues – Daytona and Indianapolis. The unknown newcomer shocked the NASCAR establishment by running fast in practice and capturing one of the two 125-mile qualifying races, earning him a front row start for the Daytona 500. However, Rutherford's real desire was focused on Indianapolis where he managed to qualify for his first 500 three months later.

The year 1965 brought his first break-through as he piloted one of the Leader Card Watson-Fords to victory in a USAC's 250-miler in Atlanta. It was a significant transition – a sprint-car, dirt track specialist winning in a rear-engined car on a paved, high-banked oval. Rutherford also capped off the season by winning USAC's sprint-car title. It was quite an accomplishment when you figure his competition came from drivers like A.J. Foyt,

Mario Andretti and Don Branson. The future was looking bright indeed. However, it nearly ended in a sprint-car accident in Eldora, Ohio, that left him with a concussion and two broken arms. He would make a comeback, but top rides and Indy-car wins would have to wait. After nearly snatching the pole at Indianapolis in 1970 and passing Al Unser for lead at the start, people took notice.

In 1973, his career got a major boost when he was signed to drive for Team McLaren. Label this Transition II. Gordon Coppuck's sleek M16 was already a winner. With Rutherford, it allowed him to show the world that he also was a winner. In 1974, he put together an epic drive that earned him his first victory at Indianapolis.

Two years later, he was a two-time winner and he opened the 80s by winning a third time at the Speedway and capturing his first national Indy-car title. By this time, Rutherford had made another transition as one of the sport's best-liked ambassadors. When he officially retired in 1994, he appropriately chose Indianapolis to make the announcement. It was a tearful farewell, but not long after, the familiar smile returned. Now active in the IRL, Rutherford continues his ambassadorship, smiling all the way.

Above: The 1974 "rookie" class comprises (from left): future winner Tom Sneva, Pancho Carter, safety equipment magnate Bill Simpson, Jan Opperman, Tom Bigelow, Larry "Boom Boom" Cannon, and Johnny Parsons, son of the 1950 winner. Interestingly, Parsons and Carter are half-brothers (having the same mother), and they were raised in the same household.

Left: Jerry Grant, who but for some rather mysterious activity during his final pit stop would have finished second in the 1972 "500," is part of Bob Fletcher's Cobre team in 1974. He will finish tenth.
Photographs: IMS

starter as to whether the attempt would take place.

In addition to that change, qualifying would be limited to two Saturdays (with each day divided in half to maintain the four-session process) and the opening week of practice was eliminated. This was in compliance with government requests that each sport cut back participation by 10 percent thanks to the energy crisis caused by the OPEC oil embargo. The opening practice time also was moved from 9 a.m. to 11 a.m. Both the opening practice week and the original opening time for practice would never be restored.

The first driver was also the first man to qualify – Foyt. One of the fastest in practice all month, Foyt turned in an average speed of 191.632 in the Gilmore Coyote-Foyt. A year earlier, Foyt's average would have been 17th fastest. With the new rule changes, Foyt wound up being quickest.

Dallenbach turned in his best-ever qualifying performance at Indy to average 189.683 in the STP Eagle-Offenhauser. It earned him a spot right next to Foyt. Hiss filled out the front row with an average of 187.490 in Roger Penske's Norton McLaren-Offenhauser.

Row 2 featured Vukovich, Andretti and Mosley all in Eagle-Offenhausers. Bobby Unser, the man most folks expected to win the pole, had to settle for the inside of Row 3 with an average of 185.176. That was nearly 13 mph slower than he had qualified the previous year.

Another pole contender, Rutherford, was unable to qualify on the first day and was relegated to 25th on the grid. Rutherford had blown an engine in morning practice and his crew was unable to make an engine change and get him into his original spot in the qualifying line. As a result, he was considered a second-session qualifier and would have to start behind the 24 drivers considered first-session qualifiers. However, his starting position was misleading. Rutherford's 190.446 average was second fastest in the field of 33.

He would be the man to watch on Race Day – provided the field could make a safe start and Foyt would not build up too big of a lead.

There would also be a controversy. With only two days earmarked for qualifying, there were a few participants left at the line when the gun went off at 6 p.m. on the final Saturday. Six teams believed the entry entitled them to have at least one chance to qualify. Binford interpreted it differently. The issue was not resolved.

Spearheaded by a crew member who happened to be an attorney, the six teams sought an injunction to block the race. A hearing was held on Tuesday, May 20, in Marion County Superior Court and a trial began the following morning. Among those testifying was track owner Tony Hulman. Ultimately, qualifying was not reopened and the race would go on as scheduled.

Eagle clearly won the battle of the numbers as 18 used them to qualify and three more drivers made the race in Eagle copies. Six drivers qualified McLarens with the rest of the field a hodge-podge of chassis. In the engine department, Offenhauser was the top choice. Twenty-eight starters had the turbocharged Offenhauser with the remaining opting for the turbocharged Foyt.

It would appear there was the most parity in this field since the era of the front-engined roadsters. But Race Day would show the 1974 race really belonged to two drivers.

For the first time in its history, the Indianapolis 500 would be held on a Sunday. With the 500 Festival Parade ensconced on Saturday and the possibility of a rain-out on a Monday race, it made more sense to run the race on Sunday and use Memorial Day Monday as a rain day.

When Vidan dropped the green flag to start the 58th Indianapolis 500, it was Dallenbach and not Foyt who jumped into the lead. The veteran of eight 500s was more than 100 yards ahead of Foyt when he came by to complete Lap 1. Dallenbach's opening lap was 184.011 mph and he followed up with a lap at 191.4 mph. The two laps represented three track records. One was a record for the opening lap. The second was a record for the fastest average of the first two laps (187.637) and the third was for what ended up being the race's fastest lap and the fastest race lap ever.

There was a reason for Dallenbach's speed in addition to the fact he was an outstanding driver (the previous fall, he captured the Ontario 500). When Dallenbach qualified, Chief Mechanic George Bignotti used a larger turbocharger blower for added horsepower. Bignotti was prohibited from replacing it with a smaller blower that would have been easier on the engine for the 500 miles. It undoubtedly contributed to his retirement on Lap 3 as he coasted into the pits with a burned piston.

Surprisingly, Dallenbach was not the first out of the race. He was actually the fourth, having been preceded into the pits by Simon, Bettenhausen and Andretti.

Now it was Foyt's turn to lead the field and like Dallenbach, he did so at a record pace. Foyt set records for the first 10 miles (185.366), the first 25 miles (185.079) and the first 50 miles (183.234) during the first 20 laps.

It was going to require a record pace because another driver was moving forward at a torrid pace of his own. From 25th starting position, Rutherford was on the move. By Lap 13, he was an incredible third place! By Lap 21, he was second, but two laps later, he was in the pits for his first stop. With only 40 gallons of fuel on board, drivers were going to have to make six to eight stops for the 500 miles.

Foyt, still maintaining a strong lead over Rutherford at this point, made his first stop on Lap 24. That gave the lead to Bobby Unser for two laps and then it was Unser's turn to make his first stop.

J.R.'s charge to the front was not without its moments.

While trying to lap Jim McElreath, Rutherford decided to use rookie Pancho Carter as a blocker to him get past both cars. Rutherford later admitted he had cut it a bit too close for comfort and Carter lost control. Fortunately, he missed the wall and McElreath's car and was able to continue. Rutherford would later apologize to Carter from Victory Lane.

Foyt, Unser and Rutherford had a lock on the first three spots and Rutherford would soon pass Unser and continue his pursuit of Foyt, who set race records for 100 miles (177.859) and 150 miles (176.627).

On Lap 64, it came to a head – in the pits. Making their stops together, Foyt spent a disastrous 54 seconds following problems with a tire change while Rutherford was in and out in 14 seconds.

The McLaren driver had caught Foyt on the track; now he got the lead in the pits. Lap 65 would be the first lap led in the Indianapolis 500 by Rutherford, twice a front-row qualifier at the Speedway. Foyt, in a serious bid to become the first four-time 500 winner, was soon behind Rutherford. No one was capitulating just yet.

For the next 76 laps, the two drivers swapped the lead on the track and in the pits. On Lap 140, Foyt received the black flag for leaking oil. He stopped only long enough for his crew to check for leaks. Finding none, Foyt returned to the track before consulting with USAC officials. They black-flagged him again and this time, Foyt turned left into the Gasoline Alley entrance and was pushed back to his garage. Foyt, who was hoping for a record fourth win, did set a record with his 17th start, breaking the old mark of 16 jointly held by Cliff Bergere and Chet Miller.

Rutherford led until his final pit stop on Lap 175, surrendering the lead to Bobby Unser. He then caught and passed Unser to score his first victory at Indianapolis. Unser finished second and Vukovich, runner-up the year before, was third. Defending race winner Gordon Johncock was fourth and Rutherford's teammate David Hobbs scored his first and only top-10 finish at Indy by placing fifth. McElreath and Carter, who nearly came to grief while being passed by the forward-marching Rutherford, finished sixth and seventh, respectively.

Bob Harkey brought the field's oldest car – the Kenyon-Foyt that started out life as a 1967 Coyote – home in eighth. Lloyd Ruby finished ninth, but it was his headgear that was making history. "Rube" was the only man in the 1974 race wearing an open-face helmet and goggles. He would be the last man to do so.

Rutherford would be a popular Indy 500 winner and a safe month of May had done much to put the tragic May of 1973 behind everyone.

1975: Awash in victory

In many ways, the outcome of the 1975 Indianapolis 500 could have been different. One man won, but one wonders who might have won had The race was prematurely ended by a near monsoon, with three former winners all trying to repeat.

For the most part, the month of May was pretty quiet at the Indianapolis Motor Speedway. With the rules unchanged, no one was going to break the 200-mile-per-hour barrier. There were few new cars and for the first time since 1961, there was a real feeling of status quo where equipment was concerned. An owner could go out and purchase an Eagle or McLaren chassis and then purchase a turbocharged Offenhauser or Foyt engine and be ready to run at Indy.

That's not to say there were only Eagles or McLaren at the track, but as it had been in 1974, the Eagle was the most popular choice among 500 entrants and McLaren was second most popular. With the exception of the new Wildcats, the Bob Riley-designed Coyote and Hopkins Riley chassis, all of the other cars at least outwardly resembled the Eagle and McLaren.

The latter Eagles provided interesting story lines for the month. Fred Gerhardt and Bettenhausen were reunited for the first time since 1971. Gary had lost his ride with Roger Penske after injuring his arm in a dirt-car race in Syracuse, N.Y. Although he had only partial use of his left arm, he could still race effectively.

The McNamara Motor Express name was back on a car for the first time since the late 1950s. Longtime owner Lee

Main photograph: After the lap-175 deluge has subsided, Bobby Unser sloshes his way down the pit lane headed for Victory Circle.

Above: On the front row for 1975: Bobby Unser, Gordon Johncock, and pole sitter A. J. Foyt.
Photographs: IMS

Elkins decided to give the Speedway one more attempt, with rookie Bill Puterbaugh. He would not be disappointed.

The McLaren ranks were led by Team McLaren, who entered brand-new cars for defending race winner Johnny Rutherford and Lloyd Ruby. Penske Racing entered cars for Tom Sneva and Bobby Allison while Dayton-Walther Racing entered a pair of McLarens for Salt Walther and Bob Harkey. John Martin was also back with his unsponsored McLaren.

A.J. Foyt decided to concentrate on the elusive fourth victory at Indianapolis and only entered cars for himself. The defending pole winner returned to the Speedway with a brand-new Coyote-Foyt.

Bob Riley's car for Lindsey Hopkins Racing also returned with driver Roger McCluskey. But there were a couple of changes to the program. The broad nose was replaced with a nosecone that resembled a McLaren. The car also had one of the more unique sponsors in 500 history – Silver Floss Sauerkraut.

Rolla Vollstedt returned with his McLaren look-alike and Grant King entered a pair of Eagle look-alike Kingfish chassis for Bentley Warren and rookie Sheldon Kinser.

Canadian driver/fabricator Eldon Rasmussen purchased a pair of the McLaren look-alike Atlanta chassis and revamped them. The cars were renamed Rascars. Rasmussen entered himself in a Foyt-powered car and sold an Offenhauser-powered version to fellow rookie Larry McCoy.

Two of the most interesting entries for 1975 were the new Wildcats for Patrick Racing Team's Gordon Johncock and Wally Dallenbach. Built by George Bignotti, the day-glo red cars were powered by a version of the 4-cylinder Offenhauser called the Drake-Goosen-Sparks. The DGS was narrower, taller and more efficient than the conventional Offenhauser.

Another car ran some test miles during practice, but for practical purposes its team was not going to run it.

Vel's Parnelli Jones Racing gave everyone a peak at the future with the new Parnelli VPJ-6. Based on the team's Formula One car they unveiled the previous autumn, the new Parnelli was powered by a Cosworth DFX, a turbocharged version of Cosworth's Formula One DFV engine.

Featuring what had to be the smallest frontal area for an Indy car, both Al Unser and Andretti spent some time in the car during the month of May before concentrating on the team's more conventional Eagle-Offenhausers. The new car showed promise, particularly in the engine department. Andretti was clocked in the traps along the straightaway at 206 mph. Only Foyt (clocked at 216) and the DGS-powered Wildcats (clocked at 210) went faster.

Driver nationality was another point of interest in the 1975 entry list. The only foreign driver was Canada's Rasmussen (whose parents were actually American) and for only the second time since 1960, every driver was from the North American continent. In fact, fewer and fewer drivers running at the Speedway had road-racing backgrounds. New Zealand's Graham McRae unsuccessfully attempted to qualify in one of Lindsey Hopkins' cars. McRae, the 1973 500 Rookie of the Year, pointed out that "the world's greatest race should have at least one representative from the rest of the world!"

With road-course events dropped from USAC's National Championship, drivers with oval-track backgrounds were replacing F1 and sports-car drivers.

There was another significant change to the Indianapolis Motor Speedway. Where renovations for the 1974 race centered on safety features, the new offering for 1975 was clearly for the fans.

Located inside the track between Turns 1 and 2 was the gleaming new IMS Hall of Fame Museum. The new facility, scheduled to open for the following year's race, was more spacious than the track's original museum with 96,000 square feet of space to display its growing collection of historic racing cars and automobiles. Equally important, the new museum would have something its predecessor has always lacked – adequate parking space.

The stage was now set for practice and qualifying (restored to four days again). Thanks to the horsepower of the turbocharged Foyt V-8, Foyt was the man to beat and he and

Johncock began a psychological war of sorts. Johncock threw down the gauntlet on Tuesday afternoon at 190.880 mph. Foyt responded the following day with a 193.924 – with more turbocharger boost than he would have been allowed in qualifying.

On Thursday, Johncock benefited from extra boost to post the month's quickest speed at 195.228. That was the fastest lap at the Speedway since 1973 when the cars had larger rear wings and unlimited boost. Speeds dropped a bit on Friday and when qualifying concluded on Saturday, Foyt was on the pole with Johncock and Bobby Unser filling out the front row. Tom Sneva, Mike Mosley and Lloyd Ruby filled the second row with defending winner Rutherford nearby in seventh starting spot.

Ruby, the last man to wear an open-face helmet in the 500, apparently couldn't quite part with the past. Although he now sported the new full-faced models, Ruby removed the face shield and continued to use goggles.

One other qualifying effort proved to be outstanding when one considered the circumstances. In the year since he last raced at Indianapolis, Jimmy Caruthers was diagnosed with cancer. Caruthers underwent successful treatment and was able to return to the cockpit. Driving Alex Morales' Eagle-Offenhauser, the gutsy Caruthers posted the 10th-best qualifying time.

Foyt's average of 193.976 mph showed what the cars could achieve with legal boost. It was nearly five mph slower than Rutherford's record of 198.413 mph but more than two mph faster than his pole speed the previous year.

Foyt also tied an Indy 500 record by capturing his fourth pole position. He now shared the distinction of being the only man besides Rex Mays to have won four poles at the Speedway. Of course, Foyt's real goal was to become its first four-time race winner.

One man looking for his first 500 victory almost missed the show completely after qualifying 18th. Pancho Carter, the top rookie in the 1974 race, was involved in a major crash during Carburetion Day, three days before the race and only two minutes before the end of the session. Carter slammed into the Turn 1 wall and then slid into the infield where it rested partially in the drainage ditch. The ditch may have prevented Carter's car from hitting the line of trees in the spectator enclave.

The heavily damaged Fletcher Racing Eagle-Offenhauser was taken to local fabricator Don Brown. Following an all-out effort by Brown and Carter's crew, the car made it to the starting grid by race time. No one was sure how the rebuilt car would run, but at least Carter was going to start his second Indy 500.

When Pat Vidan dropped the green flag, the Foyt-versus-

Above: **Defending winner Johnny Rutherford makes a stop. Purists are somewhat taken aback by the decidedly un-McLaren-like paint job.**
Photographs: IMS

Above: Following a fifth-place finish in 1971, a second in 1973, and a third in 1974, Billy Vukovich switches from the Jerry O'Connell team to that of Bob Fletcher and finishes sixth.

Bottom: Bobby Unser brings Dan Gurney his third win as a constructor and his first as a car entrant.
Photograph: IMS

Johncock battle resumed with Johncock dashing into the lead for the first eight laps. Foyt took over on Lap 9 with Johncock, Bobby Unser and Rutherford in pursuit. One other driver was in pursuit of Foyt, but few took notice until the first round of pit stops. Wally Dallenbach, who qualified 21st, didn't stay there long and was fifth by the time the leaders began to pit on Lap 22.

Foyt's first stop gave the lead to Rutherford, who pitted on Lap 24, giving the lead to Bobby Allison. Allison pitted on Lap 25 and Foyt regained the lead ahead of Rutherford, Bobby Unser and Dallenbach.

Dallenbach's run to the front culminated with a pass of Foyt for the lead on Lap 58. Dallenbach, whose first laps led at Indianapolis had been the opening two circuits of 1974, kept going this time and built a cushion over Foyt, whose car was starting to experience tire trouble.

Between Laps 100 and 160, Dallenbach only relinquished the lead when he pitted. He was in control of the race and his destiny. Another man trying to control his destiny was Sneva, who now ran in fifth in Roger Penske's McLaren-Offenhauser.

While trying to get past the lapped car of Rasmussen on Lap 125, Sneva cut it too close heading into Turn 2 and found himself launched over the right front wheel of Rasmussen's car. Sneva's McLaren flipped and flew into the wall and the fence, where the engine broke free from the tub in a flurry of smoke and flames. Sneva landed right-side up with half a car and ground to a halt. Miraculously, Sneva popped open the face shield of his helmet and tried to get out of the car.

By that time, rescue crews arrived and helped the shaken Sneva step from the car. Despite the carnage, Sneva only suffered first- and second-degree burns and was able to return to competition at Pocono the following month. The accident also showed rules governing fuel tank construction to be effective. Sneva's car had a newly mandated, aircraft break-away fuel safety system that would cut and seal the fuel lines in the event of an impact. Three gallons in the overflow tank and in the fuel lines were all that burned in the fire. The 40-gallon fuel cell in the tub had not leaked despite the severity of the accident, as evidenced when they pumped out 37 gal-

lons from the tank afterward.

However, the incident may have affected the outcome. Dallenbach was forced into the grass and ran over something that caused his left rear tire to begin losing pressure. He managed to keep the car going until Lap 162, when he retired with a burned piston.

"I had to let off the throttle and run lean into the turns," Dallenbach explained in a post-race interview. "This caused my engine to heat up and eventually it burned up on me."

The race now became a battle between Bobby Unser, Rutherford and Mother Nature as black clouds loomed over the Speedway. Foyt also had an outside chance, but running out of fuel had pretty much taken him out of contention. Unser and Rutherford both pitted on Lap 171, but with 29 laps to go, both drivers were going to require another stop.

This time, they wouldn't need it.

On Lap 174, the skies opened up and the track was quickly deluged in water, causing a number of cars to spin or stop. As the rain let up, Unser crossed the line to receive the checkered and red flags. As each car slowly crossed the line, the crowd roared in appreciation for the effort. The 59th Indianapolis 500 was history and for the fourth time, the race failed to go the distance due to rain.

Following Unser were Rutherford, Foyt, Carter (whose car must have worked fine), McCluskey, Vukovich, Puterbaugh (who garnered the award for Indy's top rookie) and Snider. Even though he had retired 12 laps from the finish, Dallenbach wound up ninth.

Naturally, the soggy ending produced a number of "what if" scenarios. For Dallenbach, he might have won had the rain come a few laps earlier. Rutherford believed he could have caught Unser had it not rained. And Foyt believed he might have been able to pull out a victory had Rutherford and Unser been forced to go the distance and make another pit stop.

It didn't matter, however. Unser joined brother Al as a two-time 500 winner and his victory gave Dan Gurney's All American Racers team its first win at Indianapolis after 11 years of trying. Unser had also given the Eagle its first Indy 500 victory when he won in 1968.

Above: **Longtime race-goers will probably feel sticky and clammyy just looking at this scene. Once again, it is back and forth, back and forth. "Do you think we'll get in any running today?" "Well, I hear there is a 'window' over Terre Haute."**
Photograph: IMS

1976: More rain, but not so much more of the same

The year 1976 was the Bicentennial of the United States and at its premier, single-day sporting event – the Indianapolis 500 – there was something of a feeling of revolution in the air. When all was said and done, history would be made in the 1976 Indianapolis 500, but not the kind anyone expected.

At the USAC Championship Division's season opener at Phoenix, Arlene Hiss made it into the record books by becoming the first woman to qualify and run in an Indy-car race. The wife of Indy's top rookie from 1972, Mike Hiss, the experiment in social progress was hardly a success.

Hiss started on the last row and finished a distant 14th. It would be her first and last Indy-car start, but she would not be the last woman to attempt to break into the all-male domain of Indy-car racing. There will be more on that later.

Equipment was pretty much unchanged although Bob Riley's influence could be seen in the updated Wildcats and Grant King's new Dragon chassis. Looking more like A.J. Foyt's Coyote, the revamped Wildcat-DGS featured a broad nose section. King's previous Kingfish chassis had been copies of the McLaren and Eagle, but his new entries were Coyote look-alikes for Sheldon Kinser and John Martin. Bob Harkey would drive one of the team's Eagle look-alike Kingfish cars.

Rolla Vollstedt's car for Dick Simon also featured a full-width, Coyote-like nose section. However, it was Vollstedt's other driver who attracted the most attention during the month.

Vollstedt obtained backing from longtime 500 sponsor Phil Hedback and invited sports-car racer Janet Guthrie to drive a second Vollstedt-Offenhauser. Prior to Indianapolis, Guthrie had become the second woman to compete in an Indy-car event by qualifying 14th and finishing 15th at Trenton. Women had first been allowed to enter the pits and the garage area only five years earlier and now one was going for

an attempt to make history at Indianapolis.

Team McLaren was back with just one entry for Johnny Rutherford, but 1976 would see the most McLarens in an Indy 500 lineup. Entering customer McLarens were Penske Racing for Tom Sneva and Mario Andretti and Dayton-Walther for David Hobbs and Salt Walther. A pair of fathers also got into the act by entering McLaren-Offenhausers for their sons. Al Loquasto, Sr., whose son and namesake had been trying (unsuccessfully) to make the race since 1969, entered a 1972 McLaren for his son. Longtime USAC sprint-car owner Carl Gehlhausen entered Peter Revson's 1971 pole-winning McLaren for his son, Daniel "Spike" Gehlhausen.

The ever-popular Eagle was unchanged, but there was a change to the All American Racers lineup. Pancho Carter took over for Bobby Unser, who was now entered in an Eagle for Fletcher Racing. For the first time since 1973, AAR had more than one driver with Australia's Vern Schuppan entered in their second car.

Another departure from the Eagle camp was designer Roman Slobodynskj, who formed a company with Lindsey Hopkins called Romlin, to design the Lightning chassis. Low and sleek, the new Lightning was entered for Roger McCluskey.

The V-8 engine had all but become a thing of the past in terms of quantity, but there were two V-8-powered cars that were considered contenders. A.J. Foyt, still trying for an elusive fourth victory at Indianapolis, continued to run his Bob Riley-designed Coyote-Foyt. The Foyt engine was a turbocharged version of the Ford DOHC V-8 that had been running at Indy since 1964. Louie Meyer had turned the distributorship of the engine over to Foyt in 1971.

Another engine with Ford ties was the Cosworth DFX, mounted to the ultra-low Parnelli VPJ-6 chassis entered by Vel's Parnelli Jones Racing for Al Unser. The car was based on the team's F1 entry and had run some practice laps a

Above: During the rain delay, Foyt engine man Howard Gilbert checks the repaired sway bar. "Gil" was the man who helped George Salih build the winning car of 1957 and 1958.

Bottom: The crew of Jerry Grant's number 73 wait out the rain delay. Just as the cars are being warmed up in the pit lane for a restart, it will rain again.

Photographs: IMS

year earlier.

For 1976, the team was regrouping and concentrating on Indianapolis and the USAC National Championship with a sponsorship deal from American Racing Equipment and one car for Unser.

And in keeping a tie to the past, veteran Jim Hurtubise returned with his front-engined Mallard-Offenhauser. In addition to eschewing the latest full-face helmet style, Hurtubise continued to run in his open-face model with goggles and a bandana for facial protection.

Speeds were expected to drop, thanks to another rule change that mandated a lower turbocharge boost level from 80 inches to 65 inches. In fact, no one would top the 190 mark during the month, although some would come close.

Rutherford, on the heels of finishing first and second in the

past two 500s, established himself as the man to beat for the pole. His chief competition came from Al Unser in the new Parnelli-Cosworth and Johncock in the Wildcat-DGS. Foyt, although among the leaders, failed to establish the dominance he exhibited the previous two years.

For qualifying, Rutherford captured his second pole in four races with an average speed of 188.957 mph. Johncock qualified second with a 188.531 average. Sneva, survivor of the terrifying accident in Turn 2 last year, rebounded to qualify third with a 186.355 average.

Al Unser gave the Cosworth engine its first 500 start by qualifying fourth at 186.258. Foyt, the polesitter in 1974 and '75, had to settle for fifth fastest in 1976 with a 186.261 average. And Carter filled out the second row with a 184.824 average.

Andretti, now concentrating on Formula One and taking a ride with Team Lotus after Vel's Parnelli Jones Racing shut down its F1 effort, had to skip the opening weekend of qualifying to run in the Belgian Grand Prix. He returned for the second weekend of qualifying and did more than safely make the show. Andretti's average of 189.404 was the fastest of the 33-car field, but because he was a third-day qualifier, the best he could start was 19th.

Throughout practice and qualifying, the eyes of most were focused on Guthrie's progress. Plagued with numerous mechanical problems, Guthrie passed her rookie test, but struggled to find speed. On the night of the third day of qualifying, the team withdrew her car. However, on the final day of qualifying, Guthrie was able to prove she had the speed as a driver.

As if to prove a point, Foyt rolled out his backup Coyote on Sunday morning and let Guthrie take a few laps. Foyt understandably was going to run only one car – his own. After all, he was pursuing a fourth 500 victory. But it was still a sporting gesture as Guthrie was able to record a top lap of 180.796 mph in only a handful of laps. At the time, it would have been fast enough to qualify but it wound up requiring an average of 181.114 to make the 1976 500 field. The world would have to wait another year to see if a woman could

qualify for the 500.

One driver who did muster the necessary speed in his car was Loquasto. After eight years of trying in some of the worst cars in history, the likable Pennsylvanian was finally in the show. Schuppan also qualified and became the first Australian to make the race since Jack Brabham in 1970.

Under threatening skies, country & western singer Marty Robbins led the 33 starters at the wheel of the pace car. Robbins was more than a celebrity pace car driver – he had raced in a number of Daytona 500s.

At the drop of the green flag, Rutherford took the lead followed in procession by Johncock, Sneva, Foyt, Carter, Unser and Dallenbach. After three laps, Foyt took over the lead and stayed there until his first stop. Andretti made the biggest improvement by the time everyone pitted on Lap 12. When the caution came out for McCluskey's accident, the 1969 winner was up to seventh. McCluskey had spun into the Turn 2 wall and it would be the only caution of the race.

Foyt's six-second stop nearly took him out of contention. A crew member attempted to adjust Foyt's rear wing with a special six-foot-long socket wrench. Foyt got away before the wrench could be disengaged. Fortunately, the wrench fell off. Had it remained on the car, Foyt would have been black-flagged.

In the meantime, Andretti's first stop would prove more costly. After experiencing a problem during a tire change, Andretti returned to the fray 44 seconds later. On this particular day, no one realized just how important each pit stop was going to be and the uncharacteristically slow stop would be a prime example.

The early stops by the leaders put Carter in front for the first time in his career, but on Lap 17, Dallenbach passed for the lead and stayed there for next two laps before losing the lead to Johncock, who held it until Lap 38. Sneva took over for a lap before making a pit stop. His stop lasted 36 seconds while repairs were made to his windscreen. Sneva's car and helmet had been hit by debris from the McCluskey incident.

Rutherford took over the lead from Sneva and remained in front until his pit stop on Lap 60. Despite his earlier problems, Foyt regained the lead for the next 19 laps. At one point, he held a 14-second margin over Rutherford, but the McLaren driver was closing.

Foyt's car was suffering from a handling problem and on Lap 80, Rutherford swept past in Turn 3 to take the lead. He would stay for the next 22 laps. And then it rained before the leaders could complete Lap 103. With the race slightly past the halfway point, it could be declared an official race.

Of course, everyone in the stands was hoping to see the full 500 miles. Everyone in the pits shared that sentiment – except, of course, the Team McLaren crew and driver Johnny Rutherford!

From the time Tony Hulman purchased the Indianapolis Motor Speedway and held the first post-war Indianapolis 500 in 1946 through 1966, only one race had been shortened due to rain. Hulman's luck with the weather in the ensuing years was not so hot. Rain made the 1967 race a two-day affair and delayed the start of the 1970 race. The 1973 race required three days before rain halted the race for good. And the 1975 race had been shortened by 26 laps.

With the red flag out, there was hope the track could be dried in time to resume to race. Foyt, in second place despite the handling problems, used the downtime to check his car. It was determined that the front sway bar had broken. Because the rules allowed repairs during a red flag period, Foyt was able to avoid what would have been a lengthy pit stop.

However, the broken sway bar became a moot point. The track had been dried and was in the final stages of being checked. With drivers in their cars and the engines being warmed up, the rains returned and the race was called very shortly thereafter. History would be made on two fronts. Rutherford would be the first man to win the Indianapolis 500 and then walk into Victory Lane. And the 1976 race would be the shortest in the Speedway's 66-year history.

"I'm proud and I'm happy to win – but I would have liked to raced for it," said Rutherford, who would collect $256,121

in cash and prizes.

Foyt finished second and recorded his seventh top-three finish since 1961. Johncock and Dallenbach, who might have provided Rutherford with his strongest challenge had the race gone the distance, were third and fourth, respectively. Carter scored his third straight top-10 at Indy by placing fifth. Sneva was sixth and Unser gave the Cosworth engine a successful debut by placing seventh. Andretti wound up eighth, but one wonders where he might have finished had he qualified on the first weekend and/or not have experienced the lengthy first pit stop.

But "what if" pretty much sums up the 1976 Indianapolis 500.

Top: Just minutes before this fairly typical Victory Circle scene was photographed, Johnny and Betty Rutherford were standing here with no car. When the race was called after yet another rain shower, they made their way here on foot, arriving two or three minutes before the crew showed up with the car.

Above: Lone Star JR, from Fort Worth, Texas, now has a first, a second, and another first in three consecutive starts.
Photographs: IMS

Top right: History is made as Tom Sneva becomes the first to turn an official lap in excess of 200 miles per hour. Longtime sponsor Phil Hedback, who poured 150 silver dollars into the helmet of Parnelli Jones after Parnelli broke the "150" barrier in 1962, returns with 200 silver dollars for Sneva.

Bottom: Highly touted "rookie," drag racer Danny Ongais, waits between practice runs.
Photograph: IMS

1977: Making history on many fronts

Following the 1976 race, the entire track was repaved in asphalt for the first time. Over the years, only portions of the track had been repaved. The Speedway also allowed the asphalt to cure and prohibited testing until the spring when the starting line area was gouged out and replaced with the yard of bricks.

The new surface resulted in faster speeds and Gordon Johncock turned in the first unofficial 200-mph lap during April tire tests.

There was also a tinge of sadness in the air with the passing of two men closely tied to the race. Longtime Safety Director Joe Quinn passed away during the winter and Sid Collins, known to millions of radio listeners as "the Voice of the 500," died by his own hand May 2 after being diagnosed with Lou Gehrig's disease.

There were new cars with one manufacturer going back for a design idea not seen at the Speedway in nearly a decade. More drivers would be using the Cosworth engine, but there would be four other types of engines in qualified cars. Contrast that to 1974 when 28 starters used Offenhausers and the other five used the Foyt V-8.

On the driver front, A.J. Foyt would be going for an unprecedented fourth victory at Indy while Johnny Rutherford and the brothers Unser would be seeking a third win in the 500. Janet Guthrie, who might have made the 1976 field had she remained in Foyt's backup car, returned with Rolla Vollstedt and teammate and mentor Dick Simon. Guthrie would drive the 1976 Lightning-Offenhauser run the previous year by Roger McCluskey.

In addition to a bid at history-making by Guthrie, for the first time in history of the track, a father and son would both attempt to qualify for the 500. Jim McElreath, an 11-time starter, was entered in the Fred Carrillo's Eagle-AMC. He entered his son, James McElreath, in his own Eagle-Offenhauser.

There was another "first" in the entry. Belgium's Teddy Pilette became the first third-generation driver to run at Indianapolis. His grandfather, Theodore

Pilette, had finished fifth in the 1913 race.

Mario Andretti took time out of his full-time F1 schedule to run at Indianapolis and was joined by fellow F1 driver Clay Regazzoni. Regazzoni came from the Italian-speaking canton of Lugano in Switzerland and was entered by Teddy Yip as a teammate to safety equipment manufacturer Bill Simpson.

For 1977, there was only one new Eagle and that was the one entered by All American Racers for Pancho Carter. The latest Eagle featured a full nose section, much like those seen on the Coyote, Wildcat and Kingfish chassis. Aerodynamic fairings were placed in front of the rear wheels to channel air. And the car featured the most significant offset suspension seen on a new Indy-car design since the Lotus 38 of 1965 and '66.

The Eagles built between 1972 and '74 were still competitive but the ranks were considerably slimmer than in previous years. In fact, when qualifying ended for the 1977 race, there would only be seven Eagles in the starting field – the fewest since 1971.

One chassis making inroads on the Eagle's domain at Indianapolis was the Lightning. Designed a year earlier by Roman Slobodynskj for Lindsey Hopkins, the Lightning became a sought-after machine after McCluskey tested it at speeds in the high 190s during winter tire testing.

In addition to McCluskey's car, Hopkins entered a new Lightning for Lloyd Ruby. Also entering new Lightnings were Bob Fletcher for Bobby Unser, Alex Morales for Bobby Olivero, Jerry O'Connell for Mike Mosley and Rolla Vollstedt for Guthrie.

After running Eagles for a number of years, A.J. Watson unveiled his first rear-engined creation since 1968. Entered for Tom Bigelow, the car bore strong resemblance to the Lightning.

With the new Cosworth DFX available, McLaren brought out its first new car since 1971 – the M24. Team McLaren entered one car for Rutherford with Team Penske entering cars for Andretti and Tom Sneva. The Theodore team had 1975 chassis for Regazzoni and Simpson and Canadian rookie Cliff Hucul also had a 1975 McLaren at his disposal (the winning car from 1976). Al Loquasto was back with his 1971-pole winning McLaren and rookie Jerry Sneva was en-

OFFICIAL 1977 PROGRAM $3

INDIANAPOLIS 500

61st 500 MILE RACE: MAY 29, 1977

COMPLETE ENTRIES
CARS & DRIVERS

FIRST WOMAN IN THE "500"?

THE 200 MPH LAP
THE SUPER SIX OF THE "500"

tered in the 1971 McLaren driven by Denis Hulme. The latter cars all used Offenhauser power.

The other Cosworths could be found in the Parnelli VPJ-6 chassis entered for Al Unser and rookie Danny Ongais. Ongais made his name as a drag racer, but more recently had been a highly successful Formula 5000 driver.

George Bignotti updated the Wildcat-DGS, which now sported a small wing between the front wheels. STP returned as a sponsor for the Patrick team and there were entries for Gordon Johncock, Wally Dallenbach and Johnny Parsons.

George Snider was assigned to a 1975 Wildcat-DGS entered by oilman Bobby Hillin. Hillin also entered an Eagle-Offenhauser for Norman "Bubby" Jones, one of the top sprint-car racers in the country.

Foyt returned in the 1975 Coyote-Foyt he had driven to third- and second-place finishes in the previous two 500s. For 1977, he would be teamed with Bill Vukovich, who was entered in the Coyote Foyt had used to win the pole in 1974.

Grant King returned with his Coyote look-alike, the Dragon. For the second year, he was partnered with longtime owner J.C. Agajanian. Cars were entered for Sheldon Kinser and Gary Bettenhausen. Bettenhausen's car had an interesting sponsor – motorcycle daredevil Evel Knievel. The Knievel car carried his trademark red, white and blue with stars paint scheme and Bettenhausen's driving suit was copied after Knievel's flamboyant riding leathers.

There were two other interesting entries of note.

Back by popular demand was Jim Hurtubise in his front-engined Mallard. Never mind that Hurtubise had not qualified the car for the 500 since 1968, both were still fan favorites.

The other entry might have become a fan favorite had it ever made it onto the track. Tucked inside one of the IMS garages was one of the 1972 Antares chassis, which was now holding a Voelker V-12 engine. Bob Olmsted, who made a living restoring Lincoln Zephyrs, was the entrant and, naturally, the chief mechanic.

Overshadowed by some better-known rookies was a veteran of off-road racing named Rick Mears. Mears and fellow rookie Teddy Pilette were assigned to Eagle-Offenhausers owned by Art Sugai.

Early in practice, it was obvious that changes in the rule that governed boost made an impact. For 1977, boost was increased from 65 inches to 80 inches. By the third day of practice, the Cosworth guys were setting a pace much faster than the previous three years. Rutherford went 196.850 in the new McLaren and Al Unser was right behind at 196.378 in the Parnelli. The new Cosworth DFX was producing enough horsepower and aided by the slippery aerodyamic shapes of the two new chassis.

On the following day of practice, Rutherford and Andretti both topped the 198 mark. Unser was right behind with a 197.628, but Foyt served notice he would be in the mix by posting a lap at 196.979. There was more to come.

On Wednesday, May 11, Andretti clocked the first unofficial 200-mph lap in May practice, but the only laps that count at Indianapolis are those during qualifying or the race itself. Shortly after, Foyt joined the unofficial 200-mph club with a lap at 200.011. The following day, Rutherford set the month's fastest lap at 200.634.

The once unthinkable 200-mph lap was about to become reality. The question was who would be first and how many would follow? There were some skeptics.

"Records are made to be broken," said Andretti. "Wait till tomorrow – everyone will be running 200. Wait until Saturday – everyone will be running 192 because everyone will be legal!"

That might have been stretching it a bit, but none of the frontrunners seemed inclined to admit to what boost level they had been using in practice. For qualifying, the United States Auto Club would be in control of the turbocharger popoff valve that controls the boost level. In a sense, the boost control was a 1970s version of nitromethane, the fuel additive that resulted in increased horsepower that was commonly used in small doses in the 1950s and early '60s.

The opening day of qualifying did verify who was legal and who wasn't – but it also produced a major surprise.

In morning warmup, Foyt topped the charts with a lap at

196.937. He was first in line to qualify and wound up with an average of 193.456. Later on, he would be granted another attempt after it was determined his popoff valve had been faulty. Foyt's second run produced an average of 194.563.

Another pole position contender, Al Unser, made his run a few minutes later. Unser averaged 195.950 with a top lap of 196.980. Those laps would have gained him the pole for 1974, '75 and '76. Now the question was whether it would hold up.

In a short time, Tom Sneva provided the answer. Overlooked thanks to the fact he had not topped 200 in practice, Sneva got everyone's attention with his opening lap of 200.401 mph. It was a new track record and the first official lap at over 200-mph. Lap 2 was faster – 200.535. Sneva slowed down to 197 on the final two laps, but his four-lap average was also a new record of 198.884. Sneva's would be the only 200-mph laps in qualifying, but at last, the barrier had fallen. Sneva had an idea he would be quick in qualifying. Although he was involved in a minor accident on Friday, he believed the lap would have been in excess of 201.

Bobby Unser showed the potential of the new Lightning with an average of 197.618 for second-fastest speed and joined his brother and Sneva on the front row.

Foyt's speed ended up being fourth quickest. Johncock and Andretti joined Foyt in Row 2 with four-lap averages in the 193-mph range. Ongais, driving a car identical to Al Unser's, was the fastest rookie with the seventh-best speed of 193.040.

And, of course, there was Janet Guthrie, whose second try at Indy seemed to be more troublesome. On the fourth day of practice, she lost control in Turn 4 and hit the wall twice. It was a 500 "first," but not the kind she was seeking.

Guthrie wasn't the only rookie having a rocky time. Regazzoni brushed the Turn 4 wall the day after Guthrie's accident, but was able to drive his car into the pits. He reportedly asked for teammate Simpson's car and shortly afterward, Simpson

217

Above: A. J. Foyt runs in the warmup lane during practice.

Main photograph: One of the Speedway's most memorable moments comes when A. J. Foyt takes his lap of honor in the pace car and invites Tony Hulman to join him. This is something Tony has never done before, and sadly, it is the last time most people will see him. He will pass away on October 27.

Far right: More history is made as A. J. Foyt becomes the first person ever to win the "500" for a fourth time.

Below: A nostalgic look at Gasoline Alley. This was the view seen by millions as they waited for the drivers and cars to make their way back and forth between the pits and the garage area.

Photographs: IMS

the third day and focused his efforts on getting son James in the field. One driver who had failed to find speed earlier was Salt Walther, survivor of the horrendous opening-lap accident in 1973.

Walther was hoping to get one more chance to qualify before 6 p.m. The only car ahead of him as the deadline drew near was McElreath. After two laps, McElreath's 182-mph average was obviously too slow to make the field. If the elder McElreath could abort the run, there would still be time for Walther to make his attempt.

To everyone's surprise, McElreath allowed his son to complete the run as the deadline expired. A "Salt didn't make the 500" party began and McElreath explained why he kept his son on the track.

The 1962 Indy 500 "Rookie of the Year" drove for Walther's father at Pocono in 1971 and was still owed money six years later. The quiet Texan decided it would be an appropriate way to collect on the debt.

For 1977, the starting field for the Indianapolis 500 was going to have its first driver to post a 200-mph qualifying lap, three sets of siblings, five former 500 winners, two Canadians, an Italian-Swiss and the first woman to make the race. Would the race itself provide something more?

The answer would be yes – in many ways.

Tony Hulman had a surprise when it came time to issue his starting command. Still keeping with tradition, Hulman said: "*In company with the first woman ever to qualify at Indianapolis, gentlemen, start your engines.*" No one was disappointed.

When the green flag was dropped, Al Unser jumped into the lead. His opening lap was a new record of 185.197 mph and he stayed in front for the first 17 laps. It marked the first laps led by a Cosworth DFX engine, which powered five of the starters.

On Lap 12, one member of the Cosworth delegation was already out. After finishing first-second-first in the previous three years, Johnny Rutherford retired with gearbox trouble and placed last. He would later quip during the following night's victory banquet: "It's chicken one year, feathers the next."

Three laps later, Guthrie made a lengthy stop. It was unscheduled and Guthrie would eventually rejoin the race but would ultimately be sidelined with engine problems.

In the meantime, Johncock took the lead and surrendered it to Foyt four laps later when he made his first pit stop. From the back of the pack, Regazzoni was on the move. Starting 29th, he was up to 13th before being sidelined with a leaking fuel cell on Lap 29.

On Lap 34, Lloyd Ruby slammed the Turn 2 wall in a big way. The car was heavily damaged and Ruby was dazed from the impact. It would be the last Indy 500 for the popular Texan known for his hard luck at the Speedway.

The race, for the most part, would become a three-way battle between Foyt, Johncock and Sneva. Those three drivers would be the only ones to lead from Lap 71 to the finish, although Foyt nearly lost it when he ran out of fuel on Lap 92.

Johncock had the lengthiest stay at the helm, leading from Lap 97-179. Foyt took over for four laps when Johncock pitted and then Foyt made his last stop of the day on Lap 182 and relinquished the lead.

The 1973 Indy 500 winner led by nearly the length of a straightaway and as he would later say, "I thought we had it in

---

announced his retirement as a driver.

On the second day of qualifying, Regazzoni blew the engine on the McLaren-Offenhauser. Fortunately, the car he had wrecked earlier in the week had been repaired. He then attempted to qualify it – in spectacular fashion. Regazzoni's first lap was 191 and the second was almost 190. On Lap 3, he lost control exiting Turn 3 and slid into the infield. The car backed into an earth bank, got airborne and began gyrating after the rear wing became entangled in the fence. The Italian-Swiss was unhurt, but the car was totaled. A few days later, Simpson would have the tub crushed into a cube.

When qualifying resumed the following weekend, Regazzoni would make the 500 field. But it was another rookie who stole the headlines. After struggling to find speed, Guthrie found it on the final day. She put together a consistent, four-lap run with an average speed of 188.403 mph to become the first woman in history to qualify for the Indianapolis 500.

The history even came with some controversy. When it was suggested Tony Hulman's famed "*Gentlemen, start your engines*" command was actually directed to the mechanic operating the starter motor and could therefore be retained, Kay Bignotti volunteered to start Guthrie's car on Race Day thereby complicating the situation. It appeared that one Speedway tradition might have to be changed to accommodate Guthrie.

Qualifying closed with another controversy of sorts. Jim McElreath had safely qualified Fred Carrillo's Eagle-AMC on the bag." The "bag" burst on Lap 184 in the form of blue smoke out of the DGS exhaust. Johncock's engine expired and he pulled down to the grass on the inside of Turn 1.

He saluted Foyt as the Texan sailed by into the lead and promptly jumped into the infield creek to cool off.

Foyt now had the race in the bag and 15 laps later, he became the first four-time winner of the Indianapolis 500. Tom Sneva came home second and Al Unser wound up third, one lap down. Dallenbach and Parsons gave the STP Patrick team fourth and fifth, respectively. Rounding out the top 10 were Tom Bigelow, Lee Kunzman, McCluskey, Steve Krisiloff and Jerry Sneva, who would be honored as the top rookie.

Louie Meyer, Wilbur Shaw and Mauri Rose all had a chance to win No. 4, but only Foyt was able to pull it off. Since winning his third in 1967, winning a fourth had been his obsession. Now he was in Victory Lane for a fourth time talking about winning a fifth 500!

It was a very emotional moment and Foyt made a most sporting gesture of inviting Hulman to accompany him on his

lap of honor around the track in the pace car. The gesture would be even more noteworthy in that it would be Hulman's last Indianapolis 500. The grand elder statesman of auto racing passed away on October 27.

Hulman's passing marked the end of an incredible era. In 32 years, the Indianapolis Motor Speedway and the 500-mile race had undergone a number of changes. The post-war 500 revived a tradition and by 1977, it had developed a stature unparalleled in any sport or facility.

One of the men responsible for the continual process of upgrading the Speedway was Clarence Cagle, superintendent of the track since 1948. One of the most respected men in the sport, he was often called upon to provide consultation to management of other tracks. Over the years, he had become an expert in such areas as paving and general racetrack construction. In July, Cagle retired from his distinguished career.

Changes were destined for the Speedway and the sport itself. It was as if a new era was about to emerge. New team owners were coming onto the scene and the success of the Cosworth revived interest in the 500 from overseas. In Formula One, Colin Chapman's Lotus team had successfully developed a concept known as ground effects. It would only be a matter of time before the concept found its way to Indy-car racing.

One had to wonder what barriers would fall in the new era.

A.J. FOYT

The winningest driver in the history of Indy-car racing with 67 victories and the first man to win four times at the Indianapolis Motor Speedway, Foyt is part of a 1960s triumverate that includes rivals Parnelli Jones and Mario Andretti. Like his two legendary cohorts, Foyt is one of those rare individuals in sport where the mere mention of his first name (or in this case his initials) makes one instantly think of auto racing. And with good reason. Between 1958 and 1992, Anthony Joseph Foyt started an incredible 35 consecutive Indianapolis 500s. In addition to the aforementioned victories, there were two runner-up finishes, three thirds and eight other top-10 placings. He started on the pole position four times and was on the front row another five times. He led 555 laps and leads the categories for most races led (13) and most competitive laps/miles in a career with 4,904 laps/12,272.5 miles.

Those are just the numbers, but A.J. Foyt has been, is and always will be more than a collection of auto racing statistics. Outspoken, Foyt seldom held back regardless of whether he was speaking to an official, a member of the media or some unfortunate track announcer who made the mistake of asking how it was out there. He could also be something of an intimidator and his reputation for holding his own in a fight was legendary – except for the fact that no one could ever seem to remember seeing him in a fight!

Foyt always maintained that Indianapolis made him and there may be a certain element of truth to that claim. However, before Foyt recorded his first of four Indy wins, he made history as the youngest driver to capture the national title for Indy cars (25), having won four of the last six races of 1960 in the process. By 1979, Foyt had chalked up a seventh national Indy-car title – another record.

Those titles accompany national titles in USAC's dirt and stock car divisions. Foyt also excelled in road racing, scoring wins at Sebring and Daytona that were overshadowed by a surprise victory with Dan Gurney in the 1967 24 Hours of Le Mans. It was his only visit to the famed French circuit.

In 1993, Foyt retired as an Indy-car driver – appropriately at Indianapolis where he ran a tearful final ceremonial lap. As he told a shocked Pole Day crowd, "This isn't the Ol' A.J. that you're used to seeing." And with that, he turned over his car to a younger driver. But his departure from the cockpit was hardly a farewell from the sport. Since that time, he concentrated on running his racing team. In 1999, Sweden's Kenny Brack gave him his first Indy 500 victory as an owner.

In every sense of the word, A.J. Foyt is an Indy 500 legend, a 500 icon and any other superlative description one can conjure up.

CHAPTER 13
TRULY FLAT OUT FOR THE FIRST TIME

1978: A Triple Crown Year for Al Unser

I N what had become an illustrious racing career, Al Unser decided to take what many might have considered a gamble. Unser had driven for the Vel's Parnelli Jones Racing team since 1969 and it was during that stint that he had his greatest success. From the middle of the 1969 season to the middle of the 1971 season, Unser won 20 out of 38 races (including back-to-back Indy 500s in 1970 and '71) and the 1970 USAC National Championship. The team's expansion to three cars for 1972 and its status as "Super Team" failed to live up to expectations and it wasn't until 1976 that Unser became a consistent frontrunner again.

Unser's return to the front was due to the Parnelli VPJ-6, based on the team's Formula One car and powered by the Cosworth DFX V-8 engine. Unser gave the Cosworth engine its first victories by winning at Pocono, Milwaukee and Phoenix in 1976 and capturing his first Ontario 500 in 1977. After the mid-'70s slump, Vel's Parnelli Jones Racing and Unser were clearly on the upswing. For 1978, Unser would be wearing No. 2 – it signified his best finish in the national championship since 1970 when he captured his first title.

However, it would be with a different team. In the off-season, Unser decided to join Jim Hall's new team that would campaign the first new Indy-car design from Lola since 1972. Hall, whose innovations rocked the world of sports-car racing in the 1960s, was planning an innovative Chaparral Indy car for the future. Interestingly, this was his second effort for Indianapolis.

"We tested here in 1965," said Hall, who took his first laps at Indianapolis when his Chaparral sports car ran during an autumn Firestone tire test. "I was interested in racing here and we did build an Indianapolis car for the 1967 race. We didn't have a proper USAC engine (which at the time was a Ford or an Offenhauser), so we planned to run a stock block-powered car with a wing. We knew if we could sneak up on the other guys, we could win. Then USAC came out with a 'no wing' rule."

Hall later embarked on a partnership with Lola distributor Carl Haas and campaigned a factory-backed Lola in Formula 5000. The Hall-Haas team dominated both Formula 5000 and the revived Can-Am series that featured F5000 cars with fenders.

For 1978, they would make an all-out assault on Indy-car racing. Unser would drive the new Lola-Cosworth; Hywel Absalom would run the team; and First National City Bank would provide the sponsorship. On paper, the team looked like a winner right out of the box.

Of course, there were several contenders who believed they had the right stuff to prevail at the Speedway.

Roger Penske unveiled his new PC-6 chassis for reigning national champion Tom Sneva, Mario Andretti and promising rookie Rick Mears. Mears had shown promise the previous season in some tired equipment and attracted the attention of Penske. While both participated in Wally Dallenbach's "Colorado 500" motorcycle ride, Penske offered Mears a ride with his team. It was the beginning of a great partnership.

The new Penske PC-6 was actually the second Penske Indy car. The first one – the PC-5 – was a McLaren copy that Sneva raced toward the end of the 1977 season. The new car, designed by Geoff Ferris, outwardly resembled the team's F1 car. The PC-5 wound up in the hands of Russ Polak's team for driver Larry Dickson.

Also unveiling a new car was Dan Gurney. The All American Racers design team retired their offset Eagle from 1977 and replaced it with a car that followed the lines of the Parnellis, Penskes and Lightnings. They also had a driver change with Bobby Unser rejoining the team after a two-year hiatus.

That was the only new Eagle, but a number of drivers were entered in Eagles built between 1972 and 1974.

Below: An entry by sports car legend Jim Hall, rumored for over a dozen years, finally becomes a reality. Al Unser prepares to take a run.
Photograph: IMS

Lindsey Hopkins' Lightning chassis was now in its third year of competition and like the Eagle, a number of competitors pinned their hopes on it. The venerable Offenhauser powered most of the Lightnings, but the Fletcher Racing entry for Pancho Carter had a Cosworth DFX engine.

Carter arrived at the Speedway something of a question mark. The previous December, he suffered serious leg injuries following a test accident at Phoenix. Still recovering, Carter would be driving an Indy car for the first time when 500 practice began.

Patrick Racing returned with its two-year-old Wildcat-DGS cars for Gordon Johncock and Steve Krisiloff and the new Sherman Armstrong team also entered one for Tom Bigelow. Bignotti's new Wildcat-DGS that was tested but not raced at Indianapolis in 1977 was now in the hands of Janet Guthrie, who had her own team and sponsorship from Texaco.

A.J. Foyt, Indy's first four-time winner, sought an unprecedented fifth 500 with Coyote-Foyts entered for himself and George Snider.

Team McLaren, hoping to rebound from last year's early exit, entered the latest version of its Cosworth-powered M24 for Johnny Rutherford. Jerry O'Connell also entered a new McLaren-Cosworth for Wally Dallenbach and Dayton-Walther entered one for Salt Walther.

Danny Ongais, who won his first Indy-car event the previous season at Michigan, was back with Ted Field and the Interscope Parnelli-Cosworth. Vel Miletich and Parnelli Jones were also significantly involved in the project.

Ongais arrived at Indianapolis on a roll. After winning the pole in the season opener at Phoenix (where he finished 12th), Ongais won back-to-back 200-milers at Ontario and Texas and finished fourth at Trenton to lead the point standings.

However, traditionalists could at least cheer the fact that the other pre-500 races had been won by Johncock with the 4-cylinder, Offenhauser-based DGS engine. More than 40 years after its introduction at the Speedway, the "Offy" was still competitive.

The past was certainly on the minds of everyone connected to the sport and the Indianapolis 500.

Track owner Tony Hulman had passed away the previous October. His passing left a considerable void that would become more significant following the airplane crash that took the lives of eight USAC officials – Frankie DelRoy (chairman of the technical committee), Stan Worley (the registrar), Shim Malone, Ray Marquette, Judy Phillips, Don Peabody, Ross Teegarden and Dr. Bruce White. The group was returning from the spring race at Trenton when the airplane crashed near Rushville, Ind., during a storm. The accident occurred only days before the opening of the Speedway and several of the victims were prominent in the day-to-day operation of USAC's involvement in the 500.

Jack Beckley, a highly respected former chief mechanic, was already in place as assistant to DelRoy. He would now take DelRoy's place as technical committee chairman.

The ensuing shock was understandable. Despite rising speeds, Indy-car racing was safer – the last fatality had been Swede Savage in 1973. It brought to reminiscence 1954, when Wilbur Shaw, the president of IMS and three-time winner of the 500, was killed in an airplane crash.

Ramifications of the latest tragedy would be felt down the road. However, racing, as always, would go on.

And at the Indianapolis Motor Speedway, it would go on in excess of 200 miles an hour. One year after becoming the first man to officially break the 200-mph barrier, Tom Sneva returned to the Speedway as the national champion and one of many contenders for the pole position. In the first four races of 1978, Sneva won two poles and finished the last three races second, second and third.

Sneva's 200-mph laps were official, but it didn't take long for some competitors to announce they intended to join him in upcoming qualifying.

On Wednesday after the track opened, Ongais set an unofficial record at 201.974. Earlier, Andretti toured the track with a top lap of 201.838.

Ongais went a little slower but still topped the 201 mark on Thursday (201.567), but Andretti became the frontrunner for the pole on Friday with a lap at 203.482. Joining them in the 200-mph club were Rutherford at 201.839, Mears at 201.703 and Foyt at 200.356. Foyt was the only driver among the leaders on the speed chart who wasn't using a Cosworth. Powering his Coyote was the Foyt V-8, a turbocharged version of the Ford DOHC that first appeared at Indianapolis in 1964.

Qualifying would have to wait another week as rains washed out the proceedings. Andretti was the driver most seriously affected by the weather. In what would turn out to be his World Championship year in Formula One, Andretti was committed to run in the Belgian Grand Prix the following weekend. (Andretti would win that race from the pole to regain the lead in the point standings and would never relinquish it en route to the title.)

A number of scenarios were considered, including flying Andretti back in between qualifying and the race at Belgium to qualify at Indy. Ultimately, former Penske driver Mike Hiss got the call and by Thursday he was on the track. On Friday, Ongais led the way with a 203.2 lap, but Foyt was close behind at 202.876.

Ongais also provided some excitement during a Tuesday practice session. While running his backup car, Ongais spun in Turn 3 and hit the wall. Ongais was shaken and bruised and the incident would be the first of many at the Speedway for the "Flyin' Hawaiian." The accident also affected Lloyd Ruby, who had been scheduled to drive the car.

As had been the case the previous year, Sneva saved his best for last. After running his first 200-mph lap in Saturday morning practice, he uncorked a 203.6.

He followed that up with qualifying records of 203.620 for one lap and 202.156 for four laps. It was the first time a driver averaged over 200-mph for a four-lap qualifying run. Mears went out next and qualified at a very respectable 200.078. Ongais, who then averaged 200.122, topped Mears' run and for the first time, Indianapolis would have a 200-mph front row. Two new Penskes and Parnelli occupied Row 1 – all powered by Cosworth.

Row 2 had a bit more diversity with Rutherford on the inside in the McLaren-Cosworth, Al Unser in the middle in the Lola-Cosworth and Gordon Johncock on the outside in the Wildcat-DGS. The third row was also somewhat diverse with Dallenbach in a McLaren-Cosworth, Johnny Parsons in a Lightning-Offenhauser and Dickson in the old (but new) Penske PC-5-Cosworth.

Hiss qualified Andretti's car at an average of 194.647. That would have placed him in the middle of Row 3, but since

Above: Retired assistant high school principal, Tom Sneva, on the pole for the second year in a row.

Below: One can almost hear the sound of the "yellow shirts" blowing their whistles as the crews trudge endlessly back and forth between the pit area and the garage area.
Photographs: IMS

Andretti would be driving the car in the race, it was destined to start in last place, as per the rule requirements.

One other first-day qualifier of note was Guthrie. Armed with a better car, the first lady of Indianapolis qualified on the outside of Row 5 at 190.325.

Bobby Unser also qualified on Saturday, but because he was unable to make an attempt from his original spot in the qualifying line, he would start on the inside of Row 7. He was considered a second-day qualifier.

Foyt, who also was unable to complete an attempt, wound up pacing the third-day qualifiers on Sunday with an average of 200.122. His average was identical to that of Ongais, and had Foyt been a first-day qualifier with that speed, he would have started third.

Qualifying two rows behind Foyt was Jim McElreath. McElreath qualified the 1974 Eagle-Offenhauser that his son James had attempted to qualify a year earlier. Sadly, James was killed the previous autumn while running in a USAC sprint- car event at Winchester.

The most bizarre story of the month centered on Jim Hurtubise, who once again entered his front-engined Mallard. "Herk" had not qualified at Indy since 1974 and that had been in the McLaren-Offenhauser that Mark Donohue drove to victory two years earlier. The effort was definitely in the Don Quixote category as Hurtubise's last Indy 500 start in the Mallard had been 1968.

Ten years after the fact, Hurtubise didn't have a prayer of making the show and was too slow to be allowed in the qualifying line on the final day. USAC had issued a bulletin during the month stating that if a car failed to practice at a minimum speed of 180, it would not be allowed to make a qualifying attempt. He wasn't being singled out as the cars of Lee Kunzman and Eldon Rasmussen were also denied the opportunity for the same reason. Hurtubise maintained that since it was not on the entry form, the bulletin was null and void.

After an argument with Chief Steward Tom Binford, Hurtubise jumped into the car of Bob Harkey (at the head of the qualifying line) and shouted: "If I can't qualify, no one can."

At this point in time, the track was about to be opened after rain had shut down the proceedings. The crowd began to cheer and encourage Hurtubise as he continued his protest. Hurtubise eventually got out of Harkey's car and Harkey got in and left the pit to begin his run. Hurtubise then jumped over the wall and ran down the main straightaway to disrupt the attempt. With a group of pit guards in pursuit, fellow driver John Martin finally tackled Hurtubise. Sadly, Hurtubise, always a favorite with Speedway crowds, was now being booed and jeered for disrupting qualifying. He was escorted from the premises by Indiana State Police and banned from the track for the remainder of the month.

With the hoopla surrounding Sneva's record run, Ongais' continued speed and the sensational rookie run by Rick Mears, it was easy to overlook Al Unser and the new Jim Hall team.

As Roger Penske pointed out: "He (Hall) has one bullet in his gun. I have three in mine." Two of those three were on the front row and everyone knew it would only be a matter of time before Andretti charged to the front.

There was another driver guaranteed to charge, although he was already on the front row. That, of course, was Ongais.

For the first time since 1955, someone other than Tony Hulman voiced the command: "Gentlemen, start your engines." In his place was his widow, Mary Fendrich Hulman, who in recognition to Guthrie, paraphrased it as: "Lady and gentlemen, start your engines."

When the green flag dropped, Ongais vaulted from second to first place – a position he would often occupy during the 1978 season – with Sneva and the others in pursuit. Sneva took the lead on Lap 12, but the fastest man on the track at the time appeared to be Andretti.

By Lap 10, Andretti was already up to 15th and 10 laps later, he was 11th. Unfortunately, his first pit stop would require eight minutes to replace an electrical coil. Andretti would run the rest of the day, but he was hopelessly out of contention after making such a fine run to the front.

By mid-race, it had become a three-way battle between

Ongais, Sneva and Al Unser. Unser moved into the lead on Lap 111 and on Lap 145, Ongais retired with a blown engine. The large plume of smoke trailing from the car provided a spectacular exit for Ongais, who would exit future races in even more spectacular fashion.

Unser continued to pace the field until his final stop on Lap 179, when he surrendered the lead to Sneva. Sneva led Lap 180 and made his final stop. Unser's final stop was not without drama. Approaching his pit box, Unser's front wing struck one of the tires placed on the pavement should a tire change be required. The contact "dinged" the front wing, but Unser returned to the track with a 30-second margin over Sneva as he regained the lead.

He also began to slow his pace and Sneva cut into the once-healthy lead. Unser later explained that the wing had nothing to do with the times on his final laps. He was simply trying to preserve the victory and was able to drive home free – scoring his third victory at Indianapolis.

Sneva wound up second only 8.09 seconds in arrears and Johncock was third. Following the lead trio were Krisiloff, Dallen-bach, Bobby Unser, Foyt, Snider, Guthrie and Parsons. Andretti ended up 12th. Mears (who retired on Lap 103 with engine trouble) and Larry Rice, who finished 11th, were named "Co-Rookie of the Year." Guthrie's finish was the highest-ever for a woman and would remain so for nearly 30 years.

At the 500 Victory Banquet, Unser celebrated his 39th birthday by collecting $290,364 in cash and prizes. Among the prizes was the 1978 Corvette that had been used as the pace car. It was the first time the Corvette had ever paced an Indy 500, but it would not be the last time.

Unser would also make history with his performance the rest of the season. He would only win two more races en route to second in the championship behind Sneva for the second straight year. However, those two races happened to be the Pocono 500 and the Ontario 500. Unser was the first and thus far only man to ever win the mythical "Triple Crown" of Indy-car racing.

And while Unser was making his mark, his owner was busy behind the scenes as well. He had a new car in the works and typically Hall, it would be revolutionary.

Main photograph: An all-200-mph front row: Rick Mears (a "rookie"), Danny Ongais, and pole sitter Tom Sneva.

Inset top left: Wally Dallenbach switches teams but finishes in the top five for the third year in a row.

Inset top right: Steve Krisiloff, Gordon Johncock's teammate, scores his highest finish ever with a fourth.

Photographs: IMS

1979: Flying On The Ground – Literally

As far as off-seasons go, the time between the 1978 season finale at Phoenix and the 1979 season opener at Phoenix was easily one of the most eventful in history.

With the death of Tony Hulman in 1977 and the void left following the deaths of eight USAC officials who perished in an airplane crash in April of 1978, there was some serious unrest involving a number of team owners. With budgets continually escalating to cover the cost of 200-mph racing cars and their operation, owners were seeking higher purses and facilities that would better accommodate the needs of their corporate partners.

As owner U.E. "Pat" Patrick pointed out, "We were showing up with multimillion-dollar operations racing for $30,000 purses."

OFFICIAL 1979 PROGRAM $3

INDIANAPOLIS 500
COMPLETE ENTRIES: CARS & DRIVERS

Owners like Patrick, Roger Penske and Dan Gurney – to name a few – were also hoping to see Indy-car racing get more exposure. Thanks to its stature in the motorsports world, Indianapolis had a place all its own. But the series was also racing in cities like Trenton, Milwaukee and Phoenix – in some cases three times a year. The owners were hoping for bigger markets.

They also sought access to accounting records of the United States Auto Club. According to the by-laws of the organization, owners were within their rights to expect such access. However, USAC President Dick King refused the request and that seemed to put the unhappy owners over the top.

During the annual Christmas party hosted by Penske in Detroit, several of the owners present decided to have a business meeting and wound up forming Championship Auto Racing Teams. Although there was hope that reconciliation could be reached, the CART group announced its schedule (with the month of May open so its team could compete at Indianapolis). In order for its members to be able to participate at Indianapolis, the Sports Car Club of America would sanction CART races.

On March 11, CART held its inaugural event at Phoenix with Gordon Johncock winning in Patrick's Penske-Cosworth. Two weeks later, USAC opened its season at Ontario with A.J. Foyt winning in a Parnelli-Cosworth. Most of the top teams in Indy-car racing opted to go with CART. Foyt had been among those planning to make the switch, but at the last moment he went back to USAC, where he would dominate against diminished competition.

Both series held races in April – CART at Atlanta and USAC at Texas – and that set the stage for one of the more interesting months of May at Indy. By the time June arrived, most members of the racing community would be highly knowledgeable about the legal profession.

The first indication it would be an atypical May was the court injunction against the "CART 6." In conjunction with the Speedway, USAC decided to reject the entries of six teams – Penske Racing, Jim Hall Racing, Team McLaren, Patrick Racing, Fletcher Racing and Interscope Racing. That represented 19 cars and drivers Al and Bobby Unser, Johnny Rutherford, Danny Ongais, Johncock, Steve Krisiloff and Wally Dallenbach.

CART responded by filing an injunction to allow their member teams and drivers to practice and race. Interestingly, CART contended that the Indianapolis Motor Speedway had already accepted its entries; USAC was simply sanctioning the race and therefore could not prohibit the participation of those entries.

On opening day of practice, Federal Judge James E.

Noland issued a temporary injunction to allow the CART entries to compete. He also enjoined each party to do nothing that would affect the other's participation and made it clear he would take a very close look at the events of the month to see if his orders were being carried out.

It was unfortunate that legal matters seemed to overshadow the racing activity. There were some interesting new cars in the 1979 entry.

Chief among them was the car they dubbed the "Yellow Submarine." After running a conventional Lola-Cosworth during his initial season of Indy-car competition, Jim Hall unveiled the latest in his line of innovative Chaparrals. Hall's Cosworth-powered car was the Chaparral 2K and the "Yellow Submarine" nickname came largely due to the yellow paint scheme of sponsor Pennzoil.

This was the first true ground effects car to run at Indianapolis. Designed by John Barnard in collaboration with Hall and built in England by Bob Sparshott's BS Fabrications, the new Chaparral featured a pair of tunnels that ran underneath, down each side of the tub. The car's nose wings and rear wing would push the car down to the ground. The tunnels, or underwings, were shaped to create a suction effect that would allow the car to corner at faster speeds than conventional designs. The fuel tank was located behind the cockpit and directly in front of the engine. Because of the location of the fuel tank, the driver was now seated further forward than ever before. In short, it was a radical design.

The conventional designs – or flat-bottomed cars – tried to achieve some degree of ground effects by the addition of skirts around the base of the tub. This had actually been tried on a number of cars in 1978, but the shape of the underwing was what gave the ground effects its advantage.

Penske also experimented with ground effects and the result was the PC-7, a design considered to be more semi-ground effects. Designed by Geoff Ferris, the new Penske followed the lines of its predecessor – the PC-6 – but sported sidepods that contained the underwing. The new car was fast, but surprisingly not as fast at the PC-6.

Three PC-7s were built for the Penske team of Bobby Unser and Rick Mears. New PC-6s were also sold to Patrick Racing for Johncock and Dallenbach and Dayton-Walther for Salt Walther. PC-6s from 1978 were sold to Bobby Hillin for Tom Bagley, and to Jim McElreath, who would pilot the car driven the previous year by Mario Andretti. Tony Bettenhausen (son of the 1950s champion), who had married McElreath's daughter, Shirley, was listed as McElreath's chief mechanic. Larry Dickson returned in Russ Polak's Penske PC-5.

Patrick Racing would ultimately put Spike Gehlhausen in its latest Wildcat-Cosworth, while Armstrong Mould and Wysard Racing had older Wildcat-DGS chassis for Howdy Holmes and Vern Schuppan, respectively.

Dan Gurney entered his latest Eagle-Cosworth for Mike Mosley.

Team McLaren had a new car for Rutherford and one for Warner Hodgdon for Roger McCluskey. O'Connell Racing returned with their year-old McLaren for Tom Sneva. Interestingly, Penske had released Sneva at the end of 1978 after Sneva won the title and the pole at Indianapolis for the team the last two years.

The Hodgdon team also had a chassis called the Spirit. It was powered by AMC and entered for NASCAR ace Neil Bonnett, but ultimately was qualified by Jerry Sneva.

Lola, which reigned supreme a year earlier with Hall and Unser, returned with updated models for Janet Guthrie and the Armstrong Mould Team and Tom Bigelow.

Various Lightning chassis designed by Roman Slobodynskj were entered by a number of teams including Morales for

Main photograph: A car is merely a blur as it enters turn 1. Note the official observer sitting somewhat precariously in front of the Armco barrier.
Photograph: IMS

Inset below: In a partnership with Vel's
Parnelli Jones, A. J. Foyt drives a VPJ
Parnelli/Cosworth to second. The engine
fails on the very last lap, and he is barely
able to trickle over the line to salvage
the position.
Photograph: IMS

Pancho Carter, Fletcher Racing for Krisiloff, Hoffman Racing for George Snider, S&M Electric for Larry Rice, and Hopkins' own entries for Johnny Parsons and rookie Hurley Haywood. The Hopkins entries were notable in that Parsons' car had the Offenhauser engine in a laydown position. The placement of the 4-cylinder engine was successfully tried in the 1950s in an attempt to give the car a lower profile. It marked the first time someone had tried the technique in a rear-engine car. The new Drake V-8 powered Haywood's car, but it would suffer serious teething problems.

A.J. Watson returned with his Lightning-like Watson-Offenhausers for Bill Vukovich and Sheldon Kinser while Rolla Vollstedt entered his sleek Vollstedt-Offenhauser for Dick Simon.

The Vel's Parnelli Jones Racing team may have departed the scene, but the team's equipment lived on with entries for A.J. Foyt, Danny Ongais and the Conqueste Team for Lee Kunzman.

There were also some "blasts from the past." Driver/fabricator Eldon Rasmussen entered a heavily renovated Antares-Offenhauser for himself. Intercomp Racing entered John Mahler in a 1973 Eagle-Offenhauser modified by Bill Finley. Despite the incident on the main straightaway from a year ago, Jim Hurtubise was back with his front-engine Mallard. And, yes, he was still wearing an open-face helmet and goggles!

Missing from the entry was Mario Andretti, the reigning F1

world champion whose contractual commitments kept him away from the Speedway in 1979.

One rule change would affect the speeds in both practice and qualifying. After witnessing the first 200-mph front row in Indianapolis history the previous May, officials decided to cut the turbocharger boost level again. As speeds had neared the 200-mph mark in 1973, a number of changes had been implemented to slow down the cars. It took them four years to get back to that range in speed, and practice times in 1978 far exceeded the 200-mph barrier. With ground effects technology in its infancy, it was probably a wise move on the part of USAC rulesmakers to lower the boost to 50 inches.

The effectiveness of the lower boost was evident in the speeds on practice days that preceded qualifying. A.J. Foyt's lap of 194.890 on Thursday was the fastest speed during the first week of practice. Rain would prevent anyone from qualifying on Pole Day, but the track was dry long enough for Ongais to crash in Turn 4. The car was heavily damaged and Ongais was hospitalized with a concussion in what was becoming an annual event for the Hawaiian driver.

Qualifying was able to proceed the following day and Al Unser became the first to top the 190-mph mark as he qualified the Chaparral at an average of 192.503. Tom Sneva, bidding for a third straight pole, topped Unser's speed with a 192.998 average in the Sugaripe McLaren-Cosworth.

No one had ever won the pole at Indianapolis three straight and it wasn't going to happen in 1979, as Mears bumped Sneva with a 194.847 average in the Penske-Cosworth. Mears' pole position run came in a PC-6 chassis and it was going to be up to Bobby Unser to run the new semi-ground-effects PC-7. Prior to Mears' run, Unser qualified his Penske at 189.913, which would be good enough for the inside of Row 2.

Johncock and Foyt would fill out the second row as 18 cars made successful qualifying runs. One of those 18 was Guthrie, who qualified 14th fastest at 185.720. A year earlier, she opined that she could probably win the race if she had Al Unser's car, engine and mechanic. Team owner Sherman Armstrong gave her that opportunity by purchasing a new Lola-Cosworth and hiring Hywel Absalom away from Hall Racing.

Controversy would plague the second weekend of qualifying. Most notable was the exclusion of rookie Dick Ferguson, who had seemingly made the race in Wayne Woodward's Eagle-Offenhauser. Ferguson qualified at 184.644, but it was later determined that the turbo popoff valve had been altered to allow the rookie more than the maximum of 50 inches of boost.

Then there was the saga of Bill Alsup. The rookie road racer tried to qualify his McLaren-Offenhauser, but failed to go fast enough. On the final day of qualifying, Alsup got the opportunity of a lifetime when Roger Penske put him in one of the team's backup PC-7s. Alsup responded by safely qualifying at 187.744. That speed made him the fastest rookie for a time. Unfortunately, when it was learned that the engine in Alsup's car was the same one used by Bobby Unser on his qualifying run, Alsup's run was nullified. The Penske team changed engines, but time expired before Alsup could get another attempt.

Qualifying was over. Or was it? The year 1979 was clearly going to be the year of the lawsuit and sure enough, another suit was filed by a group of car owners who believed they did not get a fair chance to qualify. Once again, the controversy centered on a modification to the exhaust system that reportedly affected the turbo popoff valve and enabled more boost than allowed.

Judge Nolan, once again confronted with several angry members of the racing community, refused to issue an injunction to stop the race. USAC eventually decided to give 11 cars and drivers one more chance to qualify. Anyone who could run faster than Roger McCluskey's bump speed of 183.908 would be added to the 33-car field.

On the morning before the race, eight of the eligible 11 took advantage of the situation to practice and attempt to qualify. Only Bill Vukovich and George Snider went fast enough. For Sunday's race, there would 35 starters, the most since 1933 when 42 drivers took the green flag.

Right: From shoulder-length hair, a
mustache, and a floppy hat in 1977, to a
clean-cut kid on the Penske team, Rick
Mears will soon be recognized as one of
the very best ever, as well as one of
the finest human beings ever to don
a helmet.
Photographs: IMS

Pacing the 1979 Indianapolis 500 would be the Ford Mustang. Fifteen years earlier, the sensational new Mustang paced the 1964 500 field. The Speedway seemed to be a most appropriate place to mark a milestone in the car's history. Chosen to drive the pace car was Jackie Stewart, who had nearly won the 500 in 1966.

Stewart retired in 1973 after winning three F1 World Championships. It is interesting to note that of the 1979 starting field, nine drivers had raced with Stewart in the 1966 500. Two of those drivers would dominate the 1979 race.

Al Unser jumped into the lead at the start in the Chaparral. During practice and qualifying, there had been occasional comments that Unser was "sandbagging" in the radical new Chaparral. The comments were much like those made during the years when the STP turbine cars nearly won the 500s of 1967 and '68.

Unlike Parnelli Jones' charge from sixth to first on the opening lap, Unser simply outgunned Sneva and Mears to the first corner and proceeded to drive away.

On Lap 28, the caution came out for Cliff Hucul's stalled car. It would be a historic moment because for the first time in Indianapolis 500 history, the pace car came out and the field packed up behind it. After years of the "honor system" and pacer lights, it was determined that the pack-up rule was the best idea for a caution period.

The first half of the race belonged to Unser and the "Yellow Submarine." He led 85 of the first 100 laps and only surrendered first place when he made routine pit stops. Unser's car was in its first race and had not received much test time. In fact, most of the car's testing took place during practice for the 500.

New cars tend to break and the Chaparral began spewing smoke from the rear of the car. A transmission seal had melted and the gearbox was losing its lubricant. On Lap 105, Unser was out of the race. It easily could have been Indy 500 victory No. 4 had the car remained healthy.

Now it was brother Bobby's turn to lead the race. Out in front from Lap 97 to 181, the elder Unser seemed to have his third victory at Indianapolis in the bag. With 20 laps to go, Foyt passed Mears for second to make it a three-way battle and Unser suddenly began to slow. He had lost fourth gear and on Lap 182, Mears took the lead.

Prior to that time, Mears had only led six laps, but with his teammate's car handicapped, it was left to the sophomore driver to hold off Foyt. Now it was Foyt's turn to have a problem and he slowed as smoke appeared from underneath his car.

On Lap 191, the yellow flag came out for Tom Sneva's accident in Turn 4. Regardless of what Foyt's problem might have been, the caution period allowed Foyt to cut Mears' lead from 47 seconds to 17 seconds.

The green flag came out on Lap 196, and Foyt began to close on Mears. He was six seconds behind the leader, but Mears had the advantage of having 15 cars between him and Foyt. The real drama at the finish came courtesy of Mike Mosley.

Running third, Mosley pulled up behind Mears before the start-finish line as the white flag was unfurled. Both drivers appeared to have gotten the white flag, although Mosley had been listed as being one lap down and was unlapping himself as he passed Mears. As Mears came down for the checkered flag, Mosley received the white flag again.

In the meantime, Foyt was slowing – thanks to an engine malfunction. Foyt had signaled the people in his Turn 2 VIP suite that he was losing power and as he passed by on his final lap, the engine shut down on the backstretch. The crowd that had been cheering Mears' victory was now urging on Foyt, whose car was crawling, and Mosley, who was coming on strong. Foyt managed to coax his car across the line by only 2.5 seconds ahead of Mosley.

It was soon determined that Mosley was actually unlapping himself and he wound up third behind Foyt and Mears. Ongais finished fourth, Bobby Unser limped to fifth, Johncock was sixth and rookie Howdy Holmes came home seventh. Holmes won the top rookie award, but that was a given as he was the only rookie in the starting field.

For Mears, it was a remarkable feat when one considers he had failed to qualify here two years earlier. Now he was an Indy 500 winner for Roger Penske, whose only other win at Indianapolis had come in 1972 with Mark Donohue.

It was the start of a great relationship. It was also the start of a new era. The Chaparral and the Penske PC-7 had proven that ground effects technology was clearly the wave of the future.

1980: Two For Texas

Changes on the managerial front at the Indianapolis Motor Speedway have always tended to be rather few and far between throughout the track's history.

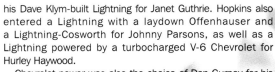

Such a change came about late in 1979 with the announcement of John Cooper being named president of the track. Since the death of Tony Hulman in 1977, Joe Cloutier had been serving as president, but continued to conduct business in Terre Haute. Cooper would be the first IMS president to effectively be on site on a full-time basis. Cooper's background included stints with USAC and NASCAR, as well as the Ontario Motor Speedway.

On the USAC-CART front, there was a temporary peace with the formation of the Championship Racing League (although the two sides would part after five races). Under the CRL banner, a 200-miler had already been staged at Ontario, California, with Johnny Rutherford coming home first.

Rutherford's victory was notable in that it underscored a driver lineup change. The Texan was now piloting Jim Hall's Chaparral.

When Al Unser left the Vel's Parnelli Jones Racing team at the end of the 1977 season, he had been with the operation for nine seasons. "I felt it was time to make a change," Unser explained later. "And since I won the 500 in 1978, I think I made the right decision."

With the radical new Chaparral, everyone expected Unser to win everything in sight in 1979. Unfortunately, the Chaparral 2K had a number of teething problems and Unser would not visit the winner's circle until the season finale at Phoenix.

So he made another decision. He switched teams again. Whether it was a good or bad decision depends on whom you ask. Unser to this day will insist he made the right move to leave Jim Hall's team because he felt Hall failed to give credit to certain people – like the designer of the car, John Barnard.

At the end of the 1979 season, Team McLaren pulled out of Indy-car racing and Unser's departure gave Rutherford a new lease on his racing life. In fact, Rutherford would embark on his best year as an Indy-car driver.

With a year of racing development under its belt, the Chaparral was ready to live up to everyone's expectations.

Penske returned with its first full ground effects design – the PC-9. Cars were entered for defending winner Rick Mears, Bobby Unser and Mario Andretti. There were a number of PC-7s with entries from Alex Morales for Pancho Carter, Mach I Racing for rookie Tim Richmond, Whittington Brothers Racing for Don Whittington and Fletcher Racing for Spike Gehlhausen. There were also PC-6s entered by Patrick Racing for Gordon Johncock, Jack Rhoades for Dennis Firestone, Steve and Richard Sanett for Dick Ferguson and Jim McElreath for himself.

A British company produced a ground effects design called the Phoenix for O'Connell Racing and Tom Sneva and Patrick Racing for rookie Gordon Smiley. The Patrick team also had it first ground effects Wildcat for Tom Bagley.

Al Unser joined Bobby Hillin's team and was entered in the Longhorn LR01, built in Indianapolis but based on the Williams F1 car. Naturally, the Cosworth-powered machine was a ground effects design, but it featured another futuristic option. The car's performance could be monitored, thanks to a computer located in the pits that would be hooked up to the car when stationary.

Armstrong Mould Inc. entered another ground effects design. Named the Orbiter II, the car was designed and built by March and entered for Howdy Holmes. AMI also had Lolas for Tom Bigelow, Greg Leffler and Jerry Sneva and a four-year-old Wildcat-DGS for Gary Bettenhausen.

Lindsey Hopkins also got into the ground effects act with

his Dave Klym-built Lightning for Janet Guthrie. Hopkins also entered a Lightning with a laydown Offenhauser and a Lightning-Cosworth for Johnny Parsons, as well as a Lightning powered by a turbocharged V-6 Chevrolet for Hurley Haywood.

Chevrolet power was also the choice of Dan Gurney for his new ground effects Eagle designed by John Ward and driven by Mike Mosley. Gurney's car had a unique approach with its ground effects system. Unlike the "conventional" ground effects designs that featured sidepods located just behind the front wheel and right in front of the rear wheel, the Eagle's ground effects system began right in front of the rear wheel and stretched beyond the rear axle line. The frontal area of the car was also pencil thin.

Arizona Racing Associates and the International Association of Machinists entered yet another ground effects design – the ARA-IAM-Chevrolet – for Phil Threshie.

Still campaigning the Parnelli chassis were Interscope Racing with Danny Ongais, A.J. Foyt Racing for Foyt and George Snider and the Whittington Brothers for Bill Whittington.

The Whittington Brothers were something of a mystery. In 1978, both brothers began racing professionally in sports cars. A year later, they teamed with Klaus Ludwig to win the prestigious 24 Hours of Le Mans. Don Whittington would

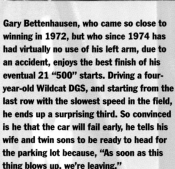

Gary Bettenhausen, who came so close to winning in 1972, but who since 1974 has had virtually no use of his left arm, due to an accident, enjoys the best finish of his eventual 21 "500" starts. Driving a four-year-old Wildcat DGS, and starting from the last row with the slowest speed in the field, he ends up a surprising third. So convinced is he that the car will fail early, he tells his wife and twin sons to be ready to head for the parking lot because, "As soon as this thing blows up, we're leaving."

Right: Innovative Jim Hall of Chaparral sports car fame finally takes on Indianapolis as a car owner, winning in two out of his first three starts (1978 with Al Unser, and 1980 with Johnny Rutherford).

Photographs: IMS

ultimately win the World Challenge for Endurance Drivers. In their third year of competition, they were tackling Indy-car racing and the 500.

And for the 14th straight year, Jim Hurtubise entered his trusty Mallard-Offenhauser, complete with a wedge-shaped nose and rear wing, but still very much a front-engined design.

Practice promised to be the domain of Rutherford and Chaparral. Even though there were a number of ground effects cars entered, Jim Hall's car was ahead of the game thanks to its design and a full year of on-track development.

Rutherford did not disappoint as he topped the charts during the first days of practice and as the opening weekend of qualifying approached, it appeared his top rivals would be the Penske team and A.J. Foyt. Few expected a brash rookie named Tim Richmond to be a contender, but he opened a lot of eyes on Friday when he recorded the month's fastest lap at 193.507.

But Richmond's challenge for the pole position ended during the pre-qualifying warmup session. Richmond spun coming out of Turn 1 and hit the wall, inflicting heavy damage on the Penske PC-7-Cosworth. The rookie was unhurt but would have to wait until the following weekend to qualify.

Despite the practice speeds, only two men would end up qualifying with averages in excess of 190 mph.

Rutherford won his third pole position since 1973 by averaging 192.256 mph. It was more than 1 mph faster than the second-fastest qualifier – Andretti – who would be making his first 500 start in two years with a 191.012 average. Bobby Unser filled out the front row with a 189.994 average.

Row 2 had some surprises. Spike Gehlhausen, who had never started better than 16th in his three previous 500s, posted the fourth-fastest average at 188.344. Jerry Sneva, whose brother Tom usually started in the front row, was fifth fastest at 187.852. Defending race winner Rick Mears, a front-row starter in his first two 500s, wound up sixth fastest at 187.490. Al Unser, who undoubtedly would have been on the pole with the Chaparral, qualified a respectable ninth fastest in the new Longhorn.

There were other good first-day stories.

Sprint-car ace Roger Rager qualified for his first 500 with a Wildcat chassis powered by an engine whose Chevrolet block was reputedly out of an old school bus. Rager maintained that many of the engine failures on the stock blocks were due to the use of too many new parts. So he sought a block with at least 30,000 miles as it would be "seated" or "broken in." Apparently, the idea had merit as Rager posted the 10th-best speed to qualify for his first Indianapolis 500.

Jim McElreath started 11th and in qualifying, became the oldest man (52) to ever make the Indianapolis 500 field. For

once, Tom Sneva was outqualified at Indianapolis by his brother Jerry. Sneva did post the 14th-fastest time in the O'Connell Racing Phoenix-Cosworth.

The week that followed would be tough on the Sneva family, however.

On Tuesday, another Sneva brother – Jan – crashed his Dayton-Walther Penske-Cosworth coming out of Turn 2. The car was heavily damaged, and Sneva was unhurt. But on his way to the infield hospital for a mandatory check, he reportedly told the ambulance driver to take him straight to the airport instead! Older brother Tom would rib younger brother Jan on TV that night.

On Wednesday, it was Tom's turn. As the Phoenix entered Turn 1, the right front tire blew and Sneva slammed into the wall. The driver was OK, but the car was heavily damaged.

When asked about what the team planned, Sneva replied: "I don't care what they do with that car. I don't want to have anything to do with it."

Sneva would ultimately jump into the team's McLaren-Cosworth originally assigned to Vern Schuppan, who failed to qualify it. The car, nicknamed "Old Hound," was the same car Sneva had qualified on the front row a year earlier. This time, he would have to start in last place.

The second weekend of qualifying allowed Richmond to show his stuff after his accident. The rookie driver posted an average of 188.344, which was fifth fastest of the starting field. Had he qualified at that average on the opening day of qualifying, he would have started in the middle of Row 2. As it was, he would be starting on the inside of Row 7. Starting alongside was an equally brash rookie – Smiley – who turned in a solid run of 186.848 in the Patrick Racing Phoenix-Cosworth.

AMI put three more cars in the field to join Jerry Sneva's entry qualified on the first day. Rookie Greg Leffler, whose father Paul was the chief mechanic for the AMI operation, and Tom Bigelow qualified their AMI Lola-Cosworths in Rows 8 and 11, respectively. Gary Bettenhausen put the team's old Wildcat-DGS in the race with the slowest average at 182.463. Howdy Holmes nearly put the new Orbiter in the field, but suffered a suspension failure in Turn 3 as he made a qualifying run.

One notable driver not making the field was Guthrie, who failed to find necessary speed in the new ground effects Lightning. Guthrie hinted that she might not be back.

With Sneva opting to run his old McLaren instead of the Phoenix he qualified, he would now occupy the last row with Bigelow and Bettenhausen.

Because of the importance of the 500, there are a number of social functions during the month that invariably honor the most successful drivers and teams. However, the Indianapolis

Above: Lining up for the start with yet another incredibly talented front row, Mario Andretti gets slightly ahead of pole sitter Johnny Rutherford and Bobby Unser.

Below: Tim Richmond, the charismatic Rookie of the Year, soon to be NASCAR-bound.

Bottom: John Cooper, an American in no way related to the F1 principal of the same name, rose from a 1950's crew member to IMS president between 1979 and 1982.

Photographs: IMS

Right: Yet another of the truly great moments at Indianapolis: Winner Rutherford stops on his "cool-off" lap to pick up an out-of-fuel Tim Richmond, whose ninth-place finish will help net him Rookie of the Year honors.

Bottom left: A final start for three legends at Indianapolis: Billy Vukovich, in his final "500," finishes 12th with the last chassis to be built by A. J. Watson and powered by the last Offenhauser engine to qualify.

Photographs: IMS

Press Club for many years hosted an annual event to pay tribute to those overlooked. The annual "Last Row Party" did just that – it honored the occupants of the last row of qualifiers.

The event is in reality a roast, with participants getting checks for 31 cents, 32 cents and 33 cents to commemorate their starting positions. In 1978, Mario Andretti was honored after Mike Hiss qualified his car while he raced in Europe. In 1979, John Mahler actually cashed his 32-cent check!

For 1980, the last row would certainly distinguish itself.

Johnnie Parsons, who won the rain-shortened Indianapolis 500 in 1950, found himself pacing the 1980 field at the wheel of the Pontiac Firebird. Earlier, Parsons had toured the Speedway during pre-race festivities behind the wheel of his 500-winning Kurtis-Offenhauser.

As expected, Rutherford jumped into the lead at the start and stayed there for the first 15 laps. Although his car was the second oldest in the field (Larry Cannon's car was the oldest), Bettenhausen was one man on the move. By Lap 3, he was up to 20th.

Bettenhausen wasn't the only one moving forward. Tom Sneva did not remain in last place for long. By Lap 20, he was up to fourth! He would remain in the lead pack for the rest of the race.

Rutherford pitted on Lap 16, with the caution out for the accident involving Dick Ferguson and Bill Whittington. Whittington slammed into the wall between Turns 1 and 2 and Ferguson hit the inside wall trying to avoid Whittington's car. Whittington suffered a broken leg in the accident.

The south end of the track appeared to be where most of the action would take place. Three laps after the green came out following the Whittington-Ferguson accident, the caution came back out after Gehlhausen crashed in Turn 1.

Thirty laps later, there was another accident, this one involving McElreath and Rager. McElreath spun in the south chute trying to control his ill-handling car and Rager spun to avoid McElreath. His car struck the inside wall. Rager had actually led a couple of laps during the shuffle for pit stops and was running 11th at the time. Both cars were out and joined the broken machines of Whittington, Ferguson and Gehlhausen in what was one of the more expensive parking lots in the world.

By this time, Rutherford was firmly in control, surrendering the lead when he pitted. The real race was for second place, but Carter seemed to have the second-best car. Unfortunately, an excellent drive was spoiled by the black flag. Carter was penalized a lap for passing the pace car under the yellow, although he maintained he had been waved by.

Regardless, the race belonged to Rutherford and the Chaparral as the Texan came home for his third Indy 500 victory and Hall's second in three years.

Rutherford now joined an elite group of three-time Indy 500 winners that included Louis Meyer, Wilbur Shaw, Mauri Rose and Al Unser. With four victories, Foyt was in a class all by himself, but Rutherford undoubtedly believed he had another 500 win or two left in his career.

Thanks to the penalty assessed to Carter, Sneva came home second. The two-time Indy pole winner actually led

Laps 74-84 and Laps 143-147 and proved that it was possible to win from the last row, although the number of cautions greatly aided his result. Rutherford still had the fastest car on the track. In fact, Rutherford was the only driver in the race with a lap in excess of 190 (190.074 on Lap 149).

Bettenhausen came home with an equally impressive third-place finish. Ironically, the hard-luck driver believed he was going to have a short race as he had barely made the field. He instructed his wife, Wavelyn, and twin sons, Cary and Todd, to be ready to leave the track as soon as the car was out of the race! Little did he know that the trusty old Wildcat would provide him with his career-best finish in the Indianapolis 500.

Johncock brought his Penske home fourth, followed by Mears, the penalized Carter and Ongais. Bigelow finished

eighth, with Richmond ninth and Leffler 10th. Richmond ran out of fuel on the final lap and actually caught a ride into the pit area from race winner Rutherford, who was taking his cool-off lap. Richmond sat down on the sidepod of Rutherford's car, patted him on the helmet and rode into the pits, waving to the crowd which responded with a thundering ovation.

It was a unique moment. The two drivers had become friends with their garages located next door to each other. Richmond garnered the top rookie honors. With Bettenhausen third, Bigelow and Leffler gave the AMI three top-10 finishes.

Rutherford's victory marked a new era for Indy-car racing. The ground effects design was here to stay and with it would come higher speeds, new track records and the fastest 500s in history.

Main photograph: The beautiful lines of the Chaparral are undoubtedly enhanced by the Pennzoil livery. Rutherford's helmet design and driver signature on the side of the car complete a stunning visual package.

Inset above left: It's three wins in the last seven starts for Johnny Rutherford.
Photographs: IMS

1981: The Longest 500 In History: Trial by Fire and Water

Call it the second phase of the second British invasion of Indy-car racing, if you will. The first, of course, came in the 1960s with the advent of rear-engined cars and a host of foreign teams and drivers dominating the proceedings.

The second "invasion" officially began in 1976 when the Vel's Parnelli Jones Racing team ran Al Unser in their F1-based Parnelli chassis powered by a British Cosworth DFX V-8. The Cosworth's power made it a viable alternative to the Offenhauser and Ford DOHC engines. In a matter of five years, the Cosworth would go from powering one starter in the Indianapolis to 29 of the 33 starters for the 1981 race.

The second phase came in the form of ground effects technology. The first successful design was the Chaparral 2K that bore strong resemblance to the Lotus 79 F1 car Mario Andretti used to capture the world title in 1978. The Chaparral's near successful debut of 1979 spawned ground effects designs in 1980 from Penske, Phoenix, Eagle, Lightning and Longhorn.

England's influence was felt in most of the early ground effects cars. The Chaparral was built in England and designed in part by Englishman John Barnard. The Penskes were designed by Englishman Geoff Ferris and built in the team's shop in Reading, Poole, England. The Phoenix was also designed and built in England and Bobby Hillin's Longhorn chassis was based on the Williams F1 car.

The slightly updated Chaparral 2K was back with Rutherford at the wheel and O'Connell Racing rebuilt Sneva's wrecked Phoenix from 1980 and entered it for rookie Kevin Cogan. (Although Sneva was wary of the car following his practice crash, he wound up winning the 1980 season finale in it at Phoenix.)

For 1981, there were updated models from the aforementioned designs (except Phoenix), and some interesting newcomers.

The most striking was the latest creation from Roman Slobodynskj, who designed the 1972 Eagle and 1977 Lightning chassis. Ted Fields' Interscope Racing underwrote Slobodnyskj's new project for Danny Ongais, who campaigned a Parnelli for the team the previous three seasons.

They called the new car the Interscope, but with its futuristic lines and gleaming black paint scheme, everyone dubbed it "The Batmobile." Like the Eagle of 1980, the car had a

pencil-thin nose section and wide bodywork from the middle of the tub to the rear of the car that held the underwing.

The car was originally built to house a Porsche engine. Interscope and Ongais had conducted tests with a flat-six Porsche engine in their Parnelli chassis and had planned to enter it in 1980. The project was abandoned after it was determined the Porsche would not be subject to a higher turbocharger boost allotted for stock-block engines.

Another new design came from overseas. Although March Engineering had built a ground effects chassis for Sherman Armstrong's AMI team, the car was called the Orbiter II (it would be driven by Tom Bagley in 1981).

For 1981, March built its own Indianapolis car with chassis going to the new Bignotti-Cotter Racing team and the Whittington Brothers. Designed by Gordon Coppuck, whose McLaren designs had been so successful in the 1970s, the project was unusual it that March was making customer cars only – there would be no March factory entry.

After campaigning Parnelli-Cosworths in 1979 and '80, A.J. Foyt brought out the first ground effects Coyote-Cosworth, designed by Bob Riley. Although it had a thinner nose section, the car somehow looked a lot like the new March.

Longhorn Racing returned with the LR02 that bore a stronger resemblance to the Williams F1 car than its predecessor. The team entered cars for Al Unser and Sheldon Kinser.

Patrick Racing introduced its first full ground effects Wildcat designed by Gordon Kimball with entries for Gordon Johncock, Gordon Smiley and Mario Andretti, who left the Penske fold at the end of the 1980 season. A new Wildcat would also be sold to Jack Rhoades for Dennis Firestone.

Penske Racing updated its PC-9 with the PC-9B for Bobby Unser, Rick Mears and Bill Alsup. The PC-9s from 1980 were sold to the new Psachie-Garza Racing team for rookies Josele Garza and Geoff Brabham, the eldest son of Jack Brabham. Psachie-Garza also had a PC-7 that ultimately was assigned to Steve Krisiloff.

Team owner David Psachie came up with an idea that would become an annual feature on the schedule – the Rookie Orientation Program (ROP). With two new drivers (Garza and Brabham), Psachie had asked the Speedway if it would be possible to hold a special practice session for rookies only. Speedway officials huddled with USAC and allotted three days in early April for such a session. Prior to that, all rookie tests had been conducted in May as part of regular practice. Under the new format, drivers could take part of the mandatory rookie test under more relaxing circumstances and complete the final test phases during official practice.

PC-7s continued to be the customer car of choice with entries from Mach I Racing for Tim Richmond, Kraco Racing for Larry Cannon, Warner Hodgdon for rookie Mike Chandler,

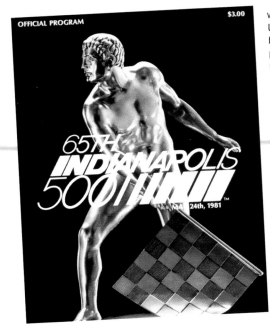

Main photograph: It is hard to believe that Danny Ongais is able to survive this horrendous accident. He will be back again to drive in 1982.

Top right: Mario Andretti chases Bobby Unser.

Inset far right: Andretti and Unser chat during practice. They have no way of knowing that they will soon be embroiled in a major controversy.

Photographs: IMS

Fletcher Racing for rookie Bob Lazier, Gohr Racing for Tim Bigelow, Machinists Union for Larry Dickson, Arciero Racing for rookie Pete Halsmer and Alex Morales for Pancho Carter.

Lindsey Hopkins had two ground effects Lightnings for Gary Bettenhausen and Johnny Parsons.

Another entry of interest was the Schkee entered for rookie Tom Klausler. Klausler's car had the only turbocharged Chevrolet on the entry list. To combat the high cost of the Cosworth, rules allowed for 355-cubic-inch production-based, stock-block engines. Because the Schkee's engine was turbocharged V-8, it was only allowed 208 cubic inches (the turbocharged Cosworths were 161 cubic inches).

Flat-bottomed cars were also in abundance at the Speedway in 1981, although the probability of one going faster than a ground effects model was slim.

Vern Schuppan entered a McLaren-Cosworth that had been Johnny Rutherford's backup car in 1978 and the new H&R Racing Team picked Tony Bettenhausen to drive "Old Hound," the McLaren that Tom Sneva had driven from last to finish second in the 1980 race.

Practice speeds showed that improvements in the ground effects design were allowing participants to creep up on the 200-mph mark.

Andretti set the pace early in the rainy first week of practice with a top lap of 195.143 set on Thursday. The following day, Bobby Unser topped 200 mph and teammate Mears was close behind, with Andretti up to 198.417. Andretti's teammates Gordon Johncock and Gordon Smiley also topped 195, setting up a Penske-versus-Patrick Racing battle in qualifying.

The 1969 500 winner looked to be a strong contender for the pole position, but as a full-time F1 driver, Andretti was faced with the annual dilemma of having a grand prix conflict with qualifying for the 500. With rain in the forecast, there was a good chance Andretti would have to find a substitute to qualify his car and start from the back row for the second time since 1978.

Rain did indeed hamper qualifying and before everyone in the line could get an opportunity, wet weather postponed everything until the following weekend. Prior to the rain, Foyt took the pole temporarily with an average of 196.078. Foyt's average would have been much higher had he not brushed the Turn 4 wall on his final lap.

Other first-day qualifiers were Rutherford at 195.837, Al Unser at 192.719, Bill Alsup at 193.154 and Pancho Carter at 191.022. Tim Richmond, a threat for the pole a year earlier, posted a shaky 185.309. Equally shaky was rookie Herm Johnson's average of 185.874. Both drivers were likely to be bumped, but with weather always a factor at Indianapolis, there was no guarantee the track – and the competition – would get faster.

The United States Auto Club denied a bid to have a special

Right: Tom Sneva is the fastest qualifier, at 200.691 mph, although he will have to start in the 20th position. His brand-new March arrived only three days before the final qualifying weekend.

Below: Australian Vern Schuppan will start 18th and finish third.

Bottom left: The faithful "yellow shirts" are here every year, some of them with 40 years of service and more.

Photographs: IMS

DANNY ONGAIS

qualifying session on Monday for Andretti. Steve Krisiloff volunteered to give up his Psachie-Garza ride to qualify Andretti's car, but ultimately that role would go to recently retired driver Wally Dallenbach.

Rain kept anyone from running until Tuesday and a new contender emerged for the pole – Ongais in "The Batmobile." The "Flyin' Hawaiian" topped 200, followed by Andretti at 199.600 and Bobby Unser at 199.159. Andretti then left for Monaco to run in the Grand Prix.

On Wednesday, Mears became first to run back-to-back laps at 200 mph – 200.312 and 200.133. Patrick Racing confirmed Dallenbach would qualify for Andretti and he topped 190 on his first day back. As Andretti would be starting last, Dallenbach only needed to find a safe average for qualifying.

Wet weather returned on Thursday, but on Friday, Bobby Unser recorded the month's quickest lap at 201.387. Also topping 200 was Sneva in the new March-Cosworth and Mike Mosley gave the stock-block crowd hope with a lap at 197.8.

On what would normally have been the third day of qualifying, the pole position was still up for grabs with a number of cars in the original qualifying line unable to make an attempt the previous weekend. This time, the weather cooperated and fans got to see a full day.

Garza became the first driver from Mexico to make the Indy 500 field with his average of 195.101. The late F1 driver

Pedro Rodriguez had nearly qualified twice – in 1963 and 1967 – but was bumped both times. Garza's teammate Brabham also qualified at 187.990.

Next up was Bobby Unser and when his run was finished, he was on the pole with a 200.546 average. It was Unser's first 500 pole position since 1972 when he smashed the track record by nearly 18 miles per hour. Surprisingly, it was the first time he had qualified in excess of 200 mph.

Mosley recorded a 197.141 average to take the middle spot of Row 1. Mears then went out and following two laps at 200 mph, he was forced to abort the run after picking up an engine vibration. Following Bob Lazier's successful qualifying attempt, first-day qualifying was over. Every driver who qualified thereafter would be considered a second-day qualifier.

The front row for the 1981 Indy 500 would be Bobby Unser, Mosley and Foyt. Mosley would be giving the Chevrolet engine its first-ever front-row start at the Speedway. Johncock would start fourth with Rutherford and Garza alongside.

Tom Sneva may have wished his run had come earlier. After a somewhat quiet month, Sneva qualified at 200.691 with a top lap of 202.420 – the fastest of the month. Likewise for Ongais, who averaged 197.694 with a top lap of 200.401 mph. If they had been considered first-day qualifiers, Sneva would have had the pole and Ongais would have started on the outside of Row 1. In fact, Sneva's car was not even at the track until the second week of practice; therefore it had not been in the first-day qualifying draw.

One of the biggest surprises in qualifying came from George Snider in Foyt's backup Parnelli-Cosworth. Snider qualified for his 17th 500 with an impressive 189.225 average. It was impressive due to the fact he only had three laps of practice in the car and had not driven any kind of race car for several months.

Another surprise came when Jim Hurtubise tried to qualify Norm Hall's Kingfish-Chevrolet. Earlier in the month, Hurtubise could be seen doing carpentry work in the garage area. For the first time since 1964, he had not entered one of his cars. "Herk" could only muster 174 in his run and it would be his last attempt to qualify at Indianapolis.

As anticipated, last year's rookie sensation was bumped. Tim Richmond's average became a liability with the improved weather and he found himself on the sidelines – for a time. Thanks to an arrangement by his sponsor, UNO, Richmond got back into the field at the expense of Snider. Foyt agreed to replace Snider with Richmond, whose sponsor was now on the car. He would start last next to Andretti, who returned from Monaco to take over his car already qualified by Dallenbach.

Once upon a time at Indianapolis, such an attempt to start the race would be frowned on. In 1981, it was tolerated, but if nothing else, it showed that the corporations participating in racing would carry considerable influence.

Perhaps the best way to describe the 1981 Indianapolis 500 is that it was a trial of fire and water. There would be plenty of fire. The race would be completed right before a major thunderstorm. And afterward, there would be THE trial.

Bobby Unser quickly established himself by leading the first 21 laps. Poor Mosley quickly dropped back and was the first to exit with a broken radiator. Already on the move was Andretti, who advanced to ninth by Lap 20. When Unser made his first stop, Rutherford led briefly until he pitted on Lap 24. Unfortunately, the Chaparral would never leave the pits. An accessory drive belt sidelined the defending winner.

Sneva was also on the move. Starting 20th, the two-time pole winner had the new March in first place by Lap 25. Unser regained the lead when Sneva pitted but Sneva passed for the lead on Lap 33 and stayed there until Lap 56. Mears, starting 22nd as a second-day qualifier, now took over the lead on Lap 57 and made his second stop of the day.

Something went wrong during the refueling and fire broke out, although there was no visible flame since it was a methanol fire. Mears was at first unaware of the fire until his face shield began to melt and he quickly exited the car. In the meantime, two of his crew members were jumping up and down in pain after being set on fire by spraying fuel. Mears was also burning and finally he and crew were doused. All three – including Penske Team Manager Derrick Walker – went to the hospital with burns.

Smiley led a lap and then Unser led until he pitted. Next, it was Ongais' turn to lead and he did so until making his second stop on Lap 63. In his haste to rejoin the fray, he may have accelerated too quickly and damaged a half-shaft. Film showed the car jerk as he left the pits. That was the start of his troubles.

Heading into Turn 3, Ongais' car suddenly swapped ends and he slammed almost head-on into the wall. The impact tore the front off the car, exposing the driver, now slumped in the cockpit as it slid along the track. The car left a wide trail of debris before it came to a stop in the short chute.

Due to the grisly nature of the accident, many were convinced Ongais had been killed in the accident. Miraculously, he would survive and although seriously injured, he would race again at Indianapolis.

Sneva's challenge ended with a broken clutch on Lap 96. The race was primarily a four-way battle between Unser, Andretti, Johncock and the rookie Garza, who led Laps 99-104.

Garza's impressive run came to an end on Lap 138 when his suspension failed between Turns 3 and 4. The Penske-Cosworth brushed the wall and the Mexican was out of the race. As Garza emerged from his car unhurt, his effort was rewarded with an appreciative ovation.

Two laps after the green came out (on Lap 144), the yellow was on again. Smiley, running a solid third, hit the wall after making contact with Tony Bettenhausen. Bettenhausen had cut a tire on debris and was trying to get out of the way when Smiley attempted to get past on the inside.

It set up the scenario that would give the 500 one of the biggest controversies in its 71-year history.

With the yellow for Smiley's accident, the leaders made their pit stops. Unser left his pit and then proceeded to pass a number of cars as he drove along the pit apron. Unser eventually blended into formation and stayed there. Andretti initially passed some cars, but dropped back.

The rule stated that when a driver would leave the pits, he was to look to his right, stay low across the short chute and run alongside the first car he spotted and then blend in as he approached Turn 2. What Unser did was to pass 11 cars before "blending in." Andretti didn't pass nearly as many and also dropped back although he may have gained a position or two.

Andretti's teammate Johncock, who was running second at the time, witnessed Unser's interesting move and radioed to the pits. USAC officials were alerted, but no action was immediately taken.

Unser took the lead for good on Lap 182 and crossed the finish line to join his younger brother Al as a three-time Indy 500 winner. Or was he?

Andretti finished second 5.2 seconds behind Unser and was followed by Vern Schuppan, Kevin Cogan and Brabham. Cogan's run was especially impressive in that he lost a wheel but managed to drive into the pits for a replacement.

Sheldon Kinser finished sixth, followed by Tony Bettenhausen and Krisiloff, Johncock and Firestone. Bettenhausen's run was pleasing to the nostalgia buffs, especially considering he had lost his father 20 years earlier.

Within an hour, the skies would open up. However, there was another storm brewing.

Throughout the garage area, rumors were rampant about a possible penalty for Unser. Traditionally, the official results were not posted until 8 a.m. the morning after the race.

The following morning, when Chief Steward Tom Binford posted the official results, Andretti had been declared the winner and Unser was penalized one position for passing under the yellow. Initially, Penske filed a protest but it was denied. He would continue trying to get Unser's victory reinstated.

Although Unser had gotten to enjoy the Victory Lane celebration, it was Andretti who got the winner's photo session on the main straightaway and the first-place awards at the victory banquet.

"For the rest of my life, I'm going to have to apologize for

winning this race," Andretti said.

Unser maintained he had simply interpreted a gray area of USAC's blend-in rule.

The elusive second victory at Indianapolis would remain in Andretti's hands for another 138 days. On October 8, the arbitration committee for the United States Auto Club voted 2-1 to reinstate Unser as the race winner. Signing for the majority, chairman Edwin Render and Reynold MacDonald held that "Unser gained a 'significant competitive edge' over Andretti by the maneuver, but they were unable to determine with any degree of certainty what would have happened had Mr. Unser blended in where he should have."

Board member Charles Brockman dissented the decision, but it would have no effect on the outcome. The longest 500 was now one for the record books and the history books.

Top: Bobby Unser enters the victory enclosure for the third time.

Above: The following day, however, when the official results are posted at 8 A.M., it is Mario Andretti who is declared the winner, Bobby having been penalized one position. At the official "day-after" photo session, it is Mario, not Bobby, who poses with the Borg–Warner trophy. In October, however, an arbitration committee will return the win to Bobby.

Photographs: IMS

Above: Rick Mears, Kevin Cogan, and A. J. Foyt lead the field into the pace lap proper.

Photograph: IMS

1982: The Closest 500 yet

In a sense, the situation for car owners in 1982 was similar to that of the mid-1970s. In the '70s, a car owner could go out and purchase a chassis from Eagle or McLaren, power it with a 4-cylinder Offenhauser and be competitive.

In 1982, things hadn't changed all that much although the names were somewhat different. An Indy-car owner circa 1982 was likely to purchase an Eagle, Penske or March chassis and power it with a turbocharged Cosworth or a stock-block Chevrolet. That owner could also expect to be competitive. There would even be cases where the customer car was faster than the factory entry. That may or may not have had something to do with the fact that there was a record of 109 entries for the race.

And so it was when the Indy-car teams arrived at Indianapolis to compete in the 66th Annual Indianapolis 500.

There was one change regarding the Speedway. Shortly before the track was scheduled to open, John Cooper surprisingly resigned as president. Joe Cloutier was back in charge.

Defending winner Bobby Unser was also back – but as a driver coach for second-year man Josele Garza. Garza attracted a nice sponsorship package from Schlitz brewery and was one of many with March-Cosworths at his disposal.

New March-Cosworths were entered by A.J. Foyt Enter-

prises for Foyt, the new Forsythe Racing Team for rookies Danny Sullivan and Hector Rebaque, Alex Morales for Pancho Carter, Bignotti-Cotter for Tom Sneva and Geoff Brabham, Shierson Racing for Howdy Holmes, Truesports Racing for rookie Bobby Rahal, H&R Racing for Tony Bettenhausen, Harry Schwartz for rookie Jim Hickman, Wysard Racing for Bob Lazier and Whittington Brothers Inc. for Don, Bill and Dale Whittington. The Whittingtons were hoping to establish a precedent of having three brothers qualify in the same 500.

Year-old March-Cosworths were also entered by Fletcher Racing for Gordon Smiley and Hoffman Racing for Jerry Sneva.

Next to the March, the most popular chassis was the Eagle usually powered by a Chevrolet stock-block engine. New Eagle-Chevrolets were entered by Dan Gurney for Mike Mosley, Menard Championship Racing for rookie Herm Johnson, Bill Freeman Racing for Mike Chandler, Arciero Racing for Pete Halsmer and BCV Racing for Dennis Firestone. Theodore Racing entered a Cosworth-powered Eagle for Desire Wilson.

A year earlier, Mosley qualified his Eagle-Chevrolet second and then made history at Milwaukee the following week by starting last and winning the 200-miler. Much was expected of this driver/car combination and for 1982, the car's Chevy engine was turbocharged.

Wilson was hoping to become the second woman to race

at Indianapolis, and the South African arrived at the Speedway with high regard. Wilson was internationally known and became the first (and thus far only) woman to win a Formula One event. (Wilson's victory came in the British Aurora AFX series for older F1 cars.)

Year-old Eagles were entered by Hall Racing for Tom Bigelow, Jamieson Racing for rookie Chip Mead and Circle Bar Auto Racing for rookie Chet Fillip. Cosworth powered the cars of Fillip and Mead.

Penskes were also prevalent – with three different models at the Speedway.

Penske Racing unveiled its latest PC-10 chassis, which featured a prow-like nose section, somewhat reminiscent of the Antares, but clearly more aerodynamic. New PC-10s were entered for Rick Mears and new teammate Kevin Cogan.

Year-old PC-9Bs were entered by Machinists Union for Roger Mears, Kraco Racing for Bill Vukovich and Vern Schuppan and Alsup Racing for Bill Alsup. Alsup also had a PC-7 as a backup.

Patrick Racing entered new Wildcats for Gordon Johncock and Mario Andretti, while Rhoades Racing entered the car driven by Andretti in 1981 for rookie Chip Ganassi. Ganassi was an exceptionally busy driver. In addition to trying to make his first Indy 500, he celebrated his 24th birthday and graduated from Duquesne University – all during the month of May. Andretti, who started on the last row in 1978 and '81 due to conflicts with his F1 schedule, was back as a full-time Indy-car driver. (As things would turn out, he might have wished he had started on the last row in 1982.)

Despite his horrific accident in 1981, Danny Ongais made a full recovery and returned with a new "Batmobile," an updated Interscope-Cosworth.

Also returning in updated versions of their ground effects cars were three-time winner Johnny Rutherford in the Chaparral 2K and Gary Bettenhausen in Lindsey Hopkins' Lightning.

After two years of running cars patterned after the Williams F1 car, Bobby Hillin turned to a new design team for the Longhorn LR-03 for three-time 500 winner Al Unser. Designed by former Eagle designer John Ward, the new Longhorn had a unique look when compared to the competition. With the driver sitting behind a rather stubby nose section, the car featured a long engine cover and rear bodywork that stretched far behind the rear axle line to form supports for the rear wing.

As unique as Unser's car was, there was no car at the Speedway as unique as Ken Hamilton's DW2-Chevrolet. Dubbed the "Eagle Aircraft Flyer" but also known as the "Crop Duster," the car easily had the longest wheelbase of any car on the entry list (140 inches). Hamilton, who allegedly mortgaged his house to finance the car, sat even farther forward than any of the ground effects designs. The wheelbase may have accounted for the car's unwieldy handling characteristics and after two spins, Hamilton wisely decided to park the car.

One noticeable change in the entry was the prevalence of teams with road-racing backgrounds. Although the United States Auto Club sanctioned only two road-course events since the 1970 season, the new CART series was starting to add more and more road-course venues to its schedule. The ultimate demise of the Can-Am series also pushed top-flight teams and drivers into Indy-car racing. The new Truesports and Forsythe teams were prime examples of the influx of road-racing talent.

Following annual opening day festivities, practice got very serious in a hurry as Rick Mears topped the charts on Sunday with a lap at 203.620. That was the fastest unofficial speed at the Speedway and came on Mears' 11th lap of practice.

A day later, Mears went 205, with teammate Cogan checking in at 202. Cogan, then paced Tuesday practice with a 204.5 and upped the ante the following day with a 206.3. Mears was close behind with a 205.8. The race for the pole position was shaping up to be a battle between the Penske teammates.

On Thursday, Mears went 206.8, but Andretti joined the fray at 206.6. Friday's "Happy Hour" produced more speed with Mears at 208.7 and Cogan at 207.8. For the fifth day in a row, an unofficial track record had been set. Of course, the

official track record could only be broken in qualifying, but that would be a foregone conclusion.

Fans didn't have to wait long on Saturday. For one thing, there would be a streamlined qualifying procedure with two warmup laps allowed instead of three. In the past, drivers had slowed down the process by running very slowly on the opening warmup lap.

First out was Cogan, who qualified for his second 500 with one- and four-lap records of 204.638 and 204.082, respectively. Cogan was actually driving Mears' backup (No. 1T) instead of his usual car (No. 4). Cogan had blown the engine in No. 4 during pre-qualifying warmup and because 1T was second in the draw, the decision was made to have Cogan qualify it. While Cogan was being interviewed following his run, Mears took to the track. He returned to the pits with his second Indy 500 pole position, a one-lap record of 207.612 and a four-lap average record of 207.004.

Roger Mears gave the field its first brother act of the year by qualifying his year-old Penske at 194.154. Joining him in the starting field were Johncock, Rahal, Rutherford, Ongais, Holmes and Sullivan.

Next up was Smiley, who had struggled to find speed in his year-old March, but nevertheless believed it to be a front-row car. On his second and final warmup lap, Smiley entered Turn 3 and got out of shape. Smiley instinctively steered into the skid, the normal procedure in any kind of racing car except a ground effects design. By correcting the skid as he did, the doomed driver steered it head-on into the wall. The car disintegrated upon impact in a ball of flame and flying debris. Smiley was killed instantly and became the first fatality at the Speedway in nine years. By coincidence, the Smiley accident was similar to the 1973 wreck that ultimately claimed the life of Swede Savage.

The accident also left the Speedway with an incredible

Below left: Of the several father-and-son combinations who have competed in the "500," the only non-Americans have been the Brabhams of Australia. Geoff, who will finish fourth in 1983, is visited by his knighted father, Sir Jack Brabham, three-time world champion and the man who brought the rear-engined Cooper–Climax to Indianapolis in 1961.

Bottom: Early arrivals to the infield stake their claim for an excellent view of the action along the backstretch.

Photographs: IMS

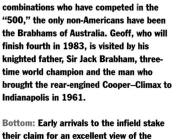

Above: Duane Sweeney, chief starter from 1980 to 1996, waves the white flag for Johncock and Mears.
Photograph: IMS

cleanup task. Not only was there the debris from the shattered March, the engine gouged the track as it bounded between Turns 3 and 4.

Qualifying eventually continued more than two hours later and when the 6 p.m. gun sounded, Foyt had joined the Penskes on Row 1. Andretti, Johncock and Bill Whittington qualified on the second row as 19 cars made successful attempts on opening day.

When qualifying closed a week later, the 33 starters averaged 197.740 mph. This was the fastest field in the history of the 500 and more than 6 mph faster than 1981.

GORDON JOHNCOCK

Gordon Johncock has been always been something of an enigma in a publicity-crazy sport full of outspoken, colorful characters. A rather quiet individual, Johncock always let his throttle foot do his talking. But the man from Hastings, Michigan, has always been the epitome of the work ethic. All his life, he has worked, whether as a lumber merchant, a rancher, a farmer or even a big-time Indy-car driver. Hard work and experience got one ahead in life. A telling example was Johncock's response to a media question about drivers coming to the Indianapolis 500 and performing there at a young age and with limited experience. "I think you should spend years preparing yourself for the Speedway. You need to race all kinds of cars for a number of years," he said.

Of course, that was what Gordon Johncock did in preparation for his first Indianapolis 500. He had raced for 10 years and was nearly 29 years of age when he first came to the Speedway. Part of the famous rookie "Class of '65" with future luminaries Mario Andretti, Joe Leonard and Al Unser, Johncock finished an impressive fifth in a front-engined Watson roadster. It would be the last top-five finish for a roadster at Indianapolis and by

the end of summer, Johncock had scored his first Indy-car victory, albeit in a new rear-engined Gerhardt-Offenhauser. The following May, he nearly scored his first Indianapolis 500 win. Caught up in the opening-lap crash that slightly damaged his car, he had to wait until the restart to get it repaired. He rejoined the race and finished fourth, but completed the 500 miles in less time than race winner Graham Hill!

Johncock's first Indianapolis 500 victory had to wait until 1973, when he won the rain-shortened, accident-filled event. Nine years later, he won again, this time dueling Rick Mears to what was then the closest finish in 500 history. It would be the pinnacle of his career and would be followed by a surprise retirement, and a pair of comebacks. One such comeback occurred in 1991 when he started last and finished sixth. He wanted to use the prize money to purchase a new tractor for his farm. Johncock's last 500 was in 1992 and although he has finally retired from racing, he hasn't completely retired. Today, he can be found in the tranquility of Michigan's woodlands, resuming his career as a lumber merchant. He's doing what he likes most – working.

On the third day, history was made as rookie Dale Whittington joined brothers Bill and Don following his successful run at 197.694. There were also three other sets of brothers – the Mearses, Bettenhausens and Snevas and half-brothers Pancho Carter and Johnny Parsons. The combined brother acts made up one-third of the starting field.

After a number of engine failures, Wilson was unable to qualify and for a time, it appeared that Garza would be unable to make his second 500 start. The Mexican driver scraped in on the last day to cap a frustrating month of engine woes and an accident in Turn 3. Bobby Unser even took some laps in Garza's car to search for speed and although he had not yet announced his retirement, these would be his final practice laps at Indianapolis.

Two other teams that failed to qualify were noteworthy. After a month of repeated engine failures, Mike Mosley did not even make a qualifying attempt. A year earlier, Mosley started on the front row. This year, he would be watching from the sidelines along with Dan Gurney, who had been involved in every 500 since 1962 as a driver and/or team owner. The new Kraco team also failed to make the field as Vukovich and Schuppan were unable to make their year-old Penskes handle properly.

The 1982 500 did have a diverse rookie field. Ganassi was the fastest qualifier of a class that included Rahal, Sullivan, Hickman, Johnson, Whittington, Halsmer, Roger Mears, Fillip and Rebaque. Rebaque was a veteran of F1, while teammate Sullivan was the reigning Can-Am champion. Also hailing from the road-racing ranks were Rahal, Hickman, Johnson, Whittington and Halsmer. Mears, like his younger brother, was a veteran of off-road racing. Fillip's pedigree was a blast from the past. His experience was in supermodifieds.

On the equipment side, there were 17 Marches, six Eagles, three Penskes, three Wildcats, a Chaparral, a Lightning, a Longhorn and one Interscope. Chevrolet had five engines in the field with Cosworth supplying the other 28 starters – sort of.

The two Penske teammates had a distinction in that their engines were "officially" listed as Fords instead of Cosworths. Technically, the engines were manufactured by Cosworth Engineering, but a deal with Ford resulted in valve covers that carried the "Ford" name.

Regardless of the engine name, the pre-race debate centered on which driver might finish third behind the Penskes. As it happened, those predictions were hasty.

Everyone was ready to go racing as Mears brought the field down for the start. Then it happened.

Cogan's car suddenly veered to the right and bumped into Foyt's car. Cogan's car rebounded and spun across the track where Andretti collected him. Most of the field was able to avoid the incident, but Dale Whittington came charging through, locked it up and spun into Roger Mears. The race was stopped.

Twenty-eight cars made it around unscathed, as Foyt's car suffered front suspension damage from the contact with Cogan. Cogan, Andretti, Roger Mears and Dale Whittington were out of the race before it started. Cogan maintained his car had broken a half-shaft. Because of the damage to his car, it was impossible to determine. In the meantime, Andretti and Foyt made sure the national TV audience knew that in their estimation the accident had been the fault of Cogan.

During the red flag period, Foyt was able to fix his car as well as he could under the circumstances. What transpired afterward might have been a testament to the power of adrenalin.

When the green flag dropped, Foyt shot into the lead and stayed there for the first 22 laps until surrendering the lead to Johncock when he pitted. In the process, Foyt set race records for the first lap, first two laps, 10 miles, 25 miles and 50 miles – all with an injured car!

Pit stops shuffled the order, but on Lap 27, Foyt was back in front for eight more circuits. Now it was Rick Mears' turn. The '79 winner passed Foyt and stayed in front until pitting on Lap 41. Tom Sneva led for three laps and then Mears and Foyt swapped the lead thanks to pit stops during a caution period.

The second half of the race was primarily between

Inset top right: Pancho Carter, who eventually will compete in 17 "500s," finishes third in this one, the best of his career. The son of Duane Carter, Pancho was raised about one mile from the track in the same household as Johnny Parsons, his half brother. They attended grade school, appropriately enough one block away at Carl G. Fisher Elementary, an old building which did not have an air-conditioner. On a hot May day, when the windows were open, they could hear the race cars running at the track.
Photograph: IMS

Johncock and Mears, although Sneva led Laps 155-159. Johncock took the lead on Lap 160 and was able to increase his margin after a slower car (Johnson) held up Mears in the pit lane during his final pit stop on Lap 183. Mears took on a full load of fuel although it was clearly more than he needed with only 17 laps remaining. Johncock came in on Lap 186 and got away five seconds faster than Mears. The Patrick crew made what is now commonly known as a timed stop – Johncock received only the amount of fuel needed to complete the distance.

Mears was now 11 seconds behind and spent the next 14 laps chasing down Johncock, who was now having handling problems. With three laps to go, the margin was down to two seconds.

After the completion of Lap 199, Mears attempted a pass on the inside in Turn 1. Mears was almost side by side with Johncock and it appeared someone was going to have to back off. Johncock kept his foot on the throttle and Mears dropped back momentarily. He was running out of time.

Coming off Turn 4, Mears closed, drafted and attempted to slingshot past Johncock as they approached the start-finish line. He came up short by .16 of a second. Johncock had captured his second Indianapolis 500 victory. It was the closest finish in 500 history, beating the 1937 record when Wilbur Shaw crossed the line 2.16 seconds ahead of Ralph Hepburn.

Sneva's race ended in a plume of white smoke, but he lost only one spot to Carter, who charged to third. Sneva wound up fourth, followed by Al Unser, Don Whittington, Jim Hickman, Rutherford, Johnson and Holmes. Hickman was named top rookie.

In some ways, it was a vindication for Johncock. He should have won the 1966 race, but lost it in the pits while his car was being repaired. He won the 1973 race, but it was shortened by rain. Somehow, this one was for real.

The real winners may have been the fans. Johncock's battle with Mears reminded the oldtimers of the classic duels between Rodger Ward and Jim Rathmann in 1959 and '60. But those two epics were nowhere near as close as the 1982 finish. Could it be any closer? Time would tell.

Above: Rick Mears draws almost level with Gordon Johncock at the white flag. He will have to back off in turn one, remount his challenge, and try it again – only to come up .16 seconds short.

Inset top left: After winning the "500" nobody wanted to remember (1973), Johncock wins the race no one will ever forget.
Photographs: IMS

1983: A Tale Of Two Rookies –
And Tom Sneva

During the month of May at the Indianapolis Motor Speedway, there are always a number of story lines. The main story of the month generally centers on the man who wins the race. That's a given due to the stature of the Indianapolis 500.

There would certainly be much to write about in 1983 – new drivers, new cars and new teams.

For starters, March was back as a full-fledged factory effort. Since 1981, the March chassis had been placed in the hands of private teams. From two teams and three cars in 1981, the car's popularity was such that more than half of the 1982 field (17 cars) was composed of March chassis. For 1983, March aligned itself with Forsythe Racing, who returned with an Italian rookie named Teo Fabi.

Joining Forsythe in the March camp were Bignotti-Cotter with entries for Tom Sneva and Kevin Cogan, Shierson Racing with Howdy Holmes, Alex Morales with Pancho Carter, Kraco Enterprises with Mike Mosley, Truesports with Bobby Rahal, Wysard Motors with Derek Daly and Desire Wilson, Whittington Brothers for Don and Bill Whittington, Menard Racing with Herm Johnson, Hoffman Racing for Jerry Sneva, Provimi Racing with Tony

Bettenhausen, Interscope Racing with Danny Ongais, Dick Simon Racing with Simon, Leader Card Racers with Rich Vogler, A.J. Foyt Enterprises with Foyt and George Snider and Brayton Racing for Scott Brayton and Patrick Bedard.

As columnist for *Car & Driver Magazine,* Bedard was hoping to give readers a true behind-the-scenes angle. An accomplished SCCA club racer, Bedard had been entered and practiced for the 1981 and '82 500s.

Bignotti-Cotter was also trying out the new Theodore chassis, based on the Theodore F1 car and designed by Morris Nunn.

Penske Racing returned with its new PC-11 for Rick Mears and Al Unser. The year-old PC-10s were sold to Arciero Racing for Pete Halsmer, VDS Racing for John Paul, Jr. and Machinists Union for Roger Mears and Josele Garza.

Patrick Racing entered its new Wildcat IX for defending race winner Gordon Johncock and Chip Ganassi. Johncock gave the car a successful debut by winning the season opener at Atlanta. Bobby Unser, who had planned to run for Patrick, did some development work on the car, but decided to retire after a test accident at Phoenix. Johnny Rutherford, who at one time was earmarked to drive for Forsythe, wound up replacing Unser.

Official Program
FOUR DOLLARS
67th INDIANAPOLIS 500

Dan Gurney did not enter a team for 1983, but 1983 Eagles were entered by Galles Racing for rookie Al Unser, Jr., and Circle Bar Auto Racing for Chet Fillip. Gohr Racing entered a 1982 Eagle for rookie Steve Chassey.

Lola introduced its first new design since 1978, the T700. The new Newman-Haas Racing team entered one for Mario Andretti with Armstrong Mould posting an entry for rookie Harry McDonald (who was subsequently replaced by veteran Steve Krisiloff).

The Newman-Haas operation was the merger of actor Paul Newman and Lola distributor Carl Haas's Can-Am teams. Newman reportedly sold Haas on the merger by guaranteeing Andretti as the team's driver.

Another new team was Primus Racing with rookie driver Chris Kneifel. The team's Primus-Cosworth was actually an updated version of the Longhorn LR03 from 1982. With Kneifel at 6'6" one of the updates involved raising the rollbar to accommodate the lanky driver.

Longtime entrant J.C. Agajanian and record producer Mike Curb joined forces with Rattlesnake Racing to enter a new Rattlesnake-Cosworth for Mike Chandler. The Rattlesnake was the latest design from Roman Slobodynskj, who previously designed cars for Eagle, Hopkins and Interscope.

Another new car at Indy was the Argo, entered by Bill Alsup. Former McLaren engineer Jo Marquart designed the new car and Alsup had captured the 1978 Super Vee title in an Argo. Unfortunately, the car arrived at Indianapolis without the benefit of testing.

Gone from the scene for the first time since 1978 was Jim Hall and his Chaparral team. After winning two of the first three Indy 500s he entered, Hall decided to call it quits. By 1982, the Chaparral 2K was becoming obsolete. In fact, before the 1982 season was over, Hall purchased a March for Johnny Rutherford. At season's end, he folded the team. Hall's revolutionary Indy car would be the last to bear the Chaparral name.

As a result of the fatal accidents of Gordon Smiley at Indianapolis and Jim Hickman at Milwaukee, rule changes were implemented to lower the speeds. Chief among them was the turbocharger boost limit that was initially lowered to 45 inches, but raised to 47 after a number of participants complained.

That meant that Rick Mears' track records from 1982 should be safe – or so everyone thought.

Practice speeds showed a noticeable drop with most of the first week's top speeds hovering around the 203-mph mark.

Below: Defending winner Gordon Johncock races Kevin Cogan, who, had it not been for the choice of gearing (according to some crew members), might have finished second to Tom Sneva, his teammate.

Inset below left: Although Al Unser, Jr. (right) appears to be about 15 years old when he participates in the Rookie Orientation Program, he is in fact on the verge of turning 21. Approximately one month from now, he will become the first person ever to compete in the "500" against his own father, who is seen here imparting some knowledge.
Photograph: IMS

On Wednesday, Don Whittington posted the month's best at 205.198 and Rick Mears responded with a 205.1 on Friday. John Paul's chances to make the race suffered a serious setback when he broke his ankle in an accident. Geoff Brabham would eventually replace Paul.

The race for the pole position would have to wait another week as rain kept anyone from qualifying.

On Monday, Halsmer crashed his car and suffered a collapsed lung. Johnny Parsons would replace him. Rahal was fastest of the day at 202.429 and Whittington topped the charts on Tuesday at 204.081.

The Speedway's unforgiving walls sidelined another driver on Wednesday. This time it was Rutherford, who suffered a broken right ankle and foot when his Wildcat slammed into the Turn 3 wall. On May 8, Rutherford had heavily damaged another new Wildcat in a Turn 1 accident.

Patrick offered the ride to Don Whittington, who crashed it on the final Friday. (Whittington returned to his own March and made the field.)

By week's end, Ongais had the best speed with a lap at 205.996 during Friday's "Happy Hour." Mosley also topped 205 and Rick Mears went 204.918.

When qualifying finally commenced on what should have been the third day of time trials, Mosley and Fabi surprised the crowd with practice laps of 206.896 and 206.043, respectively. Fabi's newfound speed took everyone but his team by surprise. The soft-spoken Italian had quietly been working up to speed and made progress each day.

He saved his best for qualifying.

Mosley temporarily occupied the pole with an average of 205.372. After missing the race in 1982 after starting third in 1981, Mosley was not only back in the race, he was back on the front row.

Al Unser, Jr., showed he had inherited his family's talent by posting a very respectable average of 202.146. Unser's Coors-sponsored Eagle featured the first spat-style wheels seen at Indy since the Jack Adams turbine car of 1969. Unser looked years younger than his listed age of 21. However, under his famous father's tutelage, he raced sprint cars at age 16, won the national Super Vee title at 19 and came to Indianapolis as the reigning Can-Am champion.

Rick Mears survived a wild qualifying run, capped by brushing the Turn 4 wall. Despite that, he still managed to average 204.301. Teammate Unser followed up with a 201.954 average and in doing so, gave the Speedway its first father-son combination in an Indianapolis 500 starting field.

Following Tom Sneva's run at 203.687, it was Fabi's turn.

His first lap was 207.273 – the month's fastest. His second lap was a new track record at 208.049. He closed his run with laps at 207.622 and 206.640 for an average speed of 207.395, another track record. So much for the rule changes to make the cars slower!

"It was flat out all the way around," Fabi said afterward. "The car was perfect, the engine was perfect, there were no problems."

Indianapolis had its first rookie pole winner since 1950, when Walt Faulkner won the pole driving for J.C. Agajanian. In the course of one qualifying run, Fabi became an instant celebrity at Indianapolis, although to look at him, one never would have guessed his occupation. Born in Italy and educated in engineering, Fabi had been a first-rate skier before trying auto racing. Diminutive and balding, one writer described him as "only looks the part when he puts on his helmet."

When qualifying closed the following day, March solidified its hold on the field with 18 of 33 starters using its chassis. Six Penskes, three Eagles, two Wildcats, two Lolas, a Rattlesnake and a Primus filled out the field. Cosworth powered 32 of the 33 qualifiers, with Chassey's Eagle the only car to use Chevrolet power. That marked the most cars to use one power-plant in a 500 field since 1962 when Offenhauser supplied power for 32 of the 33 (Buick powered Gurney's car).

As if to prove that his pole position was no fluke, Fabi brought the field down for the start and proceeded to drive off into the distance. For 23 laps, no one could touch the Italian rookie. He surrendered the lead when he pitted on Lap 24. Once the first round of stops was over, Fabi was fifth behind Al Unser, Sneva, Rahal and Rick Mears.

Unser had stayed out the longest of the leaders, but when the race's first caution came for Bedard's brush with Turn 4 wall, he was able to stop and retain the lead.

On Lap 36, Sneva passed Unser for the lead and on Lap 44, the yellow came out for Roger Mears' accident in Turn 1. That brought the leaders back into the pits. The top runners got tires and fuel and quickly returned.

Unfortunately, an overeager crewman gave Fabi the "go" sign too quickly. With the fuel apparatus still engaged, the car lurched forward and fuel began to spill out as the result of a torn cell. Fabi was out in an incident reminiscent of Lloyd Ruby in 1969.

Second-year man Rahal, who had won twice in his rookie season and finished runner-up in the point standings to Rick Mears, led his first laps at Indianapolis and swapped the lead with Unser and Sneva during the first half of the race. Rahal's strong run ended on Lap 110 with radiator problems.

That left Unser and Sneva to contest the final half of the race.

Following the final round of pit stops on Lap 173, Unser was in front, followed by Sneva and Al's son, who was several laps down. The younger Unser had been forced to stop 11 times and the extra pit time took him out of contention. However, he would figure in the drama surrounding the final laps.

On a restart on Lap 177, Al, Jr., dashed by Sneva and his father and was given an automatic two-lap penalty for jumping the start. He led the field to the start-finish for the Lap 178 restart and allowed his father past.

For the next few laps, the elder Unser tried to make a break while his son tried to inconspicuously hold up Sneva. While he was later accused of blocking, the younger Unser began taking a unique line to prevent Sneva from drafting and making a pass. For being only 21 years old and in his first Indianapolis 500, the younger displayed an incredible amount of race savvy.

Finally, on Lap 191, Sneva dispatched the younger Unser and then passed the elder Unser for the lead. Al, Sr., could not stay with Sneva, who built a seven-second margin in three laps. By the time he took the white flag, the margin was up to 10 seconds. A lap later, he had his first victory at Indianapolis after finishing second in 1977, '78 and '80.

The elder Unser finished second for the third time in his career to go with his three victories. It was his strongest performance at Indy since 1979, when he dominated the first half of the race in the new Chaparral.

Mears wound up third, followed by Brabham, Cogan, Holmes, Carter, Ganassi, Brayton and Al Unser, Jr., the highest-finishing rookie. Despite that distinction, Unser's willingness to admit he had purposely tried to help his father win a fourth 500 may have cost him Indy's top rookie honor, which went to Fabi. In other years, the two might have shared the award. Not this time.

Brabham's run was especially impressive in that he arrived at Indianapolis without a ride. With limited time in the car vacated by the injured John Paul, Jr., Brabham safely qualified 26th and then charged through the field to finish fourth.

Sneva's victory was the first for the March chassis, and there would be more to follow.

1984: March To Victory For Mears

There's an old adage that says "If you can't beat them, join them." And a prime example of this could be seen in the entry list for the 1984 Indianapolis 500.

If you wanted to go racing at the Indianapolis Motor Speedway, there was a simple plan – providing you had the wherewithal to finance the plan. A budding Indy-car owner simply needed to order a 1984 March 84C and a Cosworth DFX engine to go with it.

That may be oversimplifying things, but consider that even successful team owners like Roger Penske and Pat Patrick decided to stop building their own cars and purchased March chassis for their 1984 programs. Penske did have his latest PC-12 ready to go, but once he purchased a March, it appeared the PC-12 would be pushed aside.

In fact, entering something other than a March-Cosworth was the exception to the rule. But that's not to say there were no other new cars.

Among the "exceptions" was the new Lola T800 entered by Newman-Haas Racing for Mario Andretti.

Doug Shierson decided to build his own car, producing a pair of Shierson DSR-Cosworths for Johnny Rutherford and Danny Sullivan. Shierson hired Ian Reed away from March to design the car and it bore a strong resemblance to the March.

Dan Gurney entered a pair of new Eagle-Pontiacs for Mike Chandler with sponsorship help from Dubonnet and record producer Mike Curb.

Dubonnet and Curb were also behind the first French factory effort at Indianapolis since the early 500s. Ligier, a fairly successful participant in F1, designed a Cosworth-powered car for Kevin Cogan. The Californian was now running with a different team for the fourth time in four years. Ligier had never designed a car for oval-track racing, but in fairness, neither had John Cooper or Colin Chapman when they first came to the Speedway.

Another European team, Theodore Racing, entered a pair of 1984 Theodore-Cosworths for Italian rookie Bruno Giacomelli whilst Chris Kneifel had a new Primus after campaigning a heavily revised Longhorn the previous year. The Primus was custom made to fit Kneifel's 6'6" frame.

That was pretty much it for the others. Virtually everyone else in the entry was running a March and most teams had the latest March 84C.

Emerson Fittipaldi came out of a three-year retirement to resume his racing career. In October of 1974 shortly after clinching his second World Championship, he had actually done some test laps at Indianapolis for Team McLaren, his employer in F1 racing at the time. That test had been conducted in secret. Fittipaldi would be noticeable on two fronts – his famous name and the shocking pink color of his car and firesuit.

There were a few notable absences in 1984. Indy 500 fans mourned the passing of longtime owner J.C. Agajanian and driver Mike Mosley. Mosley had been fatally injured after flipping his van on a California highway in March. Agajanian lost a long battle to cancer on the opening weekend of practice for the 500.

Also missing were the Whittington brothers, who had competed in every race since 1980. Although Don and Bill Whittington had entered cars for the race, the brothers and their cars did not arrive and no reason was given for their absence.

The 1984 entry had a most distinctive rookie class. In addition to Fittipaldi, Roberto Guerrero also brought F1 experience with him to Indy. Al Holbert and Tom Gloy were top road racers and Michael Andretti was hoping to follow in the steps of his famous father. Five months younger than Al Unser, Jr., the two youngsters had been compared in the formative years of their respective careers. Now they would be compared at the ultimate test in motorsport – the Indianapolis 500.

Jacques Villeneuve was the younger brother of the late F1 ace Gilles Villeneuve. Like his brother, Jacques raced snowmobiles before moving up to Atlantics and sports cars. Unlike his brother, he was unable to make it in F1.

The opening practice showed that it was going to take speeds at 200 mph or better to make this year's race. Rahal recorded the fastest opening-day speed at 205.058 mph and followed with a 205.996 on Sunday. If they could go that fast on opening weekend, how fast would they be by qualifying weekend?

Mario Andretti was quickest on Monday at 207.660 and Mears topped the charts the following day at 207.039. Now it was Andretti's turn and he responded with a lap at 210.575 during Wednesday's "Happy Hour." Mears was close behind at 209.937. Both represented the fastest two unofficial speeds in track history.

Andretti was fast again on Thursday at 201.182 and that set the stage for Friday afternoon's drama.

Mears struck first with a 210.624. Andretti came back with an astounding 212.414. Johncock also posted a 211.118 but used the draft to gain speed. The proceedings were overshadowed by the accident of Mike Chandler in Turn 3. Chandler encountered some sort of suspension or tire failure and slammed into the wall. He sustained serious head injuries and even though he would recover, the accident ended his career.

The race for the pole position figured to be a battle between Mears and Andretti. Someone forgot to tell Tom Sneva and for the third time in seven years, he would surprise everyone.

Of the contenders, Mears qualified first and emerged with a one-lap record of 208.502 and a four-lap record average of 207.847. Michael Andretti then posted a very respectable 207.805 average to make his first Indianapolis 500. Now all eyes were on Mario Andretti.

His first lap was a new track record of 209.687 mph. Coming out of Turn 4 to complete his fourth and final lap, his electrical system malfunctioned and he slowed to a 202.950. That dropped his average to 207.467 and the even though it wasn't the pole, the Andretti family became the second in Speedway history to have a father and son start in the same 500.

Following the successful runs of Al Unser (204.441), Tony Bettenhausen (202.813), Chip Ganassi (201.612) and Tom Gloy (203.758), it was time for Tom Sneva. He did not disappoint.

After an opening lap of 209.113, he broke the track record on each of the next three laps – 209.898, 210.423 and 210.689 – for a record average speed of 210.029.

The new Mayer Motorsports team of ex-McLaren men Teddy Mayer and Tyler Alexander had another surprise for the qualifying crowd – Howdy Holmes. The Michigan driver posted an average speed of 207.977 to start alongside Sneva. The team had previously scored a 1-2 finish at Phoenix with Sneva winning.

Other first-day qualifiers included Al Unser, Jr., who gave Indianapolis its second father-son combination, and last year's pole winner Teo Fabi. Fabi averaged 203.600 – nearly 4 mph slower than his pole average from a year ago. A total of 26 cars qualified, including Foyt who would be making a record 27th start in the race.

There were also some lineup changes. With the new Shierson DSR-1 unable to run fast enough, Rutherford moved to Foyt's March-Chevrolet but failed to qualify. Sullivan went ahead and qualified his DSR-1 with an average speed of 196.044. That car would be withdrawn as Sullivan planned to move into a new Lola purchased by Shierson and attempt to qualify it. One other change was that Cogan would replace the injured Chandler in the Eagle-Pontiac. The Ligier project was finis.

The Canadian Tire team also suffered a setback. Although Villeneuve qualified on the first day with a speed average that would have held up, he suffered a head injury after backing into the wall on May 17 in his backup car. Villeneuve could have run his previously qualified car, but his injury was serious enough for him to miss the race. The team also could have put another driver in the car and started it last, but opted to withdraw their entry. That allowed Kneifel – the 34th-fastest qualifier – into the starting lineup. Kneifel became the first alternate to start the 500 since 1929.

March and Cosworth thoroughly dominated the lineup with March supplying chassis for 29 of the starters and Cosworth providing the power for 30. For the first time in years, there were no brother acts, but with the Andrettis and Unsers, there was still a family feel with two sets of fathers and sons.

From third position, Mears jumped into the lead at the start. A number of folks believe the third starting position is preferable for the start since the driver is already in the groove.

Mears led the first 24 laps until he pitted and Sneva led Lap 25. Mario Andretti now led and stayed there until Lap 47, when he pitted. That put Sneva in front for a couple of laps, but Andretti regained the lead on Lap 54.

On Lap 58, the most serious incident of the day occurred.

Patrick Bedard, in his second 500 start, brushed the wall between Turns 3 and 4. The car swerved into the infield where it struck an earthen bank and began to flip. Bedard's car broke in half and the tub (containing the cockpit and the driver) landed upside down. With the yellow out and debris on the track, a number of drivers slowed up. One who couldn't slow down in time was Sullivan, who launched his new Lola over the rear wheel of Fabi's car. Fabi was able to continue, but Sullivan's car damaged its suspension upon landing.

Bedard was ultimately removed from the car and although he would fully recover, he would never race at Indy again.

Fabi and Ongais each held the lead at one time during the first 100 laps and Al Unser, Jr., charged from 15th starting spot to lead Laps 83-86. Fabi would be out with fuel system problems on Lap 104 and Unser was sidelined on Lap 131 with a broken water pump.

From Lap 87 on, the battle was between Sneva and Mears.

Sneva led through Lap 109 and then Mears took over from from Laps 110-141. Sneva led the next two, but it would be Mears the rest of the way. Sneva's

Above: Howdy Holmes, who will compete in six "500s," take the checkered flag in every one, and never finish lower than 13th, surprises many by qualifying second (to teammate Tom Sneva) in 1984.

Left: All day long on every practice day, it's back and forth, back and forth.
Photographs: IMS

Above: Replacing the departed Tom Sneva at Bignotti-Cotter, at the suggestion of engineer Morris Nunn, is the Columbian, Roberto Guerrero, seen here being "coached" by George Bignotti. In his first four of fifteen "500s," Guerrero will finish second, third, fourth and second, and will continue to be what the Brits refer to as "a lovely bloke."

Opposite: Danny Sullivan hounds Mario Andretti shortly before attempting a pass.

Main photograph: Danny Sullivan takes the lead from Mario Andretti and then promptly spins directly in front of him. Mario instinctively aims left, having instantaneously experienced a flashback to the Johnny Parsons accident which had happened in exactly the same spot two years earlier. "I tried going around the right side on that one and it didn't work out very well," Mario would later explain. "So I decided to go left." This evaluation, of course, took place in just a fraction of a second.
Photographs: IMS

challenge ended on Lap 168 when he broke a CV joint. Sneva was fortunate that the failure occurred during a caution. Al Holbert had pulled alongside to warn Sneva after seeing sparks from the underside of the car. Mears was more than a lap ahead of his nearest competitor and what would have continued as an epic battle was now over.

The real battle in the closing laps was for second place between Guerrero and Al Unser. The Colombian driver was fortunate to be that highly placed, despite making a pit stop on Lap 193 and having spun on Lap 153. Coming out of Turn 2, Guerrero had executed a complete 360 without hitting anything and continued on. He was also able to overcome two stalls during pit stops. In the closing laps of the race, however, he was the fastest man on the track – turning lap after lap at 200 mph.

Guerrero ultimately finished second to Mears, but down by two laps. Unser was third, followed by Holbert and Michael Andretti. Foyt, Rahal, Johnson, Ongais and Garza filled out the top 10. Guerrero and Andretti would be named Co-Rookies of the Year.

For Mears, the sky was the limit. Since joining Penske in 1978, he had won three national titles, two Indianapolis 500s and 17 other Indy-car races. He had performed impressively in a 1980 F1 test at Riverside for Brabham. Sadly, it

would nearly come to an end for Mears when he sustained serious foot and leg injuries that summer at St. Pie, Quebec.

Mears' injuries would mark a changing of the guard. On the rise were people like Rahal, Michael Andretti and Al Unser, Jr. Another man on the rise would be Sullivan, who would win three times for Shierson in his Lola and ultimately be hired away by Penske at season's end.

Lola would seriously challenge the domination of March with Andretti and Sullivan combining for eight straight victories during the summer. It was yet another changing of the guard.

1985: The World's Biggest Spin For A Win

Sometimes, being in the right place at the right time means everything. And sometimes, it's not so much what you know, but who you know. Danny Sullivan is a good study of both theories.

The son of a wealthy construction company owner in Louisville, Kentucky, Sullivan was unsure of his life's direction. He was certain he didn't want to follow in his father's footsteps, but his uncertainty took him to New York City where he worked for a time as a taxicab driver and a waiter at several restaurants.

A family friend, a physician named Dr. Frank Faulkner, was asked to look in on Sullivan. As fate would have it, the British-born Faulkner had a number of contacts in the world of auto racing and for a time had served as timer for Ken Tyrrell's racing organization. Faulkner found that Sullivan might like to try auto racing, so he arranged for the youngster to have a job with Tyrrell's team and try his hand at racing Formula Fords in England.

Over the years, Sullivan honed his skills and in 1981, he won a number of races in the Can-Am championship. Fellow Louisville resident Garvin Brown, whose family owned a successful distillery, backed Sullivan in his Can-Am days and followed him to Indy-car racing in 1982 with the new Forsythe team.

In his first race at Atlanta, Sullivan finished third. For the next 11 years, it marked the most successful debut of a rookie driver in his first Indy-car event. He also qualified for his first Indy 500, but crashed in the race. That would be his final Indy-car race of 1982 as Forsythe concentrated its efforts on teammate Hector Rebaque.

The following year, he was back with Team Tyrrell, but this time it was as driver of one of the Benetton-sponsored F1 cars. It was not one of Tyrrell's better years and the highlight for Sullivan was a fifth-place in the prestigious Grand Prix of Monaco.

In Sullivan's case, he was with two good teams in two good series, but in each case he was there at the wrong time.

Sullivan returned to Indy-car racing in 1984 as teammate to Johnny Rutherford for Doug Shierson Racing. The team had high hopes with the new Ian Reed-designed Shierson DSR-1. Based on the ever-popular March, the car failed to meet everyone's expectations. Sullivan qualified one of the cars, but found more speed when Shierson purchased a new Lola

T800. Then Sullivan got caught up in the aftermath of Patrick Bedard's accident and was sidelined.

It appeared it was going to be more of the same. Then a couple of things happened that would affect Sullivan's career and future. Sullivan & Co. got more comfortable with the new Lola and won at Cleveland, Pocono and Sanair (St. Pie). During practice for the Sanair race, Rick Mears suffered serious foot and leg injuries and his future was suddenly in doubt. Sullivan's mid-season form vaulted him to fourth in the final point standings.

Sullivan was exactly what Roger Penske needed and he signed him to partner Al Unser. Even if Mears was able to return, his injuries were such that there was no certainty about his ability to perform on CART's numerous road circuits. Oval tracks would be another story, as history would show.

Sullivan arrived at Indianapolis in 1985 as a driver to watch. Of course, there were a few other drivers to watch at the Speedway as well.

Mario Andretti saw his career rejuvenated by dominating the 1984 season (six victories, two seconds and eight pole positions) and winning his fourth national Indy-car title. Andretti would have the latest Lola T900 chassis at his disposal and a hefty sponsorship package from Beatrice.

Like Mears, Derek Daly suffered serious foot and leg injuries the previous summer. Running at Michigan International Speedway, Daly slammed into the wall, tearing off the front of the car and exposing the driver much like it had in Danny Ongais' accident of 1981. Before Daly could hit the wall a second time, the car of John Paul, Jr., collected Daly's car. He required a lengthy recovery like Mears and it was becoming more apparent that the driver's lower extremities were vulnerable in the new ground effects designs.

Like Sullivan, Bobby Rahal was another driver on the rise and he had never been lower than fifth in the final standings since embarking upon Indy-car racing in 1982. For Rahal and the Truesports team, it was more a matter of when than if. For the fourth straight year, Rahal would be driving a March-Cosworth.

March-Cosworths were the choice of Penske Racing for the second straight year and for the first time since 1981 the team would have three drivers – Rick Mears, Al Unser and Sullivan. Mears was still recovering from injuries the previous summer and would only drive in select oval-track races in 1985. In his third year with Penske, Unser was hoping to rebound after winning the national title in 1983 but dropping to ninth in the final standings of '84. And, of course, there was Sullivan.

Second-generation drivers were also hoping to make their mark at Indy – Michael Andretti and Al Unser, Jr.

Michael Andretti duplicated Unser's rookie season by winding up seventh in the final standings (Unser was sixth). More was expected of him as he returned with the Kraco Racing team and new March-Cosworths for Andretti and teammate Kevin Cogan.

Unser, Jr., won his first Indy-car event at Portland and was signed to drive the new Lotus for Roy Winkelmann. Gerard Ducarouge designed the Lotus and the car (called the Type 96) was built, but the project was scrapped when Winkelmann failed to procure proper funding. By coincidence, Al Unser knew there was an opening at Shierson Racing and was able to get his son the Shierson ride.

After losing Unser, Galles went shopping and came up with two new drivers. Geoff Brabham took Unser's place in the Coors-sponsored March-Cosworth and Pancho Carter was signed to drive the team's Buick-powered March.

The 500 was getting more of an international flavor, thanks in part to the number of road-course races sanctioned by CART. USAC still sanctioned the 500, but CART offered points in its championship for Indianapolis.

Joining Andretti and Emerson Fittipaldi from the F1 ranks were Roberto Guerrero from Colombia, Derek Daly from Ireland, Jim Crawford from Scotland and Raul Boesel, like Fittipaldi, from Brazil. Dutch driver Arie Luyendyk started his career in Europe with an eye toward F1, but ultimately migrated to the United States where he attracted Indy-car owner Aat Groenevelt and won the 1984 Super Vee title.

One rookie who would have merited the most attention opted to pass on Indianapolis after an abbreviated test session in April. Willy T. Ribbs, one of the most promising road racers in the country, had hoped to be the first African-American driver to compete in the 500. His presence at Indianapolis in May would have drawn the same kind of attention drawn by Janet Guthrie nine years earlier.

Ribbs' test in a March-Cosworth was uneventful. But after running a few laps, Ribbs decided that he would like to get more experience before attempting to make history.

Above: Dan Gurney has his final start as an entrant and constructor, Ed Pimm finishing ninth and Tom Sneva becoming involved in an accident while running second.

Below: Danny Sullivan is completely sideways while executing this spin, which will end up being about 420 degrees before he will save it, straighten out, and keep going. Fellow competitors will be amazed that Sullivan is able to keep from hitting anything, while tire engineers will be flabbergasted that the tires show no flat spots.
Photographs: IMS

When the track opened officially for practice on May 4, Dick Simon achieved something of a double. For years, Simon made it a personal goal to be first on the track. For the umpteenth time, he achieved that goal and then he topped the speed charts on opening day with a lap at 209.302. With a full week of practice ahead, Tom Sneva's track record already appeared to be in jeopardy.

On Day 2, Herm Johnson, whose 211.2 had been quickest in April testing, posted the fastest lap at 206.706 mph. Rick Mears did not post one of the fastest speeds, but his on-track appearance was his first since being injured the previous summer at Sanair. Mears was able to walk, but used a three-wheeled electric cart to get around the Speedway.

On Day 3, Bobby Rahal led the way with a 210.910 lap, followed by Johnson at 209.937 and Mario Andretti and Roberto Guerrero, who each posted at 209.643. In one of the more unusual occurrences, Randy Lanier had his driving privileges revoked after being observed making erratic maneuvers on the track. Earlier, Lanier participated in the Rookie Orientation Program and was given clearance to run. Don Whittington would take Lanier's place.

Speeds continued to go up as Guerrero led the way with a lap of 212.816 on Tuesday. A day later, Mears went faster than anyone had ever gone at the Speedway with a lap at 213.371. Another of the leaders was something of a surprise. Pancho Carter posted a lap at 212.464, the fastest ever in a Buick-powered machine. The Buick V-6 engine had a 10-inch advantage in boost over the Cosworth V-8s and with three years of development, the powerplant was finally showing its true potential.

Jacques Villeneuve crashed after breaking a CV joint. He was uninjured, but the accident was his second in four days. The French-Canadian had been forced to withdraw from last year's race after a major crash in practice.

On Thursday, Rahal went quicker – this time with a top lap of 214.183. Andretti would top that the following day with a 214.285 although a number of pit row timers clocked him at 215.6. Andretti's fast lap was overshadowed by the serious accident of Herm Johnson and the surprise retirement announcement by Johncock.

Johnson suffered multiple chest injuries and a broken right arm after crashing in Turn 1. The soft-spoken Wisconsin driver had been among the leaders in practice speeds and appeared ready to move on to a higher level in the sport.

On the day before qualifying, Johncock made the surprise announcement that he was retiring. The two-time 500 winner told the media that "it's just not as much fun as it used to be and I decided this morning that I'd had enough." And with that, the two-time 500 winner figuratively "rode off into the sunset." Actually, Johncock wound up doing color commentary for the Speedway Radio Network on Race Day. In the meantime, team owner U.E. "Pat" Patrick named Don Whittington as his replacement.

Windy conditions on the first qualifying day would affect the runs, but there was little doubt that the track records would stand. Fans did not have to wait long as the first qualifier – Scott Brayton – did just that.

Driving his father's March-Buick, Brayton broke the track record on each of his first three laps with his third lap at 214.199 establishing a new one-lap record. Brayton would have easily set a four-lap record had his transmission not begun to pack up as he headed for the start-finish line. Brayton's car slowed dramatically and his fourth lap was only 210.256. His average was still a record of 212.354.

After the successful runs of Tom Sneva and Ongais, Carter went out for his attempt. His run was more consistent, but after four laps, he averaged 212.583 for a new four-lap record. He had the pole while Brayton was left with the one-lap record in second spot. Buicks were 1-2 on the grid. Rahal, one of the pre-qualifying favorites, joined Carter and Brayton on Row 1 with an average of 211.818.

Row 2 was somewhat eclectic with former F1 world champions Andretti and Fittipaldi joined by Don Whittington, who found speed with little time in the ex-Johncock car. Whittington reminded the press that he was used to racing airplanes at speeds in excess of 500 miles per hour so his run at Indianapolis at 210.991 should not have been so surprising.

Al Unser, Danny Sullivan and Geoff Brabham occupied Row 3 and Mears gave the fans a sentimental favorite after easily qualifying in 10th position.

The second week of practice saw another driver change. With two crashes, Villeneuve never felt comfortable in his car,

and so the search went out for a replacement. The height of the driver was a priority in the search, thanks to the alteration made to the tub to custom-fit Villenueve. Veteran Johnny Parsons. fit the bill in the height department and his experience was a definite asset.

Parsons would be one of 11 qualified on the second weekend as the 33-car field averaged 208.138 mph, faster than Teo Fabi's track record from two years ago. Derek Daly capped his comeback from injury by scraping into the field in 31st position. Three-time 500 winner Johnny Rutherford started one spot ahead of Daly and next to the "man on the bubble" – Tony Bettenhausen, whose 204.824 average in the Gurney-Curb Lola was the slowest in the field.

The 1985 starting field also had the distinction of being the first in the history of the race to be composed of 33 new cars. There were 24 March chassis, seven Lolas and two Eagles. Thirty starters used Cosworth, one used Chevrolet and the other two used Buick engines. Of course, the latter two were the two fastest cars in the field. The question was how long they could run in a 500-mile race.

At the start of the race, there was a pretty good indication that it might be a long day for the Buicks. Carter dropped back as Rahal jumped into the lead with Brayton in pursuit. In six laps, Carter's race was run as he retired with oil pump problems. Snider's Chevy expired seven laps later. Brayton would run a strong second during the early stages and even lead Lap 15, but he also would retire early. His day came to an end on Lap 31 when he was sidelined with a wheel-bearing problem.

Mario Andretti took the lead on Lap 16 and stayed there for the next 32 circuits. In the first half of the race, Andretti appeared to be in control. Fittipaldi and Sullivan each led briefly, but Andretti led 75 of the first 100 laps.

But there was one driver who seemed to be reeling in the

1969 winner – Sullivan. Andretti's car appeared to have developed a push and lap after lap, Sullivan got closer.

On Lap 120, Sullivan attempted to pass Andretti, going low in Turn 1. No sooner had he gotten ahead of Andretti, than his car started to swap ends. In a cloud of smoke, Sullivan did a 360-degree spin and then some. Andretti needed all of his ability and experience to miss the spinning March, darting to the inside and getting through unscathed. To the surprise of everyone in the stands and on the track, Sullivan also avoided contact with the wall completely and was able to continue.

Informed by Penske Team Manager Derrick Walker that the yellow was on, Sullivan replied: "I know. It's for me, I just spun but the car's OK. I'm coming in."

Sullivan pitted for new tires. Unbelievably, Sullivan's tires had not been flat-spotted in the spin. He rejoined the race still in second place behind Andretti, who also stopped during the caution.

When the green came out on Lap 122, Sullivan resumed his pursuit of Andretti. Unfazed by the previous passing attempt and spin, Sullivan hung with Andretti and on Lap 140 attempted the same move in the same place. This time Sullivan did not spin and for the next 60 laps, he kept Andretti at bay.

Andretti, whose handling got worse, could not challenge Sullivan. On Lap 200, Sullivan crossed the finish line and won the Indianapolis 500. Andretti finished second while Guerrero placed third. Al Unser brought his Penske-owned March home in fourth place, followed by Parsons, Rutherford, Luyendyk, Michael Andretti, Pimm and Howdy Holmes, who survived contact with Rich Vogler to finish in the top 10. Luyendyk was named Rookie of the Year.

For the time being, Indianapolis belonged to Sullivan. It was truly a case of being in the right place at the right time, knowing the right person and literally spinning for a win.

1986: Saving The Best for Last

In a lot of ways, the story of the 1986 Indianapolis 500 was the tale of two drivers – Bobby Rahal and Kevin Cogan.

Their careers seemed to parallel one another and yet following the '86 500, one driver's career would continue to rise while the other's career would begin a long decline.

In the late 1970s, *Road & Track Magazine* did a profile on six young road racers from America with the potential to make it to Formula One. Rahal and Cogan were among the six. They also represented the changing face of the big-name racing driver in America. Both went to college. Both were intelligent. Both were articulate.

Cogan made it to Indianapolis a year before Rahal and by season's end was the new driver to watch. Roger Penske inked Cogan to a contract and when the latter qualified next to teammate Rick Mears on the front row at Indy, the future looked bright indeed.

Of course, the bright future went away in a hurry after Cogan was involved in an accident at the start of the 1982 500 that eliminated Cogan and three other cars. For all practical purposes, Cogan's time at Penske was short-lived and by the end of the year, Al Unser was signed to take his place. Over the next three years, Cogan drove for Bignotti-Cotter, Gurney-Curb and Kraco Racing. For 1986, he signed with Patrick Racing.

Rahal, by contrast, remained with the Truesports and both improved with time. In fact, Rahal won two events in his rookie season of 1982 and scored enough high finishes to wind up second in the point standings. After that season, Rahal did fine everywhere he raced except Indianapolis.

He won races and pole positions each year and led laps at Indianapolis. But after four starts in the 500, his best finish was seventh in 1984. Despite his success as an Indy-car driver, he had to wonder if he was ever going to win at Indy.

Both came to the Speedway in 1986 with something to prove. Cogan was actually having a good year for a change. Starting fourth in the season opener at Phoenix, he went on to score his first Indy-car victory. Rahal, after winning three races and seven poles in 1985, opened the '86 season with a 16th at Phoenix and an 18th at Long Beach. On top of that, Rahal's team owner, Jim Trueman, was suffering from terminal cancer. Everyone connected with the Truesports operation knew what a victory at Indianapolis would mean to the stricken Trueman.

One thing was certain: both drivers were with good teams and each had the latest March-Cosworth.

March won 10 of 15 races in 1985 and its March 86C featured a triangular-shaped rollbar and a narrower nosecone.

Cosworth powered all of the new March chassis with the exception of the cars of Danny Ongais, Scott Brayton, Steve Chassey and John Paul, Jr., that used Buick power.

Lola's new T86/00 looked more like a March, but could be distinguished by its conventional rollbar.

Entering Lolas were Newman-Haas for Mario Andretti, Shierson Racing for Al Unser, Jr., Provimi Racing for Arie Luyendyk, Raynor Racing for Dennis Firestone, Dick Simon Racing for Simon and Raul Boesel and Galles Racing for Geoff Brabham, Pancho Carter and Roberto Moreno, a Brazilian rookie from F1 racing.

Dan Gurney's new Eagle also resembled the March and two chassis were entered for Dutch rookie Jan Lammers.

There was also a new kid on the block. After running March chassis for the past two years, Roger Penske turned to British

Above: Danny Ongais, Josele Garza, and A. J. Foyt in action, going into turn one.
Photograph: IMS

designer Alan Jenkins, who turned out the new Penske PC-15. What made this car stand out was its powerplant.

After coming up with a design for what they thought would be a better engine, former Cosworth engineers Mario Ilien and Paul Morgan approached Penske for assistance in starting up their company. Penske got Chevrolet interested and Ilmor was born. Ilmor's first project was what would ultimately become the Chevy Indy V-8 with Penske Racing getting exclusive use of the engine for the 1986 season.

Al Unser, the reigning national champion, was given the task of driving the new car. It made its debut at Phoenix, with Unser qualifying it a respectable seventh before retiring and finishing 18th. Despite winning two national titles in three years (including the previous year's by only one point over his son), Penske had Unser in a part-time role for 1986 with emphasis on developing the new chassis and engine.

The Indianapolis Motor Speedway also had a new look for 1986. Gone were the old wooden garages, some of which had been in use since the 1940s. Now facing north and south (instead of east and west) were three rows of rather nondescript concrete structures with 96 garages. Rows of buildings on three of the four sides of the complex became the new homes and hospitality suites for various accessory manufacturers.

In order to slow down the cars, new rules were once again in place for the 1986 designs and the cars were said to have 30 percent less downforce. Spring testing speeds indicated only a slight drop with Ongais topping 213 but most competitors in the range of 209-210. However, the records set in 1985 by Brayton and Carter would soon be in jeopardy.

On opening day, Michael Andretti set the pace with a 210.133 lap. Papa Mario topped the speed charts the next day with a 211.764.

Rick Mears would top 211 (211.118) on Monday, but it was his teammate, Unser, who attracted some attention. Driving the new Penske PC-15-Ilmor Chevrolet, Unser had a top lap of 208.044.

On Tuesday, Sullivan tied Andretti for top-speed honors with a 211.764. Unfortunately, the day's activities were marred by the serious accident involving Herm Johnson. Johnson lost control of the Menards March-Cosworth after a piece of the

car's bodywork flew off as he approached Turn 1. The car plowed into the wall, leaving Johnson with severe foot and ankle injuries and a lumbar spinal fracture. It was the second year in a row the Wisconsin driver was sidelined after a Turn 1 accident.

Speeds went up on Wednesday with the Penske March-Cosworths on top. Mears had the quickest lap of the day and the month at 214.694, with Sullivan close behind at 214.081. Michael Andretti was next at 213.725, followed by Rahal at 213.017 and Unser at 212.064 in the Penske-Chevy.

Fittipaldi joined Mears and Sullivan as all three topped 214 on Thursday. Mears was fastest at 214.592, followed by Sullivan at 214.285 and Fittipaldi at 214.193. Fittipaldi's teammate Cogan was right behind at 213.929.

On Friday before qualifying the Andrettis, Rahal and Sneva became the newest members of the 214-mph club. Mario had the day's fastest lap of 214.643. Mears went 214.592 with Rahal at 214.387, Michael at 214.132 and Sneva at 214.030.

Practice prior to qualifying belonged to the Penske team again. In the first group that went out at 8 a.m. on Saturday, Mears turned in an astounding 217.548. In the second practice group, Sullivan topped Mears with a 217.608. It was going to be a quick qualifying day at the Speedway.

Mario Andretti became the first to qualify and his average of 212.300 nearly eclipsed Carter's record of 212.583 for four laps. Sullivan was next.

On Lap 1, Sullivan broke the official one-lap record at 215.729. He went faster on Lap 2 at 215.755. He slowed on the next two laps at 215.636 and 214.413 but the four-lap average was a record of 215.382. He was on the pole – for now.

An hour later, it was time for Mears to run.

Mears set a new track record at 217.581 on the first lap. Lap 2 was 217.124. Lap 3 was 216.852 and the final lap was 215.765, for a new four-lap record of 216.828. Mears and Sullivan were 1-2. Michael Andretti joined them on Row 1 with an average of 214.522. The latest in a line of new rules to slow the cars did not slow them at all.

Rahal wound up fourth fastest at 213.550 and Al Unser

Paul, was able to join the 214 club with several laps in that range on Wednesday. Andretti's car suffered a suspension failure as he entered Turn 3 earlier that day. The car spun and slammed into the wall, leaving Andretti with lacerations on his left heel and abrasions on both knees.

He would be able to race in the 500, but there was question as to whether his already qualified car could be repaired. The rules stipulated that a qualified car that was wrecked would be allowed to start in its qualified position if repaired. If the car was unable to be repaired, the driver could use a backup car, but start at the rear of the field. Ultimately, the decision was made to run Andretti in the last row with a different car.

There were 24 Marches, eight Lolas and one Penske in the starting field. Cosworth powered 29 of the 33 starters with Buick powering three and the new Ilmor Chevy powering the other. With the exception of Krueger's '85 March, all other cars in the starting field were '86 models.

However, Carburetion Day's activity would alter the last two rows of the starting field.

With the 33 qualified cars and drivers using the two-hour practice session to run in a race setup, Carburetion Day had become a mini-version of the 500 with a crowded track and pit stop practice. Occasionally, a driver would have an accident.

On this particular Carb Day, Dennis Firestone had a major accident. Coming off of Turn 4, Firestone had a wheel rotor explode and hit the inside wall. His car continued to the pit entrance where it then impaled itself on the inside wall. Moreno was trailing Firestone when he spun, and he glanced off the inner retaining wall to avoid Firestone's car. Moreno's car then slid into the pits where it struck the parked cars of Snider and Garza. Moreno's car then came to a stop in his own pit! Firestone miraculously escaped with minor injuries, as did two mechanics and a spectator.

But Firestone was out of the race. He did not a have a registered backup car to substitute and although there was a spirited attempt to repair the car, it was ultimately withdrawn.

Dick Simon, who had been bumped on the final day, was back in the starting field as 34th-fastest qualifier and first alternate. It was the second time in three years an alternate would start the 500.

The accident also rearranged the starting grid as the damage to the other three cars necessitated a change to new cars. Andretti, who was to have started 33rd, was now starting 30th with Snider, Moreno and Simon on the last row.

Where the 1986 Indianapolis 500 is concerned, history was not only made in track records. Mother Nature established her own "first."

Intermittent rain forced the postponement of the race on Sunday, May 25. Rain precluded any running on Monday so a decision had to be made as to whether to hold the race on Tuesday or hold it the following weekend. Normally, race organizers attempt to hold an event that has been postponed on the next possible day. In 1973, rain turned the race into a three-day affair.

There were a number of considerations. One was television. For the first time in 37 years, the Indianapolis 500 would be televised live. In 1949, local network WFBM televised the event locally. Since 1971, ABC had offered same-day coverage of the race with the telecast aired during prime time. The belief was that the race would get better national ratings on the weekend.

Another consideration was the annual week-after-Indy race at Milwaukee. Milwaukee's promoters agreed to postpone their race (which enticed its fans by letting them be first to see the new 500 winner) and finally the decision was made to hold the race on Saturday, May 31, with Sunday as a backup day should the rain return. Fortunately, it did not.

Inset above: Rahal is the first winner to experience a new victory enclosure. This one is actually in the pit area, at the point where all winners since 1971 have turned left in order to be pushed up a ramp. The winner now drives on to a platform which is then raised into the air by a scissor-like mechanism, after which the platform can be partially rotated. At left is "500" Festival Queen Wendy Barth, whose mother, the former Diane Hunt, was the "500" Festival queen when A. J. Foyt won his first Indianapolis race in 1961.

Photograph: IMS

qualified fifth in the new Penske-Chevy at 212.295.

Cogan joined them on the second row with a 211.922 average.

A total of 23 cars qualified on Saturday and five more joined the field on Sunday. One of the second-day qualifiers provided one of the better stories of the month.

Phil Krueger had been entered in the Leader Card team's year-old March. Krueger's job was two-fold. Not only was he the driver, he also effectively served as his own chief mechanic for much of the month, making him a throwback to days long gone at Indianapolis.

The second week of practice would be highlighted by the newly found speed of Jim Crawford in the March-Buick and the accident of Mario Andretti. Crawford, who had replaced

On Friday, there was a one-hour practice session that was closed to the public. Because drivers were required to run under yellow-flag conditions, only 24 of the 33 starters took advantage of the session.

Race Day Part III was a beautiful day and everyone knew the race would be held.

But this had been an unusual year and as the cars rounded Turn 2 on the pace lap, Tom Sneva's car suddenly snapped sideways and struck the inside wall. The red flag came out. Sneva was out of the race before it even started, the apparent victim of a broken CV joint.

Finally the race got started. Like Rick Mears in 1985, Michael Andretti used the outside of Row 1 to jump into the lead, staying there for 42 laps. Andretti had scored his first Indy-car victory the previous month at Long Beach and he was eager to score one at Indianapolis.

His father was an early exit on Lap 19 with handling problems. Cogan, Al Unser, Jr., and Fittipaldi all took turns leading the race and it wasn't until Lap 49 that polesitter Mears finally got the lead. He would stay there for the next 25 laps before pit stops jumbled the standings and saw Rahal, Cogan, Al Unser, Jr., and Mears also lead.

The second half of the race featured a battle between Rahal and Mears with Cogan running a strong third.

On Lap 188, Cogan passed both and took the lead for the next seven laps. He was pulling away when Luyendyk brushed the wall inside of Turn 4 and ended up in the entrance to the pit lane. That brought the caution out for two laps and allowed Rahal and Mears to pull up behind Cogan. When Cogan brought the field down for the restart on the completion of Lap 198, Rahal moved to the inside and passed for the lead right before the start-finish line.

With no one to balk him, Rahal stood on the throttle and slowly pulled away from Cogan. In about a minute and a half, Rahal crossed the line to deliver a much-deserved victory to his terminally ill owner, who remained on the scoring stand the entire race. Ahead of Cogan by 1.441 seconds at the checker, Rahal had also set the race's fastest lap, on Lap 200 at 209.152. It was the first time in the history of the race that the fastest lap had been set by the winner on the final lap.

Mears wound up a close third (1.881 seconds behind Rahal) and it marked the closest three-way finish in the history of the 500. Guerrero finished fourth followed by Al Unser, Jr., Michael Andretti, Fittipaldi, Rutherford, Sullivan and Randy Lanier, who was named top rookie.

As Rahal reached the victory enclave, he stopped onto a checkered platform. Newly constructed at the Speedway, the platform employed a scissor-style lift system that allowed more spectators a view of the victory celebration.

On hand to greet the victor was 500 Festival Queen Wendy Barth, whose mother, Diane Hunt Barth, had been 500 Queen 25 years earlier. Joining them were Rahal's wife Debi,

and infant daughter Michaela, whose victorious father hoisted her over his head for all to see.

Knowing what lay ahead for Trueman made it hard for one to feel sorry for Cogan, who had come so close to winning racing's biggest prize. And yet, with a victory at Phoenix and a near miss at Indianapolis, one could only hope it would be the start of bigger and better things for Cogan.

Only 11 days after Rahal's victory, Jim Trueman passed away.

Rahal used the 500 victory as a springboard to five more wins and the 1986 national championship. He would go on to win the title two more times. Cogan, by contrast, would have a mixed season but still wind up sixth overall in the points, his best finish since 1982 when he drove for Penske.

Both men had saved their best for the last laps of the 1986 race.

Below: The camaraderie in the Trueman camp, combined with the crowd's awareness of Jim Trueman's declining health condition, makes the Bobby Rahal victory hugely popular.

Main photograph: Kevin Cogan passed Bobby Rahal late in the race and is apparently headed for victory until a lap-195 caution period, after which he will be outmaneuvered by Rahal.
Photographs: IMS

Above and right: Kevin Cogan is one of a handful of drivers who have led lap 197 of the "500," and not won the race. Once described as being "star-crossed," he will eventually compete in 12 "500s" and survive several spectacular accidents, but finish second in 1986, fourth as a "rookie" in 1981, and fifth in 1983.
Photographs: IMS

Chapter 14
WELCOME TO OUR SHOW FOR CHEVROLET

1987: From Hotel Lobby To Victory Lane

AL UNSER was not exactly looking at retirement in 1987, but it certainly appeared that Roger Penske intended to put his two-time national champion out to pasture. After spending part of the 1986 season developing Penske's new PC-15 chassis along with the new Ilmor Chevy Indy V-8, Unser took a back seat to Penske regulars Rick Mears and Danny Sullivan, who raced the new car/engine combination in the final events of 1986.

For the 1987 Indianapolis 500, Penske would have new PC-16s powered by the Ilmor Chevy for Mears, Sullivan and Danny Ongais, whose Panavision sponsorship helped secure the ride. The team had not planned to run four drivers, so Unser became the odd man out.

Penske also entered three March 86Cs, two of which were powered by Chevrolet. The third March, which Penske had no intention of using, was still powered by Cosworth. In fact, the car was booked for a hotel lobby in Reading, Pennsylvania, where the Penske team was based.

Unser showed up for the opening weekend of practice looking for a ride, but soon returned to Albuquerque after failing to find anything promising.

Penske Racing wasn't the only team to use the new Ilmor Chevrolet, but with Roger Penske controlling a major interest in the company, he had the say-so over which team could use it. Indy-car racing was about to enter the era of the engine lease.

First to "qualify" for an engine were Newman-Haas Racing and Patrick Racing. Newman-Haas returned to Indianapolis with the latest Lola T87/00 chassis and driver Mario Andretti, while Patrick entered Marlboro-sponsored March 87Cs for Emerson Fittipaldi and Kevin Cogan.

Lola users enjoyed a reasonable amount of success since the company's return to Indy-car racing in 1983 with Newman-Haas as its factory representative. The 1987 season looked to be somewhat of a downturn in Lola's popularity, but that would soon change.

March made some changes to its new Indy car. Most notable was the conventional rollbar that replaced the distinctive triangular version on the 86C. However, March was about to suffer from the defection of its top engineer, Adrian Newey. Newey, the most sought-after engineer amongst the March set, was heading to Formula One.

The Galles Marches stood out on the entry list. The Marches of Geoff Brabham and Jeff MacPherson used Brabham-Honda power. Developed by Englishman John Judd, the V-8 project also involved Jack Brabham and marked Honda's first "unofficial" foray into Indy-car racing. The Honda factory team had previously visited the Speedway. In 1968, Ronnie Bucknum ran John Surtees' Honda F1 car (complete with a high-strut rear wing) during an impromptu test session. It was believed the success of the Galles/Judd/Brabham project would entice Honda to make a full-fledged effort.

Despite its success in qualifying two years earlier, the Buick failed to make inroads even with a more affordable price than a Cosworth or an Ilmor Chevrolet lease.

The track opened for practice and before the weekend was over, it was evident that it would be a most eventful month. Pancho Carter set the tone of things to come.

On Sunday, Carter spun between Turns 3 and 4 and suddenly got airborne. The car turned upside down and then landed on its rollbar before coming to rest against the outside wall. Other than scrapes on his helmet and damage to the rollbar, the car was in remarkably good shape. Carter was also unhurt.

After years of testing, Goodyear finally decided to use its radial tire at Indianapolis. Thanks to Michelin, radial tires had been de rigueur in F1 since the late 1970s. Radials had been used on other tracks, but Indianapolis represented the first effort for an Indy-car superspeedway. In 1985, Goodyear's attempt to introduce them at Michigan ended in disaster with several tire-related accidents and the postponement of that year's race. They would end up playing a major role in the month of May.

For the most part, the tires worked well. That is, they worked well on the Lola chassis and the March 86C. For some reason, those using the 87C found the new tires a handful. The trouble began once practice began in earnest and the story always seemed to be the same: the driver went high in the turn and struck the wall. In most of the aforementioned cases, the driver maintained the car simply stopped turning.

Cogan was the first, hitting the wall in Turn 1 on May 6. Later that day, Brayton hit the wall in Turn 4. And before the day was over, Daly brushed the south chute. On May 8, the Turn 1 wall got Tom Sneva, who crashed his backup car there two days later. With the cars hitting speeds at over 200 mph, most were big accidents. There were complaints from other drivers who had a "moment" but were able to avoid crashing.

Not every accident could be blamed on the tire situation with the new March chassis as no less than seven drivers crashed older Marches during the month.

The numerous accidents involving the new March sent many teams scampering for their 1986 models. Of course, not everyone wrecked. Guerrero, Luyendyk and Barbazza went the entire month free of trouble.

And the March was not the only car to crash during May. The newly formed Raynor team went through three Lolas thanks to major accidents by drivers Dennis Firestone and Phil Krueger. As the final weekend of qualifying drew near, the Raynor had run out of cars and for all practical purposes withdrew from the event.

In between the unusually high number of accidents (25 for the month), there was also practice and predictably high speeds.

Mario Andretti established himself early as a pole contender with a top lap of 213.371 on opening weekend. Bobby Rahal made a Lola 1-2 with the weekend's second fastest lap at 212.464.

Two days later, the attention would focus on speed. More specifically, the attention was focused on Mario Andretti's speed after the 1969 500 winner turned in a lap at 218.204, the fastest unofficial lap in Speedway history. With three more days of practice until qualifying, the 220-mph mark suddenly seemed to be achievable.

After running only 216.502 on Wednesday, Andretti turned in the month's fastest at 218.234 mph on Thursday. Rahal once again appeared to be the only one capable of staying near Andretti. The reigning 500 winner turned in his fastest of the month at 216.502.

On Friday, the focus returned to safety as Ongais crashed heavily in the new Penske-Ilmor Chevy. Ongais slammed into the Turn 4 wall, got airborne and slid along the top of the wall for 80 feet, and then slid into the pit entrance. He sustained a serious head injury and would be sidelined for the month.

The new Penske was under assault from another front – Penske himself. With Mears the fastest in the new Penske at 211, the decision was made to see what kind of speeds he could turn with a year-old Chevrolet-powered March 86C. With little time in the car, Mears topped the 209 mark. He would qualify the March and then park the Penske.

With sunny, breezy and warm weather conditions, Mario Andretti's quest for 220 was momentarily stalled as he could only muster at 216.242. Rahal ran 215.568 but he had company. Luyendyk ran a 214.951—the fastest lap for a March 87C-Cosworth – while Jim Crawford showed the Buick's potential with a 214.438.

But instead of going faster in the pre-qualifying warmup, everyone went slower, including Andretti, whose 215.879 topped both practice groups. With a number of drivers waving off their attempts, Mario became the third qualifier and as predicted, he emerged with the pole position. Andretti's average was 215.390, but even with everyone slowing down, he

was 2 mph faster than anyone else.

After a few unsuccessful qualifying attempts and a brief practice period, Crawford returned to the qualifying line to make his second attempt of the day. He had been expected to challenge for a spot on the front row, but his run failed to go beyond Turn 1 of his first lap. The Scotsman entered the corner and did a 360-degree spin before the striking the wall almost head-on. He suffered serious leg and ankle injuries and was airlifted to Methodist Hospital for surgery by Dr. Terry Trammell.

Crawford's accident in the ARS March 86C-Buick was apparently the result of a faulty tachometer. Since Indy cars of the time did not carry speedometers, drivers would often use the tach as a reference point for speed. Crawford's team estimated he entered Turn 1 in excess of 230 mph.

Two drivers not bothered by the new March turned in solid runs to make the field. Roberto Guerrero, who scored his first Indy-car victory earlier in the season at Phoenix, had the fourth-fastest speed with an average of 210.680. Luyendyk appeared to have a 210 average, but dropped off considerably on Lap 3 and wound up with a 208.337 average, good for seventh spot.

A.J. Foyt, who had been overlooked during the month, opened his qualifying run with an electrifying 212.259. He followed up with a trio of 210 laps for an average of 210.935 that placed on the inside of Row 2. In doing so, Foyt had qualified for his 30th straight Indianapolis 500!

The second week of practice was eventful – highlighted by another major accident, a pair of driver announcements and a car change for an already qualified driver.

On May 14, Johnny Parsons slammed into the Turn 1 wall. Parsons' accident looked eerily like Crawford's wreck and like Crawford, he also suffered serious foot and leg injuries.

Two former 500 winners wound up with rides.

Named to replace the injured Ongais was Al Unser, who drove for Penske from 1983 to 1986. In all likelihood, Unser, probably the only driver the Penske team would have selected under the circumstances, was suddenly back in demand. Earlier, Unser had turned down the ride vacated by the injured Crawford. That ride would now go to Gordon Johncock, who had reconsidered his 1985 decision to retire.

Later in the week, it was confirmed that Sullivan would be withdrawing the Penske he had qualified and attempt to qualify a March 86C-Ilmor Chevrolet. With Sullivan using the team's last available Ilmor Chevrolet, Unser would be given a March 86C-Cosworth, that had started its month of May in the lobby of a hotel in Reading, Pennsylvania.

Unser and Johncock would qualify on the second weekend, with Sullivan recording the fastest average at 210.271. Unser managed to outqualify his son and namesake, who struggled all month with his new March.

The starting field was composed of 28 March chassis (11 86C models and 17 87C models) and five Lolas. Cosworth supplied power for 21 cars with five cars using the new Ilmor Chevrolet, four using the turbocharged Buick V-6, two using Honda and George Snider's car using a turbocharged V-6 Chevrolet.

After a major accident on Carburetion Day in 1986 altered the starting field, it was expected that Carburetion Day 1987 would be uneventful. But since May 1987 was a very eventful month, it was no surprise that someone would heavily damage a car on the final practice day of the month.

What was surprising was that it was two drivers of stature – Foyt and Fittipaldi. Foyt spun and hit the wall between Turns 1 and 2. He was uninjured and the car was believed to be repairable by Race Day. Fittipaldi was not so lucky. He spun and hit the wall between Turns 3 and 4 but damaged his car so severely the decision was made to use his backup and have him start last. Michael Andretti and Tony Bettenhausen also made contact in the pits with Andretti's car suffering slight suspension damage.

Predictably, Mario was quickest at 211.515 and after the two-hour session, his crew captured the Miller Pit Stop Competition. Now all Mario had to do was win the race.

At the start of the race, Mario Andretti jumped into the lead, but by the time the field got to Turn 1, the yellow came on. Josele Garza spun and was missed by everyone except

Left: Late in the race, the eliminated Danny Sullivan senses victory for his Penske teammate.

Below: The brand-new electronic signboards flash another history-making message.
Photographs: IMS

Carter, his teammate. Snider was already out of the race before it started, with an oil leak.

Andretti led the first 27 laps with Mears, Rahal and Guerrero in tow. Another driver was slowly and quietly moving up in the pack. After nearly collecting the spinning Garza on Lap 1, Al Unser settled in for one of his typically smooth Sunday afternoon drives at Indy.

Starting 20th, Unser was fifth by Lap 60 and firmly ensconced among the lead pack from that point on. Even with his forward progress, however, his year-old March was no match for the flying Andretti in his new Lola-Ilmor Chevrolet.

Andretti would only surrender the lead when he pitted and by Lap 177, he had been in front for 171 laps! Suddenly, Chief Announcer Tom Carnegie's voice boomed: "Mario is slowing down."

With a lead of more than a lap over Guerrero and two laps over Unser, now third, Andretti's engine had suffered some sort of electrical malfunction. His bid for a second 500 was over once again.

Guerrero was firmly in the lead, but his drive had not been without problems. On Lap 131, Tony Bettenhausen's car lost its right front wheel and Guerrero punted it into the stand between Turns 3 and 4. On the top row, a Wisconsin spectator named Lyle Kurtenbach was the only person standing. The unfortunate Kurtenbach was struck by the wheel and killed. He was the first spectator to lose his life in a race-related accident since 1938.

Guerrero's car suffered minor damage, but he was able to maintain second position until Andretti's demise promoted him into the lead. On Lap 182, he made his final pit stop. What Guerrero did not know was that the contact with the wheel had damaged the fluid reserve container for his clutch. With no clutch fluid (or clutch), Guerrero stalled his car.

Unser sailed past to unlap himself. He came down the front straightaway with Guerrero still stranded in the pits. From unemployed driver to substitute, Unser was now in position to win a fourth Indianapolis 500. Guerrero was finally able to rejoin the race, but the stop required 68.6 seconds and the Colombian was now a lap down to Unser. Guerrero was able to pass Unser and unlap himself, but time was running out. He needed help. He soon got it.

On Lap 192, the yellow came out for Andretti, who tried to rejoin the race, but stalled in Turn 4. Guerrero was able to go around to the back of the pack. Through most of the race, he had been ahead of Unser. With the green coming out at the completion of Lap 196, he had four laps to get by six cars and attempt to pass Unser.

It was not to be. With a clear track, Unser poured it on and crossed the line to join Foyt as the only four-time winner in Speedway history. In leading Lap 200, Unser also supplanted Ralph DePalma as the all-time lap leader with 613 laps led.

Guerrero came home runner-up for the second time in four years. Despite a spin, Barbazza finished an impressive third to capture the top rookie honor. Al Unser, Jr., brought his ill-handling March home in fourth and Gary Bettenhausen wound up fifth to record his second-best finish at Indianapolis. Dick Simon was sixth for his best Indy finish and Fox was seventh to lead the way for the Foyt team. Rounding out the top 10 were MacPherson, Mario Andretti (who still recorded enough laps to merit a ninth-place finish) and Tony Bettenhausen.

For Unser, the victory was something of a vindication. All but retired by Penske, he was now going to be back in demand as a four-time 500 winner. The Ilmor Chevrolet engine may not have won the race, but everyone knew it would be a matter of time before it did. Time would also be on the side of Lola, whose ranks were about to swell with a number of owners abandoning their March chassis. The Buick was getting stronger, Honda was there and rumor had it that Porsche was planning its own Indy project.

The win also provided a footnote of sorts. Between 1931 and 1952, Cummins Engine Co. spent thousands of dollars trying to win the 500 with a Diesel-powered vehicle. Now, at the very last minute, through its Holset turbocharger division, it was the winning sponsor

Above: Rick Mears makes it three, and Roger Penske appears uncharacteristically ecstatic. At left is IMS President Joseph R. Cloutier, a key member of the managerial staff during the entire Hulman regime.
Photographs: IMS

1988: A Pair Of Firsts For Penske

There's an old saying that the "third time's a charm." With the Penske PC-15 and -16s failing to win a race, it was time to make some changes. At Penske Racing, that meant that the new Penske PC-17 would have a new design engineer. Out went Alan Jenkins and in his place was an Englishman named Nigel Bennett. The new Penske promised to be an improvement over its predecessors.

Al Unser's victory for the team at Indianapolis in 1987 was so popular, the 48-year-old driver was "unretired" by Penske for the 1988 season – sort of. With sponsorship from Hertz, Unser would run a third Penske at select races with Rick Mears once again piloting the Pennzoil entry and Danny Sullivan continuing with Miller.

Despite some defections, March returned to the fray with its latest model, the 88C. This car was a collaborative effort between company founder Robin Herd and Alan Mertens, although the latter was about to form his own engineering firm with team owner Rick Galles.

Mertens was assigned to the Galles team that once again employed Al Unser, Jr. Galles became the latest team to be allowed to lease the Ilmor Chevy engine, now officially known as the Chevy Indy V-8.

Also using the new March chassis were Patrick Racing for Emerson Fittipaldi, Kraco Racing for Michael Andretti, Machinists Union for Kevin Cogan, Alex Morales for Howdy Holmes, Gohr Racing for rookie Billy Vukovich III and Porsche Motorsports for Teo Fabi.

The latter entry was long awaited. Porsche tested engines with the Interscope team in the early 1980s and the original Interscope chassis was supposedly designed to take the Porsche flat-six. That project fell through, but Porsche maintained an interest in running in Indy-car competition.

Near the end of the 1987 season, Porsche unveiled its new chassis and engine. The car made a less-than-impressive debut at Laguna Seca with Al Unser. Team principal Al Holbert wound up driving it at the season finale in Miami. Holbert failed to qualify the car, the chassis was scrapped and Porsche commissioned March to design a special tub to accommodate its engine.

The Honda name was gone, but the engine remained in the series. At Honda's request to avoid making it look like a factory effort, it was now called the Judd. The Truesports and Hemelgarn teams signed to use the engines.

After having five of its chassis qualify for the 1987 500, Lola made a number of gains in customers for 1988.

Mario Andretti was back in the Newman-Haas Lola-Chevrolet after nearly winning his second 500 the previous year. Other entrants running new Lolas were Truesports for Bobby Rahal, Shierson Racing for Raul Boesel, Dick Simon Racing for Simon and Arie Luyendyk, Leader Card Racers for Randy Lewis, Mike Curb Motorsports for John Andretti, Vince Granatelli Racing for Roberto Guerrero and Hemelgarn Racing for Ludwig Heimrath, Jr., Scott Brayton and Tom Sneva.

Guerrero had been seriously injured in a test crash at Indianapolis the previous fall. After striking the Turn 2 wall, Guerrero had been hit by a wheel and was in a coma for several days. He recovered and made an impressive return to the cockpit, finishing second in the season opener at Phoenix.

Lola's design team came up with a chassis for every engine. Besides the Chevrolet for Newman-Haas and the Judd engine for Rahal and Sneva, there was a Buick chassis for Brayton. All of the other new Lola users had Cosworth engines.

Despite suffering serious leg and ankle injuries the previous May, Crawford was able to recover and resumed his job as development driver for Buick. In fact, he still needed a cane to be able to walk. Indianapolis would be his only race of the year as boost rules kept the engine from being competitive on the CART circuit.

Two of the rookies on the entry list bore names from famous racing families. Billy Vukovich III was bidding to become the first third-generation starter in the Indianapolis 500. His grandfather, Bill Vukovich, was a two-time 500 winner who lost his life while leading the 1955 race. His father raced in 12 500s and finished second in the 1973 500. John Andretti was the son of Mario Andretti's twin brother, Aldo. Aldo Andretti had actually participated in tire tests prior to the 1967 500, but never got the opportunity to practice or qualify for the race. In addition to their pedigree, both rookies came to Indianapolis with strong credentials.

It didn't take long for one of the new Penskes to top the charts and grab the headlines. After posting the quickest lap on the third day of practice at 213.118 mph, Mears followed up the next day with a truly astounding 220.048. Another barrier had fallen, albeit an unofficial one.

But Mears wasn't alone in the speed department. Right behind him was Mario Andretti, who recorded a lap at 219.887 on Tuesday and then moved the goalposts on Wednesday with a 221.565. The two combatants only went 219 on Thursday and then tied for top speed honors on Friday at 221.456.

Qualifying was appearing to be more and more a battle royal between Mears and Andretti. Sullivan was the next-closest competitor on the charts at 218.446. Al Unser, in the third Penske, was biding his time with a top lap in the 215 range. But he would have a surprise for qualifying.

The three Penske drivers seemed to enjoy an unusual camaraderie for teammates and this would show when the first day of qualifying was over. In morning warmup, Mario Andretti paced the first group with a lap at 220.372. Mears went out with the second group and returned with an even more astounding 222.827. He was the man to beat for the pole, but he would have to wait until Andretti and his teammates qualified.

The 1969 500 winner turned in a disappointing run with an average of 214.692. (Andretti blamed the oil-dry left on the track from an accident in Turn 4.)

Unser was first of the Penske trio to qualify and emerged with the pole, averaging 215.270. Now it was Sullivan's turn, and the 1985 winner knocked the defending race winner off the pole. After an opening lap at 217.334, Sullivan set a new track record at 217.749. That would be his only record as he slowed on the next laps for an average of 216.214. Team Penske was 1-2 in qualifying with Mears yet to run. He would not disappoint.

Lap 1 was a new track record of 220.453. It would be his best as he slowed to 219.887, 218.7 and 217.7. The four-lap average was a record 219.198 as Mears pushed his teammates aside. Mears had captured the pole for the fourth time and in doing so, tied Rex Mays and A.J. Foyt for winning the most pole positions at Indianapolis.

The qualifying effort of the Penske team was a milestone in Speedway history. In the past, other teams had qualified their cars in the first two spots (including Penske in 1982). To have all three of its entries in the first spots was unprecedented.

The successful attempts to qualify by rookies Vukovich III and Andretti allowed them to make history. Young Vukovich became the first third-generation member of a family to qualify at the Speedway. Andretti's inclusion in the starting field meant that for the second time, three members of the same family would be starting an Indianapolis 500. However, it would be the first time that a father (Mario) would be racing against his son (Michael) and nephew (John).

Fabi, the track-record-setting pole winner in 1983, made history of sorts by qualifying the Porsche team's entry in 17th position. It marked the first factory effort at Indianapolis by a German firm since 1923.

Two other noteworthy qualifying performances belonged to Phil Krueger and Steve Chassey. In each case, the driver had unofficially served as his own chief mechanic. The teams of R. Kent Baker (Krueger's owner) and Gary Trout were what could be described as "shoestring efforts." In an age of designers, engineers, team managers, chief mechanics and crew chiefs, to have two drivers that involved in the preparation of their cars on minimal budgets was incredible.

In terms of equipment, Lola led the way with 18 of the 33 starters using either 1987 or '88 models. Dropping to second for the first time in years was March with 12 cars – seven in 88Cs, three 86Cs and two 87Cs. Penske provided the other three cars – the front row.

In the engine department, there were 20 Cosworths, six Chevy Indy V-8s, three Buicks, two Judds, one Porsche and one turbocharged Chevrolet V-6.

The starting field also featured one of the more international lineups in history with representatives from eight foreign countries: Brazil (Fittipaldi and Boesel), Scotland (Crawford), Holland (Luyendyk), Finland (Tero Palmroth), Canada (Ludwig Heimrath, Jr.), Italy (Fabi), Ireland (Daly) and Colombia (Guerrero).

Rick Mears may have been on the pole and he may have been perceived as the team leader, but when the green flag dropped, it was Sullivan in the middle of Row 1 who shot into the lead. Mears and Unser followed and the 72nd Indianapolis 500 was underway.

However, it didn't take long for the yellow to come out. Exiting Turn 2, Scott Brayton's car swapped ends and he slid into the outer wall. Guerrero had nowhere to go and was collected by Brayton's car. Further up the track, Tony Bettenhausen got on the brakes only to lose control and strike the wall all by himself. Less than one lap into the race, the 33-car field was reduced to 30 cars.

No one was injured and once the wreckage was cleared, the race resumed with Sullivan beginning to pull away. In fact, the 1985 winner had everything going his way during the first half of the race. With the new PC-17 clearly the class of the field, Sullivan poured it on and had almost a full-lap lead on his nearest rival – Mears.

Porsche's initial expedition to Indianapolis ended when Fabi's car shed its left rear wheel in the pit lane following a pit stop on Lap 32. Although the car was not yet up to speed, it sustained enough damage to merit its withdrawal from the race.

Unfortunately for Sullivan, it was not going to be his day to win. With an on-board TV camera to document his problem, his right front wing began to flutter as he entered Turn 1 on Lap

Below: Teammates Rick Mears, Danny Sullivan, and Al Unser occupy the entire front row and lead 192 of the 200 laps, the only eight they don't lead being captured by Buick V-6 driver Jim Crawford (car 15), who is still recovering from severe foot and ankle injuries sustained the previous year. He will finish sixth.

Bottom: Defending "500" champion Al Unser is chased by his namesake son.
Photographs: IMS

259

Above: **Victory-bound Mears is trailed by Dominic Dobson, Howdy Holmes, and eventual eighth-place finisher Phil Krueger, who prepared his own car almost single-handedly.**
Photograph: IMS

107. The wing finally gave way and Sullivan's car drifted right into the wall between Turns 1 and 2. The crumpled Penske came to a rest in Turn 2 and Sullivan's day was finished.

The man now firmly in command was Mears, with teammate Al Unser in second. An unprecedented 1-2-3 finish for Penske may have been spoiled, but Mears and Unser appeared to have a handle on the remainder of the field to save the team's honor.

One man would spoil that – Fittipaldi. His day was not without its pratfalls. Early in the race, the Brazilian had been penalized a lap for a pit infraction. Thanks to his speed and a little luck with some caution periods, Fittipaldi was able to get back onto the lead lap.

Unser also had a couple of "moments." While lapping his son, the younger Unser apparently did not realize his father was passing on the inside of Turn 2. The two cars nearly touched, but both continued without incident. Later, while exiting Turn 2, Unser's car collected a rabbit that unsuccessfully tried to cross the track. Unser heard the thump, but had no idea what happened. A subsequent pit stop showed no damage, only some slight remains of the unfortunate rabbit.

With two laps to go, Mears was firmly in command with Fittipaldi and Unser following. Then the caution came out for debris. Bodywork on Michael Andretti's car had come loose after flapping a number of laps, landing on the main straightaway. The yellow flag allowed Fittipaldi and Unser to close up behind Mears, but there was no time for a restart. This race would finish under caution.

Michael Andretti finished fourth with Bobby Rahal fifth and Jim Crawford sixth. Crawford, the only non-Penske driver to lead the race, ran as high as third before losing valuable track position on his final pit stop. Crawford's team was unable to change the right rear tire, but he was still able to bring the car home in sixth.

Initially, Crawford was listed on the scoring pylon as finishing third. As the post-race celebration continued, he ultimately dropped down to sixth. It didn't matter as the Scotsman was euphoric about the drive. And considering his injuries suffered a year earlier, it was an incredible performance.

Rounding out the top 10 were Boesel, Krueger, Simon and Luyendyk. Vukovich wound up 14th and earned the top rookie honor.

It would be an incredible payday for Mears, who was awarded a record $809,853. It would also be a milestone for the Speedway, which for the first time was offering a purse in excess of $5 million ($5,025,399).

Mears was now a three-time winner and Roger Penske's new car dominated at Indy. In addition to occupying the entire front row and finishing in two of the top three positions, Mears, Sullivan and Unser led a combined 192 of the race's 200 laps.

In the case of the PC-17, the third time truly was a charm.

1989: The Million-Dollar Bump

A year makes all the difference in the world, especially in the sport of Indy-car racing.

For 1989, competitors found a newly paved Indianapolis Motor Speedway that promised even faster speeds than the previous year's record-setting month of May.

There was another change to the landscape, one that tied the past to the present. The previous summer, as part of the demolition of the former Prest-O-Lite plant, the chimney that could be seen by drivers as they headed down the main straightaway was also taken down. A Speedway landmark since 1913, drivers used the direction of the smoke in lieu of a windsock to determine which way the wind was blowing. In recent years, a windsock had been added to the scoring pylon.

Lola continued making inroads in the customer-car ranks as March concentrated on making specialty chassis for Porsche and eventually Alfa Romeo.

After dominating at Indianapolis, the new Penske PC-17 failed to follow up as spectacularly in the remaining races of 1988. But Danny Sullivan put together enough strong finishes to capture the championship. For 1989, Penske would return to Indy with its latest model – the PC-18 – and its driver lineup from '88: Rick Mears, Al Unser and Sullivan. There was another Penske to consider as well.

In a multimillion-dollar deal with Philip Morris, Marlboro would sponsor Unser's car, as well as the Patrick Racing entry for Emerson Fittipaldi. Fittipaldi would join Penske for 1990, but in the meantime, his team would get to run the latest Penske chassis. Pennzoil would continue as Mears' primary sponsor with Miller sponsoring Sullivan. Patrick was also in the process of selling his team to former driver Chip Ganassi.

The Penske PC-17s were sold to Arciero Racing for Belgian rookie Didier Theys and Todd Walther Racing for Phil Krueger. Cosworths would power these older Penskes, despite the fact the car had been designed around the more compact Chevy Indy V-8.

With the lease situation governing the usage of Ilmor-designed engines, Chevrolets would go to Penske Racing's trio, Patrick Racing and Fittipaldi, Galles and Al Unser, Jr., and the newly expanded Newman-Haas team of Mario and Michael Andretti. After running for Kraco for five years, Michael fulfilled his father's dream of having the two run as teammates. They made a formidable team.

The most prevalent chassis was Lola, with the new T8900 entered by Newman-Haas for the two Andrettis, Galles for Unser, Jr., Shierson Racing for Raul Boesel, A.J. Foyt Enterprises for Foyt, Andale Racing for Mexican rookie Bernard Jourdain, Truesports Racing for rookie Scott Pruett, Protofab Racing for Canadian rookie John Jones, Raynor Racing for Derek Daly, Dick Simon Racing for Arie Luyendyk, Leader Card Racers for Pancho Carter, Kraco Racing for Bobby Rahal and TeamKar International for Randy Lewis.

One of the shockers of 1989 was the departure of Rahal from Truesports, the only Indy-car team he had raced for since 1982. Rahal and Truesports won the 1986 and '87 national titles as well as the '86 Indy 500. But the death of team owner Jim Trueman in 1986 and the team's switch to Judd engines in 1988 were enough to make Rahal consider a change of venue. Ironically, Rahal gave the Judd its only Indy-car victory at Pocono, but coming on the heels of back-to-back championships, one victory was not enough to convince Rahal to stay with the team.

Rahal was enticed to join Kraco on the promise that it would soon be leasing the much-vaunted Chevy Indy V-8. Taking his place at Truesports was Pruett, a successful Trans-Am driver who impressed in his previous Indy-car drives.

Entering Lola T88/00s were Euromotorsports for Davy Jones, Gohr Racing for Tero Palmroth, Bayside Motorsports for Dominic Dobson, Vince Granatelli Racing for Tom Sneva and John Andretti, and Hemelgarn Racing for Billy Vukovich III, Ludwig Heimrath, Jr., and Gordon Johncock.

Kenny Bernstein Racing returned with a 1987 Lola-Buick for Jim Crawford and newcomer David Mann also entered a 1987 Lola-Buick for Gary Bettenhausen.

Although the Alex Morales Autosports team entered a March-Alfa Romeo for Roberto Guerrero, the new car would not be unveiled until June in Detroit. Guerrero would be a spectator as his contract prohibited him from driving for anyone else. There was a new March at the Speedway in 1989 with its long-wheelbase 89P for the Porsche team and driver Teo Fabi. Ex-McLaren man Gordon Coppuck designed the new car exclusively for Porsche, which had used a 1988 model altered to house its engine the previous year.

The team was undergoing a transformation. Sports-car ace Al Holbert was the driving force behind the project, but perished in a private airplane crash the previous summer. Derrick Walker was now the team's principal.

Cosworth continued to power most of the entries, but the company also attempted to stem a flood of defectors with its new short-stroke version called the DFS. Dick Simon Racing had one of the new engines for Luyendyk and Kraco Racing had one for Rahal.

The track opened for practice on May 6 and was significantly affected by weather, although not the type one normally experiences at Indianapolis in May. Arie Luyendyk got the honor for top speed at 213.675, but the track was shut down early for snow! The National Weather Service measured an accumulation of .2 of an inch, the first measurable snowfall in May in 29 years.

On Sunday, it was slightly warmer but at least it was dry and Fittipaldi topped the list with a 221.347. Michael Andretti and Al Unser, Jr., were close behind at 220 and 219, respectively.

On Monday, it was Mears' turn. The three-time winner ran back-to-back laps in excess of 225 mph. Mears' laps, though unofficial, were the first recorded at under 40 seconds. Lap 1 was 39.91 seconds (225.507 mph) and 39.87 seconds (225.733 mph).

"The new surface is obviously a gain," said Mears after yet another electrifying run at Indianapolis.

It also overshadowed the laps at 224 run by Al Unser, Michael Andretti and Fittipaldi. On the same day, Mario Andretti and Sullivan topped 222 mph.

Sullivan had a major "moment" on Thursday when the rear

OFFICIAL PROGRAM
FIVE DOLLARS

73rd Indianapolis 500

Main photograph: Emerson Fittipaldi becomes the first winner whose individual portion of the purse exceeds one million dollars.

Inset below: After disappointing finishes in his first four "500" starts, Emerson Fittipaldi places second in 1988 and then wins in 1989.
Photographs: IMS

Top: With just over one and a quarter laps to go, Al Unser, Jr., and Emerson Fittipaldi touch wheels while side by side for the lead, Unser being unable to prevent himself from spinning towards the outer wall.

Above: Fittipaldi regains control while Unser hits the wall with force.

Backdrop: As Fittipaldi comes around behind the pace car on his way to the checkered flag, the sporting Unser walks to the track's edge and gives his friend applause before a "double-thumbs-up."
Photographs: IMS

cowling came off his Miller Penske-Chevy at speed. The loss of the bodywork forced Sullivan to spin into the wall. His right wrist was broken in the incident. It would be a case of wait-and-see if he could be cleared to drive.

Although he was engineer for Fittipaldi and Patrick Racing, Mo Nunn recognized a potential problem in the cowling clasp and beefed up the ones on Fittipaldi's car. Penske Racing soon followed suit.

Despite the accident, Mears continued his onslaught, topping everyone with a 226.231 on Friday. Almost simultaneously, Unser had recorded a 225.960. The 1988 records were clearly in jeopardy.

Rain managed to wash away Saturday's activity, but the weather was more cooperative on Sunday. In morning warmup, Unser topped the first group with a 224.215 lap. Mears and Fittipaldi were quickest in the second group with Mears again going 226 and the Brazilian close behind at 225. It appeared that Penske chassis would occupy the front row for a second straight year, albeit with a "customer" mixing it up with the factory entries.

Al Unser was first of the contenders to qualify. He broke the one-lap record four straight times (222.712, 223.636, 223.736 and 223.803) for a record four-lap average of 223.471. Only two years earlier, Unser had been unable to find a suitable ride. Now he was the man of the moment at Indianapolis.

Later on, Mears made his run. It would be memorable although his first lap at 223.187 was slower than Unser. Mears then broke the track record at 223.897, upped it to 224.254 and finished with a 224.204 for a record four-lap average of 223.885 mph. No one would go faster and Mears became the first man to win the pole at Indianapolis five times. His previous poles had come in 1979, 1982, 1986 and 1988, allowing him to share the record with Rex Mays (1935, 1936, 1940 and 1948) and A.J. Foyt (1965, 1969, 1974 and 1975).

When it came to qualifying at Indy, Mears was in a class all by himself. Besides his five Indy pole positions, Mears started third four times (1978, 1983, 1984 and 1987) in 12 starts. Bobby Unser also started on the front row nine times, but only captured the pole on two occasions.

Fittipaldi could only muster an average of 222.329 mph, but it was good enough for third place and for the second straight year, the front row would feature three Penske chassis.

The field was filled the following weekend and joining the 33 starters was Sullivan. Qualifying with his wrist in a cast, Sullivan put his Miller-liveried Penske in the middle of Row 9. In the official post-qualifying photo, Sullivan's crew had some fun, each man posing with his arm in a sling.

The average speed for the 33 starters was also notable. At 216.588, it was the fastest field in 500 history, more than 6 mph faster than the field average from a year ago.

When the green flag dropped on Race Day, Fittipaldi used outside position on Row 1 to his advantage, jumping into the lead and heading the field by nearly two seconds when he completed Lap 1. Fittipaldi also established an opening-lap record of 209.200, smashing Michael Andretti's 1986 mark by seven miles per hour! He followed up with another quick lap at nearly 214 mph. That established a record average for the first two laps at 211.563. The two-time F1 world champion had earlier stated that he truly felt like an Indy-car driver, having qualified on the front row. Now he was showing everyone he meant it, leading the first 34 laps of the race.

Fittipaldi's early pace was slowed when Kevin Cogan had a monumental accident on Lap 3. Coming out of Turn 4, Cogan's car did a quick half-spin and then struck the inside wall. Cogan's car disintegrated and the tub (containing the driver) and engine slid into the pit area. Miraculously, Cogan emerged from the wreckage unhurt. As safety workers reached him, he was struggling to get his harness unbuckled. He was able to exit the car and stand up unattended. A piece of metallic debris could be seen embedded in Cogan's helmet, but he was otherwise unscathed.

The caution period ended on Lap 15 and Fittipaldi continued his onslaught. After surrendering the lead for two laps following his first pit stop, he led the next 51 laps. It was looking like it was his day. In the meantime, Sullivan's one-armed comeback came to naught when he pitted with clutch trouble on Lap 41. A month later, he would decide to sit out the remainder of the racing season and let his wrist heal. Unser was out with clutch trouble on Lap 68.

Mears' bid for a fourth victory ended on Lap 113 when he was sidelined with engine problems. Despite his pace in practice and qualifying, he failed to lead a lap.

Michael Andretti seemed to be the only driver consistently staying with Fittipaldi, but his day ended on Lap 163 when his engine blew. Andretti had been leading at the time. Al Unser, Jr., was now second, but he did seem not to have anything for the flying Fittipaldi.

On Lap 181, the caution came after Tero Palmroth lost a wheel. Fittipaldi pitted the following lap, but Unser, Jr., stayed out. The Galles team was gambling on getting Unser better track position. He was still second to Fittipaldi, but much closer on the track. With the help of some late-race cautions, he might be able to go the distance, even though he had last pitted for fuel on Lap 165. Following his last stop, Fittipaldi retained the lead and stayed there until Lap 195.

Suddenly, Unser swept past Fittipaldi and now led. This particular month had been frustrating for Unser, but now all he had to do was hold off the Brazilian to score his first victory at Indianapolis and join his father and uncle as a winner of the 500. Fittipaldi may have been surprised to lose the lead, but he had not given up.

With less than two laps to go, Unser and Fittipaldi came up behind lapped traffic as they approached Turn 2. Unser was momentarily balked and Fittipaldi got a stronger run off the turn. Passing the lapped cars, Unser moved left and the Brazilian darted to the inside as they headed down the backstretch.

The two drivers were neck-and-neck as they went into Turn 3. Unser held his line, but Fittipaldi appeared to slightly drift up from the apron. Fittipaldi's right front wheel brushed Unser's left rear wheel. For a moment, Fittipaldi's car got out of shape as Unser's car began to spin. Unser's car swapped ends and he struck the Turn 3 wall before sliding into the infield.

Miraculously, Fittipaldi maintained control of his car and continued on. The caution was out as he came around to com-

plete Lap 199. The race was over. Fittipaldi would lead the parade behind the pace car for the final lap and savor what had to be the biggest racing victory of his illustrious career.

Unser was unhurt in the incident and walked to the edge of the track, where he applauded Fittipaldi, now en route to Victory Lane.

Despite the accident, Unser still finished in the runner-up position. At the time of the contact, he and Fittipaldi were a whopping six laps ahead of third-place man Boesel. It spawned a number of what-if scenarios.

Had Fittipaldi crashed with Unser, it would have been the first time since 1912 that the eventual winner had to unlap himself at the end of the race in order to pass the stricken race leader for the victory.

However, Boesel was nursing a sick engine at the time of the incident. The final two laps under caution may have allowed him to bring his car home. Had he also faltered, fourth-place finisher Mario Andretti could have scored his elusive second victory. But Andretti also had a sick engine and had he faltered, fifth-place finisher Foyt would have scored an unprecedented fifth 500 victory.

Another "what if" centered on Unser. Having made his last fuel stop on Lap 165, there was also the possibility that he might have run out of fuel had he and Fittipaldi not touched and continued on. However, the Galles team displayed some heads-up thinking by basing their gamble on the fact that Unser was six laps ahead of the third-place car. He could have run out of fuel with five laps to go and still finished second. We'll never know.

Unser also gained the distinction of being the highest-placed driver to not finish a race that went the entire 500-mile distance.

Fittipaldi's post-race festivities offered a most interesting footnote. On the day after the race, one of the Speedway's traditions has the winner, his car and crew pose on the front straightaway for a photo shoot. This year's race had a milestone with Fittipaldi becoming the first 500 winner to earn more than $1 million ($1,001,604 to be exact). And so, Fittipaldi posed proudly with the Borg-Warner trophy and his Marlboro Penske surrounded by stacks of currency representing the $1 million payout.

Below: The cars have changed greatly over the years, and so has the downtown-Indianapolis skyline, but the old creek just keeps on flowing.
Photograph: IMS

1990: The Fastest one in History

A new era was underway at the Indianapolis Motor Speedway.

Track President Joe Cloutier had passed away in Terre Haute on Dec. 11, 1989. A longtime employee of Tony Hulman, Cloutier was often credited for the success and the growth of the Indianapolis 500 following Hulman's purchase of the track in 1945. When Hulman passed away in October of 1977, Cloutier was named acting president until John Cooper assumed the position in 1979. After Cooper's departure in May of 1982, Cloutier again took over the helm and stayed there until his death at age 81.

The past few years had been spent grooming Hulman's grandson, Tony George, for the IMS presidency. On Jan. 8, George was announced as the new president. The son of former 500 driver Elmer George and IMS Chairman of the Board Mari Hulman George, the 30-year-old progeny had done some racing himself, running Super Vees and spending the 1989 season competing in the American Racing Series under the tutelage of one Anthony Joseph Foyt, Jr.

He would be taking over the world's greatest auto racing facility at a most exciting time, with track records being broken, speeds continuing to climb and an ever-increasing involvement of corporate America in the sport.

If you wanted to go Indy-car racing in 1990, there was an interesting array of engines to choose from – if you were in the position to be chosen to choose.

With engine leases in full swing, the engine most teams wanted was the Chevrolet Indy V-8 built by Ilmor Engineering. If a team was designated to be "worthy" of the honor, it would have to shell out more than $1 million to lease the engine. But with one of those engines, a team could expect to run up front.

For those left wanting, there was the venerable Cosworth V-8 (which only seven years earlier had powered 32 of the 33 starters at Indy), the Judd V-8 and the Buick V-6 (which got a 10-inch boost advantage over the V-8). There were also two other European engine providers of note – Porsche and Alfa

Romeo. The latter two were factory efforts with special chassis built by March.

The March chassis for Porsche was especially interesting and controversial, depending on whose opinion you believed. When the Porsche team unveiled its low-profile car for testing, it sent shock waves out to the Indy-car community. Designed by Tino Belli, this chassis was made entirely of the revolutionary carbon fiber that was prevalent in Formula One racing. The chassis was stiffer and stood up to crash testing better than any of its predecessors. For the drivers, who had been prone to serious foot, ankle and leg injuries with the ground effects design, the all-carbon fiber concept represented a step in the right direction.

The cars were to be driven by the two smallest drivers in Indy-car racing – Teo Fabi and John Andretti. In fact, it was rumored that the car would only fit the two jockey-sized drivers.

Carbon fiber could be found on current Indy cars, particularly the tub, but the idea of an all-carbon fiber Indy car was a novelty. It would also be temporarily ruled illegal by Championship Auto Racing Teams, the organization that sanctioned all of the Indy-car events except the Indianapolis 500.

Team principal Derrick Walker protested, but to no avail. CART – and the Indianapolis 500 – would have to wait at least one more year for the radical design. March was forced to rebuild the car with tubs containing an "acceptable" amount of carbon fiber and honeycomb aluminum.

March's exclusive design for Alfa Romeo was less spectacular than its Porsche counterpart. Designed by John Baldwin and Maurice Phillipe (designer of the wedge-shaped Lotus-Turbine and various Parnelli Indy cars), the March 90-CA had an almost bulbous appearance in contrast to the sleek March-Porsche. The car also featured the tallest rollbar hoop amongst the other Indy-car designs. These cars were assigned to Roberto Guerrero and Al Unser.

Team Penske returned to the Speedway with its latest Nigel Bennett-designed PC-19. Rick Mears was assigned to drive the Pennzoil-sponsored entry, with Emerson Fittipaldi and Danny Sullivan driving Marlboro-sponsored entries. Fittipaldi joined

Above: The diplomatic Thomas W. Binford, who would pooh-pooh any suggestion that he was an intellectual, served as chief steward for a record 22 years between 1974 and 1995.

Below: Pole sitter Emerson Fittipaldi is already out of the shot as Rick Mears leads Arie Luyendyk (number 30) and a challenging Bobby Rahal (number 18).
Photograph: IMS

Penske for 1990 as part of a pre-arranged agreement from 1989 in which Marlboro sponsored Al Unser at Penske as well as Fittipaldi at Patrick Racing. Fittipaldi also got to use the Penske chassis and wound up out-performing the factory team with a victory at Indianapolis and the national championship.

Marlboro also continued to celebrate its first Indy 500 victory from a year ago. As drivers headed west on 16th Street near the entrance to the Speedway, a large billboard undoubtedly drew everyone's attention, with a gigantic Marlboro Penske (at least three times as large as the real thing) bursting through a wall.

For the rest of the entry, the chassis of choice was the new Lola T9000 designed by Bruce Ashmore. The needle-nosed car could house the Ilmor Chevy, the Cosworth, the Judd and the Buick.

Rules changes made in the off-season affected the older cars. In an attempt to reduce the speeds, older cars were expected to install underwing inserts to reduce the height of the underwing tunnel. Any car designed prior to 1990 was expected to have what some described as "pluggers" or "diffusers."

In practice, the drivers only needed two days to top the 220-mph mark.

Mears was first at 220.788, but new Penske teammate Fittipaldi showed he was fitting right in by winding up quickest for the day at 222.607. On Monday, Mears went 224.389. On Tuesday, Fittipaldi was back on top, but only at 223.286. Windy weather slowed everyone for the next two days, but on Friday, it got very serious.

Early in the afternoon, Fittipaldi went 224.888. Mears went out later, ran a pair of 225 laps and then uncorked a 226.398. Fittipaldi went faster at 226.512. Then a third driver joined the 226-mph club. Al Unser, Jr., became a pole position contender with a 226.097. He followed up with a 226.483 and then got a tow from Foyt to uncork a 228.502! It was an unofficial track record, of course, but Unser's trap speed was only 231 mph – he was flat out the entire lap.

That would be the best of the month and the day, and the battle for the pole would have to wait until Sunday with rain washing out Saturday's proceedings.

Rain delayed Sunday's schedule, but the track was eventually dried and an abbreviated warmup session began at 2:55 p.m. There would only be two 30-minute sessions and qualifying would begin no sooner than 4:30 p.m.

There was one change to the qualifying process. The new Race Spec Qualifier was now in place. The device employed templates and fixtures to speed up the pre-qualifying tech inspection procedures.

Fittipaldi topped the brief practice session with a 228.012, but like Unser, Jr., he had the benefit of a tow. Rahal went

225.717 and Mears went 224.176. Luyendyk was next at 223.652, but Unser, Jr., could only muster a 222.668.

It was now time to qualify and Fittipaldi was first to go out.

Lap 1 was a new track record of 225.006 mph. Lap 2 was faster at 225.259. Lap 3 was still faster at 225.366. And Lap 4 was the quickest at 225.575. He was temporarily on the pole with a record four-lap average of 225.301.

It was now up to the others to unseat him. No one could do it. Mears averaged 224.215 and Rahal averaged 222.694. But by the time 6 p.m. rolled around, there were still a number of cars still in line to qualify. Among them were Unser and Luyendyk. They would now have to wait to qualify on the third day, but as remaining first-day qualifiers who still had a shot at the pole.

When qualifying resumed the following weekend, Luyendyk posted an average of 223.304 to bump Rahal off the front row. It would be the fastest speed of the first-day qualifiers and Fittipaldi could finally celebrate. The Brazilian's previous best start at Indianapolis had been third in 1989. Joining him were Mears and Luyendyk, who qualified for the front row for the first time in his career.

The second row was composed of three drivers with legitimate chances to win: Rahal, Michael Andretti and Mario Andretti. Unser, Jr., wound up seventh – a very good starting spot – but found it totally disappointing after setting the fastest practice speed ever.

Both Porsche-powered cars made the starting field, as did both Alfa Romeo-powered cars. John Andretti had the best qualifying run, winding up in 10th starting position, while Fabi struggled in 23rd spot. The Alfa Romeos were more disappointing, with Guerrero starting 28th and Unser in 30th position. What a difference was made as the four-time 500 winner had been second fastest in 1989.

Three-time winner Rutherford and Jeff Andretti failed to make the race. Both had qualified on the final day, only to be bumped out of the starting field. Had Andretti's speed been fast enough, he would have joined his father, brother and cousin in the race. The Andretti foursome would have to wait another year.

Like 1987, this month of May had seen a rash of accidents. However, this time the radial tires were not to blame. As most of the accidents occurred involving drivers in older cars using the underwing "plugger" or "diffuser," it became the point of contention. As had been the case in 1987, many of the 1990 accidents occurred when drivers would enter the turn and suddenly run wide into the concrete.

Lazier, Vukovich III and Wood all hit the wall. Chassey, Jourdain, Vogler, Jeff Andretti and Rutherford all crashed twice.

In a three-day span, there were six accidents involving older cars. It spawned a movement by teams with older cars

Above: March built special versions of its chassis to house the Porsche engine, these being among the lowest-sitting cars ever to appear at Indianapolis. The drivers are Teo Fabi (seen here) and John Andretti.

Below: Eddie Cheever, the most experienced American in Formula One racing with 132 Grand Prix starts between 1978 and 1989, turns his attention to Indianapolis and finishes eighth for Chip Ganassi.

Photographs: IMS

Above: Arie Luyendyk, poses with his family on the day after the race. At right is Arie Luyendyk, Jr., who will drive in the "500" in 2006.

Top: Bobby Rahal, who has just finished second, pulls alongside to salute winner Arie Luyendyk.

Inset right: History is made as Willy T. Ribbs becomes the first African American to qualify for the "500."

Inset bottom right: Japanese driver Hiro Matsushita is the first Asian to compete in a "500."

Photographs: IMS

to ask USAC and the Speedway to ban the "diffusers." A heated meeting was held during the first week of practice and not every owner agreed with the argument. Not every team was having problems and ultimately, the matter was dropped.

Crawford also crashed twice and spun a third time. But it was his second accident that got everyone's attention. On Friday before the first day of qualifying, Crawford spun in Turn 1 and struck the wall. Upon impact, air got underneath the car and it shot up several feet. It almost seemed to hover before dropping to the ground and sliding into the infield. Crawford was taken to Methodist Hospital for precautionary X-rays and quickly released.

Always quick with a quip, Crawford was asked about the ride height of his Lola. In the wink of an eye, he replied: "Well, at this track, anywhere from two inches to 15 feet!" It certainly gave a new meaning to the term "Flying Scotsman."

Not all accidents were limited to older cars. Guerrero survived an almighty accident when the rear wing strut broke on his new March-Alfa.

Race Day would give a true indication of the new equipment versus the older models.

From the pole, Fittipaldi shot into the lead and would stay there for the first 92 laps of the race. It broke a record held since 1927 when Frank Lockhart led the first 81 laps.

The defending race winner would have two primary challengers that day – Luyendyk and Rahal.

One man who had hoped to challenge for the lead was Danny Sullivan, who started ninth in a Marlboro-liveried Penske-Chevy. His race ended when a bearing blew on the left rear wheel as Sullivan entered Turn 1. The car swapped ends and banged into the wall very hard. It would be Sullivan's last Indy 500 as a Penske driver, and it must have given him pause for thought after mechanical failure put him into the IMS concrete for a third straight year.

When Fittipaldi pitted, Luyendyk took over the lead for two laps before pitting and handing the lead back to Fittipaldi, who would stay there through Lap 117, but a problem was surfacing that would affect his race. Blisters appeared on the rear tires of Fittipaldi's car the Brazilian was forced to pit and relinquish the lead to Rahal, who led the next four laps. Fittipaldi got the lead again, but 13 laps later, he had to stop to replace another set of blistered tires. Tire pressures set higher than the figures suggested by manufacturer Goodyear seemed to be the cause of Fittipaldi's troubles.

In the meantime, it set up a two-way battle between Luyendyk and Rahal. The 1986 Indy 500 winner appeared to have the upper hand on the Dutchman until making his final pit stop. The set of scuffed tires he received were not as good as the previous set and Luyendyk soon darted by on the inside coming out of Turn 4 to lead Lap 168 and every lap thereafter.

With few caution laps and a blazing pace set by the lead trio throughout the race, Luyendyk was about to make history in more ways than one. As Rahal's ability to challenge was diminished by his tires, Luyendyk was able to take the checker by nearly 11 seconds. Interestingly, Luyendyk was so busy racing with Fittipaldi he failed to see the white.

In winning the race, he became the first driver from Holland to capture the Indy 500. More importantly, he averaged an astounding 185.981 miles per hour en route to the victory. It was the fastest winner's speed in the history of the race. Luyendyk needed 2:41 to go 500 miles, slightly more than four hours less than Ray Harroun needed in 1911.

Rahal, who seemed poised to win his second Indy 500, wound up second. Despite his tire problems, Fittipaldi finished third. Al Unser, Jr., placed fourth and Rick Mears was fifth.

For the second straight year, the winner's take topped $1 million with Luyendyk earning a record $1,090,940 for the victory.

1991: Mears Joins The Four-timers

In many ways, the month of May 1991 would be the month of Rick Mears as the likable racer from Bakersfield, California, would come away with more records for his illustrious career. But May 1991 would also be a month of historical precedents. On top of that, it would be a milestone – the 75th running of the Indianapolis 500.

As had been the case since 1988, the Chevrolet Indy V-8 engine was the one most sought after by the competition. The winners of the lottery the previous season were UNO/Granatelli Racing (a merger of Vince Granatelli Racing and Doug Shierson Racing), Bettenhausen Motorsports and the newly formed Hall-VDS Racing team that paired Jim Hall and his former Chaparral mechanic Franz Wiess.

Thanks to its affordability, the Buick V-6 became a viable alternative to a number of teams. Buicks were the choice of Dick Simon Racing, Arciero Racing, Hemelgarn Racing, Menards Racing, Kingsports Racing, A.J. Foyt Enterprises, D.B. Mann Racing and Walker Motorsports. The latter was what was left of the now-defunct Porsche team with Derrick Walker at the helm. It was bidding to make history with rookie driver Willy T. Ribbs, who was going to attempt to be the first African American in the Indy 500 starting field.

Four teams also chose the Judd V-8 (UNO Racing, Norm Turley, Burns Racing and Truesports) and the remainder of the entry used the Cosworth DFS, a short-stroke version of the DFX model.

On the chassis front, Lola dominated the ranks with March gone from the scene entirely. Porsche pulled the plug on its Indy-car program at the end of the previous season and the March-Alfa was so dismally slow that Patrick Racing wound up purchasing a new Lola by mid-season.

The attempt to "grandfather" older cars had not succeeded as well as had been hoped and with a couple of exceptions, most of the Lolas that would qualify for the 1991 race would either be a 1990 or a 1991 model.

One man driving a new Lola-Chevrolet was simply happy to be back. That man was A.J. Foyt and the eyes of the racing world were focused on him more so than usual. The previous September, he had suffered serious foot and leg injuries in a crash at Elkhart Lake, Wisconsin. Foyt did everything possible to enhance his recovery and by May was fit to drive. Immediately after his accident, there had been fear he might lose one or both extremities and no one was even considering a

return to the cockpit.

Penske returned with its new PC-20 for Mears and Emerson Fittipaldi and Bettenhausen Motorsports purchased a pair of PC-19s for Tony Bettenhausen.

There was also a new chassis at Indianapolis and interestingly it was built in the United States.

After discovering an abandoned wind tunnel in Columbus, Ohio, Truesports' Steve Horne worked on getting it activated with the idea of using it to develop different parts and ultimately a Truesports chassis. The new Truesports design was the brainchild of Don Halliday. Judd engines powered the Truesports entries for Scott Pruett and Geoff Brabham. Truesports also purchased the rights to the Judd engine and continued its development with the aid of an in-house dynamometer.

Rain and "weepers" (water that would seep up through the asphalt surface) pretty much restricted on-track activity for opening weekend. On Monday, they finally got in a full day of practice and to no one's surprise, the pace was set by Fittipaldi at 223.981 and Mears at 223.430.

Mears picked up the pace on Tuesday with a 226.555, but later on maintained that conditions had been better the day before! Michael Andretti showed that he would be a player with a lap at 225.994. The following day (Wednesday), Mears and Andretti had company. Bobby Rahal set the pace with a top lap of 226.080 and Jim Crawford was close behind at 225.643. The latter was in a car with Buick power.

Kevin Cogan continued the Buick charge by leading the way on Thursday, with the fastest lap of the month at 226.677 in one of John Menard's Lolas. However, Fittipaldi and Mears were close behind with laps at 226.512 and 226.108, respectively. Luyendyk and Michael Andretti had identical laps at 225.649 and Mario Andretti checked in at 225.253.

Surprisingly, it had been an extremely safe month as qualifying weekend drew near. That would all change.

In Friday practice before Pole Day, Mears achieved the kind of "first" he had always managed to avoid in the past. Heading into Turn 1, Mears' car suffered some sort of wheel failure and it slammed into the wall. In 14 years of racing at Indianapolis, Mears had never wrecked a car at the Speedway.

Later in the day, rookie Mark Dismore brushed the Turn 4 wall and slid across the track. The car backed into the inside wall, reducing a five-foot section of the concrete to rubble. The car then struck the outer pit wall, whereupon it broke in half. While the engine and rear axle flipped along the pit lane, the tub (containing Dismore) also flipped and ended upside down by the pit wall. Dinsmore suffered multiple fractures, but would eventually recover.

Dismore's accident closed the track for the day. Despite the accident involving his teammate, Fittipaldi again topped the speed charts with a top lap at 226.705. Even more surprising was the 226.557 lap turned in by Mears. The three-time 500 winner had been cleared to drive following his accident and hopped into his backup car, getting the lap in a mere seven minutes.

It promised to be a memorable day of qualifying.

Pre-qualifying warmup saw Fittipaldi, Cogan and Mears all turning record laps in excess of 226 mph. All were contenders, but another driver had plans of his own and his name was A.J. Foyt.

Foyt was the first four-time winner at Indianapolis and a driver bidding to make his 34th start in the 500. It was expected to be his last and he made the most of the qualifying run.

Lap 1 was 221.174. Lap 2 was 222.211. Lap 3 was 222.932 and Lap 4 was his best at 223.469. Foyt averaged 222.443 and was on the pole. At age 56, he was the "Comeback Kid."

Three drivers qualified – Sullivan, Crawford and Goodyear – and it was Mario Andretti's turn. The 1969 winner responded with an average of 221.818, despite complaining about his

Above: Note how Rick Mears clutches the milk bottle after his fourth win. Not having realized the significance of the bottle after his first "500" victory in 1979, he allowed it to get away from him. Years later, he was approached by a fan at Nazareth, Pennsylvania, who mentioned that he had the bottle. "What do you want for it?" Mears asked excitedly. Somewhat taken aback, the fan suggested an autographed helmet. "Done," said Mears, who later recalled, "That was the best deal I ever made in my life."
Photograph: IMS

pole. Earlier in the day, Jeff Andretti had safely qualified for his first 500. With his father, brother and cousin all safely in the field, it would mark the first time that four members of the same family would race against each other in an Indianapolis 500.

With the pole already decided and 12 cars in the field, Day 2 would become a contest to see who could salvage his effort by qualifying on the fifth row. One man would clearly run fast for pride. Gary Bettenhausen went out in a second Menard car and electrified PA announcer Tom Carnegie and the crowd with four laps near or above 224 mph. Bettenhausen's four-lap average of 224.468 would be the quickest of the 33 starters. Ironically, Bettenhausen's run came on the 30th anniversary of the death of his father.

The second weekend of qualifying would see more history made at the Speedway. Despite a number of engine failures during the month, Willy T. Ribbs continued to work up to speed in Derrick Walker's Lola-Buick. On the final day, Ribbs did some electrifying of his own, putting together a solid run to average 217.358 and become the first African American starter in Indianapolis 500 history. Ribbs acknowledged an appreciative crowd by coming halfway out of the cockpit and waving as he rolled down the pit lane for his official qualifying photo.

Two former 500 winners would be noticeably missing from the starting field. Al Unser was at one time mentioned as a candidate to drive Luyendyk's backup car, but he never turned a wheel during the month. Tom Sneva drove one of Menard's older cars and turned in a wild qualifying performance, inadvertently putting both left-side wheels on the grass while ne-

popoff valve. He was second fastest. As qualifying progressed, Foyt's speed was looking better all the time. Pole contenders Rahal and Michael Andretti could only come up with speeds slower than A.J. and Mario. Cogan nearly hit the wall on his first lap and wound up aborting his run.

Now it was Mears' turn. His first lap was 223.447 – a tick slower than Foyt's fastest lap but faster than Foyt's four-lap average. Mears then reeled off three laps in excess of 224. Mears was now on the pole. His average speed was slightly below Fittipaldi's track record from the previous year (225.301), but there were still some contenders, most notably Fittipaldi.

Running late in the afternoon, Fittipaldi ran laps of 222.409, 223.899 and 223.369 before getting the yellow flag from Roger Penske. John Andretti went to qualify and completed his run despite the fact a light rain had begun on his warmup lap. More rain followed and the track was finally closed for good at 5:45 p.m. Those who had not qualified would not be considered second-day qualifiers.

Mears now owned an unprecedented sixth pole position at Indianapolis. And he headed a row of legends with Foyt and Mario Andretti starting alongside.

There was other history made in addition to Mears' sixth

gotiating one of the corners! His speed failed to stand up and he was bumped.

The 75th Indianapolis 500 had a little more pre-race fanfare than usual with the appearance of Gulf War hero General H. Norman Schwartzkopf and U.S. Vice President Dan Quayle. General Schwartzkopf had been named the grand marshal of the 500 Festival Parade while Quayle, a former two-term U.S. senator from Indiana, returned to the track he had visited a number of times previously.

Set to pace the field was the Dodge Viper. It was a most unique pace car as it was still in development and not yet available in showrooms. To mark the occasion, Chrysler also paraded its one-of-a-kind Newport concept car that had paced the 1941 race.

When the race began, Mears shot into the lead, but the yellow came out almost immediately. Gary Bettenhausen had bobbled and in an attempt to avoid him, rookie Buddy Lazier spun and grazed the Turn 1 wall with the nosecone. Bettenhausen kept going, but Lazier, whose father, Bob, had run here in 1981, headed to the pits. He was through for the day. Four laps later, Ribbs joined him on the sidelines with yet another engine failure.

Mario Andretti took over the lead on Lap 12 but the cau-

tion came out on Lap 25. Cogan and Guerrero had tangled in Turn 1 and Foyt's car was seriously damaged after running through debris. All three drivers were out and Cogan's injuries were serious enough to merit a trip to Methodist Hospital.

Andretti would lead through Lap 33 and for the next 105 laps, the lead would be swapped between Michael Andretti, Al Unser, Jr., and Fittipaldi. Mears, who had not led since Lap 11, had kept the leaders in sight, running in the top five most of the day. He finally got the lead back on Lap 139 and the race became a three-way battle between the Penske teammates and Michael.

Fittipaldi dashed into the pits on Lap 171. His day was ended because of gearbox problems. It would now be a fight to the finish between Mears and Michael Andretti.

Michael led for 12 laps and then Mears took over the lead for three circuits.

Next came "the pass." A three-lap caution for Danny Sullivan's smoking engine set up the scenario.

The restart allowed Andretti to close on the leader. As he followed Mears down the main straightaway to complete Lap 186, he didn't have quite enough draft to get the job done as the pair headed into Turn 1.

Or did he? Andretti did the unthinkable, even though Mears was hugging the inside line. He swept past Mears around the outside and took the lead. The crowd went wild.

Now it was Mears' turn.

In a repeat of the previous lap, Mears drafted Andretti as the pair entered Turn 1. And like Andretti, he swept around on the outside for the lead. Now the crowd really went wild in anticipation of what the two drivers might do for an encore.

But there would be no encore this time. Mears began to put distance between his car and Andretti's. Even Papa Mario couldn't help although he brought out the caution on Lap 191 when his car coasted to a halt inside Turn 4. Three laps were required to tow the elder Andretti's car out of harm's way. On Lap 195, the green came out.

Mears again built a small gap on Andretti, drawing away on each of the race's closing laps.

By the time the checker came out, Mears was ahead of Andretti by 3.149 seconds. The Californian joined A.J. Foyt and Al Unser as a four-time winner of the Indianapolis 500.

Defending winner Luyendyk was third, followed by Al Unser, Jr., John Andretti, Gordon Johncock, Mario, Stan Fox, Tony Bettenhausen and Sullivan, who gave Alfa Romeo its first top-10 finish at Indianapolis since 1948. Jeff Andretti finished 15th after being sidelined with engine problems on Lap 150, but he still received the top rookie award. It was the third for the Andrettis, with Mario and Michael being previously honored.

It was a copybook performance for Mears – the pole, a strong race car and another 500 victory highlighted this time by his daring pass.

RCK MEARS

On the surface, the relationship between Roger Penske and Mark Donohue seemed like the perfect racing marriage. Both men were talented drivers, well educated, articulate and determined to succeed while maintaining a quiet dignity. The relationship paid off with numerous championships in sports-car racing, Trans-Am, Can-Am and victory in the 1972 Indianapolis 500. When Donohue was tragically killed in practice for the 1975 Austrian Grand Prix, everyone wondered if Penske would ever have the same kind of relationship with a driver.

Rick Mears was not educated as an engineer like Donohue, but the two drivers had a lot in common in the form of a ready smile and boyish personality that endeared him to his crew, his fans and the media. Mears did possess an articulate style of speaking

and likewise had a quiet dignity about him. More importantly, Mears was the kind of winning driver Penske had long sought to take Donohue's place. In a chance meeting at Wally Dallenbach's Colorado 500 motorcycle ride, Penske hooked up with the former off-road racer from Bakersfield, California. Penske had noticed Mears' prowess at the wheel of an ancient Eagle-Offenhauser and saw a rough-edged talent he could shape into a race winner and champion.

Equipped with a state-of-the-art Penske-Cosworth and support from Penske's considerable operation, Mears responded by qualifying on the front row at Indianapolis and winning on ovals at Milwaukee and Atlanta and the road course of Brands Hatch, Eng-

land. By contrast, Mears' teammate Tom Sneva finished in the points enough times to win the national title for the second straight year. Running a partial schedule, Mears wound up 11th, but Penske kept Mears and fired Sneva. He was now part of the Penske family.

Mears truly showed his stuff in 1979, winning his first Indianapolis 500 from the pole and never qualifying lower than 10th or finishing lower than seventh to win the national title. In 1980, Formula One made overtures and Mears tested for Brabham at Riverside, where he would ultimately win twice in an Indy car. He would continue winning races and poles and by the end of 1982, he had two more national Indy-car titles. Earlier, he won the pole at Indy for a second time and engaged in an epic battle with Gordon Johncock. In 1984, he won at Indy again, but shortly afterward, his career was threatened after a testing accident at Sanair left him with serious foot and ankle injuries.

It would take time to heal, and Mears, once a threat on road courses, would win only one more road-course event before retiring at the end of 1992. However, the injuries failed to slow him on ovals and he saved his best for Indianapolis. By the time he finished, he had a record six poles in the 500 and won the race two more times to join the exclusive club of Indy's four-time winners, A.J. Foyt and Al Unser. And then he surprised the racing with his retirement announcement – all the while maintaining that quiet dignity.

1992: The Closest one yet

There were strong indications that May of 1992 would be the fastest in Indy history. No one realized that it would also be one of the wildest races in history. The 76th Annual Indianapolis 500 would wind up being one of the most talked-about races ever.

Thanks to some incredible laps during spring testing turned in by Kingsports Racing's Roberto Guerrero and Jim Crawford, there was no doubt that Emerson Fittipaldi's 1990 track record of 225.301 mph would be in jeopardy. Driving special Lola-Buicks engineered by John Travis, Guerrero and Crawford both topped the 230-mph mark during April tests at the track.

Accentuating the speed of the teammates was a first-ever test conducted simultaneously by the International Race of Champions (IROC), the series that pitted top drivers from different forms of motorsports in identically prepared Dodge Daytonas. The difference between the 230-mph Indy Lolas and the 160-mph IROC cars was striking.

As had been the case, the expected battle lines were drawn between the Lolas and Penskes although there was a pair of interesting newcomers on the equipment front. Lola users could count on power from the V-6 Buicks and Chevrolet Indy V-8s, but the Newman-Haas and Chip Ganassi teams had a new powerplant at their disposal. After running and developing the Cosworth DFX and DFS engines for 17 years, Cosworth produced the all-new XB.

The XB was lighter and more powerful than its predecessor, but perhaps more importantly, it was lower in profile and that

allowed Lola to design a lower-profile T92/00 model. That approach had already proved to be an advantage when Ilmor unveiled its Chevy Indy V-8 back in 1986.

Driving the new Lola-Cosworth XB combination would be Mario and Michael Andretti and Ganassi teammates Arie Luyendyk and Eddie Cheever.

There was also another new American chassis to go with the Truesports that had been unveiled the previous year. Making its debut at Indy was the Alan Mertens-designed Galmer-Chevy for Galles Racing. The Galmer had already scored its initial Indy-car victory with Danny Sullivan capturing the Long Beach GP. Sullivan was in his first season with Galles, with Al Unser, Jr., as teammate. Indianapolis would be its first superspeedway test.

Amongst the newcomers, Lyn St. James was hoping to become the first woman to qualify for the 500 since Janet Guthrie in 1979 and Philippe Gache was hoping to become the first Frenchman to race at Indianapolis since Rene LeBegue in 1940. Team Menard hired three-time F1 world champion Nelson Piquet.

The Brazilian would be one of the more heralded rookies to arrive at the Speedway. With dirt-track-bred teammate Gary Bettenhausen showing him the ropes, they truly made the "Odd Couple" of racing. However, the two racers hit it off and in no time Piquet was up to speed.

With a fast quartet like Guerrero, Crawford, Bettenhausen and Piquet, the Lola-Buick combination dominated the charts on the early days of practice.

Crawford blistered opening day with a lap at 229.609. Piquet was a respectable second quick at 225.875. Two days

later, Crawford went 233.433. Michael Andretti was second at 230.852 with Guerrero close behind at 230.432. Guerrero set the pace on the fourth day at 230.149 while Bettenhausen had his fastest lap of the month at 228.079.

On Wednesday, Crawford once again topped the charts and the 233 mark with a lap at 233.239. Guerrero was second at 231.558, but Michael and Mario Andretti also recorded laps in the 231-mph range.

Mears would remember Wednesday for other reasons. After running at Indianapolis incident-free for 14 years (not counting the pit fire of 1981), Mears had his second accident in as many years at the Speedway and nearly a year to the day of his first IMS accident. As Mears entered Turn 2, fluid could be seen coming out of his car and it swapped ends. The Penske clouted the wall and then got upside down. Mears suffered a sprained right wrist and a fracture to his left foot, but he would be cleared to practice the following day.

Guerrero was back on top on Thursday with a 232.624 lap, but things began to go awry for Team Menard.

Although he had never raced on an oval track before, the fun-loving Piquet looked very comfortable running at the incredible speeds. However, the former F1 world champion was not used to the necessity of shutting down the track for numerous inspections during the practice sessions. A modern F1 car could top 200 mph in a straight line, but at Indianapolis, there was little speed scrubbed off during a lap at 230 miles per hour.

Piquet's impatience proved to be his undoing.

After another car lost some sort of metallic part on the backstretch, the yellow came out. Piquet actually ran over the piece but continued down the backstretch at full speed. He went through Turn 3 at full speed. Partway through Turn 4 at full speed, he abruptly got out of the throttle to go into the pits. The sudden loss of speed caused his car to swap ends and the hapless Brazilian hit the Turn 4 wall nearly head-on.

He became the latest Indy-car driver to suffer serious foot, leg and ankle injuries and Dr. Terry Trammel set out performing his medical magic to allow Piquet to race again. The 1992 500 was out of the question for Piquet, of course, and team owner John Menard would ultimately replace Piquet with Al Unser.

On Friday, Bettenhausen crashed his backup car, but was uninjured. For the second straight day, a Menard car returned to the garage area on a hook. The Indianapolis Motor Speedway would also witness its first fatality in 10 years.

Rookie Jovy Marcello, a native of the Philippines, suffered a fatal head injury after hitting the wall between Turns 1 and 2. Marcello's demise came as a shock as he had previously recorded a lap in excess of 170 mph. However, telemetry showed he was going more than 215 mph prior to his accident. Ironically, it happened 10 years to the day of Gordon Smiley's fatal accident.

For the first time in a number of days, a Lola-Buick was not the fastest car. Mario Andretti took the honors with his fastest lap ever at Indianapolis – 233.202. Luyendyk was next at 232.654 and Guerrero and Crawford were third and fourth with laps in the 231-mph range.

Pole Day began with showers that delayed on-track activity until the afternoon. When the track finally opened, Crawford lost an engine in pre-qualifying warmup and spun in Turn 3. Shortly afterward, Hiro Matsushita spun on fluid left by Tony Bettenhausen's car and clobbered the Turn 1 wall. He suffered a broken thigh and would have to miss the race. When practice ended, Guerrero was back on top with a lap at 232.090.

Luyendyk became the first to qualify and smashed Fittipaldi's records in the process. Lap 1 was 228.967, a new track record. Lap 2 was another record, 229.305. Lap 3 was 228.996 and Lap 4 was 229.241. It gave the 1990 winner a record four-lap average of 229.127, breaking Fittipaldi's mark by nearly 4 mph.

Gary Bettenhausen qualified for his 20th 500 with an average speed of 228.932 mph. The fastest qualifier a year earlier, Bettenhausen set a one-lap record on Lap 3 with a speed of 229.317 mph.

Shortly after 5:30 p.m., Guerrero rolled onto the track. This is what they had come to see. Lap 1 was a new track record of 232.186. Lap 2 was another new track record at 232.516. Lap 3 was still faster, a one-lap track record of 232.618. And Lap 4 was almost as fast at 232.606. Guerrero's average of 232.482 mph smashed Luyendyk's old record by more than 3 mph. Fortunately for Guerrero, the engine went with a bang as soon as he crossed the finish line.

Unfortunately for those yet to qualify, Guerrero's engine problem temporarily shut down the track. Qualifying resumed at 5:48 p.m. (with only 12 minutes remaining) and Mears made the field with a 224.594 average, despite a bandaged wrist. Mario Andretti qualified at 229.503 to bump Luyendyk

to third. Foyt went out, but blew an engine after recording three laps with a 226 average. Foyt's demise shut the track down for the day, but Danny Sullivan, Jimmy Vasser, Michael Andretti, Eddie Cheever and Jim Crawford would all get a chance to qualify Sunday as first-day qualifiers. Guerrero's celebration would have to wait a few more hours.

Crawford would suffer a blown engine for the second time in two days and narrowly miss getting back into the first-day qualifying line. He would now be a second-day qualifier.

Cheever became the day's first qualifier and turned in a surprising run, averaging 229.639 mph. It was the second fastest speed although Cheever had been quickest in morning practice at 230.970. Michael Andretti would be last to challenge for the pole, but his average of 228.169 put him on the outside of Row 2.

Guerrero was on the pole with Cheever and Mario Andretti starting alongside. Row 2 had Luyendyk, Gary Bettenhausen and Michael Andretti.

Starting 23rd for his record 35th 500 would be Foyt, who decided after the previous year's disappointment to give it at least one more try.

It would be a welcome return for one 500 winner and something of a curtain call for another. After not even practicing the previous year, Al Unser qualified for his 26th Indianapolis 500 in 22nd position. Three-time winner Johnny Rutherford, who had not qualified since 1988, failed to get up to speed in one of Derrick Walker's cars and took what would be his final competitive laps at the Speedway.

Another driver on the sidelines was one who had qualified safely. Scott Goodyear, who had been bumped, replaced Mike

Groff, who had already qualified Goodyear's backup car. Thanks to Goodyear's Canadian sponsor, MacKenzie, contractual arrangements stipulated that the Canadian driver would be in the car regardless of who qualified it. He would start last.

The starting field for the race had an unprecedented 10 former winners on the grid: Foyt, Unser, Mears, Sullivan, Rahal, Luyendyk, Fittipaldi, Andretti, Johncock and Sneva. And if that wasn't impressive enough, Foyt, Unser and Mears

would each be bidding to become the first five-time winner in Indy history.

For the second straight year, there would be four Andrettis in the starting field and Lyn St. James would be the first woman to run in the 500 in 13 years.

Race Day dawned overcast, somewhat damp and very cold. Even though it was the end of May, the 8 a.m. temperature was 50 degrees (Fahrenheit) with a wind chill factor of 36 degrees. There would be no rain on this particular race day, but many of the frozen fans in the stands believed that snow was likely.

The cool temperatures enhanced by strong winds made for a cold racing surface. This would be a difficult day in which to get one's tires up to a proper temperature.

First to fall victim to the problem of cold tires was the pole-sitter, Guerrero, who suddenly spun on the parade lap and clouted the inside wall in Turn 2. As would be the case in the accidents that followed, Guerrero had no warning.

That left an opening on the front row and as No. 2 man Eddie Cheever brought the field down for the start, Mario and Michael Andretti decided to exploit the situation. Before Cheever knew what was happening, the two Andrettis passed him on both sides! Mario, starting third, took the high line while Michael went low to take the lead as the trio emerged from the first turn.

Michael Andretti also established a new record for the opening lap, running at 210.339. He then established a record average for the first two laps at 215.636.

Six laps into the race, the yellow came out for Eric Bachelart, whose car was smoking. When the track went green on Lap 11, the yellow almost immediately returned. This time, it was for Sneva, who was moving up in the field from his 30th starting position only to slide into the Turn 4 wall very hard.

Caution was out for nine laps and they actually got 42 laps of racing in before the track again went yellow. This time it was for Johncock, whose engine was smoking. But no sooner had the race restarted than the yellow came out as Gache spun and struck the Turn 1 wall. He began to get out of his stricken car, but ducked inside in time as Stan Fox came through and collided with Gache's car. The impact broke Gache's tub in two, but the Frenchman was unhurt.

Cleanup lasted for nine laps and the race restarted on Lap 76. But as the field made its way through Turn 1, Crawford spun and was collected by Mears and Fittipaldi. Ted Prappas drove through the grass to avoid the carnage, but was able to continue. Crawford, Mears and Fittipaldi were taken to the

Below: Lady driver Lyn St. James prepares to go into her first "500." She will finish 11th and be declared Rookie of the Year. Throughout her career, and after, St. James will continue to be one of the sport's most outstanding spokespersons.
Photograph: IMS

track hospital but later released. Both Penske entries were out in one accident.

The field came down for a restart on Lap 83, but no sooner had the green flag come out, than the yellow was back on as Mario Andretti's car swapped ends and struck the wall head-on as he exited Turn 4. Andretti suffered smashed toes on his foot, but because he was still getting up to speed for the restart, his injuries were undoubtedly not as severe. Nevertheless, they were serious enough for him to go to Methodist where he would undergo surgery by Dr. Trammel.

On Lap 94, Trammel got another "customer" when Vasser slammed into the Turn 1 wall. His injury was a broken thigh, and it would sideline him for the season.

On Lap 102, rookie Brian Bonner crashed into the Turn 4 wall. He was unhurt, but the incident kept the yellow out for nine more laps. Slightly past the race's halfway point, 10 of the 33 starters had been eliminated in accidents.

On Lap 115, Jeff Andretti lost the right rear wheel from his Lola-Chevy. Andretti made a complete spin and then struck the outer wall nearly head-on. Unable to avoid the debris from the accident, Gary Bettenhausen's car was damaged even as he tried to go through the infield.

Andretti suffered serious foot and leg injuries and was rushed straight to Methodist for surgery. His father, who was about to undergo surgery, asked Dr. Trammel to work on his son first due to the severity of his injuries.

On Lap 135, Luyendyk hit the Turn 4 wall. He was unhurt, and surprisingly, his accident would be the last of the race. Luyendyk was running in second at the time and he banged wheels with Foyt. The side mirror had fallen off Foyt's car and the two cars got together.

At this point, Michael Andretti had complete control of the race, losing the lead to second-placed Al Unser, Jr., only when making pit stops. Despite the advantage, Andretti continued to pour it on and recorded the fastest-ever race lap on Lap 166 at 229.118 mph.

With his father and brother both injured, it seemed that the only way to salvage the day would be to win the race. Oh, how he tried.

Incredibly, the unthinkable happened. On Lap 189, with a healthy lead over Unser, Andretti's car slowed to a crawl. It was a cruel day for the Andretti family as Michael limped to a halt between Turns 3 and 4 with a broken fuel pump. He had led 160 laps thus far, but he would lead no more.

Andretti's demise brought out the caution on Lap 190 and when the track went green on Lap 193, it set the stage for a potential shootout between Unser and Goodyear.

Unser, Jr., had some unfinished business. Three years earlier, he had come within two laps of joining his father and uncle as an Indianapolis 500 winner. On this day, he would not have Emerson Fittipaldi to worry about, but Goodyear was ready to give him a run for the money.

Another man was on the move after being eighth on the restart. Unser's father, who had nearly been down a lap to his son before the caution, was now moving forward in John Menard's Lola-Buick. In 1988, Crawford had given the Buick its best run to date by leading eight laps and finishing sixth. But in light of the juggernaut by Team Penske that year, it was unlikely that Crawford could have won that race. With a little more time, Unser might have reeled in his son and Goodyear.

The race was now between Unser, Jr., and Goodyear. For several laps, the Canadian driver followed Unser and with three laps to go, made an unsuccessful pass for the lead. It momentarily put some space between his car and Unser's, but he continued to close as the white flag came out.

The gap was sliced in half as Goodyear got a better run off Turn 2 and he appeared to be even faster as they emerged from Turn 4. By now, the once-frozen crowd had forgotten its misery and was on its feet, cheering the combatants.

Goodyear feinted right and then tried to slingshot past Unser as they came down the straightaway. He made the pass, but only after the pair had crossed the finish line. Unser won by the slimmest margin in history – 0.043 seconds. It was almost a photo finish, but Unser's Galmer was clearly ahead. The only son and namesake of four-time winner Al Unser had captured his first Indy 500 and given the Unser family its eighth victory at the track.

Ironically, Unser's month had gone so poorly that he showed up on Race Day for the first time in 10 starts believing he had no chance to win.

Al Unser wound up third to give the Buick its best-ever finish at Indy. Following him home was Cheever, the only other car on the lead lap. Rounding out the top 10 were Sullivan, Rahal, Boesel, John Andretti, Foyt and Paul. St. James finished 11th and garnered top rookie honors, the first woman to do so.

"You just don't know what it means to win here at Indianapolis," a tearful Unser told the crowd as he celebrated an unexpected win in Victory Circle.

Thanks to the weather and the rash of accidents, the 1992 Indy 500 may not have been the best race in the history of the Speedway, but no one could disagree that it definitely was among the best finishes ever.

Above: Al Unser, Jr., holds off Canadian Scott Goodyear by .043 of a second, for the closest finish in history.

Left: He came so close: The expression on his face and the tear rolling down his cheek says it all for Scott Goodyear, who came within less than a car length of winning.
Photographs: IMS

1993: Battle Of The World Champions

A phenomenon known to the racing world as "Mansell Mania" was about to descend upon the Indianapolis Motor Speedway.

After capturing the 1992 F1 World Championship in dominating fashion, Nigel Mansell was suddenly the hottest racing driver in the world. Mansell was the first Briton to win the world title since James Hunt in 1976 and the British media were eager to exploit the product.

Unfortunately for F1, Mansell decided his efforts were unappreciated by his team owner and sponsors and he made a surprise move to Indy-car racing. Formula One's reigning champion would be running Indy cars for 1993 while Indy-car racing's fastest driver – Michael Andretti – was heading to Europe to try his hand at F1. Mansell took over the Newman-Haas ride vacated by Andretti.

With the Cosworth XB now available to the masses, there was a significant increase in their ranks. In addition to the Newman-Haas and Target Chip Ganassi teams, other Cosworth users included Hayhoe Racing, A.J. Foyt Enterprises, Walker Motorsports and Dick Simon Racing.

All of the aforementioned teams used the Lola chassis, but Lola also had T9300s for Buick and Chevrolet engines.

Dale Coyne Racing entered older Lolas for rookies Eric Bachelart and Robbie Buhl. Bachelart's entry was of particular interest with its sponsorship from Marmon Group, a yellow-and-black paint scheme and No. 32 in honor of Marmon's last attempt at Indianapolis – its race-winning Marmon Wasp of Ray Harroun. The Marmon Group could trace its roots to the Nordyke & Marmon company that had entered the winning car in 1911.

In what would be the final year of the Ilmor Chevy Indy V-8, the 1993 version would be known as the Chevy Indy C. Naturally, Marlboro Team Penske coupled the updated engine with the latest Penske PC-22 for Emerson Fittipaldi and Paul Tracy. Penske also sold a pair of PC-22s to Bettenhausen Motorsports for Swedish rookie Stefan Johansson and Tony Bettenhausen. Noticeably missing from the Penske lineup was four-time winner Rick Mears, who shocked the racing world with his surprise retirement the previous December.

One welcome change came in the form of rules that dictated an extra bulkhead be placed in the front of the cars to minimize the danger to the drivers' feet and ankles. Future designs would move the drivers' feet behind the front axle line, while the new rule was an attempt to "grandfather" that safety aspect into the older cars. Two drivers would wind up attesting to the structural soundness of the extra bulkhead. Unfortunately for Dale Coyne, the two drivers were his. Both Bachelart and Buhl made head-on collisions with the IMS concrete. While both suffered sore feet and ankles, neither suffered the kind of injuries incurred in similar collisions the

year before.

There were also some significant changes made to the track. With the strong possibility of a NASCAR event in the future, there was a need to strengthen the outer walls around the track. A thicker, slightly taller wall with a stronger fence replaced the old wall.

Both the original and replacement walls were removed and cut into sections. Some of the sections would wind up along the bank of a new infield lake as the golf course underwent a total renovation. (At least one section of the Turn 3 wall would also end up in Albuquerque where it graced the front of property owned by Al Unser, Jr., who struck the section trying to win the 1989 race!)

In order to attempt to slow down the cars, the apron was replaced by rumble strips to keep drivers from using the apron as part of the racetrack. To replace the apron that was intended to provide a lane for cars exiting and entering the pits, separate warmup lanes were added to the inside of Turns 1 and 2 as well as Turns 3 and 4.

Practice soon became the "Nigel Mansell show" with a large entourage of overseas journalists and photographing recording his every movement. The Briton made quick work of his rookie test requirements and then proceeded to set the fourth-quickest speed for the day at 222.855. This was on a track he had never raced at before! In fact, Mansell had never raced on an oval. Although he practiced at Phoenix earlier in the season, he was knocked unconscious in a practice crash and unable to race.

Unlike the most recent years, records would not be seen at Indianapolis thanks to the new apron and rumble strips which kept drivers from cutting down as low as they had in previous years.

By the time qualifying rolled around, Arie Luyendyk had posted the month's quickest speed at 226.162 mph. It was still plenty fast, but obviously not as fast the laps in excess of 233 mph a year ago. Throughout the first week, Mario Andretti, Tracy, Luyendyk and Raul Boesel had all set the fast speeds.

Qualifying produced a number of surprises with Luyendyk capturing the pole for Ganassi with an average speed of 223.967 mph.

Mario Andretti, who showed he could still win in Indy cars by capturing the race at Phoenix, qualified an impressive second at 223.414 and was joined on Row 1 by the equally impressive Boesel at 222.379. Scott Goodyear and Al Unser, Jr., who gave Indy its closest finish in history the previous May, qualified fourth and fifth, respectively. They were joined in the final moments of Pole Day by Johansson, who managed to outqualify the factory Penskes of Tracy (seventh) and Fittipaldi (ninth) as well as highly touted fellow rookie Mansell (eighth).

But the real surprise of the day came from Foyt. After teammate Robby Gordon brushed the wall in the morning warmup, Foyt decided he needed to step out of the cockpit and put all of his effort behind the flashy Gordon.

Track announcer Tom Carnegie informed a stunned crowd that Foyt would be taking a ceremonial final lap at the Speedway and then retiring as a driver. The four-time winner received a fitting ovation as he slowly toured the track and received the checkered flag one last time by IMS President Tony George.

"I had no idea I was going to do this," Foyt said as he tried to fight back the tears. "This was the place that made A.J. Foyt. It's hard to give up what you love. It's hard to give up racing. For 35 years, I've been here, but this has been my life here."

When the field was full, Lola had the upper hand in numbers with 28 chassis. The new Penske PC-22 accounted for four positions and Dominic Dobson was the lone wolf in the pack qualifying a '92 Galmer. Chevrolet supplied the power to 13 starters, Cosworths supplied the power to 12 and Buick (or Menard) powered the remaining eight.

The field had an international flair with three Brazilians (Fittipaldi, Boesel and Nelson Piquet), two Canadians (Goodyear and Tracy), a Dutchman (Luyendyk), a Briton (Mansell), an Italian (Teo Fabi), a Belgian (Didier Theys), a Frenchman (Stephane Gregoire), a Swede (Stefan Johans-

son), a Japanese (Hiro Matsushita), an Australian (Geoff Brabham), a Scotsman (Jim Crawford) and a Colombian (Roberto Guerrero). There were also three former F1 champions (Andretti, Mansell and Piquet) and seven others who had made at least one start in F1 (Boesel, Fabi, Johansson, Eddie Cheever, Crawford, Guerrero and Danny Sullivan).

The 1993 starting field also had six former 500 winners (Fittipaldi, Luyendyk, Andretti, Al Unser, Jr., Al Unser and Sullivan), two fathers and sons (the Unsers and the Andrettis) and one set of brothers (Tony and Gary Bettenhausen).

Although the pole winner is supposed to have the best position in the starting, there is a school of thought that the outside of Row 1 has a slight advantage at the start of the race because that driver is actually on the racing line heading into the first turn. The theory goes all the way back to the 1930s and it was even suggested the pole winner be allowed to start on the outside of Row 1. Boesel proved that theory to be a sound one and quickly jumped into the lead for the first 17 laps.

A yellow for Jim Crawford's spin brought the leaders into the pits and a variety of drivers, ranging from rookie Stephan Gregoire to Al Unser and Mario Andretti, all took turns leading. On Lap 70, Mansell took over the lead for the first time and stayed there for 21 laps. For a man who had never raced on an oval, he showed he could adapt quite well, thank you.

The second half of race centered on Luyendyk, Mansell and Fittipaldi, who had quietly kept the leaders in sight during the first 100 laps.

With 25 laps to go, Mansell was back in front, followed by Fittipaldi and Luyendyk. The reigning F1 world champion was about to get an education in the fine art of restarts in an Indycar race, something he would not have experienced in a grand prix. The yellow came out on Lap 183 for a tow-in for Lyn St. James.

As Mansell brought the field down for the Lap 185 restart, he was pounced on and quickly passed by Fittipaldi and

Luyendyk. It would be a three-way battle to the finish.

On Lap 193, Mansell brushed the wall with his right front wheel as he exited Turn 2. Miraculously, his car did not appear to be damaged and the yellow came back out for two laps. Fortunately for Mansell, the new wall was exactly 90 degrees to the angle of the track. When the wheel brushed the wall, it was flush with the concrete. A year earlier, Mansell might have damaged the wheel and suspension against the old wall.

Fittipaldi and Luyendyk would hold their positions on the restart and the Brazilian crossed the finish line 2.8 seconds ahead of the Dutch driver. Mansell came home a very impressive third and would garner the top rookie honor for the race. Boesel finished fourth followed by Mario Andretti, Brayton, Goodyear, Al Unser, Jr., Fabi and John Andretti, who had replaced Foyt.

Four-time 500 winner Al Unser finished 12th, although he did manage to lead 15 laps. It would be his last 500 and the 15 laps led gave him an all-time total of 644 – the most in Indy 500 history.

The winner was exultant about his second 500 win. "I was a little faster than Nigel coming out of Turn 4," Fittipaldi said. "I was really concerned about Arie. I knew he was coming fast, but I was able to put the power down when I needed to put the power down. It's like a dream. It's fantastic. As a driver, this was the best race of my life."

"All the procedures are new to me," Mansell said. "I'm not making any excuses. I just goofed up on a couple of them. The restart was one. I'm happy. What I've gone through since the beginning of this year to sit in front of you at one of the greatest races in the world and come in third, I'm going to be happy."

Fittipaldi also provided a footnote of sorts. For the first time since 1981, the winner refused to drink the traditional bottle of milk. Thanks to his ties to Brazil's citrus industry, Fittipaldi insisted on drinking orange juice before finally accepting the milk.

Above: Mansell makes a stop. He leads as late as lap 184. In spite of the Newman-Haas team competing in every "500" between 1983 and 1995, and then again in 2004 and 2005, they do so with only six drivers, Mario Andretti, Michael Andretti, Nigel Mansell, Paul Tracy, Bruno Junqueira, and Sébastien Bourdais.

Below: After being hospitalized due to a horrendous crash during practice in 1992, three-time world champion Nelson Piquet returns for another shot. He qualifies this time, but lasts only 38 laps before being eliminated by engine trouble.
Photographs: IMS

Right: Emerson Fittipaldi becomes a two-time "500" winner.

Below: Theresa Fittipaldi wills her husband on to victory. The seahorse earrings she is wearing are of her own design.

Bottom right: Yet another victory for Roger Penske.
Photographs: IMS

1994: Penske's Very Secret Weapon

When he produced his autobiography in 1973, Mark Dono-hue entitled it "The Unfair Advantage." It was an expression taken from team owner Roger Penske, who always sought the upper hand (or unfair advantage) over the competition.

In 1994, Roger Penske took the "unfair advantage" to a new high.

In an effort to find an engine formula that would be fast but affordable, the Indianapolis Motor Speedway devised regulations for a 209-cubic-inch, turbocharged pushrod engine. The rule had been around for a few years, with only one taker – the Greenfields. For 1994, New York industrialist Peter Greenfield entered a pair of cars for his son, Michael Greenfield. The Greenfield 209C pushrod engine was listed as the power-plant. Interestingly, in addition to making its own engine, Greenfield Industries was known worldwide for manufacturing bicycle kickstands.

Well, there was another taker, although no one found out until early May of 1994. Conducting secret tests, Penske developed a V-8 pushrod engine with assistance from Mercedes-Benz. The German motor giant was about to buy Chevrolet's interests in Ilmor Engineering, making them a partner with Penske as well. Nigel Bennett designed a PC-23 to house the powerplant and the profile of the engine cowling was noticeably taller than the Ilmor V-8 that it would have required.

Somehow, Penske managed to keep the entire project secret with Paul Tracy conducting most of the tests at Nazareth Speedway, conveniently owned by Penske himself. The engine project was unveiled in early May at the Speedway and when practice began in May, more than a few anxious eyes were fixated on the new Penske-Mercedes entered for Tracy, Emerson Fittipaldi and Al Unser, Jr., who had left the Galles team after six seasons.

The son and namesake of the four-time Indy 500 winner was in the early stages of one of his most remarkable seasons. For that matter, 1994 would be perhaps the most remarkable season for Penske Racing. Fittipaldi gave the

team its first win of the season at Phoenix and Unser delivered a week later at Long Beach. But little did anyone know that the total domination by Penske's talented trio was about to begin.

Bettenhausen Motorsports also entered Ilmor-powered Penske PC-22s for Stefan Johansson and Gary Betten-hausen. No one knew it at the time, but there would be additional Penskes in the 500 starting field.

Figuring to give them the most competition were the various Lola users. Chief among them were reigning national champion Nigel Mansell and Newman-Haas teammate Mario Andretti, who was starting his final season in Indy-car racing. The Newman-Haas Lolas used the latest Cosworth XB engines.

There was another newcomer on the block: the Reynard chassis. The product of Adrian Reynard and Rick Gorne, the Reynard 94I made a successful debut in the CART series opener at Surfers Paradise with Michael Andretti, making his Indy-car comeback with Chip Ganassi's team. Reynard produced chassis to house both the Cosworth XB and the Ilmor D, the latest version of what started out life as the Ilmor Chevy Indy V-8.

There was a new look at the corner of 16th Street and Georgetown. Nearing the final phases of construction, a new administration building stood on the spot where the previous administrative offices and museum had been located. That building had been demolished the previous July. By coincidence, the building at 729 North Capitol Avenue in Indianapolis had also been demolished at approximately the same time. For seven years, it had served as the Indianapolis Motor Speedway's corporate headquarters.

Once practice got underway, two things were certain: the new Penske-Mercedes were all going to be fast and their drivers were actually having problems trying to control the excessive horsepower produced by the new powerplant. Actually, there was the usual mention of the word "sandbagging" in conjunction with the Penske.

On Tuesday, Raul Boesel actually set the quickest speed to date at 230.403, and it wasn't until Thursday that one of

Above: The number of "500" victories by the Unser family extends to nine, as Al Jr., wins his second.

Photograph: IMS

Penske trio went faster. Fittipaldi went 230.438 and Tracy was second quick at 228.444. There was no real favorite for the pole, but everyone figured the Penske team was saving its best for qualifying.

Two prominent drivers took time during practice to announce their retirements – Al Unser and Johnny Rutherford. Unser had been entered in the Arizona Motor Sport Lola-Cosworth, but quickly decided it was time to quit. Rutherford, who had not driven at Indy in two years, took a ceremonial retirement lap in one of Foyt's cars. Besides winning at Indy four times, Unser retired with the record for most top-three finishes with 11 and most laps led in the 500 at 644. Rutherford, who won three 500s, was one of the few American drivers at Indianapolis who made a successful transition from front-engined roadster to rear-engine car.

In qualifying, there was still an Unser with which to contend, but there was also rain and the schedule was delayed while they attempted to dry out the track.

Al Unser, Jr., was first to qualify and posted an average of 228.011. He spent the rest of the day playing "king of the hill." Boesel finished with a 227.618, at the time good for second fastest. In all, 21 cars qualified by 6 p.m. and four drivers – Fittipaldi, Mario Andretti, Robby Gordon and Jimmy Vasser – would be allowed to make attempts as first-day qualifiers on Sunday.

Fittipaldi wound up third fastest at 227.303. Unser was on the pole. Squeezing in between the two Penskes was Boesel, who qualified on the front row for the second straight year. It would be the first Indianapolis 500 pole for Unser and the only time he would ever start on the front row at the Speedway.

Jacques Villeneuve and Michael Andretti occupied the fourth and fifth spots, giving the Reynard contingent its highest hopes for the race. But the biggest surprise in qualifying came from St. James, who by posting the sixth fastest speed out-qualified such luminaries as Mansell, Luyendyk and Mario Andretti, who occupied the third row.

Andretti would be starting his 29th (and final) 500 and desperately wanted to add that elusive second win at Indianapolis. After dominating the scene in his early years at the track, it seemed impossible that he would only win on one occasion. Of course, there were a number of drivers in the history of the sport who would have been glad to have his record!

In a year when a lot of people might have predicted an all-Marlboro Penske front row, mechanical problems prevented Tracy from joining Unser and Fittipaldi. He became a second-weekend qualifier and started 25th, although no one expected him to stay there for long.

One team that found itself struggling for the second straight year was Rahal-Hogan, whose Honda powerplants appeared to be a liability. A year earlier, Rahal missed the show after failing to find necessary speed in the team's RH01/Chevy Cs. Then, the aging chassis was considered the culprit. This year, the problem centered on the Honda engine that seemed to lack the necessary horsepower. In spite of his contract with Honda, Rahal decided it was more important to please longtime sponsor Miller Brewing. Penske PC-22/Ilmor Ds were leased for Rahal and Groff, who qualified the race on the final weekend.

One driver who failed to make the field was fan-favorite Gary Bettenhausen. Bettenhausen was unable to find speed in his brother's Penske-Ilmor D and the 1994 effort would mark his last at the Speedway after 21 starts.

The overriding question was which Penske-Mercedes would win and whether or not Roger Penske's drivers could score an unprecedented 1-2-3 finish.

When the green flag dropped, Unser jumped into the lead for the first 23 laps, but Fittipaldi took over and led the next 38 before pitting and surrendering the lead to Jacques Villeneuve. Early on, Fittipaldi appeared to have the race in hand with only Unser and Villeneuve able to run close.

Mario Andretti's last 500 came to an early end on Lap 23 when fuel system problems sidelined his car. After finishing an impressive third in his first 500, winning back-to-back pole positions and finally capturing the race in 1969, it seemed to be a most anti-climatic final run for one of the great names in the sport.

The first major caution of the day came out on Lap 30, when Groff and Dominic Dobson went around either side of Hideshi Matsuda and made contact with each other in Turn 1. The rest of the field packed up, but Lyn St. James managed to clip Scott Goodyear's car, sidelining Goodyear and losing a number of laps in the pits for repairs. Adrian Fernandez also was sidelined after damaging his suspension on the debris. Fortunately, no one was hurt.

Lap 92 produced one of the more bizarre incidents of the day. First, Matsuda crashed in Turn 1. On the same lap, John Paul, Jr., crashed in Turn 3, apparently after cutting a tire on debris from Matsuda's accident. Tracy's car began to smoke and he headed down the warmup lane en route to the pits where he would retire the car. The caution also gave everyone else the opportunity to pit under yellow and it produced yet another incident. As Dennis Vitolo sped down the access lane in Turn 3, his car vaulted over the left rear wheel of John Andretti. Vitolo's car cleared Andretti and Scott Brayton and then landed sideways on the engine cowling of Nigel Mansell's car.

The in-car camera showed a stunned Mansell trying to figure out what had happened before a broken water line began to spray him with scalding-hot water. With the help of a safety crewman, he bailed out of the car and rolled on the grass, believing he was on fire. Mansell was running third at the time of the incident, and although he was unhurt, Indianapolis had seen him for the last time as he would ultimately return to F1 and score one more victory for the Williams team at the season-ending Australian GP.

Fittipaldi and Unser continued to control the race, with Villeneuve getting the lead whenever they would pit. Finally, the Brazilian managed to put some distance on Unser and drove away, putting his teammate down a lap as the race neared its finish. Unser was able to unlap himself, but Fittipaldi seemed obsessed with lapping the entire field.

As Fittipaldi charged, his crew urged him to slow down and with 15 laps to go, there really was no reason to lap Unser. As the two Penskes exited Turn 4 on Lap 185, Fittipaldi touched the rumble strip, fishtailed, almost gathered it up and then slammed into the wall, coming to a halt just short of the finish line.

"I'm very disappointed," Fittipaldi said later. "At that time, I had everything under control. The car was flying. I nearly corrected it, but it was too late. Going into Turn 4, I tried to go a little lower than Jr. and hit the apron."

Fittipaldi had led an amazing 145 laps at the time of his demise.

Unser, nearly a lap down at the time, was now the leader and would stay in front for the remaining 15 laps. For the second time in three years, Unser had won the Indy 500. That gave the Unser family nine wins at Indianapolis.

Villeneuve finished an impressive second by 8.6 seconds in his first 500 and Rahal, who started 28th in a borrowed car, wound up third, one lap down to Unser. To no one's surprise, the French-Canadian youngster was named Indy's top rookie.

Jimmy Vasser finished fourth, followed by Robby Gordon, Michael Andretti, Teo Fabi, Eddie Cheever, Bryan Herta and John Andretti, who was on his way to making history. Immediately after finishing 10th, Andretti left the track by helicopter, and then caught a jet to Charlotte, N.C., where he ran in NASCAR's World 600. He became the first driver to run in both races on the same day.

EMERSON FITTIPALDI

No one knew what to make of Emerson Fittipaldi when he arrived at Indianapolis in 1984 as a rookie hoping to make his first 500. It may have been the same dark-haired Brazilian with the toothy grin and familiar blue and orange helmet, but there were some doubts. Perhaps it was the pink driving suit and the pink March-Cosworth entered by an unknown, Miami-based team owned by Jose "Pepe" Romero. Perhaps it was the fact that the 36-year-old Brazilian was trying to make a comeback after retiring three years earlier – leaving one to wonder about his commitment. Or perhaps it was the consideration of whether or not Fittipaldi still possessed the level of talent that earned him two F1 world titles.

In his first Indy 500, Fittipaldi did not qualify up front. He did not lead a lap or come close to leading one. He started 23rd and finished 32nd after oil pressure problems sidelined him on Lap 37. It was hardly the stuff one found on a resume for someone named Emerson Fittipaldi. Shortly after Indianapolis, Fittipaldi left the team and Romero decided to insert himself in the cockpit for Portland. Driving for another small team at the Meadowlands, he finished a respectable seventh. The California Cooler entry was not considered a potential frontrunner, but maybe this guy they called "Emmo" still had something left.

That thought obviously crossed Pat Patrick's mind and he signed the Brazilian to run the entire 1985 season. Openly admitting he needed time to learn about Indy-car racing, he proved a quick study and even led four different times in that year's Indy 500. Two months later, he won the Michigan 500, his first oval-track victory and first in Indy-car racing. The second phase of Fittipaldi's impressive career was taking off and Indy-car racing was the beneficiary of this consummate professional racer from Sao Paolo.

It had to be more than coincidental that Philip Morris' return to America's premier auto racing series coincided with the ascending rebirth of Fittipaldi's career. Marlboro had sponsored him in his final two years with McLaren and now was poised to spend significant sponsor dollars in Indy-car racing. Fittipaldi would artfully talk about his "Marlboro car" without sounding like a commercial. And with Marlboro came fashion giant Hugo Boss. Indy-car racing was officially trendy, thanks to the worldwide fame of Fittipaldi.

In 1986, he showed his '85 Michigan win was no fluke by scoring podium finishes on the ovals of Phoenix, Sanair and Michigan. In 1989, he outlasted Al Unser, Jr., in a wheel-banging fight to the finish to win racing's biggest prize: the Indianapolis 500. He would win again in 1993 and should have won in 1994, crashing while trying to put a lap on teammate Al Unser, Jr., who went to win his second 500. No one knew it would be Fittipaldi's last 500, but all in all, it was quite a comeback.

"We had been working on the car to make it better," said Unser. "I think Emerson was the strongest player out there. His car was working really well, but mine was understeering, particularly when I was running in traffic. If you've got a heavy hitter in front of you, you do everything you can to lap him. It would have put a final nail in my coffin if he could have done that."

Several days before the race, Unser asked his father what he wanted for his 55th birthday, which would fall on Race Day. The elder Unser replied: "Win the race."

It made some kind of birthday present for the Unser family.

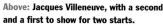

Above: Jacques Villeneuve, with a second and a first to show for two starts.

Top right: Late in the race, Scott Goodyear, Scott Pruett and Jacques Villeneuve, running first, second and third peel out of the pits.
Photographs: IMS

1995: Jacques Absorbs Two-Lap Penalty For "500" Victory

It would be a month of surprises.

For the first time since 1973, there would be cars running at the Indianapolis Motor Speedway using Firestone tires. The maker of the tire with the most wins in 500 history (52 as of 1995) disappeared from the motorsports scene more than 20 years earlier and ultimately was purchased by Bridgestone. The Japanese company decided it wanted a presence in Indy-car racing and announced it would be entering into an agreement with Pat Patrick and embarking on a year of testing and development, with Scott Pruett piloting a Lola-Ford Cosworth. Patrick and Firestone spent all of 1994 running at various tracks, including the Speedway. By 1995, they were ready to return to racing.

For the first time since the mid-1960s, Indy-car racing was about to have a tire war although not quite like the original one in which Goodyear and Firestone literally funded teams and drivers. There was some exchange of money this time around, but most teams decided to wait and see how good the Firestone tires would be before making a change.

In addition to the Patrick team, Firestone also shod the teams of Tasman Motorsports, Chip Ganassi Racing, Arciero Wells Racing, Dale Coyne Racing, Hemelgarn Racing and Greg Beck Motorsports. There were also a few Goodyear teams that would be offered Firestones during the month as they struggled to qualify. Firestone, it seems, had done its homework.

One outfit hoping to make a successful return was Honda, which supplied engines the previous year to Rahal-Hogan Racing. The Rahal team opted to run Penske-Ilmors after failing to reach competitive speeds in practice. Rahal and Honda parted company at the end of the season, but Steve Horne's Tasman operation decided to take the gamble and run the engines for 1995.

Mercedes-Benz, which appeared the previous year in the form of a pushrod V-8, purchased a share of Ilmor Engineering and badged Ilmor's latest version of its engine. Following the domination of the M-B pushrod in 1994, the United States Auto Club and the Indianapolis Motor Speedway scrapped that formula. All engines would be turbocharged V-8s and V-6s with the latter getting 10 more inches of turbo boost.

Thanks to a successful debut season in 1994, Reynard made serious inroads in Lola territory with a number of top teams using the new 95I chassis, including Players Team-Green for Jacques Villeneuve.

Although Mario Andretti had retired and Nigel Mansell had returned to F1, the 1995 entry had a very international flavor with no less than 11 drivers – both Fittipaldis (Emerson and nephew Christian), Eliseo Salazar, Mauricio Gugelmin, Teo Fabi, Danny Sullivan, Roberto Guerrero, Stefan Johansson, Raul Boesel, Michael Andretti and Eddie Cheever – boasting F1 experience. Latin America was also well represented with eight Brazilians, a Colombian, a Chilean and two Mexicans on the entry list.

Of the American contingent, only Stan Fox, Davey Hamilton and Johnny Parsons represented the USAC midget-sprint car set. It would provide fodder for discussions regarding the future of Indy-car racing.

One by-product of having more than one tire manufacturer is speed, and Arie Luyendyk showed it was going to be a fast month of May by running a lap at 233.281. Not only did it break Jim Crawford's opening-day mark of 229.609, it also eclipsed Roberto Guerrero's lap record of 232.618. Of course, Luyendyk's speed was considered unofficial since it occurred on a practice day, but the gauntlet had definitely been thrown.

Two days later, Luyendyk upped the ante by running a 234.107. The following day it would be Luyendyk's teammate, Brayton, who set the pace with a top lap of 231.410. The Menard drivers were clearly establishing themselves as the contenders for the pole position.

The next day, Luyendyk was back on top with a 232.468, but it was news off the track that dominated the headlines. Speedway President Tony George headlined a press conference in which plans were announced for the Indy Racing League, designed to run as a rival to CART. George, 500 Chief Steward Tom Binford and Jack Long (who would eventually head the IRL) were hopeful it would be a viable alternative to CART, cut the skyrocketing costs of Indy-car racing, offer more oval-track events and give more young American drivers a chance to race in the 500.

Underscoring the latter point was a notable visitor to the Speedway from NASCAR, Jeff Gordon. Displaying incredible talent in USAC midgets and sprints though only a teenager, Gordon was unable to find a ride in the CART series. His talent took him instead to NASCAR, where he instantly flourished.

Meanwhile, the Buick-engined Menard speedsters continued to set the pace in practice, topping Friday's charts with the fastest speeds of the month. Luyendyk was first at 234.913 with Brayton close behind at 234.473.

However, those speeds may have come courtesy of tows generated by running in traffic. Drivers will often try to run by themselves to get a realistic idea of how fast they can go, but during practice for the 500, it's not at all unusual for a driver to get a "flyer" by allowing another fast car to provide a tow down the straight.

Rain hampered the first day of qualifying, but a handful of drivers managed to make their runs. Leading the way was Brayton, whose average speed of 231.604 mph would prove to be the fastest of the 33 starters. Luyendyk also qualified on the first day, but his 231.031 average was slightly slower than his Menard teammate. Goodyear joined them on the front row with an average speed of 230.759.

Despite the speed of the Menard duo, the news centered on the difficulties encountered by the Penskes of Unser and Fittipaldi as the first weekend of qualifying ended. Neither was able to put together a run good enough to make the race. After dominating the 1994 season, the team opted to forgo

Above: Paul Tracy avoids the collision as Stan Fox and Eddie Cheever hit the wall in turn one of the first lap. It is believed that Cheever's striking of the out-of-control Fox actually lessened the severity of the injuries to Fox, who miraculously breaks no bones but does sustain a head injury which will prevent him from ever racing again. He will lose his life in an automobile accident in New Zealand on December 18, 2000.

Photograph: IMS

tire testing with Goodyear. The result was that Goodyear's superspeedway tire was tested and developed based on data from the Lola and Reynard chassis.

The Penske chassis might also have been a liability. A year earlier, it dominated Indianapolis thanks to the excessive horsepower of the Mercedes pushrod. Running a conventional engine later that season at Michigan, the Penske team was clearly off the pace.

Now with only one week of practice and two qualifying days remaining, there was a mad scramble in the Penske camp. Ironically, one solution centered on leasing Lolas from Rahal-Hogan Racing, which had found itself in a similar situation a year earlier. But nothing seemed to work.

On the final day of qualifying, Fittipaldi finally squeezed into the field, but with less than 15 minutes remaining, he was bumped by Johansson, whose team had abandoned its Penske-Mercedes for a Reynard-Ford Cosworth.

The gun went off at 6 p.m. and to everyone's surprise, the 1995 Indianapolis 500 starting field would not have Al Unser, Jr., Emerson Fittipaldi, the Marlboro Penske team or even a Penske chassis. It was a memorable "bump day" at Indianapolis and the closest anyone could come to a comparison would have been 30 years earlier, when Rodger Ward failed to qualify after six straight years of never finishing out of the top four.

But in racing, the show must go on and the 80th Indianapolis 500 would go on without the sport's marquee team.

Scott Goodyear showed how far the Honda had come by

jumping into the lead from the outside of the front row when the green flag dropped. Almost immediately, there was trouble in Turn 1 near the front of the pack. Stan Fox, who had started in a career-best 11th position, suddenly snapped to the right and spun backward into the wall. As Fox struck the wall, Cheever had nowhere to go and instantly collected Fox's car. The impact tore the front off of Fox's car, exposing the driver who obviously was knocked unconscious in the incident. The rest of the field happened onto the scene and by the time the smoke had cleared, the cars of St. James and Carlos Guerrero were involved in the accident. Debris also damaged de Ferran's car although he managed to limp into the pits before retiring.

Fox somehow survived the accident with a serious concussion, but no broken bones. The head injury, however, would end the racing career of the affable Wisconsin driver, who had made eight 500 starts.

Goodyear's lead ended when the race restarted on Lap 9 and Luyendyk got past for the next seven laps. Michael Andretti would lead the next 16 laps and the first half of the race would become a battle between Andretti and Goodyear. Andretti's run ended on Lap 77 when he brushed the Turn 4 wall to miss Gugelmin. The latter was leading the race at the time and suddenly slowed in front of Andretti after deciding to dash into the pits. Andretti retired with suspension trouble.

Gugelmin, who had led earlier, appeared to be the man to beat and would lead 50 laps between Laps 82 and 138. In

There was one major problem. Goodyear caught and passed the pace car before it entered the pits.

Because it was an infraction of the rules, Goodyear was given the black flag. Team owner Steve Horne decided to keep Goodyear out on the track and hopefully deal with the pace-car issue after the race. It was a gamble worth taking, but after Lap 195, race officials stopped counting Goodyear's laps. Villeneuve was now in the lead and would stay there for the next five laps. Goodyear also continued but when he completed what should have been his 200th lap, he was not given the checkered flag.

"When I was beside the pace car, I looked up and saw the green," Goodyear explained. "In my eyes, it was perfect. I think when the green light is on, it means go."

Interestingly, the problems of Pruett and Goodyear kept Firestone from making a triumphant return to Indianapolis. Villeneuve's car was shod with Goodyears. In fact, the top nine finishers used Goodyear tires.

Villeneuve crossed the line 2.4 seconds ahead of Christian Fittipaldi. Rahal was third for the second year in the row and Salazar finished a very respectable fourth. Rounding out the top 10 were Robby Gordon, Gugelmin, Luyendyk, Fabi, Sullivan and Matsushita. Fittipaldi's run earned him the top rookie honor.

For Villeneuve, the win was most unexpected thanks to the earlier penalty, but he became the beneficiary of another driver's infraction. The French-Canadian youngster seemed to especially enjoy the victor's traditional bottle of milk, taking sips for the photographers before turning around with his back to everyone and guzzling most of it. He was given a second bottle.

"We did everything we could do not to win this race and then we had to work harder, so that made it more exciting," Villeneuve said. "When I was running third or fourth, after being two laps down, I was already pretty happy even if it wasn't as good as the year before. To win the race after that, was really just a good feeling."

At the time of his victory at Indianapolis, Villeneuve and his manager were engaged in negotiations for his future. In just over a year, he would be runner-up for Williams in the F1 World Championship. A year afterward, he would be world champion.

Below: This aerial shot provides an excellent view of the golf course, revamped in 1992 by the world-renowned Pete Dye. There are now four holes inside the track and 14 to the east of the backstretch. Whereas the course originally was relatively flat, it now features an assortment of lakes and mounds.
Photograph: IMS

all, the Brazilian would wind up leading the most laps (59), but he would drop back and wind up finishing sixth.

One man overlooked by the lead group was Jacques Villeneuve, who was all but written off after getting a two-lap penalty. With a number of cars heading into the pits on Lap 36, Villeneuve was unaware he was in the lead at the time and erroneously believed he had been waved by the pace car. The infraction dropped him two laps back.

But thanks to steady driving and good pit strategy, the French-Canadian driver worked his way back onto the lead lap and took the lead on Lap 156. As the race entered its final quarter, the contenders were Goodyear, Vasser, Pruett and Villeneuve.

Vasser's day ended on Lap 171 when he crashed in Turn 3 after being passed for the lead by Pruett. Pruett was now pursued by Goodyear, who swept past on Lap 176. The two stayed together until Lap 185 when Pruett looped it in Turn 2 and struck the wall with such force, it separated the transmission and rear wheels from the rest of the car.

That brought out the yellow for five laps with Goodyear leading Villeneuve, Fittipaldi, Rahal and Salazar. With the track about to go green, Goodyear and Villeneuve engaged in a game of "thrust and pare" on the backstretch with the race leader making a mock start and his rival following suit. Finally, the pace car sped away for the restart as they approached Turn 4. Goodyear held back and then gassed it, but this time Villeneuve seemed to hang back.

THE UNSER FAMILY

MORE than any other family in the sport, the Unsers were, are and always will be the first family of auto racing. Take that to the bank. The formula is simple: Indianapolis was, is and always will be the biggest auto race in the world and no family has won it more times (9), led more laps (1,194), posted more top-three finishes (19), amassed more miles (26,702.5) and had more of its members (6) participate at the Indianapolis Motor Speedway than the offspring and grandsons of one Jerome (Jerry) Henry Unser Sr.

The Unser Indy 500 saga might have started even earlier had Jerry's brother Joe not been killed testing a car he hoped to run in the 1930 race. With the Coleman Automobile company providing three front-wheel-drive cars for Jerry, Joe and Louis, the brothers planned a three-pronged assault on Indianapolis during the summer of 1929. While testing on a Colorado highway, Joe crashed to his death. Coleman withdrew its support and Jerry would ultimately devote his attention to his four sons, Jerry, Jr., Louis, Bobby and Al. To say they were born and bred to be racers would be an understatement. All graduated from the rough-and-tumble jalopy tracks and three would make it to auto racing's pinnacle – the Indianapolis Motor Speedway.

The first member of the Unser family to run at Indy was Jerry Unser, Jr., who qualified for the 1958 race. The 1957 USAC Stock Car Champion, Unser's debut at Indianapolis ended in Turn 3 of the first lap. Caught up in the pileup that killed Pat O'Connor, Unser's car sailed over the wall. He suffered a dislocated shoulder and returned the following year, only the die from blood poisoning after receiving serious burns in a practice accident.

Physically the largest of the four Unser brothers, Jerry was easy going and something of a gentle giant. Photos show the characteristic Unser smile.

Bobby Unser would be the next of the clan to tackle Indianapolis. Blessed with the gift of gab, Unser would talk to anybody and everybody. Outspoken and somewhat cocky, Unser did have enough talent to back up his words. However, it would take time at Indianapolis for that talent to truly show. After failing to finish his first three 500s while driving the legendary Novis, Unser finally went the distance in 1966, driving Gordon Van Liew's new Huffaker-Offenhauser. Unser was lucky to even be at the race, yet alone in it. In the season opener at Phoenix, he drove Van Liew's older Huffaker-Offy through the fence! He survived and mounted the twisted

steering wheel and column on his wall.

Toward the end of the 1966 season, Unser made the wise decision of joining Bob Wilke's Leader Card team with Jud Phillips as his chief mechanic. They started winning in 1967 and by the end of the 1968 season, the partnership produced a national championship and the first victory at Indianapolis for the Unser family.

It was only the beginning and besides, there were now two Unsers competing at Indianapolis. In 1965, Al arrived with brother Louis as his chief mechanic and Frank Arciero's curious, Maserati-powered creation. That car failed to produce the necessary speed, but Unser was invited to run A.J. Foyt's new Lola-Ford. He accepted, qualified and finished ninth to give his career a strong boost.

Unlike Bobby, Al was quiet and somewhat shy, especially around strangers. He let his throttle foot do all of his talking and once he hooked up with George Bignotti, it wasn't long before he started winning races.

As each brother enjoyed success, they found themselves on the opposite sides of the tire war. Al drove for Firestone and Bobby was a Goodyear man. Someone even cut a pair of racing jackets in half and sewed them together for the parents. "Goodstone" adorned the back of father Jerry's jacket, while mother Mary Unser's jacket read "Fireyear." Racing had always been a family affair for the Unser and the parents could be found at Indy to support their sons. For a number of years, one of the highlights for the racing community was "Mom" Unser's annual chili cookout.

Al would win at Indianapolis in 1970 and made history in the process. Sets of brothers had raced together at Indy since the earliest years of the race. But Al's victory marked the first time two brothers had won. He won again in '71 and Bobby would give the family its fourth victory in the rain-shortened 1975 race. Al won for a third time in 1978 and Bobby followed with a win from the pole in 1981 that temporarily was awarded to Mario Andretti.

Although he never officially retired, Bobby Unser would never race at Indianapolis again. But two years after his final

Below right: **Brothers Jerry, Jr., Bobby, and Al, followed by Al, Jr., Robby (son of Bobby), and Johnny (son of Jerry, Jr.).**
Photographs: IMS

race, there were again two Unsers in the starting field at Indy. Al's son, Al, Jr., made history by qualifying for the 1983 race. Never before in the history of the race had a father and son raced against each other.

Al, Jr. showed some of Uncle Bobby brashness in and out of the car. A youthful look belied his age of 21, and the perpetual cigarette dangling from his mouth gave more of the appearance of a defiant kid caught smoking. On the track, he possessed a combination of Bobby's outright speed and father Al's smoothness. As he matured, he would race more and more like his father – one of the best in the business in bringing a car home.

In the closing laps of the race, he tried to delay Tom Sneva, who was attempting to close in on the race leader, Al Unser. Sneva finally got past both Unsers and went on to win the race. Afterward, Al Jr. admitted he took a different line to try "to mess up Sneva's air." It was honest and forthright – just like Bobby Unser would have handled the situation. But it was also controversial and there was the predictable backlash about Unser's "blocking" tactics. In later years, Al, Jr. would deal with the media more like his father than his uncle.

But like his father and uncle, he would also start winning, recording his first Indy-car victory in his second season of competition.

In 1987, Al Unser went home to Albuquerque after being unable to find a ride for the 500. It was only after Danny Ongais crashed and was ruled medically unfit to race that Roger Penske called. "Big Al" qualified a car that only days before had been a show car in the lobby of a hotel. In one of the more amazing 500 stories, Unser dodged a first-lap accident, moved up in the standings and then inherited the lead late in the race to win his fourth 500.

The victory certainly extended his career and while he continued to be competitive, the focus was now on his son who came close to winning in 1989. After staging a late-race charge, he overhauled Emerson Fittipaldi and had he not been balked in traffic, he would have cruised to a victory. However, the traffic allowed Fittipaldi to close and when the two drivers went into Turn 3, Fittipaldi moved up and bumped Al, Jr. into the wall. The race finished under the caution and as Fittipaldi came around to take the checker, there was Unser giving him a pair of "thumbs up." Still, one could see that extraordinary restraint was being employed, but to Unser's credit, he showed no bitterness toward Fittipaldi in the post-race press conference. It might have been his classiest moment as a driver.

Al, Jr. would join his father and uncle by holding off Scott Goodyear in 1992 and winning the closest 500 in history. Ironically, one other driver who could have won that day was Al Unser, who finished third after a slow final pit stop.

Al Unser retired during practice for the 1994 500. There was no farewell tour and Unser simply circled the track once more to receive the checkered flag for a final time. It was the kind of curtain call one would have expected from the reserved Unser. He retired as Indy's all-time lap leader with 644.

However, the family was not finished winning. Al, Jr. became a two-time victor that year giving the Unser family its ninth win at Indianapolis.

In 1996, Johnny Unser, youngest son of the late Jerry Unser, became the fifth member of the family to qualify for the 500. He would run in five races before retiring from the sport.

Bobby's youngest son, Robby, would make his first 500 start in 1998 and he finished an impressive fifth. A lengthy pit stop took him out of contention, but he ran with the leaders for most of the second half of the race. He would race at Indianapolis the following year and has since retired from the sport.

Al Unser, Jr. retired after the 2004 race, but in 2006, he returned after being bored with retirement. It remains to be seen if he will race at Indy again, but on the horizon is his son, Al, who has shown some promise in various development series.

Even if an Unser never races at Indianapolis, no one can discount the impact their family members made at the place.

285

Chapter 15
INDY RACING LEAGUE USHERS IN NEW ERA FOR SPEEDWAY

1996: Buddy Battles Back For The Win

Above: Carrying on the tradition: Tony Hulman George, IMS president, founding father of the IRL, and a tireless advocate of safety in racing.

Below: Scott Brayton and John Menard take one of the greatest gambles ever by withdrawing a qualified car from the outside of row two in order to go for the pole. It pays off. Not only is this the second consecutive pole for the historically minded Brayton, but, amazingly for a driver, he is even able to recite the names of the eight back-to-back pole winners who preceded him.

Photographs: IMS

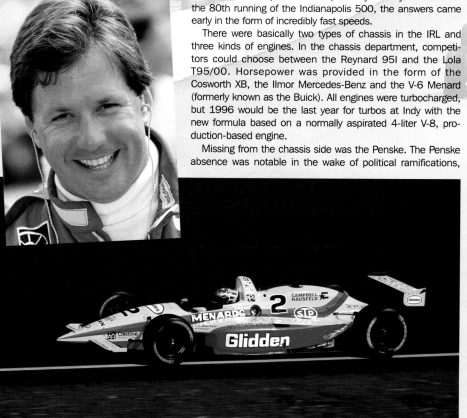

NINETEEN NINETY-SIX marked the debut of the Indy Racing League, and as anticipated, virtually every regular entrant with Championship Auto Racing Teams elected not to enter the "500." Memories of 1979 came flooding back.

Ironically, the impetus for the IRL's formation was Championship Auto Racing Teams, the organization of Indy-car team owners that had broken away from the United States Auto Club in 1979. CART sanctioned every Indy-car race except the Indianapolis 500, which remained under USAC sanction. Over the years, CART staged races in a number of big-TV-market venues like New York and Los Angeles, but its movement to street circuits was a source of concern to the Indianapolis Motor Speedway. Another source of concern was the increase in foreign drivers coupled with a significant decrease in American drivers. The stated intention of the IRL was to make some changes to address those situations. To further underscore its intentions, the Indianapolis Motor Speedway announced it would guarantee (with certain stipulations) 25 of the 33 starting positions for IRL regulars.

Understandably, there were growing pains and the starting field of the 1996 Indianapolis 500 would feature 17 rookies, the most since the 1930 race when 19 starters were newcomers. The equipment would also not be as state-of-the-art, with IRL teams using year-old Reynards and Lolas until a new car and engine package could be designed, tested and manufactured. However, even year-old cars were still competitive and the Speedway would have its fastest month in history.

The idea behind the new cars and engines was cost. IRL rules stipulated a maximum cost for chassis, while engine leases were not permitted. With the decision to officially form the IRL in 1995, there simply was not enough time to devise new chassis and engine regulations and get the new equipment ready to race in time for the 1996 season.

If there were any questions about how competitive it would be at the Indianapolis Motor Speedway in May of 1996 for the 80th running of the Indianapolis 500, the answers came early in the form of incredibly fast speeds.

There were basically two types of chassis in the IRL and three kinds of engines. In the chassis department, competitors could choose between the Reynard 95I and the Lola T95/00. Horsepower was provided in the form of the Cosworth XB, the Ilmor Mercedes-Benz and the V-6 Menard (formerly known as the Buick). All engines were turbocharged, but 1996 would be the last year for turbos at Indy with the new formula based on a normally aspirated 4-liter V-8, production-based engine.

Missing from the chassis side was the Penske. The Penske absence was notable in the wake of political ramifications,

but in fairness, the all-conquering Penske chassis of 1994 was obsolete and its 1995 predecessor proved to be a failure. If the truth were to be known, Roger Penske would have been more than happy to part with his older cars if there had been any takers.

The starting field of the 500 was guaranteed to be a mix of well-known names and a few not-so-well-known names. Leading the list were 1990 winner Arie Luyendyk and two-time 500 runner-up Roberto Guerrero. When the IRL launched its inaugural race at Disney World, Luyendyk and Guerrero were among the three drivers who had scored Indy-car victories in their careers (John Paul, Jr., was the third).

Joining them would be 500 veterans Scott Brayton, Buddy Lazier, Davy Jones, Alessandro Zampedri, Scott Sharp, Eddie Cheever, Lyn St. James, Mike Groff, Johnny Parsons, Stephan Gregoire, Eliseo Salazar, Hideshi Matsuda and Marco Greco. Brayton had captured the pole position the year before and had started on the front row in 1985. Cheever was a front-row starter in 1992 and like St. James was a former Rookie of the Year.

Danny Ongais, a veteran of 10 Indianapolis 500s and survivor of some of the most spectacular accidents in Speedway history, would be a surprise starter despite a 10-year absence from the race.

The dynamic Tony Stewart and the IRL's first-round race winner, Buzz Calkins, would lead the rookie contingent, but it would have more than a few names of interest.

Italy's Michele Alboreto, runner-up in the 1985 F1 world championship, would make his sole 500 appearance. Joining him would be Spanish sports-car ace Fermin Velez. Nineteen-year-old Michel Jourdain, Jr., would try to become one of the youngest men to start in the Indianapolis 500. Joe "Double-O" Gosek was an eastern supermodified star who gave the traditionalist something to cheer for.

Johnny Unser, whose father, Jerry, had raced in the 1958 500, would try to become the fifth member of the famed Unser family to race at Indianapolis. Also hoping to make their first 500 would be fellow rookies Robbie Buhl, Richie Hearn, Davey Hamilton, Scott Harrington, Jim Guthrie, "Bronco" Brad Murphey, Johnny O'Connell, Paul Durant, Racin Gardner and Mark Dismore. Dismore, like Ongais, had been the survivor of one of the wildest crashes in Speedway history. Fully recovered, he was hoping to make folks forget his highlight film from practice in 1991.

In order to have a full field of 33 starters, the two largest teams – Menard and Scandia – would be fielding considerably more than the normal count of two or three drivers. Menard's lineup included Brayton, Stewart, Cheever and Dismore. Scandia (formerly Dick Simon Racing) would have Zampedri, Salazar, Jourdain, Velez, Gosek, Alboreto and Gardner. All seven would qualify and would represent the most cars owned by one team starting in an Indianapolis 500.

Lazier, who captured the pole at the season opener at Disney World, was questionable for 500 duty. During practice for the Phoenix race, Lazier spun and backed into the wall. St. James was unable to avoid his spinning car and collected Lazier for a second hard impact. The result was a number of back fractures, a trip to Indianapolis to call on Dr. Trammell & Co. and an uncertain future.

However, when practice began, Lazier took part, although it was safe to say he was still very much in pain. The team wisely limited his practice time to allow the healing process to continue.

Weather hampered the first two days, but cloudy conditions and temperatures in the low 60s produced a day of incredible speed when practice began in earnest on Monday. Stewart, showing everyone that he was no ordinary rookie, set the pace in his Lola/Menard with a phenomenal lap of 237.336 mph (the official track record for one lap was 234.913 set by Luyendyk the previous year). Earlier, he had recorded a lap in excess of 231 mph after passing his rookie test.

"I told Larry (Curry, the team manager) the car felt more comfortable at 237 than it did at 231," Stewart said of his memorable lap.

Stewart would set the pace the following day with a top lap of 236.121, but this time he had some company. Menard teammates Eddie Cheever and Scott Brayton checked in at 235.997 and 235.750, respectively.

Rain would hamper the fifth day of practice, but Stewart discovered a new rival on Day 6 – Luyendyk. The 1990 500 winner set the fastest speed of the month with a lap of 237.774 in his Reynard/Cosworth. Stewart was second at 237.029.

The Friday before qualifying has been dubbed "Fast Friday" and with good reason. Drivers invariably find some extra on this day in an attempt to psyche out the competition. Luyendyk may have gone beyond that. Admitting he had help from a tow, the Dutch driver astounded everyone with a lap of 239.260.

Could 240 be possible for qualifying? With ideal weather conditions and a tow, the answer is that it probably could have been achieved. However, Mother Nature had other ideas and rain delayed the proceedings. Stewart was quickest in practice with a top lap of 235.719, more than 3 mph slower than Luyendyk's unofficial record lap. The effect of the tow also showed up when qualifying eventually got underway.

Stewart became the first of the Menard drivers to qualify, earning a spot in his first 500 with an average speed of 233.179 mph. Teammate Cheever, a fellow contender for the pole, could only muster an average of 231.781. Salazar bumped Cheever a spot with an average of 232.684 in the Scandia Lola/Cosworth.

Luyendyk went out with 33 minutes left and seemingly emerged with the pole, averaging a new track record of 233.390 mph. His second lap was also a one-lap record at 234.742. But the Menard team, despite having qualified four cars, was not finished in its quest for the pole.

In a huge gamble, John Menard and Scott Brayton decided to withdraw their safely qualified car and try for it with another. It was an extremely risky move which could easily have backfired. But it paid off, and amazingly, Brayton won the pole with a new track record of 233.718 mph. The pole was his for a second straight year, and Stewart was moved up to second spot after Luyendyk's car flunked post-qualification tech for being seven pounds underweight. Davy Jones, who qualified Rick Galles' Lola/Mercedes-Benz with an average of 232.882, joined Brayton and Stewart on Row 1.

"Nothing is more exciting than the Indianapolis Motor Speedway on Pole Day," said an elated Brayton. "To put it in the field and be happy, but disappointed because you're not on the front row... then come back a couple of hours later and have all that change... this is the most emotion I've ever been through."

Luyendyk might have lost the pole, but he stole a little of Brayton's thunder the following day when he went out to re-qualify, his Saturday run having been disallowed. Arie set marks which were destined to last for years to come. In the final year for turbocharged engines, he raised the lap mark to 236.986 mph, with a single lap at a breathtaking 237.498. Because he was a second-day qualifier, however, he would have to start in 20th position.

"I've never been on a roller coaster like this, but we achieved one thing and that's breaking the track record," Luyendyk said after his run.

Week 2 of practice is usually split between drivers yet to qualify searching for speed and drivers already in the race working on race setups. With 26 drivers already in the field, seven spots remained open although Jim Guthrie's average of 222.394 looked marginal.

Cold, rainy conditions kept the speeds down through Thursday, but Brad Murphey managed a top lap of 228.612 on Tuesday as the week's quickest lap among the non-qualifiers.

Tragedy struck on Friday. Practicing race setups in a backup car, Brayton lost control and instantaneously slammed into the Turn 2 wall. Brayton was transported to Methodist Hospital where the affable Michigan driver was pronounced dead at 12:50 p.m. The accident was blamed on a slowly deflating right rear tire and the 80th Indianapolis 500 had lost its pole position winner.

Brayton's death was the first at the Speedway since Jovy Marcelo in 1992 and left team owner John Menard in a quandary as to what he should do. One school of thought was that out of respect for Brayton, he would simply withdraw the car and let someone else qualify. Someone suggested the Speedway start 32 cars and leave the polesitter's space open in a show of respect to Brayton. Another option was to put someone else in the car and move it to the back of the field.

Menard opted for the latter and wound up putting Ongais in the car. Ongais' last attempt at making the 500 ended in a Turn 4 accident during practice for the 1987 race. He last raced in the 1986 Indianapolis 500, now he was not only getting a chance to start his 11th race, but would have the luxury of the pole winner's car at his disposal.

When qualifying finished, only Billy Boat had been bumped from the field, but it would be notable in that more than half of the 33 starters (17) were rookies.

Early morning rains threatened the proceedings on Race Day, but a concerted effort by track workers resulted in a delay of only 15 minutes.

Stewart, now on the pole, jumped into the lead and stayed there for the first 31 laps, surrendering the lead to Guerrero when he made his first stop. Guerrero led briefly, then Lazier led. Running second was Luyendyk, who had charged from 20th position. Then it was back to Stewart for Laps 42-54. However, the sensational rookie had his race hampered by a sour engine and by Lap 82, he was out of the race.

Jones and Lazier had swapped the lead through Lap 133 when Guerrero took over for 24 laps. Luyendyk's charge came to a halt on Lap 97 when he and Salazar made contact. The Chilean driver was able to continue, but damage to the Dutch driver's car ultimately sidelined him on Lap 149.

The battle was now between Jones, Lazier and Zampedri, who led Laps 170-189. The Italian's marvelous bid to win was hampered by a damaged shock absorber. Jones swept by for the lead on Lap 190, and Lazier moved past for second the following lap. In an incredible move, Lazier seemed to come out of nowhere on lap 192 to overhaul Jones and beat

Above: Alessandro Zampedri leads laps 170 through 189 and almost becomes the first-ever Italian resident to win. The delightful Zampedri, who has lived for the majority of his life in Brescia (starting and finishing point of the famed Mille Miglia), possesses one of the most infectious laughs the track has ever heard.

Top: Richie Hearn, impressive in his first start with a third-place finish.
Photographs: IMS

Top: Still battling the effects of his back injuries sustained at Phoenix, a joyful Buddy Lazier has already completely drained his bottle of milk. At left is the equally jubilant car entrant, Ron Hemelgarn.

Above: Davy Jones leads 46 laps, including laps 190 through 192, and ends up second. Just three weeks later, the underrated Jones will share the winning car in the 24-Hours of Le Mans. Conducting the interview for the IMS Radio Network is Mike King, who in 1999 will succeed Bob Jenkins as the Network's chief announcer.

Photographs: IMS

him into the first turn. The field would be bunched for a final caution on Lap 196, but the race belonged to Lazier, who led Jones to the line by .695 of a second. It was the third-closest 500 in history.

Near-tragedy struck as the checker fell. Believing he was battling for position, Guerrero lost control and slammed into the car of Zampedri, launching it into the catch fence as Salazar drove underneath. The fence ripped off the front of Zampedri's car, but fortunately no fans were injured. The Italian driver was the only casualty, suffering serious foot, ankle and leg injuries.

Earlier in the contest, poor Guerrero, who had appeared headed for a possible win, had been delayed by a pit fire and was apparently through for the day. When it was determined by his crew that he could continue, he took off not realizing that the radio in his helmet had been disconnected. He had been totally without communication.

"If I had known, I would have put it in third and coasted in," said the shocked Colombian driver, reflecting on the incident that involved two of the nicest people in the sport.

Hearn would finish third and despite the accident, Zampedri was fourth. Rounding out the top 10 were Guerrero, Salazar, Ongais (who started 33rd and survived an early-race spin), Matsuda, Buhl and Sharp.

To Eddie Cheever went the honor of setting the fastest lap ever in competition. Many laps behind due to a delay at around the midpoint, he decided to see just how fast he could run, and he was frequently the fastest person on the track. His 78th lap was turned at an amazing 236.103 mph.

It was an injured driver who won the race. Still grimacing from the pain of 16 fractures in his back, Lazier somehow managed to smile as he drank the milk and received the winner's accolades.

1997: Number Two For Arie

The scream was gone, but in its place was a very loud roar. For the first time in its 87-year history, every car entered for the Indianapolis 500 was a new machine. Designed and built under the auspices of Indy Racing League rules, chassis from G Force and Dallara would be the only choice although a Riley & Scott design was also in the works. In order to cap the rising costs of Indy cars, the IRL would have to approve a manufacturer before it could sell its cars to teams.

Likewise for engine manufacturers that were a given a 4.0-liter, normally aspirated formula that had to be based on a current production engine. Most of the field would use the Oldsmobile Aurora V-8, but Infiniti had a few takers for its powerplant. Unlike Championship Auto Racing Teams, engine leases were forbidden, but there were a number of approved engine builders who offered their services to the teams. Large teams like Menard could take their engine program in-house. The smaller teams were able to cut costs by going with one of the aforementioned concerns.

Teams were now faced with the decision to select a chassis without figuring the cost into the equation. That's because the G Force and Dallara were available at the same price. The new cars were nearly identical in appearance with the Dallara distinguished by small, upturned winglets in front of the rear wheels. Both designs required the use of airboxes as the normally aspirated V-8s needed air for the injector system.

Because they were based on production engines, the new V-8s were incredibly loud with a sound much like that of a sprint car.

One of the goals for the packages was also to cut the speeds following the incredible, record-breaking month of May in 1996. That point came home early in practice as Vincenzo Sospiri, an Italian rookie with F1 experience, paced the first dry day with a top lap of 211.964. Contrast that to Tony Stewart's first-day stunner in excess of 237 mph! The new cars would indeed be slower, but time would tell how much slower they would be as the month progressed.

On Day 4, Arie Luyendyk, the fastest man in Speedway history, upped the ante with a top lap of 218.707. He followed up with a 220.297 the next day to firmly establish himself as the man to beat for the pole. At that point, the closest competitor was Scott Sharp at 217.402. Luyendyk and British engineer Tim Wardrop clearly had something figured out the rest of the competition had yet to find.

The Dutch driver continued to set the pace, although he ended the week without topping his previous best of 220. As qualifying approached, one team decided to switch engine brands for its top driver. Although Johnny Unser and Lyn St. James would continue using the Infiniti, team owner Ron Hemelgarn purchased an Aurora for Buddy Lazier, the defending winner of the race.

Two drivers were also sidelined for the month following accidents on Friday. John Paul, Jr., sustained a broken right leg and left heel after his PDM Dallara/Aurora hit the Turn 4 wall. Later, Scott Sharp was taken to Methodist Hospital with signs of a concussion after hitting the Turn 4 wall in his Foyt Racing G Force/Aurora.

Mike Groff became first to qualify with an average of 208.943 and in doing so became the first to qualify a car powered by a normally aspirated engine since Sammy Swindell in 1987. Track conditions changed and Luyendyk would wait until mid-afternoon to make his run for the pole. He averaged 218.263, but found himself wondering if the Menard team might strike.

"The call was up to me, coming out of Turn 4, whether we wanted to keep the run and I had my mind made up that if it was over 218, we'd take it," Luyendyk said. "I'm not the world's biggest optimist because the Menard guys have run quick. You can only run so many laps around this place before you get it right and I think we're pretty close."

Sospiri impressed with an average of 216.822, second only to Luyendyk, but now it was Stewart's turn. He came close, but his average of 218.021 was only good for the middle of Row 1. The Dutchman was on the pole for the first time since 1993 and his speed was nearly 16 miles an hour slower than his track record set the year before.

Twenty-one drivers qualified on opening day and only two made the field on the second day, but one attracted more attention than your usual 500 rookie. Outlaw sprint-car king Steve Kinser averaged 210.793 to make his first Indianapolis 500. Although considered a rookie at Indianapolis, Kinser had racked up 14 World of Outlaws titles, and qualifying had to make up for the disappointment of 1981, when he practiced but failed to find the necessary speed to make the race.

Billy Boat, the only driver bumped in 1996, was named to replace the injured Scott Sharp, and set the pace during most of the second week of practice. There were still 10 spots open and Boat's lap of 215.151 was the best of the week. Boat's teammate, Johnny O'Connell, wasn't so fortunate. On Friday, the second-year driver hit the Turn 1 wall in the car Sharp had previously crashed. O'Connell suffered a dislocated arch on his left foot, requiring surgery and sidelining him for the month.

IRL Director Leo Mehl also announced that the 25-8 rule would be eliminated for 1998. With technical specifications and manufacturer participation, guidelines had been solidified and the qualifying incentive had served its purpose.

Because the controversial 25-8 rule was being rescinded for 1998 anyway, it was decided to include the runs of Lyn St James and Johnny Unser, who were not "guaranteed" a spot, but whose speeds had been among the fastest 33. Thus, for the first time since 1979, there were 35 starters instead of 33.

The 81st running of the Indianapolis 500 would have to wait as rain precluded any racing activity on Sunday.

Under overcast skies Monday, the field was given the start command and one of the more bizarre starts to a 500 was about to take place. Alessandro Zampedri, who had been bumped and then bumped his way back in only to learn he would have been included anyway, never made it to the green flag as he limped into the pits with a broken timing chain.

The fifth row didn't make it to the green flag either. Heading into Turn 4, Stefan Gregoire, Affonso Giaffone and Kenny Bräck managed to tangle and all three cars wound up against the wall. Each driver blamed another but it was a moot point as all three were out. And so the parade laps were extended for the cleanup and Sam Schmidt pitted with a smoking engine. With the green yet to drop, five cars were already eliminated.

When the race finally started, Stewart wasted no time and led the first 18 laps. Of course, rain briefly returned and the race was stopped until the following day.

Finally, they got the race in and Stewart continued his lead, pacing the field for the first 50 laps before pitting. Boat led a lap and Stewart resumed command, but now he had Luyendyk to deal with and on Lap 63, the polesitter took over for the first time.

Luyendyk would swap the lead with Stewart, Lazier and Robbie Buhl over the next 80 laps. Scott Goodyear led briefly but then rookie Jeff Ward took over for 24 laps before pitting, allowing the Treadway duo of Goodyear and Luyendyk to pass. The Dutchman took over on Lap 194 and it appeared the battle would be between teammates.

Goodyear had nearly won the race in 1992 and felt he won in 1995 when he was black-flagged for passing the pace car on a restart. Once again, he had a legitimate chance to win the 500 with only Luyendyk standing in the way. But Goodyear was destined to be a bridesmaid again because the caution came out on Lap 196 for Kinser's accident and again on Lap 198 for Stewart's brush with the wall.

Race officials decided to go green on Lap 199 and Luyendyk jumped ahead far enough to out-distance his teammate. The margin was .570 seconds over Goodyear. Jeff Ward was an impressive third and ultimate winner of the top rookie award.

Following them home were Lazier, Stewart, Davey Hamilton, Boat, Buhl, Robbie Groff and Fermin Velez.

In spite of the numerous late-race changes of lead over the years, this was the first time ever that *three different* drivers had led within the last 10 laps. In addition, Fred Treadway was the first entrant to score a one-two finish since the Leader Card team of Rodger Ward and Len Sutton in 1962, while interestingly enough, Treadway's Oldsmobile engines had been prepared under the direction of NASCAR's Jack Roush.

Below: Arie Luyendyk has to work hard for his second "500" win.

Below center: Scott Goodyear leads only two laps during the 1997 race, but one of them is lap 193. He ends up second to teammate Arie Luyendyk, the Fred Treadway team being the first to score a one–two finish since Leader Card Racers (with Rodger Ward and Len Sutton) in 1962.

Bottom: Motocross legend Jeff Ward teams up with Eddie Cheever for his first start, and finishes an impressive third. He leads 49 laps and is in front as late as lap 192.

Photographs: IMS

Main photograph: A. J. Foyt driver Billy Boat
paces the field from the pole, flanked by
Greg Ray and Kenny Bräck.
Photographs: IMS

1998: Cheever's Biggest Day

For a number of years, the only American driver competing in Formula One was Eddie Cheever. Born in Phoenix, but a resident of Rome most of his life, Cheever's career in motorsport was understandably geared at European racing and F1.

After recording an impressive number of results in various development series, Cheever entered the world of F1 with the small Osella team in 1980. He was 22 at the time and went on to run for the Tyrrell, Ligier, Renault, Alfa Romeo and Arrows teams before turning to Indy-car racing and Chip Ganassi's new team.

Driving the Penske/Chevy that Emerson Fittipaldi had used to win Indianapolis and the national championship the year before, Cheever struggled at first but ran well enough in his first Indianapolis 500 to capture top rookie honors after finishing eighth. Ganassi would ultimately buy a new Lola and Cheever began to run up front and score high finishes.

However, the marriage to Ganassi lasted through the end of 1992 and for 1993, he was searching for ride. John Menard gave him a lifeline and for 1995, he signed with A.J. Foyt. Cheever nearly scored his first Indy-car win at Nazareth, running out of fuel with two laps to go while in the lead.

But if Indy-car racing had given Cheever a lifeline, the new Indy Racing League gave him a new lease on life. He became a team owner for 1997 and opened the season with a victory in the rain-shortened Disney World event. Cheever had not won a major race since 1986, when he won at Silverstone for Jaguar in the world sports-car championship.

For 1998, he would enter two cars for Indianapolis – one for himself and the other for rookie Robby Unser, youngest son of three-time winner Bobby Unser.

Team Cheever was one of many teams to select the Dallara chassis for Indianapolis. Although the Dallara, G Force and new Riley & Scott chassis were basically identical in design, there were enough differences for certain tracks to favor certain marques. The superspeedway events seemed to suit the Dallara the best and could be distinguished by an oval-shaped opening for the airbox.

Making its Indianapolis 500 debut was the new car from Riley & Scott, designed and built just around the corner from the track. A year behind Dallara and G Force, Riley & Scott fielded a factory entry for Eliseo Salazar and sold a pair of chassis to Metro Racing Systems for rookie Stan Wattles.

On the engine front, the Aurora was clearly the top choice with only entries from McCormack, Sinden, Beck and St. James using the Infiniti.

As an additional cost-cutting measure, practice and qualifying were significantly cut. There would be only six days of practice, two days of qualifying and Carburetion Day practice for 1998.

As a result, everyone got serious in a hurry. A year of running the new cars and new formula also produced a jump in speeds as evidenced by the numbers posted on opening weekend.

Robbie Buhl paced opening day with a top lap of 219.325, faster than Arie Luyendyk's pole speed from a year ago. Buhl's Menard teammate Tony Stewart then took over and topped the Day 2 chart with a lap of 223.703. But the first serious wall-banger of the year produced a casualty. Danny Ongais, whose comeback in the 1996 race was capped by a seventh-place finish, hit the wall in Turn 3 in the Team Pelfrey Dallara. Ongais was briefly hospitalized and ultimately would not receive clearance to qualify.

Stewart topped Day 3 with another lap over 223, but Day 4 produced some challengers – Billy Boat and Scott Sharp. The second-year driver led the way with a lap of 221.691, with Sharp close behind at 221.517. Luyendyk also topped 220.

Day 5 saw Stewart back on top at 223.430, but Bräck was close with a 223.264. Greg Ray also surprised a lot of folks with his lap at 222.717. Stewart closed the week with a 223.797, but it appeared there would be several contenders for the pole.

The first qualifier of the day was John Paul, Jr., who got the ride vacated by the injured Ongais. Not lost on Paul was the fact the last man to replace Ongais was Al Unser in 1987, who went on to win the race.

Buhl was first to qualify at 220 (220.236). However, he was soon be bumped off the pole by Stewart, who averaged 220.386. Kenny Bräck then bumped Stewart with an average of 220.982. Robby Unser became the sixth member of his family to qualify at Indianapolis, making the race with a respectable 216.534 average.

After Davey Hamilton qualified at 219.748, the attention was focused on Boat. He averaged 223.503 to handily take the pole. Ray would again surprise everyone by qualifying second at 221.125. In all, there were 26 first-day qualifiers and one more day to fill the field. Foyt's cars sandwiched Ray on Row 1, with the Menard cars of Stewart and Buhl starting fourth and fifth.

"You don't want to show your hand," Boat said. "When we went out this morning, I knew we could run a 224 today. I only problem I had was in Turn 1 with the wind. I was real loose and I knew I'd have to run through because I was OK in the other turns. On the fourth lap, I lost it in Turn 1 and I held my breath three times."

In all there were 26 qualifiers and one more day to fill the field.

Inset above: A view of the IMS Hall of Fame
Museum, which opened in April 1976. On
display in the grass are the car with which
Janet Guthrie became the first lady to pass
a "rookie" test (1976) and the Louis
Meyer/Rex Mays Bowes Seal Fast car with
which Mays finished second in 1940 and
1941. The museum is open every day of the
year except for Christmas Day.

Inset right: Locally raised Tony Stewart led
the first 31 laps of the 1996 "500" and
was declared Rookie of the Year.
He will compete in five "500s," finish in
the top ten three times, and twice
undertake the "double" by flying directly
from Indianapolis to participate in the
600-mile NASCAR event at Charlotte,
North Carolina, the same night.
Photographs: IMS

Jimmy Kite would end up leading the second day's qualifiers with an average of 219.290 and Wattles put the only Riley & Scott chassis in the field with a 217.477 average. Billy Roe would be bumped, but was able to bump his way back into the field at the expense of Eliseo Salazar, who was trying to get a second Riley & Scott qualified. His last-minute attempt was thwarted when the engine began to smoke. The field was set.

Unlike the previous year, there was no rain to interrupt the proceedings and as the field took the green flag, Boat jumped into the lead where he stayed for the first 12 laps. Ray passed for first on Lap 13 but lost it to Stewart on Lap 21. Ray led the next 10 laps before Bräck moved in front from Laps 32 through 46.

At that point, the Menard team was out. Engine problems sidelined Stewart on Lap 22 and Buhl on Lap 44. One man moving up was Cheever, who had started 17th but took the lead on Lap 68. Luyendyk would succeed him at the helm after charging from 28th to first by Lap 85. Paul also moved up, starting 16th and getting his first lead on Lap 98.

It was anybody's race, but at the midway point, the strongest runners appeared to be Bräck, Lazier, Cheever, Luyendyk and Paul.

Luyendyk would be first to crack, losing valuable time as he struggled with gearbox trouble after leading Lap 147.

By Lap 157, only Cheever, Buddy Lazier and Steve Knapp were on the lead lap. Paul was fourth, a lap down, but he lost additional time after stalling in the pits. Cheever pitted for the final time on Lap 177. Lazier also pitted and was credited with leading the lap, but Cheever's team got him out of the pits in first place.

He would stay there the rest of the way, holding a 3.191-second lead over Lazier. Knapp finished an impressive third and would capture top rookie honors. Hamilton was fourth, followed by Unser (whose car had no rear brakes for most of the race), Bräck, Paul, Andy Michner, J.J. Yeley and Buzz Calkins.

"I was sure it was going to break, and I had no reason to think that, other than past history," Cheever said from Victory Circle. "When we lost the race in Nazareth for A.J. Foyt and ran out of fuel with two laps to go, it was heart-breaking. I was thinking, 'Don't break. Don't break. Please don't break.' I had to take that risk the last 20 laps of running with a shorter gear, which I knew was not very healthy for the engine. The Braytons have done one hell of a job for the engine and I ran it hard all day long."

Inset below: Dynamic owner/driver Eddie Cheever scores his biggest win.

Inset bottom: The latest in a long line of victory enclosures.
Photographs: IMS

1999: Bräck Outlasts Gordon For Win

There are times in racing when being in the right place at the right time makes all the difference in the world.

Just ask Kenny Bräck or A.J. Foyt.

In some ways, the story of the 83rd Indianapolis 500 should have been about John Menard, who first entered a car for the race in 1980. Since 1990, his team was devoted to one task – running in and trying to win the 500.

Menard bought a racing shop near the track and proceeded to pour millions of dollars into the project as his home-building supply business flourished in the Midwest. He could afford it as Forbes Magazine listed him as the wealthiest individual in Wisconsin.

Despite funding rivaled only by a program like Penske, Menard's effort had a somewhat Quixote-like quality. He hired the best crew, the best engineers and some of the best drivers. That chassis were usually the latest Lola. But Menard also invested heavily in the V-6 Buick that was given a boost advantage at Indianapolis.

Menard cars were often among the fastest, but time and time again, the Buick's reliability resulted in a DNF. In recent years the effort appeared to be geared as much toward the pole position as it was toward the race. It had not been that

long ago that Menard had withdrawn Scott Brayton's car so that Brayton could win the pole in another car. Never mind that Brayton would have started in the second row!

At that point in time, the engine was renamed the Menard, but the new regulations of 1997 changed that. Menard's cars were still fast, but he was now running Dallara/Auroras as were most of his rivals.

The Indianapolis Motor Speedway had a different look when competitors arrived for practice in May. Part of the Tower Terrace grandstand was torn down to make way for a new pit/garage complex to conform to requirements for an F1 race. The Speedway had successfully bid to put a United States Grand Prix on the calendar for the first time in 10 years. Phase 1 of the project involved demolition of the area where the new F1 pit garages would be located. In the meantime, temporary bleachers were erected for the fans that could still observe the action in the pits.

Changes to the equipment were much more subtle.

Once again, the Dallara chassis was perceived to be the car to have for a superspeedway. Earlier in the season, Scott Goodyear had won in a G Force/Aurora, but Eddie Cheever won the opener in a Dallara. Cheever's victory was also the first for the Infiniti engine.

The Riley & Scott firm continued to find adequate funds to develop its car, and only Brant Racing entered a pair of cars for Andy Michner, and Metro Racing entering one for Stan Wattles.

Oldsmobile's Aurora V-8 was again the engine of choice although Infiniti-powered cars were entered for Cheever, Robbie Buhl, Roberto Guerrero, Jaques Lazier, Scott Harrington and Jeret Schroeder. Interestingly, Aurora-powered cars were also entered for Jaques Lazier, Harrington and Cheever's teammate, Wim Eyckmans.

A popular returnee to the Speedway was none other than Tony Stewart, now ensconced in NASCAR, arriving at the Speedway with Home Depot sponsorship, a chief rival for his longtime backer John Menard. He was planning to duplicate the previous efforts of John Andretti and Robby Gordon by running in both the Indianapolis 500 and NASCAR's World 600 at Charlotte.

Year three of the new IRL formula saw the competitors inching up on the speed charts as Greg Ray opened the proceedings with a top lap of 225.887. Last year's surprise front-row qualifier was now employed by the team that specialized in the front row – Team Menard.

With the shortened schedule in effect for the second straight year, early practice days were full of on-track activity.

Ray set the pace for the first three days, but Arie Luyendyk began to emerge as his top rival for the pole. With his stated intention of running his last 500, the Dutch driver was hoping to go out on the highest note possible. Goodyear paced Day 4 with a lap at 223.842 and Stewart showed he could still handle the lightweight Indy car by topping the Day 5 charts at 226.683, the fastest of the month and the new era. Ray topped him the following day with a 227.192 and followed that up with a 227.175 on the final day of practice.

Ray was the favorite to win the pole, but Luyendyk was lurking in the background.

Stewart became the first to qualify and accepted a seemingly safe average of 220.653. Then he left the track to fly to Charlotte for NASCAR practice. Bräck qualified at 222.659 and shortly afterward, it was Luyendyk's turn. Luyendyk put together a four-lap average of 225.179 with a top lap of 225.643. That established track records for normally aspirated engines.

One by one, the challengers tried to dislodge Luyendyk from the top spot. Mark Dismore turned in a fine run at 222.963. Billy Boat went 223.469. Gordon went 223.066. But it was Ray who came the closest. For a time, he was on the pole, but his final lap of 224.439 dropped his average to 225.075 – just a tick slower than Luyendyk. Thirty-three cars would qualify on the first day and four drivers would end up being bumped on the second day. One driver who bumped his way into the field was Buhl, who hopped into one of Foyt's car and safely qualified for his fourth 500.

"When Billy Boat got hurt, Robbie helped us out," Foyt said. "If they help you out, you turn around and help them out."

"It all comes down to people," Luyendyk said after winning

the 500 pole for the third time. "The whole package of guys – there's great chemistry. They really made me look good today."

In his quest to go out a winner, Luyendyk was one leg up on the field. Historically speaking, were Luyendyk to retire from Victory Lane, he would be the third driver in history to do so, joining Ray Harroun in 1911 and Sam Hanks in 1957.

And for the first half of the race, everything appeared to fall into place for Luyendyk. He led early and often, pacing the field 63 of the first 117 laps. But that's when it all went wrong for him. Coming up to lap the slower car of Tyce Carlson, he had to brake early and spun into the Turn 3 wall.

"I went underneath Tyce," Luyendyk explained. "I thought he would give me room, but he came down on me. I had to slam on the brakes and when I touched the brakes, the car became unstable. I was driving with confidence and maybe that confidence bit me."

With Luyendyk out of the way, the battle for race began to center on Bräck and Gordon. The Swedish driver led Laps 154 through 170 and then Gordon took over when Bräck pitted. Despite a caution for Dismore's accident on Lap 169, Gordon opted to stay out on the track instead of making a "splash and dash" fuel stop.

When the green came out on Lap 173, Bräck was third behind Gordon, but he passed Jeff Ward for second with 12 laps to go and took off after Gordon.

With less than 10 laps to go, it looked like John Menard's long quest to win at Indianapolis was about to become a reality. Or was it? Gordon was repeatedly told to conserve fuel as the race neared the final laps. It was going to be close, but maybe, just maybe…

With less than two laps to go, Gordon frantically radioed his crew that he was out of fuel and on his way to the pits. Bräck swept by to take the lead and the white flag as Gordon & Co. tried to make the best of a splash-and-go. Gordon would rejoin the race, but Bräck was long gone and in slightly more than a minute, he crossed the finish line in triumph.

Jeff Ward, who finished third two years earlier, was second by 6.5 seconds. Boat was third, followed by an understandably disappointed Gordon, Robbie McGehee (who would capture the top rookie award), Buhl, Buddy Lazier, Robby Unser, Stewart and Hideshi Matsuda.

"We were one lap short," said Gordon. "It makes me sick."

"I thought he (Gordon) was going to have to go into the pits," Bräck said afterward. "We were thinking it was impossible for him to finish, but the last laps we had to pick it up."

The reigning IRL champ had picked up racing's biggest prize and no one was happier to greet the Swedish driver in Victory Circle than team owner A.J. Foyt, who announced that it was "his" fifth victory at Indianapolis.

While maintaining he was happy for Foyt, Bräck opined: "But I think I'm more happy for me. A.J. has won it four times already."

Top right: Robby Gordon is trailed here by Scott Goodyear, Eddie Cheever, Davey Hamilton, Robby Unser and Buddy Lazier. But for a late-race caution, which never comes, Gordon might well have ended up as the winner. He "stays out" when the other leaders pit for fuel during a lap-169 caution, gambling that the race will not "stay green" from lap 173 until the end. But it does. Instead of taking the white flag in the lead, he has to pit for a "splash and go."

Above: Kenny Bräck leads 66 laps in six different segments, reassuming control for the final time after Robby Gordon is forced to duck in for fuel with just over one lap to go. With A. J. Foyt having already won four times as a driver, "Super Tex" can now claim a fifth "500" victory.

Photographs: IMS

Inset above: The new pagoda is almost complete.

Bottom center: Greg Ray (left) confers with Robby Gordon. Ray has started from the second position in 1998 and 1999 prior to winning the pole this year, and he will qualify second again in 2001 – for four straight years of starting either first or second.

Inset below: John Menard, strong advocate of the V6 Buicks until turbocharged engines were no longer permitted, has fielded entries for such colorful and accomplished performers as Arie Luyendyk, Al Unser, Tony Stewart, Nelson Piquet, Tom Sneva, Eddie Cheever, Robby Gordon, Gary Bettenhausen, Scott Brayton, Kevin Cogan, Greg Ray, Jim Crawford, Buddy Lazier, Geoff Brabham, Johnny Rutherford, Raul Boesel, J.J.Yeley, Jaques Lazier, Danny Ongais, Robbie Buhl, Mark Dismore, and Herm Johnson.

Photographs: IMS

2000: Montoya Romps To Victory

Over the winter, the Indianapolis Motor Speedway had undergone a major renovation. Replacing the old scoring tower was a gleaming new, 10-story pagoda-like structure. To the south of the new tower, a complex of F1-style pit garages replaced the old Tower Terrace section. Temporary bleachers were set up on top of the garages and in front for pit viewing purposes and many of the garages served as hospitality suites during the month of May.

To the north of the tower, additional hospitality suites were built atop the old Tower Terrace stands and the media would benefit from a new press center that featured a view of the pits and the main straightaway. It was an exciting time for the Speedway and understandably so. The new construction project made an impressive racing facility look even more impressive.

There was a surprise entry for the 84th running of the Indianapolis 500. For the first time since the IRL-CART dispute, a top CART team had purchased a pair of IRL cars and entered them in the race. This was no ordinary team. Chip Ganassi, who shared the winning effort of Emerson Fittipaldi and Patrick Racing in 1989, built up an operation that dominated CART during the IRL's early years. With a talented lineup of drivers and personnel, the Ganassi team captured four straight titles between 1996 and 1999.

Ganassi temporarily employed one of racing's hottest properties – Juan Pablo Montoya – and the Colombian driver was the reigning CART champion, and a strong peformance would go nicely in his resume as he headed for Europe to go F1 racing with Williams in 2001.

For his first assault on Indianapolis, Montoya would also have the experience of teammate Jimmy Vasser, a veteran of four 500s who had finished fourth in 1994. Ganassi purchased a pair of G Force/Auroras for his first try at Indianapolis in four years.

Goodyear tires were missing for the first time in 36 years. With costs skyrocketing as the Akron firm tried to compete with Bridgestone/Firestone, Goodyear decided to devote its energies to NASCAR.

G Force and Dallara pretty much split the entry with only a handful of Riley & Scott chassis on the list.

Once again, the Aurora engine was the top choice with only Team Cheever using the Infiniti powerplant.

Al Unser, Jr., was hoping to make his first Indianapolis 500 start since winning the race in 1994. He had already tasted victory in the IRL, winning at Las Vegas the previous month, his first in any kind of Indy car since 1995. He started his month of May off on the right foot by setting the pace on opening day with a top lap of 217.223, and the following day he was second to Eddie Cheever on the list. Cheever's best lap was 220.881 while Unser was right behind at 220.686. Robby Gordon would be quickest on Day 3 at 223.120, and Scott Sharp recorded the month's quickest speed the next day at 223.936. Montoya and Vasser, in their second day on the track, were second and third at 222.102 and 221.773, respectively. Sarah Fisher, looking to become only the third woman to make the start of the 500, also went quickly, posting the seventh-fastest lap of the day at 220.881.

Montoya and Vasser were quickest the next two days, but each driver could only manage a fast lap in excess of 221. Greg Ray closed out the week of practice with the month's top speed of 223.948. Ray would be the man to beat for the pole, but everyone was cautiously eyeing the newcomer from Colombia – Montoya.

Ray went out, but was forced to abort his run after overcooking it in Turn 1.

Montoya went out next and returned with a four-lap average of 223.372. Ray got a second chance and edged Montoya with an average of 223.988. The pole was his and he would keep it after coming so close to winning it the previous year. Salazar's 223.231 average was also good enough for the front row.

In all, 23 drivers qualified on the first of two days of time trials, including Fisher and Unser, whose 220-plus averages put them safely in the field. Another rookie turned in a most impressive run. Driving for the small PDM team, rookie Sam Hornish, Jr., posted the 14th fastest time of the day to safely make his first Indianapolis 500.

"I'd be lying to you if I didn't say the pole was a big focus for us," said Ray, who delivered John Menard his third pole position at Indy since 1995. "There's no question we wanted to put the car on the pole. I'd have soon as qualified 33rd as been second again. The four laps of qualifying are the ultimate speed event. You've got to drive it for all it's worth."

For Greg Ray, it was worth more than $100,000 in cash

and prizes, along with the best starting spot in the world's biggest auto race.

The second day of qualifying concluded with 15 drivers joining the field and five being sent home for the year. Scraping into the field for a seventh time was Lyn St. James, giving Indianapolis two female starters for the first time in its history. The slowest qualifier, Andy Hillenburg, would end up adding a nostalgic touch to his effort. Sponsored by Sumar, Hillenburg's car would be painted white and blue, similar to the paint scheme used when the Sumar team raced at Indianapolis in the 1950s.

On Race Day, Ray brought the field down for the start and immediately jumped into the lead for the first 26 laps. The Colombian rookie then took over for three laps as the entire field began to make the first round of pit stops.

Montoya resumed the lead on Lap 33 and a caution came out for the first time, for Ray's accident in Turn 2. Trying to keep up to Montoya's pace, the Texan overdid it and brushed the concrete. He would return to the race but soon have another accident, this one taking him out. He suffered the dubious distinction of having traveled 67 laps in order to finish dead last. This was not a record, however, Bill Homeier having finished last in 1954 with 74 laps on the board.

Already out by this time were Lyn St. James and Sarah Fisher, who had tangled with each other in turn one, this being Sarah's first race and Lyn's seventh and final.

Montoya remained in front through Lap 175 when he pitted and Vasser took over for four laps. Only Buddy Lazier appeared to keep him in sight. Not only was Montoya quick on the track, the Ganassi crew was able to gain him time in the pits. Montoya regained the lead on Lap 180 and pulled out to a 7.184-second margin.

For the first time since 1966, a rookie had captured the Indianapolis 500. Salazar came home third, followed by Ward, Cheever, Gordon, Vasser, Gregoire, Goodyear and Sharp. Not surprisingly, Montoya also garnered the top rookie award.

"What makes this place is the people," Montoya reflected after winning the race. "It's a huge race track. I saw a lot of people standing. And it's just great to win here. It means a lot to me, to Target, to Budweiser, to everyone involved in this project. It's just over the roof."

Above: Former "500" driver Chip Ganassi (1982-1986), who finished eighth in 1983, became a partner of Pat Patrick in 1989, thus being part owner of Emerson Fittipaldi's winning car. He won as the sole entrant in 2000 with Juan Pablo Montoya, and had the second-place finishing car in 1993 with Arie Luyendyk. His cars were also on the pole in 1993 (Luyendyk), and 2002 (Bruno Junqueira).

Top: Formula One-bound Juan Pablo Montoya becomes the first Columbian to win the "500," and the first "rookie" to win since Graham Hill in 1966. Montoya is not the first Columbian to compete, however. That was Roberto Guerrero. It turns out that the fathers of Montoya and Guerrero have long been the best of friends and that Roberto used to run around with Juan Pablo's older brother.
Photographs: IMS

Left: Pole winner Greg Ray leads at the start, followed by fourth place-starting Robby Gordon, Juan Pablo Montoya, Eliseo Salazar, Scott Sharp, and Jeff Ward.
Photograph: LAT

Bottom near left: Sam Hornish, Jr., making his "500" debut with the close-knit PDM team, takes a spin. There will be better days ahead.
Photographs: IMS

2001: Castroneves Climbs Victory Ladder

Juan Pablo Montoya, who won in 2000, would not be returning to defend his victory at Indianapolis. But his team, Target Chip Ganassi Racing, would be back with Jimmy Vasser and Tony Stewart. Ganassi's new rookie drivers in CART – Bruno Junqueira and Nicolas Minassian – would ultimately join them, as well as Marlboro Team Penske with cars for Gil de Ferran and Helio Castroneves, and Team Green with a car for Michael Andretti.

All through the month of May 2000 and beyond, Ganassi & Co. maintained that the Indianapolis Motor Speedway and the IRL had treated them very well. The fans certainly welcomed Montoya and Vasser, and now they would have some newcomers to welcome for 2001.

Although he retired two years earlier, Arie Luyendyk decided to attempt a comeback. Luyendyk believed he should have won the 1999 race and undoubtedly felt he still had another 500 win left.

On the equipment front, it was once again a battle between Dallara and G Force. Due to a lack of funds needed for additional development, the Riley & Scott chassis had fallen by the wayside the previous season.

The engine situation was pretty much unchanged.

The Oldsmobile Aurora engine was again the primary choice of the competitors with only Team Cheever and Dreyer & Reinbold Racing using the Infiniti. The Oldsmobile name would also be disappearing in the future. With the demise of its division within the General Motors empire, Oldsmobile would no longer produce vehicles for the 2002 model year. In honor of the longtime manufacturer, the Speedway made a significant decision on its pace car.

For the first time in Indianapolis 500 history, a truck would pace the race. More specifically, the Olds Bravada sport-utility vehicle would represent Oldsmobile's last official appearance at the track. Adding to the historic occasion was the selection of supermodel Elaine Irwin-Mellencamp as the driver. The wife of Indiana rock star John Mellencamp, she would be the first woman to ever drive the 500 pace car.

Although he was fast all month, Scott Sharp wound up surprising everyone by capturing the pole position with an average speed of 226.037 mph.

The defending polesitter, Greg Ray, was second fastest and qualified for the front row for the fourth straight year. Joining them was Robby Gordon, who qualified for Row 1 for the first

time in seven starts.

Mark Dismore gave Kelley Racing the pole for Row 2 as well and joining him were de Ferran and Luyendyk, still racy after a two-year hiatus.

The second day of qualifying produced a pair of surprises as Ganassi decided to let Junqueira and Minassian qualify the backup cars of Vasser and Stewart. As Indianapolis was the only IRL race of the year for Ganassi, it made a lot of sense to use the equipment once the original drivers (Vasser and Stewart) were safely in the field. A year earlier, Junqueira and Minassian were battling each other for the FIA Formula 3000 championship. Now they were "500" starters.

Michael Andretti also became a second-day qualifier despite qualifying on opening day. His average of 220.747 was deemed marginal and the car was withdrawn. Qualifying his backup at a safer 223.441, he would be starting two spots behind Al Unser, Jr., in 21st position.

For the first time since 1992, the pole winner would fail to complete the first lap. Roberto Guerrero had spun out on cold tires during the pace lap for the frigid 1992 race, and Scott Sharp was to share the same disappointment.

Taking the lead at the drop of the green flag, Sharp may have clipped the grass at the apex of Turn 1 with his left side wheels, but the result was that he spun into the outside wall. Gordon passed Ray for second and found himself in the lead as the track went yellow for Lap 1. Gordon and Ray would swap the lead during the first 45 laps and pit stops elevated Stewart and Luyendyk to the point.

Andretti was on the move early from his Row 7 starting spot. In 47 laps, he went from 21st to first and stayed there for four laps. The battle became an "us versus them" proposition with Ray and Andretti taking turns leading the race.

Ray held an advantage over Andretti but the son of the 1969 winner was getting closer with every lap. Finally he was on Ray's tail and Ray inexplicably brushed the wall between Turns 3 and 4 on Lap 103. Andretti swept into the lead.

After coming close so many times, everyone wondered if it might be his year. It wasn't, as a cut tire forced him into an unscheduled stop that appeared to cost him the race. Under normal circumstances, there would have been enough time to overcome the deficit, but overcast skies made rain look more and more imminent. In fact, the track had briefly gone yellow for rain on Laps 107-118.

With the race beyond the halfway point, it could be called at any time and there was a real scramble among the front-

Main photograph: Helio Castroneves delights the crowd with his flamboyant post-victory celebration tradition (previously carried out at other tracks) of climbing the outer fencing.

Inset below: Michael Andretti lines up for his first "500" start since 1995. He will finish third.

Inset bottom left: The upper deck is a marvelous vantage point from which to view the race.

Top right: The Indianapolis Motor Speedway now features a road course which winds through the infield and hooks up with the oval. The Grand Prix of the United States Formula One race moved here in 2000.

Photographs: IMS

runners. Penske's talented duo had run up front all afternoon with de Ferran in front from Laps 110 to 136. Stewart, who was planning to run the NASCAR World 600 at Charlotte, took over for the next 12 laps and the prospect of his victory raised a dilemma. If he won the 500, he would be obligated to perform the necessary post-race ceremonies and interviews as the race winner. However, there was the matter of his contract with Joe Gibbs Racing, his full-time employer, and sponsor Home Depot.

Stewart's problems would be solved when Castroneves took the lead on Lap 149. Rain and the yellow flag returned on Lap 148 and on Lap 155, the race was halted. The shower was very brief and dampened only one portion of the huge track. Within 15 minutes, the engines were being re-fired. The show would go on, Stewart would remain in his car (there had been talk of having a relief driver so he could leave for Charlotte) and Castroneves would be in the lead when the race went green on Lap 157.

He would stay there for the next 43 laps and then introduce Speedway fans to his unique manner of celebrating.

After taking the checker 1.7 seconds ahead of his teammate, the Brazilian completed his cool-down lap but instead of entering the pits, he drove down the main straightaway. Stopping at the start-finish line, he emerged from his car and climbed up the outer fence, waving to the thrilled fans, who had never seen such antics.

Despite the cut tire, Andretti climbed back into third place. Following Andretti were Vasser, Junqueira, Stewart, Eliseo Salazar, Airton Daré, Billy Boat and Felipe Giaffone.

For the second straight year, a rookie had won the race and like Montoya ahead of him, Castroneves was awarded the top rookie honor.

Penske's Brazilian drivers also accomplished a first for the team. Although Castroneves' victory was No. 11 at Indianapo-

lis for Roger Penske, his team had never recorded a 1-2 finish at the Speedway despite a driver list over the years that rivaled a "Who's Who" of auto racing.

Castroneves also joined an elite list of drivers who won at Indianapolis on their first try (Ray Harroun, Jules Goux, René Thomas, Frank Lockhart, George Souders, Louis Meyer, Graham Hill and Juan Pablo Montoya).

Below: Special garages are now housed at pitside to accommodate the Formula One cars for the U. S. Grand Prix, complete with team suites above each garage.
Photograph: IMS

2002: Two For Two For Helio

For the first time since 1999, the Indianapolis 500 would have its reigning winner return to try for a second victory at the Speedway. But this time was slightly different as Helio Castroneves returned as a full-fledged participant in the Indy Racing League. In the off-season, team owner Roger Penske switched his Indy-car program to the IRL.

In fact, Castroneves had already tasted victory in the IRL, winning the annual spring event at Phoenix.

Other CART operations were coming back to the 500. Joining Penske at Indy would be Target Chip Ganassi, Team Green and Rahal Letterman Racing.

After an absence of eight years, the Chevrolet name was back with what had been the Aurora V-8 now bearing the Chevy bow tie. Infiniti had the usual number of takers with Team Cheever and Dreyer & Reinbold using their engine.

Another change could be seen in the physical plant.

The Indianapolis Motor Speedway had undergone a number of improvements in recent years, but they unveiled a new idea that would revolutionize the safety aspect of the sport. IMS always had concrete walls (with the exception of the backstretch, which had wooden guardrails through 1955), but engineers were trying to come up with a way to soften the impact.

The result was the SAFER Barrier. SAFER was an acronym for "Steel and Foam Energy Reduction" and the idea was to put the apparatus inside the concrete walls in each of the track's four turns. A metal barrier composed of hollow, square tubes was reinforced by sections of foam, creating a shock absorber system. It was a joint project between the Speedway, the IRL and the University of Nebraska-Lincoln's Midwest Roadside Safety Facility.

For the second straight year, a surprise polesitter emerged – Bruno Junqueira, whose average of 231.342 mph marked the fastest speed in the six-year history of the IRL's 4.0-liter, normally aspirated engine formula.

Joining the Brazilian sophomore on the front were Robbie Buhl and Raul Boesel, the latter making his first Row 1

appearance since 1994. Felipe Giaffone had an impressive run to qualify fourth, with rookie Tony Kanaan fifth and Eddie Cheever giving the Infiniti its best 500 grid position at sixth. Castroneves and Gil de Ferran wound up 13th and 14th, respectively.

Paul Tracy, who last raced at Indianapolis in 1995, managed to qualify 29th on the last day of time trials.

Although only making his second 500 start, Junqueira looked like a seasoned veteran and jumped into the lead, where he would stay for the first 32 laps. Tomas Scheckter led briefly, followed by Kanaan, Sharp, de Ferran and Al Unser, Jr.

By the midway point, Scheckter was firmly in the lead with challenges from de Ferran and Giaffone. Slowly, Tracy was moving up in the standings. He would figure into the final outcome, but that was several laps away.

Scheckter's bid to be 500's third straight rookie winner ended on Lap 173 when he went high in Turn 4 and slammed into the wall. He was leading at the time of the accident. His effort would not go unnoticed, however. He would end up sharing the top rookie honor with Alex Barron.

Giaffone led briefly, but dashed into the pits for fuel. Castroneves was now in the lead for the first time. Tracy was second.

As the laps wound down, the Canadian driver hounded the Brazilian. Ten laps to go. Five laps to go. Tracy appeared to be waiting for the right moment. With one lap to go, he believed he found it as he set up to pass Castroneves in Turn 3.

Almost simultaneously, Laurent Redon and Buddy Lazier tangled in Turn 2. The caution came out, but in the eyes of Tracy's camp, it came out after he had successfully passed Castroneves. Naturally, the Penske camp believed the yellow had come out prior to any pass, negating it.

Tracy did cross the finish line and did receive the checkered flag, but immediately afterward, it was determined that Castroneves was still the leader by virtue of the timing of the caution light.

Following them home were Giaffone, Barron, Cheever, Richie Hearn, Andretti, Gordon, Jeff Ward and de Ferran.

"I saw the yellow light on my dash and I cried: 'It's yellow,

it's yellow," said an understandably excited Castroneves after the race.

Ultimately, the issue would fall in favor of the Brazilian.

In addition to scoring Indianapolis 500 win No. 13 for Roger Penske, Castroneves also became the first driver in the history of the race to win on his first two attempts. He also joined an illustrious group of back-to-back winners that included Wilbur Shaw, Mauri Rose, Bill Vukovich and Al Unser. Could he win an unprecedented third? For only the fifth time in the history of the 500, a driver was in position to do so.

Right: New this year is a major safety innovation, soon to be seen at other tracks, but pioneered here, and spearheaded by Tony George. The SAFER barriers are designed to lessen the impact of a race car which previously would have been hitting solid concrete. SAFER is an acronym for "steel and foam energy reduction."
Photograph: IMS

Above: Tomas Scheckter, son of 1979 world champion Jody Scheckter, is very impressive in his first "500," leading on four different occasions for a total of 85 laps. He is still ahead when he slides wide and into the wall after 173 laps. He will share the Rookie of the Year honors with fourth-place-finishing Alex Barron.

Above left: Helio Castroneves, who becomes the first driver ever to be undefeated in his first two "500" starts, is joined on the fence this time by the entire Penske crew.

Main photograph: A late-race accident, involving Buddy Lazier and French "rookie" Laurent Redon, brings out the yellow as Castroneves successfully defends his title under caution.

Inset left: Paul Tracy, who believes he has won, is consoled by teammate Dario Franchitti after the finish.
Photographs: IMS

Above: In spite of Roger Penske's phenomenal success at Indianapolis, the victory by de Ferran enables him to finally tie Lou Moore's half-a-century-plus-old record of being the winning car entrant in three consecutive years.

Top: The normally tranquil Gil de Ferran is uncharacteristically euphoric in victory. The little boy at left is his amazingly look-alike son, Luke.

Photographs: IMS

2003: Three-Peat For Penske

There were a lot of new kids on block when the racers returned to the Indianapolis Motor Speedway for the 87th running of the 500.

In the off-season, the IRL's ranks swelled with the addition of Team Green, Target Chip Ganassi, Rahal-Letterman and Mo Nunn, plus the partnership of Adrian Fernandez and Aguri Suzuki.

In addition to the new teams and drivers, the most significant newcomers were engine manufacturers Honda and Toyota. Honda had briefly run at Indianapolis with the Galles team in 1987. However, that engine became the Judd and never represented a true factory-backed effort. For 2003, it would be different with both Japanese automotive giants

squaring off against the Chevrolet V-8, formerly known as the Oldsmobile Aurora.

There were also new cars from Dallara and G Force, now owned by Panoz. Each car had distinguishing characteristics. The Dallara featured a lengthy, needle nosecone while the Panoz G Force had distinctively shaped sidepods that gave the appearance of a swimmer doing the butterfly stroke.

As usual, there was debate as to which chassis to select, especially with newly designed cars in the equation. With Honda and Toyota in the fray, the engine selection would also be vital to a team's chances.

In the case of Penske, his drivers had a choice of either chassis with power from Toyota. Helio Castroneves chose the Dallara while Gil de Ferran opted for the new Panoz G Force.

The engine situation was understandably more equally divided. Team Penske, Target Chip Ganassi, Mo Nunn, Kelley Racing, A.J. Foyt Enterprises and Curb Agajanian used Toyota engines. Team Green, Ray Racing, Super Aguri-Fernandez and Rahal-Letterman Racing used Hondas. The remaining teams used the tried and true Chevrolet. Perhaps the most interesting pairing was that of Honda and Rahal-Letterman. Only nine years earlier, Rahal had been unable to get his team's Honda-powered cars up to speed and wound up leasing Penske/Ilmors for the 500. That effectively severed his ties to Honda at the year's end, but apparently all was now forgiven.

On a blustery, cool day, the field attempted to qualify under tricky conditions, Castroneves' effort seeming to be the most heroic.

Going out when no one else dared to do so, he electrified the crowd with an average speed of 231.725, a tick faster than Bruno Junqueira the previous year under much more favorable conditions. The Brazilian was intent on becoming the Speedway's first man to win three in a row. It was an important first step.

Joining him on Row 1 were Tony Kanaan and Robby Gordon, who qualified third quickest for the second time in three years. Scott Dixon, Dan Wheldon and Kenny Bräck made up the second row.

Michael Andretti, who announced he would retire after the

500, qualified a respectable 13th. Al Unser, Jr., his longtime rival, qualified in 17th position.

Race Day crowds were ready to see history in the making and Castroneves was hoping to provide them with some.

At the drop of the green flag, the Brazilian set the early pace, but he faced challenges from Dixon, Andretti and Kanaan during the first 50 laps. Tomas Scheckter and Andretti swapped the lead for most of the next 50 laps, but Michael's race and his racing career came to a halt on Lap 94 when he was sidelined with a broken throttle linkage.

Scheckter led Laps 101-128 before Castroneves took over for the next 37. In the meantime, de Ferran had quietly moved up from 10th starting position and he now found himself behind his teammate.

With 50 laps to go, it looked more and more like a Penske driver would be winning the race, but which Penske driver would it be?

Castroneves held a slim lead on de Ferran and was seeking a date with destiny by being the first man to win three in a row at Indianapolis. By contrast, de Ferran was looking for a fitting way to end a successful career. That could be achieved by victory at the Speedway.

On Lap 165, Castroneves pitted, and the lead was taken in turn by Kanaan, Scheckter and Tora Takagi. In the meantime, de Ferran had passed his teammate. With 30 laps to go, he was leading the Indianapolis 500. Obviously, Roger Penske's greatest concern was that the team maintain its 1-2 finish, regardless of which driver was ahead at the checker.

On Lap 187, the caution came out for Wheldon's terrifying accident. The British rookie slammed into the wall between Turns 3 and 4 and then flipped over. Fortunately, he was uninjured and the race went green on Lap 194.

Once he lost the lead, Castroneves seemed unable to dislodge his teammate. And so the race finished with de Ferran crossing the finish line .2990 seconds ahead.

Kanaan finished third to give the country of Brazil a 1-2-3

Left: **Michael Andretti prepares for what he has announced will be his final start as a driver. Three years later, he will reconsider.**
Photograph: IMS

finish while Scheckter wound up fourth, followed by Takagi, Alex Barron, Tony Renna, Greg Ray, Unser and Roger Yasakawa. Takagi, a veteran of F1, was given the honor for top rookie.

Castroneves may have not won three in a row, but Roger Penske got his first-ever hat trick at the Speedway. Lou Moore, whose cars won the 500 from 1947 through 1949, was the only other owner to record three in a row. But Moore's cars only won five times; Penske now had his 13th victory.

With the race in hand, it was now time for some celebrating and de Ferran copied his fellow Brazilian's antic of climbing the fence along the main straightaway. Joining de Ferran on the fence were members of he victorious crew and Castroneves, who seemed almost as happy for his teammate's victory as if it had been his own.

Above: **Still more history is made as A. J. Foyt IV (right), grandson of the legendary four-time winner, becomes the youngest driver ever to compete in the "500." He is still only 18 when he qualifies, and turns 19 on May 25, which just happens to be race day.**

Below: **Closely packed action, featuring Kenny Bräck (number 15), Vítor Meira (22), Roger Yasukawa (55), Buddy Lazier (91), and Jaques Lazier (2).**
Photographs: IMS

Above: After being on hiatus for several years, U. E. "Pat" Patrick returns with Al Unser, Jr., as driver. Patrick won three times as an entrant, in 1973 and 1982 with Gordon Johncock, and in 1989 with Emerson Fittipaldi.

Inset above center: Jim Nabors, has sung "Back Home Again in Indiana" for all but about five years since 1972. Since the tradition was created by James Melton in 1946, other notables who have offered renditions include Dinah Shore in 1955 (the only woman so far to have sung it solo), Dennis Morgan (1960), Mel Tormé (1961), Vic Damone (1964), Johnny Desmond (1965), Ed Ames (1966), and Peter Marshall (1979).
Photographs: IMS

2004: Rice splashes to 500 Win

In the sport of auto racing, there are often changes of address. Being forced to leave or choosing to switch teams is simply the nature of the beast.

Where Buddy Rice was concerned, his entry as driver of one of the Rahal-Letterman Racing cars was the opportunity for vindication. Two years earlier, the 2000 Formula Atlantic champion was something of a sensation. Signed by Red Bull Team Cheever to debut at Michigan, Rice qualified second and finished runner-up to teammate Tomas Scheckter. He went on to score three more top-10 finishes and also led at Kentucky.

For 2003, he replaced Scheckter but with three races to go, he and Team Cheever parted company. Enter Bobby Rahal, who cast Rice a lifeline. Once again, he was a replacement – this time for the injured Kenny Bräck – but he would more than vindicate himself.

Marlboro Team Penske also had a different lineup thanks to the retirement of de Ferran. Looking for the special type of driver he always looked for, Roger Penske settled on two-time IRL champion Sam Hornish, Jr. Hornish made team history by being the first new Penske driver to win in his debut race. Hornish made a daring pass of teammate Helio Castroneves on the final lap of the season opener at Homestead to give the team a 1-2.

As had been the case since 2000, teams had the choice of the Dallara or Panoz G Force chassis, whilst Honda and Toyota continued to duke it out for supremacy in the IRL with Chevrolet hoping to find a new start using a rebadged version of what started out as a Ford-Cosworth. The jury was still out for the Chevy although Hornish had turned in some impressive performances with the engine the previous season.

Thanks to a cut in engine size (3.5 liters to 3.0 liters), speeds dropped noticeably from the previous year.

Rice, making a strong statement that Rahal had made the right decision in choosing him, captured the pole position with an average speed of 222.024. It was the slowest average for a 500 polesitter since 1997, when Arie Luyendyk averaged 218.263 in the first year of the new IRL formula. Wheldon, who finished his rookie 500 upside down, turned in an impressive speed average to qualify second. Dario Franchitti gave Andretti Green Racing a second front-row with his best-ever run at the Speedway.

The previous year's polesitter, Bruno Junqueira, was fourth with Tony Kanaan and Adrian Fernandez filling out the second row. On the final day, P.J. Jones managed to squeak into the

field for the first time. Parnelli's oldest son gave the nostalgia buffs something to cheer about. The car number was appropriately 98, which adorned Parnelli's winning car in 1963, and the paint scheme was white with red and blue scallops, reminiscent of the cars the elder Jones had raced in the early 1960s at Indianapolis.

Race Day was overcast and rain was predicted. Weather would definitely play a role in this race.

Rice jumped into the lead at the drop of the green flag and stayed there for the first 12 laps. When a caution came out for A.J. Foyt IV's spin in Turn 1, the leaders dashed into the pits. That vaulted Alex Barron into the lead despite the fact he had started in 24th position. Wheldon would lead briefly but the red flag came out due to rain on Lap 27.

The track was shut down for a short time and after Wheldon led through Lap 33, Rice regained the lead. Next it was Hornish in front for nine laps. Surprisingly they were the first laps led at the track for the highly regarded Ohio driver.

Rice took the lead again on Lap 59 and stayed there until pitting near the midway point of the race. The lead shuffled between Wheldon, Kanaan, Franchitti and Junqueira before the polesitter got back on top on Lap 152. Surrendering the lead to make what would end up being his final pit stop, Bryan Herta and Fernandez led before Rice regained the top spot on Lap 172.

Rice's race wasn't against the competition so much as it was against Mother Nature as dark clouds moved in over the Indianapolis Motor Speedway. Stormy weather would hit all of Indianapolis that afternoon and tornadoes struck different parts of the city.

On lap 174, it began to rain gently, and with no signs of a letup, and with tornadoes known to be in the area, the race was red-flagged and checkered simultaneously at lap 180. Rice was the winner in the one of the better comeback stories of auto racing.

With the storms prevailing, the victory celebration was moved inside for the first time in race history. The new "green room" at the foot of the tower provided an impromptu Victory Circle as Rice and the Rahal-Letterman team celebrated his win.

Because the race finished under caution, there was no victory margin. Kanaan was second regardless of the gap and Wheldon capped a fine month off with a third-place finish. Franchitti gave Andretti Green Racing a 2-3-4 finish and Junqueira came home fifth. Rounding out the top 10 were Meira, Fernandez, Dixon, Castroneves and Roger Yasukawa. Kosuke Matsuura finished 11th and captured the top rookie honor.

Above: GO, GO, GO: Buddy Rice gets rapid servicing by the Rahal–Letterman crew.

Left: The imminent arrival of severe weather conditions results in yet another Speedway first. For the first time ever, the victory celebration is moved inside, the location being "the green room" on the ground floor of the Bombardier Pagoda.

Inset far left: Bobby Rahal's partner in the winning team is not here on a whim. Comedian and talk-show host David Letterman was raised about eleven miles from the track and became enamored of the race as a boy in the 1960s. He is quite humbled by the win and can hardly believe he will now go into the history books as the co-owner of a winning car. For many years, David's parents ran a florist's shop in Indianapolis, his mother recently revealing that one of the busiest few days they ever had was following the death of Wilbur Shaw in a plane crash on October 30, 1954. Dozens upon dozens of floral arrangements were sent down to the Vernon, Indiana funeral home by the Lettermans.
Photographs: IMS

2005: Dan wins while Danica dazzles

The 89th Indianapolis 500 may have belonged to race winner Dan Wheldon and the Andretti Green Racing team, but the month of May and the sport of Indy-car racing became the domain of a diminutive young lady from Roscoe, Ill., by the name of Danica Patrick.

Few drivers have taken the Speedway and the sport by storm like Patrick did in May of 2005. But even though Wheldon's likeness would be on the Borg-Warner Trophy, Patrick's month-long effort generated so much publicity that one might have thought she had actually won the race. Danica Patrick did not win the 500, but she certainly won the hearts and admiration of millions of fans. Pretty, 23 years of age and absolutely tiny in size, Patrick's prowess in anything she raced belied the demure, feminine image she seemed to project. Once the helmet was on, Patrick's focus was as professional as anyone who previously sat in an Indy-car cockpit.

Patrick had already demonstrated her prowess by winning the pole position at Motegi and then passing no less than Sam Hornish, Jr., for the lead. She ultimately finished fourth but the weekend performance showed that she was for real. Indianapolis fans might have been skeptical, but she silenced them in short order by posting the top times throughout most of the first days of practice.

When qualifying arrived, she was a legitimate contender for the pole position, thanks to the month's fastest practice speed at 229.880. Of course, Patrick wasn't the only driver at the track that May. She did have some company.

Teaming with her at Rahal-Letterman Racing were defending 500 winner Buddy Rice and Vitor Meira. Their chief opposition came in the form of Andretti Green Racing with reigning IRL champion Tony Kanaan, Dario Franchitti, Dan Wheldon and Bryan Herta. Rahal-Letterman used the Panoz G Force chassis, with Andretti Green opting for the Dallara. But making them the teams to beat was the Honda powerplant. Honda clearly had the legs on the rival Toyota and Chevrolet engines.

Toyota's lineup was headlined by Marlboro Team Penske for Helio Castroneves and Hornish (in Dallaras), and Target Chip Ganassi Racing for Scott Dixon, Darren Manning and Australian rookie Ryan Briscoe (in Panoz G Forces). Chevy runners were perceived as the "poor kids on the block," but five drivers would qualify for the race with the engine. Leading the

way was Panther Racing with Dallaras for Tomas Scheckter and 1996 500 winner Buddy Lazier.

Some years, drivers seem to have problems with a particular turn. In 2005, that problematic area was Turn 2. First to back in forcibly was Rice, who seemingly was OK as he got out of his wrecked car. X-rays revealed he had broken two vertebrae and he was forced to sit out the month of May. He would be replaced by Kenny Bräck, who was hoping to make his first race since being seriously injured in the 2003 season finale at Texas.

Paul Dana was next to back into the Turn 2 wall. Like Rice, he was seemingly OK and quickly out of the car. However, the likable rookie had suffered a broken neck and would be out of action for the entire season.

The Speedway unveiled a new qualifying format. With four days designated as qualifying days, the first day's runs would be for the first 11 grid positions. Day 2 qualifying would be for positions 12-22. The third day would be for the final 11 spots, with the fourth day devoted to bumping. Unlike all previous years, drivers would be allowed as many as three completed attempts to qualify on each of the days – with the same car. A driver could also requalify his previously qualified car. It would allow the top drivers more opportunities to win the pole.

Patrick was first to qualify and was understandably nervous. It showed on her first lap when she bobbled in Turn 1. But like an experienced veteran, she kept the car off the wall and recorded a very strong lap. She would follow up with three more trouble-free laps and emerge with what would end up as the fourth-best speed of the starting field. She also showed her competitive side by displaying anger rather than disappointment in her run. She believed she could have won the pole and had her first lap been as quick as her other three, she most certainly would have won it.

Tony Kanaan would wind up with the pole position honors, qualifying at an average speed of 227.566. Hornish turned in a splendid run to qualify second and Scott Sharp made the front row for the first time since 2001, when he won the pole.

Patrick was fourth, giving her the best-ever starting spot in the 500 for a woman (Lyn St. James had qualified sixth in

Above: Joie Chitwood III, grandson of the auto thrill show legend and seven-time competitor in the "500" (1940–1950), enjoys the view of downtown Indianapolis from the Bombardier Pagoda. In December 2004, Joie was named President and COO of the Indianapolis Motor Speedway.

Left: Early in the going, pole winner Tony Kanaan (number 11) has a slight edge over Dario Franchitti (27), Danica Patrick (16), Sam Hornish, Jr. (6), Helio Castroneves (3), Buddy Lazier (95), Scott Sharp (8), and Vitor Meira (17).

Top: A euphoric Danica Patrick is interviewed for ABC television by Dr. Jerry Punch. "Danicamania" is about to move into full swing.

Photographs: IMS

Hornish, Kanaan and Franchitti continued to share the lead as the race passed the halfway point. On Lap 77, the caution came out for the most serious incident of the day. Trying to pass A.J. Foyt IV, Bruno Junqueira tangled with him and slammed into the Turn 2 wall twice. The Brazilian sustained serious injuries and would be sidelined for the remainder of the year.

Patrick survived a close call when the pack checked up on a restart. With nowhere to go, she banged wheels with Tomas Enge, setting off a chain-reaction accident that eliminated the Czech, teammate Scheckter and Jeff Bucknum. Patrick suffered damage to the nosecone but was able to continue.

At this point Wheldon had moved up from 16th to take the lead for the first time. He swapped the lead with Meira and then pitted for his final time, under caution, on lap 171. Patrick's Rahal-Letterman crew, gambling that there would be further cautions, decided to "leave her out there," thus giving her the lead. She led at the restart and held on until lap 185 when passed by Wheldon, just before Matsuura caught the turn 3 wall, to bring out another caution.

Wheldon led the field down for the restart at lap 190, and to the amazement of just about everyone Danica moved to the inside and out-accelerated Dan to the first turn. The crowd's reaction was absolutely phenomenal. For four dramatic laps, she remained in front until Wheldon was able to reclaim the lead. Because it had been necessary for her to conserve fuel in order to be able to finish, she had to ease off just slightly, bowing first to Meira and then to Herta, with others coming up. Sébastien Bourdais, running fifth, was just about to move around her when he drifted into "the gray stuff," striking the wall and bringing out the caution for the final time.

The race was over and Wheldon took the checkered flag, becoming the first driver from England to do so since Graham Hill in 1966. Meira and Herta finished ahead of Patrick, who had driven one heck of a race.

Rounding out the top 10 were Buddy Lazier, Franchitti, Sharp, Kanaan, Castroneves and Briscoe. Not surprisingly, Patrick netted the top rookie honor. And equally not surprisingly, she was disappointed in fourth. She had come to win.

Above: Felipe Giaffone (number 48), who qualified at the very last moment, gets lapped by eventual winner Dan Wheldon (26), Tomas Scheckter (4), and eventual runner-up Vitor Meira (17).

Below: Dan Wheldon, the first Englishman to win since Graham Hill in 1966, positively cherishes competing at Indianapolis.
Photographs: IMS

1994). She was now a favorite to win the race. Joining her on Row 2 would be Castroneves and Franchitti.

Bräck, named to replace the injured Rice, wasted no time establishing that he was back by setting the quick speed in qualifying with an average of 227.598. Because he was a second-day qualifier, he would start 23rd.

With Janet Guthrie recording the only top-10 finish in the history of the race, it was hard to perceive that Patrick could indeed win. There would be a lot of skeptics, but Danica Patrick was not one of them.

Hornish, Kanaan and Franchitti all took turns leading the first 50 laps. Patrick kept the leaders in sight and on Lap 56, she became the first woman to lead the Indianapolis 500. A rookie mistake would cost her as she stalled during one of her first pit stops.

2006: One for the record books

After 2005, there was obviously going to be an encore for Danica Patrick as she prepared for her second Indianapolis 500. The Indianapolis Motor Speedway had rarely seen anything like the preceding year's rendition of "Danicamania," but in addition to Act II, there were a number of interesting story lines for the 90th running of the Indianapolis 500.

May would see the return of two of the 500's most popular drivers – two-time winner Al Unser, Jr., and Michael Andretti. Andretti's son, Marco, would also make his debut. Another famous name would return to the Speedway – Luyendyk, as two-time winner Arie Luyendyk was able to put together a package for his son, Arie, Jr., and longtime engineer Tim Wardrop.

There was tinge of sadness as the racers prepared their first runs. Missing from the entry list was Paul Dana, who was hoping to make his first 500 as one of the Rahal-Letterman team drivers. Dana had procured sponsorship from Ethanol, which was planning to make inroads in the sport of racing. For 2006, all cars would run on a mixture of methanol and ethanol (10% ethanol) with the promise that the 2007 fuel would be all ethanol. Sadly, Dana did not get to see that dream come to fruition as he was fatally injured during the morning warmup for the season opener at Homestead. However, the Ethanol program continued and Jeff Simmons was named to replace Dana.

The entry list would also have the most former 500 winners in quite some time with six assigned to rides – Unser, Wheldon, Buddy Rice, Buddy Lazier, Eddie Cheever and Castroneves.

On the equipment side, history would also be made. For the first time ever, every entrant would be using the same engine – the Honda V-8. Statisticians can find certain 500s in which every starter used the same engine, but there had always been more than one engine choice in the entry. To be able to properly provide the Indianapolis 500 starting field with adequate powerplants, Honda was obliged to offer a second-weekend package to some of the smaller teams. A handful of drivers would have limited mileage that would allow them to practice only after the first weekend of qualifying.

Each driver would be allowed one engine for practice and qualifying with the promise of a fresh race engine for each qualifier.

Dallara continued to be the chassis of choice, with the Rahal-Letterman team the only prominent operation still using the Panoz. Those most likely to succeed at the Speedway in 2006 – Marlboro Team Penske, Target Chip Ganassi Racing and Andretti Green Racing – all had Dallara chassis. Rahal-Letterman also added Jeff Simmons to replace Dana in the Ethanol-sponsored entry.

The Speedway continued its tradition of doing something special on opening day and 2006 featured one of the better ideas for 500 fans. Abandoning the annual free-for-all for first-on-the-track rights, track officials chose to honor one of racing's first families – the Andrettis.

Marco and Michael Andretti were strapped into their respective cars and joined on the main straightaway by 1969 winner Mario Andretti, who donned an open-face helmet and goggles as he drove the Brawner Hawk-Ford from 1967 in a ceremonial lap. Tradition is always what it's been about at Indianapolis and this gesture underscored that fact in magnificent fashion.

The Andretti Green Racing operation would be the largest at the track in 2006 with five cars for Michael and Marco Andretti, Dario Franchitti, Tony Kanaan and Bryan Herta. Reigning series champion and defending 500 winner Dan Wheldon had departed for the reorganized Target Chip Ganassi Racing team where he would partner with Scott Dixon.

Inset top: On opening day, three generations of Andretti take a lap of honor, the now un-retired Michael and his 19-year-old son, Marco, driving the cars to which they are assigned for the race, while father/grandfather Mario wheels the Dean Van Lines Brawner Hawk/Ford with which he won the pole in 1967. Mario is seen being greeted by Tom Carnegie, the legendary "voice" of the public address system, who will step down after this race, having "called" an incredible 61 "500s" in a row.
Photograph: IMS

Below: The delightful and full-of-fun Helio Castroneves visits the Hall of Fame Museum and tries out the cockpit of a car which won 90 years before he did: the Marmon "Wasp" which carried Ray Harroun to victory in the very first Indianapolis "500" in 1911. It can be clearly seen here how the Marmon cylinders were cast in pairs, so that, while offering only a "four" to the public, a larger engine could be achieved for the "Wasp" by adding a third pair.
Photograph: IMS

Right: The legend continues: Marco Andretti, the 19-year-old son of Michael Andretti and grandson of Mario, makes his "500" debut and comes within a blink of winning, being passed by Sam Hornish, Jr., with only yards to go.

Below: Brian Barnhart, president and chief operating officer of the Indy Racing League, serves in the capacity, which until 1998 carried the title chief steward. No matter how many times a driver may have made qualifying attempts over the years, the passionate and meticulous Barnhart runs through the instructions in full every time. Scott Sharp, the 2001 pole sitter who has competed in every "500" but one since 1994 (he was injured in 1997), listens just as intently as he has for the last dozen years.
Photographs: IMS

Sam Hornish, Jr., and rain would dominate the week of practice with teammate Castroneves and the Target Ganassi drivers usually right behind on the charts. Wheldon managed to top practice a couple of days, including what was then the month's best at 228.663, but it was clear the Penske drivers had the upper hand. Both were getting their top times without the benefit of a tow, while Wheldon admitted his quick time of the month had come courtesy of a tow – from Hornish.

Rain would eliminate the possibility of qualifying the first weekend, but in recent years, the Speedway had restored the second weekend of qualifying. For 2006, it would be needed. The top teams used the second week of practice for race setups and full-tank running, while the second-weekend designates devoted their practice time to qualifying.

In pre-qualifying practice, the Penske boys showed they would be tough to beat. Hornish did a 229.244 (the month's best) and would be followed on the charts by Castroneves at 228.838. Hornish, with a tow from Patrick, would go even faster at 229.930. It was time to qualify.

Vitor Meira, now piloting the Panther Racing Dallara, temporarily took the pole with a 226.156 average. Al Unser, Jr., who like Michael Andretti had decided to come out of retirement, qualified for his 18th 500 with a 219.388 average. Michael soon joined him and posted a respectable 224.508. Because Larry Foyt had qualified earlier, Andretti's successful run meant that for the first time since 1992, there would be a Foyt, an Andretti and an Unser in the starting field.

Marco Andretti put together a smooth run and averaged 224.918 to top his father. Papa Michael gave his 19-year-old son high marks for the run and for the month of May.

Now it was time for Hornish, who showed his true speed on an empty track with an average of 228.985. Could Castroneves or Wheldon bump him from the pole? Wheldon went first but could only muster a 227.338. Castroneves then averaged 228.028 to move into second. The front row would end up Hornish, Castroneves and Wheldon.

It was also a busy day with a record 29 straight successful qualifying attempts before Franchitti was forced to wave off his first run. By day's end, all 33 spots had been filled.

Hornish had his first Indianapolis 500 pole and Roger Penske his 13th.

"I told the guys we were going to run a 229 average," Hornish pointed out. "Unfortunately, we were unable to do that. I felt really comfortable out there. I had a little push in the last couple of laps (that) knocked our speed off, but our time held up so far."

One of the better qualifying efforts came from Patrick, the sensation of the 2005 season. Struggling with her Panoz G Force all month and barely able to crack the top 20 on the daily speed charts, Patrick turned in a very impressive average of 224.674 mph, good for the outside of Row 4.

There were 32 qualifiers the first day and although there were a number of rumored deals involving a variety of drivers, only Thiago Medeiros qualified on Sunday. There would be no bumping this year and 33 starters would take the green flag.

The composure of the field had some interesting statistical ramifications. In addition to having the most former winners (6) since 2002 (the record being 10 in 1992), there were also more sons (9) of former drivers in the field. The fathers of Marco Andretti (Michael), Michael Andretti (Mario), Al Unser, Jr. (Al), P.J. Jones (Parnelli), Arie Luyendyk, Jr. (Arie), Larry Foyt (A.J.), Jeff Bucknum (Ronnie) and Buddy and Jaques Lazier (Bob) all raced in previous 500s. The fathers of Michael Andretti, Unser, Jones, Luyendyk and Foyt were all former 500 winners. And Michael Andretti gained the distinction of being the first and only driver in 500 history to race against his father, his brother (Jeff), cousin (John) and now his son.

Of the 33 starters, 13 countries were represented, with the United States having 21, Brazil five (Castroneves, Kanaan, Meira, Airton Daré and Medeiros), and England (Wheldon), Scotland (Franchitti), New Zealand (Dixon), South Africa (Scheckter), Japan (Kosuke Matsuura), France (Stephan Gregoire) and Italy (Max Papis) each with one.

When the green flag dropped, Castroneves darted into the lead and stayed there for the next nine laps. Hornish ran second initially, but Wheldon was on the move and soon dispatched the polesitter for second. On Lap 10, the reigning 500 winner passed Castroneves for the lead and began to run away with the race.

The Brazilian, by contrast, began to slowly drop back with handling problems, plaguing his bid for a third 500 victory. Castroneves had never failed to finish in five previous starts, but his string snapped when he tangled with Rice between Turns 3 and 4.

Wheldon may have been slower than Hornish in practice and qualifying, but he clearly had the stronger car on this day, continually running up front with Dixon protecting him in second place for a good part of the day. Hornish was third, but his bid to win an elusive 500 appeared to come apart when he pitted on Lap 151. With the fuel coupling still attached, Hornish left his pit. That drew a drive-through penalty under the green and for all practical purposes should have taken him out of contention.

Thanks to a subsequent yellow for Simmons' accident, Hornish was able to stay on the lead lap. When the race went green on Lap 162, it was Wheldon, Dixon, Kanaan, Franchitti and Marco Andretti, who was having a very good day.

After serving his penalty, Hornish rejoined the race 29 seconds behind the leader with 34 laps to go. Marco moved into fourth while Kanaan took the fight to the Ganassi drivers. In three laps, he lopped seven seconds off the deficit, lapping in the 221 range while the leaders lapped at 217. However, the leaders upped their pace and Hornish soon found himself down by more than 30 seconds.

Dixon's protection of second place drew a warning from race officials for blocking. With Wheldon unable to draw away, it was a matter of time for Kanaan. The Brazilian dove under Dixon in Turn 3 and shortly afterward, the New Zealander drew a drive-through penalty for a second block. That would effectively end his chance to win.

Wheldon was now .2 of a second ahead of Kanaan on Lap 174. Dixon made his penalty drive-through on Lap 176 and he rejoined in seventh position. Marco Andretti was now third. Forty-one years ago, his grandfather had finished third in his rookie 500.

Wheldon managed to maintain a slight lead on Kanaan with Marco four seconds in arrears. Franchitti was fifth and Patrick, last year's fourth-place finisher, was up to sixth. There were 20 laps to go and one more round of pit stops that

There has never been a year in which the storyline of the race has changed so many times within the final minutes. Dan Wheldon, having switched from Andretti Green to Chip Ganassi, leads 148 of the 200 laps, including as late as lap 182. No driver has ever won in consecutive years for different teams. Will he be the first? But wait a moment! Tony Kanaan is leading. As the only person in history to have led in all of his first five races, and with a second and a third-place finish to his credit, will he be the winner? With six laps to go, the "un-retired" Michael Andretti takes over. Will Michael finally be able to shake his apparent "curse" here and shed the dubious distinction of never having won in spite of having led more laps than Rick Mears, who has won the "500" four times? Suddenly, just as Mears had performed a stunning outside pass of Michael for the lead late in the 1991 race, so Michael's own son is now doing the same thing. There are two laps to go. Troy Ruttman's 54-year-old record of having been the youngest-ever winner (at 22) is apparently going to be slashed by three years, and the race is going to be won for the first time by the grandson of a former winner. But wait again! They are coming out of the final corner and here comes Sam Hornish, Jr., who has had to overcome a pit accident and who has never gone the distance in any of his six previous starts. Hornish is darting for the inside! He is coming around. Who will win? Can Marco hold him off? No, it is Sam, taking over in the final few yards! In the last 18 laps, the race has been led by five different drivers. There has, quite simply, never in the 90 runnings of the Indianapolis 500, ever been anything to match this.

Photograph: LAT

Below: Sam Hornish, Jr., wins. The latest in a long line of victory enclosures, this one is at the foot of the Formula 1 Grand Prix victory rostrum, just a few feet further to the north from most of its predecessors since 1971.
Photograph: IMS

might decide the outcome.

On Lap 183, Kanaan went by on the inside to take the lead. Wheldon passed to briefly retake the lead, but then Kanaan swept past and quickly built a six-second margin. On Lap 184, Wheldon pitted for the final time. He rejoined in seventh place, the last car on the lead lap. Kanaan continued to pour it on with rookie teammate Andretti now 6.6 seconds behind. Franchitti was third and Michael Andretti fourth to give Andretti Green Racing a temporary 1-2-3-4. However, all needed one more stop. Kanaan was scheduled to pit on Lap 190. Marco pitted on Lap 191, just as the yellow came out for Felipe Giaffone's brush with the Turn 2 wall.

Patrick became the victim of an ill-timed yellow. She had pitted during the green and was once again down a lap (earlier in the race, she had pitted under green only to rejoin in time for a caution).

Kanaan led Franchitti, Michael Andretti, Dixon, Hornish, Wheldon and Marco Andretti. Kanaan ducked into the pits on Lap 193, followed by Franchitti. Michael Andretti was now in the lead. With six laps to go, it had been 34 laps since he had pitted, but some of those laps were under caution. He conceivably could stay out for the remainder of the race.

Michael was directly behind the pace car with Marco now second and three cars between them. However, Dixon, Hornish and Wheldon were right behind Marco.

On Lap 196, the green came out and Marco got past two of the lapped cars. Michael led Lap 197, and suddenly was very much a player in this drama. Could he finally win at Indianapolis? No sooner had they entered Turn 1 than Marco swept by Hornish and then passed Michael as they headed into Turn 3. By the time they came around, Hornish had displaced Michael for second and set off after the rookie. So much for Michael's late-race bid, but perhaps his son could win for the family. With two laps to go, Marco led by half a second with Hornish closing. Hornish tried, but Marco slammed the door as they headed into Turn 3. He drew away

from Hornish ever so slightly.

The white flag came out, and Marco was .9 seconds ahead of Hornish, but Sam wasn't done. Closing up and then drafting as they exited Turn 4, he pulled out and nipped him at the line on the inside. It may not have been as close as 1992 with Al Unser, Jr., and Scott Goodyear, but it was the second-closest finish with Hornish .0635 of a second ahead of Marco Andretti.

It was the first time in 500 history that the lead had changed hands on the final lap. In fact, Hornish only led the last few yards of the race – it was that close.

Understandably, the crowd went wild as the two cars crossed the start-finish line. Sam Hornish, Jr., was the 2006 Indianapolis 500 winner, Indy-car racing had another star driver of the future and the fans saw a fantastic finish to the world's greatest race.

Michael wound up third ahead of Wheldon, who led 148 laps, more than by any other driver in the race. Kanaan finished fifth, followed by Dixon, Franchitti, Patrick, Sharp and Meira. Andretti Green Racing garnered four of the top seven positions.

It was a month of comebacks and Hornish may have scored one of the greatest comebacks of them all. In less than 50 laps, he survived a pit-stop blunder that could have been worse, overcame a penalty for that blunder and still managed to stay on the lead lap, trailed the leaders by more than 30 seconds with 30 laps to go and passed two determined members of the Andretti family to snatch a victory from the jaws of defeat.

For the first time in seven Indianapolis 500s, Sam Hornish went the distance. In addition to leading the last lap, it seems that's all he ever needed to do to win the race.

There was more joy for Sam, when in addition to his momentous victory at the Speedway, he emerged as the 2006 champion of the Indy Racing League, edging out teammate Helio Castroneves and Ganassi's Dan Wheldon after a thrilling wheel-to-wheel battle at Chicagoland.

Roger Penske: Nobody does it better

ON five occasions, cars owned by former driver Lou Moore won the Indianapolis 500. Moore ranks second on the all-time list of 500-winning car owners. Mike Boyle, Bob Wilke and U.E. "Pat" Patrick each owned the winning car on three occasions. They rank equal third on the winning owners list.

But they don't even begin to come close to the man who occupies the top spot.

That distinction belongs to Roger Penske, thank you.

Mr. Penske has been the winning car owner at Indianapolis on 14 occasions at the time of this writing, with the prospect of future victories in the 500 a likely possibility.

How does one describe Roger Penske? That's a tall order for a man often in the public eye who keeps his private life private. There are no forthcoming biographies, but perhaps there is one telling story that sums up the man.

In 1988, after his cars made history by occupying the entire front row in qualifying and then dominating the race and finishing first and third, Penske was asked if he planned to celebrate.

His response: "We've got to get ready for Milwaukee next weekend. We've got a championship to win."

Enough said – the man is focused.

While building a successful career as a driver, Penske also had his eye on business. He is living proof that business and pleasure can mix, especially if you do things right. And doing things right has always been a Penske trademark. One need only look at the cleanliness of the garages, the neat appearance of the crews and the workmanship on the cars to know that Penske's way is the way to go racing.

That penchant for doing it right carried over into his business prospects and he soon developed an empire of car dealerships, franchises, distributorships, industries and even racing tracks. Occasionally mentioned as the man who ought to run General Motors, Penske never lost his enthusiasm for auto racing.

After retiring as a driver on a winning note (he swept every major event at the Nassau Speed Weeks) at the end of 1964, he spent a year as manager for Jim Hall's Chaparral team. That year was highlighted by the Chaparral's upset victory at Sebring and numerous wins in pre-Can-Am races in the United States and Canada. But more importantly, it would lay a foundation for his future plans in the sport.

By 1969, Penske and driver Mark Donohue were ready for an all-out assault on Indianapolis. Although Donohue finished seventh, his practice and qualifying effort made him one of the pre-race favorites. Perhaps more than anything, though, the tout came courtesy of the reputation that Penske had already developed by winning races and titles. In three years of racing for Penske, Donohue had done plenty of that.

It would take Penske three more tries to score that elusive first win with Donohue in 1972 and it would be seven more years before Rick Mears delivered a second victory. But again, the reputation that preceded Penske and his marvelous operation was such that he invariably was the guy to beat even in the years when he didn't win.

Over the years, his driver roster was a veritable "Who's Who" of auto racing. Supporting the drivers were some of the best engineers and mechanics in the business. The cars, still immaculately prepared, represented the best in Indy-car racing technology.

Between 1981 and 1994, Penske's drivers won eight 500s. There might have been more 500 wins had he not missed races between 1996 and 2000 due to the IRL-CART dispute. But he returned in 2001 and resumed winning – taking three in a row with Brazilian stars Helio Castroneves and Gil de Ferran. In 2006, Sam Hornish, Jr., gave Penske his 14th win at Indianapolis. Earlier, Hornish captured the pole position for Penske, the team's record 13th.

Do the math. In the last 21 Indianapolis 500s he has contested, Penske's drivers have come home first 12 times and captured 10 pole positions. Then add 132 Indy-car victories and 12 national Indy-car titles to the tally.

Nobody does it better. Nobody ever has.

Above: Roger Penske and team manager Tim Cindric celebrate with their latest winner. Cindric was raised locally, the son of Carl Cindric, a close associate of the late Herb Porter, a fixture who had a presence in the old garage area throughout the entire year. Tim, as a young boy, spent many an hour running around the complex during the summer holidays. It is common for the winning driver to hold up the appropriate number of fingers in order to indicate his number of "500" wins. Penske is apparently celebrating only that of Hornish. If he were celebrating his own as an entrant, his amazing 14 would be on the verge of requiring four HANDS, while the use of fingers only (no thumbs) would have already made that a necessity in 2003.
Photograph: LAT

RG-WAR
INDIANAPOL

GOUX
1913
M.P.H.

RENE THOMAS
1914
82.47 M.P.H.

STATISTICS

DRIVERS LISTED BY FIRST RACE START

A total of 708 different drivers have started in at least one Indianapolis 500 up through 2006. They are listed here, alphabetically, and according to the year of each driver's first start.

1911: (40) Johnny Aitken, Gil Anderson, Charles Basle, Ralph Beardsley, Fred Belcher, Charlie Bigelow, Caleb Bragg, David Bruce-Brown, Bob Burman, Arthur Chevrolet, Harry Cobe, Joe Dawson, Ralph de Palma, Ernest Delaney, Louis Disbrow, Fred Ellis, Bill Endicott, Harry Endicott, Frank Fox, Lee Frayer, Harry Grant, Art Greiner, Howard Hall, Ray Harroun, Eddie Hearne, Hughie Hughes, Joe Jagersberger, Will Jones, Harry Knight, Billy Knipper, Herb Lytle, Mel Marquette, Charlie Merz, Ralph Mulford, Lewis Strang, Teddy Tetzlaff, Jack Tower, W. H. "Bill" Turner, Howdy Wilcox, Spencer Wishart

1912: (8) Bert Dingley, Joe Horan, Johnny Jenkins, Billy Liesaw, Joe Matson, Len Ormsby, Eddie Rickenbacker, Len Zengel

1913: (10) George Clark, Robert Evans, Jules Goux, Albert Guyot, Willie Haupt, Don Herr, Joe Nikrent, Theodore Pilette, Vincenzo Trucco, Paulo Zuccarelli

1914: (15) George Boillot, S.F. Brock, Billy Carlson, Billy Chandler, Jean Chassagne, Josef Christiaens, Earl Cooper, Arthur Duray, Ernst Friedrich, Ray Gilhooly, Charles Keene, Art Klein, George Mason, Barney Oldfield, Rene Thomas

1915: (13) Tom Alley, George Babcock, Louis Chevrolet, Joe Cooper, C.C. Cox, John de Palma, George Hill, Johnny Mais, Eddie O'Donnell, Tom Orr, Jean Porporato, Dario Resta, Noel Van Raalte

1916: (8) Wilbur D'Alene, Jules DeVigne, Aldo Franchi, Ora Haibe, Pete Henderson, Art Johnson, Dave Lewis, Tom Rooney

1919: (19) Paul Bablot, Andre Boillot, Joe Boyer, W.W. Brown, Gaston Chevrolet, Cliff Durant, Denny Hickey, Kurt Hitke, Ray Howard, Charles Kirkpatrick, Louis LeCocq, J.J. McCoy, Tommy Milton, Roscoe Sarles, Elmer Shannon, Arthur Thurman, Omar Toft, Ira Vail, Louis Wagner

1920: (4) John Boling, Bennett Hill, Jimmy Murphy, Joe Thomas

1921: (6) Riley Brett, Jules Ellingboe, Louis Fontaine, Percy Ford, Eddie Miller, C.W. Van Ranst

1922: (11) E.G. "Cannonball" Baker, L.L. Corum, Jack Curtner, Peter de Paolo, Leon Duray, Frank Elliott, I.P Fetterman, Harry Hartz, Douglas Hawkes, Glenn Howard, Jerry Wonderlich

1923: (10) Martin de Alzaga, Prince de Cystria, Pierre de Viscaya, Harlan Fengler, Christian Lautenschlager, Wade Morton, Raul Riganti, Max Sailer, Christian Werner, Count Louis Zborowski

1924: (7) Ernie Ansterburg, Fred Comer, Fred Harder, Bill Hunt, Bob McDonogh, Alfred E. Moss, Antoine Mourre

1925: (8) Pietro Bordino, Earl DeVore, Ralph Hepburn, Herbert Jones, M.C. Jones, Peter Kreis, Phil Shafer, Dr. W. E. Shattuc

1926: (12) Norman Batten, John Duff, E.A.D. Eldridge, Tony Gulotta, Thane Houser, Ben Jones, Fred Lecklider, Frank Lockhart, Jack McCarver, Bon McDougall, Steve Nemesh, Cliff Woodbury

1927: (13) Dutch Baumann, Cliff Bergere, Al Cotey, Dave Evans, Fred Frame, Jimmy Hill, Al Melcher, Jack Petticord, Louis Schneider, Wilbur Shaw, Benny Shoaff, George Souders, Babe Stapp

1928: (12) Billy Arnold, C. W. Belt, Jimmy Gleason, Ira Hall, Ray Keech, Henry Kohlert, Deacon Litz, Louis Meyer, Lou Moore, Sam Ross, Johnny Seymour, Russ Snowberger

1929: (14) Frank Brisko, Louis Chiron, Wesley Crawford, Rick Decker, Frank Farmer, W.H. "Speed" Gardner, Albert Karnatz, Bill Lindau, Carl Marchese, Jules Moriceau, Herman Schurch, Bill Spence, Ernie Triplett, Fred Winnai

1930: (19) Leslie Allen, Baconin Borzachini, Claude Burton, Harry Butcher, Joe Caccia, Shorty Cantlon, Letterio Cucinotta, Bill Cummings, Bill Denver, Roland Free, Chet Gardner, Joe Huff, Mel Kenealy, Cy Marshall, J.C. McDonald, Zeke Meyer, Chet Miller, Charles Moran, Marion Trexler

1931: (12) Al Aspen, Paul Bost, Gene Haustein, George Howie, Luther Johnson, Phil Pardee, Francis Quinn, Joe Russo, Myron Stevens, Stubby Stubblefield, George Wingerter, Billy Winn

1932: (12) Ray Campbell, Bob Carey, Malcolm Fox, Juan Guadino, Al Gordon, Johnny Kreiger, Doc MacKenzie, Al Miller, Kelly Petillo, Bryan Saulpaugh, Gus Schrader, Howdy Wilcox II

1933: (5) Mark Billman, Willard Prentiss, Mauri Rose, Johnny Sawyer, Lester Spangler

1934: (7) Herb Ardinger, George Bailey, George Barringer, Charles Crawford, Dusty Fahrnow, Rex Mays, Harry McQuinn

1935: (8) George Connor, Ted Horn, Harris Insinger, Floyd Roberts, Bob Sall, Jimmy Snyder, Louis Tomei, Clay Weatherly

1936: (4) Emil Andres, Frank McGurk, Ray Pixley, Doc Williams

1937: (7) Floyd Davis, Billy DeVore, Ken Fowler, Ronney Householder, Bob Swanson, Frank Wearne, Tony Willman

1938: (4) Henry Banks, Duke Nalon, Al Putnam, Joel Thorne

1939: (1) Mel Hansen

1940: (6) Joie Chitwood, Sam Hanks, Tommy Hinnershitz, Rene LeBegue, George Robson, Paul Russo

1941: (2) Overton Phillips, Everett Saylor

1946: (10) Tony Bettenhausen, Hal Cole, Duke Dinsmore, Lewis Durant, Jimmy Jackson, Danny Kladis, Hal Robson, Bill Sheffler, Luigi Villoresi, Jimmy Wilburn

1947: (7) Fred Agabashian, Les Anderson, Walt Brown, Milt Fankhouser, Bill Holland, Pete Romcevich, Charles Van Acker

1948: (9) Bill Cantrell, Duane Carter, Mack Hellings, Johnny Mantz, Johnny Mauro, Jack McGrath, Mike Salay, Lee Wallard, Spider Webb

1949: (11) Manuel Ayulo, Myron Fohr, George Fonder, Jackie Holmes, Norm Houser, Bayliss Levrett, George Lynch, Johnny McDowell, Johnnie Parsons, Jim Rathmann, Troy Ruttman

1950: (9) Walt Ader, Jimmy Davies, Walt Faulkner, Pat Flaherty, Cecil Green, Gene Hartley, Jerry Hoyt, Dick Rathmann, Bill Schindler

1951: (12) Bobby Ball, Carl Forberg, Gene Force, Cliff Griffith, Joe James, Andy Linden, Bill Mackey, Mike Nazaruk, Carl Scarborough, Chuck Stevenson, Bill Vukovich, Rodger Ward

1952: (8) Alberto Ascari, Jimmy Bryan, Art Cross*, Eddie Johnson, Jimmy Reece, Jim Rigsby, Bob Scott, Bob Sweikert

1953: (6) Jimmy Daywalt*, Don Freeland, Ernie McCoy, Cal Niday, Marshall Teague, Johnny Thomson

1954: (6) Frank Armi, Larry Crockett*, Len Duncan, Ed Elisian, Bill Homeier, Pat O'Connor

1955: (8) Keith Andrews, Johnny Boyd, Ray Crawford, Al Herman*, Al Keller, Eddie Russo, Shorty Templeman, Chuck Weyant

1956: (5) Bob Christie, Billy Garrett, Johnnie Tolan, Jack Turner, Bob Veith*

1957: (5) Bill Cheesbourg, Don Edmunds*, Elmer George, Mike Magill, Eddie Sachs

1958: (8) George Amick*, Art Bisch, A.J. Foyt, Paul Goldsmith, Jud Larson, Len Sutton, Jerry Unser, Dempsey Wilson

1959: (5) Red Amick, Chuck Arnold, Don Branson, Bobby Grim*, Jim McWithey

1960: (4) Jim Hurtubise*, Lloyd Ruby, Bud Tingelstad, Wayne Weiler

1961: (8) Jack Brabham, Don Davis, Norman Hall, Parnelli Jones*, Bobby Marshman*, Roger McCluskey, Ebb Rose, A.J. Shepherd

1962: (5) Allen Crowe, Dan Gurney, Chuck Hulse, Jim McElreath*, Chuck Rodee

1963: (5) Jim Clark*, Art Malone, Al Miller, Johnny Rutherford, Bobby Unser

1964: (7) Ronnie Duman, Walt Hansgen, Bob Harkey, Dave MacDonald, Bob Mathouser, Bob Wente, Johnny White*

1965: (11) Mario Andretti*, Billy Foster, Jerry Grant, Masten Gregory, Gordon Johncock, Bobby Johns, Arnie Knepper, Joe Leonard, Mickey Rupp, George Snider, Al Unser

1966: (7) Gary Congdon, Larry Dickson, Graham Hill, Mel Kenyon, Jackie Stewart*, Carl Williams, Cale Yarborough

1967: (5) Wally Dallenbach, Denis Hulme*, Art Pollard, Jochen Rindt, Lee Roy Yarbrough

1968: (6) Gary Bettenhausen, Ronnie Bucknum, Jim Malloy, Mike Mosley, Sam Sessions, Billy Vukovich*

1969: (5) Sonny Ates, Mark Donohue*, George Follmer, Peter Revson, Bruce Walkup

1970: (4) Donnie Allison*, Rick Muther, Dick Simon, Greg Weld

1971: (4) David Hobbs, Steve Krisiloff, Bentley Warren, Denny Zimmerman*

1972: (8) Jimmy Caruthers, Mike Hiss*, Lee Kunzman, John Mahler, John Martin, Sam Posey, Swede Savage, Salt Walther

1973: (3) Bobby Allison, Jerry Karl, Graham McRae*

1974: (7) Tom Bigelow, Larry Cannon, Pancho Carter*, Jan Opperman, Johnny Parsons, Bill Simpson, Tom Sneva

1975: (4) Sheldon Kinser, Larry McCoy, Bill Puterbaugh*, Eldon Rasmussen

1976: (4) Spike Gehlhausen, Al Loquasto, Vern Schuppan*, Billy Scott

1977: (7) Janet Guthrie, Cliff Hucul, Bubby Jones, Bobby Olivero, Danny Ongais, Clay Regazzoni, Jerry Sneva*

1978: (5) Tom Bagley, Rick Mears*, Larry Rice*, Joe Saldana, Phil Threshie

1979: (1) Howdy Holmes*

1980: (10) Billy Engelhart, Dick Ferguson, Dennis Firestone, Hurley Haywood, Greg Leffler, Roger Rager, Tim Richmond*, Gordon Smiley, Bill Whittington, Don Whittington

1981: (10) Bill Alsup, Tony Bettenhausen, Geoff Brabham, Scott Brayton, Michael Chandler, Kevin Cogan, Josele Garza*, Pete Halsmer, Tom Klausler, Bob Lazier

1982: (9) Chet Fillip, Chip Ganassi, Jim Hickman*, Herm Johnson, Roger Mears, Bobby Rahal, Hector Rebaque, Danny Sullivan, Dale Whittington

1983: (6) Patrick Bedard, Steve Chassey, Derek Daly, Teo Fabi*, Chris Kneifel, Al Unser Jr.

1984: (5) Michael Andretti*, Emerson Fittipaldi, Tom Gloy, Roberto Guerrero*, Al Holbert

1985: (6) Raul Boesel, Jim Crawford, Arie Luyendyk*, John Paul Jr., Ed Pimm, Rich Vogler

1986: (4) Phil Krueger, Randy Lanier*, Roberto Moreno, Jacques Villeneuve (uncle)

1987: (6) Fabrizio Barbazza*, Stan Fox, Ludwig Heimrath Jr., Davy Jones, Randy Lewis, Jeff MacPherson

1988: (5) John Andretti, Dominic Dobson, Rocky Moran, Tero Palmroth, Billy Vukovich III*

1989: (4) John Jones, Bernard Jourdain*, Scott Pruett*, Didier Theys

1990: (3) Eddie Cheever Jr.*, Scott Goodyear, Dean Hall

1991: (5) Jeff Andretti*, Mike Groff, Buddy Lazier, Hiro Matsushita, Willy T. Ribbs

1992: (7) Eric Bachelart, Brian Bonner, Philippe Gache, Ted Prappas, Lyn St. James*, Paul Tracy, Jimmy Vasser

1993: (5) Robby Gordon, Stephan Gregoire, Stefan Johansson, Nigel Mansell*, Nelson Piquet

1994: (9) Adrian Fernandez, Marco Greco, Mauricio Gugelmin, Bryan Herta, Hideshi Matsuda, Scott Sharp, Brian Till, Jacques Villeneuve* (nephew), Dennis Vitolo

1995: (6) Gil de Ferran, Christian Fittipaldi*, Carlos Guerrero, Andre Ribeiro, Eliseo Salazar, Alessandro Zampedri

1996: (17) Michele Alboreto, Robbie Buhl, Buzz Calkins, Mark Dismore, Paul Durant, Racin Gardner, Joe Gosek, Jim Guthrie, Davey Hamilton, Scott Harrington, Richie Hearn, Michel Jourdain Jr., Brad Murphey, Johnny O'Connell, Tony Stewart*, Johnny Unser, Fermin Velez

1997: (13) Billy Boat, Claude Bourbonnais, Kenny Bräck, Tyce Carlson, Affonso Giaffone, Robbie Groff, Steve Kinser, Jack Miller, Greg Ray, Billy Roe, Sam Schmidt, Vincenzo Sospiri, Jeff Ward*

1998: (8) Donnie Beechler, Jack Hewitt, Jimmy Kite, Steve Knapp*, Andy Michner, Robby Unser, Stan Wattles, J.J. Yeley

1999: (4) Wim Eyckmans, John Hollansworth Jr., Robby McGehee*, Jeret Schroeder

2000: (7) Airton Daré, Sarah Fisher, Andy Hillenburg, Sam Hornish Jr., Jaques Lazier, Jason Leffler, Juan Pablo Montoya*

2001: (6) Helio Castroneves*, Felipe Giaffone, Jon Herb, Bruno Junqueira, Nicolas Minassian, Cory Witherill

2002: (9) Alex Barron*, Dario Franchitti, Shigeaki Hattori, Tony Kanaan, George Mack, Max Papis, Laurent Redon, Tomas Scheckter*, Rick Treadway

2003: (9) Scott Dixon, A.J. Foyt IV, Vitor Meira, Shinji Nakano, Tony Renna, Buddy Rice, Tora Takagi*, Dan Wheldon, Roger Yasukawa

2004: (8) Ed Carpenter, Larry Foyt, P. J. Jones, Darren Manning, Kosuke Matsuura*, Marty Roth, Jeff Simmons, Mark Taylor

2005: (6) Sébastien Bourdais, Ryan Briscoe, Jeff Bucknum, Patrick Carpentier, Tomas Enge, Danica Patrick*

2006: (5) Marco Andretti*, Townsend Bell, P.J. Chesson, Arie Luyendyk Jr., Thiago Medeiros

* Denotes the winner of the Rookie of the Year Award, first presented in 1952. Two asterisks appear in 1961, 1978, 1984, 1989, and 2002, years in which co-winners were declared.

Left: 2006 Rookie of the Year Marco Andretti comes home second only a couple of yards behind winner Sam Hornish Jr.
Photograph: IMS

OFFICIAL
BOX SCORES
1911-2006

PREPARED BY DONALD DAVIDSON & TIM SULLIVAN

Official Box Score

Inaugural Indianapolis 500-Mile Race at the Indianapolis Motor Speedway • Tuesday, May 30, 1911

FP	SP	No.		Driver	Car Name	Chassis/Engine	Laps	Status	Total Prize Money
1	28	32	R	Ray Harroun*	Marmon "Wasp"	Marmon/Marmon	200	74.602	$14,250
2	29	33	R	Ralph Mulford	Lozier	Lozier/Lozier	200	74.285	5,200
3	25	28	R	David Bruce-Brown	Fiat	Fiat/Fiat	200	72.730	3,250
4	11	11	R	Spencer Wishart*	Mercedes	Mercedes/Mercedes	200	72.648	2,350
5	27	31	R	Joe Dawson*	Marmon	Marmon/Marmon	200	72.365	1,500
6	2	2	R	Ralph DePalma	Simplex	Simplex/Simplex	200	71.084	1,000
7	18	20	R	Charlie Merz	National	National/National	200	70.367	800
8	12	12	R	W.H. Turner*	Amplex	Amplex/Amplex	200	68.818	700
9	13	15	R	Fred Belcher*	Knox	Knox/Knox	200	68.626	600
10	22	25	R	Harry Cobe	Jackson	Jackson/Jackson	200	67.899	500
11	10	10	R	Gil Anderson	Stutz	Stutz/Wisconsin	200	67.730	0
12	32	36	R	Hughie Hughes	Mercer	Mercer/Mercer	200	67.630	0
13	26	30	R	Lee Frayer*	Firestone-Columbus	Firestone Col./Firestone Col.	N/A	Running	0
14	19	21	R	Howdy Wilcox	National	National/National	N/A	Running	0
15	33	37	R	Charlie Bigelow*	Mercer	Mercer/Mercer	N/A	Running	0
16	3	3	R	Harry Endicott	Inter-State	Inter-State/Inter-State	N/A	Running	0
17	36	41	R	Howard Hall	Velie	Velie/Velie	N/A	Running	0
18	40	46	R	Billy Knipper	Benz	Benz/Benz	N/A	Running	0
19	39	45	R	Bob Burman	Benz	Benz/Benz	N/A	Running	0
20	34	38	R	Ralph Beardsley*	Simplex	Simplex/Simplex	N/A	Running	0
21	16	18	R	Eddie Hearne*	Fiat	Fiat/Fiat	N/A	Running	0
22	6	6	R	Frank Fox*	Pope-Hartford	Pope-Hartford/Pope-Hartford	N/A	Running	0
23	24	27	R	Ernest Delaney	Cutting	Cutting/Cutting	N/A	Running	0
24	23	26	R	Jack Tower	Jackson	Jackson/Jackson	N/A	Running	0
25	20	23	R	Mel Marquette	McFarlan	McFarlan/McFarlan	N/A	Running	0
26	37	42	R	Bill Endicott*	Cole	Cole/Cole	N/A	Running	0
27	4	4	R	Johnny Aitken	National	National/National	125	Rod	0
28	9	9	R	Will Jones	Case	Case/Wisconsin	122	Steering	0
29	1	1	R	Lewis Strang*	Case	Case/Wisconsin	108	Steering	0
30	7	7	R	Harry Knight	Westcott	Westcott/Westcott	90	Accident	0
31	8	8	R	Joe Jagersberger	Case	Case/Wisconsin	87	Accident	0
32	31	35	R	Herb Lytle	Apperson	Apperson/Apperson	82	Accident	0
33	17	19	R	Harry Grant	Alco	Alco/Alco	51	Bearings	0
34	15	17	R	Charles Basle	Buick	Buick/Buick	46	Mechanical	0
35	5	5	R	Louis Disbrow	Pope-Hartford	Pope-Hartford/Pope-Hartford	45	Accident	0
36	14	16	R	Arthur Chevrolet	Buick	Buick/Buick	30	Mechanical	0
37	35	39	R	Caleb Bragg	Fiat	Fiat/Fiat	23	Mechanical	0
38	21	24	R	Fred Ellis	Jackson	Jackson/Jackson	22	Fire Damage	0
39	30	34	R	Teddy Tetzlaff	Lozier	Lozier/Lozier	20	Accident	0
40	38	44	R	Art Greiner	Amplex	Amplex/Amplex	12	Accident	0

Total Purse $30,150

Time of Race: 6:42:08 Average Speed: 74.602 mph Margin of Victory: 1:43.00
Pole: #1 Lewis Strang (determined by order of entry) Fastest Race Lap: N/A
Winning Car Owner: Nordyke & Marmon Co. Winning Chief Mechanic: Harry Goetz Winning Tire: Firestone
Legend: R=Indianapolis 500-Mile Race Rookie; *=Had Relief Help
Race Notes: Winner Harroun was relieved by Cyrus Patschke for approximately 35 laps at the halfway point of the race.
Lap Leaders: Aitken 1-4, Wishart 5-9, Belcher 10-13, Bruce-Brown 14-19, DePalma 20-23, Bruce-Brown 24-72, Aitken 73-76, Bruce-Brown 77-102, Harroun 103-137, Mulford 138-142, Harroun 143-176, Mulford 177-181, Harroun 182-200.
Lap Leader Summary: Harroun 3 times for 88 laps, Bruce-Brown 3-81, Mulford 2-10, Aitken 2-8, Wishart 1-5, Belcher 1-4, DePalma 1-4.
Lead Changes: 12 among 7 drivers.

Official Box Score

Second Indianapolis 500-Mile Race at the Indianapolis Motor Speedway • Thursday, May 30, 1912

FP	SP	No.		Driver	Car Name	Chassis/Engine	Laps	Status	Total Prize Money
1	7	8		Joe Dawson*	National	National/National	200	78.719	$20,000
2	3	3		Teddy Tetzlaff*	Fiat	Fiat/Fiat	200	76.632	10,000
3	17	21		Hughie Hughes	Mercer	Mercer/Mercer	200	76.307	5,000
4	22	28		Charlie Merz*	Stutz	Stutz/Wisconsin	200	76.014	3,000
5	15	18		Bill Endicott*	Schacht	Schacht/Wisconsin	200	73.807	2,500
6	2	2	R	Len Zengel*	Stutz	Stutz/Wisconsin	200	73.088	2,000
7	11	14	R	Johnny Jenkins	White	White/White	200	72.704	1,500
8	18	22	R	Joe Horan	Lozier	Lozier/Lozier	200	71.491	1,400
9	8	9		Howdy Wilcox*	National	National/National	200	69.525	1,300
10	16	19		Ralph Mulford	Knox	Knox/Knox	200	56.285	1,200
11	4	4		Ralph DePalma	Mercedes	Mercedes/Mercedes	198	Piston	0
12	12	15		Bob Burman	Cutting	Cutting/Cutting	156	Accident	0
13	10	12	R	Bert Dingley	Simplex	Simplex/Simplex	116	Rod	0
14	21	25	R	Joe Matson	Lozier	Lozier/Lozier	107	Crankshaft	0
15	6	7		Spencer Wishart	Mercedes	Mercedes/Mercedes	82	Water line	0
16	1	1		Gil Anderson	Stutz	Stutz/Wisconsin	79	Accident	0
17	14	17	R	Billy Liesaw*	Marquette-Buick	Marquette/Buick	72	Carb. Fire	0
18	24	5		Louis Disbrow*	Case	Case/Case	67	Differ. pin	0
19	19	23		Mel Marquette	McFarlan	McFarlan/McFarlan	63	Accident	0
20	5	6		Eddie Hearne*	Case	Case/Case	54	Crankshaft	0
21	13	16	R	Eddie Rickenbacker	Firestone-Columbus	Firestone Col./Firestone Col.	44	Bearing	0
22	23	29		David Bruce-Brown	National	National/National	24	Valves	0
23	9	10		Harry Knight	Lexington	Lexington/Lexington	7	Engine trouble	0
24	20	24	R	Len Ormsby	Opel	Opel/Opel	5	Rod	0

Total Purse $47,900

Time of Race: 6:21:06 Average Speed: 78.719 mph Margin of Victory: 10:23.00
Pole: #1 Gil Anderson (determined by order of entry) Fastest Race Lap: N/A
Winning Car Owner: National Motor Vehicle Co. Winning Chief Mechanic: Harry Martin ** Winning Tire: Michelin
Legend: R=Indianapolis 500-Mile Race Rookie; *=Had Relief Help, **=Also Riding Mechanic.
Race Notes: Winner Dawson was relieved by Don Herr for laps 108-144.
Lap Leaders: Tetzlaff 1-2, DePalma 3-198, Dawson 199-200.
Lap Leader Summary: DePalma 1 time for 196 laps, Tetzlaff 1-2, Dawson 1-2.
Lead Changes: 2 among 3 drivers.

Official Box Score

Third Indianapolis 500-Mile Race at the Indianapolis Motor Speedway • Friday, May 30, 1913

FP	SP	No.		Driver	Car Name	Chassis/Engine	Laps	Status	Total Prize Money
1	7	16	R	Jules Goux	Peugeot	Peugeot/Peugeot	200	75.933	$21,165
2	19	22		Spencer Wishart*	Mercer	Mercer/Mercer	200	73.489	10,165
3	16	2		Charlie Merz*	Stutz	Stutz/Wisconsin	200	73.382	5,165
4	2	9	R	Albert Guyot	Sunbeam	Sunbeam/Sunbeam	200	70.925	3,500
5	13	23	R	Theodore Pilette	Mercedes-Knight	Mercedes/Knight	200	68.148	3,000
6	20	12		Howdy Wilcox*	Gray Fox	Pope-Hartford/Pope-Hartford	200	67.653	2,200
7	22	29		Ralph Mulford	Mercedes	Mercedes/Mercedes	200	66.951	1,800
8	23	31		Louis Disbrow*	Case	Case/Case	200	66.793	1,600
9	15	35	R	Willie Haupt*	Mason	Duesenberg/Duesenberg	200	63.481	1,500
10	27	25	R	George Clark*	Tulsa	Tulsa/Wisconsin	200	62.994	1,400
11	21	4		Bob Burman*	Keeton	Keeton/Wisconsin	N/A	Running	0
12	14	3		Gil Anderson*	Stutz	Stutz/Wisconsin	187	Camshaft	0
13	4	5	R	Bob Evans	Mason	Duesenberg/Duesenberg	158	Clutch	0
14	3	17		Billy Liesaw*	Anel	Buick/Buick	148	Rods	0
15	1	19		Caleb Bragg*	Mercer	Mercer/Mercer	128	Pump shaft	0
16	11	10		Billy Knipper*	Henderson	Knipper/Duesenberg	125	Clutch	0
17	8	27		Teddy Tetzlaff	Isotta-Fraschini	Isotta/Isotta	118	Broken chain	0
18	24	32	R	Joe Nikrent*	Case	Case/Case	67	Bearings	0
19	25	6		Jack Tower	Mason	Duesenberg/Duesenberg	51	Accident	0
20	18	28	R	Vincenzo Trucco	Isotta-Fraschini	Isotta/Isotta	39	Loose tank	0
21	10	1		Harry Endicott*	Nyberg	Nyberg/Nyberg	23	Drive shaft	0
22	26	15	R	Paolo Zuccarelli	Peugeot	Peugeot/Peugeot	18	Bearing	0
23	12	21		Ralph DePalma	Mercer	Mercer/Mercer	15	Bearings	0
24	6	26		Harry Grant	Isotta-Fraschini	Isotta/Isotta	14	Broken Tank	0
25	17	18		Johnny Jenkins	Schacht	Schacht/Schacht	13	Crankshaft	0
26	5	8	R	Don Herr	Stutz	Stutz/Wisconsin	7	Clutch shaft	0
27	9	33		Bill Endicott	Case	Case/Case	1	Drive shaft	0

Total Purse $51,495

Time of Race: **6:35:05** Average Speed: **75.933 mph** Margin of Victory: **13:8.40**
Pole: **#19 Caleb Bragg (determined by drawn order)** Fastest Race Lap: **N/A**
Winning Car Owner: **Peugeot** Winning Chief Mechanic: **Emile Begin **** Winning Tire: **Firestone**
Legend: R=Indianapolis 500-Mile Race Rookie; *=Had Relief Help, **=Also Riding Mechanic
Lap Leaders: **Bragg 1, Evans 2-3, Goux 4-14, Burman 15-55, Goux 56-95, Anderson 96-102, Goux 103-124, Anderson 125-135, Goux 136-200.**
Lap Leader Summary: **Goux 4 times for 138 laps, Burman 1-41, Anderson 2-18, Evans 1-2, Bragg 1-1.**
Lead Changes: **8 among 5 drivers.**

Official Box Score

Fourth Indianapolis 500-Mile Race at the Indianapolis Motor Speedway • Saturday, May 30, 1914

FP	SP	No.		Driver	Car Name	Chassis/Engine	Laps	Status	Total Prize Money
1	15	16	R	Rene Thomas	Delage	Delage/Delage	200	82.474	$39,750
2	10	14	R	Arthur Duray	Peugeot	Peugeot/Peugeot	200	80.994	10,450
3	11	10		Albert Guyot	Delage	Delage/Delage	200	80.210	5,425
4	19	6	W	Jules Goux	Peugeot	Peugeot/Peugeot	200	79.491	3,500
5	30	3	R	Barney Oldfield*	Stutz	Stutz/Stutz	200	78.156	3,000
6	7	9	R	Josef Christiaens	Excelsior	Excelsior/Excelsior	200	77.439	2,200
7	26	27		Harry Grant	Sunbeam	Sunbeam/Sunbeam	200	75.687	1,800
8	27	5	R	Charlie Keene*	Beaver Bullet	Keene/Wisconsin	200	74.822	1,600
9	5	25	R	Billy Carlson*	Maxwell	Maxwell/Maxwell	200	70.972	1,500
10	23	42		Eddie Rickenbacker	Duesenberg	Duesenberg/Duesenberg	200	70.827	1,400
11	6	23		Ralph Mulford	Mercedes	Mercedes/Peugeot	200	69.550	0
12	28	43		Willie Haupt	Duesenberg	Duesenberg/Duesenberg	200	66.660	0
13	12	31		Billy Knipper*	Keeton	Keeton/Wisconsin	200	65.790	0
14	29	7	R	Georges Boillot	Peugeot	Peugeot/Peugeot	148	Frame	0
15	18	34	R	Ernst Friedrich	Bugatti	Bugatti/Bugatti	134	Pinion	0
16	24	1		Louis Disbrow	Burman	Burman/Wisconsin	128	Rod	0
17	25	19		Spencer Wishart	Mercer	Mercer/Mercer	122	Camshaft	0
18	14	2	R	Earl Cooper*	Stutz	Stutz/Stutz	118	Wheel	0
19	9	21		Caleb Bragg*	Mercer	Mercer/Mercer	117	Camshaft	0
20	8	15	R	Art Klein	King	King/Wisconsin	87	Valve	0
21	4	38	R	Billy Chandler	Braender Bulldog	Mulford/Duesenberg	69	Rod	0
22	3	4		Howdy Wilcox*	Gray Fox	Fox/Pope-Hartford	67	Valve	0
23	13	13	R	George Mason*	Mason	Duesenberg/Duesenberg	66	Piston	0
24	22	17		Bob Burman	Burman	Burman/Wisconsin	47	Rod	0
25	17	26	W	Joe Dawson	Marmon	Marmon/Marmon	44	Accident	0
26	16	24		Gil Anderson	Stutz	Stutz/Stutz	42	Loose Bolts	0
27	20	49	R	Ray Gilhooly	Isotta-Fraschini	Isotta/Isotta	41	Accident	0
28	2	8		Teddy Tetzlaff	Maxwell	Maxwell/Maxwell	38	Rocker arm	0
29	1	12	R	Jean Chassagne	Sunbeam	Sunbeam/Sunbeam	20	Accident	0
30	21	48	R	S.F. Brock	Ray	Mercer/Wisconsin	5	Camshaft	0

Total Purse $70,625

Time of Race: **6:03:45** Average Speed: **82.474 mph** Margin of Victory: **6:39.00**
Pole: **#12 Jean Chassagne (determined by drawn order)** Fastest Race Lap: **N/A**
Winning Car Owner: **L. Delage Co.** Winning Chief Mechanic: **Robert Laly **** Winning Tire: **Palmer Cord**
Legend: R=Indianapolis 500-Mile Race Rookie; W=Indianapolis 500-Mile Race Former Winner; *=Had Relief Help, **=Also Riding Mechanic
Lap Leaders: **Wilcox 1, Christaens 2-4, Goux 5, Christaens 6, Bragg 7, Christaens 8-12, Thomas 13-29, Duray 30-66, Guyot 67-75, Duray 76-115, Thomas 116-200.**
Lap Leader Summary: **Thomas 2 times for 102 laps, Duray 2-77, Christaens 3-9, Guyot 1-9, Wilcox 1-1, Goux 1-1, Bragg 1-1.**
Lead Changes: **10 among 7 drivers.**

Official Box Score
Fifth Indianapolis 500-Mile Race at the Indianapolis Motor Speedway • Monday, May 31, 1915

FP	SP	No.		Driver	Car Name	Chassis/Engine	Laps	Status	Total Prize Money
1	2	2		Ralph DePalma	Mercedes	Mercedes/Mercedes	200	89.840	$22,600
2	3	3	R	Dario Resta	Peugeot	Peugeot/Peugeot	200	88.911	10,900
3	5	5		Gil Anderson*	Stutz	Stutz/Stutz	200	87.602	5,600
4	4	4		Earl Cooper*	Stutz	Stutz/Stutz	200	86.624	3,700
5	11	15	R	Eddie O'Donnell	Duesenberg	Duesenberg/Duesenberg	200	81.473	3,000
6	7	8		Bob Burman	Peugeot	Peugeot/Peugeot	200	80.359	2,200
7	1	1		Howdy Wilcox	Stutz	Stutz/Stutz	200	80.143	1,800
8	9	10	R	Tom Alley	Duesenberg	Duesenberg/Duesenberg	200	79.972	1,600
9	16	19		Billy Carlson*	Maxwell	Maxwell/Maxwell	200	78.962	1,500
10	14	7	R	Noel Van Raalte	Sunbeam	Sunbeam/Sunbeam	200	75.874	1,400
11	24	28		Willie Haupt	Emden	Emden/Emden	200	70.750	0
12	10	14		Harry Grant*	Sunbeam	Sunbeam/Sunbeam	184	Oil Pan	0
13	17	21	R	Tom Orr*	Maxwell	Maxwell/Maxwell	168	Bearing	0
14	6	6	R	Jean Porporato	Sunbeam	Sunbeam/Sunbeam	164	Piston	0
15	15	18	R	Joe Cooper	Sebring	Duesenberg/Duesenberg	154	Accident	0
16	18	22		Ralph Mulford*	Duesenberg	Duesenberg/Duesenberg	124	Rod	0
17	12	12	R	George Babcock	Peugeot	Peugeot/Peugeot	117	Cylinder	0
18	8	9		Art Klein*	Kleinart	Duesenberg/Duesenberg	111	Disqualified	0
19	19	23		Eddie Rickenbacker	Maxwell	Maxwell/Maxwell	103	Rod	0
20	23	27	R	Louis Chevrolet	Cornelian	Cornelian/Sterling	76	Valve	0
21	13	17	R	John DePalma	Delage	Delage/Delage	41	Loose flywheel	0
22	20	24	R	Johnny Mais	Mais	Mais/Mercer	23	Left track	0
23	22	26	R	George Hill	Bugatti	Bugatti/Bugatti	20	Pump gear	0
24	21	25	R	C.C. Cox	Cino-Purcell	Cino/Mercer	12	Timing gears	0

Total Purse $54,300
Time of Race: 5:33:55.51 Average Speed: 89.840 mph Margin of Victory: 3:29.43
Pole: #1 Howdy Wilcox (98.900, 1:31.00) Fastest Race Lap: N/A
Winning Car Owner: E.C. Patterson Winning Chief Mechanic: Louis Fontaine ** Winning Tire: Goodrich
Legend: R=Indianapolis 500-Mile Race Rookie; *=Had Relief Help, **=Also Riding Mechanic
Race Notes: Race was postponed from May 29 due to rain.
Lap Leaders: Resta 1, Wilcox 2-6, Anderson 7-32, Resta 33-61, DePalma 62-127, Resta 128-134, DePalma 135-200.
Lap Leader Summary: DePalma 2 times for 132 laps, Resta 3-37, Anderson 1-26, Wilcox 1-5.
Lead Changes: 6 among 4 drivers.

Official Box Score
Sixth Indianapolis 500-Mile Race at the Indianapolis Motor Speedway • Tuesday, May 30, 1916

FP	SP	No.		Driver	Car Name	Chassis/Engine	Laps	Status	Total Prize Money
1	4	17		Dario Resta	Peugeot	Peugeot/Peugeot	120	84.001	$12,000
2	10	1	R	Wilbur D'Alene	Duesenberg	Duesenberg/Duesenberg	120	83.237	6,000
3	20	10		Ralph Mulford	Peugeot	Peugeot/Peugeot	120	82.594	3,000
4	14	14		Josef Christiaens	Sunbeam	Sunbeam/Sunbeam	120	79.435	2,000
5	5	15		Barney Oldfield	Delage	Delage/Delage	120	79.185	1,700
6	9	4	R	Pete Henderson*	Maxwell	Maxwell/Maxwell	120	78.284	1,400
7	6	29		Howdy Wilcox*	Premier	Premier/Premier	120	76.754	1,200
8	17	26	R	Art Johnson	Crawford	Crawford/Duesenberg	120	74.411	1,000
9	15	24		Billy Chandler*	Crawford	Crawford/Duesenberg	120	74.161	900
10	13	9	R	Ora Haibe	Ostewig	Ostewig/Wisconsin	120	74.043	800
11	19	12		Tom Alley	Ogren	Duesenberg/Duesenberg	120	73.550	0
12	21	8		Louis Chevrolet*	Frontenac	Frontenac/Frontenac	82	Rod	0
13	3	28		Gil Anderson	Premier	Premier/Premier	75	Oil line	0
14	18	25	R	Dave Lewis	Crawford	Crawford/Duesenberg	71	Fuel tank	0
15	1	18		Johnny Aitken	Peugeot	Peugeot/Peugeot	69	Valve	0
16	12	21	R	Jules DeVigne*	Delage	Delage/Delage	61	Accident	0
17	7	27	R	Tom Rooney	Premier	Premier/Premier	48	Accident	0
18	11	7		Arthur Chevrolet	Frontenac	Frontenac/Frontenac	35	Magneto	0
19	8	19		Charlie Merz	Peugeot	Peugeot/Peugeot	25	Lubrication	0
20	2	5		Eddie Rickenbacker	Maxwell	Maxwell/Maxwell	9	Steering	0
21	16	23	R	Aldo Franchi	Peusun	Peugeot/Sunbeam	9	Engine	0

Total Purse $30,000
Time of Race: 3:34:17 Average Speed: 84.001 mph Margin of Victory: 1:57.57
Pole: #18 Johnny Aitken (96.690, 1:33.08) Fastest Race Lap: N/A
Winning Car Owner: Peugeot Auto Racing Co. Winning Chief Mechanic: Robert Dahnke ** Winning Tire: Goodrich
Legend: R=Indianapolis 500-Mile Race Rookie; *=Had Relief Help, **=Also Riding Mechanic
Race Notes: Race scheduled for 300 miles.
Lap Leaders: Rickenbacker 1-9, Aitken 10-17, Resta 18-120.
Lap Leader Summary: Resta 1 time for 103 laps, Rickenbacker 1-9, Aitken 1-8.
Lead Changes: 2 among 3 drivers.

Official Box Score

Seventh Indianapolis 500-Mile Race at the Indianapolis Motor Speedway • Saturday, May 31, 1919

FP	SP	No.		Driver	Car Name	Chassis/Engine	Laps	Status	Total Prize Money
1	2	3		Howdy Wilcox	Peugeot	Peugeot/Peugeot	200	88.050	$20,000
2	8	14		Eddie Hearne	Durant	Stutz/Stutz	200	87.087	10,000
3	22	6	W	Jules Goux	Peugeot	Peugeot/Premier	200	85.935	5,000
4	3	32		Albert Guyot	Ballot	Ballot/Ballot	200	84.443	3,500
5	28	26		Tom Alley	Bender	Bender/Bender	200	82.177	3,000
6	4	4	W	Ralph DePalma	Packard	Packard/Packard	200	81.042	2,200
7	12	7		Louis Chevrolet*	Frontenac	Frontenac/Frontenac	200	81.041	1,800
8	10	27	R	Ira Vail	Hudson	Hudson/Hudson	200	80.494	1,600
9	27	21	R	Denny Hickey	Stickle	Hoskins/Hudson	200	80.224	1,500
10	16	41	R	Gaston Chevrolet*	Frontenac	Frontenac/Frontenac	200	79.499	1,400
11	1	31	W	Rene Thomas	Ballot	Ballot/Ballot	200	78.750	0
12	9	8		Earl Cooper*	Stutz	Stutz/Stutz	200	78.600	0
13	29	23	R	Elmer Shannon*	Shannon	Shannon/Duesenberg	200	76.950	0
14	26	17		Ora Haibe	Hudson	Hudson/Hudson	200	65.740	0
15	32	37	R	Andre Boillot	Baby Peugeot	Peugeot/Peugeot	195	Accident	0
16	21	48	R	Ray Howard	Peugeot	Peugeot/Peugeot	130	Lubrication	0
17	23	22		Wilbur D'Alene	Duesenberg	Duesenberg/Duesenberg	120	Axle	0
18	25	15	R	Louis LeCocq	Roamer	Duesenberg/Duesenberg	96	Accident	0
19	7	29		Art Klein	Peugeot	Peugeot/Peugeot	70	Oil line	0
20	11	19	R	Charles Kirkpatrick	Detroit	Mercedes copy/Mercedes copy	69	Rod	0
21	6	33	R	Paul Bablot*	Ballot	Ballot/Ballot	63	Accident	0
22	5	10		Eddie O'Donnell	Duesenberg	Duesenberg/Duesenberg	60	Piston	0
23	24	12	R	Kurt Hitke	Roamer	Duesenberg/Duesenberg	56	Bearing	0
24	20	1	R	Cliff Durant	Chevrolet	Stutz/Stutz	54	Steering	0
25	31	9	R	Tommy Milton	Duesenberg	Duesenberg/Duesenberg	50	Rod	0
26	13	34	R	Louis Wagner	Ballot	Ballot/Ballot	44	Wheel	0
27	18	18	R	Arthur Thurman	Thurman	Duesenberg/Duesenberg	44	Accident	0
28	30	43	R	Omar Toft	Toft/Darco	Miller/Miller	44	Rod	0
29	15	2		Ralph Mulford	Frontenac	Frontenac/Frontenac	37	Driveshaft	0
30	33	36	R	J.J. McCoy	McCoy	McCoy/N/A	36	Oil line	0
31	14	39	R	Joe Boyer	Frontenac	Frontenac/Frontenac	30	Wheel	0
32	17	5	R	W.W. Brown	Richards	Brown/Hudson-Brett	14	Rod	0
33	19	28	R	Roscoe Sarles	Oldfield	Miller/Miller	8	Rocker arm	0

Total Purse $50,000

Time of Race: **5:40:42.87** Average Speed: **88.050 mph** Margin of Victory: **3:46.00**
Pole: **#31 Rene Thomas (104.780, 1:25.89)** Fastest Race Lap: **N/A**
Winning Car Owner: **Indianapolis Speedway Team Co.** Winning Chief Mechanic: **Maurice Becker ** ** Winning Tire: **Goodyear**
Legend: R=Indianapolis 500-Mile Race Rookie; W=Indianapolis 500-Mile Race Former Winner; *=Had Relief Help, **=Riding Mechanic: Leo Banks
Lap Leaders: DePalma 1-65, L. Chevrolet 66-74, DePalma 75-102, Wilcox 103-200.
Lap Leader Summary: Wilcox 1 time for 98 laps, DePalma 2-93, L. Chevrolet 1-9.
Lead Changes: 3 among 3 drivers.

Official Box Score

Eighth Indianapolis 500-Mile Race at the Indianapolis Motor Speedway • Monday, May 31, 1920

FP	SP	No.		Driver	Car Name	Chassis/Engine	Laps	Status	Total Prize Money
1	6	4		Gaston Chevrolet	Monroe	Frontenac/Frontenac	200	88.618	$21,800
2	18	25	W	Rene Thomas	Ballot	Ballot/Ballot	200	86.992	10,700
3	11	10		Tommy Milton	Duesenberg	Duesenberg/Duesenberg	200	86.946	5,000
4	15	12	R	Jimmy Murphy	Duesenberg	Duesenberg/Duesenberg	200	85.101	3,500
5	1	2	W	Ralph DePalma	Ballot	Ballot/Ballot	200	82.120	11,300
6	9	31		Eddie Hearne	Duesenberg	Duesenberg/Duesenberg	200	81.002	2,200
7	4	26		Jean Chassagne	Ballot	Ballot/Ballot	200	79.941	1,900
8	19	28	R	Joe Thomas*	Monroe	Frontenac/Frontenac	200	78.597	1,600
9	23	33		Ralph Mulford	Mulford	Mulford/Duesenberg	200	68.613	1,500
10	17	15		Pete Henderson*	Revere	Duesenberg/Duesenberg	200	67.583	1,400
11	14	32	R	John Boling*	Richards	Brett/Brett	199	Running	0
12	2	6		Joe Boyer*	Frontenac	Frontenac/Frontenac	192	Accident	9,500
13	10	9		Ray Howard*	Peugeot	Peugeot/Peugeot	150	Camshaft	0
14	12	29		Eddie O'Donnell	Duesenberg	Duesenberg/Duesenberg	149	Oil line	0
15	21	16	W	Jules Goux	Peugeot	Peugeot/Peugeot	148	Engine	0
16	13	34		Willie Haupt*	Meteor	Duesenberg/Duesenberg	146	Running	0
17	8	7	R	Bennett Hill*	Frontenac	Frontenac/Frontenac	115	Accident	0
18	3	3		Louis Chevrolet*	Monroe	Frontenac/Frontenac	94	Steering	0
19	20	18	W	Howdy Wilcox	Peugeot	Peugeot/Peugeot	65	Mechanical	0
20	7	5		Roscoe Sarles	Monroe	Frontenac/Frontenac	58	Accident	0
21	5	8		Art Klein	Frontenac	Frontenac/Frontenac	40	Accident	100
22	22	19		Jean Porporato	Gregoire	Gregoire/Gregoire	23	Ruled off	0
23	16	17		Andre Boillot	Peugeot	Peugeot/Peugeot	16	Engine	0

Total Purse $70,500

Time of Race: **5:38:32.00** Average Speed: **88.618 mph** Margin of Victory: **6:16.60**
Pole: **#2 Ralph DePalma (99.150, 6:03.08)** Fastest Race Lap: **N/A**
Winning Car Owner: **William Small Co.** Winning Chief Mechanic: **Johnny Bresnahan ** ** Winning Tire: **Firestone**
Legend: R=Indianapolis 500-Mile Race Rookie; W=Indianapolis 500-Mile Race Former Winner; *=Had Relief Help, **=Also Riding Mechanic
Lap Leaders: Boyer 1-11, Klien 12, Chassange 13, Boyer 14-37, DePalma 38-42, Boyer 43-62, Thomas 63-69, Boyer 70-107, Thomas 108-112, DePalma 113-186, G. Chevrolet 187-200.
Lap Leader Summary: Boyer 4 times for 93 laps, DePalma 2-79, G. Chevrolet 1-14, Thomas 2-12, Klien 1-1, Chassange 1-1.
Lead Changes: 10 among 6 drivers.

Official Box Score

Ninth Indianapolis 500-Mile Race at the Indianapolis Motor Speedway • Monday, May 30, 1921

FP	SP	No.		Driver	Car Name	Chassis/Engine	Laps	Status	Total Prize Money
1	20	2		Tommy Milton	Frontenac	Frontenac/Frontenac	200	89.621	$26,200
2	2	6		Roscoe Sarles	Duesenberg Straight 8	Duesenberg/Duesenberg	200	88.608	10,100
3	8	23	R	Percy Ford*	Chicago Frontenac	Frontenac/Frontenac	200	85.025	5,000
4	9	5	R	Eddie Miller*	Duesenberg Straight 8	Duesenberg/Duesenberg	200	84.646	3,500
5	13	16		Ora Haibe	Sunbeam	Sunbeam/Sunbeam	200	84.277	3,000
6	14	9		Albert Guyot*	Duesenberg Straight 8	Duesenberg/Duesenberg	200	83.035	2,000
7	10	3		Ira Vail	Leach	Leach/Miller	200	80.152	1,800
8	15	21		Bennett Hill*	Duesenberg Straight 8	Duesenberg/Duesenberg	200	79.132	1,600
9	21	8		Ralph Mulford	Frontenac	Frontenac/Frontenac	177	Running	1,500
10	17	15	W	Rene Thomas	Sunbeam	Sunbeam/Sunbeam	144	Water hose	0
11	18	27		Tom Alley	Frontenac	Frontenac/Frontenac	133	Rod	0
12	1	4	W	Ralph DePalma	Ballot	Ballot/Ballot	112	Rod	10,600
13	4	1		Eddie Hearne	Revere	Duesenberg/Duesenberg	111	Oil line	0
14	19	24		Jimmy Murphy*	Duesenberg Straight 8	Duesenberg/Duesenberg	107	Accident	0
15	16	17	R	Riley Brett*	Junior	Brett/Brett	91	Accident	0
16	23	28	R	C.W. Van Ranst	Frontenac	Frontenac/Frontenac	87	Water hose	0
17	3	7		Joe Boyer	Duesenberg Straight 8	Duesenberg/Duesenberg	74	Rear axle	0
18	6	19		Jean Chassagne	Peugeot	Peugeot/Peugeot	65	Lost hood	0
19	5	22	R	Jules Ellingboe	Frontenac	Frontenac/Frontenac	49	Steering	0
20	11	14		Andre Boillot	Talbot-Darracq	Sunbeam/Sunbeam	41	Bearing	0
21	7	18	R	Louis Fontaine	Junior	Brett/Brett	33	Accident	0
22	22	25		Joe Thomas	Duesenberg Straight 8	Duesenberg/Duesenberg	24	Accident	0
23	12	10	W	Howdy Wilcox	Peugeot	Peugeot/Peugeot	22	Rod	0

Total Purse $65,300

Time of Race: 5:34:44.65 Average Speed: 89.621 mph Margin of Victory: 3:49.38

Pole: #4 Ralph DePalma (100.750, 5:57.34) Fastest Race Lap: N/A

Winning Car Owner: Louis Chevrolet Winning Chief Mechanic: Henry Franck ** Winning Tire: Firestone

Legend: R=Indianapolis 500-Mile Race Rookie; W=Indianapolis 500-Mile Race Former Winner; *=Had Relief Help, **=Also Riding Mechanic

Lap Leaders: DePalma 1, Boyer 2, DePalma 3-5, Sarles 6, DePalma 7-110, Milton 111-200.

Lap Leader Summary: DePalma 3 times for 108 laps, Milton 1-90, Boyer 1-1, Sarles 1-1.

Lead Changes: 5 among 4 drivers.

Official Box Score

Tenth Indianapolis 500-Mile Race at the Indianapolis Motor Speedway • Tuesday, May 30, 1922

FP	SP	No.		Driver	Car Name	Chassis/Engine	Laps	Status	Total Prize Money
1	1	35		Jimmy Murphy	Murphy	Duesenberg/Miller	200	94.484	$28,075
2	2	12	R	Harry Hartz	Duesenberg Straight 8	Duesenberg/Duesenberg	200	93.534	10,000
3	23	15		Eddie Hearne	Ballot	Ballot/Ballot	200	93.042	5,000
4	3	17	W	Ralph DePalma	Duesenberg Straight 8	Duesenberg/Duesenberg	200	90.613	3,500
5	14	31		Ora Haibe*	Duesenberg Straight 8	Duesenberg/Duesenberg	200	90.573	3,000
6	7	24	R	Jerry Wonderlich*	Duesenberg Straight 8	Duesenberg/Duesenberg	200	88.789	2,200
7	13	21	R	I.P. Fetterman*	Duesenberg Straight 8	Duesenberg/Duesenberg	200	87.996	1,800
8	9	1		Ira Vail*	Disteel Duesenberg	Duesenberg/Duesenberg	200	86.128	1,600
9	12	26		Tom Alley	Monroe	Frontenac/Frontenac	200	84.295	1,500
10	17	10		Joe Thomas*	Duesenberg Straight 8	Duesenberg/Duesenberg	200	82.553	1,400
11	16	3	R	E. G "Cannonball" Baker	Frontenac	Frontenac/Frontenac	200	79.250	0
12	11	34		Cliff Durant*	Durant	Miller/Miller	200	77.750	0
13	19	22	R	Douglas Hawkes	Bentley	Bentley/Bentley	200	74.950	0
14	27	18	R	Jack Curtner*	Fronty-Ford	Ford T/Fronty-Ford	165	Running	0
15	18	25		Wilbur D'Alene	Monroe	Frontenac/Frontenac	160	Running	0
16	8	9	R	Frank Elliott*	Leach	Miller/Miller	195	Rear axle	0
17	15	27	R	L.L. Corum	Monroe	Frontenac/Frontenac	169	Mechanical	0
18	21	19	R	C. Glenn Howard	Fronty-Ford	Ford T/Fronty-Ford	163	Mechanical	0
19	5	5		Ralph Mulford	Frontenac	Frontenac/Frontenac	161	Rod	0
20	10	7	R	Pete DePaolo	Frontenac	Frontenac/Frontenac	110	Accident	0
21	25	6		Art Klein	Frontenac	Frontenac/Frontenac	105	Rod	0
22	4	4	R	Leon Duray	Frontenac	Frontenac/Frontenac	94	Axle	0
23	6	2		Roscoe Sarles	Frontenac	Frontenac/Frontenac	88	Rod	0
24	24	8	W	Tommy Milton	Leach	Milton/Miller	44	Fuel tank	0
25	22	14	W	Jules Goux	Ballot	Ballot/Ballot	25	Axle	0
26	20	23		Jules Ellingboe	Duesenberg Straight 8	Duesenberg/Duesenberg	25	Accident	0
27	26	16	W	Howdy Wilcox	Peugeot	Peugeot/Peugeot	7	Valve spring	0

Total Purse $58,075

Time of Race: 5:17:30.79 Average Speed: 94.484 mph Margin of Victory: 3:13.60

Pole: #35 Jimmy Murphy (100.500, 5:58.24) Fastest Race Lap: N/A

Winning Car Owner: Jimmy Murphy Winning Chief Mechanic: Ernie Olson ** Winning Tire: Firestone

Legend: R=Indianapolis 500-Mile Race Rookie; W=Indianapolis 500-Mile Race Former Winner; *=Had Relief Help, **=Also Riding Mechanic

Lap Leaders: Murphy 1-74, Duray 75-76, Hartz 77-83, DePaolo 84-86, Hartz 87-121, Murphy 122-200.

Lap Leader Summary: Murphy 2 times for 153 laps, Hartz 2-42, DePaolo 1-3, Duray 1-2.

Lead Changes: 5 among 4 drivers.

Official Box Score

11th Indianapolis 500-Mile Race at the Indianapolis Motor Speedway • Wednesday, May 30, 1923

FP	SP	No.		Driver	Car Name	Chassis/Engine	Laps	Status	Total Prize Money
1	1	1	W	Tommy Milton*	H.C.S.	Miller/Miller	200	90.954	$28,700
2	2	7		Harry Hartz	Durant	Miller/Miller	200	90.063	10,100
3	9	5	W	Jimmy Murphy	Durant	Miller/Miller	200	88.078	7,000
4	14	6		Eddie Hearne*	Durant	Miller/Miller	200	86.646	3,500
5	7	23		L.L. Corum	Barber-Warnock Ford	Ford T/Fronty-Ford	200	82.851	3,000
6	16	31		Frank Elliott*	Durant	Miller/Miller	200	82.219	2,200
7	10	8		Cliff Durant*	Durant	Miller/Miller	200	82.170	2,200
8	20	15	R	Max Sailer*	Mercedes	Mercedes/Mercedes	200	80.683	1,600
9	22	19	R	Prince de Cystria	Bugatti	Bugatti/Bugatti	200	77.637	1,500
10	24	34	R	Wade Morton*	Duesenberg	Duesenberg/Duesenberg	200	74.984	1,400
11	15	16	R	Christian Werner*	Mercedes	Mercedes/Mercedes	200	74.650	0
12	6	18	R	Pierre de Viscaya	Bugatti	Bugatti/Bugatti	166	Rod	0
13	21	28		Leon Duray*	Durant	Miller/Miller	136	Rod	0
14	3	3	W	Dario Resta*	Packard	Packard/Packard	87	Differential	0
15	11	2	W	Ralph DePalma	Packard	Packard/Packard	69	Head gasket	0
16	19	26	R	Harlan Fengler*	Durant	Miller/Miller	69	Fuel tank	0
17	8	25	W	Howdy Wilcox	H.C.S.	Miller/Miller	60	Clutch	2,000
18	13	4		Joe Boyer	Packard	Packard/Packard	59	Differential	0
19	18	35		Bennett Hill*	Miller	Miller/Miller	41	Crankshaft	0
20	5	27	R	Count Louis Zborowski	Bugatti	Bugatti/Bugatti	41	Rod	0
21	12	29		Earl Cooper*	Durant	Miller/Miller	21	Accident	0
22	23	22	R	Raul Riganti	Bugatti	Bugatti/Bugatti	19	Fuel line	0
23	17	14	R	Christian Lautenschlager	Mercedes	Mercedes/Mercedes	14	Accident	0
24	4	21	R	Martin de Alzaga	Bugatti	Bugatti/Bugatti	6	Rod	0

Total Purse $63,200

Time of Race: 5:29:50.17 Average Speed: 90.954 mph Margin of Victory: 3:15.73

Pole: #1 Tommy Milton (108.170, 5:32.81) Fastest Race Lap: N/A

Winning Car Owner: H.C.S. Motor Co. Winning Chief Mechanic: George Stiehl Winning Tire: Firestone

Legend: R=Indianapolis 500-Mile Race Rookie; W=Indianapolis 500-Mile Race Former Winner; *=Had Relief Help

Race Notes: Winner Milton was relieved by Howdy Wilcox for laps 103-151.

Lap Leaders: Murphy 1-2, Milton 3, Murphy 4, Milton 5, Murphy 6, Milton 7-15, Murphy 16-20, Milton 21-25, Wilcox 26, Milton 27, Wilcox 28, Murphy 29, Milton 30-37, Murphy 38, Wilcox 39-40, Milton 41-43, Wilcox 44-48, Milton 49-52, Wilcox 53, Milton 54-62, Durant 63, Milton 64, Durant 65-66, Milton 67-73, Durant 74, Milton 75-103, Hartz 104-109, Wilcox (for Milton) 110-150, Milton 151-200.

Lap Leader Summary: Milton 13 times for 128 laps, Wilcox (for Milton) 1-41, Murphy 6-11, Wilcox 5-10, Hartz 1-6, Durant 3-4.

Lead Changes: 28 among 6 drivers.

Official Box Score

12th Indianapolis 500-Mile Race at the Indianapolis Motor Speedway • Friday, May 30, 1924

FP	SP	No.		Driver	Car Name	Chassis/Engine	Laps	Status	Total Prize Money
1	21	15		L.L. Corum/ Joe Boyer*	Duesenberg	Duesenberg/Duesenberg	200	98.234	$20,000
2	6	8		Earl Cooper	Studebaker	Miller/Miller	200	97.788	13,700
3	1	2	W	Jimmy Murphy	Miller	Miller/Miller	200	97.269	7,800
4	2	4		Harry Hartz	Durant	Miller/Miller	200	96.544	3,500
5	5	3		Bennett Hill	Miller	Miller/Miller	200	96.463	3,000
6	13	12		Pete DePaolo	Duesenberg	Duesenberg/Duesenberg	200	94.297	2,200
7	16	14	R	Fred Comer*	Durant	Miller/Miller	200	93.424	1,800
8	15	6		Ira Vail*	Vail	Miller/Miller	200	92.450	1,600
9	9	32	R	Antoine Mourre	Mourre	Miller/Miller	200	91.764	1,500
10	18	19	R	Bob McDonogh	Miller	Miller/Miller	200	90.513	1,400
11	7	18		Jules Ellingboe	Miller	Miller/Miller	200	90.570	1,049
12	11	7		Jerry Wonderlich*	Durant	Miller/Miller	200	85.480	1,049
13	8	16		Cliff Durant*	Durant	Miller/Miller	198	Out of fuel	1,038
14	19	26	R	Bill Hunt	Barber-Warnock Ford	Ford T/Fronty-Ford	190	Running	996
15	17	31		Ora Haibe*	Schmidt	Mercedes/Mercedes	181	Running	949
16	20	28	R	A.E. Moss	Barber-Warnock Ford	Ford T/Fronty-Ford	176	Running	923
17	22	27	R	Fred Harder	Barber-Warnock Ford	Ford T/Fronty-Ford	175	Running	917
18	4	9	W	Joe Boyer*	Duesenberg	Duesenberg/Duesenberg	176	Accident	973
19	14	1		Eddie Hearne*	Durant	Miller/Miller	150	Fuel tank	787
20	12	21		Frank Elliott	Miller	Miller/Miller	150	Fuel tank	787
21	3	5	W	Tommy Milton	Miller	Miller/Miller	110	Fuel tank	577
22	10	10	R	Ernie Ansterburg	Duesenberg	Duesenberg/Duesenberg	1	Accident	5

Total Purse $66,550

Time of Race: 5:05:23.51 Average Speed: 98.234 mph Margin of Victory: 1:23.57

Pole: #2 Jimmy Murphy (108.037, 5:33.22) Fastest Race Lap: N/A

Winning Car Owner: Duesenberg Bros. Winning Chief Mechanic: John Starost Winning Tire: Firestone

Legend: R=Indianapolis 500-Mile Race Rookie; W=Indianapolis 500-Mile Race Former Winner; *=Had Relief Help

Race Notes: Joe Boyer replaced L.L. Corum in the winning car on lap 111.

Lap Leaders: Boyer 1, Murphy 2-41, Cooper 42, Murphy 43, Cooper 44-105, Murphy 106-120, Cooper 121-176, Boyer (for Corum) 177-200.

Lap Leader Summary: Cooper 3 times for 119 laps, Murphy 3-56, Boyer(for Corum) 1-24, Boyer 1-1.

Lead Changes: 7 among 4 drivers.

Official Box Score

13th Indianapolis 500-Mile Race at the Indianapolis Motor Speedway • Saturday, May 30, 1925

FP	SP	No.		Driver	Car Name	Chassis/Engine	Laps	Status	Total Prize Money
1	2	12		Pete DePaolo*	Duesenberg	Duesenberg/Duesenberg	200	101.127	$36,150
2	5	1		Dave Lewis*	Junior '8' Front Drive	Miller/Miller	200	100.823	15,000
3	22	9	R	Phil Shafer*	Duesenberg	Duesenberg/Duesenberg	200	100.185	8,750
4	3	6		Harry Hartz	Miller	Miller/Miller	200	98.892	4,300
5	11	4	W	Tommy Milton	Miller	Miller/Miller	200	97.267	3,500
6	1	28		Leon Duray*	Miller	Miller/Miller	200	96.910	2,200
7	18	8	W	Ralph DePalma*	Miller	Miller/Miller	200	96.847	1,800
8	9	38	R	Peter Kreis*	Duesenberg	Duesenberg/Duesenberg	200	96.324	2,250
9	14	15	R	Doc Shattuc	Miller	Miller/Miller	200	95.742	1,500
10	8	22	R	Pietro Bordino*	Fiat	Fiat/Fiat	200	94.747	1,400
11	12	5		Fred Comer*	Miller	Miller/Miller	200	93.670	1,096
12	10	27		Frank Elliott*	Miller	Miller/Miller	200	92.230	1,037
13	15	24	R	Earl DeVore*	Miller	Miller/Miller	198	Running	981
14	20	14		Bob McDonogh*	Miller	Miller/Miller	187	Truss rod	929
15	16	23		Wade Morton*	Duesenberg	Duesenberg/Duesenberg	156	Accident	880
16	6	17	R	Ralph Hepburn	Miller	Miller/Miller	143	Fuel Tank	2,334
17	4	2		Earl Cooper	Junior '8'	Miller/Miller	127	Accident	1,191
18	13	3		Bennett Hill*	Miller	Miller/Miller	69	Rear spring	750
19	17	29	R	Herbert Jones*	Jones & Whitaker	Miller/Miller	68	Accident	729
20	19	19		Ira Vail	R.J.	Miller/Miller	61	Rod	692
21	21	7	R	M.C. Jones*	Skelly	Ford T/Fronty-Ford	32	Transmission	657
22	7	10		Jules Ellingboe	Miller	Miller/Miller	24	Steering	625

Total Purse $88,751

Time of Race: 4:56:39.46 Average Speed: 101.127 mph Margin of Victory: 53.69 sec

Pole: #28 Leon Duray (113.196, 5:18.03) Fastest Race Lap: N/A

Winning Car Owner: Duesenberg Bros. Winning Chief Mechanic: Augie Duesenberg/H.C. "Cotton" Henning Winning Tire: Firestone

Legend: R=Indianapolis 500-Mile Race Rookie; W=Indianapolis 500-Mile Race Former Winner; *=Had Relief Help

Race Notes: Winner DePaolo was relieved by Norman Batten for laps 106-127.

Lap Leaders: DePaolo 1-54, Shafer 55-67, DePaolo 68-85, Hartz 86-88, DePaolo 89-104, Lewis 105-107, Hepburn 108-122, Cooper 123-126, Lewis 127-173, DePaolo 174-200.

Lap Leader Summary: DePaolo 4 times for 115 laps, Lewis 2-50, Hepburn 1-15, Shafer 1-13, Cooper 1-4, Hartz 1-3.

Lead Changes: 9 among 6 drivers.

Official Box Score

14th Indianapolis 500-Mile Race at the Indianapolis Motor Speedway • Monday, May 31, 1926

FP	SP	No.		Driver	Car Name	Chassis/Engine	Laps	Status	Total Prize Money
1	20	15	R	Frank Lockhart	Miller	Miller/Miller	160 (Rain)	95.904	$35,600
2	2	3		Harry Hartz	Miller	Miller/Miller	158	Running	13,900
3	14	36	R	Cliff Woodbury	Boyle	Miller/Miller	158	Running	6,700
4	13	8		Fred Comer*	Miller	Miller/Miller	155	Running	4,000
5	27	12	W	Pete DePaolo	Duesenberg	Duesenberg/Duesenberg	153	Running	3,500
6	8	6		Frank Elliott*	Miller	Miller/Miller	152	Running	2,200
7	16	14	R	Norm Batten	Miller	Miller/Miller	151	Running	1,800
8	15	19		Ralph Hepburn*	Miller	Miller/Miller	151	Running	1,600
9	28	18	R	John Duff	Elcar	Miller/Miller	147	Running	1,500
10	5	4		Phil Shafer*	Miller	Miller/Miller	146	Running	3,000
11	12	31	R	Tony Gulotta	Miller	Miller/Miller	142	Running	615
12	7	16		Bennett Hill*	Miller	Miller/Miller	136	Running	607
13	21	33	R	Thane Houser	Abell	Miller/Miller	102	Running	600
14	17	27		Douglas Hawkes*	Eldridge	Eldridge/Anzani	92	Camshaft	593
15	4	1		Dave Lewis*	Miller Front Drive	Miller/Miller	92	Valve	4,886
16	1	5		Earl Cooper	Miller Front Drive	Miller/Miller	74	Transmission	579
17	11	9		Cliff Durant*	Locomobile Junior 8	Fengler/Locomobile	61	Fuel leak	572
18	18	29	R	Ben Jones	Duesenberg (Two-Cycle)	Duesenberg/Duesenberg	54	Accident	565
19	23	26	R	E.A.D. Eldridge*	Eldridge	Eldridge/Anzani	46	Steering	558
20	24	23	W	L.L. Corum	Schmidt	Schmidt/Argyle	45	Cracked block	551
21	22	24	R	Steve Nemesh	Schmidt	Schmidt/Argyle	42	Transmission	544
22	6	7		Jules Ellingboe	Miller	Miller/Miller	39	Supercharger	538
23	3	10		Leon Duray	Locomobile Junior 8	Fengler/Locomobile	33	Fuel leak	531
24	26	17	R	Fred Lecklider	Nickel Plate	Miller/Miller	25	Piston	525
25	25	28	R	Jack McCarver	Hamlin Front Drive	Ford T/Fronty-Ford	24	Rod	519
26	9	34	R	Bon McDougall	Miller	Miller/Miller	19	Water leak	512
27	10	22		Doc Shattuc	Miller	Miller/Miller	16	Valve	506
28	19	39		Albert Guyot	Guyot	Schmidt/Argyle	9	Piston	500

Total Purse $88,101

Time of Race: 4:10:14.95 Average Speed: 95.904 mph Margin of Victory: 2 laps 35.54 sec.

Pole: #5 Earl Cooper (111.735, 5:22.19) Fastest Race Lap: N/A

Winning Car Owner: Peter Kreis Winning Chief Mechanic: Jimmy Lee Winning Tire: Firestone

Legend: R=Indianapolis 500-Mile Race Rookie; W=Indianapolis 500-Mile Race Former Winner; *=Had Relief Help

Race Notes: Race stopped on lap 71 due to rain, restarted and stopped again on lap 160.

Lap Leaders: Shafer 1-15, Lewis 16-21, Shafer 22, Lewis 23-59, Lockhart 60-100, Hartz 101-106, Lockhart 107-160.

Lap Leader Summary: Lockhart 2 times for 95 laps, Lewis 2-43, Shafer 2-16, Hartz 1-6.

Lead Changes: 6 among 4 drivers.

Official Box Score

15th Indianapolis 500-Mile Race at the Indianapolis Motor Speedway • Monday, May 31, 1927

FP	SP	No.		Driver	Car Name	Chassis/Engine	Laps	Status	Total Prize Money
1	22	32	R	George Souders	Duesenberg	Duesenberg/Duesenberg	200	97.545	$30,650
2	15	10		Earl DeVore*	Miller	Miller/Miller	200	93.868	12,800
3	27	27		Tony Gulotta*	Miller	Miller/Miller	200	93.139	6,000
4	19	29	R	Wilbur Shaw*	Jynx	Miller/Miller	200	93.110	4,000
5	28	21	R	Dave Evans*	Duesenberg	Duesenberg/Duesenberg	200	90.782	3,500
6	7	14		Bob McDonogh*	Cooper	Cooper/Miller	200	90.410	5,200
7	18	16		Eddie Hearne*	Miller	Miller/Miller	200	90.064	1,800
8	25	6	W	Tommy Milton*	Detroit	Detroit/Miller	200	85.081	1,600
9	14	25	R	Cliff Bergere*	Miller	Miller/Miller	200	79.929	1,500
10	13	5		Frank Elliott*	Junior 8	Miller/Miller	200	78.242	1,400
11	33	31	R	Fred Frame*	Miller	Miller/Miller	199	Running	750
12	32	42	R	Jimmy Hill*	Nickel Plate	Miller/Miller	197	Running	600
13	31	24	R	Benny Shoaff*	Perfect Circle Duesenberg	Duesenberg/Duesenberg	198	Drive gears	550
14	26	41		Wade Morton*	Thompson Valve	Duesenberg/Duesenberg	152	Accident	500
15	20	44	R	Al Melcher*	Miller	Miller/Miller	144	Supercharger	490
16	23	43	R	Louis Schneider*	Miller	Miller/Miller	137	Timing gears	480
17	12	9		Peter Kreis*	Cooper	Cooper/Miller	123	Front axle	470
18	1	2	W	Frank Lockhart	Perfect Circle Miller	Miller/Miller	120	Rod	11,460
19	6	15		Cliff Woodbury*	Boyle Valve	Miller/Miller	108	Supercharger	450
20	17	26	R	Dutch Baumann	Miller	Miller/Miller	90	Pinion shaft	1,340
21	29	35	R	Al Cotey*	Elcar	Miller/Miller	87	Universal joint	430
22	16	17		Doc Shattuc	Miller	Miller/Miller	83	Valve	420
23	30	23		Fred Lecklider*	Elgin Piston Pin	Miller/Miller	49	Accident	410
24	5	19		Ralph Hepburn	Boyle Valve	Miller/Miller	39	Fuel leak	400
25	4	1		Harry Hartz	Erskine Miller	Miller/Miller	38	Crankshaft	390
26	2	3	W	Pete DePaolo	Perfect Circle Miller	Miller/Miller	31	Supercharger	380
27	3	12		Leon Duray	Miller Front Drive	Miller/Miller	26	Fuel tank	370
28	9	4		Bennett Hill	Cooper	Miller/Miller	26	Shackle bolt	360
29	21	18		Jules Ellingboe	Cooper	Miller/Miller	25	Accident	350
30	10	8		Norm Batten	Miller	Fengler/Miller	24	Fire	340
31	24	38	R	Babe Stapp	Duesenberg	Duesenberg/Duesenberg	24	Universal joint	330
32	11	22	R	Jack Petticord	Boyle Valve	Miller/Miller	22	Supercharger	320
33	8	7		Dave Lewis	Miller Front Drive	Miller/Miller	21	Front axle	310

Total Purse $90,350

Time of Race: 5:07:33.08 Average Speed: 97.545 mph Margin of Victory: 12:2.87
Pole: #2 Frank Lockhart (120.100, 4:59.75) Fastest Race Lap: N/A
Winning Car Owner: William S. White Winning Chief Mechanic: Jean Marcenac Winning Tire: Firestone
Legend: R=Indianapolis 500-Mile Race Rookie; W=Indianapolis 500-Mile Race Former Winner; *=Had Relief Help
Lap Leaders: Lockhart 1-81, Baumann 82-90, Lockhart 91-119, DePaolo (for McDonough) 120-149, Souders 150-200.
Lap Leader Summary: Lockhart 2 times for 110 laps, Souders 1-51, DePaolo (for McDonough) 1-30, Baumann 1-9.
Lead Changes: 4 among 4 drivers.

Official Box Score

16th Indianapolis 500-Mile Race at the Indianapolis Motor Speedway • Wednesday, May 30, 1928

FP	SP	No.	Rookie	Driver	Car Name	Chassis/Engine	Laps	Status	Total Prize Money
1	13	14	R	Louis Meyer	Miller	Miller/Miller	200	99.482	$28,250
2	8	28	R	Lou Moore*	Miller	Miller/Miller	200	99.241	13,650
3	12	3	W	George Souders	State Auto Insurance	Miller/Miller	200	98.034	8,400
4	10	15	R	Ray Keech*	Simplex Piston Ring	Miller/Miller	200	93.320	4,300
5	15	22		Norm Batten*	Miller	Fengler/Miller	200	93.228	3,200
6	5	7		Babe Stapp*	Miller	Miller/Miller	200	92.638	3,900
7	20	43	R	Billy Arnold*	Boyle Valve	Miller/Miller	200	91.111	1,800
8	14	27		Fred Frame*	State Auto Insurance	Duesenberg/Duesenberg	200	90.079	1,600
9	9	25		Fred Comer*	Boyle Valve	Miller/Miller	200	88.889	1,500
10	4	8		Tony Gulotta*	Stutz Blackhawk	Miller/Miller	200	88.888	1,600
11	7	24		Louis Schneider*	Armacost Miller	Miller/Miller	200	87.964	652
12	23	12		Dave Evans	Boyle Valve	Miller/Miller	200	87.401	638
13	28	29	R	Henry Kohlert*	Elgin Piston Pin	Miller/Miller	180	Running	625
14	17	23	R	Deacon Litz*	Miller	Miller/Miller	161	Running	610
15	21	39	R	Jimmy Gleason*	Duesenberg	Duesenberg/Duesenberg	195	Magneto	6,196
16	18	5		Cliff Durant*	Detroit	Detroit/Miller	175	Supercharger	583
17	11	33	R	Johnny Seymour	Marmon	Cooper/Miller	170	Supercharger	568
18	24	6		Earl DeVore*	Chromolite	Miller/Miller	161	Accident	555
19	1	4		Leon Duray*	Miller	Miller/Miller	133	Overheated	6,441
20	16	38	R	Sam Ross	Aranem	Miller/Miller	132	Timing gear	526
21	27	26		Ira Hall*	Duesenberg	Duesenberg/Duesenberg	115	Accident	512
22	19	32		Peter Kreis	Marmon	Cooper/Miller	73	Rod bearing	499
23	2	10		Cliff Woodbury	Boyle Valve	Miller/Miller	55	Timing gear	484
24	6	16		Ralph Hepburn	Miller	Miller/Miller	48	Timing gear	470
25	29	1		Wilbur Shaw	Flying Cloud	Miller/Miller	42	Timing gear	456
26	26	18		Benny Shoaff	Duesenberg	Duesenberg/Duesenberg	35	Accident	442
27	25	41	R	C.W. Belt	Green	Green/Green	32	Valve	428
28	3	21		Cliff Bergere	Miller	Miller/Miller	6	Transmission	415
29	22	34	R	Russ Snowberger	Marmon	Cooper/Miller	4	Supercharger	400

Total Purse $89,700

Time of Race: 5:01:33.75 Average Speed: 99.482 mph Margin of Victory: 43.89 sec
Pole: #4 Leon Duray (122.391, 4:54.14) Fastest Race Lap: N/A
Winning Car Owner: Alden Sampson, II Winning Chief Mechanic: Ted Plaisted Winning Tire: Firestone
Legend: R=Indianapolis 500-Mile Race Rookie; W=Indianapolis 500-Mile Race Former Winner; *=Had Relief Help
Lap Leaders: Duray 1-54, Stapp 55-57, Duray 58-62, Souders 63-78, Gleason 79-82, Stapp 83-96, Gleason 97-135, Snowberger 136-148, Gulotta 149-181, Meyer 182-200.
Lap Leader Summary: Duray 2 times for 59 laps, Gleason 2-43, Gulotta 1-33, Meyer 1-19, Stapp 2-17, Souders 1-16, Snowberger 1-13.
Lead Changes: 9 among 7 drivers.

Official Box Score

17th Indianapolis 500-Mile Race at the Indianapolis Motor Speedway • Thursday, May 30, 1929

FP	SP	No.		Driver	Car Name	Chassis/Engine	Laps	Status	Total Prize Money
1	6	2		Ray Keech	Simplex Piston Ring	Miller/Miller	200	97.585	$31,950
2	8	1	W	Louis Meyer	Miller	Miller/Miller	200	95.596	20,400
3	23	53		Jimmy Gleason*	Duesenberg	Duesenberg/Duesenberg	200	93.699	7,250
4	25	43	R	Carl Marchese	Marchese	Miller/Miller	200	93.541	4,350
5	21	42	R	Freddie Winnai*	Duesenberg	Duesenberg/Duesenberg	200	88.792	3,600
6	28	48	R	Speed Gardner*	Chromolite	Miller/Miller	200	88.390	2,200
7	14	6	R	Louis Chiron	Delage	Delage/Delage	200	87.728	1,800
8	7	9		Billy Arnold*	Boyle Valve	Miller/Miller	200	83.909	1,600
9	32	25		Cliff Bergere*	Armacost Miller	Miller/Miller	200	80.703	1,500
10	22	34		Fred Frame*	Cooper	Cooper/Miller	193	Running	2,500
11	29	28	R	Frank Brisko	Burbach	Miller/Miller	180	Running	468
12	18	17		Phil Shafer*	Miller	Miller/Miller	150	Running	465
13	13	3		Lou Moore*	Majestic Miller	Miller/Miller	198	Rod	2,662
14	26	36	R	Frank Farmer*	Miller	Miller/Miller	140	Supercharger	459
15	24	49	R	Wesley Crawford*	Miller	Fengler/Miller	127	Carburetor	456
16	17	4		Peter Kreis	Detroit	Detroit/Miller	91	Engine seized	453
17	11	23		Tony Gulotta	Packard Cable	Miller/Miller	91	Supercharger	450
18	19	5		Bob McDonogh*	Miller Front Drive	Miller/Miller	74	Oil tank	447
19	33	46	R	Bill Lindau	Pittsburgh Miller	Miller/Miller	70	Valve	444
20	27	31	R	Herman Schurch*	Armacost Miller	Miller/Miller	70	Tank split	441
21	16	38		Johnny Seymour	Cooper	Cooper/Miller	65	Rear axle	438
22	2	21		Leon Duray*	Packard Cable	Miller/Miller	65	Carburetor	1,135
23	30	29	R	Rick Decker*	Miller	Miller/Miller	61	Fuel line	432
24	9	26		Deacon Litz	Rusco Durac	Miller/Miller	56	Rod	5,329
25	31	27	R	Bert Karnatz	Richards Bros.	Miller/Miller	50	Fuel leak	426
26	20	47	R	Ernie Triplett	Buckeye Duesenberg	Duesenberg/Duesenberg	48	Rod	423
27	10	12		Russ Snowberger	Cooper	Cooper/Miller	45	Supercharger	420
28	4	32		Babe Stapp	Spindler Miller	Duesenberg/Miller	40	Rear end	417
29	15	35	R	Jules Moriceau	Thompson Products	Amilcar/Amilcar	30	Accident	414
30	5	37	W	Pete DePaolo	Boyle Valve	Miller/Miller	25	Steering	411
31	3	18		Ralph Hepburn	Packard Cable	Miller/Miller	14	High gear	407
32	12	10	R	Bill Spence	Duesenberg	Duesenberg/Duesenberg	9	Accident	403
33	1	8		Cliff Woodbury	Boyle Valve	Miller/Miller	3	Accident	400

Total Purse $94,950

Time of Race: 5:07:25.42 Average Speed: 97.585 mph Margin of Victory: 6:23.79
Pole: #8 Cliff Woodbury (120.599, 4:58.51) Fastest Race Lap: N/A
Winning Car Owner: M. A. Yagle Winning Chief Mechanic: Jean Marcenac Winning Tire: Firestone
Legend: R=Indianapolis 500-Mile Race Rookie; W=Indianapolis 500-Mile Race Former Winner; *=Had Relief Help
Lap Leaders: Duray 1-7, Litz 8-56, Moore 57-60, Meyer 61, Moore 62-79, Meyer 80-94, Frame 95-105, Keech 106-108, Meyer 109-157, Keech 158-200.
Lap Leader Summary: Meyer 3 times for 65 laps, Litz 1-49, Keech 2-46, Moore 2-22, Frame 1-11, Duray 1-7. Lead Changes: 9 among 6 drivers.

Official Box Score

18th Indianapolis 500-Mile Race at the Indianapolis Motor Speedway • Friday, May 30, 1930

FP	SP	No.		Driver	Car Name	Chassis/Engine	Laps	Status	Total Prize Money
1	1	4		Billy Arnold	Miller-Hartz	Summers/Miller	200	100.448	$50,300
2	3	16	R	Shorty Cantlon*	Miller Schofield	Stevens/Miller	200	98.054	13,950
3	4	23		Louis Schneider	Bowes Seal Fast	Stevens/Miller	200	96.752	7,050
4	2	1	W	Louis Meyer	Sampson	Stevens/Miller	200	95.253	4,450
5	22	6	R	Bill Cummings*	Duesenberg	Stevens/Duesenberg	200	93.579	3,500
6	33	24		Dave Evans	Jones & Maley	Stevens/Miller	200	92.571	2,700
7	8	15		Phil Shafer	Coleman Front Drive	Coleman/Miller	200	90.921	1,800
8	7	22		Russ Snowberger	Russell "8"	Snowberger/Studebaker	200	89.166	1,600
9	9	25	R	Les Allen*	Allen Miller Products	Miller/Miller	200	85.749	1,500
10	17	27	W	L.L. Corum	Jones Stutz	Stutz/Stutz	200	85.340	1,400
11	16	38	R	Claude Burton	V8	Oakland/Oakland	196	Running	550
12	30	42	R	L.P. Cucinotta	Maserati	Maserati/Maserati	185	Running	510
13	15	41	R	Chet Miller*	Fronty Ford	Ford T/Fronty-Ford	160	Running	480
14	38	46	R	Harry Butcher	Butcher Brothers	Buick/Buick	128	Running	450
15	23	10	R	Mel Keneally	MAVV	Whippet/Miller	114	Valve	420
16	34	21	R	Zeke Meyer	Miller	Miller/Miller	115	Rod	385
17	6	17		Ernie Triplett	Guiberson	Whippet/Miller	125	Piston	380
18	13	35	R	J.C. McDonald*	Romthe	Studebaker/Studebaker	112	Fuel leak	375
19	37	28	R	Roland Free	Slade	Chrysler/Chrysler	69	Clutch	370
20	20	9		Tony Gulotta	MAVV	Whippet/Miller	79	Valve	365
21	11	33		Frank Farmer	Betholine Miller	Miller/Miller	69	Accident	360
22	35	44	R	Bill Denver	Nardi	Duesenberg/Duesenberg	41	Rod	355
23	26	34	R	Joe Huff*	Gauss Front Drive	Cooper/Miller	48	Valve	350
24	25	3		Wilbur Shaw	Empire State	Smith/Miller	54	Oil Leak	345
25	14	29	R	Joe Caccia*	Alberti	Duesenberg/Duesenberg	43	Accident	340
26	10	36	R	Cy Marshall	Duesenberg	Duesenberg/Duesenberg	29	Accident	335
27	19	32	R	Charles Moran, Jr.	DuPont	DuPont/DuPont	22	Accident	330
28	24	7		Jimmy Gleason	Waverly Oil	Miller/Miller	22	Timing gear	325
29	12	14		Lou Moore	Coleman Front Drive	Coleman/Miller	23	Accident	320
30	31	12		Deacon Litz	Duesenberg	Duesenberg/Duesenberg	22	Accident	315
31	32	8		Babe Stapp	Duesenberg	Duesenberg/Duesenberg	18	Accident	310
32	18	39		Johnny Seymour	Gauss Front Drive	Cooper/Miller	21	Accident	305
33	21	5	W	Pete DePaolo*	Duesenberg	Stevens/Duesenberg	19	Accident	300
34	29	45	R	Marion Trexler	Trexler	Auburn/Lycoming	19	Accident	295
35	27	19		Speed Gardner	Miller Front Drive	Miller/Miller	14	Bearing	290
36	28	26	R	Baconin Borzachini	Maserati	Maserati/Maserati	7	Magneto	285
37	36	48		Rick Decker	Hoosier Pete	Mercedes/Clemons	8	Oil tank	280
38	5	18	R	Chet Gardner	Buckeye	Duesenberg/Duesenberg	0	Skidded out	275

Total Purse $98,250

Time of Race: 4:58:39.72 Average Speed: 100.448 mph Margin of Victory: 7:17.36
Pole: #4 Billy Arnold (113.268, 5:17.83) Fastest Race Lap: N/A
Winning Car Owner: Harry Hartz Winning Chief Mechanic: Jean Marcenac** Winning Tire: Firestone
Legend: R=Indianapolis 500-Mile Race Rookie; W=Indianapolis 500-Mile Race Former Winner; *=Had Relief Help, **= Riding Mechanic: William "Spider" Matlock
Race Notes: Cars not finishing were awarded positions in the order in which they left the track, regardless of lap count.
Lap Leaders: Meyer 1-2, Arnold 3-200. Lap Leader Summary: Arnold 1 time for 198 laps, Meyer 1-2. Lead Changes: 1 among 2 drivers.

Official Box Score

19th Indianapolis 500-Mile Race at the Indianapolis Motor Speedway • Saturday, May 30, 1931

FP	SP	No.		Driver	Car Name	Chassis/Engine	Laps	Status	Total Prize Money
1	13	23		Louis Schneider	Bowes Seal Fast	Stevens/Miller	200	96.629	$29,500
2	8	34		Fred Frame	Duesenberg	Duesenberg/Duesenberg	200	96.406	12,650
3	10	19		Ralph Hepburn*	Harry Miller	Miller/Miller	200	94.224	6,350
4	35	21	R	Myron Stevens*	Jadson	Stevens/Miller	200	94.142	4,000
5	1	4		Russ Snowberger	Russell "8"	Snowberger/Studebaker	200	49.090	3,500
6	20	33		Jimmy Gleason*	Duesenberg	Duesenberg/Duesenberg	200	93.605	2,200
7	5	25		Ernie Triplett	Buckeye	Duesenberg/Duesenberg	200	63.041	1,800
8	9	36	R	H.W. Stubblefield	Jones-Miller	Willys-Knight/Miller	200	92.434	1,950
9	14	28		Cliff Bergere	Elco Royale	Reo/Reo	200	91.839	1,500
10	15	27		Chet Miller*	Marr	Hudson/Hudson	200	89.580	1,400
11	30	44	R	George Howie*	G. N. H.	Dodge/Chrysler	200	87.651	500
12	23	12		Phil Shafer	Shafer "8"	Rigling/Buick	200	86.391	470
13	17	8		Dave Evans	Cummins Diesel	Duesenberg/Cummins	200	86.107	450
14	31	72	R	Al Aspen*	William Alberti	Duesenberg/Duesenberg	200	85.764	425
15	37	59		Sam Ross	Miller	Rigling/Miller	200	85.139	400
16	40	69		Joe Huff*	Goldberg Brothers	Cooper/Miller	180	Running	375
17	4	5		Deacon Litz*	Maley	Duesenberg/Duesenberg	177	Accident	365
18	19	37		Tony Gulotta	Hunt	Rigling/Studebaker	167	Accident	360
19	18	1	W	Billy Arnold	Miller-Hartz	Summers/Miller	162	Accident	8,905
20	12	57	R	Luther Johnson	Bill Richards	Studebaker/Studebaker	156	Accident	350
21	36	55	R	Billy Winn*	Hoosier Pete	Rigling/Clemons	138	Running	343
22	27	16		Frank Brisko	Brisko-Atkinson	Stevens/Miller	138	Steering arm	343
23	34	26	R	Gene Haustein	Fronty-Ford	Ford T/Fronty-Ford	117	Wheel	335
24	16	41	R	Joe Russo	Russo	Rigling/Duesenberg	109	Oil	330
25	7	17		Speed Gardner*	Nutmeg State	Miller/Miller	107	Frame	325
26	38	14		Lou Moore	Boyle Valve	Miller/Miller	103	Differential	320
27	26	2		Shorty Cantlon	Harry Miller	Miller/Miller	88	Rod	315
28	2	3		Bill Cummings	Empire State	Cooper/Miller	70	Oil line	710
29	28	24		Freddie Winnai	Bowes Seal Fast	Stevens/Miller	60	Accident	303
30	11	32	R	Phil Pardee*	Duesenberg	Duesenberg/Duesenberg	60	Accident	303
31	3	31	R	Paul Bost	Empire State	Rigling/Miller	35	Crankshaft	495
32	22	35		Frank Farmer	Jones-Miller	Willys-Knight/Miller	32	Rod bearing	290
33	32	58	R	George Wingerter	Wingerter	Duesenberg/Duesenberg	29	Fuel tank	285
34	25	7	W	Louis Meyer	Sampson	Stevens/Miller	28	Oil leak	330
35	6	39		Babe Stapp	Rigling & Henning	Rigling/Duesenberg	9	Oil Leak	275
36	24	48		John Boling	Grapho Metal	Morton & Brett/M&B	7	Rod	270
37	29	54		Leon Duray	Duray	Stevens:Whippett/Duray	6	Overheating	263
38	33	49		Harry Butcher	Butcher Brothers	Buick/Buick	6	Accident	263
39	39	10		Herman Schurch	Hoosier Pete	Rigling/Clemons	5	Transmission	255
40	21	67	R	Francis Quinn	Tucker Tappett	Miller/Ford A	3	Rear axle	250

Total Purse $84,053

Time of Race: 5:10:27.93 Average Speed: 96.629 mph Margin of Victory: 43.19 sec
Pole: #4 Russ Snowberger (112.769, 5:19.16) Fastest Qualifier: #1 Billy Arnold (116.080, 5:10.13) Fastest Race Lap: N/A
Winning Car Owner: B. L. Schneider Winning Chief Mechanic: J.W. "Jigger" Johnson ** Winning Tire: Firestone
Legend: R=Indianapolis 500-Mile Race Rookie; W=Indianapolis 500-Mile Race Former Winner; *=Had Relief Help, **=Also Riding Mechanic
Lap Leaders: Bost 1-2, Cummings 3-6, Arnold 7-161, Schneider 162-200.
Lap Leader Summary: Arnold 1 time for 155 laps, Schneider 1-39, Cummings 1-4, Bost 1-2.
Lead Changes: 3 among 4 drivers.

Official Box Score

20th Indianapolis 500-Mile Race at the Indianapolis Motor Speedway • Monday, May 30, 1932

FP	SP	No.		Driver	Car Name	Chassis/Engine	Laps	Status	Total Prize Money
1	27	34		Fred Frame	Miller-Hartz	Wetteroth/Miller	200	104.144	$31,050
2	6	6	R	Howdy Wilcox (II)	Lion Head	Stevens/Miller	200	103.881	12,650
3	10	22		Cliff Bergere	Studebaker	Rigling/Studebaker	200	102.662	7,000
4	14	61	R	Bob Carey	Meyer	Stevens/Miller	200	101.363	6,050
5	4	4		Russ Snowberger	Hupp Comet	Snowberger/Hupmobile	200	100.791	3,500
6	38	37		Zeke Meyer	Studebaker	Rigling/Studebaker	200	98.476	2,500
7	5	35		Ira Hall*	Duesenberg	Stevens/Duesenberg	200	98.207	2,600
8	35	65		Freddie Winnai	Foreman Axle Shaft	Duesenberg/Duesenberg	200	97.437	2,200
9	9	2		Billy Winn*	Duesenberg	Duesenberg/Duesenberg	200	97.421	2,100
10	15	55		Joe Huff	Highway Truck Parts	Cooper/Cooper	200	87.586	2,000
11	26	33		Phil Shafer	Shafer "8""	Rigling/Buick	197	Running	725
12	40	36	R	Kelly Petillo	Jones-Miller	Miller/Miller	189	Running	700
13	20	25		Tony Gulotta	Studebaker	Rigling/Studebaker	184	Running	680
14	25	15		H.W. Stubblefield	Gilmore	Adams/Miller	178	Running	660
15	17	18		Peter Kreis	Studebaker	Rigling/Studebaker	178	Accident	635
16	11	46		Luther Johnson	Studebaker	Rigling/Studebaker	164	Wheel	620
17	22	3		Wilbur Shaw	Veedol	Miller/Miller	157	Rear axle	1,915
18	19	24		Deacon Litz	Bowes Seal Fast	Duesenberg/Duesenberg	152	Rod	610
19	12	10		Bill Cummings*	Bowes Seal Fast	Stevens/Miller	151	Crankshaft	605
20	32	57	R	Malcolm Fox	Bill Richards	Studebaker/Studebaker	132	Spring	600
21	29	9		Chet Miller*	Hudson	Hudson/Hudson	125	Engine	590
22	31	7		Ernie Triplett	Floating Power	Miller/Miller	125	Clutch	1,290
23	30	1	W	Louis Schneider*	Bowes Seal Fast	Stevens/Miller	125	Frame	590
24	21	41		Joe Russo	Art Rose	Rigling/Duesenberg	107	Rod	580
25	1	8		Lou Moore	Boyle Valve	Miller/Miller	79	Timing gear	575
26	36	14	R	Juan Gaudino*	Golden Seal	Chrysler/Chrysler	71	Clutch	570

1932 box score continued

FP	SP	No.		Driver	Car Name	Chassis/Engine	Laps	Status	Total Prize Money
27	18	29	R	Al Miller	Hudson	Hudson/Hudson	66	Engine	565
28	39	42	R	Doc MacKenzie	Brady	Studebaker/Studebaker	65	Engine	560
29	13	32		Frank Brisko	Brisko-Atkinson	Stevens/Miller	61	Clutch	555
30	34	72	R	Ray Campbell	Folly Farm	Graham/Graham	60	Crankshaft	550
31	2	5	W	Billy Arnold	Miller-Hartz	Summers/Miller	59	Accident	3,345
32	3	27	R	Bryan Saulpaugh	Harry Miller	Miller/Miller	55	Oil line	540
33	7	16	W	Louis Meyer	Sampson	Stevens/Miller	50	Crankshaft	535
34	23	21		Al Aspen	Brady & Nardi	Duesenberg/Studebaker	31	Rod	530
35	33	49	R	Johnny Kreiger	Consumers Petroleum Oil	Duesenberg/Duesenberg	30	Rod	525
36	16	48		Wesley Crawford	Boyle Valve	Miller/Duesenberg	28	Crankshaft	520
37	8	17		Paul Bost	Empire State	Cooper/Miller	18	Crankshaft	515
38	24	58		Bob McDonogh	F.W.D.	Miller/Miller	7	Oil line	510
39	28	45	R	Gus Schrader	Harry Miller	Miller/Miller	3	Accident	505
40	37	26	R	Al Gordon	Lion Tamer	Miller/Miller	2	Accident	500

Total Purse $93,850

Time of Race: 4:48:03.79 Average Speed: 104.144 mph Margin of Victory: 43.66 sec
Pole: #8 Lou Moore (117.363, 5:06.74) Fastest Race Lap: N/A
Winning Car Owner: Harry Hartz Winning Chief Mechanic: Jean Marcenac** Winning Tire: Firestone
Legend: R=Indianapolis 500-Mile Race Rookie; W=Indianapolis 500-Mile Race Former Winner; *=Had Relief Help, **= Riding mechanic: Jerry Houck
Lap Leaders: Moore 1, Arnold 2-58, Carey 59-94, Triplett 95-108, Wilcox II 109, Hall 110-115, Shaw 116-125, Frame 126-134, Shaw 135-151, Frame 152-200.
Lap Leader Summary: Frame 2 times for 58 laps, Arnold 1-57, Carey 1-36, Shaw 2-27, Triplett 1-14, Hall 1-6, Moore 1-1, Wilcox II 1-1.
Lead Changes: 9 among 8 drivers.

Official Box Score
21st Indianapolis 500-Mile Race at the Indianapolis Motor Speedway • Tuesday, May 30, 1933

FP	SP	No.	Rookie	Driver	Car Name	Chassis/Engine	Laps	Status	Total Prize Money
1	6	36	W	Louis Meyer	Tydol	Miller/Miller	200	104.162	$18,000
2	23	17		Wilbur Shaw	Mallory	Stevens/Miller	200	101.795	9,100
3	4	37		Lou Moore	Foreman Axle	Duesenberg/Miller	200	101.599	4,100
4	15	21		Chet Gardner	Sampson Radio	Stevens/Miller	200	101.182	2,400
5	10	8		H.W. Stubblefield	Abels & Fink Auto	Rigling/Buick	200	100.762	3,250
6	36	38		Dave Evans	Art Rose	Rigling/Studebaker	200	100.425	1,450
7	12	34		Tony Gulotta	Studebaker	Rigling/Studebaker	200	99.071	1,300
8	17	4		Russ Snowberger*	Russell "8"	Snowberger/Studebaker	200	99.011	1,200
9	16	9		Zeke Meyer	Studebaker	Rigling/Studebaker	200	98.122	1,150
10	20	46		Luther Johnson*	Studebaker	Rigling/Studebaker	200	97.287	1,100
11	9	6		Cliff Bergere*	Studebaker	Rigling/Studebaker	200	96.536	500
12	18	47	W	L.L. Corum	Studebaker	Rigling/Studebaker	200	96.454	475
13	40	49	R	Willard Prentiss*	Jack C. Carr	Rigling/Duesenberg	200	93.595	450
14	27	14		Raul Riganti*	Golden Seal	Chrysler/Chrysler	200	93.244	425
15	28	29		Gene Haustein	Martz	Hudson/Hudson	197	Running	380
16	14	26		Deacon Litz*	Bowes Seal Fast	Miller/Miller	197	Running	370
17	31	18		Joe Russo	Wonder Bread	Duesenberg/Duesenberg	192	Running	340
18	39	51		Doc MacKenzie	Ray Brady	Duesenberg/Studebaker	192	Rear axle	330
19	25	27		Kelly Petillo*	Sacks Bros.	Smith/Miller	168	Spun	320
20	32	28		Chet Miller*	Marr	Hudson/Hudson	163	Rod	305
21	24	19		Al Miller	Marr	Hudson/Hudson	161	Rod	295
22	19	68		Bennett Hill*	Goldberg Brothers	Cooper/Cooper	158	Rod	285
23	29	45		Babe Stapp	Boyle Products	Miller/Miller	156	Out of Fuel	1,380
24	26	32		Wesley Crawford*	Boyle Valve	Stevens/Miller	147	Accident	275
25	1	5		Bill Cummings*	Boyle Products	Miller/Miller	136	Radiator	1,065
26	7	15	R	Lester Spangler	Miller	Miller/Miller	132	Accident	260
27	35	65		Freddie Winnai*	Kemp	Duesenberg/Duesenberg	125	Mechanical	255
28	30	57		Malcolm Fox	Universal Service Garage	Studebaker/Studebaker	121	Accident	250
29	3	12	W	Fred Frame	Miller-Hartz	Wetteroth/Miller	85	Valve	645
30	22	64	R	Mark Billman	Kemp-Mannix	Duesenberg/Duesenberg	79	Accident	240
31	34	53	R	Johnny Sawyer	Lencki-Madis	Miller/Miller	77	Clutch	235
32	11	2		Peter Kreis	Frame-Miller	Summers/Miller	63	Universal joint	230
33	5	16		Ernie Triplett	Floating Power	Weil/Miller	61	Piston	225
34	13	25		Shorty Cantlon	Sullivan & O'Brien	Stevens/Miller	50	Rod	220
35	42	3	R	Mauri Rose	Gilmore	Stevens/Miller	48	Timing gear	215
36	2	58		Frank Brisko	F.W.D.	Miller/Miller	47	Oil	210
37	8	10		Ira Hall	Denny Duesenberg	Stevens/Duesenberg	37	Accident	206
38	41	23		Ralph Hepburn	Highway Truck Parts	Cooper/Cooper	33	Rod	205
39	37	59		Ray Campbell	G&D	Hudson/Hudson	24	Magneto	204
40	33	24		Paul Bost	Frame-Miller Duesenberg	Duesenberg/Miller	13	Oil	203
41	38	61		Rick Decker	Miller	Miller/Miller	13	Manifold	202
42	21	22	W	Louis Schneider	Edelweiss	Stevens/Miller	0	Stalled	200

Total Purse $54,450

Time of Race: 4:48.75 Average Speed: 104.162 mph Margin of Victory: 6:41.89
Pole: #5 Bill Cummings (118.530, 12:39.30) Fastest Race Lap: N/A
Winning Car Owner: Louis Meyer Winning Chief Mechanic: Lawson Harris ** Winning Tire: Firestone
Legend: R=Indianapolis 500-Mile Race Rookie; W=Indianapolis 500-Mile Race Former Winner; *=Had Relief Help, **=Also Riding Mechanic
Lap Leaders: Cummings 1-32, Frame 33-36, Stapp 37-38, Frame 39-50, Stapp 51-63, Frame 64-84, Stapp 85-129, Meyer 130-200.
Lap Leader Summary: Meyer 1 time for 71 laps, Stapp 3-60, Frame 3-37, Cummings 1-32.
Lead Changes: 7 among 4 drivers.

Official Box Score
22nd Indianapolis 500-Mile Race at the Indianapolis Motor Speedway • Wednesday, May 30, 1934

FP	SP	No.		Driver	Car Name	Chassis/Engine	Laps	Status	Total Prize Money
1	10	7		Bill Cummings	Boyle Products	Miller/Miller	200	104.863	$29,725
2	4	9		Mauri Rose	Leon Duray	Stevens/Miller	200	104.697	14,350
3	20	2		Lou Moore*	Foreman Axle	Miller/Miller	200	102.625	6,675
4	19	12		Deacon Litz*	Stokely Foods	Miller/Miller	200	100.749	4,250
5	24	16		Joe Russo	Duesenberg	Duesenberg/Duesenberg	200	99.893	3,600
6	8	36		Al Miller*	Shafer "8"	Rigling/Buick	200	98.264	2,200
7	18	22		Cliff Bergere*	Floating Power	Weil/Miller	200	97.818	1,850
8	9	10		Russ Snowberger	Russell "8"	Snowberger/Studebaker	200	97.297	1,650
9	3	32		Frank Brisko*	F.W.D.	Miller/Miller	200	96.787	2,850
10	14	24	R	Herb Ardinger*	Lucenti	Graham/Graham	200	95.936	1,425
11	1	17		Kelly Petillo	Red Lion	Adams/Miller	200	93.432	900
12	29	5		H.W. Stubblefield*	Cummins Diesel	Duesenberg/Cummins	200	88.566	880
13	28	49	R	Charlie Crawford	Detroit Gasket & Mfg.	Ford/Ford V8	110	Hd gskt (in pit)	860
14	11	31		Ralph Hepburn*	Art Rose	Miller/Miller	164	Rod	840
15	12	18	R	George Barringer*	Boyle Products	Miller/Miller	161	Front axle	815
16	6	26		Phil Shafer*	Shafer "8"	Rigling/Buick	130	Camshaft	790
17	7	8		Tony Gulotta	Schroeder	Cooper/Studebaker	94	Rod	770
18	13	1	W	Louis Meyer	Ring Free	Stevens/Miller	92	Oil tank	745
19	22	6		Dave Evans	Cummins Diesel	Duesenberg/Cummins	81	Transmission	720
20	15	15		Shorty Cantlon*	Sullivan & O'Brien	Stevens/Miller	76	Crankshaft	700
21	5	4		Chet Gardner	Sampson Radio	Stevens/Miller	72	Rod	675
22	17	51		Al Gordon	Abels & Fink	Adams/Miller	66	Steering	650
23	23	35	R	Rex Mays	Frame Miller-Duesenberg	Duesenberg/Miller	53	Front axle	630
24	25	42	R	Dusty Fahrnow	Superior Trailer	Cooper/Cooper	28	Rod	600
25	21	41		Johnny Sawyer	Burd Piston Ring	Miller/Lencki	27	Rods	585
26	33	33		Johnny Seymour	Streamline Miller	Adams/Miller	22	Pinion	560
27	27	45		Rick Decker	Carter Carburetor	Miller/Miller	17	Clutch	540
28	2	3		Wilbur Shaw	Lion Head	Stevens/Miller	15	Lost oil	515
29	26	73		Doc MacKenzie	Cresco	Mikan-Carson/Studebaker	15	Accident	490
30	31	29		Gene Haustein	Martz	Hudson/Hudson	13	Accident	470
31	30	63	R	Harry McQuinn	DeBaets	Rigling/Miller	13	Rod	445
32	16	58	R	George Bailey	Scott	Snowberger/Studebaker	12	Accident	420
33	32	46		Chet Miller	Bohnalite Ford	Ford/Ford V8	11	Accident	400

Total Purse $83,575
Time of Race: 4:46:05.20 Average Speed: 104.863 mph Margin of Victory: 27.25 sec
Pole: #17 Kelly Petillo (119.329, 12:34.22) Fastest Race Lap: N/A
Winning Car Owner: H. C. Henning Winning Chief Mechanic: Earl Unversaw ** Winning Tire: Firestone
Legend: R=Indianapolis 500-Mile Race Rookie; W=Indianapolis 500-Mile Race Former Winner; *=Had Relief Help, **=Also Riding Mechanic
Lap Leaders: Petillo 1-6, Brisko 7-71, Cummings 72-78, Rose 79-109, Brisko 110-113, Rose 114-124, Cummings 125-148, Rose 149-174, Cummings 175-200.
Lap Leader Summary: Brisko 2 times for 69 laps, Rose 3-68, Cummings 3-57, Petillo 1-6.
Lead Changes: 8 among 4 drivers.

Official Box Score
23rd Indianapolis 500-Mile Race at the Indianapolis Motor Speedway • Thursday, May 30, 1935

FP	SP	No.		Driver	Car Name	Chassis/Engine	Laps	Status	Total Prize Money
1	22	5		Kelly Petillo	Gilmore Speedway	Wetteroth/Offy	200	106.240	$30,600
2	20	14		Wilbur Shaw	Pirrung	Shaw/Offy	200	105.990	13,500
3	5	1	W	Bill Cummings	Boyle Products	Miller/Miller	200	104.758	6,650
4	3	22	R	Floyd Roberts	Abels & Fink	Miller/Miller	200	103.228	4,000
5	7	21		Ralph Hepburn*	Veedol	Miller/Miller	200	103.177	3,500
6	19	9		Shorty Cantlon*	Sullivan & O'Brien	Stevens/Miller	200	101.140	2,200
7	9	18		Chet Gardner	Sampson Radio	Stevens/Miller	200	101.129	1,800
8	13	16		Deacon Litz*	Sha-litz	Miller/Miller	200	100.907	1,600
9	15	8		Doc MacKenzie	Pirrung	Rigling/Miller	200	100.598	1,500
10	17	34		Chet Miller	Milac Front Drive	Summers/Miller	200	100.474	1,475
11	8	19	W	Fred Frame*	Miller-Hartz	Wetteroth/Miller	200	100.436	850
12	4	36	W	Louis Meyer	Ring Free	Stevens/Miller	200	100.256	700
13	16	15		Cliff Bergere	Victor Gasket	Rigling/Buick	196	Out of fuel	600
14	31	62	R	Harris Insinger	Cresco	Mikan-Carson/Studebaker	185	Running	535
15	21	4		Al Miller	Boyle Products	Rigling/Miller	178	Engine	520
16	26	43	R	Ted Horn	Ford V-8	Miller-Ford/Ford V8	145	Steering	505
17	1	33		Rex Mays	Gilmore	Adams/Miller	123	Spring	2,490
18	23	7		Lou Moore*	Foreman Axle	Miller/Miller	116	Rod	475
19	14	37	R	George Connor	Marks Miller	Stevens/Miller	112	Transmission	460
20	10	2		Mauri Rose*	F.W.D.	Miller/Miller	103	Studs	445
21	6	44		Tony Gulotta	Bowes Seal Fast	Stevens/Miller	102	Magneto	430
22	30	39	R	Jimmy Snyder	Blue Prelude	Snowberger/Studebaker	97	Spring	415
23	24	41		Frank Brisko	Art Rose	Rigling/Studebaker	79	Universal joint	400
24	27	42		Johnny Seymour*	Ford V-8	Miller-Ford/Ford V8	71	Grease leak	385
25	12	17		Babe Stapp	Marks Miller	Adams/Miller	70	Radiator	470
26	29	35		George Bailey	Ford V-8	Miller-Ford/Ford V8	65	Steering	355
27	11	3		Russ Snowberger	Boyle Products	Miller/Miller	59	Exhaust pipe	340
28	32	26	R	Louis Tomei	Burd Piston Ring	Miller/Lencki	47	Valve	325
29	33	46	R	Bob Sall	Ford V-8	Miller-Ford/Ford V8	47	Steering	310
30	2	6		Al Gordon	Cocktail Hour Cigarette	Weil/Miller	17	Accident	295
31	28	27		Freddie Winnai	Gyro-Duesenberg	Duesenberg/Miller	16	Rod	280
32	25	45	R	Clay Weatherly	Bowes Seal Fast	Stevens/Miller	9	Accident	265
33	18	66		Harry McQuinn	DeBaets	Rigling/Miller	4	Rod	250

Total Purse $78,925
Time of Race: 4:42:22.71 Average Speed: 106.240 mph Margin of Victory: 40.02 sec
Pole: #33 Rex Mays (120.736, 12:25.43) Fastest Race Lap: N/A
Winning Car Owner: Kelly Petillo Winning Chief Mechanic: Jimmie Dunham ** Winning Tire: Firestone
Legend: R=Indianapolis 500-Mile Race Rookie; W=Indianapolis 500-Mile Race Former Winner; *=Had Relief Help, **=Also Riding Mechanic
Lap Leaders: Mays 1-63, Stapp 64-67, Petillo 68-73, Mays 74-99, Petillo 100-139, Shaw 140-144, Petillo 145-200.
Lap Leader Summary: Petillo 3 times for 102 laps, Mays 2-89, Shaw 1-5, Stapp 1-4.
Lead Changes: 6 among 4 drivers.

Official Box Score

24th Indianapolis 500-Mile Race at the Indianapolis Motor Speedway • Saturday, May 30, 1936

FP	SP	No.		Driver	Car Name	Chassis/Engine	Laps	Status	Total Prize Money
1	28	8	W	Louis Meyer	Ring Free	Stevens/Miller	200	109.069	$31,300
2	11	22		Ted Horn	Miller-Hartz	Wetteroth/Miller	200	108.170	13,775
3	4	10		Doc MacKenzie*	Gilmore Speedway	Wetteroth/Offy	200	107.460	6,900
4	30	36		Mauri Rose	F.W.D.	Miller/Miller	200	107.272	4,000
5	3	18		Chet Miller	Boyle Products	Summers/Miller	200	106.919	3,653
6	25	41	R	Ray Pixley	Fink Auto	Miller/Miller	200	105.253	2,328
7	9	3		Wilbur Shaw	Gilmore	Shaw/Offy	200	104.233	3,650
8	14	17		George Barringer	Kennedy Tank	Rigling/Offy	200	102.630	1,650
9	32	53		Zeke Meyer	Boyle Products	Cooper/Studebaker	200	101.331	1,550
10	5	38		George Connor	Marks Miller	Adams/Miller	200	98.931	1,425
11	12	35		Freddie Winnai	Midwest Red Lion	Stevens/Offy	199	Running	850
12	24	9		Ralph Hepburn	Art Rose	Miller/Offy	195	Running	700
13	27	28		Harry McQuinn	Sampson Radio	Stevens/Miller	196	Out of fuel	600
14	10	7		Shorty Cantlon	Hamilton-Harris	Weil/Miller	194	Out of fuel	535
15	1	33		Rex Mays	Gilmore	Adams/Sparks	192	Out of fuel	920
16	23	54	R	Doc Williams	Superior Trailer	Cooper/Miller	192	Out of fuel	505
17	29	32		Lou Moore*	Burd Piston Ring	Miller/Offy	185	Out of fuel	490
18	33	19	R	Emil Andres*	Carew	Whippet/Cragar	184	Running	475
19	15	4		Floyd Roberts	Burd Piston Ring	Stevens/Offy	183	Out of fuel	460
20	20	14		Frank Brisko	Elgin Piston Pin	Miller/Brisko	180	Out of fuel	445
21	17	12		Al Miller	Boyle Products	Smith/Miller	119	Accident	430
22	7	42		Cliff Bergere*	Bowes Seal Fast	Stevens/Miller	116	Engine support	415
23	26	15		Deacon Litz*	Litz	Miller/Miller	108	Crankshaft	400
24	2	21		Babe Stapp	Pirrung	Shaw/Offy	89	Crankshaft	1,585
25	19	5		Billy Winn	Harry A. Miller	Miller/Miller	78	Crankshaft	370
26	22	52	R	Frank McGurk	Abels Auto Ford	Adams/Cragar	51	Crankshaft	355
27	8	27		Louis Tomei	Wheeler's	Wetteroth/Miller	44	Engine support	340
28	6	44		Herb Ardinger	Bowes Seal Fast	Stevens/Miller	38	Transmission	325
29	18	6		Chet Gardner	Gardner	Duesenberg/Offy	38	Clutch	310
30	16	43		Jimmy Snyder	Belanger Miller	Stevens/Miller	21	Oil leak	295
31	21	47		Johnny Seymour	Sullivan & O'Brien	Stevens/Miller	13	Clutch	280
32	31	46	W	Fred Frame	Burd Piston Ring	Miller/Miller	4	Piston	265
33	13	2	W	Bill Cummings	Boyle Products	Miller/Offy	0	Clutch	250

Total Purse $81,831

Time of Race: 4:35:03.39 Average Speed: 109.069 mph Margin of Victory: 2:17.15
Pole: #33 Rex Mays (119.644, 12:32.23) Fastest Race Lap: N/A
Winning Car Owner: Louis Meyer Winning Chief Mechanic: Lawson Harris ** Winning Tire: Firestone
Legend: R=Indianapolis 500-Mile Race Rookie; W=Indianapolis 500-Mile Race Former Winner; *=Had Relief Help, **=Also Riding Mechanic
Lap Leaders: Mays 1-12, Stapp 13-31, Shaw 32-82, Stapp 83-88, Meyer 89-130, Horn 131-146, Meyer 147-200.
Lap Leader Summary: Meyer 2 times for 96 laps, Shaw 1-51, Stapp 2-25, Horn 1-16, Mays 1-12.
Lead Changes: 6 among 5 drivers.

Official Box Score

25th Indianapolis 500-Mile Race at the Indianapolis Motor Speedway • Monday, May 31, 1937

FP	SP	No.	Rookie	Driver	Car Name	Chassis/Engine	Laps	Status	Total Prize Money
1	2	6		Wilbur Shaw	Shaw-Gilmore	Shaw/Offy	200	113.580	$35,075
2	6	8		Ralph Hepburn*	Hamilton-Harris	Stevens/Offy	200	113.565	15,937
3	32	3		Ted Horn	Miller-Hartz	Wetteroth/Miller	200	113.434	7,087
4	5	2	W	Louis Meyer	Boyle	Miller/Miller	200	110.730	4,275
5	16	45		Cliff Bergere*	Midwest Red Lion	Stevens/Offy	200	108.935	3,725
6	1	16	W	Bill Cummings*	Boyle	Miller/Offy	200	107.124	3,187
7	14	28	R	Billy DeVore*	Miller	Stevens/Miller	200	106.995	1,962
8	7	38		Tony Gulotta*	Burd Piston Ring	Rigling/Offy	200	105.015	1,787
9	12	17		George Connor	Marks Miller	Adams/Miller	200	103.830	1,862
10	18	53		Louis Tomei	Sobonite Plastics	Rigling/Studebaker	200	101.825	1,487
11	9	31		Chet Gardner*	Burd Piston Ring	Duesenberg/Offy	199	Running	912
12	10	23	R	Ronney Householder*	Topping	Viglioni/Miller	194	Running	737
13	17	62		Floyd Roberts	Thorne	Miller/Miller	194	Running	600
14	11	35		Deacon Litz*	Motorola Auto Radio	Miller/Miller	191	Out of oil	535
15	24	32	R	Floyd Davis	Thorne	Snowberger/Miller	190	Accident	520
16	25	34		Shorty Cantlon*	Bowes Seal Fast	Weil/Miller	182	Running	505
17	26	42		Al Miller*	Thorne	Snowberger/Miller	170	Carburetor	490
18	8	1		Mauri Rose	Burd Piston Ring	Miller/Offy	127	Oil line	475
19	29	41	R	Ken Fowler	Lucky Teeter	Wetteroth/McDowell	116	Car pushed	460
20	20	25	W	Kelly Petillo	Petillo	Wetteroth/Offy	109	Out of oil	1,445
21	28	43		George Bailey	Duray-Sims	Stevens/Miller	107	Clutch	430
22	3	54		Herb Ardinger*	Chicago Raw Hide Oil Seal	Welch/Offy	106	Rod	915
23	15	24		Frank Brisko	Elgin Piston Pin	Stevens/Brisko	105	No oil pressure	400
24	33	44	R	Frank Wearne	Duray	Stevens/Miller	99	Carburetor	385
25	27	26	R	Tony Willman	F.W.D.	Miller/Miller	95	Rod	370
26	4	10		Billy Winn	Harry A. Miller	Miller/Miller	85	Oil line	605
27	30	12		Russ Snowberger*	R.S.	Snowberger/Packard	66	Clutch	340
28	21	33	R	Bob Swanson	Fink Auto	Adams/Sparks	52	Carburetor	825
29	22	47		Harry McQuinn	Sullivan & O'Brien	Stevens/Miller	47	Piston	560
30	13	7		Chet Miller	Boyle	Summers/Miller	36	Ignition	295
31	31	15		Babe Stapp	Topping	Maserati/Maserati	36	Clutch	280
32	19	5		Jimmy Snyder	Sparks	Adams/Sparks	27	Transmission	3,165
33	23	14		Rex Mays	Bowes Seal Fast	Alfa Romeo/Alfa Romeo	24	Overheating	500

Total Purse $92,133

Time of Race: 4:24:07.80 Average Speed: 113.580 mph Margin of Victory: 2.16 sec
Pole: #16 Bill Cummings (123.343, 12:09.67) Fastest Qualifier: #5 Jimmy Snyder (125.287, 11:58.35) Fastest Race Lap: N/A
Winning Car Owner: W. Wilbur Shaw Winning Chief Mechanic: J.W. "Jigger" Johnson Winning Tire: Firestone
Legend: R=Indianapolis 500-Mile Race Rookie; W=Indianapolis 500-Mile Race Former Winner; *=Had Relief Help, **=Also Riding Mechanic
Lap Leaders: Ardinger 1-2, Snyder 3-26, Shaw 27-74, Hepburn 75-83, Shaw 84-129, Swanson (for Hepburn) 130-163, Shaw 164-200.
Lap Leader Summary: Shaw 3 times for 131 laps, Swanson (for Hepburn) 1-34, Snyder 1-24, Hepburn 1-9, Ardinger 1-2.
Lead Changes: 6 among 5 drivers.

Official Box Score

26th Indianapolis 500-Mile Race at the Indianapolis Motor Speedway • Monday, May 30, 1938

FP	SP	No.		Driver	Car Name	Chassis/Engine	Laps	Status	Total Prize Money
1	1	23		Floyd Roberts	Burd Piston Ring	Wetteroth/Miller	200	117.200	$32,075
2	7	1	W	Wilbur Shaw	Shaw	Shaw/Offy	200	115.580	14,425
3	5	3		Chet Miller	I.B.E.W.	Summers/Offy	200	114.946	7,350
4	6	2		Ted Horn	Miller-Hartz	Wetteroth/Miller	200	112.203	4,600
5	18	38		Chet Gardner	Burd Piston Ring	Rigling/Offy	200	110.311	4,100
6	14	54		Herb Ardinger*	Offenhauser	Miller-Ford/Offy	199	Running	2,625
7	25	45		Harry McQuinn*	Marchese	Marchese/Miller	197	Running	2,175
8	30	58		Billy DeVore	P.R.&W.	Stevens/Offy	185	Running	1,925
9	13	22	R	Joel Thorne	Thorne Engineering	Shaw/Offy	185	Running	1,775
10	17	29		Frank Wearne	Indiana Fur	Adams/Offy	181	Running	1,650
11	33	43	R	Duke Nalon	Kohlert-Miller	Fengler/Miller	178	Running	1,025
12	29	12		George Bailey	Leon Duray Barbasol	Weil/Duray	166	Clutch	825
13	9	27		Mauri Rose	I.B.E.W.	Maserati/Maserati	165	Supercharger	650
14	10	16		Ronney Householder*	Thorne-Sparks	Adams/Sparks	154	Supercharger	695
15	15	6		Jimmy Snyder	Sparks-Thorne	Adams/Sparks	150	Supercharger	3,390
16	12	5	W	Louis Meyer	Bowes Seal Fast	Stevens/Winfield	149	Oil Pump	635
17	4	17		Tony Gulotta*	Hamilton-Harris	Stevens/Offy	130	Rod	680
18	22	55		Al Miller	Domont's Pepsi-Cola	Miller/Miller	125	Clutch	625
19	19	15		George Connor	Marks Miller	Adams/Miller	119	Engine	620
20	32	9		Cliff Bergere	Kraft's Real Rye	Stevens/Miller	111	Piston	615
21	31	33	R	Henry Banks	Detroit Sporting World	Miller/Voelker	109	Rod bearing	610
22	21	35	W	Kelly Petillo	Petillo	Wetteroth/Offy	100	Camshaft	955
23	24	21		Louis Tomei	P.O.B. Perfect Seal	Miller/Miller	88	Rod	625
24	16	7	W	Bill Cummings	I.B.E.W.	Miller/Miller	72	Radiator	620
25	2	14		Russ Snowberger	D-X	Snowberger/Miller	56	Rod	640
26	8	34		Babe Stapp	McCoy Auto Service	Weil/Miller	54	Valve	585
27	26	10		Tony Willman	Belanger	Stevens/Miller	47	Valve	580
28	3	8		Rex Mays	Alfa-Romeo	A.R.-Weil/Alfa-Romeo	45	Supercharger	1,125
29	28	42		Emil Andres	Elgin Piston Pin	Adams/Brisko	45	Accident	620
30	27	37		Ira Hall	Greenfield Super Service	Nowiak/Studebaker	44	Accident	565
31	11	26		Frank Brisko	Shur-Stop Mech. Brake Equal.	Stevens/Brisko	39	Oil line	585
32	23	36	R	Al Putnam	Troy Tydol	Stevens/Miller	15	Crankshaft	555
33	20	47		Shorty Cantlon	Kamm's	Stevens/Miller	13	Supercharger	550

Total Purse $91,075

Time of Race: **4:14:58.40** Average Speed: **117.200 mph** Margin of Victory: **3:35.27**
Pole: **#23 Floyd Roberts (125.681, 11:56.10)** Fastest Qualifier: **#16 Ronney Householder (125.769, 11:45.50)** Fastest Race Lap: **N/A**
Winning Car Owner: **Lou Moore** Winning Chief Mechanic: **Lou Moore** Winning Tire: **Firestone**
Legend: **R=Indianapolis 500-Mile Race Rookie; W=Indianapolis 500-Mile Race Former Winner; *=Had Relief Help**
Lap Leaders: **Mays 1-14, Snyder 15-31, Mays 32-33, Snyder 34-74, Roberts 75-110, Snyder 111-144, Roberts 145-200.**
Lap Leader Summary: **Snyder 3 times for 92 laps, Roberts 2-92, Mays 2-16.**
Lead Changes: **6 among 3 drivers.** Official Box Score

27th Indianapolis 500-Mile Race at the Indianapolis Motor Speedway • Tuesday, May 30, 1939

FP	SP	No.		Driver	Car Name	Chassis/Engine	Laps	Status	Total Prize Money
1	3	2	W	Wilbur Shaw	Boyle	Maserati/Maserati	200	115.035	$27,375
2	1	10		Jimmy Snyder	Thorne Engineering	Adams/Sparks	200	114.245	16,100
3	10	54		Cliff Bergere	Offenhauser	Miller-Ford/Offy	200	113.698	7,400
4	4	4		Ted Horn	Boyle	Miller/Miller	200	111.879	4,750
5	16	31		Babe Stapp	Alfa Romeo	A.R.-Weil/Alfa Romeo	200	111.230	4,225
6	15	41		George Barringer	Bill White	Weil/Offy	200	111.025	2,800
7	20	8		Joel Thorne	Thorne Engineering	Adams/Sparks	200	110.416	2,150
8	8	16		Mauri Rose	Wheeler's	Shaw/Offy	200	109.544	2,150
9	17	14		Frank Wearne	Burd Piston Ring	Wetteroth/Offy	200	107.806	1,800
10	33	26		Billy DeVore*	Leon Duray-Barbasol	Weil/Duray	200	104.267	1,600
11	27	62		Tony Gulotta*	Burd Piston Ring	Stevens/Offy	200	103.938	1,000
12	2	45	W	Louis Meyer	Bowes Seal Fast	Stevens/Winfield	197	Accident	3,200
13	12	18		George Connor	Marks	Adams/Offy	195	Stalled	650
14	26	51		Tony Willman	Burd Piston Ring	Lencki/Lencki	188	Fuel pump	620
15	30	58		Louis Tomei*	Alfa-Romeo	Alfa Romeo/Alfa Romeo	186	Running	590
16	19	15		Rex Mays	Thorne Engineering	Adams/Sparks	145	Rings	685
17	9	9		Herb Ardinger*	Miller-Hartz	Wetteroth/Miller	141	Clutch	680
18	24	35	W	Kelly Petillo	Kay Jewelers	Wetteroth/Offy	141	Pistons	600
19	14	49	R	Mel Hansen	Joel Thorne, Inc.	Shaw/Offy	113	Accident	595
20	32	38		Harry McQuinn*	Elgin Piston Pin	Blume/Brisko	110	Ignition	590
21	5	3		Chet Miller	Boyle	Summers/Miller	109	Accident	635
22	13	25		Ralph Hepburn*	Hamilton-Harris	Stevens/Offy	107	Accident	605
23	23	1	W	Floyd Roberts	Burd Piston Ring	Wetteroth/Offy	106	Accident	650
24	18	37		Ira Hall	Greenfield Super Service	Nowiak/Studebaker	89	Head gasket	570
25	25	21		Russ Snowberger	D-X	Snowberger/Miller	50	Radiator	590
26	6	17		George Bailey	Miller	Miller/Miller	47	Valve	610
27	29	56		Floyd Davis	W.B.W.	Miller/Offy	43	Shock absorber	555
28	28	42		Al Miller	Kennedy Tank	Adams/Offy	41	Accelerator	575
29	11	29		Frank Brisko	National Seal	Stevens/Brisko	38	Air pump	570
30	21	44		Emil Andres	Chicago Flash	Stevens/Offy	22	Spark plugs	540
31	22	32		Bob Swanson	S.M.I.	Stevens/Sampson	19	Rear axle	510
32	7	47		Shorty Cantlon	Automotive Service	Stevens/Offy	15	Bearing	605
33	31	53		Deacon Litz	Maserati	Maserati/Maserati	7	Valve	525

Total Purse $87,100

Time of Race: **4:20:47.39** Average Speed: **115.035 mph** Margin of Victory: **1:48.22**
Pole: **#10 Jimmy Snyder (130.138, 4:36.63)** Fastest Race Lap: **N/A**
Winning Car Owner: **Boyle Racing Headquarters** Winning Chief Mechanic: **Robert T. Jackson** Winning Tire: **Firestone**
Legend: **R=Indianapolis 500-Mile Race Rookie; W=Indianapolis 500-Mile Race Former Winner; *=Had Relief Help**
Lap Leaders: **Snyder 1-36, Shaw 37-69, Meyer 70-73, Mays 74, Snyder 75-103, Meyer 104-130, Horn 131-134, Meyer 135-182, Shaw 183-200.**
Lap Leader Summary: **Meyer 3 times for 79 laps, Snyder 2-65, Shaw 2-51, Horn 1-4, Mays 1-1.**
Lead Changes: **8 among 5 drivers.**

Official Box Score

28th Indianapolis 500-Mile Race at the Indianapolis Motor Speedway • Thursday, May 30, 1940

FP	SP	No.		Driver	Car Name	Chassis/Engine	Laps	Status	Total Prize Money
1	2	1	W	Wilbur Shaw	Boyle	Maserati/Maserati	200	114.277	$30,725
2	1	33		Rex Mays	Bowes Seal Fast	Stevens/Winfield	200	113.742	15,950
3	3	7		Mauri Rose	Elgin Piston Pin	Wetteroth/Offy	200	113.572	6,688
4	4	3		Ted Horn	Boyle	Miller/Miller	199	Running	4,575
5	10	8		Joel Thorne	Thorne Donnelly	Adams/Sparks	197	Running	3,850
6	20	32		Bob Swanson	Sampson	Stevens/Sampson	196	Running	2,463
7	7	9		Frank Wearne	Boyle	Stevens/Offy	195	Running	2,038
8	5	31		Mel Hansen	Hartz	Wetteroth/Miller	194	Running	1,813
9	8	16		Frank Brisko	Elgin Piston Pin	Stevens/Brisko	193	Running	1,863
10	31	49	R	Rene LeBegue*	Lucy O'Reilly Schell	Maserati/Maserati	192	Running	1,488
11	15	41		Harry McQuinn	Hollywood Pay Day	A.R.-Weil/Alfa Romeo	192	Running	938
12	22	25		Emil Andres	Belanger-Folz	Stevens/Offy	192	Running	788
13	14	28	R	Sam Hanks	Duray	Weil/Duray	192	Running	650
14	16	6		George Barringer	Hollywood Pay Day	Weil/Offy	191	Running	620
15	26	42	R	Joie Chitwood	Kennedy Tank	Adams/Offy	190	Running	615
16	18	26		Louis Tomei	Falstaff	Miller/Offy	190	Exhaust	610
17	27	34		Chet Miller*	Alfa Romeo	Alfa Romeo/Alfa Romeo	189	Running	605
18	32	14		Billy DeVore*	Bill Holabird	Shaw/Offy	181	Running	600
19	28	44		Al Putnam	Refinoil Motor Oil	Adams/Offy	179	Running	595
20	33	61		Floyd Davis*	Lencki	Lencki/Lencki	157	Running	590
21	13	35	W	Kelly Petillo	Indiana Fur	Wetteroth/Offy	128	Bearing	660
22	25	21		Duke Nalon	Marks	Silnes/Offy	120	Rod	580
23	23	17	R	George Robson	Keller	Miller-Ford/Offy	67	Shock absorber	575
24	12	24		Babe Stapp*	Surber	Stevens/Offy	64	Oil line	595
25	19	36		Doc Williams	Quillen Bros. Refrigerator	Cooper/Miller	61	Oil line	590
26	17	10		George Connor	Lencki	Lencki/Lencki	52	Rod	610
27	6	5		Cliff Bergere	Noc-Out Hose Clamp	Wetteroth/Offy	51	Oil line	605
28	29	38	R	Paul Russo	Elgin Piston Pin	Blume/Brisko	48	Oil leak	550
29	21	54		Ralph Hepburn	Bowes Seal Fast	Miller-Ford/Offy	47	Steering	595
30	30	58		Al Miller	Alfa Romeo	Alfa Romeo/Alfa Romeo	41	Clutch	540
31	11	19		Russ Snowberger	Snowberger	Snowberger/Miller	38	Water pump	535
32	9	27	R	Tommy Hinnershitz	Marks	Adams/Offy	32	Accident	530
33	24	29		Raul Riganti	Maserati	Maserati/Maserati	24	Accident	500

Total Purse $85,529

Time of Race: 4:22:31.17 Average Speed: 114.277 mph Margin of Victory: Under Caution
Pole: #33 Rex Mays (127.850, 4:41.58) Fastest Race Lap: N/A
Winning Car Owner: Boyle Racing Headquarters Winning Chief Mechanic: H.C. "Cotton" Henning Winning Tire: Firestone
Legend: R=Indianapolis 500-Mile Race Rookie; W=Indianapolis 500-Mile Race Former Winner; *=Had Relief Help
Race Notes: Race run under caution from lap 150 to 200 due to rain.
Lap Leaders: Mays 1-33, Shaw 34-73, Mays 74-99, Rose 100-104, Shaw 105-200.
Lap Leader Summary: Shaw 2 times for 136 laps, Mays 2-59, Rose 1-5.
Lead Changes: 4 among 3 drivers.

Official Box Score

29th Indianapolis 500-Mile Race at the Indianapolis Motor Speedway • Friday, May 30, 1941

FP	SP	No.		Driver	Car Name	Chassis/Engine	Laps	Status	Total Prize Money
1	17	16		Floyd Davis/MauriRose*	Noc-Out Hose Clamp	Wetteroth/Offy	200	115.117	$29,200
2	2	1		Rex Mays	Bowes Seal Fast	Stevens/Winfield	200	114.459	14,850
3	28	4		Ted Horn	T.E.C.	Adams/Sparks	200	113.864	6,863
4	10	54		Ralph Hepburn	Bowes Seal Fast	Miller-Ford/Novi	200	113.631	4,575
5	7	34		Cliff Bergere	Noc-Out Hose Clamp	Wetteroth/Offy	200	113.528	4,375
6	9	41		Chet Miller	Boyle	Miller/Miller	200	111.921	2,438
7	4	15		Harry McQuinn*	Ziffrin	A.R.-Weil/Alfa Romeo	200	111.795	2,063
8	6	7		Frank Wearne	Bill Holabird	Shaw/Offy	200	110.818	1,788
9	18	45		Paul Russo*	Leader Card	Marchese/Miller	200	105.628	1,738
10	20	27		Tommy Hinnershitz*	Marks	Adams/Offy	200	105.152	1,538
11	24	53		Louis Tomei	H-3	Miller-Ford/Offy	200	104.437	938
12	31	55		Al Putnam*	Schoof	Wetteroth/Offy	200	101.391	763
13	26	26	R	Overton Phillips*	Phillips	Bugatti/Miller	187	Running	625
14	27	25		Joie Chitwood	Blue Crown Spark Plug	Lencki/Lencki	177	Running	620
15	30	17		Duke Nalon	Elgin Piston Pin	Maserati/Maserati	173	Running	640
16	13	14		George Connor	Boyle	Stevens/Offy	167	Transmission	660
17	12	47	R	Everett Saylor	Mark Bowles	Weil/Offy	155	Accident	605
18	3	2	W	Wilbur Shaw	Boyle	Maserati/Maserati	151	Accident	5,875
19	8	23		Billy DeVore	Hollywood PayDay Candy	Stevens/Offy	121	Rod	595
20	25	62		Tony Willman	Lyons	Stevens/Offy	117	Rod	615
21	11	42		Russ Snowberger	Hussey's Sportsman Club	Snowberger/Offy	107	Water pump	585
22	29	32		Deacon Litz	Sampson 16	Stevens/Sampson	89	Oil	555
23	22	8		Frank Brisko	Zollner Piston	Stevens/Brisko	70	Valve	600
24	5	36		Doc Williams	Indiana Fur	Cooper/Offy	68	Radiator	620
25	16	10		George Robson	Gilmore Red Lion	Weil/Duray	66	Oil leak	565
26	1	3		Mauri Rose	Elgin Piston Pin	Maserati/Maserati	60	Spark plugs	1,035
27	19	22	W	Kelly Petillo	Air Liner Sandwich Shop	Wetteroth/Offy	48	Rod	605
28	14	12		Al Miller	Miller	Miller/Miller	22	Transmission	575
29	21	9		Mel Hansen	Fageol	Miller-Ford/Offy	11	Rod	595
30	15	19		Emil Andres	Kennedy Tank	Lencki/Lencki	4	Accident	540
31	23	5		Joel Thorne	Thorne Engineering	Adams/Sparks	4	Accident	535
32	-	35		George Barringer	Miller	Miller/Miller	DNS	DNS-Gar. Fire	530
33	-	28		Sam Hanks	Tom Joyce 7-Up	Kurtis/Offy	DNS	DNS-Prac. Acc.	525

Total Purse $89,229

Time of Race: 4:20:36.24 Average Speed: 115.117 mph Margin of Victory: 1:29.95
Pole: #3 Mauri Rose (128.691, 4:39.74) Fastest Race Lap: N/A
Winning Car Owner: Lou Moore, Inc Winning Chief Mechanic: Ed Shampay Winning Tire: Firestone
Legend: R=Indianapolis 500-Mile Race Rookie; W=Indianapolis 500-Mile Race Former Winner; *=Had Relief Help
Race Notes: Mauri Rose replaced Floyd Davis in the winning car on lap 72.
Lap Leaders: Mays 1-38, Rose 39-44, Shaw 45-151, Bergere 152-161, Rose(for Davis) 162-200.
Lap Leader Summary: Shaw 1 time for 107 laps, Rose(for Davis) 1-39, Mays 1-38, Bergere 1-10, Rose 1-6.
Lead Changes: 4 among 5 drivers.

Official Box Score

30th Indianapolis 500-Mile Race at the Indianapolis Motor Speedway • Thursday, May 30, 1946

FP	SP	No.		Driver	Car Name	Chassis/Engine	Laps	Status	Total Prize Money
1	15	16		George Robson	Thorne Engineering	Adams/Sparks	200	114.820	$42,350
2	5	61	R	Jimmy Jackson	Jackson	Miller/Offy	200	114.498	13,838
3	7	29		Ted Horn	Boyle Maserati	Maserati/Maserati	200	109.759	7,988
4	11	18		Emil Andres	Elgin Piston Pin	Maserati/Maserati	200	108.902	5,425
5	12	24		Joie Chitwood*	Noc-Out Hose Clamp	Wetteroth/Offy	200	108.399	4,375
6	6	33	R	Lewis Durant	Marion Engineering	Alfa Romeo/Alfa Romeo	200	105.073	3,238
7	28	52	R	Luigi Villoresi	Maserati	Maserati/Maserati	200	100.783	2,375
8	29	7		Frank Wearne	Wolfe Motors Co., Tulsa	Shaw/Offy	197	Running	2,438
9	25	39	R	Bill Sheffler	Jack Maurer	Bromme/Offy	139	Running	2,114
10	31	17		Billy DeVore	Schoof	Wetteroth/Offy	167	Throttle	1,888
11	27	4		Mel Hansen	Ross Page	Kurtis/Duray	143	Crankshaft	1,700
12	10	25		Russ Snowberger*	Jim Hussey's Sportsman's Club	Maserati/Maserati	134	Differential	1,675
13	18	14		Harry McQuinn*	Mobilgas	Adams/Sparks	124	Out of oil	1,600
14	19	2		Ralph Hepburn	Novi Governor	Kurtis/Novi	121	Stalled	7,025
15	13	12		Al Putnam*	L.G.S. Spring Clutch	Stevens/Offy	120	Magneto	1,250
16	1	3		Cliff Bergere*	Noc-Out Clamp	Wetteroth/Offy	82	Out of oil	1,625
17	8	45	R	Duke Dinsmore	Johnston	Adams/Offy	82	Rod	1,075
18	17	5		Chet Miller*	Miller	Cooper/Offy	64	Oil line	1,000
19	16	63	R	Jimmy Wilburn	Mobiloil	A.R.-Weil/Alfa Romeo	52	Block	1,000
20	26	42	Rod	Tony Bettenhausen	Bristow-McManus	Wetteroth/Miller	47	Rod	925
21	33	59	R	Danny Kladis	Grancor V8	Miller-Ford/Ford V8	46	Towed-Disq.	875
22	32	54		Duke Nalon	Maserati	Maserati/Maserati	45	Universal joint	825
23	9	8	W	Mauri Rose	Blue Crown Spark Plug	Lencki/Lencki	40	Accident	1,675
24	30	38		George Connor	Walsh	Kurtis/Offy	38	Piston	800
25	23	48	R	Hal Robson	Phillips Miller	Bugatti/Miller	37	Rod	775
26	22	15		Louis Tomei	Boxar Tool	Stevens/Brisko	34	Oil line	750
27	21	31		Henry Banks	Automobile Shippers	Snowberger/Offy	32	Pinion shaft	725
28	20	64		Shorty Cantlon	H-3	Miller-Ford/Offy	28	Clutch	725
29	24	26		George Barringer	Tucker Torpedo	Miller/Miller	27	Gears	675
30	14	1		Rex Mays	Bowes Seal Fast	Stevens/Winfield	26	Manifold	1,025
31	3	32		Sam Hanks	Spike Jones	Stevens/Sampson	18	Oil line	675
32	4	47	R	Hal Cole	Don Lee	Alfa Romeo/Alfa Romeo	16	Fuel leak	600
33	2	10		Paul Russo	Fageol Twin Coach	Fageol/Twin Offys	16	Accident	650

Total Purse $115,679

Time of Race: 4:21:16.70 Average Speed: 114.820 mph Margin of Victory: 44.04 sec
Pole: #3 Cliff Bergere (126.471, 4:44.65) Fastest Qualifier: #2 Ralph Hepburn (133.944, 4:28.77) Fastest Race Lap: N/A
Winning Car Owner: Thorne Engineering Corp. Winning Chief Mechanic: Eddie Offut Winning Tire: Firestone
Legend: R=Indianapolis 500-Mile Race Rookie; W=Indianapolis 500-Mile Race Former Winner; *=Had Relief Help
Lap Leaders: Rose 1-8, Mays 9-11, Hepburn 12-55, G. Robson 56-68, Bergere 69-70, G. Robson 71-87, Jackson 88-92, G. Robson 93-200.
Lap Leader Summary: G. Robson 3 times for 138 laps, Hepburn 1-44, Rose 1-8, Jackson 1-5, Mays 1-3, Bergere 1-2.
Lead Changes: 7 among 6 drivers.

Official Box Score

31st Indianapolis 500-Mile Race at the Indianapolis Motor Speedway • Friday, May 30, 1947

FP	SP	No.		Driver	Car Name	Chassis/Engine	Laps	Status	Total Prize Money
1	3	27	W	Mauri Rose	Blue Crown Spark Plug	Deidt/Offy	200	116.338	$35,125
2	8	16	R	Bill Holland	Blue Crown Spark Plug	Deidt/Offy	200	116.097	31,300
3	1	1		Ted Horn	Bennett Brothers	Maserati/Maserati	200	114.997	10,115
4	4	54		Herb Ardinger*	Novi Governor Mobil	Kurtis/Novi	200	113.404	6,825
5	10	7		Jimmy Jackson	Jim Hussey	Miller/Offy	200	112.834	5,675
6	20	9		Rex Mays	Bowes Seal Fast	Kurtis/Winfield	200	111.056	4,000
7	14	33	R	Walt Brown	Permafuse	Alfa Romeo/Alfa Romeo	200	101.744	3,700
8	28	34		Cy Marshall	Tattersfield	A.R.-Weil/Alfa Romeo	197	Running	2,850
9	23	41	R	Fred Agabashian	Ross Page	Kurtis/Duray	191	Running	2,905
10	27	10		Duke Dinsmore*	Schoof	Wetteroth/Offy	167	Running	2,310
11	7	58	R	Les Anderson	Kennedy Tank	Maserati/Offy	131	Running	2,480
12	17	59	R	Pete Romcevich	Camco Motors Ford	Miller-Ford/Ford V8	167	Oil line	2,360
13	30	3		Emil Andres*	Preston Tucker Partners	Lencki/Lencki	149	Oil line	1,740
14	15	31		Frank Wearne*	Superior Industries	Miller/Offy	128	Spun out	2,020
15	9	47		Ken Fowler	Don Lee Alfa Romeo	Alfa Romeo/Alfa Romeo	119	Axle	2,050
16	18	46		Duke Nalon	Don Lee Mercedes	Mercedes/Mercedes	119	Piston	1,945
17	12	28		Roland Free	Bristow-McManus	Wetteroth/Miller	86	Rod	1,450
18	25	29		Tony Bettenhausen	Belanger	Stevens/Offy	79	Gear train	1,130
19	6	25		Russ Snowberger	Federal Engineering	Maserati/Maserati	73	Oil pump	1,500
20	16	52		Hal Robson	Palmer	Adams/Offy	67	Universal joint	1,595
21	2	18		Cliff Bergere	Novi Governor Mobil	Kurtis/Novi	63	Piston	3,815
22	22	8		Joie Chitwood	Peters	Wetteroth/Offy	50	Gears	1,135
23	5	24		Shorty Cantlon	Automobile Shippers	Snowberger/Miller	40	Accident	1,505
24	26	43		Henry Banks	Federal Engineering	Miller-Ford/Offy	36	Lost oil	1,250
25	19	66		Al Miller	Preston Tucker	Miller/Miller	33	Magneto	1,370
26	13	14		George Connor	Walsh	Kurtis/Offy	32	Fuel leak	1,465
27	29	38		Mel Hansen	Flavell-Duffy	Adams/Sparks	31	Pushed-disq.	860
28	21	15		Paul Russo	Wolfe Motors, Tulsa	Shaw/Offy	25	Accident	1,080
29	24	44	R	Charlie Van Acker	Preston Tucker Partners	Stevens/Lencki	24	Accident	800
30	11	53	R	Milt Fankhouser	Jack Maurer	Stevens/Offy	15	Stalled	1,070

Total Purse $137,425

Time of Race: 4:17:52.17 Average Speed: 116.338 mph Margin of Victory: 32.12 sec
Pole: #1 Ted Horn (126.564, 4:44.44) Fastest Qualifier: #16 Bill Holland (128.755, 4:39.60) Fastest Race Lap: N/A
Winning Car Owner: Lou Moore Winning Chief Mechanic: Lou Moore Winning Tire: Firestone
Legend: R=Indianapolis 500-Mile Race Rookie; W=Indianapolis 500-Mile Race Former Winner; *=Had Relief Help
Lap Leaders: Bergere 1-23, Holland 24-59, Rose 60-85, Holland 86-192, Rose 193-200.
Lap Leader Summary: Holland 2 times for 143 laps, Rose 2-34, Bergere 1-23.
Lead Changes: 4 among 3 drivers.

Official Box Score

32nd Indianapolis 500-Mile Race at the Indianapolis Motor Speedway • Monday, May 31, 1948

FP	SP	No.		Driver	Car Name	Chassis/Engine	Laps	Status	Total Prize Money
1	3	3	W	Mauri Rose	Blue Crown Spark Plug	Deidt/Offy	200	119.814	$42,800
2	2	2		Bill Holland	Blue Crown Spark Plug	Deidt/Offy	200	119.147	19,100
3	11	54		Duke Nalon	Novi Grooved Piston	Kurtis/Novi	200	118.034	15,675
4	5	1		Ted Horn	Bennett Brothers	Maserati/Maserati	200	117.844	16,175
5	21	35	R	Mack Hellings	Don Lee	KK2000/Offy	200	113.361	7,675
6	14	63		Hal Cole	City of Tacoma	KK2000/Offy	200	111.587	5,425
7	28	91	R	Lee Wallard	Iddings	Meyer/Offy	200	109.177	5,040
8	27	33	R	Johnny Mauro*	Phil Kraft Alfa Romeo	Alfa Romeo/Alfa Romeo	198	Running	4,115
9	23	7		Tommy Hinnershitz	Kurtis-Kraft	Kurtis/Offy	198	Running	4,270
10	4	61		Jimmy Jackson	Howard Keck	Deidt/Offy	193	Left spindle	4,120
11	12	4		Charlie Van Acker	City of South Bend	Stevens/Offy	192	Running	3,120
12	20	19		Billy DeVore	Pat Clancy (6 Wheels)	Kurtis/Offy	190	Running	2,930
13	8	98	R	Johnny Mantz	Agajanian	KK2000/Offy	185	Running	2,230
14	22	6		Tony Bettenhausen	Belanger Motors	Stevens/Offy	167	Clutch	2,560
15	18	64		Hal Robson	Palmer Construction	Adams/Offy	164	Valve	1,990
16	7	36	R	Bill Cantrell	Fageol Twin Coach	Stevens/Fageol	161	Steering	1,870
17	10	55		Joie Chitwood*	Nyquist	Shaw/Offy	138	Fuel leak	2,375
18	24	53		Bill Sheffler	Jack Maurer	Bromme/Offy	132	Spark plugs	1,830
19	1	5		Rex Mays	Bowes Seal Fast	Kurtis/Winfield	129	Fuel leak	5,775
20	19	31		Chet Miller*	Don Lee Mercedes	Mercedes/Mercedes	108	Oil trouble	2,120
21	13	52	R	Jack McGrath	Sheffler Offy	Bromme/Offy	70	Stalled	1,865
22	29	16	R	Duane Carter	Belanger Motors	Wetteroth/Offy	59	Accident	1,960
23	32	26		Fred Agabashian	Ross Page	Kurtis/Duray	58	Oil line	1,580
24	9	34		Les Anderson	Kennedy Tank	Kurtis/Offy	58	Gears	1,550
25	33	17		Mel Hansen	Schafer Gear Works	Adams/Sparks	42	Disqualified	1,420
26	15	76		Sam Hanks	Flavell	Adams/Sparks	34	Clutch	1,490
27	30	51	R	Spider Webb	Fowle Brothers	Bromme/Offy	27	Oil line	1,685
28	17	9		George Connor	Bennett Brothers	Stevens/Miller	24	Drive shaft	1,330
29	6	74		Doc Williams	Clarke Motors	Cooper/Offy	19	Ignition	1,300
30	31	86	R	Mike Salay	Terman Marine Supply	Wetteroth/Offy	13	Stalled	1,470
31	16	8		Emil Andres	Tuffy's Offy	KK2000/Offy	11	Steering	1,340
32	25	25		Paul Russo	Federal Engineering	Maserati/Maserati	7	Oil leak	1,310
33	26	65		Harry McQuinn	Frank Lynch Motors	Maserati/Maserati	1	Supercharger	1,180

Total Purse $170,675

Time of Race: 4:10:23.33 Average Speed: 119.814 mph Margin of Victory: 1:24.07
Pole: #5 Rex Mays (130.577, 4:35.70) Fastest Qualifier: #54 Duke Nalon (131.603, 4:33.55) Fastest Race Lap: N/A
Winning Car Owner: Lou Moore Winning Chief Mechanic: Roscoe Ford Winning Tire: Firestone
Legend: R=Indianapolis 500-Mile Race Rookie; W=Indianapolis 500-Mile Race Former Winner; *=Had Relief Help
Lap Leaders: Mays 1-17, Horn 18-72, Mays 73-91, Nalon 92-100, Rose 101-123, Horn 124-142, Rose 143-200.
Lap Leader Summary: Rose 2 times for 81 laps, Horn 2-74, Mays 2-36, Nalon 1-9. Lead Changes: 6 among 4 drivers. Lead Changes: 6 among 4 drivers.

Official Box Score

33rd Indianapolis 500-Mile Race at the Indianapolis Motor Speedway • Monday, May 30, 1949

FP	SP	No.		Driver	Car Name	Chassis/Engine	Laps	Status	Total Prize Money
1	4	7		Bill Holland	Blue Crown Spark Plug	Deidt/Offy	200	121.327	$51,575
2	12	12	R	Johnnie Parsons	Kurtis-Kraft	Kurtis/Offy	200	119.785	18,250
3	6	22		George Connor	Blue Crown Spark Plug	Lesovsky/Offy	200	119.595	11,675
4	13	2	R	Myron Fohr	Marchese	Marchese/Offy	200	118.791	8,575
5	16	77		Joie Chitwood	Wolfe	KK2000/Offy	200	118.757	6,950
6	7	61		Jimmy Jackson	Howard Keck	Deidt/Offy	200	117.870	5,625
7	9	98		Johnny Mantz	Agajanian	KK2000/Offy	200	117.142	4,690
8	19	19		Paul Russo	Tuffy's Offy	Silnes/Offy	200	111.862	4,940
9	32	9		Emil Andres*	Tuffy's Offy	Silnes/Offy	197	Running	4,420
10	24	71	R	Norm Houser	Troy Oil Co.	Langley/Offy	181	Running	4,075
11	21	68	R	Jim Rathmann	Pioneer Auto Repair	Wetteroth/Offy	175	Running	3,195
12	18	64	R	Troy Ruttman	Carter	Wetteroth/Offy	151	Running	3,150
13	10	3	W	Mauri Rose	Blue Crown Spark Plug	Deidt/Offy	192	Magneto strap	2,605
14	5	17		Duane Carter	Belanger Motors	Stevens/Offy	182	Steering	2,610
15	15	29		Duke Dinsmore	Norm Olson	Olson/Offy	174	Radius rod	2,565
16	14	8		Mack Hellings	Don Lee	KK2000/Offy	172	Valves	2,570
17	22	4		Bill Sheffler	Sheffler	Bromme/Offy	160	Rod	2,175
18	28	32	R	Johnny McDowell	Iddings	Meyer/Offy	142	Magneto	2,005
19	11	14		Hal Cole	Gancor	KK2000/Offy	117	Rod bearing	1,975
20	25	38	R	George Fonder*	Ray Brady	Adams/Sparks	116	Valve	1,945
21	30	74		Bill Cantrell	Kennedy Tank	Kurtis/Offy	95	Drive shaft	2,315
22	17	57	R	Jackie Holmes	Pat Clancy (6 Wheels)	Kurtis/Offy	65	Drive shaft	2,410
23	20	6		Lee Wallard	IRC Maserati	Maserati/Maserati	55	Gears	4,405
24	29	69	R	Bayliss Levrett	Wynn's Oil	KK2000/Offy	52	Drain plug	2,375
25	2	5		Rex Mays	Novi Mobil	Kurtis/Novi	48	Engine	3,470
26	3	33		Jack McGrath	City of Tacoma	KK2000/Offy	39	Oil pump	2,115
27	31	15		Fred Agabashian	IRC Maserati	Maserati/Maserati	38	Overheating	2,035
28	33	52	R	Manuel Ayulo	Sheffler	Bromme/Offy	24	Rod	1,805
29	1	54		Duke Nalon	Novi Mobil	Kurtis/Novi	23	Accident	5,650
30	23	18		Sam Hanks	Love Machine & Tool	KK2000/Offy	20	Oil leak	1,645
31	27	10		Charlie Van Acker	Redmer	Stevens/Offy	10	Accident	1,615
32	8	26	R	George Lynch	Automobile Shippers	Rassey/Offy	1	Accident	1,585
33	26	37		Spider Webb	Grancor	Bromme/Offy	0	DNS-Transmission	1,555

Total Purse $178,550

Time of Race: 4:07:15.97 Average Speed: 121.327 mph Margin of Victory: 3:11.00
Pole: #54 Duke Nalon (132.939, 4:30.80) Fastest Race Lap: N/A
Winning Car Owner: Lou Moore Winning Chief Mechanic: Charles Marant Winning Tire: Firestone
Legend: R=Indianapolis 500-Mile Race Rookie; W=Indianapolis 500-Mile Race Former Winner; *=Had Relief Help
Lap Leaders: Nalon 1-23, Mays 24-35, Wallard 36-54, Holland 55-200.
Lap Leader Summary: Holland 1 time for 146 laps, Nalon 1-23, Wallard 1-19, Mays 1-12. Lead Changes: 3 among 4 drivers.

Official Box Score

34th Indianapolis 500-Mile Race at the Indianapolis Motor Speedway • Tuesday, May 30, 1950

FP	SP	No.	Rookie	Driver	Car Name	Chassis/Engine	Laps	Status	Total Prize Money
1	5	1		Johnnie Parsons	Wynn's Friction Proofing	Kurtis/Offy	138 (Rain)	124.022	$57,459
2	10	3	W	Bill Holland	Blue Crown Spark Plug	Deidt/Offy	137	Running	21,899
3	3	31	W	Mauri Rose	Howard Keck	Deidt/Offy	137	Running	15,269
4	12	54	R	Cecil Green	John Zink	KK3000/Offy	137	Running	10,964
5	9	17		Joie Chitwood*	Wolfe	KK2000/Offy	136	Running	8,789
6	23	8		Lee Wallard	Blue Crown Spark Plug	Moore/Offy	136	Running	6,864
7	1	98	R	Walt Faulkner	Grant Piston Ring	KK2000/Offy	135	Running	7,664
8	4	5		George Connor	Blue Crown Spark Plug	Lesovsky/Offy	135	Running	5,039
9	19	7		Paul Russo	Russo-Nichels	Nichels/Offy	135	Running	4,989
10	11	59	R	Pat Flaherty	Granatelli-Sabourin	KK3000/Offy	135	Running	4,639
11	16	2		Myron Fohr	Bardahl	Marchese/Offy	133	Running	3,734
12	13	18		Duane Carter	Belanger Motors	Stevens/Offy	133	Running	3,464
13	26	15		Mack Hellings	Tuffy's Offy	Silnes/Offy	132	Running	2,979
14	6	49		Jack McGrath	Hinkle	KK3000/Offy	131	Accident	2,799
15	24	55		Troy Ruttman	Bowes Seal Fast	Lesovsky/Offy	130	Running	2,979
16	31	75	R	Gene Hartley	Troy Oil	Langley/Offy	128	Running	2,509
17	27	22	R	Jimmy Davies	Pat Clancy	Ewing/Offy	128	Running	2,339
18	33	62		Johnny McDowell	Pete Wales	KK2000/Offy	128	Running	2,769
19	20	4		Walt Brown	Tuffy's Offy	Silnes/Offy	127	Running	2,339
20	14	21		Spider Webb	Fadely-Anderson	Maserati/Offy	126	Running	2,509
21	15	81	R	Jerry Hoyt	Morris	KK2000/Offy	125	Running	2,379
22	29	27	R	Walt Ader	Sampson	Rae/Offy	123	Running	2,149
23	30	77		Jackie Holmes	Norm Olson	Olson/Offy	123	Accident	2,119
24	28	76		Jim Rathmann	Pioneer Auto Repair	Wetteroth/Offy	122	Running	2,089
25	21	12		Henry Banks*	I.R.C.	Maserati/Offy	112	Oil line	2,059
26	22	67	R	Bill Schindler	Automobile Shippers	Rassey/Offy	111	Universal joint	2,604
27	17	24		Bayliss Levrett*	Palmer	Adams/Offy	108	Oil pressure	2,424
28	2	28		Fred Agabashian	Wynn's Friction Proofing	KK3000/Offy	64	Oil line	2,444
29	32	61		Jimmy Jackson	Cummins Diesel	Kurtis/Cummins	52	Supercharger	1,939
30	25	23		Sam Hanks	Merz Engineering	KK2000/Offy	42	Oil pressure	2,134
31	8	14		Tony Bettenhausen	Blue Crown Spark Plug	Deidt/Offy	30	Wheel	1,879
32	18	45	R	Dick Rathmann	City of Glendale	Watson/Offy	25	Stalled	2,149
33	7	69		Duke Dinsmore	Brown Motor Co.	KK2000/Offy	10	Oil leak	1,844

Total Purse $200,207

Time of Race: 2:46:55.97 Average Speed: 124.022 mph Margin of Victory: Under Caution
Pole: #98 Walt Faulkner (134.343, 4:27.97) Fastest Race Lap: N/A
Winning Car Owner: Kurtis-Kraft, Inc. Winning Chief Mechanic: Harry Stephens Winning Tire: Firestone
Legend: R=Indianapolis 500-Mile Race Rookie; W=Indianapolis 500-Mile Race Former Winner; *=Had Relief Help
Race Notes: Race stopped on lap 138 due to rain.
Lap Leaders: Rose 1-9, Parsons 10-32, Rose 33, Parsons 34-104, Rose 105-109, Holland 110-117, Parsons 118-138.
Lap Leader Summary: Parsons 3 times for 115 laps, Rose 3-15, Holland 1-8.
Lead Changes: 6 among 3 drivers.

Official Box Score

35th Indianapolis 500-Mile Race at the Indianapolis Motor Speedway • Wednesday, May 30, 1951

FP	SP	No.		Driver	Car Name	Chassis/Engine	Laps	Status	Total Prize Money
1	2	99		Lee Wallard	Belanger Motors	Kurtis/Offy	200	126.244	$63,612
2	7	83	R	Mike Nazaruk	Jim Robbins	Kurtis/Offy	200	125.302	21,362
3	3	9		Jack McGrath*	Hinkle	KK3000/Offy	200	124.745	14,962
4	31	57	R	Andy Linden	Leitenberger	Silnes-Sherman/Offy	200	123.812	10,012
5	29	52	R	Bobby Ball	Blakely Oil	Schroeder/Offy	200	123.709	8,612
6	17	1		Henry Banks	Blue Crown Spark Plug	Moore/Offy	200	123.304	6,962
7	24	68	R	Carl Forberg	Automobile Shippers	KK3000/Offy	193	Running	5,862
8	4	27		Duane Carter	Mobilgas	Deidt/Offy	180	Running	5,162
9	9	5		Tony Bettenhausen	Mobiloil	Deidt/Offy	178	Spun	4,662
10	1	18		Duke Nalon	Novi Purelube	Kurtis/Novi	151	Stalled	5,062
11	22	69	R	Gene Force	Brown Motor Co.	KK2000/Offy	142	Vibration	3,182
12	12	25		Sam Hanks	Schmidt	KK3000/Offy	135	Rod	3,412
13	16	10		Bill Schindler	Chapman	KK2000/Offy	129	Rod	3,142
14	5	16	W	Mauri Rose	Pennzoil	Deidt/Offy	126	Accident	3,022
15	14	2		Walt Faulkner	Agajanian Grant Piston Ring	Kuzma/Offy	123	Crankshaft	4,552
16	27	76		Jimmy Davies	Parks	Silnes-Pawl/Offy	110	Drive gears	5,482
17	11	59		Fred Agabashian	Granatelli-Bardahl	KK3000/Offy	109	Clutch	2,862
18	15	73	R	Carl Scarborough	McNamara	KK2000/Offy	100	Axle	2,642
19	33	71	R	Bill Mackey	Karl Hall	Stevens/Offy	97	Clutch shaft	2,212
20	19	8	R	Chuck Stevenson	Bardahl	Marchese/Offy	93	Caught fire	2,182
21	8	3	W	Johnnie Parsons	Wynn's Friction Proofing	KK3000/Offy	87	Magneto	2,252
22	10	4		Cecil Green	John Zink	KK3000/Offy	80	Piston	2,622
23	6	98		Troy Ruttman	Agajanian Featherweight	KK2000/Offy	78	Crankshaft	2,092
24	32	6		Duke Dinsmore	Brown Motors Co.	Schroeder/Offy	73	Overheating	2,162
25	28	32		Chet Miller	Novi Purelube	Kurtis/Novi	56	Ignition	2,532
26	13	44		Walt Brown	Federal Engineering	KK3000/Offy	55	Magneto	2,302
27	25	48	R	Rodger Ward	Deck Manufacturing Co.	Bromme/Offy	34	Oil line	2,472
28	18	23	R	Cliff Griffith	Morris	KK2000/Offy	30	Rear axle	2,042
29	20	81	R	Bill Vukovich	Central Excavating	Trevis/Offy	29	Oil tank	1,912
30	21	22		George Connor	Blue Crown Spark Plug	Lesovsky/Offy	29	Drive shaft	1,882
31	23	19		Mack Hellings	Tuffanelli-Derrico	Deidt/Offy	18	Piston	1,852
32	26	12		Johnny McDowell	W & J	Maserati/Offy	15	Fuel tank	2,222
33	30	26	R	Joe James	Bob Estes Lincoln-Mercury	Watson/Offy	8	Drive shaft	2,092

Total Purse $207,396

Time of Race: 3:57:38.05 Average Speed: 126.244 mph Margin of Victory: 1:47.26
Pole: #18 Duke Nalon (136.498, 4:23.74) Fastest Qualifier: #2 Walt Faulkner (136.872, 4:23.02)
Fastest Race Lap: #99 Lee Wallard (Race Lap 23, 133.809 mph, 1:07.26 sec.)
Winning Car Owner: Murrell Belanger Winning Chief Mechanic: George Salih Winning Tire: Firestone
Legend: R=Indianapolis 500-Mile Race Rookie; W=Indianapolis 500-Mile Race Former Winner; *=Had Relief Help
Lap Leaders: Wallard 1-2, McGrath 3-4, Wallard 5-6, McGrath 7-15, Wallard 16-26, Green 27, Wallard 28-51, Davies 52-76, Green 77-80, Wallard 81-200.
Lap Leader Summary: Wallard 5 times for 159 laps, Davies 1-25, McGrath 2-11, Green 2-5. Lead Changes: 9 among 4 drivers.

Official Box Score

36th Indianapolis 500-Mile Race at the Indianapolis Motor Speedway • Friday, May 30, 1952

FP	SP	No.		Driver	Car Name	Chassis/Engine	Laps	Status	Total Prize Money
1	7	98		Troy Ruttman	Agajanian	Kuzma/Offy	200	128.922	$61,743
2	10	59		Jim Rathmann	Grancor-Wynn's Oil	KK3000/Offy	200	126.723	24,368
3	5	18		Sam Hanks	Bardahl	KK3000/Offy	200	125.580	14,768
4	6	1		Duane Carter	Belanger Motors	Lesovsky/Offy	200	125.259	11,818
5	20	33	R	Art Cross	Bowes Seal Fast	KK4000/Offy	200	124.292	9,718
6	21	77	R	Jimmy Bryan	Schmidt	KK3000/Offy	200	123.914	7,468
7	23	37	R	Jimmy Reece	John Zink	KK4000/Offy	200	123.312	6,368
8	14	54		George Connor	Federal Engineering	KK3000/Offy	200	122.595	6,118
9	9	22		Cliff Griffith	Tom Sarafoff	KK2000/Offy	200	122.402	5,768
10	31	5	W	Johnnie Parsons	Jim Robbins	Kurtis/Offy	200	121.789	5,518
11	3	4		Jack McGrath	Hinkle	KK3000/Offy	200	121.428	4,263
12	26	29	R	Jim Rigsby	Bob Estes	Watson/Offy	200	120.587	3,193
13	16	14		Joe James	Bardahl	KK4000/Offy	200	120.108	2,923
14	15	7		Bill Schindler	Chapman	Stevens/Offy	200	119.280	2,903
15	13	65		George Fonder	Leitenberger	Silnes-Sherman/Offy	197	Running	2,683
16	24	81	R	Eddie Johnson	Central Excavating	Trevis/Offy	193	Running	2,663
17	8	26		Bill Vukovich	Fuel Injection	KK500A/Offy	191	Steering	18,693
18	11	16		Chuck Stevenson	Springfield Welding/Clay Smith	KK4000/Offy	187	Running	2,623
19	12	2		Henry Banks	Blue Crown Spark Plug	Lesovsky/Offy	184	Running	2,693
20	28	8		Manuel Ayulo	Coast Grain Co.	Lesovsky/Offy	184	Running	2,763
21	33	31		Johnny McDowell	McDowell	Kurtis/Offy	182	Running	2,333
22	29	48		Spider Webb	Granatelli Racing Enterprises	Bromme/Offy	162	Oil line	2,603
23	22	34		Rodger Ward	Federal Engineering	KK4000/Offy	130	Oil leak	2,273
24	30	27		Tony Bettenhausen	Blue Crown Spark Plug	Deidt/Offy	93	Stalled	2,443
25	4	36		Duke Nalon	Novi Pure Oil	Kurtis/Novi	84	Supercharger	2,413
26	32	73	R	Bob Sweikert	McNamara	KK2000/Offy	77	Differential	2,183
27	1	28		Fred Agabashian	Cummins Diesel	Kurtis/Cummins	71	Supercharger	2,653
28	18	67		Gene Hartley	Mel-Rae	KK4000/Offy	65	Wheels	2,123
29	25	93	R	Bob Scott	Morris	KK2000/Offy	49	Drive shaft	2,093
30	27	21		Chet Miller	Novi Pure Oil	Kurtis/Novi	41	Supercharger	3,663
31	19	12	R	Alberto Ascari	Ferrari	Ferrari/Ferrari	40	Spun out	1,983
32	17	55		Bobby Ball	Ansted Rotary	Stevens/Offy	34	Gear case	2,003
33	2	9		Andy Linden	Miracle Power	KK4000/Offy	20	Sump pump	2,273

Total Purse $230,094

Time of Race: 3:52:41.88 Average Speed: 128.922 mph Margin of Victory: 4:2.36

Pole: #28 Fred Agabashian (138.010, 4:20.85) Fastest Qualifier: #21 Chet Miller (139.034, 4:18.93)

Fastest Race Lap: #26 Bill Vukovich (Race Lap 8, 135.135 mph, 1:06.60 sec.)

Winning Car Owner: J. C. Agajanian Winning Chief Mechanic: Clay Smith Winning Tire: Firestone Rookie of Year: Art Cross

Legend: R=Indianapolis 500-Mile Race Rookie; W=Indianapolis 500-Mile Race Former Winner

Lap Leaders: McGrath 1-6, Vukovich 7-11, Ruttman 12, Vukovich 13-61, Ruttman 62-82, Vukovich 83-134, Ruttman 135-147, Vukovich 148-191, Ruttman 192-200.

Lap Leader Summary: Vukovich 4 times for 150 laps, Ruttman 4-44, McGrath 1-6.

Lead Changes: 8 among 3 drivers.

Official Box Score

37th Indianapolis 500-Mile Race at the Indianapolis Motor Speedway • Saturday, May 30, 1953

FP	SP	No.	Rookie	Driver	Car Name	Chassis/Engine	Laps	Status	Total Prize Money
1	1	14		Bill Vukovich	Fuel Injection	KK500A/Offy	200	127.740	$89,497
2	12	16		Art Cross	Springfield Welding/Clay Smith	KK4000/Offy	200	126.827	27,297
3	9	3		Sam Hanks*	Bardahl	KK4000/Offy	200	126.465	16,422
4	2	59		Fred Agabashian*	Grancor-Elgin Piston Pin	KK500B/Offy	200	126.219	12,947
5	3	5		Jack McGrath	Hinkle	KK4000/Offy	200	124.556	10,622
6	21	48	R	Jimmy Daywalt	Sumar	KK3000/Offy	200	124.379	8,197
7	25	2		Jim Rathmann*	Travelon Trailer	KK500B/Offy	200	124.072	6,847
8	20	12	R	Ernie McCoy	Chapman	Stevens/Offy	200	123.404	5,947
9	6	98		Tony Bettenhausen*	Agajanian	Kuzma/Offy	196	Accident	5,647
10	32	53		Jimmy Davies	Pat Clancy	KK500B/Offy	193	Running	5,547
11	26	9		Duke Nalon	Novi Governor	Kurtis/Novi	191	Spun out	3,317
12	19	73		Carl Scarborough*	McNamara	KK2000/Offy	190	Running	3,147
13	4	88		Manuel Ayulo	Schmidt	Kuzma/Offy	184	Rod	3,177
14	31	8		Jimmy Bryan	Blakely Oil	Schroeder/Offy	183	Running	3,057
15	28	49	W	Bill Holland*	Crawford	KK500B/Offy	177	Cam gear	3,237
16	10	92		Rodger Ward*	M.A. Walker Electric	Kurtis/Offy	177	Stalled	2,917
17	14	23		Walt Faulkner*	Automobile Shippers	KK500A/Offy	176	Running	2,497
18	22	22	R	Marshall Teague	Hart Fullerton	KK4000/Offy	169	Oil Leak	2,377
19	18	62		Spider Webb*	Lubri-Loy	KK3000/Offy	166	Oil Leak	2,347
20	29	51		Bob Sweikert	Dean Van Lines	Kuzma/Offy	151	Radius rod	2,717
21	23	83		Mike Nazaruk	Kalamazoo	Turner/Offy	146	Stalled	2,287
22	24	77		Pat Flaherty	Schmidt	KK3000/Offy	115	Accident	2,257
23	7	55		Jerry Hoyt*	John Zink	KK4000/Offy	107	Overheating	2,227
24	27	4		Duane Carter	Miracle Power	Lesovsky/Offy	94	Ignition	2,197
25	17	7		Paul Russo	Federal Engineering	KK3000/Offy	89	Magneto	2,167
26	8	21	W	Johnnie Parsons	Belond Equa-Flow	KK500B/Offy	86	Crankshaft	2,637
27	15	38	R	Don Freeland	Bob Estes	Watson/Offy	76	Accident	2,107
28	13	41		Gene Hartley	Federal Engineering	KK4000/Offy	53	Accident	2,077
29	16	97		Chuck Stevenson	Agajanian	Kuzma/Offy	42	Fuel Leak	2,047
30	30	99	R	Cal Niday	Miracle Power	Kurtis/Offy	30	Magneto	2,317
31	11	29		Bob Scott	Belond Equa-Flow	Bromme/Offy	14	Oil Leak	2,187
32	33	56	R	Johnny Thomson	Dr. Sabourin	Del Roy-Allen/Offy	6	Ignition	1,907
33	5	32		Andy Linden	Cop-Sil-Loy	Stevens/Offy	3	Accident	2,127

Total Purse $246,301

Time of Race: 3:53:01.69 Average Speed: 127.740 mph Margin of Victory: 3:30.87

Pole: #14 Bill Vukovich (138.392, 4:20.13) Fastest Race Lap: #14 Bill Vukovich (Race Lap 27, 135.870 mph, 1:06.24 sec.)

Winning Car Owner: Howard Keck Co. Winning Chief Mechanic: Frank Coon/Jim Travers Winning Tire: Firestone Rookie of Year: Jimmy Daywalt

Legend: R=Indianapolis 500-Mile Race Rookie; W=Indianapolis 500-Mile Race Former Winner; *=Had Relief Help

Lap Leaders: Vukovich 1-48, Agabashian 49, J. Rathmann 50, Hanks 51-53, Vukovich 54-200.

Lap Leader Summary: Vukovich 2 times for 195 laps, Hanks 1-3, Agabashian 1-1, J. Rathmann 1-1. Lead Changes: 4 among 4 drivers.

Official Box Score

38th Indianapolis 500-Mile Race at the Indianapolis Motor Speedway • Monday, May 31, 1954

FP	SP	No.		Driver	Car Name	Chassis/Engine	Laps	Status	Total Prize Money
1	19	14	W	Bill Vukovich	Fuel Injection	KK500A/Offy	200	130.840	$74,935
2	3	9		Jimmy Bryan	Dean Van Lines	Kuzma/Offy	200	130.178	35,885
3	1	2		Jack McGrath	Hinkle	KK500C/Offy	200	130.086	27,410
4	11	34	W	Troy Ruttman*	Automobile Shippers	KK500A/Offy	200	129.218	12,710
5	14	73		Mike Nazaruk	McNamara	KK500C/Offy	200	128.923	10,935
6	24	77		Fred Agabashian	Merz Engineering	KK500C/Offy	200	128.711	8,035
7	6	7		Don Freeland	Bob Estes	Phillips/Offy	200	128.474	6,885
8	32	5		Paul Russo*	Ansted Rotary	KK500A/Offy	200	128.037	6,260
9	25	28	R	Larry Crockett	Federal Engineering	KK3000/Offy	200	126.899	6,985
10	13	24		Cal Niday	Jim Robbins	Stevens/Offy	200	126.895	6,310
11	27	45		Art Cross*	Bardahl	KK4000/Offy	200	126.232	5,255
12	5	98		Chuck Stevenson*	Agajanian	Kuzma/Offy	199	Running	3,710
13	22	88		Manuel Ayulo	Schmidt	KK500C/Offy	197	Running	3,465
14	9	17		Bob Sweikert	Lutes	KK4000/Offy	197	Running	3,345
15	8	16		Duane Carter*	Automobile Shippers	KK4000/Offy	196	Running	3,225
16	20	32		Ernie McCoy	Crawford	KK500B/Offy	194	Running	3,105
17	7	25		Jimmy Reece	Malloy	Pankratz/Offy	194	Running	2,985
18	31	27	R	Ed Elisian*	Chapman	Stevens/Offy	193	Running	2,865
19	33	71	R	Frank Armi*	Martin Brothers	Silnes/Offy	193	Running	2,835
20	10	1		Sam Hanks*	Bardahl	KK4000/Offy	191	Spun out	2,955
21	12	35	R	Pat O'Connor	Hopkins	KK500C/Offy	181	Spun out	3,275
22	16	12		Rodger Ward*	Dr. Sabourin	Allen/Offy	172	Stalled	2,945
23	17	31		Gene Hartley*	John Zink	KK4000/Offy	168	Clutch	2,815
24	4	43		Johnny Thomson*	Chapman	Nichels/Offy	165	Stalled	2,885
25	23	74		Andy Linden*	Brown Motor Co.	Schroeder/Offy	165	Torsion bar	3,655
26	30	99		Jerry Hoyt	Belanger Motors	Kurtis/Offy	130	Engine	2,625
27	2	19		Jimmy Daywalt	Sumar	KK500C/Offy	111	Accident	4,445
28	28	38		Jim Rathmann*	Bardahl	KK500C/Offy	110	Accident	2,765
29	21	10		Tony Bettenhausen	Mel Wiggers	KK500C/Offy	105	Bearing	2,535
30	29	65		Spider Webb*	Advance Muffler	Bromme/Offy	104	Fuel pump	2,605
31	26	33	R	Len Duncan*	Brady	Schroeder/Offy	101	Brake cylinder	2,875
32	15	15	W	Johnnie Parsons	Belond Equa-Flow Exhaust	KK500C/Offy	79	Engine died	2,745
33	18	51	R	Bill Homeier	Jones & Maley	KK500C/Offy	74	Pit Accident	2,415

Total Purse $268,680

Time of Race: 3:49:17.27 Average Speed: 130.840 mph Margin of Victory: 1:09.99

Pole: #2 Jack McGrath (141.033, 4:15.26) Fastest Race Lap: #2 Jack McGrath (Race Lap 29, 140.537 mph, 1:04.04 sec.)

Winning Car Owner: Howard Keck Co. Winning Chief Mechanic: Frank Coon/Jim Travers Winning Tire: Firestone Rookie of Year: Larry Crockett

Legend: R=Indianapolis 500-Mile Race Rookie; W=Indianapolis 500-Mile Race Former Winner; *=Had Relief Help

Lap Leaders: McGrath 1-44, Daywalt 45-50, Cross 51-54, Daywalt 55, Cross 56-59, Daywalt 60, Vukovich 61, Hanks 62, Bryan 63-88, McGrath 89-91, Vukovich 92-129, Bryan 130-149, Vukovich 150-200.

Lap Leader Summary: Vukovich 3 times for 90 laps, McGrath 2-47, Bryan 2-46, Daywalt 3-8, Cross 2-8, Hanks 1-1. Lead Changes: 12 among 6 drivers.

Official Box Score

39th Indianapolis 500-Mile Race at the Indianapolis Motor Speedway • Monday, May 30, 1955

FP	SP	No.		Driver	Car Name	Chassis/Engine	Laps	Status	Total Prize Money
1	14	6		Bob Sweikert	John Zink	KK500D/Offy	200	128.209	$76,139
2	2	10		Tony Bettenhausen*	Chapman	KK500C/Offy	200	126.733	30,089
3	10	15		Jimmy Davies	Bardahl	KK500B/Offy	200	126.299	16,989
4	33	44		Johnny Thomson	Schmidt	Kuzma/Offy	200	126.241	12,889
5	7	77		Walt Faulkner*	Merz Engineerng	KK500C/Offy	200	125.377	10,764
6	8	19		Andy Linden	Massaglia	KK4000/Offy	200	125.022	8,514
7	16	71	R	Al Herman	Martin Brothers	Silnes/Offy	200	124.794	7,564
8	19	29		Pat O'Connor	Ansted Rotary	KK500D/Offy	200	124.644	6,414
9	17	48		Jimmy Daywalt	Sumar	Kurtis/Offy	200	124.401	6,414
10	12	89		Pat Flaherty	Dunn Engineering	KK500B/Offy	200	124.086	6,114
11	18	98		Duane Carter	Agajanian	Kuzma/Offy	197	Running	3,884
12	25	41	R	Chuck Weyant	Federal Engineering	KK3000/Offy	196	Running	3,614
13	32	83		Eddie Johnson	McNamara	Trevis/Offy	196	Running	3,344
14	20	33		Jim Rathmann	Belond Miracle Power	Epperly/Offy	191	Running	3,324
15	21	12		Don Freeland	Bob Estes	Phillips/Offy	178	Transmission	4,054
16	9	22		Cal Niday	D-A Lubricant	KK500B/Offy	170	Accident	3,484
17	24	99		Art Cross	Belanger Motors	KK500D/Offy	168	Rod	6,664
18	31	81	R	Shorty Templeman	Central Excavating	Trevis/Offy	142	Transmission	2,744
19	6	8		Sam Hanks	Jones & Maley	KK500C/Offy	134	Transmission	2,914
20	28	31	R	Keith Andrews	McDaniel	Schroeder/Offy	120	Drop. In pit	2,684
21	27	16	W	Johnnie Parsons	Trio Brass Foundry	KK500D/Offy	119	Magneto	2,654
22	13	37	R	Eddie Russo	Dr. Sabourin	Allen/Offy	112	Ignition	2,724
23	23	49	R	Ray Crawford	Crawford	KK500B/Offy	111	Valve	2,894
24	11	1		Jimmy Bryan	Dean Van Lines	Kuzma/Offy	90	Fuel Pump	7,514
25	5	4	W	Bill Vukovich	Hopkins	KK500C/Offy	56	Accident	10,884
26	3	3		Jack McGrath	Hinkle	KK500C/Offy	54	Magneto	6,354
27	22	42	R	Al Keller	Sam Traylor	KK2000/Offy	54	Accident	2,874
28	30	27		Rodger Ward	Aristo Blue	Kuzma/Offy	53	Accident	2,444
29	26	39	R	Johnny Boyd	Sumar	KK500C/Offy	53	Accident	2,414
30	29	68		Ed Elisian	Westwood Gauge & Tool	KK4000/Offy	53	Stopped	2,734
31	1	23		Jerry Hoyt	Jim Robbins	Stevens/Offy	40	Oil leak	2,854
32	4	14		Fred Agabashian	Federal Engineering	KK500D/Offy	39	Spun	2,724
33	15	5		Jimmy Reece	Malloy	Pankratz/Offy	10	Rod	2,294

Total Purse $269,962

Time of Race: 3:53:59.43 Average Speed: 128.209 mph Margin of Victory: 2:43.98

Pole: #23 Jerry Hoyt (140.045, 4:17.06) Fastest Qualifier: #3 Jack McGrath (142.580, 4:12.49)

Fastest Race Lap: #4 Bill Vukovich (Race Lap 27, 141.354 mph, 1:03.67 sec.)

Winning Car Owner: John Zink Co. Winning Chief Mechanic: A.J. Watson Winning Tire: Firestone Rookie of Year: Al Herman

Legend: R=Indianapolis 500-Mile Race Rookie; W=Indianapolis 500-Mile Race Former Winner; *=Had Relief Help

Lap Leaders: McGrath 1-3, Vukovich 4-14, McGrath 15, Vukovich 16-24, McGrath 25-26, Vukovich 27-56, Bryan 57, Sweikert 58, Bryan 59-88, Sweikert 89-132, Cross 133-156, Freeland 157-159, Sweikert 160-200.

Lap Leader Summary: Sweikert 3 times for 86 laps, Vukovich 3-50, Bryan 2-31, Cross 1-24, McGrath 3-6, Freeland 1-3. Lead Changes: 12 among 6 drivers.

Official Box Score

40th Indianapolis 500-Mile Race at the Indianapolis Motor Speedway • Wednesday, May 30, 1956

FP	SP	No.		Driver	Car Name	Chassis/Engine	Laps	Status	Total Prize Money
1	1	8		Pat Flaherty	John Zink	Watson/Offy	200	128.490	$93,819
2	13	4		Sam Hanks	Jones & Maley	KK500C/Offy	200	128.303	32,919
3	26	16		Don Freeland	Bob Estes	Phillips/Offy	200	127.668	20,419
4	6	98	W	Johnnie Parsons	Agajanian	Kuzma/Offy	200	126.631	15,769
5	4	73		Dick Rathmann	McNamara	KK500C/Offy	200	126.133	10,744
6	10	1	W	Bob Sweikert	D-A Lubricant	Kuzma/Offy	200	125.489	7,594
7	23	14	R	Bob Veith	Federal Engineering	KK500E/Offy	200	125.048	7,494
8	15	19		Rodger Ward	Filter Queen	KK500C/Offy	200	124.990	6,294
9	21	26		Jimmy Reece	Massaglia Hotels	Lesovsky/Offy	200	124.938	6,044
10	30	27		Cliff Griffith	Jim Robbins	Stevens/Offy	199	Running	6,194
11	22	82		Gene Hartley	Central Excavating	KK500C/Offy	196	Running	3,714
12	7	42		Fred Agabashian	Federal Engineering	KK500C/Offy	196	Running	3,644
13	25	57	R	Bob Christie	Helse	KK500D/Offy	196	Running	3,374
14	28	55		Al Keller	Sam Traylor	KK4000/Offy	195	Running	3,254
15	32	81		Eddie Johnson	Central Excavating	Kuzma/Offy	195	Running	3,434
16	29	41	R	Billy Garrett	Greenman-Casale	Kuzma/Offy	194	Running	3,014
17	33	64		Duke Dinsmore	Shannon's	KK500A/Offy	191	Running	3,094
18	3	7		Pat O'Connor	Ansted Rotary	KK500D/Offy	187	Running	8,924
19	19	2		Jimmy Bryan	Dean Van Lines	Kuzma/Offy	185	Running	3,144
20	2	24		Jim Rathmann	Hopkins	KK500C/Offy	175	Rings	3,564
21	31	34	R	Johnnie Tolan	Trio Brass Foundry	KK500D/Offy	173	Mechanical	3,084
22	5	99		Tony Bettenhausen	Belanger Motors	KK500D/Offy	160	Accident	2,754
23	14	10		Ed Elisian*	Hoyt Machine	KK500C/Offy	160	Brakes	2,624
24	16	48		Jimmy Daywalt	Sumar	KK500C/Offy	134	Accident	2,594
25	24	54	R	Jack Turner	Travelon Trailer	KK500B/Offy	131	Mechanical	2,564
26	20	89		Keith Andrews	Dunn Engineering	KK500B/Offy	94	Transmission	2,804
27	9	5		Andy Linden	Chapman	KK500C/Offy	90	Oil leak	2,534
28	27	12		Al Herman	Bardahl	KK500B/Offy	74	Accident	2,474
29	17	49		Ray Crawford	Crawford	KK500B/Offy	49	Accident	2,444
30	12	15		Johnny Boyd	Bowes Seal Fast	KK500G/Offy	35	Oil leak	2,414
31	11	53	W	Troy Ruttman	John Zink	KK500D/Offy	22	Spun out	2,384
32	18	88		Johnny Thomson	Schmidt	Kuzma/Offy	22	Spun out	2,854
33	8	29		Paul Russo	Novi Vespa	Kurtis/Novi	21	Accident	3,974

Total Purse $281,952

Time of Race: 3:53:28.84 Average Speed: 128.490 mph Margin of Victory: 20.46 sec

Pole: #8 Pat Flaherty (145.596, 4:07.26) Fastest Race Lap: #29 Paul Russo (Race Lap 19, 141.416 mph, 1:02.32 sec.)

Winning Car Owner: John Zink Co. Winning Chief Mechanic: A.J. Watson Winning Tire: Firestone Rookie of Year: Bob Veith

Legend: R=Indianapolis 500-Mile Race Rookie; W=Indianapolis 500-Mile Race Former Winner; *=Had Relief Help

Lap Leaders: J. Rathmann 1-3, O'Connor 4-10, P. Russo 11-21, O'Connor 22-40, Flaherty 41, O'Connor 42-44, Flaherty 45, O'Connor 46-55, Parsons 56-71, Freeland 72-75, Flaherty 76-200.

Lap Leader Summary: Flaherty 3 times for 127 laps, O'Connor 4-39, Parsons 1-16, P. Russo 1-11, Freeland 1-4, J. Rathmann 1-3. Lead Changes: 10 among 6 drivers.

Official Box Score

41st Indianapolis 500-Mile Race at the Indianapolis Motor Speedway • Thursday, May 30, 1957

FP	SP	No.		Driver	Car Name	Chassis/Engine	Laps	Status	Total Prize Money
1	13	9		Sam Hanks	Belond Exhaust	Salih/Offy	200	135.601	$103,844
2	32	26		Jim Rathmann	Chiropractic	Epperly/Offy	200	135.382	38,494
3	15	1		Jimmy Bryan	Dean Van Lines	Kuzma/Offy	200	134.246	21,794
4	10	54		Paul Russo	Novi Auto Air Conditioner	Kurtis/Novi	200	133.818	19,369
5	12	73		Andy Linden	McNamara/Veedol	KK500G/Offy	200	133.645	11,094
6	5	6		Johnny Boyd	Bowes Seal Fast	KK500G/Offy	200	132.846	8,194
7	28	48		Marshall Teague	Sumar	KK500G/Offy	200	132.745	6,819
8	1	12		Pat O'Connor	Sumar	KK500G/Offy	200	132.281	8,619
9	16	7		Bob Veith	Bob Estes	Phillips/Offy	200	131.855	5,969
10	14	22		Gene Hartley	Massaglia Hotels	Lesovsky/Offy	200	131.345	5,844
11	19	19		Jack Turner	Bardahl	KK500G/Offy	200	130.906	3,639
12	11	10		Johnny Thomson	D-A Lubricant	Kuzma/Offy	199	Running	5,069
13	33	95		Bob Christie	Jones & Maley	KK500C/Offy	197	Running	3,299
14	25	82		Chuck Weyant	Central Excavating	KK500C/Offy	196	Running	3,429
15	22	27		Tony Bettenhausen	Novi Auto Air Conditioner	Kurtis/Novi	195	Running	4,059
16	17	18	W	Johnnie Parsons	Sumar	KK500G/Offy	195	Running	2,989
17	21	3		Don Freeland	Ansted Rotary	KK500D/Offy	192	Running	2,869
18	6	5		Jimmy Reece	Hoyt Machine	KK500C/Offy	182	Throttle	2,749
19	27	92	R	Don Edmunds	McKay	KK500G/Offy	170	Spun out	3,169
20	31	28		Johnnie Tolan	Greenman-Casale	Kuzma/Offy	138	Clutch	2,639
21	30	89		Al Herman	Dunn Engineering	Dunn/Offy	111	Accident	2,659
22	4	14		Fred Agabashian	Bowes Seal Fast	KK500G/Offy	107	Fuel leak	2,879
23	2	88	R	Eddie Sachs	Schmidt	Kuzma/Offy	105	Fuel pump	3,299
24	18	77	R	Mike Magill	Dayton Steel Foundry	KK500G/Offy	101	Accident	2,519
25	20	43		Eddie Johnson	Chapman	KK500G/Offy	93	Wheel bearing	2,489
26	23	31	R	Bill Cheesbourg	Schildmeier Seal Line	KK500G/Offy	81	Fuel leak	3,209
27	8	16		Al Keller	Bardahl	KK500G/Offy	75	Accident	2,429
28	29	57		Jimmy Daywalt	Helse	KK500C/Offy	53	Accident	2,449
29	7	83		Ed Elisian	McNamara	KK500C/Offy	51	Timing gear	2,369
30	24	8		Rodger Ward	Wolcott Fuel Injection	Lesovsky/Offy	27	Supercharger	2,889
31	3	52	W	Troy Ruttman	John Zink	Watson/Offy	13	Piston	3,459
32	26	55		Eddie Russo	Sclavi & Amos	KK500C/Offy	0	Accident	2,404
33	9	23	R	Elmer George	Travelon Trailer	KK500B/Offy	0	Accident	2,249

Total Purse $299,252

Time of Race: 3:41:14.25 Average Speed: 135.601 mph Margin of Victory: 21.40 sec

Pole: #12 Pat O'Connor (143.948, 4:10.09) Fastest Qualifier: #54 Paul Russo (144.817, 4:08.59)

Fastest Race Lap: #26 Jim Rathmann (Race Lap 127, 143.426 mph, 1:02.75 sec.)

Winning Car Owner: George Salih Winning Chief Mechanic: George Salih/Howard Gilbert Winning Tire: Firestone Rookie of Year: Don Edmunds

Legend: R=Indianapolis 500-Mile Race Rookie; W=Indianapolis 500-Mile Race Former Winner

Lap Leaders: O'Connor 1-4, Ruttman 5-6, O'Connor 7-9, Ruttman 10-11, P. Russo 12-35, Hanks 36-48, Thomson 49-53, Hanks 54-110, J. Rathmann 111-134, Hanks 135-200.

Lap Leader Summary: Hanks 3 times for 136 laps, J. Rathmann 1-24, P. Russo 1-24, O'Connor 2-7, Thomson 1-5, Ruttman 2-4.

Lead Changes: 9 among 6 drivers.

Official Box Score

42nd Indianapolis 500-Mile Race at the Indianapolis Motor Speedway • Friday, May 30, 1958

FP	SP	No.		Driver	Car Name	Chassis/Engine	Laps	Status	Total Prize Money
1	7	1		Jimmy Bryan	Belond A.P.	Salih/Offy	200	133.791	$105,574
2	25	99	R	George Amick	Demler	Epperly/Offy	200	133.517	38,874
3	8	9		Johnny Boyd	Bowes Seal Fast	KK500G/Offy	200	133.099	24,999
4	9	33		Tony Bettenhausen	Jones & Maley	Epperly/Offy	200	132.855	17,199
5	20	2		Jim Rathmann	Leader Card 500 Roadster	Epperly/Offy	200	132.847	11,399
6	3	16		Jimmy Reece	John Zink	Watson/Offy	200	132.443	8,699
7	13	26		Don Freeland	Bob Estes	Phillips/Offy	200	132.403	6,999
8	19	44	R	Jud Larson	John Zink	Watson/Offy	200	130.550	7,049
9	26	61		Eddie Johnson	Bryant Heating & Cooling	KK500G/Offy	200	130.156	5,999
10	33	54		Bill Cheesbourg	Novi Auto Air Conditioner	Kurtis/Novi	200	129.149	6,399
11	21	52		Al Keller	Bardahl	KK500G-2/Offy	200	128.498	3,919
12	6	45	W	Johnnie Parsons	Gerhardt	KK500G/Offy	200	128.254	3,599
13	30	19		Johnnie Tolan	Greenman-Casale	Kuzma/Offy	200	128.150	3,329
14	17	65		Bob Christie	Federal Engineering	KK500E/Offy	189	Spun out	4,209
15	32	59	R	Dempsey Wilson	Sorenson	Kuzma/Offy	151	Refueling fire	4,089
16	12	29	R	A.J. Foyt	Dean Van Lines	Kuzma/Offy	148	Spun out	2,969
17	31	77		Mike Magill	Dayton Steel Foundry	KK500G/Offy	136	Running	2,849
18	14	15		Paul Russo	Novi Auto Air Conditioner	Kurtis/Novi	122	Throttle	2,779
19	23	83		Shorty Templeman	McNamara	KK500C/Offy	116	Brakes	2,699
20	11	8		Rodger Ward	Wolcott Fuel Injection	Lesovsky/Offy	93	Magneto	2,719
21	15	43		Billy Garrett	Chapman	KK500G/Offy	80	Gears	2,639
22	18	88		Eddie Sachs	Schmidt	Kuzma/Offy	68	Transmission	3,759
23	22	7		Johnny Thomson	D-A Lubricant	Kurtis/Offy	52	Steering	2,754
24	29	89		Chuck Weyant	Dunn Engineering	Dunn/Offy	38	Accident	2,549
25	10	25		Jack Turner	Massaglia Hotels	Lesovsky/Offy	21	Fuel pump	2,569
26	4	14		Bob Veith	Bowes Seal Fast	KK500G/Offy	1	Accident	2,789
27	1	97		Dick Rathmann	McNamara	Watson/Offy	0	Accident	6,259
28	2	5		Ed Elisian	John Zink	Watson/Offy	0	Accident	3,179
29	5	4		Pat O'Connor	Sumar	KK500G/Offy	0	Accident	2,574
30	16	31	R	Paul Goldsmith	City of Daytona Beach	KK500G/Offy	0	Accident	2,369
31	24	92	R	Jerry Unser	McKay	KK500G/Offy	0	Accident	2,339
32	27	68	R	Len Sutton	Jim Robbins	KK500G/Offy	0	Accident	2,309
33	28	57	R	Art Bisch	Helse	Kuzma/Offy	0	Accident	2,279

Total Purse $304,717

Time of Race: 3:44:13.80 Average Speed: 133.791 mph Margin of Victory: 27.65 sec
Pole: #97 Dick Rathmann (145.974, 4:06.62) Fastest Race Lap: #33 Tony Bettenhausen (Race Lap 55, 144.300 mph, 1:02.37 sec.)
Winning Car Owner: George Salih Winning Chief Mechanic: George Salih/Howard Gilbert Winning Tire: Firestone Rookie of Year: George Amick
Legend: R=Indianapolis 500-Mile Race Rookie; W=Indianapolis 500-Mile Race Former Winner
Lap Leaders: Bryan 1-18, Bettenhausen 19-20, Sachs 21, Bettenhausen 22-25, Bryan 26, Amick 27-30, Bryan 31, Amick 32-34, Bettenhausen 35, Amick 36-46, Bryan 47-48, Bettenhausen 49, Bryan 50-52, Bettenhausen 53-65, Bryan 66-104, Bettenhausen 105-107, Boyd 108-125, Bryan 126-200.
Lap Leader Summary: Bryan 7 times for 139 laps, Bettenhausen 6-24, Amick 3-18, Boyd 1-18, Sachs 1-1. Lead Changes: 17 among 5 drivers.

Official Box Score

43rd Indianapolis 500-Mile Race at the Indianapolis Motor Speedway • Saturday, May 30, 1959

FP	SP	No.		Driver	Car Name	Chassis/Engine	Laps	Status	Total Prize Money
1	6	5		Rodger Ward	Leader Card 500 Roadster	Watson/Offy	200	135.857	$106,850
2	3	16		Jim Rathmann	Simoniz	Watson/Offy	200	135.619	39,800
3	1	3		Johnny Thomson	Racing Associates	Lesovsky/Offy	200	135.340	32,375
4	15	1		Tony Bettenhausen	Hoover Motor Express	Epperly/Offy	200	134.768	15,475
5	16	99		Paul Goldsmith	Demler	Epperly/Offy	200	134.573	11,975
6	11	33		Johnny Boyd	Bowes Seal Fast	Epperly/Offy	200	133.867	8,475
7	12	37		Duane Carter	Smokey's Reverse Torque	Kurtis/Offy	200	133.342	7,275
8	8	19		Eddie Johnson	Bryant Heating & Cooling	KK500G/Offy	200	133.336	6,625
9	27	45		Paul Russo	Bardahl	KK500G/Offy	200	133.331	6,325
10	17	10		A.J. Foyt	Dean Van Lines	Kuzma/Offy	200	133.297	6,575
11	9	88		Gene Hartley	Drewry's	Kuzma/Offy	200	132.434	4,795
12	7	74		Bob Veith	John Zink Heater	Moore/Offy	200	132.169	4,675
13	23	89		Al Herman	Dunn Engineering	Dunn/Offy	200	131.872	4,455
14	13	66		Jimmy Daywalt	Federal Engineering	KK500E/Offy	200	131.861	5,335
15	21	71	R	Chuck Arnold	Hall-Mar	Curtis/Offy	200	130.918	4,165
16	33	58	R	Jim McWithey	Ray Brady	KK500C/Offy	200	129.024	4,045
17	2	44		Eddie Sachs	Schmidt	Kuzma/Offy	182	Running	4,675
18	28	57		Al Keller	Helse	Kuzma/Offy	163	Pistons	3,980
19	18	64	W	Pat Flaherty	John Zink Heater	Watson/Offy	162	Accident	5,725
20	4	73		Dick Rathmann	McNamara Chiropractic	Watson/Offy	150	Fire in pit	4,045
21	30	53		Bill Cheesbourg	Greenman-Casale	Kuzma/Offy	147	Magneto	3,765
22	25	15		Don Freeland	Jim Robbins	KK500G/Offy	136	Magneto	4,485
23	32	49		Ray Crawford	Meguiar's Mirror Glaze	Elder/Offy	115	Accident	3,655
24	10	9	R	Don Branson	Bob Estes	Phillips/Offy	112	Torsion bar	3,625
25	24	65		Bob Christie	Federal Engineering	KK500D/Offy	109	Rod	4,595
26	5	48	R	Bobby Grim	Sumar	KK500G/Offy	85	Magneto	4,190
27	14	24		Jack Turner	Travelon Trailer	Christensen/Offy	47	Fuel tank	4,335
28	29	47		Chuck Weyant	McKay	KK500J/Offy	45	Accident	3,505
29	19	7		Jud Larson	Bowes Seal Fast	KK500J/Offy	45	Accident	3,650
30	31	77		Mike Magill	Dayton Steel Foundry	KK500G/Offy	45	Accident	3,445
31	26	87	R	Red Amick	Wheeler-Foutch	KK500C/Offy	45	Accident	3,915
32	22	8		Len Sutton	Wolcott Memorial	Lesovsky/Offy	34	Accident	3,385
33	20	6	W	Jimmy Bryan	Belond A.P. Muffler	Salih/Offy	1	Cam housing	3,405

Total Purse $337,600

Time of Race: 3:40:49.20 Average Speed: 135.857 mph Margin of Victory: 23.27 sec
Pole: #3 Johnny Thomson (145.908, 4:06.73) Fastest Race Lap: #3 Johnny Thomson (Race Lap 64, 145.419 mph, 1:01.89 sec.)
Winning Car Owner: Leader Cards, Inc. Winning Chief Mechanic: A.J. Watson Winning Tire: Firestone Rookie of Year: Bobby Grim
Legend: R=Indianapolis 500-Mile Race Rookie; W=Indianapolis 500-Mile Race Former Winner
Lap Leaders: Thomson 1-4, Ward 5-12, J. Rathmann 13, Ward 14-16, J. Rathmann 17-30, Flaherty 31, J. Rathmann 32-33, Flaherty 34-40, J. Rathmann 41-42, Flaherty 43-45, Ward 46-48, Thomson 49-84, Ward 85-200.
Lap Leader Summary: Ward 4 times for 130 laps, Thomson 2-40, J. Rathmann 4-19, Flaherty 3-11. Lead Changes: 12 among 4 drivers.

Official Box Score

44th Indianapolis 500-Mile Race at the Indianapolis Motor Speedway • Monday, May 30, 1960

FP	SP	No.		Driver	Car Name	Chassis/Engine	Laps	Status	Total Prize Money
1	2	4		Jim Rathmann	Ken-Paul	Watson/Offy	200	138.767	$110,000
2	3	1	W	Rodger Ward	Leader Card 500 Roadster	Watson/Offy	200	138.631	48,025
3	26	99		Paul Goldsmith	Demler	Epperly/Offy	200	136.792	24,350
4	8	7		Don Branson	Bob Estes	Phillips/Offy	200	136.785	15,475
5	17	3		Johnny Thomson	Adams Quarter Horse Farm	Lesovsky/Offy	200	136.750	15,100
6	7	22		Eddie Johnson	Jim Robbins	Trevis/Offy	200	136.137	9,200
7	12	98	R	Lloyd Ruby	Agajanian	Watson/Offy	200	135.983	7,900
8	25	44		Bob Veith	Schmidt	Meskowski/Offy	200	135.452	7,850
9	28	18	R	Bud Tingelstad	Jim Robbins	Trevis/Offy	200	133.717	6,900
10	14	38		Bob Christie	Federal Engineering	KK500D/Offy	200	133.416	6,700
11	22	27		Red Amick	King O'Lawn	Salih/Offy	200	131.946	5,520
12	27	17		Duane Carter	Thompson Industries	Kuzma/Offy	200	131.882	5,450
13	31	39		Bill Homeier	Ridgewood Builders	Kuzma/Offy	200	131.367	4,980
14	24	48		Gene Hartley	Sumar	KK500G/Offy	196	Running	5,710
15	9	65		Chuck Stevenson	Leader Card 500 Roadster	Watson/Offy	196	Running	4,740
16	21	14		Bobby Grim	Bill Forbes	Meskowski/Offy	194	Running	4,920
17	19	26		Shorty Templeman	Federal Engineering	KK500E/Offy	191	Running	5,100
18	23	56	R	Jim Hurtubise	Travelon Trailer	Christensen/Offy	185	Rod	8,880
19	10	10	W	Jimmy Bryan	Metal-Cal	Salih/Offy	152	Fuel Pump	4,400
20	6	28	W	Troy Ruttman	John Zink Heater	Watson/Offy	134	Gear	6,220
21	1	6		Eddie Sachs	Dean Van Lines	Ewing/Offy	132	Magneto	9,390
22	11	73		Don Freeland	Ross-Babcock Traveler	Kurtis/Offy	129	Magneto	4,310
23	18	2		Tony Bettenhausen	Dowgard	Watson/Offy	125	Rod	5,080
24	15	32	R	Wayne Weiler	Ansted Rotary	Kuzma/Offy	103	Accident	4,200
25	16	5		A.J. Foyt	Bowes Seal Fast	Kurtis/Offy	90	Clutch	4,220
26	29	46		Eddie Russo	Go-Kart	KK500G/Offy	84	Accident	4,140
27	13	8		Johnny Boyd	Bowes Seal Fast	Epperly/Offy	77	Piston	4,160
28	20	37		Gene Force	McKay	KK500J/Offy	74	Brakes	4,480
29	32	16		Jim McWithey	Hoover Motor Express	Epperly/Offy	60	Brakes	4,100
30	5	9		Len Sutton	S-R Racing Enterprises	Watson/Offy	47	Piston ring	4,320
31	4	97		Dick Rathmann	Jim Robbins	Watson/Offy	42	Brake Line	4,440
32	30	76		Al Herman	Joe Hunt Magneto	Ewing/Offy	34	Clutch	4,010
33	33	23		Dempsey Wilson	Bryant Heating & Cooling	KK500G/Offy	11	Magneto	4,380

Total Purse $368,650

Time of Race: 3:36:11.36 **Average Speed:** 138.767 mph **Margin of Victory:** 12.67 sec

Pole: #6 Eddie Sachs (146.592, 4:05.58) **Fastest Qualifier:** #56 Jim Hurtubise (149.056, 4:01.52)

Fastest Race Lap: #4 Jim Rathmann (Race Lap 4, 146.128 mph, 1:01.59 sec.)

Winning Car Owner: Ken-Paul, Inc. **Winning Chief Mechanic:** Takeo "Chickie" Hirashima **Winning Tire:** Firestone **Rookie of Year:** Jim Hurtubise

Legend: R=Indianapolis 500-Mile Race Rookie; W=Indianapolis 500-Mile Race Former Winner

Lap Leaders: Ward 1, Sachs 2-3, Ward 4-18, Ruttman 19-24, J. Rathmann 25-37, Ward 38-41, Sachs 42-51, Ruttman 52-56, Sachs 57-61, J. Rathmann 62-69, Sachs 70-72, J. Rathmann 73-74, Sachs 75, J. Rathmann 76-85, Thomson 86-95, J. Rathmann 96-122, Ward 123-127, J. Rathmann 128-141, Ward 142-146, J. Rathmann 147, Ward 148-151, J. Rathmann 152-162, Ward 163-169, J. Rathmann 170, Ward 171-177, J. Rathmann 178-182, Ward 183-189, J. Rathmann 190-193, Ward 194-196, J. Rathmann 197-200.

Lap Leader Summary: J. Rathmann 12 times for 100 laps, Ward 10-58, Sachs 5-21, Ruttman 2-11, Thomson 1-10. **Lead Changes:** 29 among 5 drivers.

Official Box Score

45th Indianapolis 500-Mile Race at the Indianapolis Motor Speedway • Tuesday, May 30, 1961

FP	SP	No.		Driver	Car Name	Chassis/Engine	Laps	Status	Total Prize Money
1	7	1		A.J. Foyt	Bowes Seal Fast	Trevis/Offy	200	139.130	$117,975
2	1	12		Eddie Sachs	Dean Van Lines	Ewing/Offy	200	139.041	53,400
3	4	2	W	Rodger Ward	Del Webb's Sun City	Watson/Offy	200	138.539	26,500
4	18	7		Shorty Templeman	Bill Forbes Racing Team	Meskowski/Offy	200	136.873	16,025
5	26	19		Al Keller	Konstant Hot	Phillips/Offy	200	136.034	13,725
6	28	18		Chuck Stevenson	Metal-Cal	Epperly/Offy	200	135.742	9,875
7	33	31	R	Bobby Marshman	Hoover Motor Express	Epperly/Offy	200	135.534	9,550
8	25	5		Lloyd Ruby	Autolite Dealer's Assn.	Epperly/Offy	200	134.860	8,750
9	13	17	R	Jack Brabham	Kimberly Cooper-Climax	Cooper/Climax	200	134.116	7,250
10	32	34	R	Norm Hall	Federal Engineering	KK500E/Offy	200	134.104	8,250
11	15	28		Gene Hartley	John Chalik	Trevis/Offy	198	Running	5,820
12	5	98	R	Parnelli Jones	Agajanian Willard Battery	Watson/Offy	192	Running	10,350
13	6	97		Dick Rathmann	Jim Robbins	Watson/Offy	164	Fuel Pump	5,580
14	17	10		Paul Goldsmith	Racing Associates	Lesovsky/Offy	160	Oil Leak	5,210
15	12	15		Wayne Weiler	Hopkins Coral Harbour	Watson/Offy	147	Wheel	5,040
16	31	35		Dempsey Wilson	Lysle Greenman	Kuzma/Offy	145	Fuel Pump	4,920
17	16	32		Bob Christie	North Electric	Kurtis/Offy	132	Piston	4,850
18	10	33		Eddie Johnson	Jim Robbins	Kuzma/Offy	127	Accident	4,730
19	8	8		Len Sutton	Bryant Heating & Cooling	Watson/Offy	110	Transmission	4,650
20	22	52	W	Troy Ruttman	John Zink Trackburner	Watson/Offy	105	Clutch	6,970
21	20	41		Johnny Boyd	Leader Card 500 Roadster	Watson/Offy	105	Clutch	4,650
22	3	99		Jim Hurtubise	Demler	Epperly/Offy	102	Piston	10,410
23	19	86	R	Ebb Rose	Meyer Speedway	Porter/Offy	93	Oil line	4,530
24	30	26		Cliff Griffith	McCullough Engineering	Elder/Offy	55	Piston	4,750
25	21	45		Jack Turner	Bardahl	Kurtis/Offy	52	Accident	5,720
26	14	73	R	A.J. Shepherd	Travelon Trailer	Christensen/Offy	51	Accident	4,440
27	29	22	R	Roger McCluskey	Racing Associates	Moore/Offy	51	Accident	4,710
28	9	14		Bill Cheesbourg	Dean Van Lines	Kuzma/Offy	50	Accident	4,430
29	27	83	R	Don Davis	Dart-Kart by Rupp	Trevis/Offy	49	Accident	4,950
30	11	4	W	Jim Rathmann	Simoniz	Watson/Offy	48	Magneto	5,270
31	23	55		Jimmy Daywalt	Schultz Fueling Equipment	KK500G/Offy	27	Brakes	4,890
32	24	16		Bobby Grim	Thompson Industries	Watson/Offy	26	Fuel Injection	4,660
33	2	3		Don Branson	Hoover Motor Express	Epperly/Offy	2	Valves	5,080

Total Purse $397,910

Time of Race: 3:35:37.49 **Average Speed:** 139.130 mph **Margin of Victory:** 8.28 sec

Pole: #12 Eddie Sachs (147.481, 4:04.10) **Fastest Race Lap:** #52 Troy Ruttman (Race Lap 91, 147.589 mph, 1:00.98 sec.)

Winning Car Owner: Bignotti-Bowes Racing Associates **Winning Chief Mechanic:** George Bignotti **Winning Tire:** Firestone **Rookie of Year:** Parnelli Jones/Bobby Marshman

Legend: R=Indianapolis 500-Mile Race Rookie; W=Indianapolis 500-Mile Race Former Winner

Lap Leaders: Hurtubise 1-35, J. Rathmann 36-41, Jones 42-44, Sachs 45-51, Jones 52-75, Foyt 76-83, Ruttman 84-88, Foyt 89, Ruttman 90-94, Foyt 95-124, Sachs 125-137, Foyt 138, Sachs 139-141, Foyt 142-146, Sachs 147-151, Foyt 152-160, Ward 161-167, Sachs 168-169, Foyt 170-183, Sachs 184-197, Foyt 198-200.

Lap Leader Summary: Foyt 8 times for 71 laps, Sachs 6-44, Hurtubise 1-35, Jones 2-27, Ruttman 2-10, Ward 1-7, J. Rathmann 1-6. **Lead Changes:** 20 among 7 drivers.

Official Box Score

46th Indianapolis 500-Mile Race at the Indianapolis Motor Speedway • Wednesday, May 30, 1962

FP	SP	No.		Driver	Car Name	Chassis/Engine	Laps	Status	Total Prize Money
1	2	3	W	Rodger Ward	Leader Card 500 Roadster	Watson/Offy	200	140.293	$125,015
2	4	7		Len Sutton	Leader Card 500 Roadster	Watson/Offy	200	140.167	44,566
3	27	2		Eddie Sachs	Dean-Autolite	Ewing/Offy	200	140.075	26,591
4	12	27		Don Davis	J.H. Rose Truck Line	Lesovsky/Offy	200	139.768	16,716
5	3	54		Bobby Marshman	Bryant Heating & Cooling	Epperly/Offy	200	138.790	14,316
6	7	15	R	Jim McElreath	Schulz Fueling Equipment	KK500G/Offy	200	138.653	10,366
7	1	98		Parnelli Jones	Agajanian Willard Battery	Watson/Offy	200	138.534	32,966
8	24	12		Lloyd Ruby	Thompson Industries	Watson/Offy	200	138.182	8,541
9	23	44	W	Jim Rathmann	Simoniz Vista	Watson/Offy	200	136.913	8,041
10	28	38		Johnny Boyd	Metal-Cal	Epperly/Offy	200	136.600	8,841
11	6	4		Shorty Templeman	Bill Forbes Racing Team	Watson/Offy	200	135.844	6,461
12	11	14		Don Branson	Mid-Continent Securities	Epperly/Offy	200	135.836	6,041
13	29	91		Jim Hurtubise	Jim Robbins	Watson/Offy	200	135.655	6,621
14	32	86		Ebb Rose	J.H. Rose Truck Line	Porter/Offy	200	134.001	6,001
15	10	5		Bud Tingelstad	Konstant Hot	Phillips/Offy	200	133.170	5,631
16	9	17		Roger McCluskey	Bell Lines Trucking	Watson/Offy	168	Spun out	5,911
17	17	21		Elmer George*	Sarkes Tarzian	Lesovsky/Offy	146	Engine	5,341
18	30	26	W	Troy Ruttman	Jim Robbins	Kuzma/Offy	140	Piston	5,871
19	15	18		Bobby Grim	Morcroft	Trevis/Offy	96	Oil Leak	5,191
20	8	34	R	Dan Gurney	Thompson Harvey Aluminum	Thompson/Buick	92	Rear End	5,161
21	16	19	R	Chuck Hulse	Federal Engineering	KK500E/Offy	91	Fuel Pump	5,531
22	33	79		Jimmy Daywalt	City of Albany, NY	Kurtis/Offy	74	Transmission	5,351
23	5	1	W	A.J. Foyt	Bowes Seal Fast	Trevis/Offy	69	Lost wheel	5,721
24	13	9		Dick Rathmann	Chapman	Watson/Offy	51	Magneto	5,091
25	18	32		Eddie Johnson	Polyaire Foam	Trevis/Offy	38	Magneto	6,261
26	26	53		Paul Goldsmith	American Rubber & Plastics	Epperly/Offy	26	Magneto	5,031
27	20	88		Gene Hartley*	Drewry's	Watson/Offy	23	Steering	6,201
28	14	62		Paul Russo	Denver-Chicago Trucking	Watson/Offy	20	Piston	4,921
29	25	45		Jack Turner	Bardahl	Kurtis/Offy	17	Accident	5,141
30	31	29		Bob Christie	North Electric	Kurtis/Offy	17	Accident	5,311
31	22	83	R	Allen Crowe	S-R Racing Enterprises	Watson/Offy	17	Accident	5,431
32	21	67	R	Chuck Rodee	Travelon Trailer	Christensen/Offy	17	Accident	5,601
33	19	96		Bob Veith	Meguiar's Mirror Glaze	Elder/Offy	12	Piston	5,871

Total Purse $425,652

Time of Race: 3:33:50.33 Average Speed: 140.293 mph Margin of Victory: 11.52 sec
Pole: #98 Parnelli Jones (150.370, 3:59:41) Fastest Race Lap: #98 Parnelli Jones (Race Lap 56, 148.295 mph, 1:01.00 sec.)
Winning Car Owner: Leader Cards, Inc. Winning Chief Mechanic: A.J.. Watson Winning Tire: Firestone Rookie of Year: Jim McElreath
Legend: R=Indianapolis 500-Mile Race Rookie; W=Indianapolis 500-Mile Race Former Winner; *=Had Relief Help
Lap Leaders: Jones 1-59, Foyt 60-61, McCluskey 62-64, Jones 65-125, Ward 126-160, Sutton 161-169, Ward 170-200.
Lap Leader Summary: Jones 2 times for 120 laps, Ward 2-66, Sutton 1-9, McCluskey 1-3, Foyt 1-2. Lead Changes: 6 among 5 drivers.

Official Box Score

47th Indianapolis 500-Mile Race at the Indianapolis Motor Speedway • Thursday, May 30, 1963

FP	SP	No.		Driver	Car Name	Chassis/Engine	Laps	Status	Total Prize Money
1	1	98		Parnelli Jones	Agajanian Willard Battery	Watson/Offy	200	143.137	$148,513
2	5	92	R	Jim Clark	Lotus powered by Ford	Lotus/Ford	200	142.752	56,238
3	8	2	W	A.J. Foyt	Sheraton-Thompson	Trevis/Offy	200	142.210	32,614
4	4	1	W	Rodger Ward	Kaiser Aluminum	Watson/Offy	200	141.090	21,288
5	3	4		Don Branson	Leader Card 500 Roadster	Watson/Offy	200	140.866	18,588
6	6	8		Jim McElreath	Bill Forbes Racing Team	Watson/Offy	200	140.862	14,888
7	12	93		Dan Gurney	Lotus powered by Ford	Lotus/Ford	200	140.071	18,063
8	11	10		Chuck Hulse	Dean Van Lines	Ewing/Offy	200	140.064	12,163
9	31	84	R	Al Miller	Thompson Harvey Aluminum	Thompson/Chevrolet	200	139.524	12,513
10	17	22		Dick Rathmann	Chapman	Watson/Offy	200	138.845	10,463
11	30	29		Dempsey Wilson	Vita Fresh Orange Juice	Kuzma/Offy	200	138.574	8,300
12	33	17	W	Troy Ruttman	Robbins Autocrat Seat Belt	Kuzma/Offy	200	138.244	8,450
13	18	65		Bob Christie	Travelon Trailer	Christensen/Offy	200	136.104	7,900
14	32	32		Ebb Rose	Sheraton-Thompson	Watson/Offy	200	132.347	7,550
15	14	14		Roger McCluskey	Konstant Hot	Watson/Offy	198	Spun out	7,100
16	7	5		Bobby Marshman	Econo-Car Rental	Epperly/Offy	196	Rear End	6,300
17	10	9		Eddie Sachs	Bryant Heating & Cooling	Watson/Offy	181	Accident	7,100
18	9	99		Paul Goldsmith	Demler	Watson/Offy	149	Crankshaft	7,350
19	19	52		Lloyd Ruby	John Zink Trackburner	Watson/Offy	126	Accident	6,350
20	21	88		Eddie Johnson	Drewry's	Watson/Offy	112	Accident	6,300
21	22	45		Chuck Stevenson	Bardahl	Watson/Offy	110	Cylinder	5,700
22	2	56		Jim Hurtubise	Hotel Tropicana, Las Vegas	Kurtis/Novi	102	Oil Leak	7,400
23	15	83		Duane Carter	Thompson Harvey Aluminum	Thompson/Chevrolet	100	Rod	5,700
24	29	16	W	Jim Rathmann	Hopkins Coral Harbour	Watson/Offy	99	Fuel system	5,650
25	20	26		Bobby Grim	Morcroft	Trevis/Offy	79	Oil tank leak	5,900
26	24	86		Bob Veith	Sheraton-Thompson	Porter/Offy	74	Valve	5,600
27	13	35		Allen Crowe	Gabriel Shocker	Trevis/Offy	47	Accident	5,700
28	25	54		Bud Tingelstad	Hoover, Inc.	Epperly/Offy	46	Accident	5,500
29	26	37	R	Johnny Rutherford	US Equipment Co.	Watson/Offy	43	Transmission	5,400
30	28	21		Elmer George	Sarkes Tarzian	Lesovsky/Offy	21	Handling	5,350
31	23	75	R	Art Malone	STP	Kurtis/Novi	18	Clutch	5,150
32	27	23		Johnny Boyd	Bowes Seal Fast	Epperly/Offy	12	Oil	5,300
33	16	6	R	Bobby Unser	Hotel Tropicana, Las Vegas	Kurtis/Novi	2	Accident	6,250

Total Purse $492,631

Time of Race: 3:29:35.40 Average Speed: 143.137 mph Margin of Victory: 33.84 sec
Pole: #98 Parnelli Jones (151.153, 3:58.17) Fastest Race Lap: #98 Parnelli Jones (Race Lap 114, 151.541 mph, 59.39 sec.)
Winning Car Owner: J. C. Agajanian Winning Chief Mechanic: Johnny Pouelsen Winning Tire: Firestone Rookie of Year: Jim Clark
Legend: R=Indianapolis 500-Mile Race Rookie; W=Indianapolis 500-Mile Race Former Winner
Lap Leaders: Hurtubise 1, Jones 2-63, McCluskey 64-67, Clark 68-95, Jones 96-200.
Lap Leader Summary: Jones 2 times for 167 laps, Clark 1-28, McCluskey 1-4, Hurtubise 1-1. Lead Changes: 4 among 4 drivers.

Official Box Score
48th Indianapolis 500-Mile Race at the Indianapolis Motor Speedway • Saturday, May 30, 1964

FP	SP	No.		Driver	Car Name	Chassis/Engine	Laps	Status	Total Prize Money
1	5	1	W	A.J. Foyt	Sheraton-Thompson	Watson/Offy	200	147.350	$153,650
2	3	2	W	Rodger Ward	Kaiser Aluminum	Watson/Ford	200	146.339	56,925
3	7	18		Lloyd Ruby	Bill Forbes Racing Team	Watson/Offy	200	144.320	35,650
4	21	99	R	Johnny White	Demler	Watson/Offy	200	143.206	21,200
5	13	88		Johnny Boyd	Vita Fresh Orange Juice	Kuzma/Offy	200	142.345	17,625
6	19	15		Bud Tingelstad	Federal Engineering	Trevis/Offy	198	Running	15,425
7	12	23		Dick Rathmann	Chapman	Watson/Offy	197	Running	13,500
8	27	4	R	Bob Harkey	Wally Weir Mobilgas	Watson/Offy	197	Running	12,200
9	32	68	R	Bob Wente	Morcroft-Taylor	Trevis/Offy	197	Running	11,350
10	20	16		Bobby Grim	Konstant-Hot	Kurtis/Offy	196	Running	10,000
11	30	3		Art Malone	Studebaker-STP	Kurtis/Novi	194	Running	9,200
12	9	5		Don Branson	Wynn's Friction Proofing	Watson/Offy	187	Transmission	7,600
13	10	53	R	Walt Hansgen	MG Liquid Suspension	Huffaker/Offy	176	Running	7,150
14	11	56		Jim Hurtubise	Tombstone Life	Watson/Offy	141	Lost oil	6,650
15	8	66		Len Sutton	Bryant Heating & Cooling	Vollstedt/Offy	140	Magneto	6,450
16	33	62		Bill Cheesbourg	Arizona Apache Airlines	Epperly/Offy	131	Gear box	6,400
17	6	12		Dan Gurney	Lotus powered by Ford	Lotus/Ford	110	Withdrawn-tires	6,450
18	18	14	W	Troy Ruttman	Dayton Steel Wheel	Watson/Offy	99	Spun out	6,500
19	23	54		Bob Veith	MG Liquid Suspension	Huffaker/Offy	88	Piston	6,550
20	25	52		Jack Brabham	Zink-Urschel Trackburner	Brabham/Offy	77	Fuel Tank	6,000
21	26	28		Jim McElreath	Studebaker-STP	Kurtis/Novi	77	Filter system	5,850
22	28	77	R	Bob Mathouser	Dayton Disc Brake	Walther/Offy	77	Spun out	5,450
23	4	98	W	Parnelli Jones	Agajanian Bowes Seal Fast	Watson/Offy	55	Pit fire	8,200
24	1	6		Jim Clark	Lotus powered by Ford	Lotus/Ford	47	Suspension	12,400
25	2	51		Bobby Marshman	Pure Oil Firebird	Lotus/Ford	39	Transmission	12,000
26	24	84		Eddie Johnson	Thompson-Sears Allstate	Thompson/Ford	6	Fuel Pump	5,900
27	15	86		Johnny Rutherford	Bardahl	Watson/Offy	2	Accident	5,200
28	29	95		Chuck Stevenson	Diet Rite Cola	Watson/Offy	2	Accident	5,200
29	14	83	R	Dave MacDonald	Thompson-Sears Allstate	Thompson/Ford	1	Accident	5,100
30	17	25		Eddie Sachs	American Red Ball	Halibrand/Ford	1	Accident	6,300
31	16	64	R	Ronnie Duman	Clean Wear Service Co.	Trevis/Offy	1	Accident	5,000
32	22	9		Bobby Unser	Studebaker-STP	Ferguson/Novi	1	Accident	6,750
33	31	26		Norm Hall	Hurst Floor Shift	Watson/Offy	1	Accident	5,750

Total Purse $505,575
Time of Race: 3:23:35.83 Average Speed: 147.350 mph Margin of Victory: 1:24.35
Pole: #6 Jim Clark (158.828, 3:46.66) Fastest Race Lap: #51 Bobby Marshman (Race Lap 15, 157.646 mph, 57.09 sec.)
Winning Car Owner: Ansted-Thompson Racing Winning Chief Mechanic: George Bignotti Winning Tire: Firestone Rookie of Year: Johnny White
Legend: R=Indianapolis 500-Mile Race Rookie; W=Indianapolis 500-Mile Race Former Winner
Lap Leaders: Clark 1-6, Marshman 7-39, Clark 40-47, Jones 48-54, Foyt 55-200.
Lap Leader Summary: Foyt 1 time for 146 laps, Marshman 1-33, Clark 2-14, Jones 1-7. Lead Changes: 4 among 4 drivers.

Official Box Score
49th Indianapolis 500-Mile Race at the Indianapolis Motor Speedway • Monday, May 31, 1965

FP	SP	No.	Rookie	Driver	Car Name	Chassis/Engine	Laps	Status	Total Prize Money
1	2	82		Jim Clark	Lotus powered by Ford	Lotus/Ford	200	150.686	$166,621
2	5	98	W	Parnelli Jones	Agajanian Hurst	Kuzma-Lotus/Ford	200	149.200	64,661
3	4	12	R	Mario Andretti	Dean Van Lines	Brawner/Ford	200	149.121	42,551
4	7	74		Al Miller	Jerry Alderman Ford	Lotus/Ford	200	146.581	26,641
5	14	76	R	Gordon Johncock	Weinberger Homes	Watson/Offy	200	146.417	21,981
6	15	81	R	Mickey Rupp	G.C. Murphy	Gerhardt/Offy	198	Running	18,971
7	22	83	R	Bobby Johns	Lotus powered by Ford	Lotus/Ford	197	Running	16,886
8	18	4		Don Branson	Wynn's	Watson/Ford	197	Running	16,376
9	32	45	R	Al Unser	Sheraton-Thompson	Lola/Ford	196	Running	14,416
10	28	23		Eddie Johnson	Chapman	Watson/Offy	195	Running	14,656
11	9	7		Lloyd Ruby	Dupont Golden 7	Halibrand/Ford	184	Blown Engine	11,846
12	12	16		Len Sutton	Bryant Heating & Cooling	Vollstedt/Ford	177	Running	11,586
13	29	14		Johnny Boyd	George R. Bryant & Staff	BRP/Ford	140	Rear gears	11,976
14	21	53		Walt Hansgen	MG-Liquid Suspension	Huffaker/Offy	117	Overheating	10,566
15	1	1	W	A.J. Foyt	Sheraton-Thompson	Lotus/Ford	115	Gearbox	20,517
16	24	5		Bud Tingelstad	American Red Ball	Lola/Ford	115	Accident	9,596
17	6	66	R	Billy Foster	Jim Robbins	Vollstedt/Offy	85	Water line	9,936
18	19	18	R	Arnie Knepper	Konstant Hot	Kurtis/Offy	80	Cylinder	10,326
19	8	9		Bobby Unser	STP Gas Treatment	Ferguson/Novi	69	Oil Fitting	9,216
20	13	52		Jim McElreath	Zink-Urschel Trackburner	Brabham/Offy	66	Gear chain	8,656
21	16	94	R	George Snider	Gerhardt	Gerhardt/Offy	64	Rear end	8,696
22	25	65		Ronnie Duman	Travelon Trailer/H&H Bookbinding	Gerhardt/Offy	62	Rear end	8,786
23	31	41	R	Masten Gregory	George R. Bryant & Staff	BRP/Ford	59	Oil Pressure	9,076
24	10	54		Bob Veith	MG-Liquid Suspension	Huffaker/Offy	58	Piston	8,266
25	26	88		Chuck Stevenson	Vita Fresh Orange Juice	Kuzma/Offy	50	Piston	8,306
26	3	17		Dan Gurney	Yamaha	Lotus/Ford	42	Timing Gears	9,596
27	17	48	R	Jerry Grant	Bardahl/MG Liquid Susp.	Huffaker/Offy	30	Magneto	7,786
28	30	19		Chuck Rodee	Wally Weir's Mobilgas	Halibrand/Offy	28	Rear End	8,726
29	27	29	R	Joe Leonard	All American Racers	Halibrand/Ford	27	Oil Leak	7,816
30	23	25		Roger McCluskey	All American Racers	Halibrand/Ford	18	Clutch	8,106
31	11	24		Johnny Rutherford	Racing Associates	Halibrand/Ford	15	Rear End	7,596
32	33	47		Bill Cheesbourg	WIFE Good Guy	Gerhardt/Offy	14	Magneto	7,836
33	20	59		Jim Hurtubise	STP-Tombstone Life	Kurtis/Novi	1	Transmission	8,626

Total Purse $627,199
Time of Race: 3:19:05.34 Average Speed: 150.686 mph Margin of Victory: 1:59.98
Pole: #1 A.J. Foyt (161.233, 3:43.28) Fastest Race Lap: #1 A.J. Foyt Jr. (Race Lap 2, 157.508 mph, 57.14 sec.)
Winning Car Owner: Team Lotus (Overseas), Ltd. Winning Chief Mechanic: David Lazenby Winning Tire: Firestone Rookie of Year: Mario Andretti
Legend: R=Indianapolis 500-Mile Race Rookie; W=Indianapolis 500-Mile Race Former Winner
Lap Leaders: Clark 1, Foyt 2, Clark 3-65, Foyt 66-74, Clark 75-200.
Lap Leader Summary: Clark 3 times for 190 laps, Foyt 2-10. Lead Changes: 4 among 2 drivers.

Official Box Score

50th Indianapolis 500-Mile Race at the Indianapolis Motor Speedway • Monday, May 30, 1966

FP	SP	No.		Driver	Car Name	Chassis/Engine	Laps	Status	Total Prize Money
1	15	24	R	Graham Hill	American Red Ball	Lola/Ford	200	144.317	$156,297
2	2	19	W	Jim Clark	STP Gas Treatment	Lotus/Ford	200	143.843	76,992
3	7	3		Jim McElreath	Zink-Urschel-Slick	Brabham/Ford	200	143.742	42,586
4	6	72		Gordon Johncock	Weinberger Homes	Gerhardt/Ford	200	143.084	26,381
5	17	94	R	Mel Kenyon	Gerhardt	Gerhardt/Offy	198	Running	21,987
6	11	43	R	Jackie Stewart	Bowes Seal Fast	Lola/Ford	190	Oil Pressure	25,767
7	29	54		Eddie Johnson	Valvoline II	Huffaker/Offy	175	Stalled	17,615
8	28	11		Bobby Unser	Vita Fresh Orange Juice	Huffaker/Offy	171	Running	16,562
9	20	6		Joe Leonard	Yamaha Eagle	Eagle/Ford	170	Stalled	15,822
10	10	88		Jerry Grant	Bardahl-Pacesetter Homes	Eagle/Ford	167	Running	15,055
11	5	14		Lloyd Ruby	Bardahl Eagle	Eagle/Ford	166	Cam	24,926
12	23	18		Al Unser	STP Oil Treatment	Lotus/Ford	161	Accident	14,965
13	21	8		Roger McCluskey	G.C. Murphy	Eagle/Ford	129	Oil Leak	13,123
14	4	98	W	Parnelli Jones	Agajanian's Rev 500	Shrike/Offy	87	Wheel Bearing	13,462
15	13	26	W	Rodger Ward	Bryant Heating & Cooling	Lola/Offy	74	Handling	11,857
16	25	77	R	Carl Williams	Dayton Steel Wheel	Gerhardt/Ford	38	Valve, oil	12,171
17	22	56		Jim Hurtubise	Gerhardt	Gerhardt/Offy	29	Oil	11,604
18	1	1		Mario Andretti	Dean Van Lines	Brawner/Ford	27	Valve	25,121
19	3	82		George Snider	Sheraton-Thompson	Coyote/Ford	22	Accident	12,075
20	8	12		Chuck Hulse	Wynn's	Watson/Ford	22	Accident	10,463
21	27	22		Bud Tingelstad	Federal Engineering	Gerhardt/Offy	16	Overheating	10,470
22	14	28		Johnny Boyd	Prestone	B.R.P./Ford	5	Accident	9,896
23	9	4		Don Branson	Leader Cards Racer	Gerhardt/Ford	0	Accident	9,791
24	12	27		Billy Foster	Jim Robbins	Vollstedt/Ford	0	Accident	9,554
25	16	53	R	Gary Congdon	Valvoline	Huffaker/Offy	0	Accident	9,386
26	18	2	W	A.J. Foyt	Sheraton-Thompson	Lotus/Ford	0	Accident	10,887
27	19	31		Dan Gurney	All American Racers	Eagle/Ford	0	Accident	9,806
28	24	66	R	Cale Yarborough	Jim Robbins	Vollstedt/Ford	0	Accident	9,794
29	26	37		Arnie Knepper	Sam Liosi	Cecil/Ford	0	Accident	9,301
30	30	75		Al Miller	Jerry Alderman Ford	Lotus/Ford	0	Accident	8,876
31	31	39		Bobby Grim	Racing Associates	Watson/Offy	0	Accident	8,720
32	32	34	R	Larry Dickson	Michner Petroleum	Lola/Ford	0	Accident	9,933
33	33	96		Ronnie Duman	Harrison	Eisert/Ford	0	Accident	9,564

Total Purse $690,809

Time of Race: 3:27:52.53 Average Speed: 144.317 mph Margin of Victory: 41.13 sec
Pole: #1 Mario Andretti (165.899, 3:37.00) Fastest Race Lap: #19 Jimmy Clark (Race Lap 18, 159.179 mph, 56.54 sec.)
Winning Car Owner: John Mecom, Jr. Winning Chief Mechanic: George Bignotti Winning Tire: Firestone Rookie of Year: Jackie Stewart
Legend: R=Indianapolis 500-Mile Race Rookie; W=Indianapolis 500-Mile Race Former Winner
Lap Leaders: Andretti 1-16, Clark 17-64, Ruby 65-75, Clark 76-86, Ruby 87-132, Clark 133-139, Ruby 140-150, Stewart 151-190, Hill 191-200.
Lap Leader Summary: Ruby 3 times for 68 laps, Clark 3-66, Stewart 1-40, Andretti 1-16, Hill 1-10. Lead Changes: 8 among 5 drivers.

Official Box Score

51st Indianapolis 500-Mile Race at the Indianapolis Motor Speedway • Tuesday, May 31, 1967

FP	SP	No.		Driver	Car Name	Chassis/Engine	Laps	Status	Total Prize Money
1	4	14	W	A.J. Foyt	Sheraton-Thompson	Coyote/Ford	200	151.207	$171,527
2	9	5		Al Unser	Retzloff Chemical	Lola/Ford	198	Running	67,127
3	5	4		Joe Leonard	Sheraton-Thompson	Coyote/Ford	197	Running	43,177
4	24	69	R	Denis Hulme	City of Daytona Beach	Eagle/Ford	197	Running	28,177
5	11	2		Jim McElreath	John Zink Trackburner	Moore/Ford	197	Running	22,957
6	6	40	W	Parnelli Jones	STP Oil Treatment	Granatelli/Pratt & Whitney	196	Bearing	55,767
7	27	8		Chuck Hulse	Hopkins	Lola/Offy	195	Accident	18,397
8	13	16	R	Art Pollard	Thermo-King Auto Air Conditioning	Gerhardt/Offy	195	Running	16,928
9	8	6		Bobby Unser	Rislone	Eagle/Ford	193	Running	15,773
10	23	41		Carl Williams	George R. Bryant	B.R.P./Ford	189	Accident	16,173
11	28	46		Bob Veith	Thermo-King Auto Air Conditioning	Gerhardt/Offy	189	Running	14,461
12	3	3		Gordon Johncock	Gilmore Broadcasting	Gerhardt/Ford	188	Accident	15,518
13	12	39		Bobby Grim	Racing Associates	Gerhardt/Offy	187	Accident	13,244
14	25	10		Bud Tingelstad	Federal Engineering	Gerhardt/Ford	182	Spun out	13,376
15	21	22		Larry Dickson	Vita Fresh Orange Juice	Lotus/Ford	180	Spun out	12,565
16	14	15		Mel Kenyon	Thermo-King Auto Air Conditioning	Gerhardt/Offy	177	Spun out	12,273
17	20	21		Cale Yarborough	Bryant Heating & Cooling	Vollstedt/Ford	176	Accident	11,900
18	29	24		Jackie Stewart	Bowes Seal Fast	Lola/Ford	168	Engine	12,796
19	22	12		Roger McCluskey	G.C. Murphy	Eagle/Ford	165	Engine	12,961
20	30	42		Jerry Grant	All American Racers	Eagle/Ford	162	Radiator	11,845
21	2	74		Dan Gurney	Wagner Lockheed Brake Fluid	Eagle/Ford	160	Black flag	15,498
22	18	19		Arnie Knepper	M.V.S. Racers	Cecil/Ford	158	Engine	10,570
23	17	98		Ronnie Duman	Agajanian's Rev 500	Shrike/Offy	154	Fuel trouble	10,261
24	32	48	R	Jochen Rindt	Wagner Lockheed Brake Fluid	Eagle/Ford-Weslake	108	Mechanical	10,571
25	19	45		Johnny Rutherford	Weinberger Homes	Eagle/Ford	103	Accident	10,000
26	10	26		George Snider*	Wagner Lockheed Brake Fluid	Mongoose/Ford	99	Accident	9,898
27	26	67	R	Lee Roy Yarbrough	Jim Robbins Seat Belt	Vollstedt/Ford	87	Accident	10,015
28	33	32		Al Miller	Cleaver-Brooks	Gerhardt/Ford	74	Oil filter	9,951
29	15	53	R	Wally Dallenbach	Valvoline	Huffaker/Offy	73	Accident	9,406
30	1	1		Mario Andretti	Dean Van Lines	Hawk/Ford	58	Lost wheel	21,049
31	16	31	W	Jim Clark	STP Oil Treatment	Lotus/Ford	35	Piston	9,373
32	31	81	W	Graham Hill	STP Oil Treatment	Lotus/Ford	23	Piston	9,935
33	7	25		Lloyd Ruby	American Red Ball	Mongoose/Offy	3	Valves	9,666

Total Purse $733,135

Time of Race: 3:18:24.22 Average Speed: 151.207 mph Margin of Victory: Under Caution
Pole: #1 Mario Andretti (168.982, 3:33.04) Fastest Race Lap: #40 Parnelli Jones (Race Lap 6, 164.926 mph, 54.57 sec.)
Winning Car Owner: Ansted-Thompson Racing Winning Chief Mechanic: A.J. "Tony" Foyt Sr. Winning Tire: Goodyear Rookie of Year: Denis Hulme
Legend: R=Indianapolis 500-Mile Race Rookie; W=Indianapolis 500-Mile Race Former Winner; *=Had Relief Help
Race Notes: Race stopped on lap 19 (May 30th) due to rain and was completed the next day (May 31).
Lap Leaders: Jones 1-51, Gurney 52-53, Jones 54-79, Foyt 80-83, Jones 84-130, Foyt 131-149, Jones 150-196, Foyt 197-200.
Lap Leader Summary: Jones 4 times for 171 laps, Foyt 3-27, Gurney 1-2. Lead Changes: 7 among 3 drivers.

Official Box Score

52nd Indianapolis 500-Mile Race at the Indianapolis Motor Speedway • Thursday, May 30, 1968

FP	SP	No.		Driver	Car Name	Chassis/Engine	Laps	Status	Total Prize Money
1	3	3		Bobby Unser	Rislone	Eagle/Offy	200	152.882	$175,140
2	10	48		Dan Gurney	Olsonite	Eagle/Ford-Weslake	200	152.187	65,095
3	17	15		Mel Kenyon	City of Lebanon	Gerhardt/Offy	200	149.224	44,960
4	20	42		Denis Hulme	Olsonite	Eagle/Ford	200	149.140	26,625
5	5	25		Lloyd Ruby	Gene White Company	Mongoose/Offy	200	148.529	30,365
6	26	59		Ronnie Duman	Cleaver-Brooks	Brabham/Offy	200	148.232	19,205
7	23	98	R	Bill Vukovich II	Wagner-Lockheed	Shrike/Offy	198	Running	18,520
8	27	90	R	Mike Mosley	Zecol-Lubaid	Watson/Offy	197	Running	17,490
9	31	94	R	Sam Sessions	Valvoline	Finley/Offy	197	Running	15,730
10	25	6		Bobby Grim	Gene White Company	Mongoose/Offy	196	Running	15,170
11	24	16		Bob Veith	Thermo-King Auto Air Conditioning	Gerhardt/Offy	196	Running	14,510
12	1	60		Joe Leonard	STP Oil Treatment	Lotus/Pratt & Whitney	191	Fuel Shaft	37,520
13	11	20		Art Pollard	STP Oil Treatment	Lotus/Pratt & Whitney	188	Fuel Shaft	12,950
14	13	82		Jim McElreath	Jim Greer	Coyote/Ford	179	Stalled	12,910
15	28	84		Carl Williams	Sheraton-Thompson	Coyote/Ford	163	Accident	14,255
16	18	10		Bud Tingelstad	Federal Engineering	Gerhardt/Ford	158	Oil Pressure	12,670
17	12	54		Wally Dallenbach	Valvoline	Finley/Offy	146	Engine failure	11,530
18	21	18		Johnny Rutherford	City of Seattle	Eagle/Ford	125	Collision	11,585
19	2	70	W	Graham Hill	STP Oil Treatment	Lotus/Pratt & Whitney	110	Accident	13,810
20	8	1	W	A.J. Foyt	Sheraton-Thompson	Coyote/Ford	86	Rear End	11,130
21	19	45	R	Ronnie Bucknum	Weinberger Homes	Eagle/Ford	76	Fuel Leak	10,970
22	14	27	R	Jim Malloy	Jim Robbins Co.	Vollstedt/Ford	64	Rear End	10,130
23	15	78		Jerry Grant	Bardahl Eagle	Eagle/Ford	50	Oil Leak	9,760
24	22	11	R	Gary Bettenhausen	Thermo-King Auto Air Conditioning	Gerhardt/Offy	43	Damage	9,860
25	32	21		Arnie Knepper	Bryant Heating & Cooling	Vollstedt/Ford	42	Hit wheel	9,760
26	6	24		Al Unser	Retzloff Chemical	Lola/Ford	40	Accident	10,120
27	9	4		Gordon Johncock	Gilmore Broadcasting	Gerhardt/Offy	37	Rear End	9,480
28	33	64		Larry Dickson*	Overseas National Airways	Hawk II/Ford	24	Piston	9,160
29	7	8		Roger McCluskey	G.C. Murphy	Eagle/Offy	16	Oil Filter	9,460
30	30	56		Jim Hurtubise	Pepsi-Frito Lay	Mallard/Offy	9	Piston	9,330
31	29	29		George Snider	Vel's Parnelli Jones	Mongoose/Ford	9	Oil Leak	9,470
32	16	35		Jochen Rindt	Repco-Brabham	Brabham/Repco-Brabham	5	Piston	9,830
33	4	2		Mario Andretti	Overseas National Airways	Hawk III/Ford	2	Piston	9,960

Total Purse $708,460

Time of Race: 3:16:13.76 Average Speed: 152.882 mph Margin of Victory: 53.81 sec
Pole: #60 Joe Leonard (171.559, 3:29.84) Fastest Race Lap: #25 Lloyd Ruby (Race Lap 94, 168.666 mph, 53.36 sec.)
Winning Car Owner: Leader Cards, Inc. Winning Chief Mechanic: Jud Phillips Winning Tire: Goodyear Rookie of Year: Billy Vukovich II
Legend: R=Indianapolis 500-Mile Race Rookie; W=Indianapolis 500-Mile Race Former Winner; *=Had Relief Help
Lap Leaders: Leonard 1-7, B. Unser 8-56, Ruby 57-89, B. Unser 90-112, Leonard 113-119, B. Unser 120-165, Ruby 166-174, Leonard 175-191, B. Unser 192-200.
Lap Leader Summary: B. Unser 4 times for 127 laps, Ruby 2-42, Leonard 3-31. Lead Changes: 8 among 3 drivers.

Official Box Score

53rd Indianapolis 500-Mile Race at the Indianapolis Motor Speedway • Friday, May 30, 1969

FP	SP	No.		Driver	Car Name	Chassis/Engine	Laps	Status	Total Prize Money
1	2	2		Mario Andretti	STP Oil Treatment	Hawk III/Ford	200	156.867	$206,727
2	10	48		Dan Gurney	Olsonite	Eagle/Weslake-Ford	200	155.337	67,732
3	3	1	W	Bobby Unser	Bardahl	Lola/Offy	200	154.090	45,647
4	24	9		Mel Kenyon	Krohne Grain Transport	Gerhardt/Offy	200	152.177	30,612
5	33	92	R	Peter Revson	Repco-Brabham	Brabham/Repco	197	Running	25,722
6	11	44		Joe Leonard	City of Daytona Beach	Eagle/Ford	193	Running	21,602
7	4	66	R	Mark Donohue	Sunoco-Simoniz	Lola/Offy	190	Running	21,512
8	1	6	W	A.J. Foyt	Sheraton-Thompson	Coyote/Ford	181	Running	50,252
9	31	21		Larry Dickson	Bryant Heating & Cooling	Vollstedt/Ford	180	Running	17,426
10	32	97		Bobby Johns	Wagner-Lockheed	Shrike/Offy	171	Running	19,841
11	13	10		Jim Malloy	Jim Robbins Co.	Vollstedt/Offy	165	Running	17,358
12	23	11		Sam Sessions	Valvoline	Finley/Offy	163	Running	15,846
13	22	90		Mike Mosley	Zecol-Lubaid	Eagle/Offy	162	Piston	14,755
14	6	82		Roger McCluskey	G.C. Murphy	Coyote/Ford	157	Split Header	15,493
15	18	15		Bud Tingelstad	Vel's Parnelli Jones	Lola/Offy	155	Engine	13,894
16	15	84		George Snider	Sheraton-Thompson	Coyote/Ford	152	Running	14,016
17	14	59	R	Sonny Ates	Krohne Grain Transport	Brabham/Offy	146	Magneto	13,609
18	25	42		Denis Hulme	Olsonite Eagle	Eagle/Ford	145	Clutch	12,823
19	5	12		Gordon Johncock	Gilmore Broadcasting	Gerhardt/Offy	137	Piston	13,585
20	20	4		Lloyd Ruby	Wynn's Spitfire	Mongoose/Offy	105	Fuel Hose	13,864
21	19	22		Wally Dallenbach	Sprite	Eagle/Offy	82	Clutch	12,991
22	21	29		Arnie Knepper	M.V.S.	Cecil/Ford	82	Accident	12,189
23	8	67		Lee Roy Yarbrough	Jim Robbins Co.	Vollstedt/Ford	65	Split Header	12,258
24	29	95		Jack Brabham	Repco-Brabham	Brabham/Repco	58	Ignition	11,725
25	30	57		Carl Williams	STP Gas Treatment	Gerhardt/Offy	50	Clutch	11,809
26	9	8		Gary Bettenhausen	Thermo-King Auto Air Conditioner	Gerhardt/Offy	35	Piston	11,541
27	27	62	R	George Follmer	Retzloff Chemical	Gilbert/Ford	26	Engine failure	11,994
28	7	38		Jim McElreath	Jack Adams Airplanes	Hawk II/Offy	24	Engine Fire	11,768
29	17	36		Johnny Rutherford	Patrick Petroleum	Eagle/Offy	24	Oil Tank	10,963
30	16	45		Ronnie Bucknum	Weinberger Homes	Eagle/Offy	16	Piston	10,929
31	12	40		Art Pollard	STP Oil Treatment	Lotus/Offy	7	Drive Line	10,816
32	26	98		Bill Vukovich II	Wagner Lockheed	Mongoose/Offy	1	Rod	11,974
33	28	16	R	Bruce Walkup	Thermo-King Auto Air Conditioner	Gerhardt/Offy	0	Transmission	11,353

Total Purse $804,626

Time of Race: 3:11:14.71 Average Speed: 156.867 mph Margin of Victory: 1:53.02
Pole: #6 A.J. Foyt (170.568, 3:31.06) Fastest Race Lap: #82 Roger McCluskey (Race Lap 20, 166.512 mph, 54.05 sec.)
Winning Car Owner: STP Corporation Winning Chief Mechanic: Clint Brawner/Jim McGee Winning Tire: Firestone Rookie of Year: Mark Donohue
Legend: R=Indianapolis 500-Mile Race Rookie; W=Indianapolis 500-Mile Race Former Winner
Lap Leaders: Andretti 1-5, Foyt 6-51, Dallenbach 52-58, Foyt 59-78, Ruby 79-86, Andretti 87-102, Ruby 103-105, Andretti 106-200.
Lap Leader Summary: Andretti 3 times for 116 laps, Foyt 2-66, Ruby 2-11, Dallenbach 1-7. Lead Changes: 7 among 4 drivers.

Official Box Score

54th Indianapolis 500-Mile Race at the Indianapolis Motor Speedway • Saturday, May 30, 1970

FP	SP	No.		Driver	Car Name	Chassis/Engine	Laps	Status	Total Prize Money
1	1	2		Al Unser	Johnny Lightning 500	P.J. Colt/Ford	200	155.749	$271,698
2	5	66		Mark Donohue	Sunoco	Lola/Ford	200	155.317	86,427
3	11	48		Dan Gurney	Olsonite Eagle	Eagle/Ford	200	153.201	58,977
4	23	83	R	Donnie Allison	Greer	Eagle/Ford	200	152.777	36,002
5	33	14		Jim McElreath	Sheraton-Thompson	Coyote/Ford	200	152.182	32,577
6	8	1	W	Mario Andretti	STP Oil Treatment	McNamara/Ford	199	Running	28,202
7	29	89		Jerry Grant	Nelson Iron Works	Eagle/Offy	198	Running	26,977
8	15	38	R	Rick Muther	The Tony Express	Hawk II/Offy	197	Running	25,302
9	19	75		Carl Williams	McLaren	McLaren/Offy	197	Running	22,352
10	3	7	W	A.J. Foyt	Sheraton-Thompson	Coyote/Ford	195	Running	24,902
11	7	3	W	Bobby Unser	Wagner-Lockheed	Eagle/Ford	192	Running	20,552
12	32	67		Sam Sessions	Jim Robbins Co.	Vollstedt/Ford	190	Running	19,752
13	26	32		Jack Brabham	Gilmore Broadcasting-Brabham	Brabham/Offy	175	Piston	20,227
14	31	44	R	Dick Simon	Bryant Heating & Cooling	Vollstedt/Ford	168	Running	18,427
15	27	19		Ronnie Bucknum	M.V.S.	Morris/Ford	162	Accident	18,602
16	22	23		Mel Kenyon*	Sprite	Coyote/Offy	160	Accident	17,552
17	24	22		Wally Dallenbach	Sprite	Eagle/Ford	143	Coil	17,077
18	2	18		Johnny Rutherford	Patrick Petroleum	Eagle/Offy	135	Header	18,327
19	13	27		Lee Roy Yarbrough	Jim Robbins Co.	Vollstedt/Ford	107	Turbo Gear	16,302
20	10	84		George Snider	Greer	Coyote/Ford	105	Suspension	16,002
21	12	9		Mike Mosley	G.C. Murphy	Eagle/Offy	96	Radiator	15,627
22	16	73		Peter Revson	McLaren	McLaren/Offy	87	Magneto	16,627
23	30	58		Bill Vukovich II	Sugaripe Prune	Brabham/Offy	78	Clutch	15,252
24	18	15		Joe Leonard	Johnny Lightning 500	P.J. Colt/Ford	73	Ignition Switch	15,452
25	4	11		Roger McCluskey	Quickick	Scorpion/Ford	62	Suspension	15,727
26	20	16		Gary Bettenhausen	Thermo-King Auto Air Conditioner	Gerhardt/Offy	55	Valve	14,677
27	25	25		Lloyd Ruby	Daniels Cablevision	Mongoose/Offy	54	Drive Gear	17,252
28	17	5		Gordon Johncock	Gilmore Broadcasting	Gerhardt/Ford	45	Piston	14,902
29	14	97		Bruce Walkup	Wynn's Spit-Fire	Mongoose/Offy	44	Timing Gear	13,927
30	6	10		Art Pollard	Art Pollard Car Wash Systems	Kingfish/Offy	28	Piston	14,427
31	21	20		George Follmer	STP Oil Treatment	Hawk III/Ford	18	Oil Gasket	14,002
32	28	93	R	Greg Weld	Art Pollard Car Wash Systems	Gerhardt/Offy	12	Piston	14,102
33	9	31		Jim Malloy	Stearns Mfg. Transi-Trend	Gerhardt/Offy	0	Accident	13,677

Total Purse $991,887

Time of Race: **3:12:37.04** Average Speed: **155.749 mph** Margin of Victory: **32.19 sec**
Pole: **#2 Al Unser (170.221, 3:31.49)** Fastest Race Lap: **#15 Joe Leonard (Race Lap 50, 167.785 mph, 53.64 sec.)**
Winning Car Owner: **Vel's Parnelli Jones Ford** Winning Chief Mechanic: **George Bignotti** Winning Tire: **Firestone** Rookie of Year: **Donnie Allison**
Legend: R=Indianapolis 500-Mile Race Rookie; W=Indianapolis 500-Mile Race Former Winner; *=Had Relief Help
Lap Leaders: A. Unser 1-48, Foyt 49, Ruby 50-51, Donohue 52, Brabham 53, A. Unser 54-100, Foyt 101, Donohue 102-105, A. Unser 106-200.
Lap Leader Summary: A. Unser 3 times for 190 laps, Donohue 2-5, Foyt 2-2, Ruby 1-2, Brabham 1-1. Lead Changes: 8 among 5 drivers.

Official Box Score

55th Indianapolis 500-Mile Race at the Indianapolis Motor Speedway • Saturday, May 29, 1971

FP	SP	No.		Driver	Car Name	Chassis/Engine	Laps	Status	Total Prize Money
1	5	1	W	Al Unser	Johnny Lightning	P.J. Colt/Ford	200	157.735	$238,454
2	1	86		Peter Revson	McLaren	McLaren/Offy	200	157.419	103,198
3	6	9	W	A.J. Foyt	ITT Thompson	Coyote/Ford	200	156.069	64,753
4	10	42		Jim Malloy	Olsonite Eagle	Eagle/Offy	200	154.577	38,669
5	11	32		Bill Vukovich II	Sugaripe Prune	Brabham/Offy	200	154.563	32,447
6	20	84		Donnie Allison	Purolator	Coyote/Ford	199	Running	30,093
7	17	58		Bud Tingelstad	Sugaripe Prune	Brabham/Offy	198	Running	28,206
8	28	43	R	Denny Zimmerman	Fiore Racing	Vollstedt/Offy	189	Running	27,658
9	22	6		Roger McCluskey	Sprite	Kuzma/Ford	188	Running	22,980
10	13	16		Gary Bettenhausen	Thermo-King	Gerhardt/Offy	178	Running	24,419
11	7	12		Lloyd Ruby	Utah Stars	Mongoose/Ford	174	Gears	21,866
12	3	2	W	Bobby Unser	Olsonite Eagle	Eagle/Offy	164	Accident	24,842
13	19	4		Mike Mosley	G.C. Murphy	Eagle Watson/Ford	159	Accident	20,345
14	33	44		Dick Simon	TraveLodge Sleeper	Vollstedt/Ford	151	Running	18,870
15	29	41		George Follmer	Grant King Racers	Kingfish/Offy	147	Piston	18,281
16	14	21		Cale Yarborough	Gene White Firestone	Mongoose/Offy	140	Cam Cover	17,370
17	4	85		Denis Hulme	McLaren	McLaren/Offy	137	Valve	17,887
18	24	18		Johnny Rutherford	Patrick Petroleum	Eagle/Offy	128	Running	16,682
19	8	15		Joe Leonard	Samsonite	P.J. Colt/Ford	123	Turbocharger	19,906
20	16	68	R	David Hobbs	Penske Products	Lola/Ford	107	Accident	16,009
21	18	38		Rick Muther	Arkansas Aviation	Hawk II/Offy	85	Accident	16,190
22	32	99		Bob Harkey	Joe Hunt Magneto	Gerhardt/Offy	77	Gears	15,399
23	15	95	R	Bentley Warren	Classic Wax	Eagle/Offy	76	Gears	14,486
24	23	22		Wally Dallenbach	Sprite	Kuzma/Offy	69	Valve	14,602
25	2	66		Mark Donohue	Sunoco	McLaren/Offy	66	Gears	26,697
26	31	64		Art Pollard	Gilmore Broadcasting	Scorpion/Ford	45	Valve	14,770
27	25	98		Sam Sessions	Wynn's Kwik-Kool	Lola/Ford	43	Valve	13,721
28	26	45		Larry Dickson	Grant King Racers	Kingfish/Offy	33	Engine failure	13,600
29	12	7		Gordon Johncock	Norris Industries	McLaren/Ford	11	Accident	13,458
30	9	5	W	Mario Andretti	STP Oil Treatment	McNamara/Ford	11	Accident	13,245
31	27	20	R	Steve Krisiloff	STP Gas Treatment	McNamara/Ford	10	Oil-Spun out	13,260
32	30	23		Mel Kenyon	Sprite	Kuzma/Ford	10	Accident	14,153
33	21	80		George Snider	G.C. Murphy	Eagle/Offy	6	Stalled	13,974

Total Purse $1,000,490

Time of Race: **3:10:11.56** Average Speed: **157.735 mph** Margin of Victory: **22.48 sec**
Pole: **#86 Peter Revson (178.696, 3:21.46)** Fastest Race Lap: **#66 Mark Donohue (Race Lap 66, 174.961 mph, 51.44 sec.)**
Winning Car Owner: **Vel's Parnelli Jones Ford** Winning Chief Mechanic: **George Bignotti** Winning Tire: **Firestone** Rookie of Year: **Denny Zimmerman**
Legend: R=Indianapolis 500-Mile Race Rookie; W=Indianapolis 500-Mile Race Former Winner
Lap Leaders: Donohue 1-50, Leonard 51-52, B. Unser 53-64, Donohue 65-66, A. Unser 67-72, Leonard 73-82, A. Unser 83-87, Leonard 88-94, A. Unser 95-98, Ruby 99-101, B. Unser 102-110, A. Unser 111-115, Leonard 116-117, A. Unser 118-200.
Lap Leader Summary: A. Unser 5 times for 103 laps, Donohue 2-52, Leonard 4-21, B. Unser 2-21, Ruby 1-3. Lead Changes: 13 among 5 drivers.

Official Box Score

56th Indianapolis 500-Mile Race at the Indianapolis Motor Speedway • Saturday, May 27, 1972

FP	SP	No.		Driver	Car Name	Chassis/Engine	Laps	Status	Total Prize Money
1	3	66		Mark Donohue	Sunoco McLaren	McLaren/Offy	200	162.962	$218,763
2	19	4	W	Al Unser	Viceroy	Parnelli/Offy	200	160.192	95,258
3	6	1		Joe Leonard	Samsonite	Parnelli/Offy	200	159.327	58,793
4	24	52		Sam Sessions	Gene White Firestone	Lola/Ford	200	158.411	39,583
5	7	34	R	Sam Posey	Norris Eagle	Eagle/Offy	198	Running	37,411
6	11	5		Lloyd Ruby	Wynn's	Atlanta/Foyt	196	Running	29,557
7	25	60	R	Mike Hiss	STP Pylon Windshield Wiper Blade	Eagle/Offy	196	Running	30,814
8	5	9	W	Mario Andretti	Viceroy	Parnelli/Offy	194	Out of fuel	24,822
9	31	11	R	Jimmy Caruthers	US Armed Forces/Steed	Scorpion/Foyt	194	Running	23,094
10	32	21		Cale Yarborough	Bill Daniels GOP	Atlanta/Foyt	193	Running	22,133
11	21	84		George Snider	ITT-Thompson	Coyote/Foyt	190	Running	23,080
12	15	48		Jerry Grant	Mystery Eagle	Eagle/Offy	188	Penalty	24,156
13	23	44		Dick Simon	TraveLodge Sleeper	Lola/Foyt	186	Out of Fuel	19,759
14	4	7		Gary Bettenhausen	Sunoco McLaren	McLaren/Offy	182	Ignition	41,284
15	33	40		Wally Dallenbach	STP Oil Treatment	Lola/Foyt	182	Running	19,645
16	14	89	R	John Martin	Unsponsored	Brabham/Offy	161	Fuel Leak	18,084
17	30	37	R	Lee Kunzman	Caves Buick Company	Gerhardt/Offy	131	Lost Tire	17,901
18	12	23		Mel Kenyon	Gilmore Racing	Coyote/Ford	126	Fuel Injection	17,146
19	28	17		Denny Zimmerman	Bryant Heating & Cooling	Coyote/Offy	116	Ignition Rotor	17,320
20	26	24		Gordon Johncock	Gulf McLaren	McLaren/Offy	113	Exhaust Valve	17,823
21	10	15		Steve Krisiloff	Ayr-Way/Lloyd's	Kingfish/Offy	102	Ignition Rotor	15,954
22	29	31	R	John Mahler	Harbor Fuel Oil	McLaren/Offy	99	Piston	16,013
23	13	56		Jim Hurtubise	Miller High Life	Coyote/Foyt	94	Penalty	15,350
24	20	14		Roger McCluskey	American Marine Underwriters	Antares/Offy	92	Valve	15,016
25	17	2	W	A.J. Foyt	ITT-Thompson	Coyote/Foyt	60	Turbocharger	15,611
26	16	98		Mike Mosley	Vivitar	Eagle/Offy	56	Accident	15,984
27	8	18		Johnny Rutherford	Patrick Petroleum	Brabham/Offy	55	Rod	14,535
28	18	3		Bill Vukovich II	Sugaripe Prune	Eagle/Offy	54	Rear End	14,364
29	22	95		Carl Williams	City of Terre Haute	Eagle/Offy	52	Oil Cooler	14,022
30	1	6	W	Bobby Unser	Olsonite Eagle	Eagle/Offy	31	Ignition Rotor	30,830
31	2	12		Peter Revson	Gulf McLaren	McLaren/Offy	23	Gearbox	15,924
32	9	42	R	Swede Savage	Michner Industries	Eagle/Offy	5	Rod	13,767
33	27	33	R	Salt Walther	Dayton Disc Brakes	P.J. Colt/Foyt	0	Magneto	14,538

Total Purse $1,008,334

Time of Race: 3:04:05.54 Average Speed: 162.962 mph Margin of Victory: 3:10.55
Pole: #6 Bobby Unser (195.940, 3:03.73) Fastest Race Lap: #66 Mark Donohue (Race Lap 150, 187.539 mph, 47.99 sec.)
Winning Car Owner: Roger Penske Enterprises Winning Chief Mechanic: Karl Kainhofer Winning Tire: Goodyear Rookie of Year: Mike Hiss
Legend: R=Indianapolis 500-Mile Race Rookie; W=Indianapolis 500-Mile Race Former Winner
Lap Leaders: B. Unser 1-30, Bettenhausen 31-53, Mosely 54-56, Bettenhausen 57-161, Grant 162-165, Bettenhausen 166-175, Grant 176-187, Donohue 188-200.
Lap Leader Summary: Bettenhausen 3 times for 138 laps, B. Unser 1-30, Grant 2-16, Donohue 1-13, Mosely 1-3. Lead Changes: 7 among 5 drivers.

Official Box Score

57th Indianapolis 500-Mile Race at the Indianapolis Motor Speedway • Monday, May 28, 1973

FP	SP	No.		Driver	Car Name	Chassis/Engine	Laps	Status	Total Prize Money
1	11	20		Gordon Johncock	STP Double Oil Filter	Eagle/Offy	133 (Rain)	159.036	$236,023
2	16	2		Bill Vukovich II	Sugaripe Prune	Eagle/Offy	133	157.262	97,513
3	14	3		Roger McCluskey	Lindsey Hopkins Buick	McLaren/Offy	131	Running	60,753
4	19	19		Mel Kenyon	Atlanta Falcons	Eagle/Foyt	131	Running	34,488
5	5	5		Gary Bettenhausen	Sunoco DX	McLaren/Offy	130	Running	37,966
6	7	24		Steve Krisiloff	Elliott-Norton Spirit	Kingfish/Offy	129	Running	30,862
7	25	16		Lee Kunzman	Ayr-Way/Lloyd's	Eagle/Offy	127	Running	26,350
8	24	89		John Martin	Unsponsored	McLaren/Offy	124	Running	25,377
9	1	7		Johnny Rutherford	Gulf McLaren	McLaren/Offy	124	Running	29,904
10	21	98		Mike Mosley	Lodestar	Eagle/Offy	120	Rod Bolt	23,675
11	22	73		David Hobbs	Carling Black Label	Eagle/Offy	107	Running	20,935
12	30	84		George Snider*	Gilmore Racing Team	Coyote/Foyt	101	Gearbox	21,511
13	2	8	W	Bobby Unser	Olsonite	Eagle/Offy	100	Blown Engine	30,264
14	27	44		Dick Simon	TraveLodge	Eagle/Foyt	100	Piston	19,489
15	3	66	W	Mark Donohue	Sunoco DX	Eagle/Offy	92	Piston	19,950
16	13	60	R	Graham McRae	STP Gas Treatment	Eagle/Offy	91	Header	19,039
17	26	6		Mike Hiss	Thermo-King	Eagle/Offy	91	Drive Train	18,156
18	29	1		Joe Leonard	Samsonite	Parnelli/Offy	91	Hub bearing	17,301
19	18	48		Jerry Grant	Olsonite	Eagle/Offy	77	Blown Engine	16,675
20	8	4	W	Al Unser	Viceroy	Parnelli/Offy	75	Piston	20,628
21	9	21		Jimmy Caruthers	Cobre	Eagle/Offy	73	Suspension	16,009
22	4	40		Swede Savage	STP Oil Treatment	Eagle/Offy	57	Accident	19,368
23	33	35		Jim McElreath	Norris Eagle	Eagle/Offy	54	Blown Engine	15,655
24	20	62		Wally Dallenbach	Olsonite	Eagle/Offy	48	Broken Rod	14,971
25	23	14	W	A.J. Foyt	Gilmore Racing Team	Coyote/Foyt	37	Rod Bolt	14,716
26	28	30	R	Jerry Karl	Oriente Express	Eagle/Chevrolet	22	Running	17,689
27	15	18		Lloyd Ruby	Commander Motor Homes	Eagle/Offy	21	Piston	14,290
28	32	9		Sam Sessions	M.V.S.	Eagle/Foyt	17	Out of Oil	14,719
29	31	28		Bob Harkey	Bryant Heating & Cooling	Kenyon-Eagle/Foyt	12	Seized Engine	14,777
30	6	11	W	Mario Andretti	Viceroy	Parnelli/Offy	4	Piston	14,564
31	10	15		Peter Revson	Gulf McLaren	McLaren/Offy	3	Accident	13,779
32	12	12	R	Bobby Allison	Sunoco DX	McLaren/Offy	1	Rod	13,722
33	17	77		Salt Walther	Dayton-Walther	McLaren/Offy	0	Accident	13,963

Total Purse $1,005,081

Time of Race: 2:05:26.59 Average Speed: 159.036 mph Margin of Victory: Under Caution
Pole: #7 Johnny Rutherford (198.413, 3:01.44) Fastest Race Lap: #3 Roger McCluskey (Race Lap 55, 186.916 mph, 48.15 sec.)
Winning Car Owner: Patrick Racing Team Winning Chief Mechanic: George Bignotti Winning Tire: Goodyear Rookie of Year: Graham McRae
Legend: R=Indianapolis 500-Mile Race Rookie; W=Indianapolis 500-Mile Race Former Winner; *=Had Relief Help
Race Notes: Race stopped on May 28 due to 1st lap accident, rain further delayed race until May 30th.
Lap Leaders: B. Unser 1-39, Johncock 40-42, Savage 43-54, A. Unser 55-72, Johncock 73-133.
Lap Leader Summary: Johncock 2 times for 64 laps, B. Unser 1-39, A. Unser 1-18, Savage 1-12. Lead Changes: 4 among 4 drivers.

Official Box Score

58th Indianapolis 500-Mile Race at the Indianapolis Motor Speedway • Sunday, May 26, 1974

FP	SP	No.		Driver	Car Name	Chassis/Engine	Laps	Status	Total Prize Money
1	25	3		Johnny Rutherford	McLaren	McLaren/Offy	200	158.589	$245,032
2	7	48	W	Bobby Unser	Olsonite Eagle	Eagle/Offy	200	158.278	99,504
3	16	4		Bill Vukovich II	Sugaripe Prune	Eagle/Offy	199	Running	63,811
4	4	20	W	Gordon Johncock	STP Double Oil Filter	Eagle/Offy	198	Running	37,079
5	9	73		David Hobbs	Carling Black Label	McLaren/Offy	196	Running	32,074
6	30	45		Jim McElreath	Thermo-King	Eagle/Offy	194	Running	27,970
7	21	11	R	Pancho Carter	Cobre Firestone	Eagle/Offy	191	Running	27,758
8	31	79		Bob Harkey	Peru Circus	Kenyon/Foyt	189	Running	23,985
9	18	9		Lloyd Ruby	Unlimited Racing	Eagle/Offy	187	Out of fuel	23,182
10	17	55		Jerry Grant	Cobre Firestone	Eagle/Offy	175	Running	22,016
11	22	89		John Martin	Sea Snack Shrimp Cocktail	McLaren/Offy	169	Running	21,393
12	23	27	R	Tom Bigelow	Bryant Heating & Cooling	Vollstedt/Offy	166	Running	20,769
13	20	18	R	Bill Simpson	American Kids Racer	Eagle/Offy	163	Piston	19,922
14	3	68		Mike Hiss	Norton Spirit	McLaren/Offy	158	Running	21,697
15	1	14	W	A.J. Foyt	Gilmore Racing Team	Coyote/Foyt	142	Oil Fitting	38,674
16	27	1		Roger McCluskey	English Leather	Riley/Offy	141	Rear End	19,097
17	14	77		Salt Walther	Dayton-Walther	McLaren/Offy	141	Piston	18,197
18	26	15	W	Al Unser	Viceroy	Eagle/Offy	131	Valve	17,492
19	19	42		Jerry Karl	Ayr-Way/Lloyd's	Eagle/Offy	115	Accident	17,333
20	8	24	R	Tom Sneva	Raymond Companies	Kingfish/Offy	94	Drive Gear	19,136
21	32	51	R	Jan Opperman	Viceroy Parnelli	Parnelli/Offy	85	Spun out	15,617
22	15	60		Steve Krisiloff	STP Gas Treatment	Eagle/Offy	72	Clutch	16,026
23	12	21		Jimmy Caruthers	Cobre Firestone	Eagle/Offy	64	Gearbox	16,063
24	33	59	R	Larry Cannon	American Financial Corp.	Eagle/Offy	49	Differential	15,429
25	28	56		Jim Hurtubise	Miller High Life	Eagle/Offy	31	Blown Engine	15,324
26	29	94	R	Johnny Parsons	Vatis	Finley/Offy	18	Turbocharger	14,497
27	24	61		Rick Muther	Eisenhour/Brayton	Coyote/Foyt	11	Piston	14,748
28	13	82		George Snider	Gilmore Racing Team	Atlanta/Foyt	7	Valve	14,027
29	6	98		Mike Mosley	Lodestar	Eagle/Offy	6	Blown Engine	16,435
30	2	40		Wally Dallenbach	STP Oil Treatment	Eagle/Offy	3	Piston	16,222
31	5	5	W	Mario Andretti	Viceroy	Eagle/Offy	2	Valve	15,587
32	11	8		Gary Bettenhausen	Score	McLaren/Offy	2	Valve	14,230
33	10	44		Dick Simon	TraveLodge	Eagle/Foyt	1	Valve	14,551

Total Purse $1,014,877

Time of Race: 3:09:10.06 Average Speed: 158.589 mph Margin of Victory: 22.32 sec
Pole: #14 A.J. Foyt (191.632, 3:07.86) Fastest Race Lap: #40 Wally Dallenbach (Race Lap 2, 191.408 mph, 47.02 sec.)
Winning Car Owner: McLaren Cars, Ltd. Winning Chief Mechanic: Denis Daviss Winning Tire: Goodyear Rookie of Year: Pancho Carter
Legend: R=Indianapolis 500-Mile Race Rookie; W=Indianapolis 500-Mile Race Former Winner
Lap Leaders: Dallenbach 1-2, Foyt 3-24, B. Unser 25-26, Foyt 27-49, B. Unser 50-52, Foyt 53-64, Rutherford 65-125, Foyt 126-135, Rutherford 136-137, Foyt 138-140, Rutherford 141-175, B. Unser 176, Rutherford 177-200.
Lap Leader Summary: Rutherford 4 times for 122 laps, Foyt 5-70, B. Unser 3-6, Dallenbach 1-2. Lead Changes: 12 among 4 drivers.

Official Box Score

59th Indianapolis 500-Mile Race at the Indianapolis Motor Speedway • Sunday, May 25, 1975

FP	SP	No.		Driver	Car Name	Chassis/Engine	Laps	Status	Total Prize Money
1	3	48	W	Bobby Unser	Jorgensen Eagle	Eagle/Offy	174 (Rain)	149.213	$214,032
2	7	2	W	Johnny Rutherford	Gatorade	McLaren/Offy	174	148.308	97,886
3	1	14	W	A.J. Foyt	Gilmore Racing Team	Coyote/Foyt	174	147.684	74,677
4	18	11		Pancho Carter	Cobre Tire	Eagle/Offy	169	Running	33,424
5	22	15		Roger McCluskey	Silver Floss	Riley/Offy	167	Running	31,002
6	8	6		Bill Vukovich II	Cobre Tire	Eagle/Offy	166	Running	28,473
7	15	83	R	Bill Puterbaugh	McNamara-D.I.A.	Eagle/Offy	165	Running	28,786
8	24	97		George Snider	Leader Card Lodestar	Eagle/Offy	165	Running	24,688
9	21	40		Wally Dallenbach	Sinmast Wildcat	Wildcat/SGD	162	Piston	42,712
10	23	33		Bob Harkey*	Dayton-Walther	McLaren/Offy	162	Running	22,899
11	29	98		Steve Krisiloff	Leader Card Lodestar	Eagle/Offy	162	Running	22,796
12	26	19	R	Sheldon Kinser	Spirit of Indiana	Kingfish/Offy	161	Running	20,772
13	20	30		Jerry Karl	Jose Johnson	Eagle/Chevrolet	161	Running	19,975
14	10	78		Jimmy Caruthers	Alex Foods	Eagle/Offy	161	Running	19,350
15	19	45		Gary Bettenhausen	Thermo-King	Eagle/Offy	158	Accident	19,811
16	11	4	W	Al Unser	Viceroy	Eagle/Offy	157	Rod	18,300
17	25	36		Sam Sessions	Commander Motor Homes	Eagle/Offy	155	Engine	18,117
18	33	17		Tom Bigelow	Bryant Heating & Cooling	Vollstedt/Offy	151	Magneto	18,162
19	12	93		Johnny Parsons	Ayr-Way WNAP Buzzard	Eagle/Offy	140	Transmission	16,936
20	14	73		Jerry Grant	Spirit of Orange County	Eagle/Offy	137	Piston	16,539
21	30	44		Dick Simon	Bruce Cogle Ford	Eagle/Foyt	133	Running	17,070
22	4	68		Tom Sneva	Norton Spirit	McLaren/Offy	125	Accident	17,829
23	17	24		Bentley Warren	THE BOTTOMHALF	Kingfish/Offy	120	Running	15,516
24	32	58	R	Eldon Rasmussen	Anacomp-Wild Rose	Ras-Car/Foyt	119	Valve	16,432
25	13	16		Bobby Allison	CAM2 Motor Oil	McLaren/Offy	112	Gearbox	14,827
26	5	12		Mike Mosley	Sugaripe Prune	Eagle/Offy	94	Engine	16,550
27	16	89		John Martin	Unsponsored	McLaren/Offy	61	Radiator	14,551
28	27	21	W	Mario Andretti	Viceroy	Eagle/Offy	49	Accident	15,880
29	31	94		Mike Hiss	Ayr-Way WNAP Buzzard	Finley/Offy	39	Accident	14,538
30	28	63	R	Larry McCoy	Shurfine Foods	Ras-Car/Offy	24	Piston	14,925
31	2	20	W	Gordon Johncock	Sinmast Wildcat	Wildcat/SGD	11	Ignition	18,120
32	6	7		Lloyd Ruby	Allied Polymer	McLaren/Offy	7	Piston	15,583
33	9	77		Salt Walther	Dayton-Walther	McLaren/Offy	2	Ignition	14,954

Total Purse $996,112

Time of Race: 2:54:55.08 Average Speed: 149.213 mph Margin of Victory: Under Caution
Pole: #14 A.J. Foyt (193.976, 3:05.59) Fastest Race Lap: #20 Gordon Johncock (Race Lap 2, 187.110 mph, 48.10 sec.)
Winning Car Owner: All American Racers Winning Chief Mechanic: Wayne Leary Winning Tire: Goodyear Rookie of Year: Bill Puterbaugh
Legend: R=Indianapolis 500-Mile Race Rookie; W=Indianapolis 500-Mile Race Former Winner; *=Had Relief Help
Race Notes: Race stopped on lap 174 due to rain.
Lap Leaders: Johncock 1-8, Foyt 9-21, Rutherford 22-23, Allison 24, Foyt 25-58, Dallenbach 59-69, Foyt 70, Dallenbach 71-94, Foyt 95-96, Dallenbach 97-120, Foyt 121-123, B. Unser 124, Dallenbach 125-161, Rutherford 162-164, B. Unser 165-174.
Lap Leader Summary: Dallenbach 4 times for 96 laps, Foyt 5-53, B. Unser 2-11, Johncock 1-8, Rutherford 2-5, Allison 1-1. Lead Changes: 14 among 6 drivers.

Official Box Score

60th Indianapolis 500-Mile Race at the Indianapolis Motor Speedway • Sunday, May 30, 1976

FP	SP	No.		Driver	Car Name	Chassis/Engine	Laps	Status	Total Prize Money
1	1	2	W	Johnny Rutherford	Hy-Gain	McLaren/Offy	102 (Rain)	148.725	$255,321
2	5	14	W	A.J. Foyt	Gilmore Racing Team	Coyote/Foyt	102	148.355	103,097
3	2	20	W	Gordon Johncock	Sinmast	Wildcat/DGS	102	146.238	67,676
4	7	40		Wally Dallenbach	Sinmast	Wildcat/DGS	101	Running	38,050
5	6	48		Pancho Carter	Jorgensen	Eagle/Offy	101	Running	33,778
6	3	68		Tom Sneva	Norton Spirit	McLaren/Offy	101	Running	30,960
7	4	21	W	Al Unser	American Racing	Parnelli/Cosworth	101	Running	27,442
8	19	6	W	Mario Andretti	CAM2 Motor Oil	McLaren/Offy	101	Running	28,331
9	22	77		Salt Walther	Dayton-Walther	McLaren/Offy	100	Running	23,728
10	12	3	W	Bobby Unser	Cobre Tire	Eagle/Offy	100	Running	23,992
11	30	51		Lloyd Ruby	Fairco Drugs	Eagle/Offy	100	Running	23,039
12	14	93		Johnny Parsons	Ayr-Way/WIRE	Eagle/Offy	98	Running	21,215
13	27	23		George Snider	Hubler Chevrolet	Eagle/Offy	98	Running	20,718
14	32	24		Tom Bigelow	Leader Card Racers	Eagle/Offy	98	Running	20,193
15	11	12		Mike Mosley	Sugaripe Prune	Eagle/Offy	98	Running	20,954
16	33	8		Jan Opperman	Routh Meat Packing	Eagle/Offy	97	Running	18,943
17	10	69		Larry Cannon	American Financial Corp.	Eagle/Offy	97	Running	18,060
18	17	9	R	Vern Schuppan	Jorgensen	Eagle/Offy	97	Running	18,605
19	29	97		Sheldon Kinser	THE BOTTOMHALF	Dragon/Offy	97	Running	17,179
20	28	96		Bob Harkey	Dave McIntire Chevy/Ford Centers	Kingfish/Offy	97	Running	16,782
21	15	98		John Martin	Genesse Beer	Dragon/Offy	96	Running	17,213
22	18	83		Bill Puterbaugh	McNamara Motor Express	Eagle/Offy	96	Running	16,072
23	21	28	R	Billy Scott	Spirit of Public Enterprise	Eagle/Offy	96	Running	17,859
24	23	92		Steve Krisiloff	1st National City Travelers Checks	Eagle/Offy	95	Running	15,775
25	24	86	R	Al Loquasto	Frostie Root Beer	McLaren/Offy	95	Running	15,420
26	26	63		Larry McCoy	Shurfine Foods	Ras-Car/Offy	91	Running	14,993
27	20	73		Jerry Grant	California/Oklahoma	Eagle/AMC	91	Running	15,594
28	8	45		Gary Bettenhausen	Thermo-King	Eagle/Offy	52	Turbocharger	15,623
29	31	33		David Hobbs	Dayton-Walther	McLaren/Offy	10	Water Leak	15,281
30	13	7		Roger McCluskey	Hopkins	Lightning/Offy	8	Accident	15,468
31	9	5		Bill Vukovich II	Alex Foods	Eagle/Offy	2	Rod	15,283
32	16	17		Dick Simon	Bryant Heating & Cooling	Vollstedt/Offy	1	Rod	15,926
33	25	19	R	Spike Gehlhausen	Spirit of Indiana	McLaren/Offy	0	Oil Pressure	14,197

Total Purse $1,032,767

Time of Race: 1:42:52.48 Average Speed: 148.725 mph Margin of Victory: Under Caution
Pole: #2 Johnny Rutherford (188.957, 3:10.52) Fastest Qualifier: #6 Mario Andretti (189.404, 3:10.07)
Fastest Race Lap: #14 A.J. Foyt Jr. (Race Lap 2, 186.027 mph, 48.38 sec.)
Winning Car Owner: Team McLaren, Ltd. Winning Chief Mechanic: Denis Daviss Winning Tire: Goodyear Rookie of Year: Vern Schuppan
Legend: R=Indianapolis 500-Mile Race Rookie; W=Indianapolis 500-Mile Race Former Winner
Race Notes: Race stopped on lap 102 due to rain.
Lap Leaders: Rutherford 1-3, Foyt 4-13, Carter 14-16, Dallenbach 17-19, Johncock 20-37, Sneva 38, Rutherford 39-60, Foyt 61-79, Rutherford 80-102.
Lap Leader Summary: Rutherford 3 times for 48 laps, Foyt 2-29, Johncock 1-18, Carter 1-3, Dallenbach 1-3, Sneva 1-1. Lead Changes: 8 among 6 drivers.
Caution Laps: 4-6, #17 Simon, stopped. 10-13, #7 McCluskey, accident. 14-16, Debris. 60-64, #93 Parsons, lost wheel. 91-94, #73 Grant, stopped. 101-102, Rain. Cautions: 6 for 21 laps.

Official Box Score

61st Indianapolis 500-Mile Race at the Indianapolis Motor Speedway • Sunday, May 29, 1977

FP	SP	No.		Driver	Car Name	Chassis/Engine	Laps	Status	Total Prize Money
1	4	14	W	A.J. Foyt	Gilmore Racing Team	Coyote/Foyt	200	161.331	$259,791
2	1	8		Tom Sneva	Norton Spirit	McLaren/Cosworth	200	160.918	109,947
3	3	21	W	Al Unser	American Racing	Parnelli/Cosworth	199	Running	67,232
4	10	40		Wally Dallenbach	STP Oil Treatment	Wildcat/DGS	199	Running	41,192
5	11	60		Johnny Parsons	STP Wildcat	Wildcat/DGS	193	Running	33,170
6	22	24		Tom Bigelow	Thermo-King	Watson/Offy	192	Running	30,466
7	24	65		Lee Kunzman	City of Syracuse	Eagle/Offy	191	Running	29,129
8	18	11		Roger McCluskey	1st National City Travelers Checks	Lightning/Offy	191	Running	27,256
9	25	92		Steve Krisiloff	Dave McIntire Chevrolet	Eagle/Offy	191	Running	26,653
10	16	36	R	Jerry Sneva	21st Amendment	McLaren/Offy	187	Running	26,617
11	5	20	W	Gordon Johncock	STP Double Oil Filter	Wildcat/DGS	184	Crankshaft	45,014
12	28	16		Bill Puterbaugh	Dayton-Walther	Eagle/Offy	170	Valve	22,890
13	32	58		Eldon Rasmussen	Rent-a-Racer, Inc.	Ras-Car/Foyt	168	Running	21,093
14	31	42		John Mahler*	Mergard 20th Century	Eagle/Offy	157	Running	20,668
15	8	48		Pancho Carter	Jorgensen	Eagle/Offy	156	Engine	21,679
16	21	98		Gary Bettenhausen	Agajanian/Evil Knievel	Kingfish/Offy	138	Clutch	19,718
17	23	84		Bill Vukovich II	Gilmore Racing Team	Coyote/Foyt	110	Wing Strut	19,885
18	2	6	W	Bobby Unser	Cobre Tire/Clayton Dyno-Tune	Lightning/Offy	94	Oil Leak	22,130
19	9	5		Mike Mosley	Sugaripe Prune	Lightning/Offy	91	Timing Gear	19,154
20	7	25	R	Danny Ongais	Interscope Racing	Parnelli/Cosworth	90	Header	21,257
21	33	72	R	Bubby Jones	Bruce Cogle Ford	Eagle/Offy	78	Valve	17,388
22	27	29	R	Cliff Hucul	Team Canada	McLaren/Offy	72	Gearbox	17,747
23	20	73		Jim McElreath	Carrillo Rods	Eagle/AMC	71	Turbocharger	22,434
24	13	18		George Snider	Melvin Simon Greenwood Center	Wildcat/DGS	65	Valve	16,650
25	14	78	R	Bobby Olivero	Alex Foods	Lightning/Offy	57	Piston	17,245
26	6	9	W	Mario Andretti	CAM2 Motor Oil	McLaren/Offy	47	Header	17,468
27	19	10		Lloyd Ruby	1st National City Travelers Checks	Lightning/Offy	34	Accident	16,619
28	15	86		Al Loquasto	Frostie Root Beer	McLaren/Offy	28	Magneto	17,448
29	26	27	R	Janet Guthrie	Bryant Heating & Cooling	Lightning/Offy	27	Timing Gear	16,556
30	29	38	R	Clay Regazzoni	Theodore Racing Hong Kong	McLaren/Offy	25	Fuel Cell	15,643
31	30	17		Dick Simon	Bryant Heating & Cooling	Vollstedt/Offy	24	Overheating	16,458
32	12	97		Sheldon Kinser	Genesee Beer	Kingfish/Offy	14	Piston	15,101
33	17	2	W	Johnny Rutherford	1st National City Travelers Checks	McLaren/Cosworth	12	Gearbox	19,472

Total Purse $1,111,170

Time of Race: 3:05:57.16 Average Speed: 161.331 mph Margin of Victory: 28.63 sec
Pole: #8 Tom Sneva (198.884, 3:01.01) Fastest Race Lap: #25 Danny Ongais (Race Lap 42, 192.678 mph, 46.71 sec.)
Winning Car Owner: A.J. Foyt Enterprises Winning Chief Mechanic: A.J. "Tony" Foyt Sr./Jack Starne Winning Tire: Goodyear Rookie of Year: Jerry Sneva
Legend: R=Indianapolis 500-Mile Race Rookie; W=Indianapolis 500-Mile Race Former Winner; *=Had Relief Help
Lap Leaders: A. Unser 1-17, Johncock 18-21, Foyt 22-23, Snider 24-25, Vukovich 26, Foyt 27-51, Johncock 52-68, B. Unser 69-70, Johncock 71-93, Sneva 94-96, Johncock 97-179, Foyt 180-182, Johncock 183-184, Foyt 185-200.
Lap Leader Summary: Johncock 5 times for 129 laps, Foyt 4-46, A. Unser 1-17, Sneva 1-3, B. Unser 1-2, Snider 1-2, Vukovich 1-1. Lead Changes: 13 among 7 drivers.
Caution Laps: 36-44, #10 Ruby, accident. 49-51, #58 Rasmussen, spin. 69-72, #18 Snider, tow-in. 159-160, #48 Carter, tow-in. 163-166, #60 Parsons, tow-in. Cautions: 5 for 22 laps.

Official Box Score

62nd Indianapolis 500-Mile Race at the Indianapolis Motor Speedway • Sunday, May 28, 1978

FP	SP	No.		Driver	Car Name	Chassis/Engine	Laps	Status	Total Prize Money
1	5	2	W	Al Unser	1st National City Travelers Checks	Lola/Cosworth	200	161.363	$290,364
2	1	1		Tom Sneva	Norton Spirit	Penske/Cosworth	200	161.244	112,704
3	6	20	W	Gordon Johncock	North American Van Lines	Wildcat/DGS	199	Running	61,769
4	13	40		Steve Krisiloff	Foreman Industries	Wildcat/DGS	198	Running	39,504
5	7	6		Wally Dallenbach	Sugaripe Prune	McLaren/Cosworth	195	Running	35,632
6	19	48	W	Bobby Unser	ARCO Graphite	Eagle/Cosworth	195	Running	29,478
7	20	14	W	A.J. Foyt	Gilmore Racing/Citicorp	Coyote/Foyt	191	Running	29,628
8	23	84		George Snider	Gilmore Racing/Citicorp	Coyote/Foyt	191	Running	25,818
9	15	51		Janet Guthrie	Texaco Star	Wildcat/DGS	190	Running	24,115
10	8	16		Johnny Parsons	1st National City Travelers Checks	Lightning/Offy	186	Running	26,129
11	30	35	R	Larry Rice	Bryant Heating/WIBC	Lightning/Offy	186	Engine	24,276
12	33	7	W	Mario Andretti	Gould Charge	Penske/Cosworth	185	Running	23,252
13	4	4	W	Johnny Rutherford	1st National City Travelers Checks	McLaren/Cosworth	180	Running	31,805
14	28	88		Jerry Karl	Machinists Union	McLaren/Offy	176	Running	20,930
15	24	69	R	Joe Saldana	Mr. Wize Buys Carpet Shop	Eagle/Offy	173	Running	20,691
16	31	98		Gary Bettenhausen	Oberdorfer	Kingfish/Offy	147	Engine	20,130
17	25	78		Mike Mosley	Alex XLNT Foods	Lightning/Offy	146	Turbocharger	20,247
18	2	25		Danny Ongais	Interscope Racing	Parnelli/Cosworth	145	Blown Engine	33,242
19	10	17		Dick Simon	La Machine	Vollstedt/Offy	138	Wheel Bearing	18,516
20	26	26		Jim McElreath	Circle City Coal	Eagle/Offy	132	Engine	19,119
21	18	43		Tom Bigelow	Armstrong Mould	Wildcat/DGS	107	Rod	18,000
22	9	80		Larry Dickson	Polak/Stay-On Car Glaze	McLaren/Cosworth	104	Oil Pressure	22,659
23	3	71	R	Rick Mears	CAM2 Motor Oil	Penske/Cosworth	103	Engine	22,396
24	21	8		Pancho Carter	Budweiser	Lightning/Cosworth	92	Header	20,262
25	11	11		Roger McCluskey	National Engineering Co.	Eagle/AMC	82	Clutch	18,707
26	17	39		John Mahler	Tibon	Eagle/Offy	58	Timing gear	16,330
27	14	22	R	Tom Bagley	Kent Oil	Watson/Offy	25	Oil Leak	16,281
28	22	77		Salt Walther	Dayton-Walther	McLaren/Cosworth	24	Clutch	16,560
29	16	19		Spike Gehlhausen	Hubler Chevrolet/WIRE Radio	Eagle/Offy	23	Accident	15,968
30	29	47	R	Phil Threshie	Circle City Chevrolet/Tutweiler Cadillac	Lightning/Offy	22	Oil Pressure	15,705
31	32	30		Jerry Sneva	Smock Material Handling	McLaren/Offy	18	Transmission	18,120
32	12	24		Sheldon Kinser	Thermo-King	Watson/Offy	15	Oil Pressure	15,813
33	27	29		Cliff Hucul	Wendy's Hamburgers	McLaren/Offy	4	Oil Line	15,534

Total Purse $1,139,684

Time of Race: 3:05:54.99 Average Speed: 161.363 mph Margin of Victory: 8.09 sec
Pole: #1 Tom Sneva (202.156, 2:58.08) Fastest Race Lap: #7 Mario Andretti (Race Lap 75, 193.924 mph, 46.41 sec.)
Winning Car Owner: Chaparral Racing, Ltd Winning Chief Mechanic: Hywel Absalom Winning Tire: Goodyear Rookie of Year: Rick Mears/Larry Rice
Legend: R=Indianapolis 500-Mile Race Rookie; W=Indianapolis 500-Mile Race Former Winner
Lap Leaders: Ongais 1-11, Sneva 12, Ongais 13-25, Krisiloff 26-30, Sneva 31, Ongais 32-75, A. Unser 76-107, Ongais 108-110, A. Unser 111-179, Sneva 180, A. Unser 181-200.
Lap Leader Summary: A. Unser 3 times for 121 laps, Ongais 4-71, Krisiloff 5-5, Sneva 3-3. Lead Changes: 10 among 4 drivers.
Caution Laps: 2-4, #24 Kinser, tow-in. 9-11, #24 Kinser, tow-in. 26-31, #19 Gelhausen, accident T2. 48-51, Debris. 84-85, Debris. 114-118, #71 Mears, #43 Bigelow, tow-in. Cautions: 6 for 23 laps.

Official Box Score

63rd Indianapolis 500-Mile Race at the Indianapolis Motor Speedway • Sunday, May 27, 1979

FP	SP	No.		Driver	Car Name	Chassis/Engine	Laps	Status	Total Prize Money
1	1	9		Rick Mears	The Gould Charge	Penske/Cosworth	200	158.899	$270,401
2	6	14	W	A.J. Foyt	Gilmore Racing Team	Parnelli/Cosworth	200	158.260	107,291
3	12	36		Mike Mosley	Theodore Racing	Eagle/Cosworth	200	158.228	65,031
4	27	25		Danny Ongais	Interscope Racing	Penske/Cosworth	199	Running	41,197
5	4	12	W	Bobby Unser	Norton Spirit	Penske/Cosworth	199	Running	62,319
6	5	3	W	Gordon Johncock	North American Van Lines	Penske/Cosworth	197	Running	34,815
7	13	46	R	Howdy Holmes	Armstrong Mould/Jiffy Mix	Wildcat/Cosworth	195	Running	38,503
8	34	22		Bill Vukovich II	Hubler/WNDE/Thermo-King	Watson/Offy	194	Running	31,305
9	15	11		Tom Bagley	Dairy Queen/Kent Oil	Penske/Cosworth	193	Running	26,927
10	31	19		Spike Gehlhausen	Sta-On Car Glaze/WIRE	Wildcat/Cosworth	192	Running	26,366
11	28	7		Steve Krisiloff	Frosty Acres/Winton Sales	Lightning/Offy	192	Running	25,713
12	16	77		Salt Walther	Dayton-Walther	Penske/Cosworth	191	Running	24,739
13	25	72		Roger McCluskey	National Engineering Co.	McLaren/Cosworth	191	Running	26,392
14	30	44		Tom Bigelow	Armstrong Mould	Lola/Cosworth	190	Running	25,817
15	2	1		Tom Sneva	Sugaripe Prune	McLaren/Cosworth	188	Accident	30,578
16	26	69		Joe Saldana	KBHL/Spirit of Nebraska	Eagle/Offy	186	Running	24,467
17	29	97		Phil Threshie	Guiffre Brothers Crane	King/Chevrolet	172	Running	24,634
18	8	4	W	Johnny Rutherford	Budweiser	McLaren/Cosworth	168	Running	30,729
19	23	31		Larry Rice	S&M Electric	Lightning/Offy	142	Accident	21,053
20	17	10		Pancho Carter	Alex XLNT Foods	Lightning/Offy	129	Wheel Bearing	21,656
21	22	34		Vern Schuppan	Wysard Motor Co.	Wildcat/DGS	111	Transmission	20,537
22	3	2	W	Al Unser	Pennzoil	Chaparral/Cosworth	104	Transmission	39,646
23	33	50		Eldon Rasmussen	Vans by Bivouac/WFMS	Antares/Offy	89	Header Pipe	19,433
24	24	80		Larry Dickson	Russ Polak	Penske/Cosworth	86	Fuel Pump	19,149
25	32	92		John Mahler	Intercomp/Sports Magazine	Eagle/Offy	66	Fuel Pump	18,894
26	20	17		Dick Simon	Sanyo	Vollstedt/Offy	57	Clutch	19,267
27	7	6		Wally Dallenbach	Foreman Industries	Penske/Cosworth	43	Lost Wheel	19,768
28	10	24		Sheldon Kinser	Genesee Beer	Watson/Offy	40	Piston	18,297
29	18	29		Cliff Hucul	Hucul Racing	McLaren/Offy	22	Rod	21,605
30	11	89		Lee Kunzman	Vetter Windjammer	Parnelli/Cosworth	18	Scavenger Pump	18,042
31	21	73		Jerry Sneva	National Engineering Co.	Spirit/AMC	16	Piston	18,357
32	9	15		Johnny Parsons	Hopkins	Lightning/Offy	16	Piston	18,900
33	35	59		George Snider	KBHL/Spirit of Nebraska	Lightning/Offy	7	Fuel Pump	18,921
34	14	45		Janet Guthrie	Texaco Star	Lola/Cosworth	3	Piston	18,121
35	19	23		Jim McElreath	Amax Coal	Penske/Cosworth	0	Valves	18,671

Total Purse $1,267,541

Time of Race: 3:08:47.97 Average Speed: 158.899 mph Margin of Victory: 45.69 sec
Pole: #9 Rick Mears (193.736, 3:05.82) Fastest Race Lap: #36 Mike Mosley (Race Lap 184, 193.216 mph, 46.58 sec.)
Winning Car Owner: Penske Racing, Inc. Winning Chief Mechanic: Darrell Soppe Winning Tire: Goodyear Rookie of Year: Howdy Holmes
Legend: R=Indianapolis 500-Mile Race Rookie; W=Indianapolis 500-Mile Race Former Winner
Lap Leaders: A. Unser 1-24, Mears 25-27, Foyt 28, A. Unser 29-69, B. Unser 70-73, Mears 74-76, A. Unser 77-96, B. Unser 97-181, Mears 182-200.
Lap Leader Summary: B. Unser 2 times for 89 laps, A. Unser 3-85, Mears 3-25, Foyt 1-1. Lead Changes: 8 among 4 drivers.
Caution Laps: 28-31, #29 Hucul, stalled. 43-48, #24 Kinser, stalled. 94-98, #80 Dickson, stalled. 103-107, #97 Threshie, stalled. 156-162, #31 Rice, accident T2. 191-195, #1 T. Sneva, accident T4. Cautions: 6 for 32 laps.

Official Box Score

64th Indianapolis 500-Mile Race at the Indianapolis Motor Speedway • Sunday, May 25, 1980

FP	SP	No.		Driver	Car Name	Chassis/Engine	Laps	Status	Total Prize Money
1	1	4	W	Johnny Rutherford	Pennzoil	Chaparral/Cosworth	200	142.862	$318,820
2	33	9		Tom Sneva	Bon Jour Action Jeans	McLaren/Cosworth	200	142.524	128,945
3	32	46		Gary Bettenhausen	Armstrong Mould	Wildcat/DGS	200	142.485	86,945
4	17	20	W	Gordon Johncock	North American Van Lines	Penske/Cosworth	200	142.482	56,495
5	6	1	W	Rick Mears	The Gould Charge	Penske/Cosworth	199	Running	45,505
6	8	10		Pancho Carter	Alex XLNT Foods	Penske/Cosworth	199	Running	39,175
7	16	25		Danny Ongais	Interscope/Panasonic	Parnelli/Cosworth	199	Running	37,414
8	31	43		Tom Bigelow	Armstrong Mould/Jiffy Mix	Lola/Cosworth	198	Running	44,707
9	19	21	R	Tim Richmond	UNO/Q95 Starcruiser	Penske/Cosworth	197	Out of fuel	43,447
10	23	44	R	Greg Leffler	Starcraft R.V.	Lola/Cosworth	197	Running	39,047
11	22	29	R	Billy Engelhart	Master Lock	McLaren/Cosworth	193	Running	32,303
12	30	2		Bill Vukovich II	Hubler Chevrolet/WFMS	Watson/Offy	192	Running	31,087
13	18	96	R	Don Whittington	Sun System	Penske/Cosworth	178	Running	30,928
14	12	14	W	A.J. Foyt	Gilmore Racing Team	Parnelli/Cosworth	173	Valve	29,512
15	21	16		George Snider	Gilmore Racing Team	Parnelli/Cosworth	169	Engine	30,351
16	24	18	R	Dennis Firestone	Scientific Drilling Controls	Penske/Cosworth	137	Transmission	28,776
17	5	7		Jerry Sneva	Hugger's Beverage Holders	Lola/Cosworth	130	Accident	30,271
18	25	99	R	Hurley Haywood	Sta-On Car Glaze/KISS99/Guarantee Auto	Lightning/Chevrolet V6	126	Fire	28,273
19	3	11	W	Bobby Unser	Norton Spirit	Penske/Cosworth	126	Turbo	37,432
20	2	12	W	Mario Andretti	Essex	Penske/Cosworth	71	Engine	33,611
21	28	38		Jerry Karl	Tonco Trailer	McLaren/Chevrolet	64	Clutch	26,747
22	29	8		Dick Simon	Vermont American/Shihouette Spas/Regal 8 Inns	Vollstedt/Offy	58	Lost wheel	26,411
23	10	66	R	Roger Rager	Advance Clean Sweep/Carpenter Bus	Wildcat/Chevrolet	55	Accident	26,503
24	11	23		Jim McElreath	McElreath	Penske/Cosworth	54	Accident	26,323
25	20	70	R	Gordon Smiley	Valvoline/Diamond Head Ranch	Phoenix/Cosworth	47	Turbo	26,771
26	7	15		Johnny Parsons	Wynn's	Lightning/Offy	44	Piston	26,597
27	9	5	W	Al Unser	Longhorn Racing	Longhorn/Cosworth	33	Cylinder	25,151
28	13	40		Tom Bagley	Kent Oil	Wildcat/Cosworth	29	Pump	25,983
29	4	35		Spike Gehlhausen	Winton Sales	Penske/Cosworth	20	Accident	26,143
30	27	94	R	Bill Whittington	Sun System	Parnelli/Cosworth	9	Accident	24,361
31	15	26	R	Dick Ferguson	AMS Oil	Penske/Cosworth	9	Accident	26,647
32	26	48		Mike Mosley	Theodore Racing	Eagle/Chevrolet	5	Gasket	24,591
33	14	95		Larry Cannon	Kraco Car Stereo	Wildcat/DGS	2	Camshaft	25,063

Total Purse $1,490,335

Time of Race: 3:29:59.56 Average Speed: 142.862 mph Margin of Victory: 29.92 sec
Pole: #4 Johnny Rutherford (192.256, 3:07.25) Fastest Race Lap: #4 Johnny Rutherford (Race Lap 149, 190.074 mph, 47.35 sec.)
Winning Car Owner: Chaparral Racing, Ltd Winning Chief Mechanic: Steve Roby Winning Tire: Goodyear Rookie of Year: Tim Richmond
Legend: R=Indianapolis 500-Mile Race Rookie; W=Indianapolis 500-Mile Race Former Winner
Lap Leaders: Rutherford 1-15, Rager 16-17, Snider 18, Johncock 19-24, B. Unser 25-30, Johncock 31-35, Carter 36-39, Rutherford 40-46, Andretti 47-56, Carter 57, Rutherford 58-72, Richmond 73, Sneva 74-84, B. Unser 85-103, Rutherford 104-113, Mears 114-116, B. Unser 117, Rutherford 118-142, Sneva 143-147, Rutherford 148-171, Mears 172-178, Rutherford 179-200.
Lap Leader Summary: Rutherford 7 times for 118 laps, B. Unser 3-26, Sneva 2-16, Johncock 2-11, Mears 2-10, Andretti 1-10, Carter 2-5, Rager 1-2, Snider 1-1, Richmond 1-1.
Lead Changes: 21 among 10 drivers.
Caution Laps: 4-6, #95 Cannon, stopped T1. 10-18, #26 Ferguson, #94 B. Whittington, accident T2. 21-24, #35 Gelhausen, accident T1. 30-33, #40 Bagley, stopped backstretch. 45-49, #15 Parsons, stopped T1. 57-62, #66 Rager, #23 McElreath, accident south short chute. 72-75, #12 Andretti, stopped backstretch. 85-90, #96 D. Whittington spun T4. 118-124, #8 Simon, lost front wheel. 132-137, #7 J. Sneva, accident T1. 142-146, #18 Firestone, stopped backstretch. 157-159, Debris. 177-179, #14 Foyt, stopped T3. Cautions: 13 for 65 laps.

Official Box Score

65th Indianapolis 500-Mile Race at the Indianapolis Motor Speedway • Sunday, May 24, 1981

FP	SP	No.		Driver	Car Name	Chassis/Engine	Laps	Status	Total Prize Money
1	1	3	W	Bobby Unser	Norton Spirit	Penske/Cosworth	200	139.184	$299,124
2	32	40	W	Mario Andretti	STP Oil Treatment	Wildcat/Cosworth	200	139.029	128,974
3	18	33		Vern Schuppan	Red Roof Inns	McLaren/Cosworth	199	Running	87,974
4	12	32	R	Kevin Cogan	Jerry O'Connell Racing	Phoenix/Cosworth	197	Running	59,024
5	15	50		Geoff Brabham	Psachie/Garza/ESSO	Penske/Cosworth	197	Running	55,684
6	23	81		Sheldon Kinser	Sergio Valente Jeans	Longhorn/Cosworth	195	Running	44,754
7	16	16	R	Tony Bettenhausen Jr.	Provimi Veal	McLaren/Cosworth	195	Running	44,064
8	17	53		Steve Krisiloff	Psachie/Garza/ESSO	Penske/Cosworth	194	Running	39,986
9	4	20	W	Gordon Johncock	STP Oil Treatment	Wildcat/Cosworth	194	Engine	62,501
10	28	4		Dennis Firestone	Rhoades Aircraft Sales	Wildcat/Cosworth	193	Engine	36,376
11	7	7	R	Bill Alsup	AB Dick Pacemaker	Penske/Cosworth	193	Running	35,632
12	25	74	R	Michael Chandler	National Engineering Co.	Penske/Cosworth	192	Running	34,116
13	3	14	W	A.J. Foyt	Valvoline-Gilmore	Coyote/Cosworth	191	Running	35,795
14	33	84		Tim Richmond	UNO/WTTV/Guarantee Auto	Parnelli/Cosworth	191	Running	33,612
15	31	38		Jerry Karl	Tonco Trailer	McLaren/Chevrolet	189	Running	35,480
16	29	37	R	Scott Brayton	Forsythe Industries	Penske/Cosworth	173	Engine	32,176
17	9	88	W	Al Unser	Valvoline-Longhorn	Longhorn/Cosworth	166	Running	31,600
18	19	31		Larry Dickson	Machinist Union	Penske/Cosworth	165	Piston	30,652
19	13	35	R	Bob Lazier	Montgomery Ward Auto Club	Penske/Cosworth	154	Engine	33,732
20	14	56		Tom Bigelow	Genesee Beer	Penske/Cosworth	152	Engine	30,140
21	27	90		Bill Whittington	Kraco Car Stereo	March/Cosworth	146	Stalled	31,243
22	8	60		Gordon Smiley	Intermedics	Wildcat/Cosworth	141	Accident	29,240
23	6	55	R	Josele Garza	Psachie/Garza/ESSO	Penske/Cosworth	138	Accident	40,282
24	24	79	R	Pete Halsmer	Hubler Chevrolet/KISS 99/Colonial Bread	Penske/Cosworth	123	Accident	30,702
25	20	2		Tom Sneva	Blue Poly	March/Cosworth	96	Clutch	38,000
26	11	8		Gary Bettenhausen	Hopkins	Lightning/Cosworth	69	Rod	27,976
27	21	25		Danny Ongais	Interscope Racing	Interscope/Cosworth	64	Accident	30,380
28	10	5		Pancho Carter	Alex Foods	Penske/Cosworth	63	Compression	27,712
29	30	51	R	Tom Klausler	IDS Idea	Schkee/Chevrolet	60	Gearbox	27,972
30	22	6	W	Rick Mears	The Gould Charge	Penske/Cosworth	58	Pit Fire	28,560
31	26	91		Don Whittington	Whittington Brothers	March/Cosworth	32	Accident	28,743
32	5	1	W	Johnny Rutherford	Pennzoil	Chaparral/Cosworth	25	Fuel Pump	29,620
33	2	48		Mike Mosley	Pepsi Challenger	Eagle/Chevrolet	16	Radiator	31,392

Total Purse $1,593,218

Time of Race: 3:35:41.78 Average Speed: 139.184 mph Margin of Victory: 5.18 sec
Pole: #3 Bobby Unser (200.546, 2:59.51) Fastest Qualifier: #2 Tom Sneva (200.691, 2:59.38) Fastest Race Lap: #20 Gordon Johncock (Race Lap 159, 196.937 mph, 45.70 sec.)
Winning Car Owner: Penske Racing, Inc. Winning Chief Mechanic: Laurie Gerrish Winning Tire: Goodyear Rookie of Year: Josele Garza
Legend: R=Indianapolis 500-Mile Race Rookie; W=Indianapolis 500-Mile Race Former Winner
Lap Leaders: B. Unser 1-21, Rutherford 22-24, Sneva 25, B. Unser 26-32, Sneva 33-56, Mears 57, Smiley 58, B. Unser 59, Ongais 60-63, Johncock 64-91, B. Unser 92-95, Johncock 96, Andretti 97-98, Johncock 99-104, Johncock 105-112, B. Unser 113-118, Johncock 119-122, Andretti 123-125, Garza 126-132, Johncock 133-140, B. Unser 141, Andretti 142-148, B. Unser 149-178, Johncock 179-181, B. Unser 182-200.
Lap Leader Summary: B. Unser 8 times for 89 laps, Johncock 6-52, Sneva 2-25, Garza 2-13, Andretti 3-12, Ongais 1-4, Rutherford 1-3, Mears 1-1, Smiley 1-1. Lead Changes: 24 among 9 drivers.
Caution Laps: 5-7, Debris. 26-29, #1 Rutherford, stalled backstretch. 33-43, #91 D. Whittington, accident backstretch. 67-81, #25 Ongais, accident T3. 130-136, #79 Halsmer, accident T3. 140-144, #55 Garza, accident north short chute. 146-151, #60 Smiley, accident T3. 152-156, #90 B. Whittington, stalled backstretch. 162-165, #56 Bigelow, stalled T1. 180-184, #14 Foyt, stalled backstretch. 185-188, Debris. Cautions: 11 for 69 laps.

Official Box Score

66th Indianapolis 500-Mile Race at the Indianapolis Motor Speedway • Sunday, May 30, 1982

FP	SP	No.		Driver	Car Name	Chassis/Engine	Laps	Status	Total Prize Money
1	5	20	W	Gordon Johncock	STP Oil Treatment	Wildcat/Cosworth	200	162.029	$290,609
2	1	1	W	Rick Mears	The Gould Charge	Penske/Cosworth	200	162.026	215,859
3	10	3		Pancho Carter	Alex Foods	March/Cosworth	199	Running	103,559
4	7	7		Tom Sneva	Texaco Star	March/Cosworth	197	Engine	88,309
5	16	10	W	Al Unser	Longhorn Racing	Longhorn/Cosworth	197	Running	60,326
6	8	91		Don Whittington	The Simoniz Finish	March/Cosworth	196	Running	57,159
7	24	42	R	Jim Hickman	Stroh's March	March/Cosworth	189	Running	59,209
8	12	5	W	Johnny Rutherford	Pennzoil	Chaparral/Cosworth	187	Engine	50,329
9	14	28	R	Herm Johnson	Menard Cashway Lumber	Eagle/Chevrolet	186	Running	53,454
10	18	30		Howdy Holmes	Domino's Pizza	March/Cosworth	186	Running	48,679
11	17	19	R	Bobby Rahal	Red Roof Inns	March/Cosworth	174	Engine	47,989
12	30	8		Gary Bettenhausen	Kraco Car Stereo	Lightning/Cosworth	158	Engine	49,679
13	15	52	R	Hector Rebaque	Carta Blanca	March/Cosworth	150	Fire	55,116
14	13	53	R	Danny Sullivan	Forsythe-Brown Racing	March/Cosworth	148	Accident	46,889
15	11	12	R	Chip Ganassi	First Commercial Corp.	Wildcat/Cosworth	147	Engine	45,819
16	6	94		Bill Whittington	Whittington/Warner W. Hogdon	March/Cosworth	121	Engine	43,779
17	22	68		Michael Chandler	Freeman Gurney Eagle	Eagle/Chevrolet	104	Gearbox	48,269
18	31	27		Tom Bigelow	H.B.K. Racing	Eagle/Chevrolet	96	Engine	44,289
19	3	14	W	A.J. Foyt	Valvoline/Gilmore	March/Cosworth	95	Transmission	71,239
20	25	34		Johnny Parsons	Silhouette Spas/WIFE/Tombstone Pizza	March/Cosworth	92	Spin	42,919
21	26	35		George Snider	Cobre Tire/Intermedics	March/Cosworth	87	Engine	41,529
22	9	25		Danny Ongais	Interscope Racing	Interscope/Cosworth	62	Accident	41,319
23	28	69		Jerry Sneva	Great American Spirit	March/Cosworth	61	Accident	40,839
24	29	39	R	Chet Fillip	Circle Bar Truck Corral	Eagle/Cosworth	60	Accident	40,539
25	32	66		Pete Halsmer	Colonial Bread/Pay Less	Eagle/Chevrolet	38	Transmission	41,269
26	27	16		Tony Bettenhausen Jr.	Provimi Veal	March/Cosworth	37	Accident	40,429
27	21	75		Dennis Firestone	B.C.V. Racing	Eagle/Chevrolet	37	Rear End	41,319
28	20	21		Geoff Brabham	Pentax Super	March/Cosworth	12	Engine	42,139
29	33	55		Josele Garza	Schlitz Gusto	March/Cosworth	1	Engine	40,489
30	2	4		Kevin Cogan	Norton Spirit	Penske/Cosworth	0	Accident	44,769
31	4	40	W	Mario Andretti	STP Oil Treatment	Wildcat/Cosworth	0	Accident	44,279
32	19	31	R	Roger Mears	Machinist's Union	Penske/Cosworth	0	Accident	41,719
33	23	95	R	Dale Whittington	Whittington/Warner W. Hogdon	March/Cosworth	0	Accident	40,356

Total Purse $2,064,473

Time of Race: 3:05:09.14 Average Speed: 162.029 mph Margin of Victory: 0.16 sec
Pole: #1 Rick Mears (207.004, 2:53.91) Fastest Race Lap: #1 Rick Mears (Race Lap 122, 200.535 mph, 44.88 sec.)
Winning Car Owner: Patrick Racing Team Winning Chief Mechanic: George Huening Winning Tire: Goodyear Rookie of Year: Jim Hickman
Legend: R=Indianapolis 500-Mile Race Rookie; W=Indianapolis 500-Mile Race Former Winner
Lap Leaders: Foyt 1-22, Johncock 23, Don Whittington 24-25, Ongais 26, Foyt 27-35, Sneva 36-41, Sneva 42-59, Mears 60-63, Foyt 64, Mears 65-94, Johncock 95-108, Mears 109-127, Johncock 128, Mears 129-141, Sneva 142-154, Mears 155-159, Johncock 160-200. Lead Changes: 16 among 6 drivers.
Lap Leader Summary: Mears 6 times for 77 laps, Johncock 4-57, Foyt 3-32, Sneva 2-31, Don Whittington 1-2, Ongais 1-1.
Caution Laps: Pace Lap-Pace Lap, #4 Cogan, #40 Ma. Andretti, #31 Ro. Mears, #95 Da. Whittington, accident frontstretch. 40-45, #16 T. Bettenhausen, accident frontstretch. 63-70, #25 Ongais, #69 J. Sneva, accident T2. 96-102, #35 Snider, stalled. 132-135, #94 B. Whittington, tow-in. 138-141, #34 Parsons, stalled T4. 154-158, #53 Sullivan, accident T4. Cautions: 7 for 35 laps.

Official Box Score

67th Indianapolis 500-Mile Race at the Indianapolis Motor Speedway • Sunday, May 29, 1983

FP	SP	No.		Driver	Car Name	Chassis/Engine	Laps	Status	Total Prize Money
1	4	5		Tom Sneva	Texaco Star	March/Cosworth	200	162.117	$385,886
2	7	7	W	Al Unser	Hertz Penske	Penske/Cosworth	200	161.954	179,086
3	3	2	W	Rick Mears	Pennzoil Penske	Penske/Cosworth	200	161.799	135,086
4	26	12		Geoff Brabham	UNO/British Sterling	Penske/Cosworth	199	Running	108,286
5	22	16		Kevin Cogan	Caesar's Palace/Master Mechanic	March/Cosworth	198	Running	73,856
6	12	30		Howdy Holmes	Domino's Pizza	March/Cosworth	198	Running	71,696
7	14	21		Pancho Carter	Alex Foods Pinata	March/Cosworth	197	Running	77,491
8	16	60		Chip Ganassi	Sea Ray Boats	Wildcat/Cosworth	195	Running	60,580
9	29	37		Scott Brayton	SME Cement	March/Cosworth	195	Running	57,085
10	5	19	R	Al Unser Jr.	Coors Light Silver Bullet	Eagle/Cosworth	192	Out of Fuel	59,110
11	19	56	R	Steve Chassey	Genesee Beer Wagon/Sizzler/WLHN	Eagle/Chevrolet	192	Running	60,982
12	25	72	R	Chris Kneifel	Primus/C.F.I	Primus/Cosworth	191	Running	53,690
13	2	18		Mike Mosley	Kraco Car Stereo	March/Cosworth	169	Accident	61,484
14	10	20	W	Gordon Johncock	STP Oil Treatment	Wildcat/Cosworth	163	Gearbox	53,442
15	20	22		Dick Simon	Vermont American	March/Cosworth	161	Running	56,758
16	30	29		Michael Chandler	Agajanian/Mike Curb	Rattlesnake/Cosworth	153	Gearbox	50,610
17	9	10		Tony Bettenhausen Jr.	Provimi Veal	March/Cosworth	152	Half Shaft	49,998
18	15	94		Bill Whittington	Whittington Brothers	March/Cosworth	144	Gearbox	49,922
19	28	34	R	Derek Daly	Wysard Motor Co.	March/Cosworth	126	Engine	48,882
20	6	4		Bobby Rahal	Red Roof Inns	March/Cosworth	110	Radiator	55,378
21	21	25		Danny Ongais	Interscope Racing	March/Cosworth	101	Handling	48,588
22	23	66		Johnny Parsons	Colonial Bread/Arciero	Penske/Cosworth	80	Accident	47,478
23	11	3	W	Mario Andretti	Budweiser/Electrolux	Lola/Cosworth	79	Accident	47,082
24	33	90		Dennis Firestone	Simpson Sports	March/Cosworth	77	Oil Leak	49,222
25	18	55		Josele Garza	Machinists Union/Silhouette	Penske/Cosworth	64	Oil Leak	59,898
26	1	33	R	Teo Fabi	Skoal Bandit	March/Cosworth	47	Fuel Gasket	84,960
27	27	91		Don Whittington	The Simoniz Finish	March/Cosworth	44	Ignition	45,858
28	8	9		Roger Mears	Machinists Union	Penske/Cosworth	43	Accident	45,642
29	31	43		Steve Krisiloff	Armstrong Mould	Lola/Cosworth	42	U-Joint	45,462
30	17	35	R	Patrick Bedard	Escort Radar Warning	March/Cosworth	25	Accident	45,818
31	24	14	W	A.J. Foyt	Valvoline-Gilmore	March/Cosworth	24	Shift Linkage	44,888
32	13	1		George Snider	Calumet Farms	March/Cosworth	22	Ignition	45,138
33	32	38		Chet Fillip	Circle Bar Truck Corral	Eagle/Cosworth	11	Black Flagged	50,102

Total Purse $2,409,444

Time of Race: 3:05:03.06 Average Speed: 162.117 mph Margin of Victory: 11.174 sec
Pole: #33 Teo Fabi (207.395, 2:53.58) Fastest Race Lap: #33 Teo Fabi (Race Lap 3, 197.507 mph, 45.568 sec.)
Winning Car Owner: Bignotti-Cotter, Inc. Winning Chief Mechanic: George Bignotti Winning Tire: Goodyear Rookie of Year: Teo Fabi
Legend: R=Indianapolis 500-Mile Race Rookie; W=Indianapolis 500-Mile Race Former Winner
Lap Leaders: Fabi 1-23, Mosley 24, Mears 25-26, A. Unser 27-35, Sneva 36-46, A. Unser 47-52, Rahal 53-66, Sneva 67-73, Rahal 74, A. Unser 75-80, Sneva 81-89, A. Unser 90-108, Sneva 109-143, A. Unser 144-146, Sneva 147-172, A. Unser 173-190, Sneva 191-200.
Lap Leader Summary: Sneva 6 times for 98 laps, A. Unser 6-61, Fabi 1-23, Rahal 2-15, Mears 1-2, Mosley 1-1. Lead Changes: 16 among 6 drivers.
Caution Laps: 27-32, #35 Bedard, accident T4. 43-51, #9 Ro. Mears, accident T1. 82-90, #3 Andretti, #66 Parsons, accident T1. 156-161, #94 B. Whittington, tow-in. 172-175, #18 Mosley, accident T1. Cautions: 5 for 34 laps.

Official Box Score

68th Indianapolis 500-Mile Race at the Indianapolis Motor Speedway • Sunday, May 27, 1984

FP	SP	No.		Driver	Car Name	Chassis/Engine	Laps	Status	Total Prize Money
1	3	6	W	Rick Mears	Pennzoil Z-7	March/Cosworth	200	163.612	$434,061
2	7	9	R	Roberto Guerrero	Master Mechanic Tools	March/Cosworth	198	Running	171,666
3	10	2	W	Al Unser	Miller High Life	March/Cosworth	198	Running	117,416
4	16	21	R	Al Holbert	CRC Chemical	March/Cosworth	198	Running	106,261
5	4	99	R	Michael Andretti	Electrolux/Kraco	March/Cosworth	198	Running	119,231
6	12	14	W	A.J. Foyt	Gilmore/Foyt	March/Cosworth	197	Running	79,276
7	18	5		Bobby Rahal	7-Eleven/Red Roof Inns	March/Cosworth	197	Running	74,996
8	9	28		Herm Johnson	3M/Menard Cashway	March/Cosworth	194	Running	73,560
9	11	25		Danny Ongais	Interscope Racing	March/Cosworth	193	Running	68,085
10	24	55		Josele Garza	Schaefer/Machinist's Union	March/Cosworth	193	Running	66,910
11	31	4		George Snider	Calumet Farms	March/Cosworth	193	Running	69,357
12	32	50		Dennis Firestone	Hoosier Transportation	March/Cosworth	186	Running	62,765
13	2	41		Howdy Holmes	Jiffy Mixes	March/Cosworth	185	Running	85,209
14	13	77	R	Tom Gloy	Simoniz Finish	March/Cosworth	179	Engine	62,467
15	33	73		Chris Kneifel	Spa*erobics/Living Well	Primus/Cosworth	175	Transmission	61,683
16	1	1	W	Tom Sneva	Texaco Star	March/Cosworth	168	CV Joint	112,935
17	6	3	W	Mario Andretti	Budweiser Lola	Lola/Cosworth	153	Nose cone	72,323
18	26	37		Scott Brayton	Buick Dealers of America	March/Buick	150	Transmission	64,397
19	21	10		Pancho Carter	American Dream	March/Cosworth	141	Engine	59,057
20	27	98		Kevin Cogan	Dubonnet/Curb Racing	Eagle/Pontiac	137	Wheel	65,853
21	15	7		Al Unser Jr.	Coors Light Silver Bullet	March/Cosworth	131	Water Pump	67,985
22	30	84	W	Johnny Rutherford	Gilmore/Greer/Foyt	March/Cosworth	116	Engine	56,453
23	20	22		Dick Simon	Break Free	March/Cosworth	112	In Pits	64,057
24	14	33		Teo Fabi	Skoal Bandit	March/Cosworth	104	Fuel System	71,197
25	5	20	W	Gordon Johncock	STP Oil Treatment	March/Cosworth	103	Accident	61,373
26	17	16		Tony Bettenhausen Jr.	Provimi Veal	March/Cosworth	86	Piston	55,585
27	29	61		Derek Daly	Provimi Veal	March/Cosworth	76	Handling	55,333
28	22	40		Chip Ganassi	Old Milwaukee	March/Cosworth	61	Engine	54,617
29	28	30		Danny Sullivan	Domino's Pizza	Lola/Cosworth	57	Broken Wheel	57,937
30	19	35		Patrick Bedard	Escort Radar Warning	March/Buick	55	Accident	56,793
31	25	57		Spike Gehlhausen	Little Kings	March/Cosworth	45	Spun out	54,185
32	23	47	R	Emerson Fittipaldi	W.I.T. Promotions	March/Cosworth	37	Oil Pressure	53,800
33	8	18		Geoff Brabham	Kraco Car Stereo	March/Cosworth	1	Fuel Line	54,077

Total Purse $2,790,900

Time of Race: 3:03:21.66 Average Speed: 163.612 mph Margin of Victory: Two Laps

Pole: #1 Tom Sneva (210.029, 2:51.405) Fastest Race Lap: #20 Gordon Johncock (Race Lap 52, 204.815 mph, 43.942 sec.)

Winning Car Owner: Penske Cars, Ltd Winning Chief Mechanic: Peter Parrott Winning Tire: Goodyear Rookie of Year: Michael Andretti/Roberto Guerrero

Legend: R=Indianapolis 500-Mile Race Rookie; W=Indianapolis 500-Mile Race Former Winner

Lap Leaders: Mears 1-24, Sneva 25, Ma. Andretti 26-47, Sneva 48-49, Ma. Andretti 50-53, Mears 54-59, Sneva 60, Ma. Andretti 61-63, Fabi 64-70, Ongais 71-73, Fabi 74-80, Sneva 81-82, Unser, Jr. 83-86, Sneva 87-109, Mears 110-141, Sneva 142-143, Mears 144-200. Lead Changes: 16 among 6 drivers.

Lap Leader Summary: Mears 4 times for 119 laps, Sneva 6-31, Ma. Andretti 3-29, Fabi 2-14, Unser, Jr. 1-4, Ongais 1-3.

Caution Laps: 42-52, #57 Gelhausen, accident T1. 58-67, #35 Bedard, accident north short chute. 107-114, #20 Johncock, accident frontstretch. 153-157, #9 Guerrero, spin T2. 163-167, #37 Brayton, tow-in. Cautions: 5 for 39 laps.

Official Box Score

69th Indianapolis 500-Mile Race at the Indianapolis Motor Speedway • Sunday, May 26, 1985

FP	SP	No.		Driver	Car Name	Chassis/Engine	Laps	Status	Total Prize Money
1	8	5		Danny Sullivan	Miller American	March/Cosworth	200	152.982	$517,663
2	4	3	W	Mario Andretti	Beatrice Foods	Lola/Cosworth	200	152.950	290,363
3	16	9		Roberto Guerrero	Master Mechanics/True Value	March/Cosworth	200	152.832	157,113
4	7	11	W	Al Unser	Hertz	March/Cosworth	199	Running	102,533
5	26	76		Johnny Parsons	Canadian Tire	March/Cosworth	198	Running	98,863
6	30	21	W	Johnny Rutherford	Vermont American	March/Cosworth	198	Running	119,583
7	20	61	R	Arie Luyendyk	Dutch Treat/Provimi Veal	Lola/Cosworth	198	Running	99,233
8	15	99		Michael Andretti	Electrolux/Kraco	March/Cosworth	196	Running	76,813
9	22	98	R	Ed Pimm	Skoal Bandit	Eagle/Cosworth	195	Running	79,463
10	19	33		Howdy Holmes	Jiffy Mixes	Lola/Cosworth	194	Running	88,088
11	32	18		Kevin Cogan	Kraco/Wolff Sun Systems	March/Cosworth	191	Running	73,663
12	31	29		Derek Daly	Kapsreiter Bier	Lola/Cosworth	189	Running	77,963
13	5	40		Emerson Fittipaldi	7-Eleven	March/Cosworth	188	Fuel Line	78,163
14	12	12		Bill Whittington	Arciero Wines	March/Cosworth	183	Accident	69,333
15	24	43	R	John Paul Jr.	STS/Indianapolis Heliport	March/Cosworth	164	Accident	68,563
16	27	34	R	Jim Crawford	Wysard/Canadian Tire	Lola/Cosworth	142	Electrical	72,383
17	17	25		Danny Ongais	Interscope Racing	March/Cosworth	141	Engine	64,913
18	23	23	R	Raul Boesel	Break Free	March/Cosworth	134	Radiator	83,633
19	9	7		Geoff Brabham	Coors Light Silver Bullet	March/Cosworth	130	Engine	66,871
20	13	2	W	Tom Sneva	Skoal Bandit	Eagle/Cosworth	123	Accident	63,163
21	10	1	W	Rick Mears	Pennzoil Z-7	March/Cosworth	122	Linkage	67,333
22	25	84		Chip Ganassi	Calumet Farms	March/Cosworth	121	Fuel Line	57,833
23	33	60	R	Rich Vogler	Byrd's Kentucky Fried Chicken	March/Cosworth	119	Accident	71,183
24	6	20		Don Whittington	STP Oil Treatment	March/Cosworth	97	Engine	60,683
25	11	30		Al Unser Jr.	Domino's Pizza	Lola/Cosworth	91	Engine	60,133
26	14	22		Dick Simon	Break Free	March/Cosworth	86	Oil Pressure	64,833
27	3	10		Bobby Rahal	Budweiser	March/Cosworth	84	Waste Gate	83,463
28	21	14	W	A.J. Foyt	Copenhagen-Gilmore	March/Cosworth	62	Front Wing	53,863
29	29	97		Tony Bettenhausen Jr.	Skoal Bandit	Lola/Cosworth	31	Wheel Bearing	63,613
30	2	37		Scott Brayton	Hardee's 37	March/Buick	19	Cylinder Wall	86,863
31	18	55		Josele Garza	Schaefer/Machinists	March/Cosworth	15	Engine	59,083
32	28	44		George Snider	A.J. Foyt Chevrolet	March/Chevrolet	13	Engine	53,263
33	1	6		Pancho Carter	Valvoline Buick	March/Buick	6	Oil Pump	121,533

Total Purse $3,252,042

Time of Race: 3:16:06.06 Average Speed: 152.982 mph Margin of Victory: 2.477 sec

Pole: #6 Pancho Carter (212.583, 2:49.346) Fastest Race Lap: #1 Rick Mears (Race Lap 14, 204.937 mph, 43.916 sec.)

Winning Car Owner: Penske Cars Winning Chief Mechanic: Chuck Sprague Winning Tire: Goodyear Rookie of Year: Arie Luyendyk

Legend: R=Indianapolis 500-Mile Race Rookie; W=Indianapolis 500-Mile Race Former Winner

Lap Leaders: Rahal 1-14, Brayton 15, Ma. Andretti 16-48, Fittipaldi 49-51, Sullivan 52-57, Ma. Andretti 58-73, Fittipaldi 74, Ma. Andretti 75-104, Fittipaldi 105-109, Ma. Andretti 110-119, Fittipaldi 120-121, Ma. Andretti 122-139, Sullivan 140-200. Lap Leaders Summary: Ma. Andretti 5 times for 107 laps, Sullivan 2-67, Rahal 1-14, Fittipaldi 4-11, Brayton 1-1. Lead Changes: 12 among 5 drivers.

Caution Laps: 15-18, #44 Snider, engine. 22-28, #37 Brayton, stalled T3. 74-77, #29 Daly, tow-in. 120-121, #5 Sullivan, spin south short chute. 124-133, #2 Sneva, #60 Vogler, accident T1. 146-149, #25 Ongais, tow-in. 170-175, #43 Paul Jr., accident T2. 193-196, #12 B. Whittington, accident T3. Cautions: 8 for 41 laps.

Official Box Score

70th Indianapolis 500-Mile Race at the Indianapolis Motor Speedway • Saturday, May 31, 1986

FP	SP	No.	Rookie	Driver	Car Name	Chassis/Engine	Laps	Status	Total Prize Money
1	4	3		Bobby Rahal	Budweiser	March/Cosworth	200	170.722	$581,063
2	6	7		Kevin Cogan	7-Eleven	March/Cosworth	200	170.698	253,363
3	1	4	W	Rick Mears	Pennzoil Z-7	March/Cosworth	200	170.691	332,263
4	8	5		Roberto Guerrero	True Value	March/Cosworth	200	170.551	139,513
5	9	30		Al Unser Jr.	Domino's Pizza	Lola/Cosworth	199	Running	113,463
6	3	18		Michael Andretti	Kraco/STP/Lean Machine	March/Cosworth	199	Running	171,763
7	11	20		Emerson Fittipaldi	Marlboro	March/Cosworth	199	Running	104,563
8	12	21	W	Johnny Rutherford	Vermont American	March/Cosworth	198	Running	97,513
9	2	1	W	Danny Sullivan	Miller American	March/Cosworth	197	Running	134,088
10	13	12	R	Randy Lanier	Arciero Racing	March/Cosworth	195	Running	103,438
11	29	24		Gary Bettenhausen	Vita Fresh Orange Juice/Timex	March/Cosworth	193	Running	108,913
12	20	8		Geoff Brabham	Valvoline Spirit	Lola/Cosworth	193	Running	94,613
13	22	22		Raul Boesel	Duracell Copper Top	Lola/Cosworth	192	Running	90,063
14	33	23		Dick Simon	Duracell Copper Top	Lola/Cosworth	189	Running	93,463
15	19	61		Arie Luyendyk	MCI/Race For Life	Lola/Cosworth	188	Accident	86,013
16	14	15		Pancho Carter	Coors Light	Lola/Cosworth	179	Wheel Bearing	84,713
17	10	66		Ed Pimm	Skoal/Pace Electronics	March/Cosworth	168	Ignition	83,863
18	17	55		Josele Garza	Schaefer/Machinists	March/Cosworth	167	Running	88,363
19	32	9	R	Roberto Moreno	Valvoline Spirit II	Lola/Cosworth	158	Engine	82,301
20	15	81	R	Jacques Villeneuve (U)	Living Well/Labatts	March/Cosworth	154	Main Bearing	81,613
21	25	59		Chip Ganassi	Bryant Heating & Cooling	March/Cosworth	151	Blown Engine	81,163
22	5	11	W	Al Unser	Hertz	Penske/Ilmor	149	Vibration	81,563
23	16	25		Danny Ongais	GM Goodwrench	March/Buick	136	Ignition	79,713
24	21	14	W	A.J. Foyt	Copenhagen/Gilmore	March/Cosworth	135	Spun in pits	97,713
25	27	6		Rich Vogler	Byrd's Ky Fr Ckn/Vermont American	March/Cosworth	132	Accident	90,563
26	31	84		George Snider	Copenhagen/Gilmore	March/Cosworth	110	Ignition	80,163
27	28	95		Johnny Parsons	Pizza Hut/Machinists	March/Cosworth	100	CV Joint	78,013
28	18	16		Tony Bettenhausen Jr.	Bettenhausen & Associates	March/Cosworth	77	Valve	77,713
29	26	31		Jim Crawford	American Sunroofs Inc.	March/Buick	70	Head Gasket	95,263
30	23	71		Scott Brayton	Hardee's/Living Well/WTTV	March/Buick	69	Engine	78,263
31	24	42	R	Phil Krueger	Squirt/Moran Electric	March/Cosworth	67	Engine	82,413
32	30	2	W	Mario Andretti	Newman-Haas Racing	Lola/Cosworth	19	Ignition	77,013
33	7	33	W	Tom Sneva	Skoal Bandit	March/Cosworth	0	Accident	76,963

Total Purse $4,001,467

Time of Race: 2:55:43.48 Average Speed: 170.722 mph Margin of Victory: 1.441 sec

Pole: #4 Rick Mears (216.828, 2:46.030) Fastest Race Lap: #3 Bobby Rahal (Race Lap 200, 209.152 mph, 43.031 sec.)

Winning Car Owner: Truesports Winning Chief Mechanic: Steve Horne Winning Tire: Goodyear Rookie of Year: Randy Lanier

Legend: R=Indianapolis 500-Mile Race Rookie; W=Indianapolis 500-Mile Race Former Winner

Race Notes: Race scheduled to run on May 25 but rain forced postponement until May 31.

Lap Leaders: Mi. Andretti 1-42, Cogan 43, Unser, Jr. 44-47, Fittipaldi 48, Mears 49-74, Rahal 75, Cogan 76-77, Unser, Jr. 78-79, Mi. Andretti 80-82, Rahal 83-101, Mears 102, Rahal 103-135, Mears 136-165, Rahal 166, Mears 167, Guerrero 168, Mears 169-186, Rahal 187, Cogan 188-197, Rahal 198-200.

Lap Leader Summary: Mears 5 times for 76 laps, Rahal 6-58, Mi. Andretti 2-45, Cogan 3-13, Unser, Jr. 2-6, Guerrero 1-1, Fittipaldi 1-1. Lead Changes: 19 among 7 drivers.

Caution Laps: 15-19, #2 Ma. Andretti, stalled T3. 52-56, Debris. 102-106, #95 Parsons, accident backstretch. 136-141, #6 Vogler, accident T3. 166-169, #9 Moreno, stalled T3. 195-198, #61 Luyendyk, accident pit entry. Cautions: 6 for 29 laps.

Official Box Score

71st Indianapolis 500-Mile Race at the Indianapolis Motor Speedway • Sunday, May 24, 1987

FP	SP	No.		Driver	Car Name	Chassis/Engine	Laps	Status	Total Prize Money
1	20	25	W	Al Unser	Cummins/Holset Turbo	March/Cosworth	200	162.175	$526,763
2	5	4		Roberto Guerrero	True Value/STP	March/Cosworth	200	162.109	305,013
3	17	12	R	Fabrizio Barbazza	Arciero Winery	March/Cosworth	198	Running	204,663
4	22	30		Al Unser Jr.	Domino's Pizza	March/Cosworth	196	Running	142,963
5	15	56		Gary Bettenhausen	Genesee Beer Wagon	March/Cosworth	195	Running	132,213
6	6	22		Dick Simon	Soundesign	Lola/Cosworth	193	Running	131,813
7	26	41	R	Stan Fox	Kerker Exhaust/Skoal Classic	March/Cosworth	192	Running	111,263
8	12	11	R	Jeff MacPherson	McHoward Leasing	March/Brab./Hon.(Judd)	182	Running	117,313
9	1	5	W	Mario Andretti	Hanna Auto Wash	Lola/Chevrolet Indy	180	Ignition	368,063
10	27	16		Tony Bettenhausen Jr.	Nationwise/Payless	March/Cosworth	171	Running	105,838
11	8	21	W	Johnny Rutherford	Vermont American	March/Cosworth	171	Running	104,313
12	13	91		Scott Brayton	Amway/Autostyle	March/Cosworth	167	Engine	103,063
13	16	3	W	Danny Sullivan	Miller American	March/Chevrolet Indy	160	Engine	120,713
14	21	33	W	Tom Sneva	Skoal Bandit	March/Buick	143	Accident	103,313
15	19	77		Derek Daly	Scheid Tire/Superior Training/Metrolink	March/Buick	133	Engine	100,763
16	33	20		Emerson Fittipaldi	Marlboro	March/Chevrolet Indy	131	Engine	98,263
17	25	55		Josele Garza	Bryant Heating & Cooling/Schaefer	March/Cosworth	129	Running	103,350
18	7	71		Arie Luyendyk	Living Well/Provimi Veal/WTTV	March/Cosworth	125	Suspension	97,113
19	4	14	W	A.J. Foyt	Copenhagen/Gilmore	Lola/Cosworth	117	Oil Seal	102,963
20	11	81		Rich Vogler	Byrd's Kentucky Fried Chicken/Living Well	March/Buick	109	Rocker Arm	98,263
21	30	98		Ed Pimm	Skoal Classic	March/Cosworth	109	Turbocharger	95,513
22	18	2	W	Gordon Johncock	STP Oil Treatment	March/Buick	76	Valve	94,913
23	3	8	W	Rick Mears	Pennzoil Z-7	March/Chevrolet Indy	75	Coil Wire	112,463
24	14	15		Geoff Brabham	Team Valvoline	March/Brab./Hon.(Judd)	71	Oil Pressure	92,963
25	32	87		Steve Chassey	United Oil/Life of Indiana	March/Cosworth	68	Engine	97,913
26	2	1	W	Bobby Rahal	Budweiser	Lola/Cosworth	57	Ignition	123,013
27	29	29		Pancho Carter	Hardee's	March/Cosworth	45	Valve	93,263
28	28	44	R	Davy Jones	Skoal Classic/Gilmore/UNO	March/Cosworth	34	Engine	115,463
29	9	18		Michael Andretti	Kraco/STP	March/Cosworth	28	Pit Fire	91,113
30	10	23	R	Ludwig Heimrath, Jr.	MacKenzie Financial/Tim Horton Doughnuts	Lola/Cosworth	25	Spun out	111,513
31	24	7		Kevin Cogan	Marlboro	March/Chevrolet Indy	21	Oil Pump	90,763
32	23	24	R	Randy Lewis	Toshiba/Altos/Oracle	March/Cosworth	8	Gearbox	90,763
33	31	84		George Snider	Calumet/Copenhagen	March/Chevrolet	0	Engine fire	92,713

Total Purse $4,480,391

Time of Race: 3:04:59.14 Average Speed: 162.175 mph Margin of Victory: 4.496 sec

Pole: #5 Mario Andretti (215.390, 2:47.139) Fastest Race Lap: #4 Roberto Guerrero (Race Lap 57, 205.011 mph, 43.900 sec.)

Winning Car Owner: Penske Racing Winning Chief Mechanic: Clive Howell Winning Tire: Goodyear Rookie of Year: Fabrizio Barbazza

Legend: R=Indianapolis 500-Mile Race Rookie; W=Indianapolis 500-Mile Race Former Winner

Lap Leaders: Ma. Andretti 1-27, Guerrero 28, Ma. Andretti 29-60, Sullivan 61-64, Ma. Andretti 65-80, Guerrero 81, Ma. Andretti 82-96, Guerrero 97, Ma. Andretti 98-177, Guerrero 178-182, A. Unser 183-200. Lap Leader Summary: Ma. Andretti 5 times for 170 laps, Guerrero 4-8, A. Unser 1-18, Sullivan 1-4. Lead Changes: 10 among 4 drivers.

Caution Laps: 1-5, #55 Garza, #29 Carter, contact T1. 27-33, #23 Heimrath, spun/lost wheel T4. 39-42, Debris. 62-67, Debris. 81-84, #3 Sullivan, spin T4. 96-101, #22 Simon, stopped. 131-134, #16 Bettenhausen, lost wheel T3. 150-158, #33 Sneva, accident T3. 162-166, #12 Barbazza, spin T4. 192-196, #5 Ma. Andretti, stalled T4. Cautions: 10 for 55 laps.

Official Box Score

72nd Indianapolis 500-Mile Race at the Indianapolis Motor Speedway • Sunday, May 29, 1988

FP	SP	No.		Driver	Car Name	Chassis/Engine	Laps	Status	Total Prize Money
1	1	5	W	Rick Mears	Pennzoil Z-7	Penske/Chevrolet Indy	200	144.809	$809,853
2	8	20		Emerson Fittipaldi	Marlboro	March/Chevrolet Indy	200	144.726	337,603
3	3	1	W	Al Unser	Hertz	Penske/Chevrolet Indy	199	Running	228,903
4	10	18		Michael Andretti	Kraco	March/Cosworth	199	Running	192,953
5	19	4	W	Bobby Rahal	Budweiser	Lola/Judd	199	Running	151,553
6	18	15		Jim Crawford	Mac Tools/King/Protofab	Lola/Buick	198	Running	170,503
7	20	30		Raul Boesel	Domino's Pizza	Lola/Cosworth	198	Running	148,403
8	15	97		Phil Krueger	CNC Systems/Taylor Dist.	March/Cosworth	196	Running	131,053
9	16	22		Dick Simon	Uniden/Soundesign	Lola/Cosworth	196	Running	127,428
10	6	7		Arie Luyendyk	Provimi Veal	Lola/Cosworth	196	Running	123,028
11	13	11		Kevin Cogan	Schaefer/Playboy Fashions	March/Cosworth	195	Running	141,278
12	33	21		Howdy Holmes	Jiffy Mixes	March/Cosworth	192	Running	123,728
13	5	3		Al Unser Jr.	Team Valvoline/Strohs	March/Chevrolet Indy	180	Running	117,753
14	23	56	R	Bill Vukovich III	Genesee Beer/EZ Wider	March/Cosworth	179	Running	125,603
15	11	24		Randy Lewis	Toshiba/Oracle/Altos	Lola/Cosworth	175	Running	115,478
16	28	48	R	Rocky Moran	Skoal/Trench Shoring	March/Cosworth	159	Engine	107,228
17	32	29		Rich Vogler	Byrd's/Pepsi/Bryant	March/Cosworth	159	Accident	106,053
18	21	92	R	Dominic Dobson	Moore Industries/Columbia Helecopters	Lola/Cosworth	145	Coolant	107,753
19	25	23	R	Tero Palmroth	Bronson/Neste/Editor	Lola/Cosworth	144	Engine	103,728
20	4	6	W	Mario Andretti	Amoco/Kmart	Lola/Chevrolet Indy	118	Electrical	130,828
21	27	98	R	John Andretti	Skoal Bandit	Lola/Cosworth	114	Engine	106,703
22	30	17	W	Johnny Rutherford	Mac Tools/King/Protofab	Lola/Buick	107	Accident	102,303
23	2	9	W	Danny Sullivan	Miller High Life	Penske/Chevrolet Indy	101	Accident	214,378
24	26	35		Steve Chassey	Kasale Recycling	March/Cosworth	73	Accident	99,128
25	31	71		Ludwig Heimrath, Jr.	MacKenzie Funds	Lola/Cosworth	59	Accident	100,253
26	22	14	W	A.J. Foyt	Copenhagen-Gilmore	Lola/Cosworth	54	Accident	98,853
27	14	81	W	Tom Sneva	Pizza Hut/WRTV	Lola/Judd	32	Accident	97,328
28	17	8		Teo Fabi	Quaker State/Porsche	March/Porsche Indy	30	Wheel off	101,878
29	9	10		Derek Daly	Raynor Garage Doors	Lola/Cosworth	18	Gearbox	97,503
30	29	84		Stan Fox	Copenhagen/Calumet Farms	March/Chevrolet	2	Engine	113,703
31	7	91		Scott Brayton	Amway Spirit/Lifecycle	Lola/Buick	0	Accident	96,078
32	12	2		Roberto Guerrero	STP/Dianetics	Lola/Cosworth	0	Accident	100,828
33	24	16		Tony Bettenhausen Jr.	Hardee's/Sony	Lola/Cosworth	0	Accident	95,753

Total Purse $5,025,399

Time of Race: 3:27:10.204 Average Speed: 144.809 mph Margin of Victory: Under Caution
Pole: #5 Rick Mears (219.198, 2:44.235) Fastest Race Lap: #5 Rick Mears (Race Lap 166, 209.517 mph, 42.956 sec.)
Winning Car Owner: Penske Racing Winning Chief Mechanic: Peter Parrott Winning Tire: Goodyear Rookie of Year: Billy Vukovich III
Legend: R=Indianapolis 500-Mile Race Rookie; W=Indianapolis 500-Mile Race Former Winner
Lap Leaders: Sullivan 1-30, A. Unser 31-33, Sullivan 34-94, Crawford 95-101, Mears 102-103, Crawford 104, A. Unser 105-112, Mears 113-121, A. Unser 122, Mears 123-200.
Lap Leader Summary: Sullivan 2 times for 91 laps, Mears 3-89, A. Unser 3-12, Crawford 2-8. Lead Changes: 9 among 4 drivers.
Caution Laps: 1-5, #2 Guerrero, #16 T. Bettenhausen, #91 Brayton, accident T1. 34-39, #81 Sneva, accident pit entrance. 58-63, #14 Foyt, accident T2. 64-70, #71 Heimrath, accident T4. 82-88, #35 Chassey, #29 Vogler, accident T4. 93-95, Debris. 102-106, #9 Sullivan accident T2. 109-111, Rabbit on track. 117-120, #17 Rutherford, accident T1. 140-145, #6 Ma. Andretti, tow-in. 160-163, #23 Palmroth, tow-in. 167-170, #48 Moran, pulled off track. 175-179, #29 Vogler, accident T3. 198-200, #18 Mi. Andretti, lost sidepod frontstretch.
Cautions: 14 for 68 laps.

Official Box Score

73rd Indianapolis 500-Mile Race at the Indianapolis Motor Speedway • Sunday, May 28, 1989

FP	SP	No.		Driver	Car Name	Chassis/Engine	Laps	Status	Total Prize Money
1	3	20		Emerson Fittipaldi	Marlboro	Penske/Chevrolet Indy	200	167.581	$1,001,604
2	8	2		Al Unser Jr.	Valvoline	Lola/Chevrolet Indy	198	Accident	390,453
3	9	30		Raul Boesel	Domino's Pizza	Lola/Judd	194	Running	306,603
4	5	5	W	Mario Andretti	Kmart/Havoline	Lola/Chevrolet Indy	193	Running	193,853
5	10	14	W	A.J. Foyt	Copenhagen/Gilmore	Lola/Cosworth DFX	193	Running	177,403
6	6	22		Scott Brayton	Amway/Speedway/Uniden	Lola/Buick	193	Running	190,903
7	31	50		Davy Jones	Euromotorsport/UNO	Lola/Cosworth DFX	192	Running	151,328
8	33	29		Rich Vogler	Byrd's/Bryant/Saturday Evening Post	March/Cosworth DFX	192	Running	153,203
9	20	69	R	Bernard Jourdain	Corona-Monarch	Lola/Cosworth DFX	191	Running	150,153
10	17	3	R	Scott Pruett	Budweiser	Lola/Judd	190	Running	141,053
11	25	65	R	John Jones	Labatt's	Lola/Cosworth DFX	189	Running	134,103
12	30	81		Bill Vukovich III	Hemelgarn/Consani/Sierra	Lola/Judd	186	Running	147,203
13	18	71		Ludwig Heimrath, Jr.	MacKenzie Funds	Lola/Judd	185	Running	123,803
14	28	33		Rocky Moran	Skoal Classic	March/Cosworth DFX	181	Running	122,503
15	24	10		Derek Daly	Raynor Garage Doors	Lola/Judd	167	Running	125,103
16	16	56		Tero Palmroth	Neste/Rotator/Nanso	Lola/Cosworth DFX	165	Spindle	122,803
17	21	6		Michael Andretti	Kmart/Havoline	Lola/Chevrolet Indy	163	Engine	164,353
18	29	86		Dominic Dobson	Texaco Havoline Star	Lola/Cosworth DFX	161	Drive Train	113,003
19	4	15		Jim Crawford	Mac Tools/Planters	Lola/Buick	135	Drive Train	119,403
20	19	12	R	Didier Theys	Arciero MacPherson	Penske/Cosworth DFX	131	Engine	111,503
21	15	9		Arie Luyendyk	Provimi/Dutch Boy	Lola/Cosworth DFS	123	Engine	110,203
22	32	24		Pancho Carter	Hardee's	Lola/Cosworth DFX	121	Electrical	108,503
23	1	4	W	Rick Mears	Pennzoil Z-7	Penske/Chevrolet Indy	113	Engine	267,903
24	2	25	W	Al Unser	Marlboro	Penske/Chevrolet Indy	68	Clutch	132,903
25	12	70		John Andretti	Tuneup Masters/Granatelli/STP	Lola/Buick	61	Engine	104,503
26	7	18	W	Bobby Rahal	Kraco	Lola/Cosworth DFS	58	Valve	103,703
27	22	7	W	Tom Sneva	STP/Granatelli	Lola/Buick	55	Pit Fire	106,003
28	26	1	W	Danny Sullivan	Miller High Life	Penske/Chevrolet Indy	41	Clutch	125,903
29	11	28		Randy Lewis	Toshiba-Oracle	Lola/Cosworth DFX	24	Wheel Bearing	101,903
30	13	8		Teo Fabi	Quaker State/Porsche	March/Porsche	23	Ignition	113,753
31	23	91	W	Gordon Johncock	STP/Pizza Hut/WRTV	Lola/Buick	19	Engine	103,703
32	27	11		Kevin Cogan	Schaefer/Playboy Fashions	March/Cosworth DFX	2	Accident	102,503
33	14	99		Gary Bettenhausen	ATEC Environmental	Lola/Buick	0	Bent valve	101,903

Total Purse $5,723,725

Time of Race: 2:59:01.049 Average Speed: 167.581 mph Margin of Victory: Under Caution
Pole: #4 Rick Mears (223.885, 2:40.797) Fastest Race Lap: #20 Emerson Fittipaldi (Race Lap 85, 222.469 mph, 40.455 sec.)
Winning Car Owner: Patrick Racing Winning Chief Mechanic: Tom Anderson Winning Tire: Goodyear Rookie of Year: Bernard Jourdain/Scott Pruett
Legend: R=Indianapolis 500-Mile Race Rookie; W=Indianapolis 500-Mile Race Former Winner
Lap Leaders: Fittipaldi 1-34, Ma. Andretti 35, Boesel 36, Fittipaldi 37-87, Mi. Andretti 88-92, Fittipaldi 93-112, Mi. Andretti 113-123, Fittipaldi 124-129, Mi. Andretti 130-139, Fittipaldi 140-153, Mi. Andretti 154-162, Fittipaldi 163, Unser, Jr. 164-165, Fittipaldi 166-195, Unser, Jr. 196-198, Fittipaldi 199-200.
Lap Leader Summary: Fittipaldi 8 times for 158 laps, Mi. Andretti 4-35, Unser, Jr. 2-5, Ma. Andretti 1-1, Boesel 1-1. Lead Changes: 15 among 5 drivers.
Caution Laps: 5-14, #11 Cogan, accident T4. 61-65, #18 Rahal, stalled. 128-131, #9 Luyendyk, engine. 139-149, #15 Crawford, slowed. 162-166, #6 Mi. Andretti, engine. 181-186, #56 Palmroth, lost tire T4. 199-200, #2 Unser, Jr., accident T4. Cautions: 7 for 43 laps.

Official Box Score

74th Indianapolis 500-Mile Race at the Indianapolis Motor Speedway • Sunday, May 27, 1990

FP	SP	No.		Driver	Car Name	Chassis/Engine	Laps	Status	Total Prize Money
1	3	30		Arie Luyendyk	Domino's Pizza	Lola/Chevrolet Indy	200	185.981	$1,090,940
2	4	18	W	Bobby Rahal	STP/Kraco	Lola/Chevrolet Indy	200	185.772	488,566
3	1	1	W	Emerson Fittipaldi	Marlboro	Penske/Chevrolet Indy	200	185.183	592,874
4	7	5		Al Unser Jr.	Team Valvoline	Lola/Chevrolet Indy	199	Running	227,691
5	2	2	W	Rick Mears	Pennzoil Z-7	Penske/Chevrolet Indy	198	Running	201,610
6	8	14	W	A.J. Foyt	Copenhagen	Lola/Chevrolet Indy	194	Running	184,804
7	26	22		Scott Brayton	Amway/Speedway	Lola/Cosworth DFS	194	Running	201,448
8	14	25	R	Eddie Cheever Jr.	Target Stores	Penske/Chevrolet Indy	193	Running	172,786
9	15	11		Kevin Cogan	Tuneup Masters	Penske/Buick	191	Running	150,472
10	21	28	R	Scott Goodyear	Mackenzie/O'Donnell	Lola/Judd	191	Running	146,970
11	20	70		Didier Theys	Tuneup Masters	Penske/Buick	190	Running	142,384
12	16	23		Tero Palmroth	Hoechst/Celanese/Neste	Lola/Cosworth DFS	188	Running	138,756
13	30	40	W	Al Unser	Miller High Life	March/Alfa Romeo	186	Running	136,387
14	12	12		Randy Lewis	AMP/Oracle	Penske/Buick	186	Running	134,275
15	29	15		Jim Crawford	Glidden Paints	Lola/Buick	183	Running	130,022
16	32	93		John Paul Jr.	ATEC Environmental	Lola/Buick	176	Radiator	150,276
17	24	39	R	Dean Hall	Insight	Lola/Cosworth DFS	165	Suspension	134,306
18	23	4		Teo Fabi	Foster's/Quaker State	March/Porsche	162	Transmission	156,060
19	19	21		Geoff Brabham	Mac Tools Distributors	Lola/Judd	161	Running	131,688
20	5	3		Michael Andretti	Kmart/Havoline	Lola/Chevrolet Indy	146	Vibration	130,942
21	10	41		John Andretti	Foster's/Quaker State	March/Porsche	136	Accident	118,320
22	11	86		Dominic Dobson	Texaco Havoline Star	Lola/Cosworth DFS	129	Engine	116,823
23	28	20		Roberto Guerrero	Miller Genuine Draft	March/Alfa Romeo	118	Suspension	115,129
24	31	81		Bill Vukovich III	Hemelgarn	Lola/Buick	102	Engine	119,503
25	33	56		Rocky Moran	Glidden Paints	Lola/Buick	88	Engine	124,580
26	13	16		Tony Bettenhausen Jr.	AMAX	Lola/Buick	76	Engine	112,083
27	6	6	W	Mario Andretti	Kmart/Havoline	Lola/Chevrolet Indy	60	Engine	111,209
28	17	19		Raul Boesel	Budweiser	Lola/Judd	60	Engine	110,461
29	22	29		Pancho Carter	Hardee's/Machinists	Lola/Cosworth DFS	59	Accident	110,837
30	25	9	W	Tom Sneva	RCA	Penske/Buick	48	CV Joint	110,338
31	18	51		Gary Bettenhausen	Glidden Paints	Lola/Buick	39	Wheel Bearing	109,464
32	9	7	W	Danny Sullivan	Marlboro	Penske/Chevrolet Indy	19	Accident	109,778
33	27	97		Stan Fox	Miyano/CNC Systems	Lola/Buick	10	Gearbox	108,021

Total Purse $6,319,803

Time of Race: 2:41:18.404 Average Speed: 185.981 mph Margin of Victory: 10.878 sec
Pole: #1 Emerson Fittipaldi (225.301, 2:39.786) Fastest Race Lap: #1 Emerson Fittipaldi (lap 91) & Arie Luyendyk (lap 162) (Race Lap 91 and 162, 222.574 mph, 40.436 sec.)
Winning Car Owner: Doug Shierson Racing Winning Chief Mechanic: Michael Battersby Winning Tire: Goodyear Rookie of Year: Eddie Cheever Jr.
Legend: R=Indianapolis 500-Mile Race Rookie; W=Indianapolis 500-Mile Race Former Winner
Lap Leaders: Fittipaldi 1-92, Luyendyk 93-94, Fittipaldi 95-117, Rahal 118-122, Fittipaldi 123-135, Rahal 136-167, Luyendyk 168-200.
Lap Leader Summary: Fittipaldi 3 times for 128 laps, Rahal 2-37, Luyendyk 2-35. Lead Changes: 6 among 3 drivers.
Caution Laps: 20-25, #7 Sullivan, accident T1. 43-51, #16 T. Bettehnausen, stopped pit entry. 63-69, #29 Carter, accident T4. 141-146, #41 J. Andretti, accident T1.
Cautions: 4 for 28 laps.

Official Box Score

75th Indianapolis 500-Mile Race at the Indianapolis Motor Speedway • Sunday, May 26, 1991

FP	SP	No.	Rookie	Driver	Car Name	Chassis/Engine	Laps	Status	Total Prize Money
1	1	3	W	Rick Mears	Marlboro	Penske/Chevrolet Indy A	200	176.457	$1,219,704
2	5	10		Michael Andretti	Kmart/Havoline	Lola/Chevrolet Indy A	200	176.402	607,753
3	14	1	W	Arie Luyendyk	RCA/UNO Granatelli	Lola/Chevrolet Indy A	199	Running	317,053
4	6	2		Al Unser Jr.	Valvoline	Lola/Chevrolet Indy A	198	Running	223,916
5	7	4		John Andretti	Pennzoil Z-7	Lola/Chevrolet Indy A	197	Running	205,153
6	33	92	W	Gordon Johncock	Jack's Tool Rental/Bryant	Lola/Cosworth DFS	188	Running	275,690
7	3	6	W	Mario Andretti	Kmart/Havoline	Lola/Chevrolet Indy A	187	Engine	203,478
8	17	91		Stan Fox	Byrd's Cafeteria/Bryant	Lola/Buick	185	Running	201,090
9	20	16		Tony Bettenhausen Jr.	AMAX Coal	Penske/Chevrolet Indy A	180	Running	170,016
10	9	20	W	Danny Sullivan	Miller Genuine Draft/Patrick	Lola/Alfa Romeo	173	Engine	194,403
11	15	5	W	Emerson Fittipaldi	Marlboro	Penske/Chevrolet Indy A	171	Gearbox	183,728
12	27	19		Scott Pruett	Budweiser/Truesports	Truesports/Judd	166	Engine	159,191
13	30	66		Dominic Dobson	Coors/Kroger/Burns	Lola/Judd	164	Running	159,190
14	31	39		Randy Lewis	AMP/Orbit/Jenn-Air/Epson	Lola/Cosworth DFS	159	Running	150,490
15	11	86	R	Jeff Andretti	Texaco Havoline Star	Lola/Cosworth DFS	150	Engine	167,490
16	24	7	R	Hiro Matsushita	Panasonic	Lola/Buick	149	Running	145,891
17	19	22		Scott Brayton	Amway/Hoechst Celanese	Lola/Chevrolet Indy A	146	Engine	172,191
18	21	48		Bernard Jourdain	Monarch/Foyt/Deutz	Lola/Buick	141	Gearbox	140,190
19	4	18	W	Bobby Rahal	STP/Kraco	Lola/Chevrolet Indy A	130	Engine	153,741
20	22	21		Geoff Brabham	Mac Tools	Truesports/Judd	109	Electrical	136,491
21	32	12		Pancho Carter	Arciero/Alfa LAVAL	Lola/Buick	94	Engine	139,703
22	13	51		Gary Bettenhausen	Glidden Paints	Lola/Buick	89	Radiator	177,890
23	26	23		Tero Palmroth	Neste/Rotator	Lola/Cosworth DFS	77	Engine	131,990
24	18	50	R	Mike Groff	Fendi-Hawaiian Tropic	Lola/Cosworth DFS	68	Water leak	133,290
25	25	93		John Paul Jr.	ATEC Environmental	Lola/Buick	53	Oil leak	130,690
26	8	26		Jim Crawford	Quaker State	Lola/Buick	40	Engine	133,690
27	12	15		Scott Goodyear	Mackenzie Financial	Lola/Judd	38	Engine	127,791
28	2	14	W	A.J. Foyt	Foyt/Gilmore/Copenhagen	Lola/Chevrolet Indy A	25	Suspension	153,591
29	16	9		Kevin Cogan	Glidden Paints	Lola/Buick	24	Accident	127,391
30	28	40		Roberto Guerrero	Sharp's/Patrick	Lola/Alfa Romeo	23	Accident	125,203
31	10	8		Eddie Cheever Jr.	Target/Scotch Video	Lola/Chevrolet Indy A	17	Electrical	125,591
32	29	17	R	Willy T. Ribbs	McDonalds/Cosby	Lola/Buick	5	Engine	147,791
33	23	71	R	Buddy Lazier	Vail Beaver Creek	Lola/Buick	1	Accident	162,690

Total Purse $7,004,150

Time of Race: 2:50:00.791 Average Speed: 176.457 mph Margin of Victory: 3.149 sec
Pole: #3 Rick Mears (224.113, 2:40.633) Fastest Qualifier: #51 Gary Bettenhausen (224.468, 2:40.379)
Fastest Race Lap: #1 Arie Luyendyk (Race Lap 109, 222.178 mph, 40.508 sec.)
Winning Car Owner: Penske Racing Winning Chief Mechanic: Richard Buck Winning Tire: Goodyear Rookie of Year: Jeff Andretti
Legend: R=Indianapolis 500-Mile Race Rookie; W=Indianapolis 500-Mile Race Former Winner
Lap Leaders: Mears 1-11, Ma. Andretti 12-33, Mi. Andretti 34-54, Unser, Jr. 55, Mi. Andretti 56-79, Unser, Jr. 80-82, Mi. Andretti 83-108, Fittipaldi 109-112, Rahal 113, Fittipaldi 114-138, Mears 139-140, Fittipaldi 141-153, Mi. Andretti 154-165, Fittipaldi 166-169, Mears 170, Mi. Andretti 171-183, Mears 184-186, Mi. Andretti 187, Mears 188-200.
Lap Leader Summary: Mi. Andretti 6 times for 97 laps, Fittipaldi 4-46, Mears 3-20, Ma. Andretti 1-22, Unser, Jr. 2-4, Rahal 1-1. Lead Changes: 18 among 6 drivers.
Caution Laps: 1-3, #71 Lazier, accident T1. 20-23, #8 Cheever Jr., stopped T4. 25-33, #40 Guerrero, #9 Cogan #14 Foyt, accident T1. 84-89, #23 Palmroth, car fire backstretch. 148-153, #22 Brayton, engine, #48 Jourdain, tow-in. 184-186, #20 Sullivan, smoking. 191-194, #6 Ma. Andretti, stopped. Cautions: 7 for 35 laps.

Official Box Score

76th Indianapolis 500-Mile Race at the Indianapolis Motor Speedway • Sunday, May 24, 1992

FP	SP	No.		Driver	Car Name	Chassis/Engine	Laps	Status	Total Prize Money
1	12	3		Al Unser Jr.	Valvoline	Galmer/Chevrolet Indy A	200	134.477	$1,244,184
2	33	15		Scott Goodyear	Mackenzie Financial	Lola/Chevrolet Indy A	200	134.476	609,333
3	22	27	W	Al Unser	Menard-Conseco	Lola/Chevrolet Indy A	200	134.375	368,553
4	2	9		Eddie Cheever Jr.	Target-Scotch Video	Lola/Ford Cosworth XB	200	134.374	271,103
5	8	18	W	Danny Sullivan	Molson/Kraco/STP	Galmer/Chevrolet Indy A	199	Running	211,803
6	10	12	W	Bobby Rahal	Miller Genuine Draft	Lola/Chevrolet Indy A	199	Running	237,703
7	25	11		Raul Boesel	Panasonic	Lola/Chevrolet Indy A	198	Running	191,503
8	14	8		John Andretti	Pennzoil	Lola/Chevrolet Indy A	195	Running	186,203
9	23	14	W	A.J. Foyt	Copenhagen	Lola/Chevrolet Indy A	195	Running	189,883
10	18	93		John Paul Jr.	D.B. Mann Development	Lola/Buick	194	Running	171,403
11	27	90	R	Lyn St. James	Agency Rent-A-Car /JC Penney	Lola/Chevrolet Indy A	193	Running	187,953
12	29	68		Dominic Dobson	Burns/Tobacco Free America	Lola/Chevrolet Indy A	193	Running	179,983
13	6	1		Michael Andretti	Kmart/Texaco Havoline	Lola/Ford Cosworth XB	189	Fuel Pressure	295,383
14	24	21		Buddy Lazier	Leader Cards	Lola/Buick	139	Engine	164,283
15	4	6	W	Arie Luyendyk	Target/Scotch Video	Lola/Ford Cosworth XB	135	Accident	166,953
16	32	31	R	Ted Prappas	PIG/Say No To Drugs	Lola/Chevrolet Indy A	135	Gear Box	163,253
17	5	51		Gary Bettenhausen	Glidden Paints	Lola/Buick	112	Accident	150,803
18	20	48		Jeff Andretti	Gillette/Carlo	Lola/Chevrolet Indy A	109	Accident	153,703
19	26	39	R	Brian Bonner	Applebee's	Lola/Buick	97	Accident	156,953
20	19	7	R	Paul Tracy	Mobil 1	Penske/Chevrolet Indy A	96	Engine	160,053
21	28	47	R	Jimmy Vasser	Kodalux	Lola/Chevrolet Indy A	94	Accident	170,853
22	7	22		Scott Brayton	Amway/Northwest Airlines	Lola/Buick	93	Engine	173,683
23	3	2	W	Mario Andretti	Kmart/Texaco Havoline	Lola/Ford Cosworth XB	78	Accident	156,633
24	11	5	W	Emerson Fittipaldi	Marlboro	Penske/Chevrolet Indy B	75	Accident	138,703
25	21	26		Jim Crawford	Quaker State	Lola/Buick	74	Accident	167,503
26	9	4	W	Rick Mears	Marlboro	Penske/Chevrolet Indy B	74	Accident	136,403
27	13	91		Stan Fox	Jonathan Byrd's Cafeteria	Lola/Buick	63	Accident	136,683
28	16	44	R	Philippe Gache	Rhone-Poulenc Rorer	Lola/Chevrolet Indy A	61	Accident	136,128
29	31	92	W	Gordon Johncock	STP/Jacks Tool Rental	Lola/Buick	60	Engine	136,003
30	17	10		Scott Pruett	Budweiser	Truesports/Chevrolet Indy A	52	Engine	143,503
31	30	59	W	Tom Sneva	Glidden Paints	Lola/Buick	10	Accident	139,778
32	15	19	R	Eric Bachelart	Royal Oak Charcoal	Lola/Buick	4	Engine	144,228
33	1	36		Roberto Guerrero	Quaker State	Lola/Buick	0	Accident	286,378

Total Purse $7,527,450

Time of Race: 3:43:05.148 Average Speed: 134.477 mph Margin of Victory: 0.043 sec

Pole: #36 Roberto Guerrero (232.482, 2:34.881) Fastest Race Lap: #1 Michael Andretti (Race Lap 166, 229.118 mph, 39.281 sec.)

Winning Car Owner: Galles/Kraco Racing Winning Chief Mechanic: Owen Snyder III Winning Tire: Goodyear Rookie of Year: Lyn St. James

Legend: R=Indianapolis 500-Mile Race Rookie; W=Indianapolis 500-Mile Race Former Winner

Lap Leaders: Mi. Andretti 1-6, Ma. Andretti 7, Mi. Andretti 8-13, Cheever, Jr. 14-20, Mi. Andretti 21-46, Cheever, Jr. 47, Luyendyk 48, Mi. Andretti 49-87, Cheever, Jr. 88, Mi. Andretti 89-107, Unser, Jr. 108-109, Mi. Andretti 110-115, Mi. Andretti 117-140, Unser, Jr. 116, Mi. Andretti 141-151, A. Unser 152-173, Mi. Andretti 178-189, Unser, Jr. 190-200.
Lap Leader Summary: Mi. Andretti 9 times for 160 laps, Unser, Jr. 4-25, Cheever, Jr. 3-9, A. Unser 1-4, Ma. Andretti 1-1, Luyendyk 1-1. Lead Changes: 18 among 6 drivers.
Caution Laps: 6-10, #19 Bachelart, smoking. 12-20, #59 Sneva, accident T4. 62-66, #92 Johncock, smoking. 67-75, #91 Fox, #44 Gache, accident T1. 76-83, #26 Crawford, #4 Mears, #31 Prappas, #5 Fittipaldi, accident T2. 83-89, #2 Ma. Andretti, accident T4. 94-96, #22 Brayton, engine. 97-102, #7 Tracy, smoking. 102-109, #39 Bonner, accident T4. 115-122, #48 J. Andretti, #51 Bettenhausen, Accident T2. 137-143, #6 Luyendyk, accident T4. 150-155, #21 Lazier, lost power backstretch. 190-193, #1 Mi. Andretti, stopped north short chute. Cautions: 13 for 85 laps.

Official Box Score

77th Indianapolis 500-Mile Race at the Indianapolis Motor Speedway • Sunday, May 30, 1993

FP	SP	No.		Driver	Car Name	Chassis/Engine	Laps	Status	Total Prize Money
1	9	4	W	Emerson Fittipaldi	Marlboro	Penske/Chevrolet Indy C	200	157.207	$1,155,304
2	1	10	W	Arie Luyendyk	Target/Scotch Video	Lola/Ford Cosworth XB	200	157.168	681,303
3	8	5	R	Nigel Mansell	Kmart/Texaco Havoline	Lola/Ford Cosworth XB	200	157.149	391,203
4	3	9		Raul Boesel	Duracell/Mobil 1/Sadia	Lola/Ford Cosworth XB	200	157.142	317,903
5	2	6	W	Mario Andretti	Kmart/Texaco Havoline	Lola/Ford Cosworth XB	200	157.133	313,953
6	11	22		Scott Brayton	Amway/Byrd's Cafeteria	Lola/Ford Cosworth XB	200	157.117	248,253
7	4	2		Scott Goodyear	Mackenzie Financial	Lola/Ford Cosworth XB	200	157.099	234,953
8	5	3	W	Al Unser Jr.	Valvoline	Lola/Chevrolet Indy C	200	157.070	243,253
9	17	8		Teo Fabi	Pennzoil	Lola/Chevrolet Indy C	200	156.968	206,703
10	24	84		John Andretti	Copenhagen/Marmon Group	Lola/Ford Cosworth XB	200	156.964	228,303
11	6	16	R	Stefan Johansson	AMAX Energy & Metals	Penske/Chevrolet Indy C	199	Running	186,020
12	23	80	W	Al Unser	Budweiser King	Lola/Chevrolet Indy C	199	Running	194,870
13	19	18		Jimmy Vasser	Kodalux/STP	Lola/Ford Cosworth XB	198	Running	188,003
14	14	11		Kevin Cogan	Conseco	Lola/Chevrolet Indy C	198	Running	180,603
15	28	50		Davy Jones	Agip/Andrea Moda/Marcelo	Lola/Chevrolet Indy A	197	Running	166,003
16	33	59		Eddie Cheever Jr.	Glidden/Menard/Quorum	Lola/Buick	197	Running	184,403
17	18	51		Gary Bettenhausen	Glidden Paints	Lola/Menard	197	Running	155,053
18	26	15		Hiro Matsushita	Panasonic	Lola/Ford Cosworth XB	197	Running	157,503
19	15	36	R	Stephan Gregoire	Formula Project/Maalox	Lola/Buick	195	Running	189,603
20	22	76		Tony Bettenhausen Jr.	AMAX Energy & Metals	Penske/Chevrolet Indy C	195	Running	151,063
21	30	75		Willy T. Ribbs	Cosby/Service Merchandise	Lola/Ford Cosworth XB	194	Running	146,653
22	32	92		Didier Theys	Kinko's/Delta Faucet	Lola/Buick	193	Running	176,053
23	27	66		Dominic Dobson	Coors Light/Indy Parks	Galmer/Chevrolet Indy A	193	Running	146,203
24	31	60		Jim Crawford	Budweiser King	Lola/Chevrolet Indy C	192	Running	148,270
25	21	90		Lyn St. James	JCPenney/Nike/Amer. Woman	Lola/Ford Cosworth XB	176	Stalled	146,403
26	29	27		Geoff Brabham	Glidden/Menard	Lola/Menard	174	Engine	139,203
27	25	41	R	Robby Gordon	Copenhagen/Foyt	Lola/Ford Cosworth XB	165	Gearbox	155,453
28	10	40		Roberto Guerrero	Budweiser King	Lola/Chevrolet Indy C	125	Accident	137,303
29	16	21		Jeff Andretti	Interstate Batt/Gillette/Taesa	Lola/Buick	124	Accident	154,370
30	7	12		Paul Tracy	Marlboro	Penske/Chevrolet Indy C	94	Accident	136,003
31	20	91		Stan Fox	Delta Faucet-Jacks Tool Rental	Lola/Buick	64	Engine	136,703
32	13	77	R	Nelson Piquet	ARISCO/STP	Lola/Menard	38	Engine	137,219
33	12	7	W	Danny Sullivan	Molson	Lola/Chevrolet Indy C	29	Accident	137,203

Total Purse $7,671,300

Time of Race: 3:10:49.860 Average Speed: 157.207 mph Margin of Victory: 2.862 sec

Pole: #10 Arie Luyendyk (223.967, 2:40.738) Fastest Race Lap: #4 Emerson Fittipaldi (Race Lap 198, 214.867 mph, 41.898 sec.)

Winning Car Owner: Penske Racing Winning Chief Mechanic: Rick Rinaman Winning Tire: Goodyear Rookie of Year: Nigel Mansell

Legend: R=Indianapolis 500-Mile Race Rookie; W=Indianapolis 500-Mile Race Former Winner

Lap Leaders: Boesel 1-17, Gregoire 18, Cogan 19-22, A. Unser 23-31, Ma. Andretti 32-46, Luyendyk 47-57, A. Unser 58-63, Jo. Andretti 64-65, Gordon 66-67, Goodyear 68-69, Mansell 70-91, Ma. Andretti 92-128, Mansell 129-130, Luyendyk 131-132, Ma. Andretti 133, Luyendyk 134, Unser, Jr. 135-151, Ma. Andretti 152-168, Goodyear 169-171, Ma. Andretti 172, Boesel 173, Ma. Andretti 174, Fittipaldi 185-200. Lap Leader Summary: Ma. Andretti 6 times for 72 laps, Mansell 3-34, Boesel 2-18, Unser, Jr. 1-17, Fittipaldi 1-16, A. Unser 2-15, Luyendyk 3-14, Goodyear 2-5, Cogan 1-4, Jo. Andretti 1-2, Gordon 1-2, Gregoire 1-1. Lead Changes: 23 among 12 drivers.
Caution Laps: 16-20, #60 Crawford, spin backstretch. 31-37, #7 Sullivan, accident north short chute. 89-93, Debris. 95-103, #12 Tracy, accident T3. 128-138, #21 J. Andretti, #40 Guerrero accident T3. 169-174, #41 Gordon, lost power. 183-185, #90 St. James, tow-in. 193-195, #5 Mansell, brushed wall T2. Cautions: 8 for 49 laps.

Official Box Score

78th Indianapolis 500-Mile Race at the Indianapolis Motor Speedway • Sunday, May 29, 1994

FP	SP	No.		Driver	Car Name	Chassis/Engine	Laps	Status	Total Prize Money
1	1	31	W	Al Unser Jr.	Marlboro Penske	Penske/Mercedes Benz	200	160.872	$1,373,813
2	4	12	R	Jacques Villeneuve	Player's Ltd.	Reynard/Ford Cosworth XB	200	160.749	622,713
3	28	4	W	Bobby Rahal	Miller Genuine Draft	Penske/Ilmor D	199	Running	411,163
4	16	18		Jimmy Vasser	Conseco/STP	Reynard/Ford Cosworth XB	199	Running	295,163
5	19	9		Robby Gordon	Valvoline/Cummins	Lola/Ford Cosworth XB	199	Running	227,563
6	5	8		Michael Andretti	Target/Scotch Video	Reynard/Ford Cosworth XB	198	Running	245,563
7	24	11		Teo Fabi	Pennzoil	Reynard/Ilmor D	198	Running	216,563
8	11	27		Eddie Cheever Jr.	Quaker State	Lola/Menard	197	Running	238,563
9	22	14	R	Bryan Herta	AJ Foyt/Copenhagen	Lola/Ford Cosworth XB	197	Running	212,213
10	10	33		John Andretti	Byrd's Cafeteria/Bryant	Lola/Ford Cosworth XB	196	Running	191,750
11	29	88	R	Mauricio Gugelmin	Hollywood	Reynard/Ford Cosworth XB	196	Running	182,063
12	21	19	R	Brian Till	The Mi-Jack Car	Lola/Ford Cosworth XB	194	Running	180,763
13	13	91		Stan Fox	Delta Faucet-Jacks Tools	Reynard/Ford Cosworth XB	193	Accident	186,313
14	18	22		Hiro Matsushita	Panasonic/Duskin	Lola/Ford Cosworth XB	193	Running	177,013
15	27	16		Stefan Johansson	Alumax Aluminum	Penske/Ilmor D	192	Running	164,113
16	17	71	R	Scott Sharp	PacWest	Lola/Ford Cosworth XB	186	Running	161,663
17	3	2	W	Emerson Fittipaldi	Marlboro Penske	Penske/Mercedes Benz	184	Accident	298,163
18	8	28	W	Arie Luyendyk	Indy Regency Racing	Lola/Ilmor D	179	Engine	161,412
19	6	90		Lyn St. James	Spirit of American Woman/JC Penney	Lola/Ford Cosworth XB	170	Running	161,212
20	23	59		Scott Brayton	Glidden Paints	Lola/Menard	116	Engine	177,112
21	2	5		Raul Boesel	Duracell Charger	Lola/Ford Cosworth XB	100	Water Pump	173,112
22	7	1		Nigel Mansell	Kmart/Texaco/Havoline	Lola/Ford Cosworth XB	92	Accident	153,312
23	25	3		Paul Tracy	Marlboro Penske	Penske/Mercedes Benz	92	Turbo	151,612
24	14	99	R	Hideshi Matsuda	Beck Motorsports	Lola/Ford Cosworth XB	90	Accident	150,362
25	30	45		John Paul Jr.	Pro Formance Team Losi	Lola/Ilmor D	89	Accident	168,812
26	15	79	R	Dennis Vitolo	Hooligans/Carlo	Lola/Ford Cosworth XB	89	Accident	143,862
27	32	25	R	Marco Greco	International Sports, Ltd.	Lola/Ford Cosworth XB	53	Electrical	171,762
28	26	7	R	Adrian Fernandez	Tecate/Quaker State	Reynard/Ilmor D	30	Suspension	146,612
29	12	17		Dominic Dobson	Columbia Helecopters	Lola/Ford Cosworth XB	29	Accident	139,912
30	33	40		Scott Goodyear	Budweiser	Lola/Ford Cosworth XB	29	Mechanical	159,312
31	31	10		Mike Groff	Motorola	Penske/Ilmor D	28	Accident	138,812
32	9	6	W	Mario Andretti	Kmart/Texaco/Havoline	Lola/Ford Cosworth XB	23	Fuel System	138,512
33	20	21		Roberto Guerrero	Interstate Batteries	Lola/Buick	20	Accident	143,912

Total Purse $7,864,800

Time of Race: 3:06:29.006 Average Speed: 160.872 mph Margin of Victory: 8.600 sec
Pole: #31 Al Unser Jr. (228.011, 2:37.887) Fastest Race Lap: #2 Emerson Fittipaldi (Race Lap 121, 220.680 mph, 40.783 sec.)
Winning Car Owner: Penske Racing, Inc. Winning Chief Mechanic: Richard Buck/Clive Howell Winning Tire: Goodyear Rookie of Year: Jacques Villeneuve
Legend: R=Indianapolis 500-Mile Race Rookie; W=Indianapolis 500-Mile Race Former Winner
Lap Leaders: Unser, Jr. 1-23, Fittipaldi 24-61, Villeneuve 62-63, Fittipaldi 64-124, Villeneuve 125-129, Fittipaldi 130-133, Unser, Jr. 134-138, Fittipaldi 139-164, Unser, Jr. 165-168, Fittipaldi 169-184, Unser, Jr. 185-200.
Lap Leader Summary: Fittipaldi 5 times for 145 laps, Unser, Jr. 4-48, Villeneuve 2-7. Lead Changes: 10 among 3 drivers.
Caution Laps: 7-9, #79 Vitolo, spin T4. 21-27, #21 Guerrero, accident T2. 30-40, #17 Dobson, #10 Groff, accident T1. 92-100, #99 Matsuda, accident T1, #45 Paul Jr., accident T2, #79 Vitolo, #1 Mansell, accident T3. 137-139, Debris. 185-190, #2 Fittipaldi, accident T4. 197-200, #91 Fox, accident T1. Cautions: 7 for 43 laps.

Official Box Score

79th Indianapolis 500-Mile Race at the Indianapolis Motor Speedway • Sunday, May 28, 1995

FP	SP	No.		Driver	Car Name	Chassis/Engine	Laps	Status	Total Prize Money
1	5	27		Jacques Villeneuve	Player's LTD/Team Green	Reynard/Ford Cosworth XB	200	153.616	$1,312,019
2	27	15	R	Christian Fittipaldi	Marlboro Chapeco	Reynard/Ford Cosworth XB	200	153.583	594,668
3	21	9	W	Bobby Rahal	Miller Genuine Draft	Lola/Mercedes Benz	200	153.577	373,267
4	24	7	R	Eliseo Salazar	Cristal/Mobil 1/Copec	Lola/Ford Cosworth XB	200	153.553	302,417
5	7	5		Robby Gordon	Valvoline/Cummins	Reynard/Ford Cosworth XB	200	153.420	247,917
6	6	18		Mauricio Gugelmin	Hollywood/PacWest	Reynard/Ford Cosworth XB	200	153.392	284,667
7	2	40	W	Arie Luyendyk	Glidden/Quaker State	Lola/Menard V6	200	153.067	247,417
8	15	33		Teo Fabi	ABB/Indeck	Reynard/Ford Cosworth XB	199	Running	206,853
9	18	17	W	Danny Sullivan	VISA Bank of America/PacWest	Reynard/Ford Cosworth XB	199	Running	193,453
10	10	25		Hiro Matsushita	Panasonic Duskin YKK	Reynard/Ford Cosworth XB	199	Running	196,053
11	17	34	R	Alessandro Zampedri	The Mi-Jack Car	Lola/Ford Cosworth XB	198	Running	199,153
12	13	21		Roberto Guerrero	Upper Deck/General Components	Reynard/Mercedes Benz	198	Running	181,203
13	33	4		Bryan Herta	Target/Scotch Video	Reynard/Ford Cosworth XB	198	Running	175,903
14	3	24		Scott Goodyear	LCI/Motorola/CNN	Reynard/Honda Indy	195	Penalty	246,403
15	20	54		Hideshi Matsuda	Beck Motorsports/Taisan/Zunne Group	Lola/Ford Cosworth XB	194	Running	200,503
16	31	16		Stefan Johansson	Team Alumax	Reynard/Ford Cosworth XB	192	Running	182,703
17	1	60		Scott Brayton	Quaker State/Glidden	Lola/Menard V6	190	Running	306,503
18	12	31	R	Andre Ribiero	LCI International	Reynard/Honda Indy	187	Running	176,753
19	8	20		Scott Pruett	Firestone Patrick Racing	Lola/Ford Cosworth XB	184	Accident	164,953
20	22	11		Raul Boesel	The Duracell Charger	Lola/Mercedes Benz	184	Oil Line	169,053
21	25	10		Adrian Fernandez	Tecate Beer/Quaker State/Galles	Lola/Mercedes Benz	176	Engine	183,903
22	9	12		Jimmy Vasser	Target/STP	Reynard/Ford Cosworth XB	170	Accident	162,003
23	32	77		Davy Jones	Jonathan Byrd's Cafeteria/Bryant H. & C.	Lola/Ford Cosworth XB	161	Accident	182,303
24	16	3		Paul Tracy	Kmart/Budweiser/Newman-Haas Racing	Lola/Ford Cosworth XB	136	Electrical	149,703
25	4	6		Michael Andretti	Kmart/Texaco Havoline/Newman/Haas	Lola/Ford Cosworth XB	77	Suspension	192,053
26	30	41		Scott Sharp	AJ Foyt/Copenhagen Racing	Lola/Ford Cosworth XB	74	Accident	158,003
27	23	80		Buddy Lazier	Glidden/Quaker State	Lola/Menard V6	45	Fuel System	145,903
28	26	19		Eric Bachelart	The AGFA Car	Lola/Ford Cosworth XB	6	Mechanical	155,003
29	19	8	R	Gil de Ferran	Pennzoil Special/Hall Racing	Reynard/Mercedes Benz	1	Accident	149,453
30	11	91		Stan Fox	Delta Faucet/Bowling/Hemelgarn	Reynard/Ford Cosworth XB	0	Accident	143,603
31	14	14		Eddie Cheever Jr.	AJ Foyt/Copenhagen Racing	Lola/Ford Cosworth XB	0	Accident	144,103
32	28	90		Lyn St. James	Whitlock Auto Supply	Lola/Ford Cosworth XB	0	Accident	157,803
33	29	22	R	Carlos Guerrero	Herdez-Viva Mexico!	Lola/Ford Cosworth XB	0	Accident	172,853

Total Purse $8,058,550

Time of Race: 3:15:17.561 Average Speed: 153.616 mph Margin of Victory: 2.481 sec
Pole: #60 Scott Brayton (231.604, 2:35.438) Fastest Race Lap: #24 Scott Goodyear (Race Lap 179, 224.009 mph, 40.177 sec.)
Winning Car Owner: Team Green Winning Chief Mechanic: Kyle Moyer Winning Tire: Goodyear Rookie of Year: Christian Fittipaldi
Legend: R=Indianapolis 500-Mile Race Rookie; W=Indianapolis 500-Mile Race Former Winner
Lap Leaders: Goodyear 1-9, Luyendyk 10-16, Mi. Andretti 17-32, Goodyear 33-35, Villeneuve 36-38, Mi. Andretti 39-66, Goodyear 67, Gugelmin 68-76, Mi. Andretti 77, Goodyear 78-81, Gugelmin 82-116, Goodyear 117-120, Rahal 121, Boesel 122-123, Gugelmin 124-138, Goodyear 139, Vasser 140-155, Villeneuve 156-162, Pruett 163-165, Gordon 166, Vasser 167-170, Pruett 171-175, Goodyear 176-195, Villeneuve 196-200. Lap Leader Summary: Gugelmin 3 times for 59 laps, Mi. Andretti 3-45, Goodyear 7-42, Vasser 2-20, Villeneuve 3-15, Pruett 2-8, Luyendyk 1-7, Boesel 1-2, Gordon 1-1, Rahal 1-1. Lead Changes: 23 among 10 drivers.
Caution Laps: 1-9, #91 Fox, #14 Cheever Jr., #90 St.James, #22 C. Guerrero, #8 de Ferran, accident T1. 37-44, Debris. 80-86, #41 Sharp, accident T4. 89-95, #16 Johansson, spin T4. 123-126, #31 Ribeiro, tow-in. 138-141, #3 Tracy, tow-in. 163-169, #77 Jones, accident T4. 171-176, #12 Vasser, accident T3. 185-190, #20 Pruett, accident T2. Cautions: 9 for 58 laps.

Official Box Score
80th Indianapolis 500-Mile Race at the Indianapolis Motor Speedway • Sunday, May 26, 1996

FP	SP	No.		Driver	Car Name	Chassis/Engine	Laps	Status	Total Prize Money
1	5	91		Buddy Lazier	Hemelgarn Racing-Delta Faucet-Montana	Reynard/Ford Cosworth XB	200	147.956	$1,367,854
2	2	70		Davy Jones	Delco Electronics High Tech Team Galles	Lola/Mercedes Ilmor	200	147.948	632,503
3	15	4	R	Richie Hearn	Della Penna Mtspts. Ralph's Food 4 Less Fuji	Reynard/Ford Cosworth XB	200	147.871	375,203
4	7	8		Alessandro Zampedri	Mi-Jack/AGIP/Xcel	Lola/Ford Cosworth XB	199	Accident	270,853
5	6	21		Roberto Guerrero	WavePhore/Pennzoil	Reynard/Ford Cosworth XB	198	Accident	315,503
6	3	7		Eliseo Salazar	Cristal/Copec Mobil	Lola/Ford Cosworth XB	197	Accident	226,653
7	33	32		Danny Ongais	Glidden Menards	Lola/Menard V6	197	Running	228,253
8	30	52		Hideshi Matsuda	Team Taisan/Beck Motorsports	Lola/Ford Cosworth XB	197	Running	233,953
9	23	54	R	Robbie Buhl	Original Coors/Beck Motorsports	Lola/Ford Cosworth XB	197	Running	195,403
10	21	11		Scott Sharp	Conseco AJ Foyt Racing	Lola/Ford Cosworth XB	194	Running	202,053
11	4	3		Eddie Cheever Jr.	Quaker State Menards	Lola/Menard V6	189	Running	206,103
12	10	14	R	Davey Hamilton	AJ Foyt Copenhagen Racing	Lola/Ford Cosworth XB	181	Running	184,003
13	8	22	R	Michel Jourdain Jr.	Herdez Quaker State/Viva Mexico!	Lola/Ford Cosworth XB	177	Running	193,653
14	18	45		Lyn St. James	Spirit of San Antonio	Lola/Ford Cosworth XB	153	Accident	182,603
15	32	44	R	Scott Harrington	Gold Eagle/Mechanics Laundry/Harrington/LP	Reynard/Ford Cosworth XB	150	Accident	190,753
16	20	5	W	Arie Luyendyk	Jonathan Byrd's Cafeteria/Bryant H. & C.	Reynard/Ford Cosworth XB	149	Damage	216,503
17	9	12	R	Buzz Calkins	Bradley Food Marts/Hoosier Lottery	Reynard/Ford Cosworth XB	148	Brake	173,553
18	19	27	R	Jim Guthrie	Team Blueprint Racing	Lola/Menard V6	144	Engine	168,453
19	14	30	R	Mark Dismore	Quaker State Menards	Lola/Menard V6	129	Engine	161,253
20	11	60		Mike Groff	Valvoline Cummins Craftsman	Reynard/Ford Cosworth XB	122	Tire	158,503
21	28	34	R	Fermin Velez	Scandia/Xcel/Royal Purple	Lola/Ford Cosworth XB	107	Engine Fire	176,653
22	31	43		Joe Gosek	Scandia/Fanatics Only/Xcel	Lola/Ford Cosworth XB	106	Radiator	169,653
23	26	10	R	Brad Murphey	Hemelgarn Racing-Delta Faucet	Reynard/Ford Cosworth XB	91	Suspension	177,853
24	1	20	R	Tony Stewart	Menards/Glidden/Quaker State	Lola/Menard V6	82	Engine	222,053
25	25	90	R	Racin Gardner	Team Scandia/Slick Gardner Enterprises	Lola/Ford Cosworth XB	76	Suspension	149,853
26	22	41		Marco Greco	AJ Foyt Enterprises	Lola/Ford Cosworth XB	64	Engine	153,303
27	13	9		Stephan Gregoire	Hemelgarn Racing/Delta Faucet	Reynard/Ford Cosworth XB	59	Coil fire	147,103
28	27	16		Johnny Parsons	Team Blueprint Racing	Lola/Menard V6	48	Radiator	161,203
29	29	75	R	Johnny O'Connell	Mechanics Laundry/Cunningham	Reynard/Ford Cosworth XB	47	Fuel system	145,553
30	12	33	R	Michele Alboreto	Rio Hotel & Casino/Perry Ellis/Royal Purple	Reynard/Ford Cosworth XB	43	Gear Box	144,953
31	17	18		John Paul Jr.	V-Line/Earl's Perf. Prod./Crowne Plaza/Keco	Lola/Menard V6	10	Ignition	144,203
32	24	96	R	Paul Durant	ABF Motorsports/Sunrise Rentals	Lola/Buick	9	Engine	149,153
33	16	64	R	Johnny Unser	Ruger-Titanium/Project Indy	Reynard/Ford Cosworth XB	0	Transmission	143,953

Total Purse $7,969,100

Time of Race: 3:22:45.753 Average Speed: 147.956 mph Margin of Victory: 0.695 sec
Pole: #20 Tony Stewart (233.718, 2:34.440) Fastest Qualifier: #5 Arie Luyendyk (236.986, 2:31.908) Fastest Race Lap: #3 Eddie Cheever Jr. (Race Lap 78, 236.103 mph, 38.119 sec.)
Winning Car Owner: Hemelgarn Racing, Inc. Winning Chief Mechanic: Mark Shambarger Winning Tire: Firestone Rookie of Year: Tony Stewart
Legend: R=Indianapolis 500-Mile Race Rookie; W=Indianapolis 500-Mile Race Former Winner
Lap Leaders: Stewart 1-31, Guerrero 32-37, Lazier 38-41, Stewart 42-54, Guerrero 55-70, Jones 71-86, Lazier 87-97, Jones 98-120, Lazier 121-133, Guerrero 134-158, Jones 159-160, Lazier 161-167, Jones 168-189, Zampedri 170-189, Jones 190-192, Lazier 193-200.
Lap Leader Summary: Guerrero 3 times for 47 laps, Jones 5-46, Stewart 2-44, Lazier 5-43, Zampedri 1-20. Lead Changes: 15 among 5 drivers.
Caution Laps: 3-5, Debris. 11-16, #96 Durant, spin T3. 18-20, #32 Ongais, spin T3. 50-55, #16 Parsons, smoking. 69-73, Debris. 94-105, #10 Murphy, brushed wall T2. 119-124, #34 Velez, engine fire. 132-139, #30 Dismore, stopped backstretch. 162-168, #44 Harrington, #45 St. James, accident T2. 196-198, #11 Sharp, accident T2. Cautions: 10 for 59 laps.

Official Box Score
81st Indianapolis 500-Mile Race at the Indianapolis Motor Speedway • Tuesday, May 27, 1997

FP	SP	No.		Driver	Car Name	Chassis/Engine	Laps	Status	Total Prize Money
1	1	5	W	Arie Luyendyk	Wavephore/Sprint PCS/Miller Lite/Provimi	G Force/Oldsmobile Aurora	200	145.827	$1,568,150
2	5	6		Scott Goodyear	Nortel/Sprint PCS/Quebecor Printing	G Force/Oldsmobile Aurora	200	145.820	513,300
3	7	52	R	Jeff Ward	FirstPlus Team Cheever	G Force/Oldsmobile Aurora	200	145.779	414,250
4	10	91	W	Buddy Lazier	Delta Faucet-Montana-Hemelgarn	Dallara/Oldsmobile Aurora	200	145.705	279,250
5	2	2		Tony Stewart	Glidden/Menards	G Force/Oldsmobile Aurora	200	145.490	345,050
6	8	14		Davey Hamilton	AJ Foyt PowerTeam Racing	G Force/Oldsmobile Aurora	199	Running	214,000
7	22	11	R	Billy Boat	Conseco A.J. Foyt Racing	Dallara/Oldsmobile Aurora	199	Running	269,700
8	4	3		Robbie Buhl	Quaker State/Menards	G Force/Oldsmobile Aurora	199	Running	235,200
9	21	30	R	Robbie Groff	Alfa-Laval/Team Losi/McCormack Mtspts.	G Force/Oldsmobile Aurora	197	Running	222,350
10	29	33		Fermin Velez	Old Navy Scandia Royal Purple Alta Xcel	Dallara/Oldsmobile Aurora	195	Running	216,400
11	16	12		Buzz Calkins	Bradley Food Marts	G Force/Oldsmobile Aurora	188	Half Shaft	201,000
12	18	10		Mike Groff	Jonathan Byrd's Cafeteria/Visionaire/Bryant	G Force/Oldsmobile Aurora	188	Running	197,300
13	34	90		Lyn St. James	Lifetime TV-Cinergy-Delta Faucet-Hemelgarn	Dallara/Nissan Infiniti Indy	186	Accident	188,000
14	20	44	R	Steve Kinser	SRS/One Call/Menards/Quaker St./St. Elmo's	Dallara/Oldsmobile Aurora	185	Accident	193,250
15	28	54		Dennis Vitolo	SmithKline Beechman/Kroger/Beck Mtspts.	Dallara/Nissan Infiniti Indy	173	Running	210,000
16	27	22		Marco Greco	Side Play Int'l Sport Scandia Alta Xcel	Dallara/Oldsmobile Aurora	166	Gear Box	193,000
17	3	8	R	Vincenzo Sospiri	Old Navy Scandia Royal Purple Alta Xcel	Dallara/Oldsmobile Aurora	163	Running	196,250
18	35	9		Johnny Unser	Delta Faucet-Montana-Cinergy-Hemelgarn	Dallara/Nissan Infiniti Indy	158	Oil Pressure	158,000
19	26	18	R	Tyce Carlson	Klipsch Tnemec Overhead Door Pyle V-Line	Dallara/Nissan Infiniti Indy	156	Accident	173,250
20	17	40		Jack Miller	AMS/Crest Racing/Trane/Spot-On	Dallara/Nissan Infiniti Indy	131	Accident	171,250
21	33	1		Paul Durant	Conseco A.J. Foyt Racing	G Force/Oldsmobile Aurora	111	Accident	178,000
22	24	50	R	Billy Roe	Sega/Progressive Elect./KECO/U.J.T./Euroint'l	Dallara/Oldsmobile Aurora	110	Accident	150,250
23	11	51		Eddie Cheever Jr.	FirstPlus Team Cheever	G Force/Oldsmobile Aurora	84	Timing Chain	176,000
24	9	7		Eliseo Salazar	Copec/Cristal/Scandia	Dallara/Oldsmobile Aurora	70	Accident	164,000
25	30	97	R	Greg Ray	Tobacco Free Kids	Dallara/Oldsmobile Aurora	48	Water Pump	171,250
26	6	27		Jim Guthrie	Blueprint/Jacuzzi/Armour Golf/ERTL	Dallara/Oldsmobile Aurora	43	Engine	164,500
27	19	21		Roberto Guerrero	Pennzoil-Pagan Racing	Dallara/Nissan Infiniti Indy	25	Steering	160,000
28	25	28		Mark Dismore	Kelley Auto./Mech Laundry/Bombardier	Dallara/Oldsmobile Aurora	24	Accident	159,000
29	12	42		Robby Gordon	Coors Light	G Force/Oldsmobile Aurora	19	Fire	139,500
30	32	72	R	Claude Bourbonnais	Blueprint/Jacuzzi/Armour Golf/ERTL	Dallara/Oldsmobile Aurora	9	Engine	152,250
31	13	77		Stephan Gregoire	Chastain Motorsports-Estridge-Miller Eads	G Force/Oldsmobile Aurora	0	Accident	158,000
32	14	17	R	Affonso Giaffone	General Motors Brazil Chitwood	Dallara/Oldsmobile Aurora	0	Accident	158,250
33	15	4	R	Kenny Brack	Monsoon Galles Racing	G Force/Oldsmobile Aurora	0	Accident	202,250
34	23	16	R	Sam Schmidt	Blueprint/HOPE Prepaid Fuel Card	Dallara/Oldsmobile Aurora	0	Engine	150,250
35	31	34		Alessandro Zampedri	Mi-Jack Scandia Royal Purple	Dallara/Oldsmobile Aurora	0	Oil Leak	145,000

Total Purse $8,587,450

Time of Race: 3:25:43.388 Average Speed: 145.827 mph Margin of Victory: 0.570 sec
Pole: #5 Arie Luyendyk (218.263, 2:44.939) Fastest Race Lap: #2 Tony Stewart (Race Lap 105, 215.626 mph, 41.739 sec.)
Winning Car Owner: Treadway Racing, LLC Winning Chief Mechanic: Skip Faul Winning Tire: Firestone Rookie of Year: Jeff Ward
Legend: R=Indianapolis 500-Mile Race Rookie; W=Indianapolis 500-Mile Race Former Winner
Race Notes: Race was postponed from May 25 to May 26 due to rain. Race stopped on May 26 after 15 laps due to rain and restarted the next day.
Lap Leaders: Stewart 1-50, Boat 51, Stewart 52-62, Luyendyk 63-78, Stewart 79, Lazier 80-82, Luyendyk 83-109, Stewart 110-111, Lazier 112-115, Buhl 116-131, Luyendyk 132-140, Goodyear 141, Ward 142-166, Luyendyk 167-168, Ward 169-192, Goodyear 193, Luyendyk 194-200.
Lap Leader Summary: Stewart 4 times for 64 laps, Luyendyk 5-61, Ward 2-49, Buhl 1-16, Lazier 2-7, Goodyear 2-2, Boat 1-1. Lead Changes: 16 among 7 drivers.
Caution Laps: Pace Lap-, #17 Giaffone, acc. T4. #4 Brack, #77 Gregoire, acc. T4. 10-10, #72 Bourbonnais, smoke. 11-14, Rain. 15-15, Red Flag. 16-18, Race restart. 20-28, #42 Gordon, stopped T3. #28 Dismore, #7 Salazar, #44 Kinser, acc. T4(Lap 24). 59-62, #27 Guthrie, stopped. 94-99, #7 Salazar, stopped T2. 114-123, #50 Roe, #1 Durant, acc. T3. 137-142, #40 Miller, acc. T3. 165-169, #18 Carlson, acc. T2. 189-193, #44 Kinser, acc. T4. 196-197, Debris. 199-199, Debris. Cautions: 14 for 58 laps.

Official Box Score

82nd Indianapolis 500-Mile Race at the Indianapolis Motor Speedway • Sunday, May 24, 1998

FP	SP	No.	Rookie	Driver	Car Name	Chassis/Engine	Laps	Status	Total Prize Money
1	17	51		Eddie Cheever Jr.	Rachel's Potato Chips	Dallara/Oldsmobile Aurora	200	145.155	$1,433,000
2	11	91	W	Buddy Lazier	Delta Faucet/Coors Light/Hemelgarn	Dallara/Oldsmobile Aurora	200	145.118	483,200
3	23	55	R	Steve Knapp	Primadonna Resorts/Miller Milling/ISM	G Force/Oldsmobile Aurora	200	145.076	338,750
4	8	6		Davey Hamilton	Reebok/Nienhouse Motorsports	G Force/Oldsmobile Aurora	199	Running	301,650
5	21	52	R	Robby Unser	Team Cheever	Dallara/Oldsmobile Aurora	198	Running	209,400
6	3	14		Kenny Brack	AJ Foyt PowerTeam Racing	Dallara/Oldsmobile Aurora	198	Running	310,750
7	16	81		John Paul Jr.	Team Pelfrey	Dallara/Oldsmobile Aurora	197	Running	216,350
8	19	17	R	Andy Michner	Konica/Syan Racing	Dallara/Oldsmobile Aurora	197	Running	182,050
9	13	44	R	J.J. Yeley	One Call Comm. Quaker State Menards SRS	Dallara/Oldsmobile Aurora	197	Running	198,550
10	18	12		Buzz Calkins	Int'l Star Registry/Bradley Food Marts	G Force/Oldsmobile Aurora	195	Running	248,500
11	26	7	R	Jimmy Kite	Royal Purple Synthetic/Synerlec/Scandia	Dallara/Oldsmobile Aurora	195	Running	287,300
12	22	18	R	Jack Hewitt	Parker Machinery	G Force/Oldsmobile Aurora	195	Running	265,800
13	27	35		Jeff Ward	Team Tabasco/Superflo/Prolong/ISM	G Force/Oldsmobile Aurora	194	Running	242,050
14	14	16		Marco Greco	Int. Sports Ltd. Phoenix Racing	G Force/Oldsmobile Aurora	183	Engine	167,800
15	32	10		Mike Groff	Jonathan Byrd's VisionAire Bryant H. & C.	G Force/Oldsmobile Aurora	183	Running	237,600
16	7	8		Scott Sharp	Delphi Automotive Systems	Dallara/Oldsmobile Aurora	181	Gearbox	234,800
17	31	77		Stephan Gregoire	Blue Star/Tokheim/Estridge/Miller-Eads	G Force/Oldsmobile Aurora	172	Running	225,300
18	2	97		Greg Ray	TMS/TNN/True Value/Dixie Chopper	Dallara/Oldsmobile Aurora	167	Gearbox	175,400
19	30	30		Raul Boesel	Beloit/Fast Rod/Team Losi/TransWorld	G Force/Oldsmobile Aurora	164	Gearbox	221,300
20	28	5	W	Arie Luyendyk	Sprint PCS/Radio Shack/Qualcomm	G Force/Oldsmobile Aurora	151	Gearbox	242,100
21	15	40		Jack Miller	Crest Racing	Dallara/Nissan Infiniti Indy	128	Running	159,800
22	9	21		Roberto Guerrero	Pagan Racing	Dallara/Oldsmobile Aurora	125	Running	165,300
23	1	11		Billy Boat	Conseco AJ Foyt Racing	Dallara/Oldsmobile Aurora	111	Drive Line	364,200
24	10	4		Scott Goodyear	Pennzoil Panther	G Force/Oldsmobile Aurora	100	Clutch	253,300
25	25	9		Johnny Unser	Hemelgarn Racing	Dallara/Oldsmobile Aurora	98	Engine	136,300
26	6	99		Sam Schmidt	Best Western Gold Crown Racing	Dallara/Oldsmobile Aurora	48	Accident	215,300
27	12	28		Mark Dismore	Kelley Automotive	Dallara/Oldsmobile Aurora	48	Accident	209,300
28	29	19	R	Stan Wattles	Metro Racing Systems/NCLD	Riley & Scott/Oldsmobile Aurora	48	Accident	138,550
29	20	53		Jim Guthrie	Delco Remy/Goodyear/ISM Racing Aurora	G Force/Oldsmobile Aurora	48	Accident	133,300
30	33	33		Billy Roe	Royal Purple/ProLink/Scandia	Dallara/Oldsmobile Aurora	48	Accident	137,300
31	5	3		Robbie Buhl	Johns Manville/Menards	Dallara/Oldsmobile Aurora	44	Engine	222,300
32	24	98	R	Donnie Beechler	Cahill Auto Racing	G Force/Oldsmobile Aurora	34	Engine	132,300
33	4	1		Tony Stewart	Glidden/Menards	Dallara/Oldsmobile Aurora	22	Engine	220,250

Total Purse $8,709,150

Time of Race: 3:26:40.524 Average Speed: 145.155 mph Margin of Victory: 3.191 sec
Pole: #11 Billy Boat (223.503, 2:41:503) Fastest Race Lap: #1 Tony Stewart (Race Lap 19, 214.746 mph, 41.910 sec.)
Winning Car Owner: Team Cheever Winning Chief Mechanic: Owen Snyder III Winning Tire: Goodyear Rookie of Year: Steve Knapp
Legend: R=Indianapolis 500-Mile Race Rookie; W=Indianapolis 500-Mile Race Former Winner
Lap Leaders: Boat 1-12, Ray 13-20, Stewart 21, Ray 22-31, Brack 32-46, Calkins 47-50, Brack 51-61, Brack 62-67, Cheever, Jr. 68-84, Luyendyk 85, Brack 86-87, Lazier 88-93, Cheever, Jr. 94-97, Paul 98-113, Hamilton 114-116, Cheever, Jr. 117-122, Lazier 123, Paul 124-146, Luyendyk 147-149, Cheever, Jr. 150-153, Lazier 154, Cheever, Jr. 155-176, Lazier 177, Cheever, Jr. 178-200.
Lap Leader Summary: Cheever, Jr. 6 times for 76 laps, Paul 2-39, Brack 3-23, Lazier 5-20, Ray 2-18, Boat 1-12, Luyendyk 2-4, Calkins 1-4, Hamilton 1-3, Stewart 1-1. Lead Changes: 23 among 10 drivers.
Caution Laps: 1-3, #44 Yeley, Spin T1. 22-26, #1 Stewert, stopped T1. 34-38, #98 Beechler, engine. 45-48, #3 Buhl, stopped on backstretch. 49-63, #33 Roe, #53 Guthrie, #19 Wattles, #28 Dismore, #99Schmidt, accident T3. 96-99, #7 Kite, stalled. 122-127, #40 Miller, stalled. 132-135, #11 Boat, stalled. 153-156, #5 Luyendyk, stalled. 176-179, #77 Gregoire, brushed wall T4. 180-182, #18 Hewitt, spin T1. 191-194, #16 Greco, smoking. Cautions: 12 for 61 laps.

Official Box Score

83rd Indianapolis 500-Mile Race at the Indianapolis Motor Speedway • Sunday, May 30, 1999

FP	SP	No.	Rookie	Driver	Car Name	Chassis/Engine	Laps	Status	Total Prize Money
1	8	14		Kenny Brack	A.J. Foyt PowerTeam Racing	Dallara/Oldsmobile Aurora	200	153.176	$1,465,190
2	14	21		Jeff Ward	Yahoo/MerchantOnline	Dallara/Oldsmobile Aurora	200	153.091	583,150
3	3	11		Billy Boat	A.J. Foyt Racing	Dallara/Oldsmobile Aurora	200	152.853	435,200
4	4	32		Robby Gordon	Glidden/Menards	Dallara/Oldsmobile Aurora	200	152.180	253,270
5	27	55	R	Robby McGehee	Energizer Advanced Formula	Dallara/Oldsmobile Aurora	199	Running	247,750
6	32	84		Robbie Buhl	A.J. Foyt Racing	Dallara/Oldsmobile Aurora	199	Running	257,500
7	22	91	W	Buddy Lazier	Delta Faucet/Coors Light/Tae-Bo/Hemelgarn	Dallara/Oldsmobile Aurora	198	Running	285,100
8	17	81		Robby Unser	PetroMoly/Team Pelfrey	Dallara/Oldsmobile Aurora	197	Running	195,500
9	24	22		Tony Stewart	The Home Depot	Dallara/Oldsmobile Aurora	196	Running	186,670
10	10	54		Hideshi Matsuda	Mini Juke-Beck Motorsports	Dallara/Oldsmobile Aurora	196	Running	186,000
11	11	9		Davey Hamilton	Galles Racing Spinal Conquest	Dallara/Oldsmobile Aurora	196	Running	220,500
12	33	3		Raul Boesel	Brant Racing R&S MKV	Riley & Scott/Olds. Aurora	195	Running	248,600
13	12	42	R	John Hollansworth Jr.	pcsave.com/Lycos	Dallara/Oldsmobile Aurora	192	Running	265,400
14	15	20		Tyce Carlson	Pennzoil/Damon's/Bluegreen	Dallara/Oldsmobile Aurora	190	Running	247,000
15	21	96	R	Jeret Schroeder	Purity Farms/Cobb Racing	G Force/Infiniti Indy	175	Engine	176,250
16	5	28		Mark Dismore	MCI WorldCom	Dallara/Oldsmobile Aurora	168	Accident	235,300
17	20	19		Stan Wattles	Metro Racing Systems/NCLD	Dallara/Oldsmobile Aurora	147	Running	158,000
18	16	51	W	Eddie Cheever Jr.	Team Cheever/Children's Beverage Group	Dallara/Infiniti Indy	139	Engine	246,800
19	26	12		Buzz Calkins	Bradley Food Marts/Sav-O-Mat	G Force/Oldsmobile Aurora	133	Running	228,000
20	23	33		Roberto Moreno	Truscelli Team Racing/Warner Bros.	G Force/Oldsmobile Aurora	122	Gearbox	225,670
21	2	2		Greg Ray	Glidden/Menards	Dallara/Oldsmobile Aurora	120	Accident Pits	204,900
22	1	5	W	Arie Luyendyk	Sprint PCS/Meijer	G Force/Oldsmobile Aurora	117	Accident	382,350
23	29	52	R	Wim Eyckmans	EGP/Beaulieu of America	Dallara/Oldsmobile Aurora	113	Timing Chain	145,250
24	28	30		Jimmy Kite	Alfa Laval/Team Losi/Fastrod	G Force/Oldsmobile Aurora	111	Engine	228,000
25	25	50		Roberto Guerrero	Cobb Racing	G Force/Infiniti Indy	105	Engine	217,000
26	13	35		Steve Knapp	Delco Remy-ThermoTech-Microphonics	G Force/Oldsmobile Aurora	104	Handling	216,000
27	9	4		Scott Goodyear	Pennzoil Panther	G Force/Oldsmobile Aurora	101	Engine	217,500
28	6	8		Scott Sharp	Delphi Automotive Systems	Dallara/Oldsmobile Aurora	83	Transmission	221,500
29	19	98		Donnie Beechler	Cahill Racing/Big Daddy's BBQ	Dallara/Oldsmobile Aurora	74	Engine	143,000
30	7	99		Sam Schmidt	Unistar Auto Insurance	G Force/Oldsmobile Aurora	62	Accident	213,800
31	31	17		Jack Miller	Dean's Milk Chug	Dallara/Oldsmobile Aurora	29	Clutch	146,000
32	30	92		Johnny Unser	Tae-Bo/Hemelgarn/Homier Tool/Delta Faucet	Dallara/Oldsmobile Aurora	10	Brakes	161,000
33	18	6		Eliseo Salazar	FUBU Nienhouse Racing	G Force/Oldsmobile Aurora	7	Accident	141,000

Total Purse $8,984,150

Time of Race: 3:15:51.182 Average Speed: 153.176 mph Margin of Victory: 6.562 sec
Pole: #5 Arie Luyendyk (225.179, 2:39.873) Fastest Race Lap: #2 Greg Ray (Race Lap 101, 218.882 mph, 41.118 sec.)
Winning Car Owner: A.J. Foyt Enterprises Winning Chief Mechanic: Bill Spencer Winning Tire: Goodyear Rookie of Year: Robby McGehee
Legend: R=Indianapolis 500-Mile Race Rookie; W=Indianapolis 500-Mile Race Former Winner
Lap Leaders: Luyendyk 1-32, Ray 33, Schmidt 34-37, Luyendyk 38-44, Ray 45-59, Brack 60-64, Luyendyk 65-69, Brack 70-82, Ray 83-95, Brack 96-98, Luyendyk 99-117, Ray 118-120, Cheever, Jr. 121-124, Brack 125-150, Ward 151-153, Brack 154-170, Gordon 171-198, Brack 199-200.
Lap Leader Summary: Brack 6 times for 66 laps, Luyendyk 4-63, Ray 4-32, Gordon 1-28, Schmidt 1-4, Cheever, Jr. 1-4, Ward 1-3. Lead Changes: 17 among 7 drivers.
Caution Laps: 9-14, #6 Salazar, accident T2. 35-39, #54 Matsuda, stalled. 63-68, #99 Schmidt, accident T1. 93-98, #35 Knapp, accident T2. 102-105, #4 Goodyear, engine. 118-124, #5 Luyendyk, accident T3. #2 Ray, #28 Dismore, accident pits. 162-164, #30 Kite, stalled. 169-173, #28 Dismore, accident T2. Cautions: 8 for 42 laps.

Official Box Score

84th Indianapolis 500-Mile Race at the Indianapolis Motor Speedway • Sunday, May 28, 2000

FP	SP	No.		Driver	Car Name	Chassis/Engine	Laps	Status	Total Prize Money
1	2	9	R	Juan Pablo Montoya	Target	G Force/Oldsmobile	200	167.607	$1,235,690
2	16	91	W	Buddy Lazier	Delta Faucet/Coors Light/Tae-Bo/Hemelgarn	Dallara/Oldsmobile	200	167.495	574,600
3	3	11		Eliseo Salazar	Rio A.J. Foyt Racing	G Force/Oldsmobile	200	167.362	474,900
4	6	14		Jeff Ward	Harrah's A.J. Foyt Racing	G Force/Oldsmobile	200	167.320	361,000
5	10	51	W	Eddie Cheever Jr.	#51 Excite@Home Indy Race Car	Dallara/Nissan Infiniti	200	167.315	364,500
6	4	32		Robby Gordon	Turtle Wax/Burger King/Moen/JM	Dallara/Oldsmobile	200	167.309	216,355
7	7	10		Jimmy Vasser	Target	G Force/Oldsmobile	199	Running	207,505
8	20	7		Stephan Gregoire	Mexmil/Tokheim/Viking Air Tools	G Force/Oldsmobile	199	Running	306,900
9	13	4		Scott Goodyear	Pennzoil Panther	Dallara/Oldsmobile	199	Running	348,800
10	5	8		Scott Sharp	Delphi Automotive Systems/MCI WorldCom	Dallara/Oldsmobile	198	Running	313,000
11	11	28		Mark Dismore	On Star/GM BuyPower/Bryant H. & C.	Dallara/Oldsmobile	198	Running	294,500
12	15	98		Donnie Beechler	Cahill Racing	Dallara/Oldsmobile	198	Running	283,000
13	26	33	R	Jaques Lazier	Miles of Hope/Truscelli Team Racing	G Force/Oldsmobile	198	Running	290,250
14	29	6		Jeret Schroeder	Kroger/Tri Star Motorsports Inc.	Dallara/Oldsmobile	198	Running	279,000
15	31	41		Billy Boat	Harrah's A.J. Foyt Racing	G Force/Oldsmobile	198	Running	211,000
16	24	55		Raul Boesel	Epson	G Force/Oldsmobile	197	Running	213,000
17	17	50	R	Jason Leffler	UnitedAuto Group	G Force/Oldsmobile	197	Running	170,905
18	22	12		Buzz Calkins	Bradley Motorsports/Team CAN	Dallara/Oldsmobile	194	Running	169,000
19	27	23		Steve Knapp	Dreyer & Reinbold Racing	G Force/Nissan Infiniti	193	Running	167,000
20	28	16		Davey Hamilton	FreeInternet.com/TeamXtreme	G Force/Oldsmobile	188	Running	166,500
21	12	5		Robby McGehee	Meijer/Energizer Advanced Formula/Mall.com	G Force/Oldsmobile	187	Running	281,400
22	30	22		Johnny Unser	Delco Remy/Microdigicom/Homier Tools	G Force/Oldsmobile	186	Running	161,000
23	8	92		Stan Wattles	Hemelgarn/Metro Racing	Dallara/Oldsmobile	172	Engine	159,000
24	14	18	R	Sam Hornish Jr.	Hornish Bros. Trucking/APC	Dallara/Oldsmobile	153	Accident	268,250
25	21	88	R	Airton Daré	TeamXtreme/USACredit.com/FreeInternet.com	G Force/Oldsmobile	126	Engine	262,250
26	9	24		Robbie Buhl	Team Purex Dreyer & Reinbold Racing	G Force/Oldsmobile	99	Engine	258,500
27	23	75		Richie Hearn	Pagan Racing	Dallara/Oldsmobile	97	Electrical	155,000
28	33	48	R	Andy Hillenburg	SUMAR Special by Irwindale Speedway	Dallara/Oldsmobile	91	Wheel Bearing	154,250
29	18	3	W	Al Unser Jr.	Galles ECR Racing Tickets.com Starz	G Force/Oldsmobile	89	Overheating	256,000
30	25	27		Jimmy Kite	Big Daddy's BBQ/Founders Bank	G Force/Oldsmobile	74	Engine	164,000
31	19	15	R	Sarah Fisher	Walker Racing Cummins	Dallara/Oldsmobile	71	Accident	165,750
32	32	90		Lyn St. James	Yellow Freight Systems	G Force/Oldsmobile	69	Accident	152,000
33	1	1		Greg Ray	Team Conseco/Quaker State/Menards	Dallara/Oldsmobile	67	Accident	388,700

Total Purse $9,473,505

Time of Race: 2:58:59.431 Average Speed: 167.607 mph Margin of Victory: 7.184 sec
Pole: #1 Greg Ray (223.471, 2:41.095) Fastest Race Lap: #91 Buddy Lazier (Race Lap 198, 218.494 mph, 41.191 sec.)
Winning Car Owner: Target/Chip Ganassi Racing Winning Chief Mechanic: Steve Gough Winning Tire: Firestone Rookie of Year: Juan Pablo Montoya
Legend: R=Indianapolis 500-Mile Race Rookie; W=Indianapolis 500-Mile Race Former Winner
Lap Leaders: Ray 1-26, Montoya 27-29, Vasser 30, McGehee 31-32, Montoya 33-175, Vasser 176-179, Montoya 180-200.
Lap Leader Summary: Montoya 3 times for 167 laps, Ray 1-26, Vasser 2-5, McGehee 1-2. Lead Changes: 6 among 4 drivers.
Caution Laps: 66-70, #1 Ray, accident T2. 74-84, #90 St. James, #15 Fisher, accident T1. 99-102, Debris. 127-130, Oil on Track. 144-150, #1 Ray, accident T2. 158-161, #18 Hornish Jr., accident T2. 174-177, Oil on Track. Cautions: 7 for 39 laps.

Official Box Score

85th Indianapolis 500-Mile Race at the Indianapolis Motor Speedway • Sunday, May 27, 2001

FP	SP	No.		Driver	Car Name	Chassis/Engine	Laps	Status	Total Prize Money
1	11	68	R	Helio Castroneves	Marlboro Team Penske	Dallara/Oldsmobile	200	141.574	$1,270,475
2	5	66		Gil de Ferran	Marlboro Team Penske	Dallara/Oldsmobile	200	141.555	482,775
3	21	39		Michael Andretti	Motorola/Archipelago	Dallara/Oldsmobile	200	141.510	346,225
4	12	44		Jimmy Vasser	Target Chip Ganassi Racing	G Force/Oldsmobile	200	141.419	233,325
5	20	50	R	Bruno Junqueira	Target Chip Ganassi Racing	G Force/Oldsmobile	200	141.271	255,825
6	7	33		Tony Stewart	Target Chip Ganassi Racing	G Force/Oldsmobile	200	141.157	218,825
7	28	14		Eliseo Salazar	Harrah's A.J. Foyt Racing	Dallara/Oldsmobile	199	Running	356,300
8	30	88		Airton Daré	1-800-BAR NONE TeamXtreme	G Force/Oldsmobile	199	Running	320,325
9	32	98		Billy Boat	CURB Records	Dallara/Oldsmobile	199	Running	337,325
10	33	21	R	Felipe Giaffone	Hollywood	G Force/Oldsmobile	199	Running	211,575
11	14	10		Robby McGehee	Cahill Racing Cure Autism Now	Dallara/Oldsmobile	199	Running	290,825
12	24	12		Buzz Calkins	Bradley Food Marts/Sav-O-Mat	Dallara/Oldsmobile	198	Running	286,025
13	6	5	W	Arie Luyendyk	Meijer	G Force/Oldsmobile	198	Running	182,275
14	13	4		Sam Hornish Jr.	Pennzoil Panther	Dallara/Oldsmobile	196	Running	308,825
15	9	24		Robbie Buhl	Team Purex Dreyer & Reinbold Racing	G Force/Infiniti	196	Running	300,325
16	4	28		Mark Dismore	Delphi Auto. Systems/Bryant H. & C.	Dallara/Oldsmobile	195	Running	287,375
17	2	2		Greg Ray	Johns Manville/Menards	Dallara/Oldsmobile	192	Running	335,325
18	10	91	W	Buddy Lazier	Tae-Bo/Coors Light/Delta Faucet	Dallara/Oldsmobile	192	Running	262,325
19	31	16	R	Cory Witherill	Radio Shack	G Force/Oldsmobile	187	Running	159,575
20	23	9		Jeret Schroeder	Purity Products	Dallara/Oldsmobile	187	Running	256,325
21	3	41		Robby Gordon	Team Conseco/Foyt/RCR Childress Racing	Dallara/Oldsmobile	184	Running	173,225
22	17	77		Jaques Lazier	Classmates.com/Jonathan Byrd's Cafeteria	G Force/Oldsmobile	183	Running	161,325
23	26	99		Davey Hamilton	Sam Schmidt Motorsports Racing	Dallara/Oldsmobile	182	Engine	280,325
24	8	35		Jeff Ward	Aerosmith/Heritage Motorsports/Menards	G Force/Oldsmobile	168	Running	248,325
25	27	84		Donnie Beechler	Harrah's A.J. Foyt Racing	Dallara/Oldsmobile	160	Running	172,325
26	25	51	W	Eddie Cheever Jr.	#51 Excite@Home Indy Race Car	Dallara/Infiniti	108	Electrical	247,325
27	18	6	R	Jon Herb	Tri Star Motorsports Inc.	Dallara/Oldsmobile	104	Accident	245,575
28	29	36		Stephan Gregoire	Heritage Motorsports/Delco Remy/Menards	G Force/Oldsmobile	86	Oil Leak	154,325
29	22	49	R	Nicolas Minassian	Target Chip Ganassi Racing	G Force/Oldsmobile	74	Gearbox	149,575
30	19	3	W	Al Unser Jr.	Galles Racing Starz SuperPak Budweiser	G Force/Oldsmobile	16	Accident	255,825
31	15	15		Sarah Fisher	Walker Racing Kroger	Dallara/Oldsmobile	7	Accident	247,325
32	16	52		Scott Goodyear	#52 Thermos Grill2Go Cheever Indy Racing	Dallara/Infiniti	7	Accident	143,325
33	1	8		Scott Sharp	Delphi Automotive Systems	Dallara/Oldsmobile	0	Accident	427,325

Total Purse $9,608,325

Time of Race: 3:31:54.1800 Average Speed: 141.574 mph Margin of Victory: 1.7373 sec
Pole: #8 Scott Sharp (226.037, 2:39.265) Fastest Race Lap: #4 Sam Hornish Jr. (Race Lap 130, 219.830 mph, 40.9407 sec.)
Winning Car Owner: Penske Racing Winning Chief Mechanic: Rick Rinaman Winning Tire: Firestone Rookie of Year: Helio Castroneves
Legend: R=Indianapolis 500-Mile Race Rookie; W=Indianapolis 500-Mile Race Former Winner
Lap Leaders: Gordon 1-22, Ray 23-45, Stewart 46, Luyendyk 47, Mi. Andretti 48-52, Dismore 53-74, Ray 75-80, Mi. Andretti 81-84, Dismore 85-91, Ray 92-102, Mi. Andretti 103-109, de Ferran 110-136, Stewart 137-148, Castroneves 149-200.
Lap Leader Summary: Castroneves 1 time for 52 laps, Ray 3-40, Dismore 2-29, de Ferran 1-27, Gordon 1-22, Mi. Andretti 3-16, Stewart 2-13, Luyendyk 1-1. Lead Changes: 13 among 8 drivers.
Caution Laps: 1-5, #8 Sharp, accident T1. 8-16, #15 Fisher, #52 Goodyear, accident T2. 18-21, #3, Unser Jr., accident T4. 90-95, Track Inspection. 107-118, Rain. 134-138, #16 Witherill, accident T4. 148-157, Track Inspection, Rain, Red Flag on lap 155. 166-170, #24 Buhl, accident T2. Cautions: 8 for 56 laps.

Official Box Score

86th Indianapolis 500-Mile Race at the Indianapolis Motor Speedway • Sunday, May 26, 2002

FP	SP	No.		Driver	Car Name	Chassis/Engine	Laps	Status	Total Prize Money
1	13	3	W	Helio Castroneves	Marlboro Team Penske	Dallara/Chevrolet	200	166.499	$1,606,215
2	29	26		Paul Tracy	Team Green 7-Eleven	Dallara/Chevrolet	200	166.484	489,315
3	4	21		Felipe Giaffone	Hollywood Mo Nunn Racing	G Force/Chevrolet	200	166.482	480,315
4	26	44	R	Alex Barron	Rayovac Blair Racing	Dallara/Chevrolet	200	166.477	412,115
5	6	51	W	Eddie Cheever Jr.	Red Bull Cheever Racing	Dallara/Infiniti	200	166.461	348,515
6	22	20		Richie Hearn	Grill 2 Go Sam Schmidt Motorsports	Dallara/Chevrolet	200	166.450	330,815
7	25	39		Michael Andretti	Motorola/Archipelago	Dallara/Chevrolet	200	166.444	218,715
8	11	31		Robby Gordon	Menards/Childress/Cingular	Dallara/Chevrolet	200	166.405	204,000
9	15	9		Jeff Ward	Target Chip Ganassi Racing	G Force/Chevrolet	200	166.383	308,815
10	14	6		Gil de Ferran	Marlboro Team Penske	Dallara/Chevrolet	200	166.061	293,165
11	21	22	W	Kenny Brack	Target Chip Ganassi Racing	G Force/Chevrolet	200	165.995	188,315
12	12	7	W	Al Unser Jr.	Corteco/Bryant	Dallara/Chevrolet	199	Running	288,765
13	30	14		Airton Daré	Harrah's A.J. Foyt Racing	Dallara/Chevrolet	199	Running	281,815
14	24	55	W	Arie Luyendyk	Meijer	G Force/Chevrolet	199	Running	338,815
15	20	91	W	Buddy Lazier	Coors Light/Life Fitness/Tae-Bo/Delta Faucet	Dallara/Chevrolet	198	Accident	277,615
16	2	24		Robbie Buhl	Team Purex/Aventis/Dreyer & Reinbold Racing	G Force/Infiniti	198	Running	288,315
17	32	30	R	George Mack	310 Racing	G Force/Chevrolet	198	Running	283,565
18	23	98		Billy Boat	CURB Records	Dallara/Chevrolet	198	Running	286,315
19	28	27	R	Dario Franchitti	Team Green 7-Eleven	Dallara/Chevrolet	197	Running	153,565
20	27	12	R	Shigeaki Hattori	Epson	Dallara/Infiniti	197	Running	161,565
21	3	2		Raul Boesel	Menards/Johns Manville	Dallara/Chevrolet	197	Running	268,315
22	16	34	R	Laurent Redon	Mi-Jack	Dallara/Infiniti	197	Accident	256,565
23	18	53	R	Max Papis	Red Bull Cheever Racing	Dallara/Infiniti	196	Running	153,565
24	9	23		Sarah Fisher	Team Allegra/Dreyer & Reinbold Racing	G Force/Infiniti	196	Running	163,315
25	7	4		Sam Hornish Jr.	Pennzoil Panther	Dallara/Chevrolet	186	Running	253,815
26	10	52	R	Tomas Scheckter	Red Bull Cheever Racing	Dallara/Infiniti	172	Accident	294,815
27	8	8		Scott Sharp	Delphi	Dallara/Chevrolet	137	Accident	255,665
28	5	17		Tony Kanaan	Hollywood Mo Nunn Racing	G Force/Chevrolet	89	Accident	167,665
29	17	5	R	Rick Treadway	Sprint/Kyocera Wireless/Airlink Enterprises	G Force/Chevrolet	88	Accident	147,565
30	19	19		Jimmy Vasser	Miller Lite/Rahal Letterman Racing	Dallara/Chevrolet	87	Gearbox	151,315
31	1	33		Bruno Junqueira	Target Chip Ganassi Racing	G Force/Chevrolet	87	Gearbox	282,715
32	33	99		Mark Dismore	Grill 2 Go Sam Schmidt Motorsports	Dallara/Chevrolet	58	Handling	145,315
33	31	11		Greg Ray	AJ Foyt Racing/Harrah's	Dallara/Chevrolet	28	Accident	245,315

Total Purse $10,026,580

Time of Race: 3:00:10.8714 Average Speed: 166.499 mph Margin of Victory: Under Caution

Pole: #33 Bruno Junqueira (231.342, 2:35.6136) Fastest Race Lap: #52 Tomas Scheckter (Race Lap 20, 226.499 mph, 39.7353 sec.)

Winning Car Owner: Marlboro Team Penske Winning Chief Mechanic: Rick Rinaman Winning Tire: Firestone Rookie of Year: Tomas Scheckter/Alex Barron

Legend: R=Indianapolis 500-Mile Race Rookie; W=Indianapolis 500-Mile Race Former Winner

Lap Leaders: Junqueira 1-32, Scheckter 33-63, Kanaan 64-66, Sharp 67, de Ferran 68, Unser, Jr. 69, Kanaan 70-89, Giaffone 90-91, Scheckter 92-120, de Ferran 121-124, Sharp 125-126, Giaffone 127-129, Barron 130-131, Scheckter 132-149, de Ferran 150-157, Giaffone 158-160, Barron 161-165, Scheckter 166-172, Giaffone 173-176, Castroneves 177-200.

Lap Leader Summary: Scheckter 4 times for 85 laps, Junqueira 1-32, Castroneves 1-24, Kanaan 2-23, de Ferran 3-13, Giaffone 4-12, Barron 2-7, Sharp 2-3, Unser, Jr. 1-1.

Lead Changes: 19 among 9 drivers.

Caution Laps: 30-36, #11 Ray, Accident T1. 79-87, Debris. 90-98, #17 Kanaan, #5 Treadway, accident T3. 173-180, #52 Scheckter, accident T4. 199-200, #91 Lazier, #34 Redon, Accident T2. Cautions: 5 for 35 laps.

Official Box Score

87th Indianapolis 500-Mile Race at the Indianapolis Motor Speedway • Sunday, May 25, 2003

FP	SP	No.		Driver	Car Name	Chassis/Engine	Laps	Status	Total Prize Money
1	10	6		Gil de Ferran	Marlboro Team Penske	Panoz G Force/Toyota	200	156.291	$1,353,265
2	1	3	W	Helio Castroneves	Marlboro Team Penske	Dallara/Toyota	200	156.287	739,665
3	2	11		Tony Kanaan	Team 7-Eleven	Dallara/Honda	200	156.274	486,465
4	12	10		Tomas Scheckter	Target Chip Ganassi Racing	Panoz G Force/Toyota	200	156.268	448,415
5	7	12	R	Tora Takagi	Pioneer Mo Nunn Racing	Panoz G Force/Toyota	200	156.264	363,515
6	25	20		Alex Barron	Meijer Mo Nunn Racing	Panoz G Force/Toyota	200	156.209	297,265
7	8	32	R	Tony Renna	Cure Autism Now/HomeMed	Dallara/Honda	200	156.189	206,315
8	14	13		Greg Ray	TrimSpa	Panoz G Force/Honda	200	156.134	299,065
9	17	31	W	Al Unser Jr.	Corteco	Dallara/Toyota	200	156.055	296,565
10	11	55	R	Roger Yasukawa	Panasonic ARTA	Dallara/Honda	200	155.320	288,815
11	19	52	R	Buddy Rice	Red Bull Cheever Racing	Dallara/Chevrolet	199	Running	323,315
12	26	22	R	Vitor Meira	Metabolife/Johns Manville/Menards	Dallara/Chevrolet	199	Running	192,315
13	32	18		Jimmy Kite	Denny Hecker's Auto Connection	Dallara/Chevrolet	197	Running	273,565
14	15	54	R	Shinji Nakano	Beard Papa's	Dallara/Honda	196	Running	269,315
15	18	4		Sam Hornish Jr.	Pennzoil Panther	Dallara/Toyota	195	Engine	271,065
16	6	15	W	Kenny Brack	Rahal/Letterman/Miller Lite/Pioneer	Dallara/Honda	195	Running	271,065
17	4	9	R	Scott Dixon	Target Chip Ganassi Racing	Panoz G Force/Toyota	191	Accident	304,315
18	23	14	R	A.J. Foyt IV	Conseco/A.J. Foyt Racing	Dallara/Toyota	189	Running	264,315
19	5	26	R	Dan Wheldon	Klein Tools/Jim Beam	Dallara/Honda	186	Accident	161,815
20	9	8		Scott Sharp	Delphi	Dallara/Toyota	181	Accident	257,815
21	21	91	W	Buddy Lazier	Victory Brand/Delta Faucet/Life Fitness	Dallara/Chevrolet	171	Engine	276,065
22	3	27		Robby Gordon	Archipelago/Motorola	Dallara/Honda	169	Gearbox	256,250
23	22	24		Robbie Buhl	Purex/Aventis/Dreyer & Reinbold	Dallara/Chevrolet	147	Engine	252,065
24	33	41		Airton Daré	Conseco A.J. Foyt Racing	Panoz G Force/Toyota	125	Accident	166,065
25	31	44		Robby McGehee	Pedigo Chevrolet Panther Racing	Dallara/Chevrolet	125	Steering	151,565
26	27	19		Jimmy Vasser	Argent Rahal/Letterman Racing	Dallara/Honda	102	Gearbox	161,265
27	13	7		Michael Andretti	Team 7-Eleven	Dallara/Honda	94	Throttle Linkage	259,415
28	28	99		Richie Hearn	Contour Hardening/Curb Agajanian/SSM	Panoz G Force/Toyota	61	Accident	142,565
29	20	2		Jaques Lazier	Menards/Johns Manville	Dallara/Chevrolet	61	Accident	240,315
30	30	5		Shigeaki Hattori	Epson/A.J. Foyt Racing	Dallara/Toyota	19	Fuel System	240,065
31	24	23		Sarah Fisher	AOL/GMAC/Raybestos/DRR	Dallara/Chevrolet	14	Engine/Accident	244,065
32	29	98		Billy Boat	Pedigo Chevrolet Panther Racing	Dallara/Chevrolet	7	Engine	139,065
33	16	21		Felipe Giaffone	Hollywood Mo Nunn Racing	Panoz G Force/Toyota	6	Electrical	242,815

Total Purse $10,139,830

Time of Race: 3:11:56.9891 Average Speed: 156.291 mph Margin of Victory: 0.2990 sec

Pole: #3 Helio Castroneves (231.725, 2:35.3564) Fastest Race Lap: #11 Tony Kanaan (Race Lap 100, 229.188 mph, 39.2692 sec.)

Winning Car Owner: Marlboro Team Penske Winning Chief Mechanic: Matt Jonsson Winning Tire: Firestone Rookie of Year: Tora Takagi

Legend: R=Indianapolis 500-Mile Race Rookie; W=Indianapolis 500-Mile Race Former Winner

Lap Leaders: Castroneves 1-16, Dixon 17-31, Mi. Andretti 32-49, Kanaan 50, Scheckter 51-57, Mi. Andretti 58-67, Scheckter 68-94, Castroneves 95-99, Vasser 100, Scheckter 101-128, Castroneves 129-165, Kanaan 167, Takagi 168-169, de Ferran 170-200.

Lap Leader Summary: Scheckter 4 times for 63 laps, Castroneves 3-58, de Ferran 1-31, Mi. Andretti 2-28, Dixon 1-15, Kanaan 2-2, Takagi 1-2, Vasser 1-1. Lead Changes: 14 among 8 drivers.

Caution Laps: 9-13, #98 Boat, smoke T1. 16-21, #23 Fisher, accident T3. 53-60, #24 Buhl, spin pit exit. 62-65, #99 Hearn, #2 J. Lazier, accident T2. 104-108, #19 Vasser, spray backstretch. 127-133, #41 Dare, accident T2. 172-174, #27 Gordon, tow-in. 182-185, #8 Sharp, accident T1. 187-193, #26 Wheldon, accident T3. Cautions: 9 for 49 laps.

Official Box Score

88th Indianapolis 500-Mile Race at the Indianapolis Motor Speedway • Sunday, May 30, 2004

FP	SP	No.		Driver	Car Name	Chassis/Engine	Laps	Status	Total Prize Money
1	1	15		Buddy Rice	Rahal-Letterman Argent/Pioneer	Panoz G Force/Honda	180 (Rain)	138.518	$1,761,740
2	5	11		Tony Kanaan	Team 7-Eleven	Dallara/Honda	180	138.516	659,240
3	2	26		Dan Wheldon	Klein Tools/Jim Beam	Dallara/Honda	180	138.491	533,040
4	23	7		Bryan Herta	XM Satellite Radio	Dallara/Honda	180	138.489	366,440
5	4	36		Bruno Junqueira	PacifiCare/Secure Horizons	Panoz G Force/Honda	180	138.474	296,240
6	7	17		Vitor Meira	Rahal-Letterman Team Centrix	Panoz G Force/Honda	180	138.463	301,240
7	6	5		Adrian Fernandez	Quaker State Telmex Tecate	Panoz G Force/Honda	180	138.459	294,740
8	13	1		Scott Dixon	Target Chip Ganassi Racing	Panoz G Force/Toyota	180	138.431	283,740
9	8	3	W	Helio Castroneves	Marlboro Team Penske	Dallara/Toyota	180	138.414	311,990
10	12	16		Roger Yasukawa	Rahal-Letterman Racing Sammy	Panoz G Force/Honda	180	138.401	261,740
11	9	55	R	Kosuke Matsuura	Panasonic ARTA	Panoz G Force/Honda	180	138.386	294,740
12	24	51		Alex Barron	Red Bull Cheever Racing	Dallara/Chevrolet	180	138.325	269,240
13	20	8		Scott Sharp	Delphi	Dallara/Toyota	180	138.309	253,990
14	3	27		Dario Franchitti	Arca/Ex	Dallara/Honda	180	138.297	255,740
15	25	24		Felipe Giaffone	Team Purex/Dreyer & Reinbold	Dallara/Chevrolet	179	Running	249,490
16	29	21	R	Jeff Simmons	Pioneer Mo Nunn Racing	Dallara/Toyota	179	Running	224,990
17	17	20	W	Al Unser Jr.	Patrick Racing	Dallara/Chevrolet	179	Running	220,740
18	10	4		Tomas Scheckter	Pennzoil Panther	Dallara/Chevrolet	179	Running	234,240
19	26	12		Tora Takagi	Pioneer Mo Nunn Racing	Dallara/Toyota	179	Running	230,740
20	30	33		Richie Hearn	Lucas Oil Products/Sam Schmidt	Panoz G Force/Toyota	178	Running	207,740
21	19	39		Sarah Fisher	Bryant Heating & Cooling/Cure Autism Now	Dallara/Toyota	177	Running	208,740
22	33	18		Robby McGehee	Burger King Angus Steak Burger PDM	Dallara/Toyota	177	Running	202,740
23	28	91	W	Buddy Lazier	LifeFitness DRR/Hemelgarn Racing	Dallara/Chevrolet	164	Fuel System	212,240
24	32	25	R	Marty Roth	Roth Racing	Dallara/Toyota	128	Accident	203,990
25	15	10	R	Darren Manning	Target Chip Ganassi Racing	Panoz G Force/Toyota	104	Accident	227,490
26	11	6		Sam Hornish Jr.	Marlboro Team Penske	Dallara/Toyota	104	Accident	223,240
27	27	13		Greg Ray	Access Motorsports	Panoz G Force/Honda	98	Accident	239,735
28	31	98	R	PJ Jones	CURB Records	Dallara/Chevrolet	92	Accident	195,490
29	18	70		Robby Gordon*	Meijer/Coca-Cola Robby Gordon	Dallara/Chevrolet	88	Mechanical	192,420
30	14	2	R	Mark Taylor	Menards/Johns Manville Racing	Dallara/Chevrolet	62	Accident	211,990
31	16	52	R	Ed Carpenter	Red Bull Cheever Racing	Dallara/Chevrolet	62	Accident	212,485
32	22	41	R	Larry Foyt	A.J. Foyt Racing	Panoz G Force/Toyota	54	Accident	192,485
33	21	14		A.J. Foyt IV	Conseco/A.J. Foyt Racing	Dallara/Toyota	26	Handling	215,735

Total Purse $10,250,580

Time of Race: 3:14:55.2395 Average Speed: 138.518 mph Margin of Victory: Under Caution
Pole: #15 Buddy Rice (222.024, 2:42.1445) Fastest Race Lap: #17 Vitor Meira (Race Lap 173, 218.401 mph, 41.2086 sec.)
Winning Car Owner: Rahal Letterman Racing Winning Chief Mechanic: Ricardo Nault Winning Tire: Firestone Rookie of Year: Kosuke Matsuura
Legend: R=Indianapolis 500-Mile Race Rookie; W=Indianapolis 500-Mile Race Former Winner; *=Had Relief Help
Race Notes: Race stopped on lap 27 due to rain and stopped again on lap 180 due to rain.
Lap Leaders: Rice 1-12, Barron 13-15, Herta 16, Wheldon 17-33, Rice 34-49, Hornish, Jr. 50-58, Rice 59-97, Wheldon 98-103, Kanaan 104-116, Wheldon 117-119, Kanaan 120-133, Franchitti 134, Junqueira 135-150, Kanaan 151, Herta 152-166, Fernandez 169-171, Rice 172-180.
Lap Leader Summary: Rice 5 times for 91 laps, Kanaan 3-28, Wheldon 3-26, Junqueira 1-16, Hornish, Jr. 1-9, Herta 2-3, Barron 1-3, Fernandez 1-3, Franchitti 1-1. Lead Changes: 17 among 9 drivers.
Caution Laps: 11-15, #14 Foyt IV, accident T1. 22-29, Rain, Red Flag on lap 27. 56-61, #41 Foyt, accident T2. 63-69, #2 Taylor, #52 Carpenter, accident T3. 95-102, #98 Jones, accident back stretch. 106-115, #6 Hornish Jr., #10 Manning, #13 Ray, accident frontstretch. 132-136, #25 Roth, accident T4. 174-180, Rain, Red Flag on lap 180. Cautions: 8 for 56 laps.

Official Box Score

89th Indianapolis 500-Mile Race at the Indianapolis Motor Speedway • Sunday, May 29, 2005

FP	SP	No.		Driver	Car Name	Chassis/Engine	Laps	Status	Total Prize Money
1	16	26		Dan Wheldon	Klein Tools/Jim Beam	Dallara/Honda	200	157.603	$1,537,805
2	7	17		Vitor Meira	Rahal Letterman Menards Johns Manville	Panoz/Honda	200	157.602	656,955
3	18	7		Bryan Herta	XM Satellite Radio	Dallara/Honda	200	157.601	457,505
4	4	16	R	Danica Patrick	Rahal Letterman Racing Argent Pioneer	Panoz/Honda	200	157.541	378,855
5	9	95	W	Buddy Lazier	Panther/Jonathan Byrd's/ESPN 950 AM	Dallara/Chevrolet	200	157.537	288,805
6	6	27		Dario Franchitti	ArcaEx	Dallara/Honda	200	157.532	309,055
7	3	8		Scott Sharp	Delphi	Panoz/Honda	200	157.526	295,305
8	1	11		Tony Kanaan	Team 7-Eleven	Dallara/Honda	200	157.516	467,105
9	5	3	W	Helio Castroneves	Marlboro Team Penske	Dallara/Toyota	200	157.496	277,805
10	24	33	R	Ryan Briscoe	Target Chip Ganassi Racing	Panoz/Toyota	199	Running	273,555
11	26	20		Ed Carpenter	Vision Racing	Dallara/Toyota	199	Running	258,305
12	15	37	R	Sebastien Bourdais	Newman Haas Racing Team Centrix	Panoz/Honda	198	Accident	234,555
13	22	51		Alex Barron	Red Bull Cheever Racing	Dallara/Toyota	197	Running	254,805
14	14	5		Adrian Fernandez	Investment Properties of America	Panoz/Honda	197	Running	226,305
15	33	48		Felipe Giaffone	A.J. Foyt Racing	Panoz/Toyota	194	Running	247,305
16	27	21		Jaques Lazier	Playa Del Racing	Panoz/Toyota	189	Running	219,305
17	8	55		Kosuke Matsuura	Panasonic ARTA	Panoz/Honda	186	Accident	236,305
18	17	24		Roger Yasukawa	Dreyer & Reinbold Racing	Dallara/Honda	167	Mechanical	233,305
19	10	2	R	Tomas Enge	ROCKSTAR Panther Racing	Dallara/Chevrolet	155	Accident	232,055
20	11	4		Tomas Scheckter	Pennzoil Panther	Dallara/Chevrolet	154	Accident	257,305
21	25	83	R	Patrick Carpentier	Red Bull Cheever Racing	Dallara/Toyota	153	Mechanical	231,055
22	21	44	R	Jeff Bucknum	Investment Properties of America	Dallara/Honda	150	Accident	222,555
23	2	6		Sam Hornish Jr.	Marlboro Team Penske	Dallara/Toyota	146	Accident	391,455
24	13	9		Scott Dixon	Target Chip Ganassi Racing	Panoz/Toyota	113	Accident	225,805
25	20	70		Richie Hearn	Meijer/Coca-Cola Racing Special	Panoz/Chevrolet	112	Accident	202,305
26	23	15	W	Kenny Brack	Rahal Letterman Racing Argent Pioneer	Panoz/Honda	92	Mechanical	275,805
27	31	22		Jeff Ward	Vision Racing	Dallara/Toyota	92	Handling	194,805
28	28	14		A.J. Foyt IV	A.J. Foyt Racing	Dallara/Toyota	84	Handling	218,805
29	19	10		Darren Manning	Target Chip Ganassi Racing	Panoz/Toyota	82	Mechanical	212,805
30	12	36		Bruno Junqueira	Newman Haas Racing Team Centrix	Panoz/Honda	76	Accident	192,205
31	29	25		Marty Roth	Roth Racing/PDM Racing	Dallara/Chevrolet	47	Handling	195,305
32	32	91		Jimmy Kite	Ethanol Hemelgarn Racing	Dallara/Toyota	47	Handling	210,305
33	30	41		Larry Foyt	ABC Supply Co.	Dallara/Toyota	14	Accident	189,305

Total Purse $10,304,815

Time of Race: 3:10:21:0769 Average Speed: 157.603 mph Margin of Victory: Under Caution
Pole: #11 Tony Kanaan (2:38.1961, 227.566) Fastest Qualifier: #15 Kenny Brack (227.598, 2:38.1737)
Fastest Race Lap: #11 Tony Kanaan (Race Lap 167, 228.102 mph, 39.4560 sec.)
Winning Car Owner: Andretti Green Racing Winning Chief Mechanic: Mike Horvath Winning Tire: Firestone Rookie of Year: Danica Patrick
Legend: R=Indianapolis 500-Mile Race Rookie; W=Indianapolis 500-Mile Race Former Winner
Lap Leaders: Hornish Jr. 1-2, Kanaan 3, Hornish Jr. 4-7, Kanaan 8-25, Franchitti 26, Kanaan 27-37, Hornish Jr. 38-54, Franchitti 55, Patrick 56, Junqueira 57-58, Hornish Jr. 59-97, Kanaan 98-100, Hornish Jr. 101-111, Kanaan 112-115, Hornish Jr. 116-119, Kanaan 120-122, Franchitti 123, Kanaan 124-135, Franchitti 136-143, Kanaan 144-145, Franchitti 146-149, Wheldon 150-161, Meira 162-164, Wheldon 165-171, Patrick 172-185, Wheldon 186-189, Patrick 190-193, Wheldon 194-200.
Lap Leader Summary: Hornish Jr. 6 times for 77 laps, Kanaan 8-54, Wheldon 4-30, Patrick 3-19, Franchitti 5-15, Meira 1-3, Junqueira 1-2. Lead Changes: 27 among 7 drivers.
Caution Laps: 18-24, #41 Foyt, accident T1. 77-86, #14 Foyt IV, #36 Junqueira, accident T2. 114-119, #9 Dixon, #70 Hearn, accident T1. 147-154, #6 Hornish Jr., accident T1. 155-161, #2 Enge, #4 Scheckter, #16 Patrick, #44 Bucknum, accident T4. 171-173, #24 Yasukawa, car smoking. 187-189, #55 Matsuura, accident T3. 199-200, #37 Bourdais, accident T4. Cautions: 8 for 46 laps.

Official Box Score

90th Indianapolis 500-Mile Race at the Indianapolis Motor Speedway • Sunday, May 28, 2006

FP	SP	No.		Driver	Car Name	Chassis/Engine	Laps	Status	Total Prize Money
1	1	6		Sam Hornish Jr.	Marlboro Team Penske	Dallara/Honda	200	Running	$1,744,855
2	9	26	R	Marco Andretti	NYSE Group	Dallara/Honda	200	Running	688,505
3	13	1		Michael Andretti	Jim Beam/Vonage	Dallara/Honda	200	Running	455,105
4	3	10	W	Dan Wheldon	Target Chip Ganassi Racing	Dallara/Honda	200	Running	571,405
5	5	11		Tony Kanaan	Team 7-Eleven	Dallara/Honda	200	Running	340,405
6	4	9		Scott Dixon	Target Chip Ganassi Racing	Dallara/Honda	200	Running	361,005
7	17	27		Dario Franchitti	Klein Tools/Canadian Club	Dallara/Honda	200	Running	307,905
8	10	16		Danica Patrick	Rahal Letterman Racing Team Argent	Panoz/Honda	200	Running	285,805
9	8	8		Scott Sharp	Delphi	Dallara/Honda	200	Running	283,805
10	6	4		Vitor Meira	Harrah's Panther	Dallara/Honda	200	Running	267,705
11	12	20		Ed Carpenter	Vision Racing	Dallara/Honda	199	Running	264,805
12	25	5	W	Buddy Lazier	Dreyer & Reinbold Racing	Dallara/Honda	199	Running	274,805
13	19	51	W	Eddie Cheever Jr.	Cheever Racing	Dallara/Honda	198	Running	255,805
14	18	52		Max Papis	Cheever Racing	Dallara/Honda	197	Running	229,305
15	7	55		Kosuke Matsuura	Panasonic ARTA	Dallara/Honda	196	Running	247,805
16	28	12		Roger Yasukawa	Playa Del Racing	Panoz/Honda	194	Running	228,805
17	24	21		Jaques Lazier	Playa Del Racing	Panoz/Honda	193	Running	219,305
18	29	88		Airton Dare	OCTANE Motors/Sanitec/SSM	Panoz/Honda	193	Running	216,805
19	32	98	R	P.J. Jones	CURB Records	Panoz/Honda	189	Running	214,305
20	16	7		Bryan Herta	XM Satellite Radio	Dallara/Honda	188	Running	234,805
21	21	14		Felipe Giaffone	ABC Supply Co./A.J. Foyt Racing	Dallara/Honda	177	Accident	227,305
22	15	90	R	Townsend Bell	Rock & Republic	Dallara/Honda	161	Suspension	204,555
23	26	17		Jeff Simmons	Rahal Letterman Racing Team Ethanol	Panoz/Honda	152	Accident	222,305
24	27	31	W	Al Unser Jr.	A1 Team USA Geico Dreyer & Reinbold	Dallara/Honda	145	Accident	200,305
25	2	3	W	Helio Castroneves	Marlboro Team Penske	Dallara/Honda	109	Accident	290,355
26	14	15	W	Buddy Rice	Rahal Letterman Racing Team Argent	Panoz/Honda	108	Accident	224,805
27	11	2		Tomas Scheckter	Vision Racing	Dallara/Honda	65	Accident	215,305
28	31	61	R	Arie Luyendyk Jr.	CheapCaribbean.com/Blue Star Jets	Panoz/Honda	54	Handling	196,055
29	30	97		Stephan Gregoire	Effen Vodka Team Leader Special	Panoz/Honda	49	Handling	193,305
30	23	41		Larry Foyt	AJ Foyt Racing	Dallara/Honda	43	Handling	192,305
31	33	18	R	Thiago Medeiros	PDM Racing	Panoz/Honda	24	Electrical	227,555
32	22	92		Jeff Bucknum	Life Fitness	Dallara/Honda	1	Accident	193,805
33	20	91	R	P.J. Chesson	Carmelo Hemelgarn Racing	Dallara/Honda	1	Accident	211,555

Total Purse $10,518,565

Time of Race: **3:10:58.7590** Average Speed: **157.085 mph** Margin of Victory: **0.0635 sec**

Pole: **#6 Sam Hornish Jr. (228.985, 2:37.2155)** Fastest Race Lap: **#9 Scott Dixon (Race Lap 41, 221.251 mph, 40.6777 sec.)**

Winning Car Owner: **Marlboro Team Penske** Winning Chief Mechanic: **Matt Jonsson** Winning Tire: **Firestone** Rookie of Year: **Marco Andretti**

Legend: **R=Indianapolis 500-Mile Race Rookie; W=Indianapolis 500-Mile Race Former Winner**

Lap Leaders: Castroneves 1-9, Wheldon 10-34, Hornish Jr. 35-37, Kanaan 38, Wheldon 39-107, Dixon 108-110, Wheldon 111-124, Dixon 125-127, Wheldon 128-129, Hornish Jr. 130-144, Wheldon 145-182, Kanaan 183-193, Andretti Mi. 194-197, Andretti Ma. 198-199, Hornish Jr. 200.

Lap Leader Summary: Wheldon 5 times for 148 laps, Hornish Jr. 3-19, Kanaan 2-12, Castroneves 1-9, Dixon 2-6, Andretti Mi. 1-4, Andretti Ma. 1-2. Lead Changes: **14 among 7 drivers.**

Caution Laps: 2-6, #91 Chesson, #92 Bucknum, accident T2. 67-75, #2 Scheckter, accident T4. 111-122, #3 Castroneves, #15 Rice, accident T4. 149-161, #31 Unser Jr., accident T3, #17 Simmons, accident T3. 191-195, #14 Giaffone, brushed wall T2. Cautions: **5 for 44 laps.**

Above: **2006 winner Sam Hornish, Jr. kisses the line of bricks.**

Photograph: IMS